D0422415

DICTIONARY OF **INSURA**

DICTIONARY OF **INSURANCE**

Second Edition

C. Bennett

An imprint of Pearson Education

London • New York • Toronto • Sydney • Tokyo • Singapore • Hong Kong
Cape Town • New Delhi • Madrid • Paris • Amsterdam • Munich • Milan

PEARSON EDUCATION LIMITED

Edinburgh Gate
Harlow CM20 2JE
Tel: +44 (0)1279 623623
Fax: +44 (0)1279 431059
Website: www.pearsoned.co.uk

First published 1992
Second edition published in Great Britain 2004

ISBN-10: 0-273-66365-8

ISBN-13: 978-0-273-66365-2

British Library Cataloguing-in-Publication Data
A catalogue record for this book is available from the British Library

Library of Congress Cataoging-in-Publication Data
Bennett, Carol S. C.
Dictionary of insurance/C. Bennett.—2nd ed.
p. cm. — (Financial Times series)
Contents: Common abbreviations used—The dictionary—Appendices: Marine abbreviations; Abbreviations and short forms - pensions; Glossary of special terms; Insurance industry associations, bodies, and related organisations.
ISBN 0-273-66365-8 (alk. paper)
1. Insurance—Dictionaries. I. Title. II. Series.

HG8025.B446 2004
368'.003—dc22

2004044472

10 9 8 7 6 5 4 3 2
08 07 06

Typeset by 70
Printed and bound in Great Britain by Bell and Bain Ltd, Glasgow

The Publishers' policy is to use paper manufactured from sustainable forests.

Contents

Foreword

What book do you keep at your elbow? Company handbook? Telephone directory? For the past 12 years my elbow-book has been the first edition of Carol Bennett's *Dictionary of Insurance.* My copy of the book looks as though it's been chewed by a hungry rodent and it's turning into a looseleaf manual. It's in the nature of my work that I need a wide-ranging knowledge of the whole of insurance, particularly the concepts and terminology. Unlike many technical dictionaries, which tend to disappoint as often as they come up with the goods, Carol's excellent work has rarely failed me. The vocabulary ranges over the whole area of insurance, including the many related subjects insurance people need to know about. It lists an amazingly large number of terms, at the same time providing generously detailed entries on each.

The language of insurance is a particularly complex one and rich in ambiguities. A simple word like 'risk' can have a surprisingly wide range of meanings: the possibility of loss, the peril which might cause a loss and the person, premises etc which might sustain a loss. Like other languages insurance even has its own dialects. To the marine insurance practitioner 'average' means something quite different to what's understood in property insurance, while in life assurance they tend to agree with the general public on what it means. Faced with such confusion, how can we possibly make ourselves understood? A dictionary is clearly vital.

But like all fields insurance moves on – new terms emerge and new uses arise for existing terms. And the 12 years which have passed since the first edition was published have been a period of great change for the insurance industry. In 1992 the Financial Services Authority didn't exist, income protection insurance was called permanent health insurance and alternative risk transfer was just an insurance executive's bad dream. So in 2002 I begged Carol to think about a new edition. As it turned out this is just what Carol had been doing and soon he started work in earnest on the revision. His original estimate that the new text would be ready 'by Christmas' soon turned to years as the full scale dawned on him of the changes the insurance industry had wrought on the English language over the past decade. But Carol knuckled down to some gruelling hard work and at last it's ready – and I'm delighted to see the second edition of this superb dictionary in print.

As the leading professional body in the insurance and related financial services industry with a mission to develop excellence in business conduct, the Chartered Insurance Institute welcomes the updated version of this book. Insurance is becoming an increasingly complex industry and it's vitally important that all who work in the industry or whose work brings them into contact with it should have a good understanding of its terminology as well as the underlying concepts.

Robert Cunnew
Head of Information Services, Chartered Insurance Institute

Preface to the Second Edition

The second *Dictionary of Insurance* is a totally new edition to cater for the many new terms that have entered the insurance world since the original version was published in 1992.

Its purpose is to provide a quick, one stop, first point of reference to help insurance practitioners and commercial insurance buyers through the modern maze of financial and risk management terms and to provide the ordinary consumer with a better understanding of the insurance products they may buy.

The sources of change that have resulted in this new edition have been many. The convergence of the banking and insurance markets accelerated throughout the 1990s bringing with it new products and new risk management techniques under the broad heading of alternative risk transfer (ART).

All of this has run alongside significant changes in the regulatory processes which are now the domain of the Financial Services Authority whose own glossary is a mere 196 pages! The creation of the Single European Market has been achieved by a series of Insurance Directives implemented by domestic regulations bringing the challenge of many new terms. Many other new terms have their origin in new policy forms, important legal developments and the changing business and political environment.

The changes will continue, so at no time will a book of this type ever be completely up to date. The current edition is the outcome of wide-ranging and painstaking research. As with the first edition, it includes a variety of non-insurance terms that are in some way related to the insurance industry.

The book sets out the terms in alphabetical sequence and uses abbreviations wherever possible. The Appendices consist of: marine abbreviations; abbreviations and short forms – pensions; glossary of special terms; and insurance industry associations, bodies and related organisations.

Following each term is the definition or explanation of the term. It has also been decided to introduce diagrams of which, but for space, there could have been more.

Finally, the author wishes to thank his wife, Maureen, for her patience, support and encouragement throughout the preparation of the book. He is also grateful to his friend, Peter Martin, FCII, formerly UK Commercial Marketing Manager of Eagle Star, now in great demand as an insurance and business trainer and consultant. Peter kindly read some parts of the text and gave sound advice on the project as a whole. The author also wishes to thank the staff of Pearson

Education. In the early stages he received first-class advice from Laurie Donaldson, followed up in the same way by his successor, Kate Salkilld. They have combined with their colleagues, Lisa Reading, Laura Brundell and Chris Shaw, to give the author professional support throughout the project. He is indebted to them and their senior editor Richard Stagg, like himself an old boy of Cheltenham Grammar School.

Acknowledgements

We are grateful to the following for permission to reproduce copyright material:

Figure 1 from Swiss Reinsurance Company, (Swiss Re, sigma No. 1/2003); Figure 2 from Swiss Reinsurance Company (Swiss Re, *Business Interruption Insurance* 06/98); Figure 6 from *www.ifsl.org.uk*, International Financial Services London and Diagram of insurance at Lloyd's © Lloyd's 2003.

In some instances we have been unable to trace the owners of copyright material, and we would appreciate any information that would enable us to do so.

Common abbreviations used

ABI	Association of British Insurers
ART	Alternative Risk Transfer
BIBA	British Insurance Brokers Association
CII	Chartered Insurance Institute
COB	Conduct of Business Rules
COSHH	Control of Substances Hazardous to Health
DWP	Department of Work and Pensions
FSA	Financial Services Authority
FSMA	Financial Services and Marketing Act 2000
FSAVC	Free Standing Additional Voluntary Contribution
HSC	Health and Safety Commission
HSE	Health and Safety Executive
HSWA	Health and Safety at Work, etc., Act 1974
IFA	Independent Financial Adviser
ICTA88	Income and Corporation Taxes Act 1988
ICOB	Insurance: Conduct of Business Rules
IPRU (INS)	Interim Prudential Sourcebook: Insurers
IR	Inland Revenue
IUA	International Underwriters' Association of London
MHSW	Management of Health and Safety at Work Regulations 1999
MIA	Marine Insurance Act 1906
OPB	Occupational Pensions Board
P&I	Protection & Indemnity
PA95	Pensions Act 1995
PMI	Pensions Management Institute
PN12	Inland Revenue Practice Note 12
PSA93	Pensions Scheme Act 1993
PUWER	Provision and Use of Work Equipment Regulations 1998
SERPS	State Earnings Related Pensions Scheme
SOFA	Society of Financial Advisers
SPV	Special Purpose Vehicle
S2P	State Second Pension
s.	Section (of an Act)

A1 The highest classification for seaworthiness of a vessel accorded by Lloyd's Register (qv). 'A' means that the vessel's hull is strong and seaworthy and '1' means that its rigging and gear are in perfect order.

A priori Describes a situation where all possible outcomes of an event are known in advance enabling their respective probabilities to be calculated, e.g. throwing a dice, tossing a coin.

Ab initio Insurance policies are void or voidable 'ab initio', i.e. from the beginning, if there is a breach precedent to the policy. *See* UTMOST GOOD FAITH.

Abandonment The right of a marine insured to relinquish ownership of the insured property to the underwriter in exchange for a constructive total loss (qv) payment. The underwriter is not bound to accept abandonment but, in doing so, he accepts responsibility for the property and liabilities attaching thereto, in addition to paying the full sum insured. *See* CONSTRUCTIVE TOTAL LOSS CLAUSE.

Abandonment of events A contingency insurance (qv) protecting promoters of events (e.g. exhibitions, fetes) against financial loss following cancellation, abandonment, interruption, rescheduling, postponement through circumstances (fires, storms) beyond their control. Judicial intervention that causes abandonment is sometimes included in the cover. Non-appearance cover (qv) is also available.

ABI 1996 method A method to check whether the benefits paid by an approved money purchase pension scheme (qv) exceed the Inland Revenue limits (qv).

ABI General Terms of Agreement An agreement between the insurers and credit organisations regarding the provision of replacement vehicles to innocent third parties and, where appropriate, the undertaking of repairs. Insurers agree to pay the credit hire organisations (CHOs) certain fixed rates for the supply of replacement cars plus certain other costs and the CHOs agree to supply vehicles. The agreement smoothes the process of uninsured loss claims by the innocent third parties and simplifies the negotiations between the CHOs and insurers.

ABI Genetic Testing Code of Practice The Association of British Insurers (ABI) (qv) has agreed that its members must not ask insurance-seeking applicants for genetic tests. Up to November 2006 applicants can apply for amounts to £500,000 life insurance and £300,000 health insurance without giving details of previously taken predictive genetic tests. Above those levels insurers need the results of any previously taken tests that have been specifically approved by the Genetics and Insurance Committee (qv). The only test approved (June 2003) is for Huntington's Disease. Other tests may follow and will be listed on *www.abi.org.uk*.

Absolute assignment The complete sale of a life assurance policy by the policyholder to the assignee, who then becomes the owner and an assignee for value. Usually the consideration is the surrender value or other agreed price, but it may be nominal or for 'natural love and affection', in which case it is called a voluntary assignment. The Policies of Assurance Act 1867 (qv) gives the statutory form of assignment. The assignee may covenant to pay future premiums and can give a good discharge for the policy proceeds.

Absolute net rate A rate quoted by an insurer to a broker, which makes no allowance for commission. The broker charges his client a fee. Absolute net rates are often quoted in extended warranty insurance (qv).

Absolute net retention The amount of a loss which the reinsured retains net for its own account after deducting all reinsurance recoveries. A reinsurer may oblige the reinsured to retain a minimum amount so that further reinsurance purchases do not leave the reinsured with a strictly nominal interest.

Abstainers' insurance Insurance on preferential terms exclusive to total abstainers from the consumption of alcohol. Applies to life, health and motor vehicle insurances.

Accelerated accrual A pension scheme accrual rate (qv) greater than one-sixtieth of pensionable earnings for each year of pensionable service. Also called 'uplifted sixtieths'.

Acceptance 1. Act of assenting to an offer to create a contract. It occurs, for example, when an underwriter initials a slip (qv) or the proposer for a life policy pays the premium after receiving an offer, i.e. the acceptance letter. 2. Acceptance of goods within the Sale of Goods Act 1979, s.35 is (a) where the buyer intimates to the seller that he has accepted them; or (b) where the goods have been delivered and the buyer does any act with them that is inconsistent with the ownership of the seller; or (c) when, after a reasonable lapse of time, the buyer retains them without intimating to the seller his rejection of them. After acceptance the only remedy under the Act for breach of contract by the seller will be an action for damages.

Accepted value A value on property that the insurer has accepted and will not dispute in the future unless there is proof of fraud.

Accepting office An insurance company that accepts a reinsurance.

Access to Justice Act 1999 Reformed the law relating to conditional fee agreements (qv) and *after the event legal insurance* (AEI). The court can order a losing party to pay any uplift on both the successful party's lawyer's normal fee and the premium paid by the successful party for insurance against being ordered to pay the other side's costs. Solicitors when instructed must inform their clients of the availability of alternative funding such as AEI.

Access to Medical Records Act 1988 Gives life insurance proposer the right to see medical reports. The insurer must obtain the proposer's written consent to approach his doctor for a report, but the proposer is entitled to see the report before it is submitted to the insurer. The proposer can request changes if he considers the report to be misleading. If the doctor refuses, the proposer can withdraw permission and risk losing the offer of insurance or add comments to the report.

Accessory *See* MOTOR ACCESSORIES.

Accident A sudden, unplanned and unlooked for mishap or untoward event, not under the control of the insured, resulting in injury or damage. There has to be an element of fortuity. Personal accident policies may cover injury *caused by an accident* or *accidental injury* (*accidental bodily injury*) (qv). *See* ACCIDENTAL MEANS; ACCIDENTAL OCCURRENCE.

Accident Book Workplaces with more than 10 employees and all factories must by law have an accident book in which employees, or others on their behalf, can record accident and work-related sickness details. Entries count as formal notice to the employer who may make his own entry if he believes that the employee's entry is inaccurate. The entries may be relevant in subsequent claims against the employer. The latest Accident Book (HSE-published) complies with the Data Protection Act 1998 (qv). Accidents are recorded but details of the individuals involved are stored separately and securely.

Accident frequency A measure of the incidence of accidents over a period of time. It indicates the effectiveness of loss prevention measures.

Accident severity A measure of the severity or seriousness of losses rather than the number of losses. It measures the amounts of losses and lost time, etc. Like accident frequency (qv) it checks on the loss prevention and minimisation measures.

Accident, Sickness and Unemployment policies (ASU) Creditor insurance (qv) where cover is triggered by accident, sickness or unemployment. *See also* LIFE, ACCIDENT, SICKNESS AND UNEMPLOYMENT INSURANCE (LASU).

Accident year The calendar or accounting year in which an accident or loss occurred.

Accidental bodily injury An unexpected, unintended injury to the human body caused by an accident (qv) or by ordinary means that produced an unexpected outcome. Reckless conduct leading to an expected but unintended bodily injury is not accidental for the purposes of a legal liability policy; the injury must be both unexpected and unintended from the insured's standpoint. Accidental injury generally occurs at a specific time and place, but the concept of the *slow accident* (qv) now exists and conditions such as deep vein thrombosis (qv) have to be considered in the light of policy definitions and court decisions. Under a personal accident policy a person injured under a car when a jack slips has suffered an accidental injury, but back strain from an uneventful tyre change lacks fortuity and is not therefore accidental.

Accidental damage In the absence of a precise policy definition, the term will be construed as a matter of ordinary English language usage. *Accidental damage usually means* 'unintended and unexpected damage caused by sudden and external means subject to certain exclusions, e.g. electrical and mechanical derangement, inherent vice, and action of insects, moths, vermin and the like'. A common wording, also subject to exclusions to put certain matters beyond doubt, is 'visible damage not caused on purpose'. 'Damage' includes accidental destruction but not necessarily 'accidental loss' although where the loss is of an integral part of an item, e.g. covers on a settee, the resultant 'impairment' is likely to be regarded as 'accidental damage'.

Accidental damage cover Cover under a household or a commercial policy that provides all the benefits of standard named peril policy plus accidental damage (qv) cover, e.g. spilling paint on a carpet or computer. Under a named peril policy a loss has to be matched to a named peril.

Accidental damage excess An alternative term to *own damage excess.* It is the excess (qv) in the loss or damage section of comprehensive motor policies and applies only to claims involving loss or damage to the insured vehicle. The excess is overridden in regard to loss or damage caused by fire or theft. All motor policies contain an accidental damage excess that applies to young and inexperienced drivers (qv).

Accidental damage to property Under a liability policy the damage is *accidental* if unexpected and unintended from the insured's standpoint. *Property* means 'material property' but not property or rights in intellectual property (qv). For first party policies see *accidental damage.* *See* ACCIDENTAL BODILY INJURY.

Accidental death As an insured event under a personal accident insurance it is 'death caused by violent, accidental, external and visible means which shall solely and independently of any other cause result in death occurring within 12 months'. The time limit is arbitrary but the longer the period between the injury and subsequent death the greater will be the likelihood of an intervening cause. There is no payment by the insurer if the accidental death is caused by an excepted risk. *See* ACCIDENT; ACCIDENTAL MEANS.

'Accidental fire' The Fire Prevention (Metropolis) Act 1774 (qv), s.86 enacts that no action can be brought against any person in whose premises a fire begins accidentally. In *Filliter* v. *Phippard* (1847) accidental fire was defined as 'fire produced by mere chance or incapable of being traced to any particular cause'. Thus, when fire is traced to negligence, nuisance or a *Rylands* v. *Fletcher* (qv) object, the fire is not 'accidental' and the defence under s.86 will not apply. It was seemingly intended that any liability for fire should be fault-based.

Accidental injury A bodily injury that is unexpected and unintended.

Accidental means Appears in some personal accident policies and means an unexpected and unintended cause of an accident involving at least an element of fortuity. Modern courts are unlikely to distinguish between 'accidental bodily injury' (qv) and 'bodily injury caused by accidental means'. The term is usually qualified in that the 'bodily injury' has to be caused by 'accidental means *solely and independently of any other cause*' (qv).

Accidental occurrence An event or series of events happening fortuitously or unexpectedly that causes injury or damage. An occurrence can be the result of continuous or repeated exposure to harmful conditions, with no single event causing the injury. More often an 'accident' is generally sudden and at a definite place in time and location. *See* SLOW ACCIDENT.

Accidents only policy A personal accident policy (qv) under which cover is restricted to death or disablement (as defined) caused by accidental bodily injury. No sickness cover is provided.

Accommodation business (or line) Unattractive business that an insurer accepts to 'accommodate' an existing connection (broker or insured) to preserve the goodwill of that connection.

Accommodation line *See* ACCOMMODATION BUSINESS.

Accord and satisfaction If a claim has been settled and a binding discharge obtained, it cannot be re-opened. The liability insurer who has obtained a suitable discharge in the name of his or her policyholder will have provided a good defence against future claims based on the same cause of action (qv).

Account sales A cargo claim document required when the goods have been sold. It shows the proceeds of the sale.

Accountants' clause A clause in a business interruption policy (qv) which indemnifies the insured in respect of the cost of an accountant's fee in respect of preparing and submitting the claim. Without the clause, the cost falls upon the insured.

Accreditation Process of registering an applicant as a Lloyd's broker (qv). Re-accreditation occurs after three years. Prior to applying to Lloyd's a UK-based applicant must be authorised by the FSA (qv). The new accreditation scheme allows overseas brokers to become accredited Lloyd's brokers without having a UK-based registered company. Overseas applicants have to demonstrate that they meet FSA-equivalent requirements in the matters of insurance money segregation, solvency and professional indemnity insurance. There are also requirements for reporting, monitoring, complaints handling, training and competence and codes of practice, all of which *may* take account of local requirements.

Accrual rate The rate (e.g. 1/60th) at which the pension benefit increases for each year of pensionable service in a defined benefit scheme (qv). *See* ACCELERATED ACCRUAL.

Accruals concept A pensions term referring to the accounting practice whereby revenues and costs are recognised as they are earned or incurred, rather than when money is received or paid out.

Accrued benefits Accumulated benefits in a pension scheme for a member in respect of his service up to a given time, whether vested or not. The calculation may take account of the member's current or projected earnings. Allowance may also be made for revaluation (qv) and/or pension increases (qv).

Accrued benefits funding methods Major category of funding methods in which the actuarial liability (qv) for active members (qv) is based on pensionable service accrued up to the valuation date or to the end of the control period (qv), as appropriate. The treatment of benefits not directly linked to pensionable service is not specified but left to actuarial judgement, subject to the need for consistency between successive valuations. The standard contribution rate (qv) is derived from the definition of the actuarial liability appropriate to the accrued benefits funding method selected. It is the rate sufficient, after taking into account the actuarial liability at the beginning of the control period, and the benefits expected to be paid during that period, to provide for the actuarial liability at the end of the control period.

Accrued rights The benefits an occupational pension scheme (qv) member has as of right. They include *accrued benefits* (qv). The rights for an active member (qv) can be based on the scenario that he has left service or he could have the right to link benefits to future salary increases. Specific definitions of the term are set out in PSA93 for the purposes of *preservation* (qv), *contracting out* (qv) and the *Disclosure Regulations.* PA95 contains a specific definition in relation to scheme amendments. *See* DISCLOSURE 1.

Accrued rights premium A type of state scheme premium payable in respect of a member when a defined benefit scheme ceases to be contracted out. In return the state scheme takes over the obligation to provide the member's guaranteed minimum pension (qv).

Accumulated contributions Total of a member's pension scheme contributions plus investment earnings. In a money purchase scheme (qv), the employer's contributions plus investment earnings are added to give the overall figure.

Accumulation 1. The accumulation risk arises when a large number of individual risks are so situated, e.g. within a given location, that a single occurrence, such as a windstorm, may affect many or all of these risks. The occurrence may be defined in an hours clause (qv). *See* ACCUMULATION CONTROL. 2. Life insurance term to reflect the increase in value and therefore subsequent benefits available under with profits policies (qv) as the life of the policy progresses and investment income accrues.

Accumulation Control The monitoring of any actual or potential accumulation of risk (e.g. number of properties in a locality exposed to the same loss event, e.g. flood) in order to ensure that underwriting capacity is not exceeded and/or adequate reinsurance (qv) or suitable co-insurance (qv) is arranged.

Accumulation factor Life insurance term referring to the accumulation of a single premium of 1 over a period of time taking account of the interest the premium will earn and the probability of the insured surviving.

Accumulation in risk A combination of hazardous risk factors affecting an insured risk, e.g. poorly constructed building, hazardous trade or poor claims experience.

Accumulation units Units issued by a unit trust (qv) derived from the net income when it is automatically used to buy more units in the same fund. The unitholder benefits from not having to pay an initial charge on his reinvested income.

ACORD (Association for Cooperative Operations Research and Development) Non-profit insurance association that facilitates the development use of global insurance standards for insurance-related financial services industries. ACORD is committed to improving efficiency and expanding market reach by reducing costs; reducing duplication of work and ambiguous communication exchanges; improving accuracy; facilitating e-commerce; and supporting multiple distribution models. WISE (qv) ceded the promotion of electronic data standards to the organisation in July 2001. ACORD has offices in New York and London. Visit *www.acord.org*.

Acquisition costs Expenses incurred by an insurer in obtaining new business and issuing policies. Commission to intermediaries accounts for the largest portion of acquisition costs.

Act of God Natural occurrences (earthquake, typhoon, etc.) that no amount of human foresight could have avoided. It is a defence against strict liability (qv) in tort, e.g. *Rylands* v. *Fletcher* (qv). In *Nichols* v. *Marsland* (CA 1876) the defendant was not liable when exceptionally violent storms caused his artificial lakes to flood his neighbour's land, but the defence is of very restricted application.

Act only policy Third party motor insurance policy issued by an authorised insurer under which the cover is limited to the minimum cover required to comply with the compulsory requirements of the Road Traffic Act 1988, s.145.

Actio personalis moritur cum persona 'A personal action dies with the person,' meaning that, at common law, a right of action in tort (qv) ceases on death of the claimant or defendant. Following the Law Reform (Miscellaneous Provisions) Act 1934, causes of action survive death and keep claims alive on both sides. Liability insurers grant an indemnity to a deceased insured's legal personal representatives.

Active breaches of utmost good faith Actual statements that convey false or misleading information relating to a material fact (qv). Innocent misrepresentation is the unintentional misrepresentation of a material fact; fraudulent misrepresentation is deliberate. *See* UTMOST GOOD FAITH.

Active investment management Occurs when pension funds are used to purchase and sell *particular* investments to secure growth above the level of a chosen benchmark.

Active member A current employee of a pension scheme engaged in building up pension benefits in an occupational pension scheme. During a contribution holiday (qv) a member may still accumulate extra pension benefits without payments into the scheme.

Active underwriter The person at the underwriting box at Lloyd's with principal authority from the managing agent (qv) to accept risks on behalf of the syndicate he represents.

Actively at work Group life or health policy term requiring a new member (or a member increasing cover) to be at work or on holiday on the day of joining or increasing the cover, and not absent due to sickness or industrial action. Cover may begin on the employee's return to work, either automatically or with the insurer's consent.

Activities of daily living (ADLs) Everyday living functions and activities normally performed unaided by individuals. They include eating, dressing, bathing, climbing stairs, etc. ADLs are the basis for assessing claims under long-term care insurances (qv) and similar disability contracts. A claim is triggered when an individual is unable to perform activities of this type unaided.

Activities of daily working (ADWs) A health policy term that may be used to define incapacity or *disability* (qv) for manual workers. A worker unable to perform activities that include skills such as dexterity, mobility and communication may be disabled for the purpose of the policy while able to undertake other activities not dependent on those skills.

Actual cash value (ACV) Method for placing value on property at the time of its loss or damage. ACV is usually the cost less depreciation. The market value of the property may help determine its actual cash value.

Actual total loss According to the Marine Insurance Act, s.57, this occurs in three ways: (a) destruction of the subject-matter; (b) subject-matter so damaged that it ceases to be a thing of the kind insured ('loss of specie', e.g. cement becomes concrete); (c) the insured is irretrievably deprived of the subject-matter. A fourth way (s.58) provides that if, after a reasonable time, there is no news of a missing ship (qv), actual total loss is presumed.

Actuarial assumptions Assumptions made by an actuary as a basis for the figures and estimates needed for an actuarial valuation (qv). The assumptions are based around life expectancy, inflation, earnings levels and income from pension scheme investments. *See* ACTUARIAL REPORT.

Actuarial basis Indicates either or both of the *valuation method* (qv) and the *actuarial assumptions* (qv) made for the purpose of an *actuarial valuation* (qv).

Actuarial certificate Issued by an actuary arising out of actuarial work. The work may include: (a) carrying out the solvency test required by some contracted out (qv) schemes; (b) certifying to the IR that pension scheme surpluses have been dealt with as required under ss.599A–602, ICTA 1988; (c) the position on the minimum funding requirement (qv) under the Pensions Act 1995 ss.56–60; (d) the bulk transfer (qv) certificate under Regulation 12 of the Occupational Pension Schemes (Preservation of Benefit) Regulations 1991 (SI 1991/167).

Actuarial deficiency Amount by which the actuarial valuation (qv) of a pension scheme's assets is less than the actuarial liability (qv).

Actuarial firm For FSMA purposes, it is a firm (including a sole practitioner) that is managed and/or controlled by individuals who are members of the Institute of Actuaries or Faculty of Actuaries and who are entitled to practise the profession of actuary (typically a consulting firm). Actuarial firms that carry on regulated activities (qv) must either become an *authorised professional firm* (qv) to carry on regulated activities, or apply to the Institute for a designated professional body (DPB) licence (qv). The activities are then classed as *exempt regulated activities* as set out in the DPB Handbook as they are incidental to the firm's professional services.

Actuarial function A required FSA (qv) function. *See* APPOINTED ACTUARY.

Actuarial increase The extra pension granted to a pension scheme member who has deferred his pension beyond normal retirement age.

Actuarial liability The amount, using actuarial assumptions and methods, a pension scheme will have to pay out as pension benefits and expenses after the date of the actuarial valuation (qv). It includes the present value of instalments of pensions in payment and related contingency benefits, the present value of future payments in respect of deferred pensioners and a provision for all active members (qv).

Actuarial reduction The reduction in a pension scheme member's accrued pension benefits because he has retired early. The reduction helps to cover the additional costs brought about by early retirement.

Actuarial report A report in the format required by the FSA (qv) on an actuarial valuation (qv). The name is also used when an actuary reports how changes to a pension scheme might affect it financially.

Actuarial statement Statement required by the *Disclosure Regulations* to be included in the annual report (qv). It must show, in the prescribed form, the security of the accrued and prospective rights of pension scheme members and be signed by an actuary (qv). *See* DISCLOSURE 1.

Actuarial surplus The excess of the actuarial valuation (qv) of a pension scheme's assets over the scheme's actuarial liability (qv).

Actuarial valuation Investigation by an actuary, usually every three years, to ascertain the ability of a defined pension scheme (qv) to meet its liabilities. This means assessing the level of funding required and recommending a contribution rate (qv) based on a comparison of the actuarial value of assets and the actuarial liability (qv). Actuaries also carry out annual valuations of the liabilities of life insurance companies.

Actuarial value of assets The value, following actuarial practice, placed on the assets of a pension scheme, for the purpose of the actuarial valuation (qv). It could be an assessed value, the market value or some other value.

Actuary Professional person who applies probability and other statistical theories to insurance. His work covers rates, reserves, dividends and other valuation while also conducting statistical studies, making reports and advising on solvency. PA95 obliges the trustees of occupational pension schemes to appoint an actuary to advise on funding aspects and ensure that the scheme meets the minimum funding requirement (qv).

Ad valorem bill of lading A bill recording the amount that the shipper has declared to the carrier as the cargo's value. If the carrier is liable for loss or damage to cargo his liability will be for the amount in the bill.

Ad valorem freight rate Freight based on the cargo's value rather than weight or volume.

Added years The years added to the 'actual membership years' to enhance the benefits for the member of a defined benefit scheme (qv). It may be the outcome of a transfer payment (qv) received by the pension scheme, an additional voluntary contribution (qv), or the employer or the scheme improving the member's benefits.

Addendum A document that notes alterations agreed between the parties to a reinsurance contract.

Addition to age A method used by life underwriters when charging an extra premium to under average (qv) lives. The underwriter adds a number of years to the proposer's age in order to determine the actual premium that will be charged.

Additional commission The commission at a fixed or variable rate that the reinsurer pays to the reinsured if the loss ratio (qv) is below a specified percentage.

Additional cost clauses Fire policy clauses covering additional costs such as the cost of removing debris or complying with public authorities requirements. Cover is subject to the adequacy of the sum insured. *See* PUBLIC AUTHORITIES CLAUSE; DEBRIS REMOVAL CLAUSE.

Additional Increase in Cost of Working An optional extension under a business interruption insurance (qv). It allows the insured to incur reasonable *additional* expenditure to avoid or diminish any further reduction in turnover following a loss even though the amount payable exceeds the loss thereby avoided. Without this extension the insured's recovery for 'increase in cost of working' (qv) will not be permitted to exceed the loss of gross profit avoided by such expenditure. The extra cover is for a specific sum.

Additional pension/component The earnings-related part of the state pension scheme. It is additional to the basic state pension (qv). The current additional scheme, the state second pension (qv), replaced SERPS in April 2002.

Additional perils Also called *special perils* they add to the scope of a standard *fire policy*. They include: 1. Dry perils: aircraft (qv); explosion (qv); riot and civil commotion (qv); malicious damage (qv); earthquake (qv). 2. Wet perils: storm (qv); burst pipes (qv); flood (qv); sprinkler leakage (qv). 3. Miscellaneous perils: impact (qv); subsidence (qv); subterranean fire (qv); spontaneous combustion (qv).

Additional premium (AP) An extra charge made by the insurer for improving the cover, changing the risk or extending the period of insurance, or under an adjustable policy where the record shows that the actual activity exceeded the initial estimate.

Additional voluntary contributions (AVCs) Voluntary contributions by pension scheme members to boost their eventual retirement income. Tax relief on AVCs is subject to the normal limits, but they cannot be commuted to a tax-free lump sum. AVCs are 'in-house', or set up as an FSAVC (qv) (free standing AVC) from a provider of the individual's choice. *See* HEADROOM CHECK.

Additions and deletions clause A clause applicable to certain aviation hull insurances under which the cover is automatically extended to include further aircraft owned or operated by the insured of the same type and value of the aircraft already insured.

Adequate plant, machinery and equipment At common law an employer must take reasonable care to provide adequate plant and machinery and see that it is properly maintained. This includes the provision of protective devices and clothing and, where appropriate, a warning or exhortation to use such equipment. The employer may also have to take account of any special disabilities of the workman (*Paris* v. *Stepney B.C.* (1951)). Under the Employers' Liability (Defective Equipment) Act 1969 (qv) the employer is strictly liable for injury caused by a latent defect in a tool, even though the fault is that of the manufacturer. *See* PUWER.

Adjudication A quasi-arbitration where a neutral adjudicator issues an award or decision, binding on the parties, unless unenforceable by the court or an arbitrator. The Housing, Grants, Construction and Regeneration Act 1996 provides a compulsory adjudication scheme in most construction contracts to resolve disputes on an interim basis, to minimise site delays. The adjudicator reaches a decision within 28 days of referral. The decision is binding unless the dispute is finally decided by agreement, or until, on occasions only, there is a fresh hearing by litigation or arbitration. Otherwise the court intervenes if the losing party refuses to honour the adjudicator's decision. *See* ALTERNATIVE DISPUTE RESOLUTION.

Adjustable policies Policies where, at inception, the insured estimates the size of the risk in terms of a key variable such as turnover or wages as in employers' liability insurance. The premium is based on this estimate but adjusted up or down at the end of the year when the actual figure is declared by the insured. Any return made to the insured is subject to a minimum premium.

Adjustable premiums *See* ADJUSTABLE POLICIES.

Adjusted CETV The cash equivalent transfer value (qv), worked out in the prescribed manner (the Welfare Reform and Pensions Act 1999), to establish a member's pensions rights on divorce. The CETV is a lump sum value in current terms of the rights accrued within a member's pension scheme.

Adjusted indemnity limit The initial indemnity limit under a reinsurance contract minus the losses paid during the current contract period. It is the amount of cover remaining unless re-instatement applies.

Adjuster *See* LOSS ADJUSTER (qv).

Adjustment The process of dealing with a claim starting with its investigation and concluding with its settlement or disposal. The work can be carried out by the insurer's own claims staff or by a loss adjuster (qv).

Adjustment premium An additional premium payable under the terms of the contract as a result of claims experienced under a policy of insurance or reinsurance.

Administration bond A bond (qv) issued to the Principal Probate Registrar against defaults by the person (i.e. the administrator (qv)) appointed to administer the estate of another.

Administration of Justice Act 1969 An Act compelling the courts to award interest on damages for personal injuries for the period from date of service of claim to the date of judgement at a standard rate. Interest is only awarded on those cases that proceed to court and payments into court should include interest.

Administration of Justice Act 1982 Section 1 abolished the right to damages for loss of expectation of life (qv) while s.3 replaced it with an action for bereavement (qv) by close relatives by amending the Fatal Accidents Act 1976 (qv). Section 4(2) abolished claims for a deceased person's 'lost years', i.e. no claim for loss of the deceased's income after the date of death. Section 2 abolished action for loss of services. Section 5 lays down that maintenance provided at public expense is to be taken into account in assessing personal injury damages. Section 6 allows, where the claimant's condition may deteriorate, for the award of provisional damages (qv) and a subsequent further award where deterioration actually occurs.

Administrative reinsurance (Admin Re) Life reinsurance under which closed blocks of business from both active and inactive primary insurers are accepted by reinsurers. It allows the primary insurers to realise value and release capital as well as ease their administrative constraints.

Administrator 1. A person appointed by the court to administer the estate of another who died intestate or without an executor. Section 167 of the Judicature Act 1925 obliges the administrator to enter into an administration bond (qv). 2. The person or persons regarded by the Inland Revenue and, where relevant the Occupational Pensions Board, as responsible for the management of a pension scheme. 3. An insolvency practitioner managing the affairs of a company when it goes into administration.

Admissible asset An asset, under rule 4.1(3) of IPRU (INS), that may be brought into account in determining the value of an insurer's net assets for margin of solvency (qv) purposes. Goodwill and stock-in-trade, for example, are not admissible assets and certain assets are admissible only to a specified extent. *See* ASSET VALUATION RULES.

Admissibility *See* ADMISSIBLE ASSET.

Admission of age In life insurance the insured may have his policy endorsed 'age admitted' by supplying the insurer with his birth certificate (qv). This may occur at inception or during the currency of the policy. When age has been admitted, the insured or his representatives will not to have to prove the insured's age when a claim is made.

Admission of liability 1. An admission by an insurer or reinsurer that they are liable for a claim under their contract. 2.

An admission by an insured that he is liable for injury or damage caused to a third party. In a liability policy the insurer's *conduct of proceedings clause* (qv) and *non-admission of liability clause* (qv) prevent the insured from negotiating with the claimant or admitting liability without the insurer's consent. The clauses are conditions precedent to liability (qv).

Admitted insurer An insurer authorised to transact business from within a foreign country. The insurance transacted is known as establishment business (qv).

Admitted liability insurance (automatic personal accident cover). A personal accident insurance for aircraft passengers offering benefits in return for which they waive any rights they may have at law. The maximum sum payable usually corresponds with the limits of either the Warsaw Convention, the Hague Protocol or the 1967 Carriage by Air (Applications and Provisions) Order.

Advance An agreed percentage increase applied to the total invoice plus freight for unknown expenses at the time of shipment and also for a portion of the insured's profit.

Advance freight Freight paid in advance by cargo owners to shipowners on the basis that it is 'not repayable in case of loss'. The cargo owner insures the risk by merging the advance freight with the value of the goods. Unless arranged in this way, English law insists that freight is only payable on right delivery of the goods. A charterer (qv) may also insure advance freight.

Advance or arrears Option at retirement whereby the individual's pension payment (monthly, quarterly or some other period) may be payable at the beginning or end of the relevant period. Payments in advance attract a small cost.

Advance payment bond Similar to a performance bond (qv). It safeguards the principal, who has made advance payments to the contractor, against loss due to poor performance or default by the contractor.

Advance profits insurance A form of business interruption insurance (qv) relating to a new business or a new activity for an existing business. It covers loss of gross profit following delay consequent upon damage insured under a contractor's all risks (qv) or erection all risks policy (qv). The delay in starting the activity may be due to damage to: (a) the new works, extension or machinery; (b) suppliers' premises; (c) machinery in transit. The indemnity period (qv) commences on the date production was intended to start and continues until it does actually start, but any increase in cost of working is calculated from the date of loss.

Advance rent insurance Cover for a property owner against loss of rental income due to an insured event delaying the letting of his property. The sum insured is the annual rent multiplied by the number of years representing the maximum delay period. A loss is measured by the rent that would have been paid by the tenant during the period of delay.

Advance underwriting System that may be used for underwriting members of group schemes. Once a group member has been accepted at ordinary rates he becomes entitled to increases in cover up to a pre-arranged percentage without further evidence of health or underwriting scrutiny. Also called *guaranteed insurability.*

Advanced Diploma in Insurance The CII's 'professional' qualification awarded to experienced and expert market practitioners. Candidates can choose from 46 modules each attracting a designated number of credits. Successful candidates achieve a 290 credit threshold at the culmination of which they will have an enhanced understanding of insurance practice both in terms of technical subjects and overall management skills. Holders are entitled to use the designation ACII and apply for a *Chartered title* (qv) and in due course proceed to Fellowship status.

Advanced Financial Planning Certificate (AFPC). CII qualification that gives financial advisers a broad understanding of the core disciplines needed to give high quality financial advice. The wide subject choice includes two FSA-approved subjects for regulatory compliance purposes. Pensions (G60) is an approved qualification to be held by a nominated person in a firm that carries out *pensions transfer* and *opt-out* business. *Investment portfolio management* (G70) is a recognised examination for fund management and certain other investment advice activities.

Adventure *See* MARINE ADVENTURE.

Adverse development loss cover A retrospective financial reinsurance (qv) providing cover for past losses that exceed loss reserves and loss portfolio transfer contracts (qv) on losses that are incurred but not reported (INBR) and the development on reported losses (IBNeR) (qv). The premium reflects the net present value of the expected future ceded loss payment and a risk premium in respect of underwriting, timing and investments. The main benefit is that cover facilitates mergers and takeovers by removing the risk of adverse loss developments for the acquiring company.

Adverse selection The tendency of poorer than average risks to buy and maintain insurance. It occurs when insureds select only those coverages that are most likely to have losses. Insurers respond by making *adverse underwriting decisions,* i.e. those not favourable to the insured by termination, declining acceptance, higher rates or reduction in cover. *See* SELECTION OF LIVES.

Advertising agent's indemnity Comprehensive contingency insurance for an agency and its client when a film or campaign is interrupted or abandoned due to a cause beyond the control of the agency or its client.

Advice In regulating the UK insurance where the sales process involves giving advice, the essential elements in a 'private customer advised sale' must be (a) on the advantages and disadvantages of the customer buying or selling, and (b) a particular insurance contract(s). Generic advice, e.g. recommending that someone should buy a household policy, would not fall within the definition of advice. *See* ADVISING AND SELLING STANDARDS.

Advice risk The risk of liability attaching to the insured as a result of giving advice. Solicitors, etc., are liable when 'negligent' advice leads to financial loss. The risk is insurable under professional indemnity insurance (qv). Advice for which a fee is normally payable is excluded under public and products liability insurances. Advice that is incidental to supplying a product or carrying out work is not excluded but any resultant loss will only normally be within public/product liability cover if the third party suffers accidental bodily injury or damage to property.

Advised sales *See* ADVISING AND SELLING STANDARDS.

Adviser A financial adviser (qv); representative (qv); appointed representative (qv).

Advising and selling standards FSA requirements laid down in ICOB (qv) which categorises sales into *advised sales* and *non-advised sales.* The former occurs where the customer is given an opinion or recommendation to buy or sell a specific non-investment insurance contract. The customer must be given a statement setting out the reasons for the recommendation as well as a *demands and needs statement* (qv). *Non-advised sales* occur when the sales process only involves providing information and no advice. The customer must be given a demands and needs statement unless the policy is sold directly to a commercial customer. *See* ADVISING ON INVESTMENTS; ARRANGING INSURANCE.

Advising on investments A regulated activity which occurs when the person advised is: (a) an investor or potential investor, or is acting as agent for such a person; (b) in receipt of advice on the merits of doing any of the following (whether as principal or agent): buying, selling, subscribing for or underwriting a particular security or relevant investment, ((i) *designated investment* (qv), funeral plan contract, pure protection contract (qv), general insurance contract, or right to, or interest in, a funeral plan contract; or (ii) exercising any right conferred by such an investment, other than a pure protection contract (qv), to buy, sell, subscribe for or underwrite such an investment.)

Aerial devices Balloons, rockets, space vehicles and space satellites. The term refers to an additional peril (qv) covering 'destruction or damage by Aircraft and other Aerial Devices or articles dropped therefrom'. Damage by sonic bang is excluded.

Aerospace project completions coverage Covers insureds while building a new hush kit or developing a new aerospace product whose success depends on obtaining a standard type certificate (STC) or regulatory approval. The trigger event for payment is the client's inability to obtain an STC. Deposits placed by the insured's customers to fund the project can be returned to fund research and development provided the return of the deposit to the policyholder can be insured.

Affreightment *See* CONTRACT OF AFFREIGHTMENT.

After the event legal expenses insurance (AEI) Covers the risk of the unsuccessful litigation. Cover is arranged *after* the insured becomes aware of the need to litigate. The insurance pays both the party's own and opponent's fees and disbursements (e.g. expert reports) if the action is unsuccessful and the insured is ordered to pay them or fails to recover them from his opponent. The insurance is marketed as a *conditional fee agreement* (qv) *insurance. Both Sides Insurance,* an alternative, is not linked to conditional fees. It pays both sides' legal fees and disbursements regardless of the outcome of the action. Proposals forms call upon the insured's legal representative to confirm a minimum 65 per cent chance of success. The successful insured can, at the court's discretion, recover his AEI premium from the loser.

Age 75 rule IR rule allowing members of defined contribution pension arrangements to defer the compulsory purchase of an annuity until age 75. During the deferment period the member may take 'income drawdown' (qv) within prescribed limits.

Age admitted *See* ADMISSION OF AGE.

Age attained The age last birthday of a proposer for life insurance.

Age limits The limits set by insurers as to the maximum and minimum ages at which cover will be offered, maintained or made subject to special conditions. Age limits are commonly applied to health/accident insurances including travel, certain life policies and motor insurance.

Age related payment/rebate Payment made by the IR National Insurance Contributions Office to an appropriate scheme, contracted out money purchase scheme or contracted out mixed benefit scheme from April 1997 for members who have contracted out (qv). The payments increase with the age of the member.

Agent One who solicits, negotiates or effects contracts on behalf of another such as an insured or insurer. His right to exercise various functions, his authority and his obligations are subject to the terms of the agency contract and subject to certain legal principles such as the exercise of care and skill and observing good faith. *See* INSURANCE BROKER; LLOYD'S AGENT; MANAGING AGENTS; INSURANCE INTERMEDIARY.

Agent-owned captive A captive insurance company (qv) formed in the US by insurance agents singly or in groups to insure selected risks from their own accounts.

Agent's authority The authority to act on behalf of his principal. An insurance broker (qv) may act at one time for the insured (i.e. placing insurance as instructed) and at other times for the insurer, e.g. collecting the premium. In order to determine who is bound by the agent's act it is necessary to ascertain for whom he was acting in regard to the relevant issue. An agent's authority may be express as when acting on specific instructions or it may be implied (actions taken in accordance with prevailing custom) or apparent (or ostensible) authority (actions based on appearances). Where the agent acts without authority and the principal becomes obligated the agent may be liable to his principal. *See* IMPUTED KNOWLEDGE.

Aggravated burglary A person is guilty of this offence if he commits any burglary (qv) and at the time has with him any firearm or imitation firearm, any weapon of offence or any explosive (Theft Act 1968, s.10).

Aggregate deductible *See* ANNUAL AGGREGATE DEDUCTIBLE.

Aggregate excess of loss A form of excess of loss reinsurance loss (qv) where both the deductible (qv) and reinsurer's limit of liability are expressed as annual aggregate amounts rather than on a per risk or per occurrence basis. The cover, unlike a stop loss treaty (qv) is expressed in cash sums not loss ratios. The arrangement is suitable for a reinsured whose concern is protection against cumulative losses on an account, e.g. medical insurances and not against a major 'per occurrence' exposure.

Aggregate franchise deductible Reinsurance contract provision meaning that when the reinsured's losses exceed the annual aggregate deductible the reinsurer pays the whole of the loss without deduction.

Aggregate limit of indemnity The maximum amount that the insurer will pay in respect of all insured losses that occur during the policy term. No further claim is payable once the limit has been exhausted unless it has been reinstated by policy condition or agreement. Aggregate limits are common to professional indemnity insurance (qv) and product liability insurance (qv). Under some covers the insurer may also impose a limit per claim or occurrence.

Aggregate method A prospective benefits funding method used to calculate contributions required to secure pension benefits. No standard contribution rate (qv) is determined. Instead a modified contribution rate is calculated as that which, if paid over the expected future membership of the active members (qv), would be sufficient, taking account of the actuarial value of assets (qv), to provide for the benefits. The modified contribution rate is also called the recommended contribution rate.

Aggregate monitoring System used by insurer or managing agent (qv) to record, monitor and control their total aggregate exposures by country of risk, class of business, years of exposure or other appropriate variable. For example, in the exempted classes of financial guarantee insurance (qv) Lloyd's calls upon managing agents to run systems that enable syndicates to avoid excessive exposure to any one obligor, industrial sector, location or insured nationality, in any one obligor country. The totals are regularly monitored to ensure that any limits are not exceeded.

Aggregate mortality table A table based on the rate of mortality according to age. No allowance is made for the duration of the insurance. Aggregate tables are used for the valuation of life contracts.

Aggregate retention The aggregate amount of risk retained by the insured, i.e. losses up to the level that are self-insured rather than assumed by an insurer.

Aggregation clause *See* CLAIMS SERIES CLAUSE.

'Agony of the moment'/the principle of alternative danger Where the defendant pleads contributory negligence (qv), the claimant's contribution to the accident may be excused if he acted 'in the agony of the moment'. In *Jones* v. *Boyce* (1816) the claimant, fearing that a fast-driven coach would overturn, broke his leg when jumping for safety. The coach did not overturn but his action was justified. The principle of 'alternative danger' applies to emergencies generally and may apply even when property is under threat.

Agreed return Marine insurer's clause agreeing to return a certain part of their premium in return for a subsequent improvement in the character of the risk or in respect of a reduction in their potential liability under the policy. For example, cargo may be carried by a safer route than the one initially contemplated.

Agreed value policy *See* VALUED POLICY (qv).

Agreed Values (aviation) Aviation insurers pay total losses on aircraft on an agreed value basis (qv) rather than on the basis of the replacement value of the aircraft taking account of its age and condition. The agreed value is also used as the basis of settling partial loss claims. Insurers normally allow an agreed value of 10 per cent more or less than the market value when arranging the cover.

Agricultural and forestry vehicles These vehicles, including trailers when attached, are separately rated and insured by motor insurers depending on the nature of the machine and its value.

Agricultural produce Stocks held by farmers. As values fluctuate the item is made subject to the *special condition of average* (qv).

AIDS (Acquired Immune Deficiency Syndrome) A disease that progressively weakens the immune system, making it impossible to combat infections. The causative agency is called *the human immunodeficiency virus* (HIV), which is transmitted in body fluids such as blood and semen. The onset of AIDS or having an HIV blood test has no effect on existing life policies. Having a test is not a bar to obtaining new life cover but anyone who has AIDS or is HIV positive will not in present circumstances be able to obtain cover. It is possible for medical personnel at risk of becoming infected by contact with patients or fluid specimens to arrange health care protection.

Air Accident Investigation Branch (AAIB) Part of the Department of Transport, Environment and the Regions, AAIB is responsible for the investigation of civil air accidents and serious incidents within the UK. AAIB's home page provides accident report procedures and the text of the Civil Aviation (Investigation of Air Accidents and Incidents) Regulations 1996 plus report bulletins. *www.aaib.dft.gov.uk.*

Air travel Travel as a fare-paying passenger with recognised airlines is not excluded under personal accident policies. Private flying is excluded, but cover can be specially arranged.

Air waybill The contract of carriage between a shipper and an air carrier. It serves the same purpose as a bill of lading (qv) on a vessel but is not a negotiable instrument.

Aircraft and waterborne craft exclusion Public liability policy exclusion ensuring that aviation and marine risks are not covered unwittingly. The exclusion is overridden in respect of any liability attaching to the insured arising out of business entertainment on or in craft belonging to others, or in hand-propelled boats. Work by the insured in or on aircraft or vessels (e.g. cleaning) should not normally be excluded.

Aircraft damage (aircraft or aerial devices) *See* AERIAL DEVICES.

Aircraft insurance Specified in paragraph 5 of Part I of Schedule 1 to the Regulated Activities Order (Contracts of general insurance) as the insurance upon aircraft or upon the machinery, tackle, furniture or equipment of aircraft.

Aircraft liability Specified in paragraph 5 of Part I of Schedule 1 to the Regulated Activities Order (Contracts of general insurance) as insurance against damage arising out of or in connection with the use of aircraft, including third party risks and carrier's liability.

Aircraft loss of use/aircraft unavailability Covers airlines for a pre-agreed daily amount in the event of the aircraft being out of use due to an 'intervening peril' (peril covered under hull all risks and war risks covers), but can extend to mechanical breakdown, groundings, air traffic control strikes, etc. Cover does not apply to total loss situations. Financiers may insist that cover is arranged to fund lease payments during periods of repair. Claims payments may be sufficient to help the insured meet other fixed costs. *See* TOTAL LOSS ONLY INSURANCE.

Aircraft repossession insurance Protects aircraft lessor against confiscatory acts (typically by the country of domicile of owner and/or country of registration) and inability to enforce possessory rights following a default under the lease. The insurance may be extended through a contingent war policy to cover damage to the aircraft whilst awaiting repossession.

Airline insurance Main policies are aviation hull all risks (qv) and aviation liability (qv). Other special forms of aviation insurance effected by airlines are: war risks; deductible insurance; unearned premium; mechanical breakdown; loss of use. Airlines also need a full range of non-marine policies covering ground property, vehicles, risks and liabilities related to ground operations. There are standard aviation wordings (*see* AVNIC) but most airlines have individual 'manuscript' wordings devised with brokers to reflect their particular circumstances. Premiums are based on 'own experience', regional and global airline experience, type of aircraft, route structure, passenger make-up and individual legal situations.

Airline Liability *See* WARSAW CONVENTION.

Airliner A large passenger aircraft plying in an airline on scheduled services over regular routes. Travel as a passenger on such aircraft is not normally excluded under personal accident insurance policies.

Airport owners' and operators' liability policy An aviation policy covering: 1. *Premises legal liability* to protect the insured against claims arising out of the use of his premises by third parties or passengers; 2. *Hangar-keepers' legal liability* in respect of the insured's liability as a bailee (qv) for aircraft and equipment on the ground; 3. *Products' legal liability* to cover the risk associated with servicing or repairing aircraft or sale of fuel; 4. '*Control tower liability*' is also covered. Cover can be extended to cover consequential loss following unexpected closure of the airport.

'Airside' Means being on the 'apron' of an airport making contact with aircraft possible. A motor insurer might in some circumstances exclude all liability from accidents while the insured vehicle is airside. In contract works insurance (qv) where the site of the work is at an airport, insurers will take a more stringent view of the work than the same work landside (no contact with aircraft).

Airworthiness Requirements Board (ARB) ARB advises the Civil Aviation Authority (qv) on 'design, construction, and maintenance of aircraft and all related matters'.

Airworthiness Warranty It is implied in all aviation policies that aircraft are maintained to specified standards following procedures laid down by the aircraft manufacturers in conjunction with the relevant civil aviation authority. The airline must keep maintenance records. Aircraft and engine manufacturers also specify the parameters for an aircraft's operation. If an airline breaches any of these requirements the policy may be invalidated.

ALARM (Association of Local Authority Risk Managers) ALARM assists, advises and represents public sector organisations in the development of risk management (qv) strategies. In collaboration with the Association of Insurance and Risk Managers (qv) and the Institute of Risk Management (qv) ALARM has developed a new Risk Management Standard (qv).

'Alarm system *in operation*' Policy may warrant that an *approved alarm system* (qv) be kept *in operation*. In *De Maurier (Jewels) Ltd* v. *Bastion Insurance Co. Ltd* and *Coronet Insurance Co. Ltd* (1967), a warranty in a jewellers' 'all risks' insurance stated 'alarms on road vehicles be kept *in operation* . . .' Held: 'in operation means the system must be switched on in circumstances where the user has reason to believe that switching it on makes it fully operative. It does not mean "fully operative". If, because of an unknown fault, it fails to operate there will be no breach of warranty by the insured.

Aleatory contract Any form of contract involving chance. Insurance contracts involve chance if they are of an aleatory nature, but the legal requirements as to insurable interest (qv) prevent them from being used for wagering.

Aligned member Corporate member of a Lloyd's syndicate under common control with the managing agent of that syndicate.

All-in policy An alternative name for an in and out insurance policy (qv).

All other contents clause A phrase in the basic specification wording of the standard fire policy to extend cover to forms of property otherwise excluded. The term includes money and stamps, national insurance stamps, documents, manuscripts and business books, computer systems records, patterns, moulds, plans and designs, employees' pedal cycles and personal effects. Monetary limits are usually applied to the majority of these items and cover in respect of plans, documents, etc., is limited to the cost of labour in writing them up and not their market values.

All other costs and expenses *See* OTHER COSTS AND EXPENSES (qv).

'All practicable steps' This means something 'possible of accomplishment regardless of cost but dependent on the state of knowledge at the time'. For example, regulations under the Health and Safety at Work Act 1974 provide that 'all practicable steps shall be taken to ensure that no person employed shall be in the space between any moving part of a self-acting spinning mule and any fixed part of the machine towards which it is traversing'. Compare with properly maintained (qv) and reasonably practicable (qv).

All risks A term describing a property insurance covering *any* fortuitous loss or damage that is not specifically excluded. This contrasts with a policy covering physical loss or damage caused by a named peril, e.g. fire. The 'all risks' exclusions relate to inevitable forms of loss, such as depreciation and wear and tear, and other losses due to gradually operating causes. 'All risks' cover is available for personal possessions, cameras, jewellery, industrial equipment and goods in transit, and applies to Institute Cargo Clauses A (qv). Under household and commercial policies on buildings and contents, and cover on motor vehicles, the term has given way to 'accidental loss or damage' as a means of going beyond named perils cover.

Allied perils Group of perils commonly added to a standard fire policy. They are otherwise called additional perils (qv), defined perils or special perils. They embrace dry perils (aircraft, explosion, riot, etc.), wet perils (storm, flood, burst pipes, etc;) and miscellaneous perils (impact, subsidence, etc).

Allocated capacity The part of a Lloyd's member's overall premium limit that is allocated to a syndicate in the relevant year of account (qv).

Allocated premium limit The limit as to the premiums that may be accepted on behalf of a Lloyd's underwriting member, i.e. Name (qv) or corporate member. It is expressed as the maximum permissible amount of a member's premium income which can be allocated to any year of account. *See* OVERWRITING OF PREMIUMS.

Allocation A directors' and officers' liability (qv) term dealing with the division of defence costs and loss payments when a claim is made against: (a) insured directors and officers *and* a non-covered entity such as the company; or (b) insured individuals in respect of covered *and* non-covered allegations. Some policies contain no express words dealing with the situation, while in others the insurer undertakes to use his 'best effort' to allocate defence costs proportionately between the insured individuals and the uninsured company. However, the modern tendency is for the insurer to advance 100 per cent of defence costs for both the company and the individual insureds. In the case of (b), where only part of the allegations are insured, the insurer usually seeks to 'negotiate in good faith' to secure a fair and equitable allocation of the loss taking account of the relative legal exposure of the parties. Disputes are referred to a QC.

Allocation of surplus The allocation and division of a life insurer's divisible surplus to shareholders and eligible policyholders (i.e. those holding with profits policies).

Allocation option Allows a pension scheme member to opt for a lower pension in return for a lifetime pension benefit for the member's wife, husband or dependants, if surviving at time of member's death. The member can exercise this option at the time the pension is taken. *See* OVERLAP.

Allocation rate The percentage of an investment in a financial product that is actually invested (e.g. 80 per cent) after initial charges have been taken into account.

Allotment of bonus The apportionment or division of a life office's surplus amongst its policyholders.

Allowable maximum *See* EARNINGS CAP.

Alternative accommodation clause (loss of rent). A clause in both household buildings and contents insurances to cover the insured if his home becomes uninhabitable due to insured damage. The buildings insurer will pay the reasonable cost of: any necessary alternative accommodation, loss of rent due to the insured and a maximum of two years ground rent for which the insured is liable, subject to a maximum of 10 per cent of the amount insured. The contents insurer covers the cost of alternative accommodation and rent payable by the insured up to 20 per cent of the sum insured.

Alternative basis clause A business interruption policy (qv) clause to provide the insured with an alternative basis for adjusting a claim when the interruption is short and the turnover method impractical. The practice is for the insurer and the loss adjuster (qv) to calculate the loss on a 'sales value of output' basis, provided that the lost output cannot be regained within the indemnity period. Insurers are sufficiently flexible in their approach to allow this practice to be adopted even if the clause is not included.

Alternative dispute resolution (ADR) A generic term meaning all methods of dispute resolution other than the court. ADR embraces: arbitration (qv), adjudication (qv), conciliation, early neutral evaluation, expert determination, executive tribunal (or mini-trial) or mediation (qv). ADR is actively encouraged as a part of the pre-action protocols in the Civil Procedure Rules (qv).

Alternative risk financing An ART (qv) term describing techniques that provide a funding source other than conventional (re)insurance to meet defined risks. The insured may seek to smooth his earnings over a period of years and seek committed funding to deal with prospective loss and/or secure post-loss funding. The insurer taking the risk combines discounted cashflow techniques with actuarial risk analysis. Techniques include: finite reinsurance (qv), financial reinsurance (qv) and contingent capital (qv).

Alternative risk transfer (ART) Generic phrase to denote various non-traditional forms of (re)insurance and techniques where risk is transferred to the capital markets. More broadly it refers to the *convergence* (qv) of (re)insurance, banking and capital markets. *See* FINANCIAL REINSURANCE; FINITE REINSURANCE; SECURITISATION; ALTERNATIVE RISK FINANCING; WEATHER DERIVATIVES. (See Figure 1).

Always open A term used in connection with open covers (qv) to signify that the insurance will remain continuously in force until ended by cancellation.

Ambiguity *See* CONTRA PROFERENTEM RULE.

American agency system Well-established US system under which insurance companies grant to independent contractors the right to effect all insurances and generally represent insurers in their areas or localities. The agents own the records and expirations of the policies issued through them.

American Bureau of Shipping A classification society (qv). It grants vessels their 'class' if the vessel meets the standards of

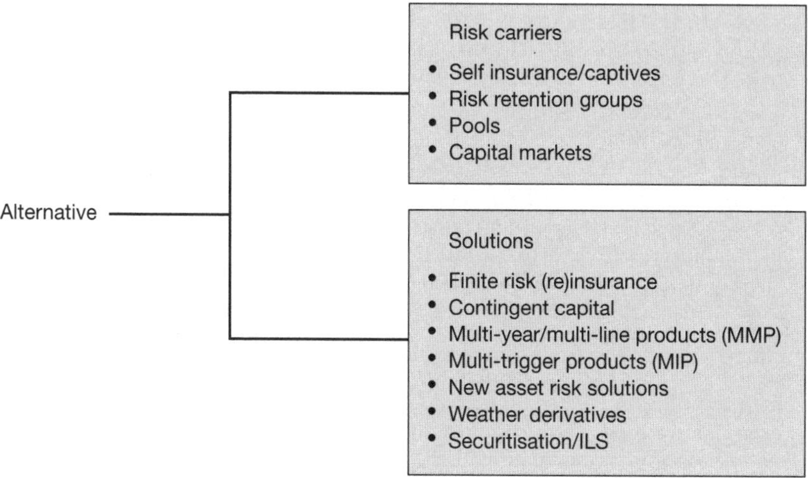

Figure 1. Classification of the ART market
Source: Swiss Re, sigma no. 1/2003

construction, material and workmanship, and maintenance to be certificated as 'seaworthy'. ABS publishes the RECORD, an alphabetical register of vessels with detailed information on construction, dimensions, etc.

American exposures Liability insurers regard any US exposure as material and therefore all known exposures should be disclosed. The exposure may arise through: (a) having employees and/or representation in the US; (b) products exported to the US; (c) US business trips. The concern has its origin in: (i) strict liability in many states; (ii) jury awards; (iii) an established contingent fee system (lawyers work on a 'no win, no fee' basis); (iv) punitive damages awards; (v) liberal interpretations of policies; (vi) reluctance to take contributory negligence into account.

American forms Marine policy forms and clauses that are the US equivalent of Institute Clauses (qv). They are approved and issued by the American Institute of Marine Underwriters (qv).

American Institute of Marine Underwriters A New York-based association of marine underwriters. They discuss problems common to their business and operate many technical committees that produce marine forms and clauses.

American trust fund A fund established in New York to hold all Lloyd's dollar premiums, whether originating in the US or not, and from which dollar claims are met. The fund, managed for Lloyd's underwriters by Citibank, makes Lloyd's one of the largest customers of one of the world's largest banks. Most of the fund is invested in US Treasury Bonds making Lloyd's one of the largest private investors in the US government.

Amortisation Periodical reduction in the value of a lease or other time-related asset until the asset is written down to nil. In insurance it is the ability to match the cost of cover to the actuarial probability of risk over time. Pension scheme actuaries spread an actuarial surplus (qv) or actuarial deficiency (qv) over an appropriate period.

Amount at risk The difference between the face value of a life policy and the mathematical reserve that has accrued. The net amount at risk declines throughout the duration of the contract while the reserve and its cash value increase. The amount at risk is the sum that an insurer would have to draw from its own funds rather than the policy reserve in the event of having to pay a claim for death.

Amounts made good The sums contributed as general average contributions (qv) to make good general average sacrifices. The allowances or amounts to be made good are formula-based to ensure equity in the adjustment. With expenditure, the amount made good is the expenditure itself.

Amounts paid in error Payment of a claim in error by an insurer is recoverable if the mistake is of a fact, but not if the payment is by mistake of law. Failure to deduct excesses or apply average are mistakes of fact and can be recovered.

Ancillary activities clause Support activities so closely related to the 'Business' of the insured that they are regarded as integral to it. The definition of 'Business' in liability policies extends to include ownership, maintenance and repair of premises, the provision and management of canteens, social, sports or welfare organisations for the benefit of employees and the insured's ambulance, first aid (excluding medical practitioners) and fire services. The *private work clause* brings in a non-business situation, i.e. cover applies to the execution of private work by employees for any director or senior official of the insured.

Ancillary risk For an insurer, authorised by the FSA to insure a principal risk under one of the *general classes of insurance* (qv), it means a risk included in another class that is connected with the principal risk. Ancillary risks can be insured (a) when concerned with the object covered against the principal risk, and (b) when included in the same policy covering the principal risk. However, risks arising under credit insurance, suretyship and legal expense insurance cannot be treated as ancillary risks but legal expenses cover is permitted as ancillary in travel policies, or when connected with the use of sea-going vessels.

And arrival In marine insurance practically all return premiums by agreement are 'and arrival'. This means that an underwriter will not be liable to pay the return unless the ship is safe *at expiry* of the policy.

Anglers' insurance Anglers insure their liability for accidents to the public, personal accident benefits for the anglers themselves and loss or damage to tackle up to a specified limit. Where the angler engages a gillie in the course of a business, employers' liability cover is compulsory. If the gillie is a 'domestic' employee, the liability section of the household contents policy applies.

Animals Act 1971 Provides that, where damage is caused by an animal of dangerous species (qv) the keeper, subject to exceptions, will be strictly liable. In the case of an animal of non-dangerous species (qv) the keeper will be liable for the damage that, to the keeper's knowledge, that particular animal is likely to cause (s.2). A trespasser cannot generally recover damages (s.5(3)). The keeper of a dog is strictly liable for killing or injuring livestock subject to certain defences.

Annexes clause The clause in a standard fire policy on buildings that brings outbuildings and the like within the scope of the cover.

Annual aggregate deductible A non-proportional reinsurance provision stipulating that the reinsured will retain, in addition to its retention per risk or per occurrence, an annual aggregate amount that would otherwise be recoverable from the reinsurer. The annual aggregate deductible is usually expressed as an amount or a percentage of the reinsured's subject premium for the period.

Annual aggregate limit *See* ANNUAL AGGREGATE DEDUCTIBLE.

Annual compliance review 1. All listed companies should conduct an annual review to confirm that the company, through its directors and officers, has followed sound practices in terms of corporate governance (qv). The directors must report on key risks facing the company and state how the risks are controlled or avoided. *See* TURNBULL REPORT (qv). 2. An annual review is also required of managing and members' agents at Lloyd's to demonstrate their commitment to, and achievement of, recognised compliance standards.

Annual pensions estimate/benefit statement Statement issued each year of the benefits a member has earned and, based on forecasts, it estimates the pension benefits at retirement age.

Annual percentage rate (APR) This is the official formula for measuring the price of money – the true interest rate. APR is the total credit cost expressed as an annual percentage rate of charge.

Annual premium method A method of determining the premiums payable under an insurance contract with the object of keeping the premium of each life insured or member of a pension scheme at a constant rate until there is a change in circumstances.

Annual return Financial statements that insurers must submit to the FSA after the end of the financial year in the prescribed format (volume 2 of IPRU (INS)). The returns are made up of: balance sheet and profit and loss account; general business revenue account and additional information; long-term business revenue account and additional information; abstract of the actuary's annual valuation report;

auditor's report under Companies Act 1985, s.235, for companies incorporated in the UK or the equivalent for companies not so incorporated. Certificates must accompany the report from the directors, the appointed actuary (qv) and the auditors. The returns must also include statements about major reinsurers and cedants, the company's policy on investing in derivatives (qv) and a statement of the controllers (qv) of the company. Companies engaging in cross-border EEA business must provide separate statistics on this business.

Annual solvency test Lloyd's carries out *two annual solvency tests.* 1. Lloyd's as a whole (as if a single insurance company) must demonstrate that the total eligible assets of members, coupled with centrally held assets such as the Lloyd's central fund (qv), exceed their liabilities by the required minimum margin (qv). 2. Lloyd's must also show that each member has sufficient assets to meet his liabilities and that any shortfall can be covered by centrally held assets. Also each *member's assets* must exceed its liabilities by the prescribed margin. This is the higher of 16 per cent of total annual premiums or 23 per cent of average claims, incurred over a three-year period, less a credit for reinsurance recoverables. Lloyd's must show that it has sufficient central assets to cover any aggregate shortfall from this test. *See* MEMBER'S MARGIN.

Annual turnover Defined in a business interruption policy (qv) as the turnover during the 12 months immediately before date of damage (where the indemnity period is for 12 months or less).

Annual venture Lloyd's practice of allocating a risk to the year in which it incepted, linked to the practice of syndicates reforming each year allowing members to leave or join. The syndicate underwriting the risk during the year of inception remains liable even though the year of insurance may straddle two years of account. The year of account is closed after 36 months by a *reinsurance to close* (qv). The annual venture approach will come to an end when Lloyd's introduce GAAP (qv) accounting; premiums will then be apportioned to particular calendar years with premiums for unexpired periods being carried forward.

Annuitant *See* ANNUITY.

Annuity A contract that provides an income to an *annuitant* for a specified term (an *annuity certain*) or for life (*life annuity*) in return for a series of contributions or a single premium. *Compulsory purchase annuities* (qv) are purchased at retirement on converting pension fund savings into a pension income. At death, there is usually no payment to the estate, although many annuities include a provision to pay an income to the spouse and some are *guaranteed annuities* (qv). *Immediate annuities* provide an income from the date of acceptance, and *deferred annuities* at a future date. Unless part of the investment risk is transferred to the annuitant (e.g. with-profits annuity), annuity business is non-profit business and is usually matched with fixed income investments. Longevity risk is an issue for insurance companies, and a possible source of losses if annuitants live longer than expected. *See* AGE 75 RULE; EXEMPT APPROVED PENSION SCHEMES; IMMEDIATE CARE ANNUITY.

Annuity deferral *See* INCOME DRAWDOWN; AGE 75 RULE.

Annuity taxation The taxation of annuity and pension payments. The annuitant (qv) is taxed on only that part of his or her annuity which is regarded as interest. The balance, a return of capital, is tax-free. Retirement annuities (pensions) are taxed as earned income, but part of the benefits can be commuted to a tax free lump sum, often used to purchase an immediate life annuity a part of which is a return of capital and therefore tax free.

Anti-selection *See* ADVERSE SELECTION.

'Any driver policy' A motor insurance policy that has no special restriction as to the persons entitled to drive. The standard car policy permits driving by the insured and any other person driving on his order or with his permission.

'Any member of the assured's household' An exclusion in *English* v. *Western* (1940) 2 All ER 515 was construed by the Court of Appeal as meaning 'any member of a household of which the insured is head'. The exclusion did not apply when a sister sued her brother for injuries. They were members of the same household but the brother was not its head. The Court applied the contra proferentem rule (qv).

Any one accident/event/cause/occurrence The definition of the conditions under which a reinsurer or insurer becomes liable for a loss or multiple related losses under an excess of loss treaty or underlying policy. Most definitions provide for the aggregation of individual losses arising from the same event or originating cause to be treated as a single claim so that the (re)insured bears only one deductible. Where weather-related losses persist over a period the *hours clause* (qv) defines the loss occurrence. Latent disease liability claims may produce multiple claims over a period due to continued exposure of workers to the same harmful working conditions. Insurers may seek (perhaps with difficulty) to define the continuing working conditions as the single event or originating cause. *See* CLAIMS SERIES CLAUSE.

'Any one occurrence' *See* ANY ONE ACCIDENT/EVENT, etc.

APF Exemptions *See* AUTHORISED PROFESSIONAL FIRM EXEMPTIONS.

Applicant's form The form used in fidelity guarantee insurance by the person, e.g. the employee, against whose dishonesty insurance is sought by the insured employer. The form elicits details of name, address, age, salary, present post within the firm and financial status of the employee. Details are also elicited about previous employment history and any previous guarantees.

Appointed actuary The person appointed to a company carrying out long-term business (qv) as required by the FSA (qv). The main statutory role of the appointed actuary is to carry out regular valuations (qv) of the insurer's reserves needed to meet future liabilities. He must also advise the board on actuarial matters, including the fair treatment of policyholders. The person appointed must hold a prescribed professional qualification. The FSA plans to change the role of the actuary and place more responsibility on directors. However, the FSA proposes a new required *actuarial function* headed by an individual to advise the directors, calculate the insurer's liabilities and liaise closely with the appointed actuary who, like the individual, will require *approved person status* (qv).

Appointed adviser A legal expenses insurances (qv) term meaning 'the solicitor, accountant, counsel or other expert appointed under the terms and conditions of the policy to represent the insured's interests'.

Appointed representative (AR) A firm that undertakes *regulated activities* (qv) as an agent for an *authorised person* (qv) and is therefore exempt from *authorisation* (qv). An AR can act for one principal (*single principal model)* for all regulated business. An AR with multiple principals is allowed only one principal for their investment business, both packaged (qv) and non-packaged policies, in regard to business with private customers (or equivalent). In regard to non-investment insurance (general insurance and pure protection) ARs are not restricted as to number of principals (i.e. product providers, intermediary or network). The principal takes responsibility for the AR's compliance with FSA rules. Multiple principals work together on issues potentially damaging to clients via a *multiple principal agreement* with one taking the 'lead' for customer complaints. When an individual becomes an AR in regard to investment products he also becomes a financial adviser (qv). *See* APPOINTED PERSON REGULATIONS; APPOINTED REPRESENTATIVE ACTIVITIES; INTRODUCER APPOINTED REPRESENTATIVES.

Appointed representative activities ARs are permitted to carry on the following regulated activities: *arranging (*bringing about) deals in relevant investments, including general insurance and pure protection; *making arrangements* with a view to the foregoing deals; giving *advice* (qv) on such deals; *agreeing* to carry on any of the regulated activities. General insurance ARs may also deal as agents in relation to a contract of general insurance and assist in the performance or administration of such a contract.

Appointed Representative Regulations Full title: The Financial Services and Markets Act 2000 (Appointed Representatives) Regulations 2001 (SI 2001/1217). They describe the business for which appointed representatives (qv) are exempt and set out the requirements that apply to contracts between authorised persons (qv) and appointed representative (*www.hmso.gov.uk/si/si/2001/20011217.htm*)

Apportionable annuity A life annuity under which the annuity is payable up to the date of death of the annuitant (qv), i.e. payment is made on a pro rata basis for the period between the last regular payment and the date of death. Under an annuity curtate, no account is taken of this period as the annuity terminates on the last payment date preceding death.

Apportionment and oversight function The FSA *controlled function* (qv) of acting in the capacity of director or senior manager responsible for either or both the apportionment function and the oversight function. The function entails the allocation of significant responsibilities among senior managers and overseeing the establishment and maintenance of the firm's systems and controls. Where there is a chief executive he/she must be one of the individuals appointed unless the functions are allocated to someone more senior.

Apportionment of value In cargo insurances different species may be insured under a single valuation. In a partial loss of cargo the insurer is liable for such proportion of the insured value as the insurable value of the part lost bears to the insured value as a whole (Marine Insurance Act 1906, s.72). In practice, the apportionment of the insured value is normally based on the invoiced value of the various goods.

Appropriate personal pension (APP) A personal pension plan (qv) approved by the Occupational Pensions Board (qv) for the purpose of contracting out of the state second pension (qv). The plan receives contributions from the Inland Revenue National Insurance Contributions Office. This Office will only contribute to one APP for a person at any time.

Appropriate personal pension stakeholder pension (APPSHP) The stakeholder version of an approved personal pension (qv).

Appropriate scheme A personal pension plan or FSAVC (qv) granted an *appropriate scheme certificate* (qv) that has met the conditions for contracting out of the state second pension (qv).

Approval The granting of tax exempt status by the Inland Revenue Savings, Pensions and Share Schemes Office to pension arrangements that meet the legislative requirements. Members will then be able to set all or part of their pension contributions against their income tax liability. Schemes meeting certain conditions get mandatory (automatic) approval (qv) while in other cases discretionary approval (qv) may be given. Most occupational schemes are *exempt approved schemes.*

Approval categories Following changes made in 1987 and 1989 Inland Revenue approval of pension schemes falls into three different categories of membership: Class A (qv); Class B (qv); Class C (qv). New schemes may only be approved under the 1989 rules following the Finance Act of that year.

Approved alarm systems Household contents insurers may give discounts to insureds who install and maintain an intruder alarm approved by NACOSS – the National Approval Council for Security Systems. It is common practice in commercial policies to include an intruder alarm warranty requiring the installation and maintenance of a NACOSS approved alarm. The alarm system has to be kept *in operation* (qv).

'Approved merchandise or H/C' Merchandise approved by an insurer for cover under an open cargo policy on the terms and conditions agreed. Other goods are 'held covered' subject to the payment of an additional premium.

Approved occupations/recognised occupations IR list of occupations (e.g. professional footballers, jockeys) whose members can receive a pension prior to age 50, e.g. the lowest age, 35 for footballers, reflects short careers.

Approved packing Packaging meeting the packaging industry standards of sufficient design and construction to protect the cargo from the normal hazards expected during the intended voyage. This includes hazards associated with normal domestic handling and storage from point of origin to final destination.

Approved pension scheme *See* APPROVED SCHEME.

Approved person A person upon whom the FSA has conferred approved person status, allowing them to undertake a controlled function (qv), having passed the *fitness and propriety test* (FIT). Approved persons must abide by the Statement of Principles and Code of Practice for Approved Persons. *See* SIGNIFICANT INFLUENCE (*www.fsa.gov.uk*).

Approved policy 1. An employers' liability policy that does not contain *prohibited conditions* (qv), i.e. certain conditions allowing an insurer to repudiate a claim. This does not preclude a condition allowing the insurer to reclaim from any employer any amounts paid by the insurer following injury to an employee when a condition, otherwise prohibited, has been breached. The prohibited conditions are set out in the Employers' Liability (Compulsory Insurance) Regulations 1998. 2. The term is also used in contracts that impose an obligation to insure one of the parties to the effect that the policy has to be approved by the party imposing the obligation.

Approved repairers Motor vehicle garages listed by motor insurers as having been approved by them for the purpose of repairing damage. The insurer secures improved terms and streamlines its administrative procedures in return.

Approved scheme Retirement benefits scheme approved by the IR under ICTA 1988, Chapter I, Part XIV, including an FSAVC scheme. The term also applies to personal pension schemes or occupational pension schemes approved under Chapter IV. Approval is given when the scheme is: established under an irrevocable trust; the administrator and the company are in the UK; the employer pays at least 10 per cent of total contributions; contributions and benefits are within IR limits (qv); cash commutation must not exceed three-eightieths of the final remuneration for each year of service; the maximum retirement benefit cannot exceed the one-sixtieth accrual rate (qv); the eligible employees must be given written notice of the scheme's terms and conditions. The strict conditions cause most employers to seek the greater flexibility of exempt approved schemes (qv).

'Approved vessel or H/C' A vessel deemed adequate to carry the insured cargo at the agreed rate of premium. In the American market a cargo-carrying vessel over 1,000 net registered tons and under 20 years of age is approved by insurers to carry cargo without additional premium. The London market uses a different standard. Where the vessel is not approved, the risk is held covered (H/C) subject to payment of an additional premium.

Arbitrage Financial transaction involving the simultaneous purchase and sale of identical or equivalent financial instruments in different markets in order to profit from price differences. Per-transaction profit is small but financial institutions such as banks and (re)insurers enter into large transactions at relatively low costs.

Arbitration An alternative to going to court for the settlement of a dispute. An independent arbitrator hears the case and makes an award in accordance with the Arbitration Act 1996. *See* ALTERNATIVE DISPUTE RESOLUTION.

Arbitration clause A policy condition that commits the insured and the insurer to use arbitration as a means of settling disputes as to the amount of a claim liability otherwise being admitted. The clause does not appear in liability policies.

Architects', surveyors' and consulting engineers' fees These fees are covered when relating to insured property damage either by making due allowance in the sum insured or by a special item. The fees are payable for plans, specifications, etc., and general supervision of rebuilding in the event of fire or other insured perils. Increasing the buildings sum insured by 12.5 per cent and the machinery sum insured by 7.5 per cent often provides cover, but insureds with very large sums insured may insure the fees on a first loss basis (qv). Fees paid by the insured for preparing the claim are not covered.

Armoured car insurance Covers loss of customers' money carried in armoured cars and physical loss or damage to customers' property whilst on insured premises, in transit, on a pavement or at an automatic telling machine. Underwriting and rating takes account of: premises to be insured; company's history; five-year loss history; number of armoured vehicles; physical security measures applied to vehicles and premises; annual revenue figures; estimated value of cash to be carried during year.

Arranged total loss/comprised total loss Marine term describing a settlement agreed between the insurer and the insured where the cost of carrying out repairs is uneconomical nothwithstanding that the cost is less than the full insured value. When appropriate the principle is also adopted in other forms of property insurance.

Arranging deals in investments A regulated activity order which means making arrangements for another person (as principal or agent) to buy, sell, subscribe for or underwrite a particular investment which is: a designated investment (qv), funeral plan contract, underwriting capacity of a Lloyd's syndicate, a pure protection contract, general insurance contract or rights to or interests in particular investment categories.

Arranging insurance Defined in the Financial Services and Markets Act 2000 (Regulated Activities) Order 2001 as 'arranging for a person to enter a particular insurance contract with an insurer [and] making arrangements with a view to another person, who takes part in these arrangements, buying an unspecified insurance contract'. 'Arranging insurance' is distinguished from *intro-*

ducing insurance. The FSA decides case by case what constitutes 'introducing'. Those who arrange insurance will be regulated by the FSA in 2005. *See* INTRODUCER APPOINTED REPRESENTATIVES.

Arrests, restraints and detainments 'Arrests, restraints and detainments of all kings, princes and people, of what nation, condition, or quality whatsoever' are defined in the Rule for Construction of the Policy (No. 10) as referring to political or executive acts, and not including a loss caused by riot or by ordinary judicial process. As goods were held to be lost when they could not be forwarded to their destination because of these perils (e.g. siege of a city), insurers introduced the frustration clause (qv), the effect of which is to relieve the insurer of liability for a claim based on 'arrests' etc.

Arrival, arrived (arrd.) A note on a report or claim to indicate that the vessel has completed the voyage or part-voyage, or cargo has reached its destination after the transit covered by the policy. Sometimes the term is used colloquially to refer to the successful completion, with no loss or claim, of a non-marine cover.

Arrived damage value The depreciated value of cargo on arrival at the place where the voyage terminates following damage in transit. A formula is used to establish the percentage depreciation.

Arrived sound value Gross wholesale value after freight, import charges, duty, etc., to represent the value that cargo would have had if it had arrived safely at the place where the adventure ended.

Arson The criminal act of setting fire to property deliberately. The resultant damage is covered by a fire policy unless the insured is the arsonist.

Arson Prevention Bureau (APB) Funded by the ABI, APB coordinates a national campaign to reduce arson (qv), raise awareness of the problem and bring together private and public sector organisations sharing these objectives. APB is an active member of the government's Arson Control Forum. The Bureau also, inter alia, gives guidance on best practice arson investigation and prevention. *www.arsonpreventionbureau.org.uk.*

ART *See* ALTERNATIVE RISK TRANSFER.

Art Loss Register A computerised art index set up to log stolen works of art and compare their description against auction catalogues world-wide.

Articles of Association Document setting out the internal regulations and bye-laws of a company. It covers procedures, shares, meetings, directors and other administrative issues. The document is deposited with the Registrar of Companies. Alternatively the company can elect to be bound by one of the model conditions (Table A is commonly chosen) that form part of the Companies Acts (1985 and 1989). The 'contract' that directors have with their company is based on the Articles. *See* DIRECTORS' AND OFFICERS' LIABILITY.

As expiry A term that indicates that an insurance should, on expiry, be renewed on its pre-expiry terms.

'As is where is' The terms under which property, e.g. salvage (vessel or cargo), is sold, meaning that it is to be sold at its present location and in its present condition without warranty as to quality or quantity. *See* SALVAGE VALUE.

'As original' Term that denotes that a reinsurance contract will follow the underlying risk. It does not mean following the insurance terms and conditions in their entirety. 'As original' serves to define the risk (e.g. period of cover, geographical limits, the nature) so that reinsurers and insurers face exactly the same risk (*Pine Top* v. *Unione Italiana Anglo Saxon*). There is a presumption against incorporation into the reinsurance contract of collateral clauses (e.g. jurisdiction clause) from the underlying contract. However, the term is presumed to make warranties as significant to the reinsurance policy as to the insurance contract (*Groupama Navigation et Transport & Others* v. *Caiaiumbo CA Seguros*).

Asbestos Any of the fibrous amphibole and serpentine minerals, especially chrysolite and tremolite that are incombustible and resistant to chemicals. It was formerly widely used in the form of fabric or board as a heat-resistant structural material. Inhalation of asbestos fibres can cause asbestosis (qv) or mesothelioma (qv). *See* CONTROL OF ASBESTOS AT WORK REGULATIONS 2002.

Asbestos surveys Under the Control of Asbestos at Work Regulations 2002 (qv), owners of non-domestic premises contemplating major refurbishment or demolition must arrange a survey sufficient to become alerted to any asbestos that may be disturbed. Guidance on what constitutes a survey is in HSE document MDHS 100.

Asbestosis A characteristic fibrotic condition of the lungs caused by inhalation of asbestos dust or fibres. The disease makes breathing difficult and is often fatal after being latent for between 20 and 40 years. Sometimes the term is used to include all asbestos-related diseases, e.g. mesothelioma (qv) intersitial pulmonary fibrosis and bronchial or laryngeal carcinomas. The disease produces long-tail liability claims (qv) in employers' liability insurance and in public liability. *See* TRIPLE TRIGGER THEORY.

Assessmentism Alternative term for 'pay as you go', a method of calculating life insurance risk premiums on a year-by-year basis. Each premium reflects the chance that the policyholder will die in the following year plus an allowance for expenses. It is suitable where term (temporary) insurance (qv) is purchased on a year-by-year basis, e.g. as group life cover (qv). The influx of new members helps to stabilise the overall annual cost. The level annual premium system (qv) is more appropriate for individual lives.

Asset allocation strategy The way in which the assets of a pension fund are distributed across a range of alternative investments, such as equities, fixed interest securities or cash. The strategy is based on the fund's long-term needs but shifts towards particular assets may occur to take advantage of short-term opportunities.

Asset-backed securities Debt securities that depend on a pool of underlying assets. In *alternative risk transfer* (qv) they refer to insurance-linked securities. *See* INSURITISATION; SECURITISATION.

Asset identification rules An insurer has to identify assets belonging to him that he maintains for a particular aspect of his business, e.g. separate funds for long-term business. The UK Treasury is empowered to pass regulations that prevent unauthorised parent undertakings of insurers, or others specified by the Treasury, from doing anything (e.g. payment of dividends or creation of charges) that lessens the effectiveness of the asset identification rules (FMSA s.142 (1)(2)).

Asset/liability matching Pensions term where the aim is to invest in assets likely to generate the cash flow needed to meet the liabilities of the scheme as they occur under varying economic conditions.

Asset valuation rules Special rules governing the way in which insurance company assets should be valued for the purpose of government returns and matters relating to solvency. Assets representing long-term funds are separated from those representing general business funds. Further sub-divisions are required. The basic rules call for 'break up values' and not, as is the case with ordinary commercial companies, 'going concern' figures. In this context no value can be placed on goodwill. *See* ADMISSIBILITY; ASSET/LIABILITY MATCHING.

Assets Cash, investments and property owned by insurance companies and other entities. They include equity investments, bonds, property, money owed by debtors (if collectable) and anything else with a monetary value. FSA regulations require insurers to put a conservative value on their admissible assets (qv).

Assigned risk A US term to describe a risk that is not ordinarily acceptable to insurers and therefore by law is assigned to an insurer participating in an assigned risk pool or plan. Each insurer in the pool accepts its share of all of the pooled risks.

Assignee The party to whom a policy is assigned, i.e. transferred. He may be an assignee for value, or a voluntary assignee to whom the policy has been assigned by way of gift. The term assignee also applies to the party to whom a lease on premises is transferred. *See* ASSIGNOR'S LEASEHOLD LIABILITY INSURANCE.

Assignment Transfer of a policy from one person to another. Generally, the insurer's consent is required as insurance contracts are personal contracts (qv). Marine policies are freely assignable unless expressly prohibited as in the case of hulls. Cargo changes hands and it is desirable that the cargo policy is assignable with the goods. The Policies of Assurance Act 1867 (qv) makes the insurer's consent unnecessary in life insurance, but the assignee has no right to sue the insurer unless written notice of the assignment has been given. Assignment of a life policy changes its ownership but not the identity of the life insured.

Assignment by operation of the law The assignment of rights and obligations under a contract, which arises automatically by operation of the law without the consent of either party to the contract (e.g. on death or in the event of bankruptcy).

Assignor The party who transfers (i.e. assigns) his rights in a policy, property or rights to another party called the Assignee (qv).

Assignor's leasehold liability insurance Covers ongoing liability of a tenant to a landlord after assigning the lease. The outgoing tenant, i.e. the assignor, may be liable to the landlord for defaults by the new tenant. The standard policy is premises-specific and is for one year, but up to three years can be arranged. Cover is in respect of liability to pay rent, interest on rent and damages and claimant's costs and 'own costs'. There is an annual aggregate limit of indemnity in the range £50,000 to £500,000. The underwriter assesses the lease, the assignment, the financial history of the new tenant and references.

Assisting An FSA regulated activity in so far as it relates to the administration and performance of insurance policies. It includes helping policyholders make insurance claims, such as notifying a claim to an insurer and negotiating the settlement on behalf of the policyholder.

Associated employers Two or more closely associated employers who are allowed to participate in the same pension scheme arrangements. An employee who transfers from one company to another company associated in this is treated as having had continuous service (qv).

Associated employments Where a person has worked for more than one of the associated employers (qv). This means that the service and salary of that person are amalgamated for pension purposes.

Associateship of the Chartered Insurance Institute (ACII) The ACII designation is available to CII (qv) members who have successfully completed the Advanced Diploma in Insurance qualification (qv). (*www.cii.co.uk*).

Association captive Captives (qv) that underwrite the risks of members of an industry or trade association.

Association of Average Adjusters An association of independent practitioners. It sets examinations for those engaged in marine insurance as average adjusters (qv). Founded in 1869, it promotes the 'correct principles in the adjustment of Averages and uniformity among Average Adjusters'. The association's expert committees serve the marine insurance community, and may, by a panel of referees, act as arbitrators in the case of dispute. All members are practising average adjusters. *See also* UK SOCIETY OF UK AVERAGE ADJUSTERS.

Association of British Insurers (ABI) The trade association for insurance companies, whose 400 members transact 95 per cent of the business of UK insurers. It speaks out on issues of common interest, participates in debates on public policy issues and promotes high standards of service. Its policy work centres on: general insurance, life and pensions, financial regulation, taxation and investment affairs. It has expert committees and represents the industry externally, involving central government, media affairs, European and international activities. (*www.abi.org.uk*).

Association of Independent Financial Advisers (AIFA) Trade association for independent financial advisers (IFAs). It is the key point of contact between the IFA community and the FSA (qv). AIFA's principal objective is to influence the nature and shape of policies affecting its members. It also monitors the regulatory and political issues and keeps members informed as to how those issues will affect them.

Association of Insurance and Risk Managers (AIRMIC) A forum for the exchange of data and opinion between insurance and risk managers in industry and commerce. AIRMIC has over 160 corporate members and nearly 1,000 individual members. It updates members on technical matters and current practice. It promotes the understanding of the nature and purpose of risk management and represents a body of informed opinion in dealings with trade and market associations and with government. In 2002 AIRMIC collaborated with ALARM (qv) and the Institute of Risk Managers (qv) to produce a new Risk Management Standard (qv).

Association of Lloyd's Members A company formed to improve the understanding of Lloyd's amongst its members and prospective members.

Association of Run Off Companies (ARC). 'Not for profit' organisation run for, and by, its membership. ARC began in 1998 as an informal talking shop helping companies manage the tail of their insurance and reinsurance operations in the London Insurance Market. It now has a formal structure, and an active agenda providing information of relevance to its members, colleagues, partners and clients. (*www.aroc.org.uk*).

Association of Unit Trusts and Investment Funds Trade body of unit trusts and investment management companies.

Assumed/Inward Reinsurance Reinsurance underwritten by Lloyd's syndicates and insurance companies, for other syndicates and UK and overseas insurance companies.

Assumed portfolio *See* PREMIUM PORTFOLIO; LOSS PORTFOLIO.

Assurance Means an insured event that is certain to happen, e.g. in an endowment policy (qv), the life assured will either survive the policy term or die within it. In contrast insurance is taken to mean events, e.g. road accidents that may or may not happen to the individual. The terms have often been used interchangeably although insurance is now the main term.

Assured Means the same as insured but is most commonly used in life and marine business.

Assurer Means the same as insurer, but is most commonly used in life business.

Atomic Energy Authority A government body which, with its licensees, incurs a strict liability for injury, loss or damage arising from the operation of nuclear establishments. *See* NUCLEAR PERILS.

Attach In regard to the policy it means its inception, i.e. coming into force. In regard to legal liability, liability attaches when a party is legally responsible for some injury, loss or damage to a third party.

Attachment date/inception date The date on which the risk attaches, i.e. begins to run.

Attachment point The point at which the liability of an excess layer insurer or re-insurer is triggered. The reinsured may carry losses up to £1m with the reinsurer carrying the excess up to £3 million. £1 million is the attachment point, otherwise called the excess point.

Attained age method A prospective benefits funding method (qv) for pension schemes in which the actuarial liability makes allowance for projected earnings. The standard contribution rate is the rate that, if payable over the expected future membership of the active members (qv), would generate their expected benefits related to future service. The value of their future service is treated as the difference between the value of total benefits and the value of past benefits calculated by the project unit method. This means that the attained age method and the projected unit method have the same actuarial liability but different standard contribution rates.

Attendance expense cover A form of cover available under legal expenses cover and certain liability policies. It provides a financial benefit to defray the cost of time lost by the insured and employees having to attend court or tribunal as defendants or witnesses on behalf of the insured. The amount payable is based on a stated fraction (e.g. a 250th part of the person's annual salary) for each day's absence or is a fixed amount per day.

Attestation clause/signature clause The final part of a policy signed by certain officers of the insurance company according to the Deed of Settlement or Memorandum and Articles of Association by which the company is constituted and business transacted. Also known as the Signature Clause.

Auditors' charges *See* ACCOUNTANTS' CLAUSE.

Augmentation Provision of additional benefits for particular members of an occupational pension scheme. The cost normally falls on the employer.

Authorised insurer A firm with FSA permission to effect and carry out insurance contracts (other than a bank). *See* AUTHORISATION.

Authorised person A person who has been authorised by the FSA to have a Part IV permission of the FSMA to undertake one or more of the regulated activities. Persons must meet the threshold conditions (qv) detailed in the Threshold Conditions Manual. Insurance applicants must be a body corporate excluding limited liability partnerships, registered friendly societies or members of Lloyd's (qv).

Authorised professional firm (APF) Professional firm that is an authorised person (qv) and therefore has a Part IV permission from the FSA (qv) to carry on one or more regulated activities (qv). When undertaking non-mainstream regulated activity (qv), APF exemptions (qv) apply.

Authorised professional firm (APF) exemptions The disapplications and modifications of the FSA's Handbook that apply in respect of APFs when undertaking non-mainstream regulated activity (qv).

Authorised unit trust *See* UNIT TRUST.

Automatic escalation clause *See* ESCALATION CLAUSE; INDEX-LINKING.

Automatic personal accident cover *See* ADMITTED LIABILITY INSURANCE.

Automatic reinstatement clause Also called a self-renewing clause. A clause under which the sum insured or limit of indemnity is automatically restored to its original level following a claim.

Average 1. In *non-marine property insurance* if a sum insured is 'subject to average', and the sum insured is less than the value at risk at the time of loss, the claim will be reduced in the same proportion. The measure combats underinsurance. Agricultural products and ecclesiastical property are subject to the *special condition of average* (the 75 per cent condition) as values fluctuate or are difficult to assess. If the sum insured is 75 per cent or more than the value at the time of loss no deduction is made for partial losses. The *two conditions of average* applies where property (e.g. A) is insured under both a specific policy *and* a more general policy covering property that includes additional property (e.g. A, B and C) under an inclusive sum insured. The first condition is *pro rata average* while the second is initially 'non-contribution', i.e. the more specific insurance pays first, leaving only any uninsured balance to be recovered under the general policy on the basis of pro rata average. *See* also REINSTATEMENT AVERAGE; DAY ONE AVERAGE; FIRST LOSS POLICIES. 2. In *marine insurance* 'average' means 'loss' in different ways, notably *general average* (qv) and *particular average* (qv) but the non-marine approach is also used. A cargo claim is based on the percentage of depreciation calculated by comparing the actual damaged value at destination with the actual sound value at destination and applying this percentage to the agreed insured value (Marine Insurance Act 1906, s.71). *See* WITH AVERAGE; FREE OF PARTICULAR AVERAGE.

Average adjuster Impartial specialist entrusted by the shipowner with the adjustment of general average losses. In practice adjusters handle all types of marine claims sometimes excepting straightforward cargo claims. Underwriters pay the adjuster's fee when they are liable for the claim. If no liability attaches, the adjuster waives his fee. *See* ASSOCIATION OF AVERAGE ADJUSTERS (qv).

Average agreement *See* GENERAL AVERAGE BOND.

Average/average clauses (marine) *See* AVERAGE 2.

Average disbursements *See* GENERAL AVERAGE EXPENDITURE.

Average earnings scheme A pension scheme where the benefit for each year of membership is related to the pensionable earnings for that year.

'Average irrespective of percentage' Marine insurance term meaning that loss or damage due to an insured peril can be claimed in full without a franchise having been reached or a deductible applied.

Average rate insurances When dealing with very large risks, fire insurers may charge a flat rate for all buildings and contents. The rate – an 'average' – is presumed to take account of the good and bad features of each risk. Contrary to the practice with blanket policies (qv) separate sums insured are set against each separate risk.

Average temperature/average daily temperature The average of the maximum temperature (Tmax) and minimum temperature (Tmin) for a given day as defined 12.00 a.m. to 12.00 p.m. The average temperature is compared with the reference temperature (qv) of a weather derivative (qv) each day.

Average temperature contract A weather derivative (qv) whose payout is based on a deviation from the average temperature for a given period, e.g. summer of 2003. This single measure contract contrasts with payouts based on the cumulative deviations centred on cooling degree days (qv) and heating degree days (qv).

Aviation hazard/risk Risk of death/injury due to participation in aeronautics other than as a fare-paying passenger in licensed aircraft. The risk is excluded from personal accident policies (qv) but cover can be arranged. Aircraft personnel obtain cover in the aviation department.

Aviation Hull All Risks Insurance Insurance covering 'all risks' of loss or damage to an aircraft subject to exclusions. There is no cover for grounding due to directives from the relevant authority or the manufacturer's directives, or consequential loss of income. The main exclusions are as follows: radioactive contamination/nuclear causes; war and allied perils (strikes, hijacking, sabotage, terrorism, confiscation, etc.); wear and tear; mechanical breakdown (i.e. fixing the broken part but not damage due to accidents caused by the breakdown); progressive damage. There are standard deductibles, e.g. $1 million for 'wide-bodied' aircraft. Geographical limits may apply. *See* AVIATION HULL WAR AND ALLIED PERILS INSURANCE.

Aviation hull deductible insurance policy Insures the amount an airline has at risk as a result of its hull policy deductible. Cover applies up to the deductible level, so it becomes an insurance of the actual deductible, subject to a small deductible itself. The intention is to cover ingestion damage to engines by foreign objects but it also covers damage to landing gear and fuselage. The policy follows the overlying hull 'all risks' cover subject to an annual aggregate limit.

Aviation hull war and allied perils insurance Covers aircraft damage resulting from the war and allied perils that are excluded under *aviation all risks insurance* (qv). The principal exclusions are as follows: nuclear war; war between five major powers (UK, US, France, Russian Federation, China); confiscation, seizure due to debt, failure to provide a bond or other financial causes; repossession or attempt thereat. Geographical limits may apply. War policies for large fleets attract an overall annual aggregate limit. The policies are not usually subject to a deductible.

Aviation insurance The main policies are: 1. *AVN1C 21/12/98* (qv). 2. *Aerial form* – an airport owners' and operators' liability policy (qv). 3. *Air displays policy* – principally a public liability (qv) policy for promoters of air meetings and displays. 4. *Cargo policy.* An 'all risks' cover that, like a voyage policy, runs from start to finish and is not confined solely to the air travel part of the journey. 5. *Deductible policy. See* AVIATION HULL DEDUCTIBLE INSURANCE; DEDUCTIBLES. 6. *Loss of licence policy.* Compensates commercial pilots who lose their flying licence or suffer suspension for medical reasons. Cover can be standalone or added to other policies. 7. *Loss of use policy.* Covers loss of earnings when an aircraft is laid-up following accidental damage. 8. *Personal accident insurance.* Group personal accident cover can be arranged for both passengers and aircraft crew. Policies are effected by employers for their aircrew whose income is at risk through being 'grounded' by an accident. Policies effected by individual travellers for their own protection are often arranged in the accident department or by admitted liability personal accident insurance (qv) in the aviation department. 9. *Satellite (or space) insurance* (qv) is another development.

Aviation Insurance Offices Association (AIOA) Promotes and protects the interests of UK aviation insurance companies. It provides a means of consultation and cooperation when drawing up standard policy and clause wordings in association with other aviation insurance interests at home or overseas.

Aviation legal liability insurance Covers operator's liability to passengers, passengers' baggage, cargo, mail and third parties plus legal defence costs. Airlines normally extend cover to include 'personal injury' claims defined as false arrest, malicious prosecution, invasion of privacy, discrimination, slander/false advertising and medical malpractice. Cover can extend to liability arising from war perils, excepting nuclear risks and war between major powers. Deductibles apply only to baggage and cargo claims. Cover in respect of noise, seepage and pollution is restricted. Exclusions include fines, flight delays, liability to pilots/crew and 'own' property.

Aviation mechanical breakdown insurance Covers operating loss due to breakdown of engine as excluded under *aviation hull all risks* (qv) and *spares insurances* (qv). The need for cover is mitigated if a strong manufacturer's warranty applies. Financiers may compel small airlines to insure this risk.

Aviation unearned premium insurance (UPI) Following an aircraft total loss, unpaid instalment premiums become payable in full. UPI covers the pro rata premium for the unexpired term. Cover can be included under aviation hull policies (qv).

AVN1C 21/12/98 The London Aircraft Insurance Policy used worldwide, except by large airline insurances (qv) who use 'manuscript' policies. Cover under the 98 form: (a) accidental loss/damage (including disappearance), emergency safety expenses; (b) legal liability to third parties excluding passengers; (c) legal liability to passengers excluding the employer's liability risk. There are section-specific exclusions and general exclusions. *See* AVIATION HULL ALL RISKS; AVIATION LEGAL LIABILITY INSURANCES.

Avoidance of certain terms and rights of recovery Clause in motor insurance and employers' liability policies compulsory insurances (Road Traffic Act and Employers' Liability (Compulsory Insurance) Act 1969). The legislation restricts the right of insurers to rely upon breaches of certain policy conditions to avoid a claim. The conditions mainly relate to matters that should or should not be done by the insured after the event, e.g. giving proper notice and not admitting liability. The insurer is entitled to recover his loss from the insured where payment is made solely because of the legislation. *See* APPROVED POLICY; PROHIBITED CONDITIONS.

Award in Insurance *See* FOUNDATION INSURANCE TEST.

B

Back-dating Occurs when a policy is expressed as operating from a date before final agreement has been reached on its terms. Cover begins before the date cover is issued and will cover any losses in the intervening period. It is illegal to backdate compulsory motor insurance, but acceptable in life insurance where the insured may wish to date from his previous birthday or other specific date.

Back-service The period of previous service in employment with which a new member of a company pension scheme can be credited.

Back-to-back arrangement A combination of an annuity (qv) and whole life policy (qv) on the same life whereby a single payment purchases the annuity, the instalments from which pay the whole life premiums. The annuity purchase reduces the purchaser's estate, but the life policy proceeds paid on death are tax-free and replace the initial single payment. Life premiums payable out of normal income are an exempt transfer and therefore exempt from inheritance tax.

Back-to-back cover Occurs where the terms and conditions of a primary insurance policy match those of its counterpart reinsurance policy. There is a presumption that facultative reinsurance (qv) is back-to-back with the original insurance (*Vesta* v. *Butchers and Others*). It is also presumed that proportional reinsurances are back-to-back with the insurance policies, but this is not true of excess of loss treaties. Where by express terms the risk presented to the reinsurer is materially different from that assumed by the reinsured, there is no presumption of back-to-back cover (*Gan Insurance and Another* v. *Tai Ping*).

Back Up Policy/Layer An excess of loss (qv) layer that provides for further reinstatements of cover after the exhaustion of the automatic reinstatements of the original contract. The policy defines which basic contracts come within its scope and how many reinstatements (qv) they contain. *Top and drop* (qv) is a development of the back up layer, but the reinsured who relies upon it runs the risk that the top layer may have been exhausted by earlier calls upon it.

Bad debts insurance *See* CREDIT INSURANCE.

Baggage insurance 'All risks' cover on personal effects and luggage generally insured under travel insurance policies (qv).

Bail bond Guarantees the appearance of a person in court enabling them to be released on bail. If the person fails to appear, the 'bondsman' pays the amount of the bond to the court. Spain requires visiting motorists to provide bail bonds from their insurers as a means of ensuring that funds will be available to meet any damages payable after road accidents.

Bail clause Provides members of P & I Clubs (qv) with the backing needed to secure bail when their vessels are *in rem* (qv) for a tortious or contractual liability leading to a maritime or statutory lien over the vessel. The club's *letter of undertaking* secures the release of the vessel long before a court could rule on the case, thus enabling the released vessel to trade.

Bailee One who has possession of another's property under contract of *bailment* (qv) or agreement. A *bailee for reward* receives payment (e.g. garage owner for repairing a car) and must use the care that a prudent man would use over his own goods. Where there is no common benefit the person in possession is a *gratuitous bailee* who must exercise the care that a vigilant person would over his own goods. Bailees for reward may seek to exempt themselves or limit their liability. *See* UNFAIR CONTRACT TERMS ACT 1997.

Bailee clause Institute Cargo Clause (qv) obliging the insured to ensure that his rights against the shipowner or other bailees (qv) are not allowed to lapse by reason of his tardiness in lodging a claim or any other default. The insurer is entitled to avoid claims where their subrogation rights have been prejudiced by the conduct of the insured. The insurer is not liable for expenses incurred by the insured in complying with the clause.

Bailment A contract or an agreement under which one person entrusts his property to another, the bailee (qv), on the understanding that it will later be returned or otherwise accounted for, e.g. delivered to a prescribed destination. The bailee can insure the property on a material damage or a liability basis, or as agent or trustee on behalf of the owner. As public liability policies exclude property in the insured's custody or control, special policies, overriding the exclusion, are written for hotel proprietors, garage owners, etc.

Balance table A table showing the balance of pension that the employer has to purchase for each employee under a pension scheme.

Balanced portfolio Insurers may seek to arrange their insurance and reinsurance so that their total business constitutes a well-balanced range of risks and so do not become unduly committed in a limited number of areas, activities or types of risk. The aim is to spread the exposure by a controlled underwriting approach.

Balancing charge A tax payable by a shipowner who receives a claim payment in excess of the book value of the ship. The excess is deemed to be a taxable profit.

Bancassurance Selling insurance through a bank's established distribution channels often in association with the bank's own insurance subsidiaries. It means that banks can offer banking, insurance, lending and investment products to customers. The term has also been used to describe separate banks and insurance companies each selling the other's products.

Band earnings The band of total earned income between lower and upper earnings limits (qv) on which *state second pension* (qv) and personal NI contributions are based.

Bankers' blanket bond Broad policy protecting the first-party liability of leading financial institutions. Key areas of cover embrace: fidelity – dishonesty of employees; fraud; forgery of cheques or other instruments; theft or robbery of valuables from own premises or in transit; damage to premises and contents during theft; counterfeit securities and counterfeit currency. The policy may be extended to cover computer fraud, safe deposit liability and kidnap and ransom (qv). Cover is available for banks and financial institutions such as central depositories, processing centres and clearing houses. Standard wordings and manuscript wordings (qv) are available.

Banking policy A reinsurance contract under which premiums are 'banked' with the reinsurer for later return to the reinsured with interest.

Bankruptcy and liquidation bond A bond (qv) to guarantee the trustee in bankruptcy appointed by the creditors.

If the trustee, who controls the assets of the insolvent party, fails to carry out his duties properly, the surety (e.g. an insurer) will make good the loss.

Banks'/Lessors' Hull and Liability Insurance A contingency cover to protect banks and lessors against their inability to secure full or part payment in respect of their interest under the operator's aviation policy. It also covers aircraft in the custody or control of the bank or lessor.

Barber Judgment European Court of Justice (ECJ) decision in *Barber* v. *Guardian Royal Exchange* (1990) means that pensions count as equal pay for the purposes of Article 119 (now Article 141(qv) following the Amsterdam Treaty). GRE's scheme allowed redundant females to get an immediate pension at age 50 while for males the age was 55. Mr Barber was made redundant at 52 and received only cash benefits and redundancy pay, but a woman would have received a pension. ECJ held that he was the victim of discrimination in breach of Article 119 and that 'equal pay' included an occupational pension. The Barber rule was held only to apply to service after 17 May 1990. *See* EQUAL TREATMENT.

Barratry A marine insurance peril meaning any wrongful act wilfully committed by the master or crew to the detriment of the vessel's owner or charterer.

Base-line The given value, e.g. 18 degrees C (i.e. the reference temperature), from which a deviation is measured in a weather derivative (qv). *See* COOLING DEGREE DAYS; HEATING DEGREE DAYS.

Base premium The reinsured's premiums (written or earned, depending on the contract) to which the reinsurance premium rate is applied to produce the reinsurance premium in non-proportional contracts (qv). The term is also called *subject premium, premium base* or *underlying premium.*

Base value The value of property at the inception of a valuation-linked insurance (qv).

Basic rate A fundamental rate applied to a whole class of policies of a given description and often published in rating guides. This rate is subject to modification depending on the characteristics of the particular risk under consideration.

Basic state pension (BSP) Flat rate state pension unrelated to earnings. It is unfunded; current taxpayers pay for the retirement income of an earlier generation. Membership is compulsory for all employed and self-employed with earnings above the lower earnings limit (qv). Pension entitlement is built up through national insurance contributions. The state pension age for women is 60 (progressively increasing to 65 between 2010 and 2020) and 65 for men. BSP is increased annually for married couples and single persons in line with prices.

Basis The price differential between a financial position held and the benchmark instrument used to hedge or price that position. The basis may reflect different time periods, product forms, qualities or locations. *See* BASIS RISK.

Basis clause A clause at the foot of a proposal form making the proposal form and declaration the whole basis of the contract. It converts representations (qv) into warranties (qv) so that any inaccuracy in the form will entitle the insurer to avoid the contract regardless of materiality. The insured's answers may be subject to his 'best knowledge and belief'.

Basis of valuation clause A clause in an open cover (qv) which sets out a basis for the valuation of cargo which has been declared and added to the policy and is the subject of a loss.

Basis risk The risk that actual losses exceed the payout as measured by the hedge instrument benchmarking the risk. For example, a weather derivative payout based on movements in an index recorded at London Heathrow may fall short because of adverse deviations occurring in the real location. Under indemnity contracts there is no basis risk as payments are based on actual losses.

Basket Two or more reference stations (qv) that are used in determining the specific of a transaction as in a weather derivative (qv).

Batch clause A product liability (qv) clause providing that all claims, whenever made, arising out of the same prepared or acquired batch of the product, shall be treated as resulting from one occurrence. The 'occurrence' could be defective design, bench error, error in distribution, etc. The clause protects the insurer from multiple claims, all of which have a common cause, being treated separately for the purpose of the per-occurrence limit, or occurring in separate years for the purpose of the aggregate limit. In terms of a deductible, it may benefit the insured to have the individual claims aggregated.

Bench error Product liability (qv) term describing an error or omission that occurs during manufacture or assembly. The risk of such errors underlies much of the demand product liability cover.

Beneficiary Party named in an insurance contract, including a life policy, to receive any benefit payment if the insured event occurs; usually, not always, identical with the policyholder. Also refers to a person who will benefit under a will.

Benefit Describes the amount to be paid upon the happening of the insured event. The benefit is agreed at the inception of the contract and, not being based on actual losses, is not subject to the principle of indemnity (qv). *See* BENEFIT POLICY.

Benefit basis A group life and/or pension scheme that varies the benefits for members according to categories of membership. Life cover for one category might be three times income, but four times for another. Each category is carefully defined in order to ensure that there is no discrimination against individuals.

Benefit of insurance clause Marine clause meaning that the bailee (qv) of goods gets the benefit of any insurance policy effected by the cargo owner should an insured loss occur while the goods are in the bailee's care. If the contract of carriage is subject to the US Carriage of Goods by Water Act, the clause is void.

Benefit policy Policies such as personal accident and life insurances where the amount to be paid is a pre-agreed *benefit* (qv) and is not based on actual losses as with indemnity contracts. Individuals are free to put their own value on life and limb; the main constraint is their ability to pay.

Benefits in kind Non-cash benefits for employees, such as private medical insurance. The amount paid for such benefits is added to the employee's taxable income for tax purposes. The benefits are shown on form P11D and their value counts towards the calculation of maximum Inland Revenue pension benefits.

Bermuda Global insurance centre focusing on reinsurance and insurance services for large companies. It accommodates captive insurance companies (qv). ACE and XL, set up to self-insure the asbestosis risk of US companies, and other Bermudan companies, have become independent and grown through acquisition into large diversified global insurance and reinsurance companies. Attractions of Bermuda: the absence of corporate or profits taxation; a flexible legal regulatory regime.

Berne Union The union, through its 51 members from 42 countries and locations, works for international acceptance of sound principles of *export credit insurance* (qv) and foreign *investment insurance* (qv). The union is a vital forum for the exchange of information, experience and expertise between members. Visit *www.berneunion.org.uk*.

Best advice rule Under FSMA anyone selling pensions, life insurance or investments must give clients and prospective clients 'best advice'. The financial adviser (qv) needs to be aware of the client's circumstances and show, where possible, that the recommendations are based on an unbiased evaluation.

Best's Rating Rating system (developed by rating agency A.M. Best Co.) that evaluates those factors that affect the overall performance of insurance companies. Provides a weighted measure of a company's financial strength, performance level, competitive position and ability to meets its obligations to policyholders. A qualitative and quantitative assessment.

Betterment The amount of the increase in the value of property after it has been reinstated or repaired by the insurer under a contract of indemnity (qv). Insurers make a deduction from the claims payment as the insured's contribution to 'betterment'.

Bid/offer spread The spread is the difference between the bid (the buy-back price payable to holders of unitised funds by fund managers) and the offer (the higher selling price at which the managers will offer the units for sale on the same day). This is normally 5–7 per cent, and covers the costs and profit of the fund.

Bid (or tender) bond *See* BONDS (SURETY BONDS)/CONSTRUCTION BONDS.

Bilateral netting Legally enforceable agreement under which two parties involved in swaps (qv) agree to exchange only the net difference in their obligations to each other rather than making full payments one to the other.

Bill of exchange The authorisation by the buyer for the seller to draw the price of the goods on a due date, on the buyer's bank, usually when the goods reach their destination. The bank will not discount the bill unless the specified goods are insured against marine risks and the policy lodged with the bank as collateral security.

Bill of lading An international shipping document issued by a carrier to a cargo exporter. It serves three purposes: (a) definition of the contract between the parties, including details of the shipowner's duties and responsibilities for the property (as defined) from the port of shipment to the port of destination; (b) receipt for the goods delivered for shipment; (c) evidence of title, and as such is transferable by endorsement and delivery. A *clean bill* carries no qualifying endorsement; a 'dirty bill' may be endorsed, for example, 'badly packed'. Copies are kept by the master, the shipper and the consignee.

Bill of lading freight The amount payable to the shipowner for the carriage of cargo and by common law earned only on completion, unless otherwise agreed. *See* ADVANCE FREIGHT.

Bill payment protection (BPP) Pays agreed sums to fund household bills following accident, sickness and unemployment. The insurance is not linked to a credit agreement and therefore stands alone.

Binding authority An agreement whereby an insurer or reinsurer delegates underwriting authority to another party known as a *coverholder*, usually a broker or underwriting agent. Binding authorities assume a particular importance at Lloyd's as a means of enabling coverholders at home and abroad to accept risks for syndicates while circumventing the rule about business only in the Room (qv). Regulations at Lloyd's lay down procedures for the registration of binding authorities and the approval of coverholders.

Blanket motor insurance certificate A certificate that sets out a general description of vehicles rather than identifying the vehicles covered by their registration numbers. Particularly useful for fleet insurances, it obviates the need for fresh certificates when a fleet owner buys or sells vehicles.

Blanket motor insurance policy A motor policy describing the vehicles in general terms rather than specifying them individually. The policy usually refers to any motor vehicle, details of which have been notified to the insurer. When a change of vehicles takes place the substitution does not have to be endorsed on the policy. The Motor Insurance Database (qv) does not preclude blanket policies or certificates, but for tracing purposes, under the European Directive, the policyholder must maintain a record of vehicles.

Blanket policy A policy with a single sum insured covering a number of separate items of property without sub-division of the amount. The approach is used in fire insurance for large risks and in fidelity guarantee insurance for unnamed employees.

Blanket rate *See* AVERAGE RATE INSURANCE.

Blast furnace clause A liability insurance *restrictive endorsement* (qv) excluding work on blast furnaces. The clause is equally a gasometer clause, or a towers clause, given the other buildings (hangars, steeples, bridges, viaducts and roofs other than private dwellings and/or shops of not more than three floors) also named. They all call for close scrutiny from the underwriter because of their height or other physical characteristics.

Blended covers/integrated covers The combining of conventional insurance with financial losses in a single programme, as in multi-line insurance. Risks can be priced on a portfolio basis – and therefore cover may be available for risks that, in isolation, would be too costly to insure. The financial losses are based on falls in a specified index and not the actual portfolio.

Blind treaty Reinsurance treaty under which the cedant (qv), instead of notifying individual risks routinely, supplies periodical summaries of premiums and claims. The reinsurer rarely exercises his right to examine the cedant's books in relation to any risk or claim.

Block limit The limit used by a property insurer to put a ceiling on the maximum amount of business he will write in respect of any one block of buildings.

Block policy Property insurance covering inland transit risks on infrequent 'shipments' by rail, parcel post or road conveyance. The policy may be 'all risks' or named perils subject to a per-shipment limit and exclusions. Cover includes the property of others in the insured's custody or control. As the premium is fixed, the insured is not required to make regular declarations of shipments. The jeweller's block policy (qv) is a particular form of block policy.

Block transfer *See* BULK TRANSFER.

Blood relative clause An industrial life policy clause that legally enables the insurer to pay the sum due under the policy to the spouse of the insured or another relative by blood or marriage. It is also known as the Da Costa clause.

'Blue Book' Published by Lloyd's Aviation as *Lloyd's Confidential Record of Civil Aviation*. It lists owners of aircraft and gives fleet details, accident history and other information of value to underwriters and others.

Blue List A term referring to Lloyd's Shipping Index (qv).

Boat insurance Marine insurance to provide *loss or damage cover, third party cover* and *passenger liability cover* for all types of small vessels used for private purposes or carrying passengers for hire. They include yachts, sailing dinghies, cabin cruisers, motorboats, houseboats, speedboats, skiffs, etc. In some cases, a standard clause (e.g. Institute Yacht Clauses) may be used. Cover for some vessels can be added to a household policy.

Bodily injury Injury, sickness or disease sustained by a person, including death resulting therefrom. Personal accident policies cover *bodily injury* caused 'by accidental, violent and visible means solely resulting in death or disablement'. *Post traumatic stress order* (qv) may amount to bodily injury, particularly where bodily harm has also occurred or where the policyholder has been in an accident. Public liability insurers cover legal liability for *bodily injury* but some use the term *personal injury* and define it as including 'illness'. 'Injury to feelings' is clearly contemplated by insurers covering liability due to wrongful arrest or false imprisonment or similarly specified events.

Boiler and pressure plant cover A general term for all steam or fluid pressure plant subject to the risks of explosion and collapse, including steam boilers, economisers and superheaters. The policy covers damage to the plant itself, surrounding property and liability for third party injury. Business interruption risks can also be covered under *engineering consequential loss* (qv). Boiler and pressure plant equipment has to be examined at prescribed intervals. *See* INSPECTION CLASSES.

Bond switching The switching of money in a life insurance bond from one fund to another controlled by the same insurer. *See* SWITCHING FACILITIES.

Bonded goods Dutiable goods in respect of which a bond (qv) for the payment of the duty has been given to Customs and Excise. *See* CUSTOMS AND EXCISE BOND.

Bonded value Where goods are normally sold in bond, the bonded price is considered to be the 'gross value'. However, The Marine Insurance Act 1906, s.71(4) defines gross value as the wholesale price or estimated value ruling on the day of sale after freight, landing charges and duty have been paid.

Bonded warehouse An approved warehouse for goods upon which excise duty has not been paid. The warehouse owner becomes the subject of a government bond (qv), i.e. a general or warehouse bond or a removal bond. This guarantees payment of the duty to HM Customs & Excise in the event that goods are removed from the warehouse without payment of the duty.

Bonds (investment/insurance) Single savings contracts issued by insurance companies. They are collective investments that create a fund whose manager aims to secure growth. An increase or decrease in the value of the fund is reflected in the value of the investors' units. The fund is treated differently in terms of taxation from unit trust funds as most taxation (income tax and capital gains) takes place within the fund. These single premium bonds are either: income/distribution bonds (qv); with profits bonds (qv); equity bonds (investing exclusively in company shares); managed bonds (spread risk by investing in shares, gilts (qv) and property).

Bonds (securities) Fixed interest securities issued by governments (gilts), financial institutions and companies (corporate bonds) to investors. The issuer pays a fixed rate of interest for a fixed number of years (e.g. 7.5 per cent for five years), at the end of which the capital is repaid. Bonds are traded in the open market in the same way as shares. Insurance companies and pensions funds are substantial investors in UK government bonds. Distinguish BONDS (SURETY BONDS) and BONDS (INVESTMENT/INSURANCE).

Bonds (surety bonds)/construction bonds A surety bond involves three parties, a surety, a principal (often a contractor) and an obligee (often a project owner). The surety guarantees under seal that the principal will carry out his obligations or alternatively compensate the obligee for losses due to the contractor's breach. In the construction industry this is known as a *performance bond*. The surety has recourse against his principal (the obligor). A *retention bond* is required when the developer releases the amount retained for defects before the contractor has completed the defects. A *pre-payment bond* guarantees any advance payment for the contractor's mobilisation. *Bid bonds* guarantee that the contractor's bid or tender is made in good faith and he is capable of entering into the contract. If the contractor fails to proceed, the surety pays for the project owner's costs in scrutinising another tender. *Payment bonds* guarantee payment for project labour and materials. *See* COURT BONDS; LOCAL AUTHORITY BONDS; GOVERNMENT BONDS.

Bonus 1. A non-guaranteed benefit added to with profits life policies periodically from the divisible surplus (qv). Once allocated, the bonuses are guaranteed and become payable at the same time as the sum insured, i.e. they are reversionary bonuses. A *uniform simple reversionary* bonus is proportionate to the sum insured; a *uniform compound reversionary bonus* is proportionate to the sum insured and accrued bonuses. *Interim bonuses* are added to policies becoming claims in between two declarations. A *terminal bonus* is added when the policy ends by death or maturity. 2. *See* NO CLAIM BONUS.

Bonus declaration Declaration by a life insurer as to the rate at which bonuses will be allotted to 'with profits' policies. The periodic declarations are usually annual and the amount declared depends on the insurer's decision as to the amount they wish to take from profit as divisible surplus. *See* NO CLAIM BONUS.

Bonus loading The amount added to a life insurance premium to distinguish 'with profits' policies from those without profits. The higher payment entitles the policyholder to participate in any divisible surplus available for bonus distribution at any bonus valuation.

Bonus-malus system A motor insurance system that gives discounts for claims-free driving and makes surcharges for claims. *See* NO CLAIMS BONUS.

Bonus reserve A reserve created by life insurers for the payment of future bonuses to with profits policyholders.

Bonus reserve valuation A type of gross premium valuation that allows explicitly for future bonuses under with profits contracts. The terms *bonus reserve valuation* and *gross premium valuation* are regarded as alternative phrases. For some purposes (certain solvency investigations) a gross premium technique will be used with no allowance for future bonuses.

Bonus sacrifice The sacrifice by an employee of all or part of his bonus payment. His employer pays an equivalent amount into an *executive pension plan* (qv) for the employee.

Book debts insurance Insurance against inability to collect money owing, following the destruction of books by an insured peril. Cover includes the cost of reproducing records and tracing debtors. Bad debts, being a credit risk, are not covered. The sum insured is the estimated maximum debt outstanding at any one-time subject to average (qv) and the premium is adjustable at the end of year. As book debts relate to pre-interruption transactions they are not covered under business interruption insurance (qv).

Book of Business Total of policies that an insurance company or agent has in force in a specific line for its business as a whole.

Book reserve scheme A pension scheme under which the employer is responsible for the payment of the benefits that are financed by a provision in the employer's accounts.

Bordereaux Lists of premiums and claims prepared monthly or quarterly by cedants (qv) or coverholders (qv) for reinsurers or underwriters to advise them of risks accepted and claims incurred under treaties or binding authorities. Bordereaux are not always required in reinsurance treaties.

Borrowed employees/servants Employees who are lent or hired out by their general employer to other employers for specific purposes. There is a presumption that the general employer will remain liable for the torts of that servant while hired or lent to the special employer unless the general employer can show that control has passed to the special employer (*Mersey Docks & Harbour Board* v. *Coggins & Griffiths* (1947). Condition 8 of the Contractors Plant-hire Association's Conditions (CPA) makes the hirer responsible for all claims from the operation of plant by the driver/operator who is supplied with it.

Both to Blame Collision Clause An Institute Cargo Clause indemnifying the cargo owner against the cost of reimbursing the shipowner who is compelled under foreign law to pay 50 per cent of a third party's cargo loss to a third party shipowner following a collision in which both were blameworthy. Under US law the shipowners are held of equal blame and the cargo owner can recover in full from the third party shipowner who then recovers 50 per cent from the ship carrying the cargo. Provisions in the *running down clause* (qv) prevent the shipowner recovering in full under the hull policy, nor is the Protection and Indemnity Club (qv) liable, causing the shipowner to pass the risk to the cargo owner under the affreightment.

Both Sides Cover *See* AFTER THE EVENT LEGAL EXPENSES INSURANCE.

Bottom limit The maximum value at risk per shipment/sending/aircraft.

Bottom painting clause An Institute Time/International Hull Clause relieving the insurer in all circumstances from the normal running costs of scraping or painting the vessel's bottom.

Bottomry A loan raised by the ship's master when other methods of raising money for a voyage have failed. The loan, secured on the vessel or vessel and cargo, is not repayable if the venture is lost. The term, now academic, illustrates an early form of risk transfer (qv).

Bouquet Treaty Reinsurance treaty combining contracts from different classes of business; the package often includes both desirable and undesirable business.

Box The space occupied by an underwriter and his staff in the Room at Lloyd's (qv).

Bracketed provisions *See* SPECIAL CIRCUMSTANCES CLAUSE.

Breach of statutory duty A tort (qv) where the defendant has committed a breach of duty imposed by statute or regulation and Parliament intended to confer a statutory remedy on the claimant. HSWA 1974, s.47, provides that breaches of the Act do not create civil remedies but a breach of regulations, (e.g. PUWER 1998 (qv)) is actionable unless the regulation indicates otherwise. Where the statute is silent on civil remedies, the courts have to enquire into the intention of Parliament.

Breach of warranty *See* WARRANTY.

Breach of Warranty Clause/Navigation provisions International Hull Clause 11 indicating that the insured is held covered for breach of warranty as to cargo, trade, locality, towage, salvage services or date of sailing, provided notice is given and any additional premium paid.

Breach of warranty insurance Insurance covering banks for the outstanding amount of loans that funded the purchase of aircraft. If the hull insurance is invalidated by the airline's breach of warranty, the bank may suffer loss notwithstanding a lien on the aircraft. Cover is separate or by endorsement of the hull policy.

Breach of warranty of authority Occurs where an agent, acting in excess of his actual or apparent authority, 'contracts' with or commits, a third party. The breach does not bind his principal and is actionable against the agent by the third party. 'Breach of warranty of authority' is insured as a 'wrongful act' under a directors' and officers' liability policy (qv) and is covered under professional indemnity policies (qv).

Breakdown/Breakdown insurance Boilers, pressure vessels, cranes, lifts and other lifting equipment, engines, electrical equipment may be insured against breakdown under the engineering policy. Breakdown generally means the breaking or burning of any part of the plant while it is running that causes a sudden stoppage that necessitates repair before resuming work although there may be specific definitions for particular forms of plant. Basic breakdown cover relates to self-damage, but cover is usually extended to damage to surrounding property, public liability, fragmentation (qv), consequential loss, hired-in plant damage and deterioration of stock.

Breakdown recovery Cover sometimes added to motor insurance whereby the insurer recovers vehicles from the scene of a breakdown as distinct from the scene of an accident. Recovery following an accident is an integral part of the cover under comprehensive motor policies. Extended warranty insurances (qv) often include breakdown recovery.

Bridging pension An additional pension taken from a pension scheme to 'bridge' the gap between actual retirement and state pensionable age at which time it is replaced by the state pension so there is no loss of income.

British Insurance (Atomic Energy) Committee The body that set up the pool of insurers to cover nuclear perils (qv).

British Insurance Brokers Association (BIBA) Represents 2,000 brokerage members, representing 37,000 employees. Its interests cover home, motor, travel and the commercial and industrial insurance markets. It aims to enhance the status and recognition of members through the maintenance of high standards, public relations, government and parliamentary contacts. (*www.biba.org.uk*).

British Insurance Law Association Brings together members from insurers, brokers, other intermediaries, academics, solicitors and barristers, all interested in insurance law. BILA holds regular talks and conferences on insurance law topics. It produces technical papers for various bodies including the UK government and the Law Reform Commission. It has initiated many changes to the world of insurance. BILA is also the British Chapter of Association International de Droit des Assurances (AIDA) and is an active participant in its quadrennial world congress.

British Maritime Law Association The organisation which coordinates the various sectors of the shipping industry, and includes both the London marine market, underwriting hull and cargo business, and the Protection and Indemnity Clubs (qv) underwriting shipowners' liabilities in mutual associations.

British Waterways Act 1995 Requires all boat owners to have third party cover with a minimum £1 million indemnity on most inland waterways. The British Waterways Authority seeks evidence of insurance before issuing the boat owner's annual licence to use its waterways.

Brokerage 1. The commission and fee income received by an insurance broker. Normally commission is received from the insurer, but brokers may also charge fees to their clients. 2. A US term for an insurance broking company, firm or office. 3. The fee paid to a broker who arranges reinsurance cover for a ceding office.

Broker's cover note A document issued by an insurance broker confirming that an insurance has been effected. It warrants to the client that his or her instructions have been carried out, but imposes no liability on an insurer who has not actually entered into any agreement. If the cover note is issued in anticipation of making an agreement that does not materialise the broker will be liable for breach of warranty.

Broker's lien In marine insurance the broker is liable to the insurer for the premium even though not collected from the insured. Consequently, the Marine Insurance Act, s.53(2), grants him a lien, i.e. the right to retain the policy until paid by the insured. The lien is valuable as no claim can be collected without production of the policy; the insured may wish to deposit the policy with his bank, or pass it to another interested party. The lien applies not only to the premium on the policy but the balance of any insurance account due to the broker. The lien has been held to apply in other classes of insurance in respect of the premium but not the balance due on any insurance account.

Broker's open cover A variation of ordinary facultative reinsurance (qv) method, whereby a reinsurer agrees in advance to accept reinsurance from a reinsurance broker. The reinsurer becomes obliged to accept a share of any business ceded to it through the broker, who thus acquires a facility for automatic reinsurance.

Buffer Layer A stratum of cover between the upper limit of the primary insurer and the attachment point of the excess or umbrella insurer. The 'buffer layer' fills the gap. Example: total policy limit of £10 million is arranged as follows: primary layer = £1 million; buffer layer is £1 million in excess of £1 million and the excess/umbrella layer is £8 million in excess of £2 million. In reinsurance terms the buffer layer sits between the *working cover/layer* and the *catastrophe layer*. It absorbs relatively large losses that do not occur annually, but do so with some regularity.

Builder's risks Policy covering a ship during construction, including launching and trial trips, until delivery to her owners. Construction of small commercial craft, e.g. fishing vessels, work boats, etc., can be insured under an *open cover* (qv).

Building rate Fire insurances are often rated separately for the buildings and contents. The terms 'building rate' and 'contents rate' have emerged as a result.

Building Research Establishment Ltd (BRE) UK's leading centre of expertise on building construction, energy, environment, fire and risk. It provides consultancy, testing and commissioned research services covering all aspects of the built environment and associated industries. BRE makes significant contributions to the development of national and international standards and codes for construction and fire safety. Its sister company, BRE Certification, provides certification to UK, European and international standards as well as CE marking and product approval. (*www.bre.co.uk*).

Building Society block policy A block or master policy under which a large number of buildings, mainly private dwellings, are insured on a 'householders' comprehensive' basis. The buildings insured at any one time are those listed in a schedule maintained by the society. Individual property owners are not given a policy but are supplied with full details of the cover. The insurance is index-linked (qv).

Building Society indemnities/mortgage guarantee insurance Where a mortgagee grants a high loan in relation to value (e.g. in excess of 75 per cent of property price) the mortgagee insures the excess against loss due to borrower default. The premium, known as the 'high value to loan' fee or indemnity guarantee premium, is passed on to the borrower.

Building Society linked life assurance An alternative to a conventional 'with profits' policy. The investment element of the premium is concentrated in designated building society investments.

Buildings 1. In household policies it is the *home* (the dwelling, outbuildings and garage), fixtures and fittings, patios, terraces, footpaths, tennis courts, drives, walls, swimming pools, fences, gates, hedges, service tanks, pipes, permanently connected cables and central heating oil tanks, within the boundaries of the home. Trees and plants are not included unless the policy has been extended to cover damage to garden. 2. Under the standard fire policy used by businesses, buildings are defined as: buildings including the landlord's fixtures and fittings therein and thereon, unless otherwise stated constructed of brick stone or concrete and roofed with slates tiles metal concrete asphalt or sheets or slabs composed entirely of incombustible mineral ingredients. Unless specifically insured, Buildings includes annexes, small outside buildings, conveyors, wires, service pipes and other equipment that is the property of the insured (or for which he responsible), walls and gates and fences.

Bulk transfer The transfer of a group of members from one occupational pension scheme to another. A transfer payment (qv) is made to the new scheme based on the transfer of assets and liabilities. The transfer may occur when members of a closed final salary scheme are given the chance to join a new money purchase scheme. More usually it occurs when the business changes ownership. The consent of the members is required as they could opt for a pension transfer to a personal pension, a section 32 policy or no transfer at all. The transfer payment (qv) usually exceeds the individual's cash equivalent transfer value (qv).

Burden of proof The onus is upon the insured to prove that his loss is within the *operative clause* (qv). It is for the insurer to prove that the loss has been caused by an excepted peril. If the insurer has cut down the scope of the operative clause by qualifying the insured peril (*see* QUALIFIED PERILS) the insured must prove that the loss was caused by the peril as qualified.

Burglary According to the Theft Act 1968, a person is guilty of burglary in two circumstances. Section 9(1)(a) applies when a person enters a property as a trespasser, with intention to commit theft, rape or grievous bodily harm. Section 9(1)(b) refers to the person who enters property as a trespasser and, having entered, commits or attempts to commit theft, rape or grievous bodily harm. Insurers avoid the use of the term 'burglary' in *theft insurance* (qv). The usual practice is to insure theft, 'following forcible and violent entry into or exit from the premises' (qv).

Burner policy A term sometimes used in aviation insurance to describe a policy covering potentially exceptional risk situations, as with helicopters, etc.

Burning cost Premium calculation method used for non-proportional reinsurances mainly or large industrial liability risks. The premium is calculated from the percentage of premiums 'burnt up' by losses in the reinsurance layer or primary insurance over a number of previous years. The calculation is adjusted for inflation and other factors subject to change and the final figure is loaded, e.g. by 100/70, for administrative costs and profit. The premium is normally adjustable based on actual experience.

Burning of debris condition A liability insurance condition to ensure that the burning of debris away from the insured's premises is properly conducted. Fires should (a) be in a cleared area and at a distance (e.g. at least 8 metres) from any property; (b) not be left unattended. A suitable fire extinguisher should be kept available for immediate use. It may also require that fires be extinguished at least one hour before leaving the site at the end of each working day.

Burning ratio The ratio of actual losses (i.e. excluding IBNR) to the amount of earned premiums.

Burning warranty/Hot Work/Use of Heat Clause Public liability (qv) clause imposing strict conditions on the insured's involvement in 'hot work'. Typically where electric oxy-acetylene or similar welding equipment or cutting equipment is used the area of work must be adequately cleared and combustible materials moved at least 6 metres from the work. The warranty also requires, inter alia, that fire extinguishers should be available. Upon completion of each period of work and at regular intervals for at least one hour after the completion of the work there should be thorough fire safety checks. Other conditions govern the use of blowlamps and blowtorches. The use of asphalt, bitumen, tar, pitch or lead heaters is also controlled. *See* HOT WORK; BURNING OF DEBRIS CONDITION.

Burst pipes An additional peril (qv) added to fire and household policies to cover damage caused by an escape of water from any tank, apparatus or pipe. The repair of the item that burst, overflowed or leaked, is not covered. The insurance is subject to an excess (qv) and cover is usually suspended when the building is unoccupied for a defined period, usually 30 days.

Business 1. The term means the insured's activities as specified in the policy Schedule and will depend on details submitted by the insured. Activities outside the description will not be covered. The policy extends the definition to include *ancillary activities* (qv). 2. For the purposes of the Employers' Liability (Compulsory Insurance) Act 1969, 'business' means a trade or profession or any activity conducted by a body of persons (whether incorporated or not). Certain activities not normally regarded as businesses (e.g. members' tennis clubs) are within the definition. Domestic 'servants' in private households are not employed in a business for the purpose of the Act.

Business and pleasure A general aviation rating class applicable when the aircraft owner is an individual, business or corporation owning and operating an aircraft for both business and pleasure but not employing full-time, professional pilots.

Business books Books of accounts and other business books, documents, etc., can be insured under material damage insurances such as fire policies as a special item. The insurer restricts liability to the cost of stationery plus the cost of writing up.

Business cancellation See abandonment of events (qv). Some businesses may be able to insure against delay or abandonment of certain events, e.g. royal visits, royal occasions, in respect of which they incur costs in advance, e.g. design and manufacture of souvenirs.

Business Continuity Management (BCM) BCM is concerned with anticipating threats to business survival and the achievement of objectives. It means conducting a business impact analysis to identify the key processes and functions within and beyond organisational boundaries that are essential for continuity. A business continuity plan (BCP) sets out the recovery strategies, priorities and actions that will be needed if a crisis occurs. A crisis could arise from a pure risk (qv) such as fire, or loss of a major customer or supplier. BCM reduces the likelihood of a disaster and minimises impact if one occurs. A BCP is distinguished from a disaster recovery plan (qv), which concentrates on the restoration of facilities *after* a disaster has occurred.

Business Interruption Insurance Covers loss of gross profit following reduced *turnover* (qv) resulting from, and occurring after, insured property damage. The gross profit indemnity enables the business to pay its standing charges (qv), including payroll, and recover its net profit during the *indemnity period* (qv), the period selected as being the time needed to restore normal trading levels. *Specified working expenses* (qv) are not at risk and are therefore deducted from turnover before arriving at the gross profit, the item to be insured. The policy also covers *increased cost of working* (qv), e.g. renting alternative premises, subject to the cost not exceeding the amount of loss thereby avoided. *Additional increased cost of working* (qv) can be insured. The policy may extend to interruptions caused by damage at the premises to customers or suppliers, or resulting from *loss of attractions* (qv), murder, suicide, food poisoning or infectious/contagious diseases. (See Figure 2). *See* AUDITORS' CHARGES; SPECIAL CIRCUMSTANCES CLAUSE; CUSTOMERS' EXTENSION; MATERIAL DAMAGE PROVISO; SUPPLIERS' EXTENSION.

Business plan The plan sets out a firm's objectives and shows in a systematic way how it will approach marketing, operations, finance, management and control. It also includes details of key personnel and covers strengths, weaknesses, threats and opportunities. The FSA (qv) sees syndicate business plans as central to the ability of Lloyd's to control and monitor the activities of managing agents (qv). Consequently the FSA monitors the way in which Lloyd's monitors syndicate business plans. Business plans are also required from most intermediaries seeking FSA authorisiation. *See* LLOYD'S BUSINESS PLAN; FRANCHISE; FRANCHISE BOARD.

Business travel Insurance for business people travelling abroad. It is similar in range of cover to the travel insurance (qv) arranged for holidays. As a business traveller travels regularly, at short notice, annual cover may be arranged.

Business use One of three classes of use (class 2) often used by motor insurers in

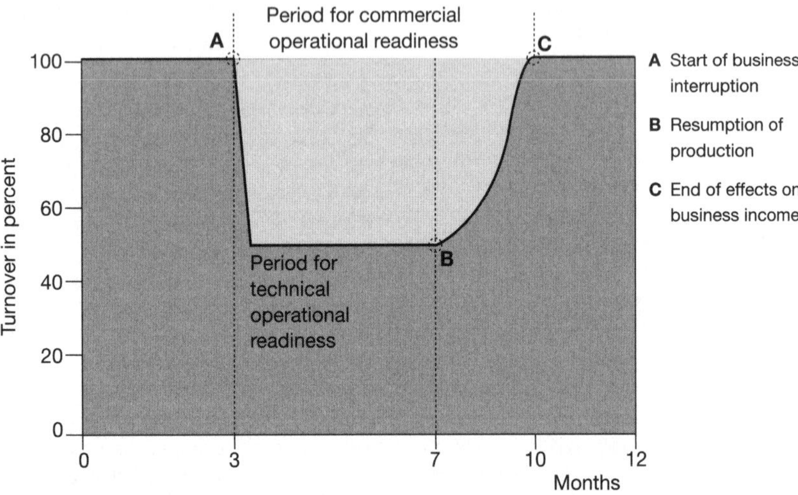

Figure 2. Technical and commercial operational readiness
Source: Swiss Re. *Business Interruption Insurance*, 06/98

fixing car insurance premiums. The policy covers social, domestic and pleasure use and business use. It excludes commercial travelling and carrying passengers for hire or reward but car sharing is allowed as long as 'lifts' where money changes hands are not part of a business arrangement. This limited business class is more costly than Class 1, where the business use element is limited to the policyholder in person, but lower than Class 3 which includes commercial travelling as defined in the policy.

'But for test' A test to help determine whether the claimant's injury was in fact caused by the defendant's negligence (qv). It assists the court in rejecting those factors that could not have had any causal effect and should therefore be regarded as being too remote. 'If the damage would not have happened but for a particular fault then that fault is the cause of the damage; if it would have happened just the same, fault or no fault, the fault is not the cause of the damage' (per Denning L.J. in *Cork* v. *Kirby Maclean Ltd* (CA, 1952). The test does not work when there are two concurrent causes each of which is sufficient to cause the damage. The test would eliminate both causes and that cannot be correct, as both could have produced the result.

Buy back 1. A payment to reinstate a contracted out person into the state second pension (qv). 2. Reinstatement of life insurance cover after payment of a critical illness claim (qv) that would terminate the policy unless the death risk is bought back. 3. The payment of additional premium to secure cover in respect of a risk (e.g. motor cycling under a personal accident policy (qv)) specifically excluded from the cover.

Buy out (Section 32 policy) The policy bought by pension scheme trustees to transfer an individual's accrued benefits to a standalone insurance policy. Unlike a personal pension plan, the policy guarantees that if a transfer payment (qv) includes an element relating to contracting out of the state second pension (qv), then a guaranteed minimum pension (qv) will be provided at retirement age. Also, unlike a personal pension plan, benefits in retirement from an s.32 policy are subject to maxima based on the limits laid down in the occupational pension scheme from which the entitlement was transferred.

Byelaw The means whereby the Council of Lloyd's (qv) under s.6 of Lloyd's Act 1982 (qv) lays down the rules of the Lloyd's community. The term extends to any direction, regulation or other instrument (including any regulation ratified by the Council by special resolution) and any associated condition or requirement. Lloyd's is expected to give the FSA (qv) adequate notice of all proposed byelaw changes affecting supervision and regulation of the Lloyd's market. The FSA also requires copies of regulatory and market bulletins and all byelaw amendments as soon as they are published. *See* LLOYD'S MARKET CONDUCT.

By way of business test FSMA, s.22, specifies that a selling or administration activity is a regulated activity (qv) only if it is carried on 'by way of business'. In effect this means that the activity provides a direct financial benefit to the business. Financial benefit need not be in the form of money or a profit element. An employer who arranges health cover for his staff but receives no commission does not generally carry on insurance mediation by way of business.

C

1992 CLC The International Convention for Civil Liability for Oil Pollution Damage 1992, a Protocol to the 1969 CLC. Makes shipowners strictly liable for oil pollution damage resulting from spills of persistent oil from tankers. Liability is based on tonnage. CLC creates compulsory insurance and facilitates direct claims against the insurer. It is supplemented by the 1992 Fund (the IOPC 1992 Fund (qv)). Bunkers on non-tankers fall under the International Liability for Bunker Oil Pollution Damage 2001. *See* MERCHANT SHIPPING (SALVAGE AND POLLUTION) ACT 1994; POLLUTION CLAUSE.

1992 Fund Fund supplementing the insurance-backed liabilities of tanker owners' CLC (qv) when CLC (qv) compensation is inadequate. The Fund's origin is the International Convention on the Establishment of International Fund for the Compensation for Oil Pollution Damage 1992. The Fund is a worldwide intergovernmental organisation. The maximum payable by the Fund in respect of one incident increased in November 2003 to £203m. Special Drawing Rights (equivalent to £180m.). The Fund is financed by oil industry levies. *See* 1992 CLC.

Cadbury Report (1992) The Committee's recommendations focused on the control and reporting functions of boards, particularly of listed companies, and on the role of auditors. Its purpose was to review those aspects of *corporate governance* (qv) specifically related to financial reporting and accountability. Has impacted upon the *Combined Code on Corporate Governance* (qv).

Calendar Year of Experience Reinsurance experience calculated by matching the total value of all losses and movements in reserves during a given 12-month period, regardless of the date of loss, with the premiums earned during the same period. Calendar year statistics are suitable for financial considerations but not for assessing results.

Call A payment to cover losses and management expenses made by a member of a protection and indemnity club (qv) in consideration of a right to indemnity. The 'calls' are based on the tonnage entered in the club by shipowners. Initial payment may be followed by supplementary calls.

Call option The right, not the obligation, to buy the underlying asset or take cash, based on movements in an underlying index as in a weather derivative (qv). Compare with *put option* (qv).

Cancellation clause A general insurance clause permitting the insurer to terminate insurance cover during the policy term. The clause sets out the notice procedure the insurer must follow, and the basis for refunding the unexpired premium. Some policies also give the insured the right of cancellation. *See* CANCELLING CLAUSE.

Cancellation rights The FSA's ICOB Rules require retail customers to be given a cancellation period of 14 days for general insurance contracts and distance non-investment mediation contracts, and 30 days for pure protection contracts (qv), or, if later, the date of receipt of the policy documents.

Cancelling clause A clause giving both parties to marine *open covers* (qv) the right to give 30 days' notice of cancellation. Where war and strike risks are covered, insurers may give seven days' notice, (in some cases less), of cancellation without disturbing the tenure of the open cover itself. When the clause is invoked, shipments that have gone or will go forward before the notice expires remain covered until arrival. Cancelling clauses also appear in floating policies (qv).

Capacity Amount of insurance or reinsurance that can be underwritten by an entity or a market. The maximum amount of business that may be accepted by a Lloyd's member is equivalent to his overall premium income limit. *See* CAPACITY BOOSTING; CAPACITY TRANSFER MARKET.

Capacity auctions A method of transferring capacity (qv) from one Lloyd's member to another. Syndicate participants in one year have the right to remain in that syndicate in the following year or transfer their capacity to other members by auction. The auctions have particularly helped *integrated Lloyd's vehicles* (qv) to increase their capacity. Sellers of capacity are called *tenderers, buyers* are called *subscribers.* The auctions are governed by Auction Byelaw (14/97). *See* CAPACITY TRANSFER MARKET.

Capacity boosting Primary insurers boost their ability to accept larger or more risks, by availing themselves of reinsurance facilities.

Capacity transfer market Market for the transfer of syndicate capacity at Lloyd's. The transfer is usually from names (qv) to aligned corporate members (qv) through capacity auctions (qv) or *bilateral agreements (byelaw 8/98). See* MANDATORY OFFERS.

Capacity Transfer Panel (CTP) The part of Lloyd's created by the Franchise Board (qv) that administers the capacity transfer market (qv). It is concerned with capacity auctions and, in particular, mandatory offers (qv) and minority buyouts (qv). CTP has three independent members – a nominated member of the Council (qv) as chairman, a lawyer and a financial expert. They also have a Lloyd's Members' Association nominee and one nominee from the third party capital providers; both can be changed on a case-by-case basis.

Capital additions clause A property insurance clause providing automatic cover for buildings and contents acquired during the period of insurance up to the lesser of 10 per cent of the sum insured or £500,000 provided they are not otherwise insured. The insured is required to give particulars of additions and to arrange specific insurance retrospectively.

Capital annuity *See* SPLIT ANNUITY.

Capital at risk Term denoting the amount payable on death under life policies, less the mathematical reserves in respect of the relevant contracts. The term is used in connection with life solvency margins.

Capital benefit The single payment of a lump sum as opposed to smaller regular payments (as with temporary disablement). Personal accident policies pay lump sums for death, dismemberment, loss of sight.

Capital content An annuity (qv) term referring to that part of an annuity payment that is paid tax-free to the annuitant. It is treated as a return of capital while the balance of the payment is taxed at the annuitant's marginal income tax rate.

Capital market A market where debt and equity are traded. By selling securitised bonds (re)insurers transfer insurance risk to the capital market. *See* CATASTROPHE BONDS; SECURITISATION.

Capital protected annuity An annuity (qv) under which the insurer guarantees to make total gross annuity payments equal to the purchase price regardless of the date of death.

Capital redemption policy Policies, unrelated to human life, whereby a company regularly sets aside money so that on maturity it can retire its bonds, debentures or preferred stock. The so-called 'sinking fund' also enables the company to replace wasting assets such as leases (leasehold redemption policies). The policies are *long-term business* (qv) but not part of the life fund.

Capital unit A charging device used by unit trust managers. In the early years (e.g. up to three) premiums are allocated to capital units in order to recover expenses.

Capitalised value The amount used for underwriting in relation to occupational pension schemes policies when a pension provision is to be made for a member's spouse or other dependants.

Captain's Room The restaurant at Lloyd's.

Captive insurance company Company owned and operated by the corporation it insures. Usually registered and domiciled in tax havens, e.g. Bermuda (qv), captives combine tax efficiency with the benefit of self-insurance (qv) and/or mutual insurance. Most captives have a presence in the reinsurance market (inward and outward) and some have become substantial writers of third party business. *See* PROTECTED CELL COMPANIES; RENT-A-CAPTIVE.

Capture and seizure 'War risks' covered under the Institute War Clauses (qv). Capture, taking the enemy in wartime or by rebels or insurgents. Seizure, a wider term embracing every act of forcible possession. *See* FREE OF CAPTURE AND SEIZURE CLAUSE.

Car groups The 20 groups used by motor insurers for rating purposes; the higher the group number, the higher the premium. Groups reflect the cost of replacement parts, ease of carrying out repairs, purchase price, performance and level of security. Expensive high performance cars are in the highest group.

Car sharing Where the passenger receiving a 'lift' pays the driver. The Road Traffic Act 1988, s.150, allows the car user to share the running costs with his passenger(s) without this being regarded as 'hire or reward' and therefore the subject of a policy exclusion. The vehicle must not be adapted for more than eight passengers and the contributions must not exceed running costs.

Care, custody and control exclusion *See* CUSTODY AND CONTROL.

Career average revalued scheme Career average scheme (qv) under which the benefits are revalued each year by reference to an appropriate index during pensionable service.

Career average scheme Pension scheme under which the benefits for each year of membership are related to the pensionable earnings for that particular year. *See* CAREER AVERAGE REVALUED SCHEME.

Cargo Goods transported aboard a vessel or other conveyance not being provisions, stores, equipment or bunker fuel for use on the vessel. The cargo owner's insurable interest (qv) continues for so long as he has title to the goods. There are other *cargo interests* (qv). The risk factors in marine insurance: mode of transportation; type of goods; packing; size/weight/value; trip route; trip duration; season; socio-economic environment.

Cargo insurance Cover is defined by standard clauses. Institute Cargo Clauses (qv), have three main sets, Clauses A, B and C, selected according to the nature of the goods, and specific to the type of cargo, e.g. coal, oil, jute, frozen food, etc. All sets cover *general average* (qv) and *salvage charges* (qv) and contain the War Exclusion Clause (qv) and the Strikes Exclusion Clause (qv).

Cargo interests Insurable interest relating to: (a) ownership; (b) freight; (c) insurance charges (qv); (d) anticipated profit, i.e. profit the seller loses when goods perish; (e) partial ownership (Marine Insurance Act 1906, s.8); defeasible interest (qv); (f) contingent interest (qv); (g) bottomry (qv) and respondentia (qv); (h) forwarding charges (qv); (i) commission insurable by an agent (Marine Insurance Act 1906, s.5).

Cargo specie *See* SPECIE.

Cargo value The value placed on cargo for insurance purposes when insured under a valued policy (qv). It normally extends to include all charges and profit.

Carpenter plan A name for *spread loss reinsurance* (qv) first introduced in the US by a broker named Carpenter.

Carriage by Air Act 1961 Enacts the Hague Protocol (qv) in the UK.

Carriage by Rail *See* CIM.

Carriage of Goods by Road Act 1965 Enacts the CMR (qv) so far as it relates to the rights and liabilities of persons concerned in the carriage of goods by road under a contract to which the Convention applies.

Carriage of Goods by Sea Act 1971 Enacts the Hague-Visby rules (qv) by specifying the respective responsibilities, liabilities and immunities of carriers and cargo owners.

Carriage of Goods by Sea Act 1992 Replaces the Bill of Lading Act 1855 in transferring rights and liabilities with bills of lading, sea waybills and ship's delivery orders. The Act transfers rights to all 'lawful holders' (e.g. the holder of the bill of lading, the receiver of the goods, persons identified in the ship's delivery order) (s.2). The removal of certain technicalities makes it easier for them to sue the carrier when goods are lost or damaged at sea. The Act also applies similar principles to electronic documentation.

Carrier 1. The railway, shipowner, haulier, airline or other transporter of goods. *See* COMMON CARRIER. 2. The insurer or reinsurer carrying the risk.

Carrying out contracts of insurance The regulated activity (qv) specified in art. 10(2) of the Regulated Activity Order (Effecting and Carrying out Insurance Contracts), of carrying out insurance contracts of insurance as a principal.

Case method/case reserve Method of calculating the reserve for the outstanding reported claims. Each claim is assessed individually on the basis of the information available and the aggregated figure is included in the balance sheet.

Cash accumulation policy Pensions term, referring to an insurance policy under which contributions net of expenses are accumulated in a pool to which bonuses and interest are added. The proceeds are used to buy pension benefits as they become due.

Cash call/loss clause A proportional reinsurance clause that permits a cedant (qv), on settling a loss above a given sum, to obtain immediate settlement to avoid waiting for the periodic payment. The clause cannot be implemented if the cedant owes outstanding balances to the reinsurer.

Cash equivalent transfer value (CETV) The cash equivalent of accrued benefits under a *defined benefit scheme* (qv) that may be used as a *transfer payment* (qv) to another approved pension arrangement or to purchase a section 32 policy (qv). The *minimum funding requirement* (qv) applies to CETV.

Cash flow underwriting Underwriting approach emphasising rapid premium growth rather than selective, profitable underwriting. The insurer expects that the investment income from the enhanced revenue will more than offset any reasonable underwriting loss. An insurer who anticipates a rise in short-term interest rates may adopt this approach.

Cash fund Funds invested by their managers, e.g. unit trust managers, exclusively in short term deposits with banks and local authorities. The interest secured is usually better than the amount that could have been achieved by individual investors.

Cash-in value *See* SURRENDER VALUE.

Cash ISA An ISA (qv) that invests in cash only and is therefore also a Mini ISA. Cash is defined widely and can include bank and building society accounts, cash unit trusts, national savings products (excluding national savings certificates and premium bonds) and money market deposits. As with other ISAs, the cash ISA is free of all taxes. *See* CAT STANDARDS.

Cash loss *See* CASH CALL.

Cash option *See* COMMUTATION.

Cashing-in Occurs where the holder of a unit-linked policy takes the cash value of his units on the maturity date. The cash value in any given year is affected by both the market trends and by investment management decisions. The holder may be allowed to defer his 'cash-in' for a period without having to pay more premiums.

***Castellain* v. *Preston* (1883)** The leading case on indemnity (qv). Defendant contracted to sell property but, before completion, the property sustained fire damage (£330), which the defendant recovered from his insurer. On completion, the defendant received the full purchase price from the purchaser despite not having repaired the damage. The insurer recovered the £330 payment as the defendant, having received the full price, had suffered no loss and the fire policy was one of indemnity.

Casualty A term describing a loss, particularly used in the insurance of marine hulls. *See* CASUALTY BOOK; CASUALTY INSURANCE.

Casualty book Stands in the centre of the underwriting room at Lloyd's into which details of vessels that are, or likely to become, total losses are entered with a quill pen.

Casualty insurance A US term most associated with general liability but also embraces such diverse forms as plate glass, crime, boiler and machinery, surety bonds and aviation insurance. The term distinguishes these forms of insurance from those written in the US property insurance sector.

Cat Bonds *See* CATASTROPHE BOND.

CAT ISA Any ISA that has been awarded the UK Treasury's CAT mark. *See* CAT STANDARDS.

CAT Marked *See* CAT STANDARDS.

CAT Standards Stands for fair Charges, easy Access and decent Terms. Voluntary government-initiated standards to help savers identify straightforward ISAs (qv) that offer a reasonable deal. Firms adopting or exceeding these standards market their ISAs as 'CAT marked'. All three types of ISA components (Cash ISAs (qv), Life Insurance ISAs (qv) and Stocks and Shares ISAs) qualify for CAT marking. The cost varies with each type of investment but is controlled.

Catastrophe The possibility of exceptionally heavy loss due to an occurrence, often of short duration, e.g. Hurricane Betsey. Most occurrences are natural disasters, but certain 'catastrophic events', e.g. downfall of Barings Bank, have been man-made. *See* CATASTROPHE BONDS; CATASTROPHE EXCESS OF LOSS.

Catastrophe bond/Act of God Bond Corporate bonds (qv) issued by a reinsurer/insurer through a *special purpose vehicle* (qv) to capital market investors who supply capital in return for periodic interest payments. The interest payments and/or the return of principal are linked to the occurrence of a defined catastrophe event. The investors sacrifice (or defer) all or part of their principal and/or interest if the catastrophe occurs and a specified claims threshold is breached. The (re)insurer is then able to use the retained funds to pay for claims based on a specific insurance portfolio, a catastrophe loss index or a formula linked to a parametric trigger (qv). Bonds thus transfer insurance risk to the capital market whose investors are attracted by high yields and an investment unrelated to general economic conditions. *See* SECURITISATION.

Catastrophe equity put (CatEPut) Put options (qv) that enable incorporated insurers to sell shares (equity) to capital market investors at pre-negotiated prices when catastrophe losses exceed the levels specified in the options. CatEPuts therefore provide insurers with access to additional equity in the wake of catastrophic losses. This is alternative risk financing (qv) by way of post-loss funding that obviates the need for the insurer to 'sit on' on large amounts of capital waiting for the loss event to occur and thereby improves the insurer's return on assets. These instruments are also traded on the Chicago Board of Trade and the Bermuda Commodities Exchange.

Catastrophe excess of loss *See* CATASTROPHE REINSURANCE.

Catastrophe layer Non-proportional reinsurance layer of cover with an excess point (qv) so high that the layer will only be affected by rare catastrophic losses.

Catastrophe options Options traded on the Chicago Board of Trade (CBOT) and the Bermuda Commodities Exchange (BCOE) the value of which is linked to the occurrence of defined losses caused by natural disasters.

Catastrophe reinsurance An *excess of loss reinsurance* (qv) which, subject to a specified limit, indemnifies the reinsured for the amount of loss in excess of a specified retention, the excess point (qv), with regard to an accumulation of losses caused by a catastrophic event (e.g. a hurricane) or series of events. The reinsurance document is referred to as a catastrophe cover. *See* HOURS CLAUSE.

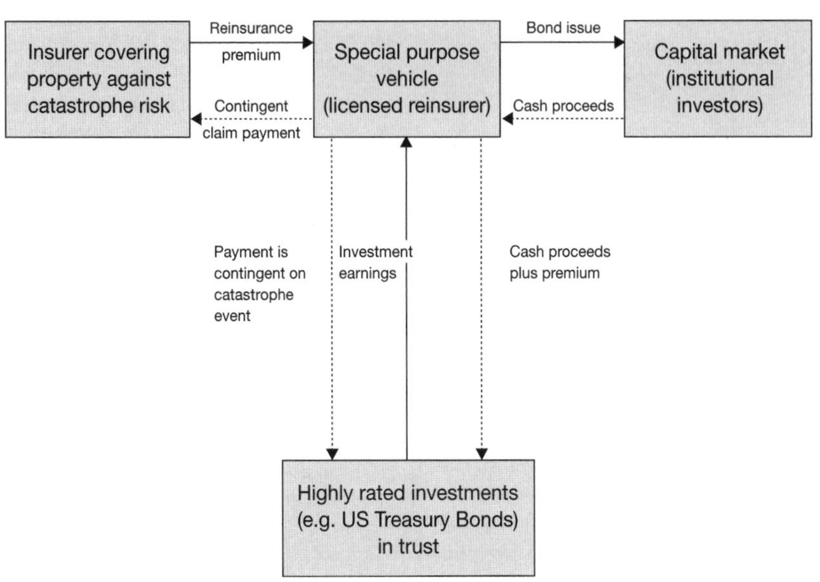

Figure 3. Basic structure of a catastrophe bond
An alternative to reinsurance (for a reinsurer it is an alternative to a retrocession)

'Catastrophe' reserves A reserve created by an insurer as a safeguard against exceptionally poor claims experience. The reserve is created out of prudence and not in pursuance of regulatory requirements. The term is used colloquially.

Catastrophe securitisation *See* CATASTROPHE BONDS.

Catastrophe swaps A reinsurer swaps part of his portfolio, e.g. earthquake in Japan, with the Florida hurricane exposure of another reinsurer, each wishing to diversify his or her portfolio. The term also describes an arrangement between an insurer and an investor. The insurer agrees to make periodic payments to another party who agrees to make payments to the insurer if defined catastrophes occur, but there is no exchange of principal. *See* WEATHER SWAPS.

Causa causans The immediate cause – the last link in the chain, the nearest in time but not necessarily the nearest in efficiency. The nearest in efficiency is the proximate cause (qv) of a loss.

Cause of action The fact or combination of facts giving rise to a right of legal action.

Caveat emptor Common law rule meaning 'let the buyer beware'. The principle is that the buyer of goods had the opportunity to satisfy himself as to the suitability of the article and therefore no liability attaches to the vendor. However, the Sale of Goods Act 1979 (qv) provides a measure of 'buyer' protection and the Defective Premises Act 1972, s.3 (qv), abolishes caveat emptor in claims based on a vendor's negligence in certain building work done pre-sale or pre-letting of property. Insurance contracts are subject to utmost good faith (qv) and not caveat emptor. The FSA calls upon the seller of financial products to give '*best advice*' (qv).

CDD *See* COOLING DEGREE DAY.

CDOs (Collateralised Debt Obligations) Bonds whose income payments and principal repayments are dependent on a pool of instruments such as a diversified pool of commercial loans or bond instruments bought in the secondary market or from the balance sheet of a bank. The cash flows are sold as securities and the risk of default is transferred accordingly. Banks may benefit from early repayment of the underlying loans and so create risk-related layers in bond format and offer them via an SPV (qv). Investors, such as reinsurers who take up high-risk layers, are compensated by high yields on the securities. *See* INSURITISATION; SECURITISATION.

Ceasing age The age at which an income protection payment (qv) comes to an end.

Cedant/ceding office An insurance company buying reinsurance cover by ceding part of its business to the reinsurer under proportional reinsurance (qv). The term is also used more informally to describe a reinsured entering into *excess of loss treaties* (qv).

Cede To purchase reinsurance.

Ceding Commission The reinsurer's payment to the reinsured as a reimbursement of all or part of the reinsured's expenses on the original business, plus a contribution to overheads.

Ceding office *See* CEDANT.

Ceiling point *See* EXIT POINT.

Centre Write Ltd Subsidiary of the Society of Lloyd's established in order to make reinsurance available to underwriting members participating in run-off syndicates and underwrite estate reinsurance protection.

Certificate in Insurance The CII's 'core' level qualification suitable for those entering the industry and gaining the essential basic knowledge of the market, key disciplines and products. Six units accumulating a 40 credit threshold achieve a pass and the entitlement to use the designation

'Cert CII'. Candidates are also able to proceed to the *Diploma in Insurance* (qv), subject to continuing professional development requirements, gaining recognition for their accumulated credits.

Certificate in IT for Insurance Professionals Examination-based qualification awarded jointly by the CII and the British Computer Society for insurance professionals seeking a greater awareness of potential IT applications in the insurance industry. The award gives credit towards other CII qualifications and the BCS Professional Examination.

Certificate of eligibility Confirmation by an employee that he is not a member of an occupational pension scheme and is eligible to pay into a personal pension scheme (qv).

Certificate of entry The policy issued by a Protection and Indemnity Club (qv) when a vessel is entered in the club.

Certificate of existence A survival certificate certifying that an annuitant (qv) is still alive.

Certificate of insurance Document evidencing the existence of insurance. Certificates are legally required in the following classes: employers' liability insurance; motor insurance (Road Traffic Act cover); oil carrying vessels (pollution liability cover). *See also* MARINE INSURANCE CERTIFICATE.

Certificate of Origin Documentary evidence to the import country's customs authorities that the cargo: (a) is not from an embargoed or restricted country; (b) genuinely comes from the country specified; (c) is included in official statistics; (d) is included or may be included with other documents.

Certificate T Certification by the scheme actuary that in a contracted out salary-related pension scheme, certain liabilities are 100 per cent funded in accordance with the valuation method (qv) specified for the minimum funding requirement (qv).

Cession A specific item of reinsurance under a reinsurance treaty (qv).

Cession limit Reinsurance term meaning a limit that restricts the total sums insured ceded for a whole country or specified zone.

CFR (C & F) Cost and Freight means that the seller *delivers* when the goods pass the ship's rail at the port of shipment and pays the costs and freight to take the goods to the port of destination. The buyer carries the risk of loss/damage during transit and therefore arranges cargo insurance.

CFS-CFS Notes on a bill of lading (qv) showing that cargo was consolidated at one *container freight station* (qv), transported to another station and deconsolidated at that CFS.

Chain ladder method A method used in general insurance by claims reserving practitioners to estimate the loss development of outstanding claims. It involves calculating ratios of adjacent 'ladders' (columns of figures) in a table.

Chain of events A *proximate cause* (qv) term referring to a sequence of events preceding a loss.

Chain of indemnity The right of a supplier of an injurious product to recover the amount paid in damages from his own supplier. A retailer, liable under the Sale of Goods Act 1979 (qv) for product-induced injuries to a customer, may seek an indemnity under the Act from the relevant wholesaler or manufacturer who breached an implied term (fitness for purpose (qv) and satisfactory quality (qv)). However, as it is a non-consumer contract (qv) an exclusion of these implied terms is permitted if the supplier can show that the exemption passes the *test of reasonableness* (qv). In turn a wholesaler can look to the manufacturer for a Sale of Goods Act 1979 breach.

Chairman's Strategy Group 2002 The committee that recommended the replacement of the regulatory and market boards at Lloyd's by a single franchise board (qv). Lloyd's acts as franchisor and the managing agents as franchisees. Another key outcome was the replacement of the three-year accounting system with GAAP accounting (qv).

Chance The probability or likelihood that an event will occur.

Chancery bonds A court bond (qv) guaranteeing the performance of receivers and managers appointed by the Chancery Division of the High Court. The receivers and managers may deal with the preservation of property or collection revenue arising from property. Receivership may arise: pending litigation; during the minority of an infant; to prevent dissipation of assets by persons having immediate or partial interest in it, or to whom it is entrusted by law. The Chancery division fixes the amount of the guarantee and the remuneration of the receiver.

Change in temperature clause Fire policy exclusion in respect of damage to perishable goods caused by a change in temperature resulting from destruction or disablement by an insured peril of the cold store or refrigerating plant. The risk can be bought back for an additional premium.

Change of interest endorsement Signifies that the original insured's interest in subject matter of insurance (qv) has been taken over by a new party who is the new insured. The latter normally completes a new proposal form prior to being accepted. *See* NOVATION; PERSONAL CONTRACTS.

Change of ownership clause An Institute Time/International Hull Clause enabling the insurer to cancel the policy in the event of the vessel being sold or transferred to new management during the currency of the policy if they do not approve the change. If the vessel has sailed, the cancellation is suspended until arrival at the port of final discharge.

Change of Underwriting Policy Clause Requires that the reinsured does not, after arranging the reinsurance treaty, change its underwriting practices with regard to the business covered by the treaty without the reinsurer's consent.

Change of voyage Voluntary change of the ship's destination from the contemplated voyage that occurs after the commencement of the risk, under a hull or cargo voyage policy. The insurer's liability ends immediately the decision is made and it is immaterial that a loss occurs when the ship is still on the original course. Institute Cargo Clauses provide that a change of voyage is held covered at a premium to be agreed if prompt notice is given to the insurer.

Chapter I pension schemes Occupational schemes approved under ICTA 1988, Chapter I, part XIV. They include: individual arrangements (qv); Hancock annuities (qv); ex-gratia benefits, i.e. lump sum payments when an employee is not already a member of an occupational or personal pension scheme in respect of the employment giving rise to the payment; earmarked schemes (qv); self-invested personal pension schemes (qv); small self-administered schemes (qv); self-managed funds (qv); simplified defined contribution schemes; unfunded schemes (qv); FSAVCs (qv); death in service life or group life schemes (qv); statutory schemes, e.g. public sector schemes e.g. schemes for the Civil Service, NHS, Police, Local Government, Teachers, etc.

Chapter IV ICTA 1988, part XIV, sets out the approval requirements for personal pensions, including stakeholder pensions (qv). Defined contribution occupational schemes can be approved under Chapter IV or Chapter I. Most occupational schemes are approved under Chapter I (qv).

Chargeable events Occur when certain payments are made from packaged life and investment products, e.g. certain life policy payments, bond withdrawals. They may or may not give rise to a tax charge but if they do, any resultant tax liability falls within normal income tax rules.

Chargeable gains The gains made on a chargeable event (qv), i.e. the excess of returns over investment from certain package products. The gains are chargeable to higher rate income tax but not the basic rate or capital gains tax (see top slicing (qv)).

Charter An agreement for the hire of a vessel or aircraft. *See* CHARTER PARTY.

Charter party Contract between the owner of a vessel and the charterer (qv). The contract covers, inter alia, the charterer's responsibility for loss/damage to the vessel, duration of the agreement, freight rate and ports involved during the voyage(s).

Chartered freight The freight payable by the charterer to the shipowner under the charter party (qv) whereby the vessel (or space therein) is hired for a voyage or period. *See* FREIGHT INSURANCE.

Chartered Insurance Institute The insurance industry's professional educational body open to individuals wholly or mainly engaged in insurance. Examinations lead to the designations of Cert CII, Dip CII and ACII. Fellowship (FCII) (qv) is based on knowledge, experience and achievement. The chief objective is to promote efficiency and improvement in insurance practice. There are 90 local institutes in the UK with 50 affiliated institutes overseas. *See* SOCIETY OF FINANCIAL ADVISERS; DIPLOMA IN INSURANCE; ADVANCED DIPLOMA IN INSURANCE.

Chartered Insurer/Chartered Insurance Practitioner/Chartered Insurance Broker *See* CHARTERED TITLES.

Chartered titles The CII offers Fellows and Associates Chartered Titles. A *Chartered Insurer* (qv) applies to members working for insurance companies and Lloyd's underwriting agents. *Chartered Insurance Practitioner* applies to those working as intermediaries or loss adjusters, in trade or professional bodies and in other insurance-related occupations. *Chartered Insurance Broker* applies to members who are carrying on business as an insurance broker. Chartered titles are granted to individual qualified members and are not used as applying to firms, partnerships or corporate bodies.

Charterer The party who acquires the whole of the carrying capacity of ship for the transportation of cargo or passengers in accordance with the agreement made with the shipowner.

Charterer's legal liability Liability to/in respect of: third parties, including cargo owners; the shipowner; indemnity to owner for liability to third parties; general average and salvage (time charterers only). Insurance cover is available on a fixed premium basis and cover is limited to the amount the charterer would have been able to limit his liability had he been the shipowner. Shortfalls in cover may be arranged in P & I Clubs, a charterers' club or in the London market.

'Cheatline' Set up by the ABI to enable members of the public to report cases of insurance fraud by freephone. Receives an average of 50 calls a week.

Chicago Mercantile Exchange (CME) The largest futures exchange in the US. CME offered the world's first exchange-traded weather derivatives (qv) based on 10 US cities in 1999. By 2003, the number increased to 15 to include five European cities (Amsterdam, Berlin, London, Paris and Stockholm.) (*www.cme.com*).

Child's deferred insurance Life policy under which, until the agreed 'vesting age' (e.g. 18), the premium is paid by the parent. At 'vesting' the child takes over the policy on a whole life or endowment basis in his own name at the insurer's normal rates regardless of health. Alternatively the child may take the cash sum or defer the benefits. If the parent dies before the 'vesting age' premiums are suspended until the child takes over the policy.

Chinese wall The separation of key functions of a business to ensure that no conflicts of interest arise, and to prevent the inappropriate transfer of sensitive or regulatory information to another part of the business.

CIM Convention The International Convention on Carriage of Goods by Rail (CIM) establishes a measure of uniformity in Europe. It is necessary in the case of rail imports or exports involving the UK to incorporate the terms of the convention into the contract of rail carriage as shown by the consignment note. The carrier's liability is similar to that of CMR (qv).

City spread The sale of a contract struck on one city against the purchase of another contract struck on another. It is a means of hedging against the weather risk.

Civil Aviation Act 1982 Sets out duties, functions and objectives of the Civil Aviation Authority (qv). Deals with aerodromes, the regulation of civil aviation and the design, construction and maintenance of aircraft. Protects aircraft operators against trespass and nuisance claims whilst engaged in 'normal flight'. Section 76 imposes a strict liability in respect of loss or damage on water or land when an article, person or animal is caused to fall from an aircraft during flight, take-off or landing. The loss is recoverable from the aircraft operator.

Civil Aviation Authority (CAA) Operates under the Civil Aviation Act 1982 (amended 1996). Responsibilities include air safety and registration of aircraft. Issues Air Operators Certificates to those who can demonstrate their competence to run an aircraft safely and show that they are adequately financed and insured for passenger and third party risks. CAA collaborates internationally on air safety.

Civil Aviation (Investigation of Air Accidents) Regulations 1996 Implements Council Directive 94/56/EC and the fundamental principles governing the investigation of civil aviation accidents and incidents. Also re-enacts the 1989 Regulations. The Inspectors of Air Accidents of the Air Accidents Investigation Branch of the Department of Transport are identified as the investigating body. The Chief Inspector can delegate investigation to another member state, or, in some cases, to a state that is a party to the Chicago Convention. An inspector's report must be published and any safety recommendations in the report are not to create a presumption of blame or liability.

Civil aviation risk The life or personal accident term for the extra risk due to a proposer engaging significantly in flying as a passenger or as a pilot in private aircraft.

Civil commotion A risk excluded under the standard fire policy and other property insurances along with riot (qv) and similar perils. It means the severe and prolonged disturbances by people 'out of hand'. Civil commotion is an intermediate state between a riot (qv) and civil war (qv). An element of turbulence or tumult is essential. Riot and civil commotion can be insured as additional perils (qv). The insurer imposes strict time limits for the notification of claims.

Civil engineering The design and construction of roads, railways, bridges, aqueducts, canals, ports, harbours, moles, breakwaters, lighthouses and drainage works. The term originated in the distinction between these engineering activities and those associated with military operations, e.g. fortification, ordnance, etc. The General Conditions of Contract for Civil Engineering Construction include insurance obligations.

Civil Liability (Contribution Act) 1978 Replaces and extends the Law Reform (Married Women and Tortfeasors) Act

1935 which abolished the common law rule that a judgment in favour of a claimant against one of a number of joint tortfeasors (qv) barred subsequent proceedings against the others. The 1978 Act gives a tortfeasor the right to secure a contribution from other tortfeasors where the legal basis of their respective liabilities lies in tort, breach of contract, breach of trust or otherwise. The Act also abolished the rule that if the claimant's action against one tortfeasor succeeded the damages awarded set a limit for any subsequent actions against other defendants.

Civil Procedure Rules (CPR) The Civil Procedure Act 1997 implemented much of the Woolf Report and unified the civil claims procedure in the UK courts. The objective is to ensure that the parties are on an equal footing, save expense and have their cases dealt with quickly and fairly. Litigation is seen as a last resort as the parties are encouraged to explore alternative dispute resolution (qv) methods and display greater cooperation at the pre-action stage under the pre-action protocols (qv). *See* ACCESS TO JUSTICE ACT 1999.

Civil war 'War between two or more portions of a country or state, each contending for mastery of the whole and each claiming to be the legitimate government. The term is also applied to war or rebellion when the rebellious portions of the state are contiguous to those containing the seat of Government'. (F.H. Jones).

Claim A demand by the insured for an indemnity or benefit under the policy. The claim will be met, subject to any limits, if the loss event is caused by an insured peril and is not excluded.

Claims advice clause *See* CLAIMS COOPERATION CLAUSE.

Claims condition A condition setting out what the insured has to do in the event of a claim. It covers notice of loss, assistance to the insurer (qv) and proofs of loss (qv), and in the case of liability policies there is a control of proceedings clause (qv) and a non-admission of liability clause (qv).

Claims Cooperation Clause Requires the reinsured (qv) to give prompt or immediate notice to the reinsurer on becoming aware of a loss likely to involve the reinsurer. The reinsured must at all times cooperate with the reinsurer in the negotiation and settlement of the loss. In liability claims the reinsured must not admit liability without the reinsurer's consent.

Claims equalisation reserve An insurer's reserve for smoothing out fluctuations in claims costs where the incidence is of an uneven nature. Produces a greater level of consistency in the revenue account.

Claims expenses/claims handling expenses Direct costs of investigation and settlement as distinct from the payments of the claims themselves. Includes loss adjusters' fees, court fees, etc. The indirect expenses, *claims handling expenses,* relate to the salaries and overheads associated with running a claims department.

Claims experience The insured's claims history with regard to the cost and frequency of previous claims. It is material for an insured to disclose his claims experience when proposing insurance. The term also describes the relationship between premium and claims experienced by an insurer for a particular class of business over a period of time.

Claims handling agreements Agreements between insurers involved in the same incidents or losses to settle matters between them by way of a prescribed formula rather than resort to costly and regular litigation. The knock-for-knock agreement (qv) has been replaced by the memorandum of agreement (qv).

Claims-made policy A liability policy covering all claims first notified during the policy year or any applicable *extended* *reporting period* (qv) regardless of when the injury or loss occurred. However, if the policy has a *retroactive date* (qv) the policy will not respond to events occurring before that date. Unlike the losses-occurring policies, the policy 'runs off' at the end of the extended reporting period (qv). *See* CLAIMS-MADE REINSURANCE; LIABILITY SEQUENCE.

Claims-made reinsurance An excess of loss reinsurance contract under which the reinsurer pays losses if the claim is made during the policy period in respect of occurrences after the retroactive date (qv). It overcomes the difficulty associated with long tail cases of having to ascertain the time of the occurrence. The treaty usually incorporates an *extended reporting period* (qv) and incorporates the claims-made trigger of the underlying liability policy. Compare with LOSSES-OCCURRING REINSURANCE and *see* RISKS ATTACHING.

Claims-related method A method of dividing the cost of insurance purchased for the organisation and apportioning it among the cost centres based on claims experience. The aim is to ensure that each part of the company contributes to total insurance costs in a manner reflecting its own claims record. It encourages loss prevention.

Claims reserve The provision made in the accounts of an insurer in respect of claims notified but not yet settled. *See* CHAIN LADDER METHOD.

Claims series clause A clause in a liability or reinsurance contract designed to treat a series of loss occurrences *unified* by a common cause as a single loss. This means that any deductible or retention will be applied only to the aggregate of individual claims arising from the common cause and not to the claims individually. For example, individual claims originating in the same product design fault would be aggregated and might breach the deductible while each one individually might fall below it. The clause also has a bearing on the application of limits of indemnity. *See* HOURS CLAUSE; ORIGINATING CAUSE.

Claims Underwriting and Exchange (CUE). Database containing details of nearly all household and private motor claims over a six-year period. The purpose is to combat fraud such as multiple claims for the same loss or the staging of a series of incidents. Underwriters may search CUE at the underwriting stage and avoid 'bad risks'. More usually they search CUE when checking the validity of claims.

Clash cover/contingency cover An excess of loss treaty (qv) with a retention higher than the limits on any one reinsured policy or contract. The agreement covers the reinsured's exposure to multiple retentions when two or more policies (perhaps from different lines of business) are involved in the same occurrence in an amount that exceeds *the clash cover* retention.

Class A member Any pension scheme member who is not a Class B or Class C member. Class A embraces members of schemes established on or after 14 March 1989 and all new members of earlier schemes joining on or after 1 June 1989. The maximum retirement benefit for Class A on retiring between ages 50 and 75 is two-thirds of final remuneration (qv). The earnings cap (qv) applies. The tax-free lump sum on retirement is 3/80ths of final salary for each year of service (not exceeding 40 years) or, if greater, 2.25 times the annual pension.

Class Action/group litigation A legal procedure one party, or group, brings against a defendant as representative of a larger group. Deep vein thrombosis (qv) sufferers have acted against airlines in this way. The Civil Procedure Rules (qv) use the term 'group litigation' while the Legal Services Commission refers to 'multi-party actions'. UK proceedings are issued under the Group Litigation Order.

Class B member Any pension scheme member who, on or after 17 March 1987 and before 1 June 1989, joined the scheme, being a scheme which commenced before 14 March 1989, or whom the IR has agreed to be a Class B member by virtue of previous membership of a relevant scheme and, in either case has not opted to be a Class A member. The earnings cap (qv) does not apply to Class B.

Class C member A pension scheme member who joined before 17 March 1987 or who joined subsequently and whom the IR has agreed to be a Class C member by virtue of previous membership of a relevant scheme, and, in either case, has not opted to be a Class A member. The earnings cap (qv) does not apply to Class C members.

Class of insurance Defined by the FSA (qv) as 'any class of insurance listed in Schedule 1 to the Regulated Activities Order (Contracts of insurance) 2001. *See* REGULATED CLASSES OF INSURANCE; LONG-TERM BUSINESS; GENERAL INSURANCE BUSINESS.

Class of use Private car insurance rating factor reflecting the extent of use of the car. Use solely for social, domestic and pleasure purposes is the most lightly rated with little difference in premium to include commuting to work. The highest rated category (known as class 3) is full business use including commercial travelling. The intermediate classes include more restricted *business use* (qv).

Classification clause 1. Hull clause providing that an insured, who fails to maintain the ship's agreed classification or follow the classification society's recommendations in regard to seaworthiness or maintenance recommendations, faces automatic termination of hull and machinery cover. Innocent mortgagees may be protected for a limited time. 2. Floating policy (qv) or open cover (qv) clause specifying the minimum class of vessel required to carry the insured cargo. If the vessel is below the class specified, an additional premium is charged.

Classification societies Organisations that survey, classify and grade ships according to their condition for insurance and other purposes. The classification clause (qv) lists nine societies including Lloyd's Register (qv) and the American Bureau of Shipping. *See* A1.

Clause 21.2.1. Non-negligent cover *See* JCT 21.2.1 NON-NEGLIGENT COVER.

Claused bill/dirty bill A bill of lading endorsed to note some defect in the products or packaging of the goods to be shipped.

Clauses descriptive of the risk *See* DESCRIPTION OF RISK CLAUSES.

Clawback 1. A practice whereby a pension scheme will offset an amount equivalent to the state pension against a target pension so as to arrive at the amount payable by the scheme. 2. Commission paid to an intermediary for introducing business may be 'clawed back' if the policy does not stay in force for a specific period of time. 3. *See* DELAYED TURNOVER.

Clean cut basis The method of transferring *premium portfolios* (qv) and *loss portfolio* (qv) from one year to another in a manner that simplifies the preparation reinsurance treaty accounts when a treaty is cancelled or transferred. *See* LOSS PORTFOLIO TRANSFER.

Clean-up costs Financial loss due to pollution (qv). Costs may include: cleaning up land, water courses, buildings, machinery, etc., and generally removing the effects of pollution. The insured may cover his liability for third party clean-up costs incurred by a third party and for the cost of cleaning up his own property under a first party policy. It is possible to extend existing liability policies but one approach is to arrange a separate environmental impairment policy (qv) that also covers cleaning up one's own site.

Cleanliness Accumulated trade waste and rubbish is a fire hazard indicative of lax management and poor moral hazard (qv). Greasy waste is liable to spontaneous heating. In some cases a warranty (qv) may require the insured to keep waste/scraps in metals bins and remove them from the building at the end of each day.

Client agreement FSA rule (Conduct of Business 4.2.7 R) requires a firm intending to conduct designated forms of investment business with UK private clients to enter into a client agreement. The client must sign the terms of business or he must have consented to them in writing.

Client money Authorised firms are bound, unless risk transfer (qv) applies, by the FSA to segregate all client money on a daily basis in accordance with the client money rule 4 in the Client Asset Sourcebook for designated investment business and rule 5 for general insurance. For investment business this means segregating money belonging to the client held either as free money or settlement money. For general insurance, client money usually means premiums received from a customer but also covers return premiums and claims money if received for the client. Money received by general insurance intermediaries, other than under a risk transfer (qv) agreement, must be segregated in a statutory or non-statutory trust (qv) meaning the money is 'ring-fenced' and therefore beyond the reach of the intermediary's creditors.

Clinical trial Research to ensure that new vaccines, drugs, treatments, etc., are safe and effective. Participants must be advised of their rights to compensation in the event of consequential injury, illness or impairment otherwise the trial will not be authorised under European legislation or by an ethics committee. *See* CLINICAL TRIAL INSURANCE.

Clinicial trial insurance Claims-made policy (qv) for research organisations, drug manufacturers, hospitals, universities, etc., involved in clinical trials (qv). The insurer indemnifies the policyholder in the sums they have agreed to pay to trial participants for injuries regardless of fault. Claimants may prefer to make normal legal liability claims rather than use the agreed arbitration/compensation processes. If so, the policyholder's legal liability is covered under a second section of the policy.

Close links A linkage between an FSA-authorised firm and another firm or entity falling into one of a number of defined categories, viz: a parent company; a subsidiary; a subsidiary of a parent company; entities or persons owning or controlling 20 per cent of the voting rights or capital; companies in respect of which the firm owns 20 per cent or more of the voting rights or capital. The FSA is concerned to satisfy itself that, taking account of *close links,* it can exercise its supervisory function effectively.

Closed fund A life insurance fund maintained for a particular group of policies with no new business being accepted for the fund.

Closed scheme A pension scheme that does not admit new members.

Closed year Where the accounting basis is for a two-year period or longer, a closed year is the year of account for which a result has been ascertained. This can only be done after providing for all outstanding claims. At Lloyd's a year of account closes after 36 months, but this will end as Lloyd's moves to annual accounting.

Closing Completion of an insurance.

Closing instructions An advice sent by a broker to an insurer who has taken a line on a slip specifying the actual proportion of risk allocated to the insurer and the actual premium receivable. If a slip is oversubscribed, the broker scales down and apportions the risk pro rata. *See* SHORT CLOSING.

Closing slip *See* CLOSING INSTRUCTIONS (qv).

Clubs *See* MEMBERS' CLUBS.

Cluster policy A life policy consisting of a number of equally valued smaller policies. Each policy in the cluster is treated separately for tax and administrative purposes. The holder can transfer each individual policy separately into a personal pension scheme to secure pension benefits and take them at different times to phase in retirement. The holder is able to retain the maximum tax-free investment and secure a lump sum return on death. *Clustering* can also be applied to investment bonds or endowments enabling the holder to take benefits as required over a period.

CMOs (Collateralised Mortgage Obligations) Similar to CDOs (qv) except that they are backed exclusively by mortgages rather than diversified loans. The cash inflows of the SPV are also divided into layers or tranches, each of which has a different payback period and seniority profile based on security.

CMR Convention (Contract de Merchandises par Route). Governs cross-border European road carriage and was enacted in the UK by the Carriage of Goods by Road Act 1965 (qv). CMR applies to the carriage of goods by road when the place of taking over the goods and the delivery place are in two different countries at least one of which is a contracting party. Any road journey for *hire or reward* (not own goods carriage) that starts or ends in the UK is subject to CMR unless an exception (e.g. furniture removal, postal despatch) applies. The carrier is liable for loss or damage from taking charge of the goods until delivery subject to a compensation limit based on a rate per kilo. There is no liability if a defence (e.g. wrongful act or neglect of the claimant) applies.

Code for Managing Underwriting Risk Guidance for a Lloyd's managing agent (qv) who must have a suitable risk management system in order to satisfy Lloyd's Core Principle 9. This Principle calls upon the agent to 'organise and control its internal affairs in a responsible manner, maintaining proper records and systems for the conduct of its business and the management of risk'.

Code for the Disposal of Motor Vehicle Salvage Created by the ABI, Lloyd's, salvage industry interests and the government, the Code gives directions on the treatment of vehicle salvage and recovered stolen vehicles. The intention is to make it difficult for criminals to ring vehicles or return dangerously repaired vehicles to the road. The Code must be complied with by insurers and salvage agents.

Code of Practice for Tracing Employers' Liability Insurance Policies Created by insurance interests and the government, it helps employees/former employees trace the employers' liability insurer on risk at the time their long-tail liability (qv) was caused. The employer may have ceased trading or insurance records may not exist or be inadequate. The Code requires insurers to maintain records to improve access to information. Insurers must state how their records can be searched, keep all records for 60 years, appoint a designated contact to handle enquiries, meet prescribed timescales and state annually that they have complied with the Code. There are two versions of this voluntary Code – the ABI Code for Insurance Companies and the NMA Code for syndicates at Lloyd's.

Co-insurance/co-insurer 1. Where two or more insurers share the same risk. A co-insurer is not bound to follow the decision of another co-insurer, except where he has given authority for the other insurer to act on his behalf. Each co-insurance is a separate contract with the insured. 2. Where an insured shares a part of the risk, e.g. 10 per cent of each claim (co-insurance clause), the insured is said to be a co-insurer.

Cold call An uninvited personal visit or oral communication. They are allowed for life insurance, unit trusts and personal pensions but the caller must present a business card stating his name, position, firm's name and address and the FSA (qv) authorisation logo. Telephone calls must not be made at an unsociable hour and no misleading information given. The caller must make it clear to the client that he will be entering into a contract for the purchase of investments. No undue pressure may be used.

Cold explosion An explosion caused by the sudden release of pressure as in the case of a ruptured steam boiler. The risk is generally covered under boiler and pressure plant policies (qv) but cover exists under the standard fire policy for damage caused by explosions (including hot explosions) of domestic boilers.

Cold storage clause *See* CHANGE IN TEMPERATURE CLAUSE.

Collapse 1. An insured risk under boiler and pressure plant insurance. It means 'the sudden and dangerous distortion (whether or not attended by rupture) of any part of the plant caused by crushing stress by force of steam or other fluid pressure (other than pressure of chemical action, or chemical action or ignition of the contents of ignited flue gases)'. 2. Under a buildings policy, collapse has been held to mean: 'falling, shrinking together with breaking down or giving way through external pressure, or loss of rigidity or support'. It is commonly the outcome of subsidence (qv). Collapse does not cover intentional demolition unless necessary in the course of remedial work consequent upon an insured event such as subsidence.

'Collapse' risk A construction/demolition term referring to damage to property caused by the removal or weakening of support accorded to any land, building or structure. The risk is excluded under the liability sections of contractors' all risks and erection all risk policies but can be bought back subject to a hefty excess (qv) and the exclusion of the contract works.

Collar Combination of *put options* (qv) and *call options* (qv) used, for example, by energy producers and end users to hedge against extreme price movements by keeping price within a defined range. The downside risk is limited at the cost of the upside potential. If price falls below the 'floor', the end user pays the energy company under the contract. If the 'ceiling' is exceeded the energy company pays the end user.

Collateral The security offered by a borrower for a loan. Life insurance policies that have acquired a surrender value are often acceptable as collateral security.

Collecting societies Registered friendly societies which operate almost exclusively in the field of industrial life insurance.

Collective investment schemes (CIS) Unit trust and similar schemes that provide for the collective holding, management and investment of a pool of assets from which the earnings or gain on disposition are shared among investors. These attributes are reflected in the definition of a CIS set out in FSMA, s.235(1). A distinct characteristic of UK schemes is that they are based on the concept of trusts. An open-ended investment company (OEIC) is a CIS.

Collective life policy A life insurance effected by credit companies to cover the loans they have advanced. The benefits are payable on death. This policy is distinguished from *group* life policies effected by employers or affinity groups.

Collective policy 1. A single policy on behalf of several co-insurers (*see* CO-INSURANCE). 2. A fidelity guarantee policy (qv) embracing a number of employees with a separate amount guaranteed for each.

Collision In marine insurance, a vessel striking another vessel or floating object but not a stationary object. The collision clause insuring a ship's legal liability is known as the Running Down Clause (qv). *See* BOTH TO BLAME CLAUSE.

Collision clause Hull policy clause known as the *Running Down Clause* (qv).

Collision damage waiver Cover for a person renting a car where the rental firm waives any right to recover the amount of damage to the car from the renter regardless of fault.

Collusion Deception perpetrated by two or more parties. Theft insurers exclude theft by collusion when a member of staff is involved. Such a theft has little to do with the security of the premises. Cover may be available under fidelity guarantee insurance (qv).

Combined Code on Corporate Governance Re-published in 2003 following the Higgs Report and the Smith Guidance on Audit Committees. The Code raises corporate governance standards for listed companies, and incorporates the Turnbull report on internal control (qv), the Smith guidance and good practice guidance from Higgs. Directors should at least annually conduct a review of the effectiveness of all internal controls including financial, operational, compliance and risk management. The FSA's Listing Rules underpin the Code by obliging companies to state in their annual reports how they have applied the principles of the Code (*www.frc.org.uk*).

Combined liability policy Policy combining two or more types of liability insurance in one document, e.g. public liability, products liability and employers' liability.

Combined Ratio The sum of two ratios: (a) incurred loss ratio (the ratio of losses incurred as a percentage of the net earned premium); and (b) the expense ratio (ratio of expenses incurred as a percentage of the net earned premium). If below 100 per cent it means an underwriting profit without taking account of investment income.

Combined single limit A single limit of protection on a liability policy for all sections of cover, i.e. bodily injury, property damage and passenger liability, in contrast to a policy with split limits, i.e. specific limits for each section. This approach applies in aviation insurance where one overall limit applies to three separate sections.

Combustible materials Materials likely to take fire and burn. The actual materials that insurers consider will ignite first are: waste and rubbish; combustible elements in structure and fittings; electrical insulation; textiles; flammable liquids; packing and wrapping.

Commercial all risks insurance *See* INDUSTRIAL ALL RISKS INSURANCE.

Commercial customer For FSA purposes, it is a policyholder or potential policyholder who is not a *retail customer* (qv). At the pre-sale stage commercial customers must be given sufficient information to enable them to make an informed decision about the proposed contract including details of premiums, fees and charges. Post-sale the policy document must be supplied promptly and notification of renewal or non-renewal must be given in good time before expiry. Intermediaries must also disclose their commission if requested. Certain commercial customers are *eligible complainants* (qv) from a complaints perspective. *See* CUSTOMER TYPES.

Commercial guarantees Fidelity guarantee insurances (qv) indemnifying the insured against financial loss resulting from acts of dishonesty by employees. *Collective policies* cover named employees with separate amounts for each. *Floating policies* cover unnamed employees up to one overall amount. *Blanket policies* guarantee the staff generally. *Positions policies* guarantee the position (e.g. chief accountant) and not the individual by name. The insurer considers the previous history of named employees and, in all cases, the type of work undertaken and the system of check.

Commercial legal expenses Provides businesses with legal advice and covers legal expenses to enforce or defend legal rights in a range of disputes. Cover is available under various sections: court attendance expenses; tax/VAT disputes; prosecution defence; data protection liability; contract disputes; personal injury or property claims; premises disputes; employment disputes and awards; licence disputes.

Commercial vehicle insurance A general term referring to the insurance of goods-carrying vehicles, buses and coaches, agricultural and forestry vehicles, mobile plant and other special types.

Commission disclosure ICOB Rules require insurance intermediaries dealing with general commercial customers to disclose, if requested to do so, their commission plus any commission received by any affiliated companies. *See* DISCLOSURE 4.

Common carrier A person who carries goods for 'all and sundry' willing to pay a reasonable charge. Such a carrier may be of a particular product over a particular route but if he limits the service to a particular sector he becomes a private carrier. A common carrier's liability at common law for the goods is strict, subject only to the defences of: action of the Queen's enemies, Act of God, fault of the owner, inherent vice. Railways are not common carriers and many road hauliers use the *Road Haulage Association Conditions of Carriage* (qv).

Common charges The shipowner ordinarily carries the cost of hauling the vessel for maintenance, but the insurer pays when the ship is brought in for insurance repairs. Consequently when the shipowner arranges maintenance to coincide with insurance repairs, the haulage charge is 'common' to both causes and is therefore shared between the shipowner and the insurer.

Common inn Defined in the Hotel Proprietors Act 1956 (qv). Essentially an establishment open to 'all and sundry', which does not pick and choose its guests. Special responsibilities attach to its proprietor including strict liability in respect of the property of guests who have booked sleeping accommodation. However, innkeepers who have displayed a statutory notice in pursuance of the Act benefit from limited liability.

Common investment fund (CIF) Refers to the investment of two or more pension schemes being managed by a single employer or a group of associated employers (qv). It does not create a pooled fund (qv).

Common Law The law that has been founded upon immemorial usage, established custom and legal precedents as distinct from statute law. Broadening down from precedent to precedent has developed the common law.

Common trust funds Feature: (a) pooling of all assets in a central fund, (b) payment of benefits from the central funds, and (c) trustees having wide powers of investment. The scheme may be insured so the funds are held centrally in insurance policies only. Alternatively, the fund is self-administered as in the case of small self-administered schemes (qv) where the funds are held centrally in investments such as commercial property, shares and cash deposits. Large schemes, i.e. those with 12 or more members, can also be self-administered.

Community Company An insurance company whose head office is within a member state of the European Community.

Commutation 1. Occurs when an individual, on reaching retirement, exchanges a part of his pension for a tax-free lump sum. In approved final salary schemes (qv) the maximum tax-free lump sum permitted is 1.5 times (based on 3/80ths for each year of service) final salary. For approved defined contribution schemes (qv) it is 25 per cent of the accumulated pension fund.

Commutation clause Reinsurance contract clause facilitating the termination of all obligations between the parties, normally accompanied by a final cash payment in respect of reinsured losses incurred. The clause is usually optional but can be mandatory.

Commutation factor The rate of exchange that determines the amount of pension that needs to be sacrificed to provide a given lump sum benefit at retirement. The commutation factor indicates how much cash is available for each £1 of pension exchanged. Scheme rules specify the commutation factor that will apply either to all members or specifically to individuals. The commutation factor is a ratio, e.g. 12:1 mean a pension of £883 per annum can be exchanged for a lump sum of £10,000.

Companies collective signing agreement (CCSA) A single market agreement (qv) used in the non-marine market. The agreement authorises the leading CCSA company to sign a collective policy on behalf of all other CCSA companies on risk. The agreement indemnifies the signatory company in respect of any liability that attaches that would not have attached had the policy been individually signed by all companies.

Company Directors Disqualification Act 1986 Enables a court to make a disqualification order against a director convicted of an indictable offence connected with promotion, formation, management or liquidation.

Company reimbursement *See* DIRECTORS' AND OFFICERS' LIABILITY INSURANCE.

Complete annuity *See* APPORTIONABLE ANNUITY.

Completed construction insurance Renewable engineering policy on completed civil engineering works, e.g. bridges, dams and tunnels, which constitute a low fire risk. Policy covers accidental physical loss from external perils excluding inherent defects.

Compliance The process of following agreed or regulated procedures such as those laid down by the FSA (qv) concerning authorisations (qv), regulated activities (qv), conduct of business, etc. At Lloyd's, the managing and members' agents (qv) must comply with the requirements imposed upon them by Lloyd's and supervised by the FSA (*www.fsa.gov.uk*).

Compliance audit 1. An audit instigated by the IR to ensure that the pension scheme has complied with IR requirements. 2. An audit to ensure that an authorised party has complied with FSA requirements under powers granted under FSMA.

Compliance oversight officer The *approved person* (qv), having *significant influence* (qv) and acting in the capacity of director or senior manager, who is allocated the compliance oversight function. He or she must ensure that the firm acts in accordance with FSA rules. He or she needs unfettered access to all individuals and information in order to further the sound and prudent management of the firm.

Composite company An insurance company that transacts all or several of the major classes of insurance.

Composite panels (sandwich panels) Building products used for cladding and insulation but creating a significant fire hazard. Materials such as expanded polystyrene, extruded polystyrene and polyurethane are more combustible than safer but more expensive alternatives. The risk is exacerbated when 'warehouse damage' lowers the fire resistance of panels. The higher the level of combustibility the harder it is to obtain insurance. Expert advice is available from the Building Research Establishment Ltd (qv).

Compound reversionary bonus A life insurance bonus payable at the same time and in the same circumstances as the sum insured which is declared periodically as an addition to the sum insured and accrued bonuses.

Comprehensive A term describing a policy with a number of different types of cover in one document (e.g. a private car comprehensive policy has sections providing material damage cover, third party cover, personal accident cover, medical expenses, etc.).

Compromised total loss An arranged settlement on a hull policy (qv) where there is no actual or constructive total loss but where repair of the vessel is impracticable.

Compulsory insurance Insurance that has to be effected to comply with the law. Failure to comply is a criminal offence. The aim is to ensure that an injured person does not have to rely upon the defendant's wealth to secure his compensation. Examples of compulsory insurance legislation include the Road Traffic Act 1988 (qv) and the Employers' Liability (Compulsory Insurance) Act 1969 (qv). Obligations to insure may arise under contracts as with the Joint Contract Tribunal (qv), or the rules of professional institutions or regulatory bodies, e.g. FSA.

Compulsory purchase annuity (CPA) An annuity that must be purchased with funds from a personal pension or an occupational pension scheme to provide a retirement income by age 75. *See* AGE 75 RULE.

Computer consultants' insurance A combined liability policy for computer consultants not engaged in manufacture, installation or servicing of hardware covering: professional indemnity insurance (qv), public and products liability (qv) and employers' liability (qv).

Computer Insurance Covers 'all risks', theft and breakdown included, on computer and ancillary equipment. Chips and standard software are included automatically. Other key features: 'new for old' settlements; cover in UK premises and in transit; negotiable excesses; loss of data; Data Protection Act liability; and consequential loss following an insured breakdown or loss. Liability insurance may be included. Exclusions are minimal but special precautions have to be taken when computer equipment is left in an unattended vehicle. Policies may apply to personal computers, laptops and mainframe systems. (See Figure 4). *See* INTERNET LIABILITY INSURANCE.

Computer system records Insured as 'contents' under commercial material damage policies up to £10,000 in respect of the material costs and the cost of reproducing them. Liability for loss of such records is similarly insured under 'Loss of Documents' cover for computer consultants.

Concealed damage *See* UNDISCOVERED LOSS CLAUSE.

Concealment The wilful failure to disclose a material fact (qv) before the insurance contract is concluded. It is a breach of utmost good faith (qv) rendering the contract void ab initio (qv) and entitling the insurer to sue for damages for deceit. If fraud is proved the insured is not entitled to a return of premium.

Concentration of investment The placing of a significant proportion of the assets of a pension fund in any single investment. PA95 lays down compulsory reporting requirements for specific amounts and levels of concentration.

Conciliation Employment dispute resolution method originating in the Employment Act 1975 that set up the Advisory, Conciliation and Arbitration Service (ACAS). Use of ACAS is voluntary but if used, and an agreement is secured, it becomes legally binding. If the conciliation officer feels that the process has failed, recourse may be made to arbitration. Conciliation is relevant to employment practices liability insurance (qv) or legal expenses insurance (qv).

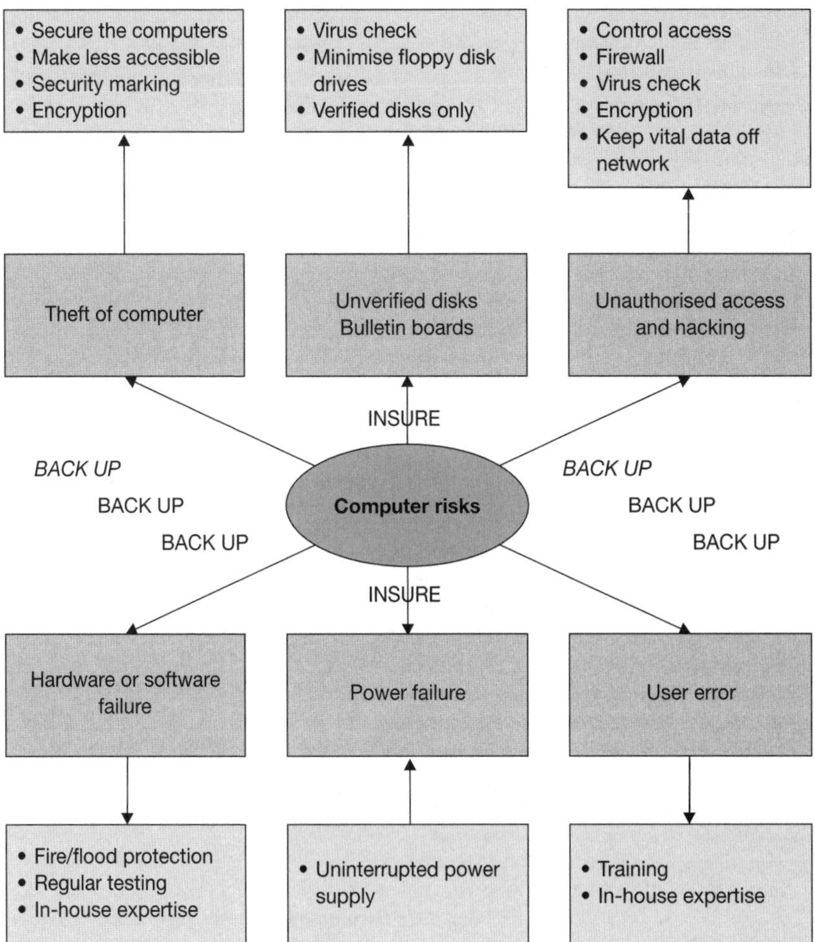

Figure 4. Managing computer risk

Concluding a contract Occurs when one party (the customer or the insurer/intermediary) accepts an offer made by the other, e.g. when a customer accepts an insurer's quotation.

Concurrency Means that members of an occupational pension scheme may contribute concurrently, subject to conditions, up to £3,600 each year into a stakeholder (qv) or personal pension. The contribution limits for occupational schemes remain the same, i.e. 15 per cent of remuneration, but contributions to a stakeholder/personal pension are capped at £3,600 gross (£2,808 net) for 2001/2002.

Concurrent causes Two or more causes operating together to produce the loss. If an insured peril combines with an excepted peril and the effects cannot be separated, the excepted peril applies. If an insured peril combines with an uninsured peril, the insured peril applies unless the insurer has modified the operation of *proximate cause* (qv) by covering 'losses solely and independently' caused by the insured peril as in the case of personal accident policies (qv). *See* CONSECUTIVE CAUSES.

Concurrent insurance Cover of the same particular risk under two or more policies although they may vary in amount or policy period.

Concussion damage Damage caused by a violent shock as in the case of an explosion. The standard fire policy covers explosion damage caused by domestic boilers (qv) or the explosion of gas used for domestic purposes or used for lighting or heating the building (provided it is not a part of a gas works).

Conditional assignment Assignment of a life policy that is not absolute but is dependent upon certain conditions. It typically happens when a policy is given as security for a loan or mortgage as on repayment the original insured has the right to have the policy reassigned to him.

Conditional fee agreement The Courts and Legal Services Act 1990 permits conditional fee agreements in certain categories of proceedings under which solicitors and counsel only receive a fee, and then at an enhanced rate, if the case is won (no win, no fee). Conditional fees are most commonly employed in personal injury cases. In *all* litigation solicitors are permitted to act whereby they receive no fee if the case is lost but *the usual fee* if they win. *See* ACCESS TO JUSTICE ACT 1999; AFTER THE EVENT INSURANCE.

Conditions Parts of a policy that must be complied with by one party or the other. Conditions may be implied by law or expressed, i.e. set out in the policy. The effect of a breach by the insured depends upon whether it relates to a *condition precedent* (things to be done before the contract is concluded, e.g. utmost good faith (qv)); a *condition subsequent* (things to be done during the policy term, e.g. maintaining certain standards); a *condition precedent to liability* (things to be done before the insurer is liable for a particular loss, e.g. proper notification). *See* WARRANTY.

Conduct of business rules (COB) FSA rules that relate primarily to the marketing of products and the advice that financial advisers give to customers concerning financial products (*www.fsa.gov.uk*). *See* KNOW YOUR CUSTOMER; SUITABILITY.

Conduct of proceedings clause Liability policy clause (a) restraining the insured from making an admission of liability and (b) enabling the insurer to take over conduct and control of all proceedings, including the defence or settlement of any claim that may be within the policy. Enables the insurer to use the name of the insured to enforce claims against third parties, effectively permitting the exercise of subrogation rights (qv) before any indemnity payment has been made.

Connected contract Certain non-investment insurance contracts that are sold by providers of non-motor goods (domestic electrical goods) and services related to travel, e.g. non-motor extended warranties (qv) and travel insurance sold with a holiday that are not subject to FSA rules on selling and administration.

Connected persons rule Pension scheme rule under SSASs (qv) preventing the scheme from dealing with members or connected persons in terms of buying, selling, leasing, etc. In the case of past members three years must elapse before the scheme can purchase an investment owned by a previous member or connected person.

Consecutive causes 1. *Broken sequence of events.* If an insured peril has been preceded by excepted perils, they will be disregarded given the break in the chain of causation. If the insured peril intervenes and causes the loss it is the *proximate cause* (qv). 2. *Unbroken sequence of events.* When the insured peril is the natural and probable consequence of an excepted peril, the excepted peril is the *proximate cause.* When the excepted peril is the natural and probable consequence of the insured peril the latter is the proximate cause of the loss. *See* CONCURRENT CAUSES.

Consensus ad idem Means 'in perfect agreement', i.e. of the same mind. Contracts are founded upon agreement although the parties will be judged by what they appeared to mean and not what they may have intended to mean.

Consequential loss The term, unless defined in a contract, follows the rule for contractual damages and embraces losses flowing directly from the breach, e.g. late delivery that increases costs. Consequential losses are generally regarded as the more remote consequences that were not reasonably foreseeable by the parties. Contracts that define consequential are more likely to limit a person's rights than a clause that simply excludes liability for consequential loss without definition. In insurance the term is used to refer to expenses such as the cost of temporary relocation, while fire damaged property is being repaired. The term 'consequential loss insurance' has been replaced by 'business interruption insurance' (qv). Consequential loss is not covered under material damage insurances.

Consequential loss insurance The former term for business interruption insurance (qv).

Consequential loss (satellites) *See* SATELLITE CONSEQUENTIAL LOSS INSURANCE (qv).

Consignee The party (usually the buyer) named in a bill of lading (qv) or waybill (qv), who is entitled to receive cargo that is shipped by the consignor and delivered by the carrier. Under CFR (qv) terms the consignee arranges the transit insurance, but under CIF (qv) he pays the premium in the price of the goods.

Consolidation The combining of separate shipments from two or more shippers for one or more consignees (qv) into one container. *See* CONSOLIDATION CLAUSE.

Consolidation clause Clause in an open cargo policy providing cover at an agreed premium on goods while in transit to, or while at, a common consolidation point for the purpose of preparing or consolidating the goods for export.

Consortium underwriting Underwriters/insurance companies working as a group to offer chosen target markets particular forms of business on a group basis, e.g. travel insurance sold through travel agents. Each consortium member taking a preset share of the business accepted by one leading, member named underwriter, on behalf of the consortium. Lloyd's issued consortium underwriting guidance notes in Regulatory Bulletin 43/99.

Constat Amiable *See* EUROPEAN ACCIDENT STATEMENT (qv).

Constant extra risk Life underwriter's term describing an impaired life (qv) where the additional risk will remain unchanged, i.e. proposer's medical condition will neither worsen nor improve. *See* INCREASING EXTRA RISK; REDUCING EXTRA RISK.

Construction (Design and Management) Regulations 1994 CDM Regulations are aimed at improving the overall management and coordination of health and safety throughout all stages of a construction product. They place duties on the client, the designer, the principal contractor and the planner supervisor (a creation of CDM). They also introduce new documents – health and safety plans and the health and safety file. The planning supervisor must notify HSE of projects that will last more than 30 days or more than 500 person days of work.

Construction of buildings The types of material used in the building and roofing of a structure. Construction types, e.g. brick or timber built, affect the risk as do the number of fire divisions in the building. Other construction factors affecting the risk include age and condition of electrical circuits, number of storeys, the building's age and the type of heating system. Underwriters grade risks according to construction features.

Construction of Policy 1. The rules governing the interpretation of a policy which include the contra proferentem rule (qv), the ordinary meaning rule (qv), the ejusdem generis rule (qv), the whole policy rule (qv), the technical words rule (qv) and the written words prevail rule (qv). 2. The First Schedule of the Marine Insurance Act 1906 contains the Rules for the Construction of the Policy.

Construction Owner's Cost Overrun Policy Protects project owners against the risk of the ultimate cost of construction exceeding the original price and contingency allowances. Policy wordings are customer and contract specific.

Construction risks (ships) *See* BUILDER'S RISKS.

Constructive Total Loss The position which exists when a marine insured abandons the subject-matter to the insurer either because it is an actual total loss (qv) or the cost of repairing or recovering the property would exceed the property's value when repaired or recovered. The total loss is commercial rather than actual. *See* ABANDONMENT; CONSTRUCTIVE TOTAL LOSS CLAUSE.

Constructive Total Loss Clause 1. Institute Cargo Clauses 1/1/82 provide that no constructive total loss claim will be recoverable unless an actual total loss appears unavoidable, or because costs of recovering the property and forwarding it to its destination would exceed its value on arrival. 2. International Hull Clauses 01/11/02 permits the insured to claim a constructive total loss (qv) if the repair costs exceed 80 per cent of the repaired value, i.e. insured value, of the property. This makes it easier for the insured to establish a constructive total loss but nothing obliges the insurer to accept the insured's notice of abandonment. *See* ABANDONMENT.

Consumer Credit Act 1974 Provides a uniform system of controlling all forms of credit supplied to individuals (including sole traders and partners). Controls lending through licensing and also controls individual credit agreements. Policy loans, 'topping up loans' and house purchase loans are within the Act.

Consumer legal expenses cover Often an extension in household policies covers the insured and his family in respect of legal expenses involved in taking or defending legal action in a range of civil disputes (personal injury/personal goods; consumer protection; residential; employment; tax) up to £50,000. Defending certain criminal proceedings, e.g. motoring offences, may also be covered. Motoring prosecutions are also covered under *motor legal expenses policies* (qv).

Consumer Protection Act 1987 Part I imposes strict liability on producers (manufacturers, raw material suppliers, importers being first importers into the EC, 'own branders' and 'forgetful suppliers', e.g. a retailer who fails to supply the identity of the producer) for defective goods that cause personal injury and damage to private property over £275. Section 4 sets out six defences to strict liability, notably the 'state of the art' defence. Part II has been largely superseded by the General Product Safety Regulations 1994 under which safety is assessed by factors such as relevant British or European standards. A breach is a criminal offence; product liability insurance covers prosecution defence costs.

Consumer sale A sale when the person buying 'deals as a consumer' with a business. Exclusion clauses of the implied terms of fitness for purpose (qv) and satisfactory quality (qv) are not permitted (Unfair Contract Terms Act 1977). The Unfair Contract Terms Act 1977 (qv), s.12 : a person deals as a consumer if (a) he neither makes the contract in the course of business nor holds himself out as doing so; and (b) the other party makes the contract in the course of business; and (c) the goods are of a type ordinarily supplied for private use or consumption.

Containers Rectangular metal boxes used to transport cargo between two or more modes of transit, i.e. road vehicle, train, vessel or aircraft. The containers themselves are insured under the Institute Container Clauses (qv).

Contaminated Land Land appearing to the local authority to be 'in such a condition, by reasons of substances in, or under the land, that significant harm is being caused or there is a significant possibility of such harm being caused' (Environment Act 1995, s.57). *See* POLLUTER PAYS PRINCIPLE.

Contents A household contents policy covers such items as furniture, furnishings, household goods, personal effects, high-risk items (qv), business equipment and money owned by the insured or any member of his family or for which he is responsible. In terms of commercial policies, contents include plant, machinery, equipment, stock, tenant's fixtures and fittings all contained in the premises.

Continental scale A scale of benefits under a personal accident policy (qv) as an alternative to fixed sum benefits. A maximum amount is fixed for payment on death but all other benefits for dismemberment and other forms of disablement are expressed as varying percentages of the death benefit.

Contingency An uncertain event.

Contingency fund A reserve fund set aside by an insurer or other entity as a safeguard against heavy and unexpected losses that could not be covered out of other funds.

Contingency insurances A term describing those policies that do not fall naturally into one of the principal classes of insurance business. The term embraces insurances such as abandonment of events (qv), pluvius insurance (qv) and others often of an unusual nature.

Contingency loading An allowance in the insurer's premium calculation for possible fluctuations in claims costs. It is added to the risk premium (qv) that covers the 'average claims' cost for the year. Wide fluctuations in claims experience necessitate a greater contingency cushion than narrow range fluctuations. Other premium computation elements: expenses loading (qv) and profit loading.

Contingency reserve An amount reserved in the books of a company or other entity in respect of a specific future liability, e.g. payment of taxes.

Contingent business interruption insurance Term describing *business interruption insurance* (qv) extensions to cover external dependencies, e.g. suppliers.

Contingent capital A post-loss funding method based on an agreement between a (re)insurer and a bank (or other investor), whereby the latter will provide a loan or equity capital after the trigger event, e.g. windstorm, has occurred. The bank/investor charges a commitment fee for their pre-agreed standby capital. Contingent capital is less costly than conventional (re)insurance in fee terms if the trigger event never occurs. *See* CATASTROPHE EQUITY PUTS; CONTINGENT SURPLUS NOTE.

Contingent credit *See* CONTINGENT CAPITAL.

Contingent funding *See* CONTINGENT CAPITAL.

Contingent liability Liability that arises in a secondary way as in the case of vicarious liability (qv). *See* CONTINGENT LIABILITY COVER.

Contingent liability cover Fallback cover that does not replace a primary cover but is triggered if the intended primary cover is non-existent or ineffective. An employer normally relies upon an indemnity under the employees' car insurances, when employees use their cars on his business. If an employee's policy is invalid, the employer's indemnity fails but the motor contingent liability section of his public liability policy fills the gap. Others who need contingent liability cover include principals relying on cover arranged by contractors and hire car operators relying on insurance arranged by hirers.

Contingent (or survivorship) annuity Also known as a reversionary annuity. The payments to the *annuitant* (qv) start on the death of a named person. One spouse can use this type of annuity to make provision for a surviving spouse.

Contingent (or survivorship) insurance Life policy under which the sum insured is payable on the death of one person (the life insured), provided it occurs during the lifetime of another (the counter life). The ages of both lives must be proved, but only the life insured is required to prove his state of health.

Contingent surplus note (CSN) A form of contingent capital (qv) giving the (re)insurer the right to issue debt to investors or a bank if specified events take place although the arrangement may be unconditional. CSNs are equivalent to overdrafts and ensure the solvency of the (re)insurer in times of high claims.

Continuation clause Institute Time Clause/International Hull Clause by which the vessel is held covered until arrival at her destination should she be at sea or a port of distress, at the time the policy expires. It rarely applies as the succeeding policy comes into operation immediately at the expiry date.

Continuation option Occupational pension scheme offers members who leave the scheme the opportunity to continue any life insurance benefit they were entitled to as members of the scheme. An ex-member is able to effect cover without producing evidence of health within a limited period.

Continuing Duty of Utmost Good Faith The revival or continuation of the pre-contractual duty of *utmost good faith* (qv). The duty may be revived by policy conditions in regard to defined changes in risk or situations calling for fresh information as when cover applies under 'held covered' clauses. Where the change goes to the root of the contract, the insurer may come off risk, so the duty revives if the insurer is to continue the policy with a newly defined risk. The duty revives at the renewal of a contract. In addition *good faith*, meaning an absence of fraud, applies in the matter of claims.

Continuing warranty A warranty (qv) whereby the insured promises that a state of affairs will exist for the duration of the policy, e.g. disposing of waste at the end of each day. The policy is voidable from the date of the breach unless the court interprets the insurer's words as being insufficient to amount to a continuing warranty, preferring to classify the words as a *description of risk clause* (qv).

Continuous service When a member leaves his occupational pension scheme but keeps his benefits in the fund, and subsequently resumes membership, the periods of service before and after the break may be aggregated. Aggregation also occurs when an employee moves from one employer to another employer in the same scheme.

Continuous Treaty A reinsurance contract that, once incepted, continues indefinitely until one of the parties gives notice of their intention to terminate the arrangement. Cancellation may be on a cut-off or run-off basis.

Continuous Trigger Theory *See* OCCURRENCE TRIGGER THEORIES.

Contra proferentem rule Any ambiguity in the wording of a contract will be construed against the person who drew up the wording, i.e. in insurance against the insurer. The rule will only be applied where there is real ambiguity.

Contraband of war Goods that a belligerent may lawfully seize on the way to his enemy's territory. When used in a marine insurance policy the term applies only to goods or merchandise. It does not extend to persons (officers of a belligerent power) even though their presence on ship may increase the risk of an attack. If a policy is warranted 'no contraband' the policy may be avoided if any part of the goods carried is contraband.

Contract cover A commercial legal expenses insurance (qv) providing for the legal costs and expenses incurred in pursuing or defending contract disputes. Cover may be confined to disputes with customers or suppliers or give full contract cover. Policies are subject to a waiting period (qv) of 90 days.

Contract loss of profits Covers airlines against the estimated loss of profit following their inability to complete a specific project due to force majeure, war, repudiation or aircraft failure.

Contract of Affreightment Contract evidencing the terms of carriage between a shipper and carrier normally expressed in the bill of lading (qv) or waybill (qv).

Contract price clause Clause whereby if damage to undelivered goods leads to cancellation of the contract, the insurer will settle on the contract price rather than production costs. The profit element, otherwise irretrievably lost, becomes a part of the indemnity.

Contract price repairs Motor claims situation where the insurer agrees to pay the repairer a guaranteed fixed price. Protects insurers against the risk of incurring any higher costs that come to light during the repair process, particularly as higher costs may make the whole repair package uneconomic.

Contract works/contractors' all risks insurance (annual or single project) Covers temporary and permanent works executed in the performance of contracts, and materials for incorporation therein, plus own and hired plant, and tools and equipment while on sites or in transit. Cover is arranged for house extensions through to multi-storey office blocks. Premiums are based on annual turnover with a maximum value of any one contract. Various extensions are available (e.g. continuing hire charges following plant damage). Key exclusions relate to existing structures and defective design. Cover may have to accord with standard term contracts (e.g. Joint Contract Tribunal).

Contract works insurance on machinery installation contracts *See* MACHINERY MOVEMENT ERECTION INSURANCE.

Contracted in money purchase scheme (CIMPS) An approved defined pension scheme (qv) whose members remain in the state second pension (qv). Employers must contribute to the approved scheme. Employee contributions are subject to both the contributions limit of 15 per cent of earnings in any tax year (qv) and the earnings cap (qv). The maximum allowable pension is two-thirds of final pensionable salary. The maximum lump sum at retirement is 2.25 times the pension income or, if greater, 3/80ths for each year of service times final remuneration capped at 1.5 times final remuneration. CIMPS is covered by Opra (qv).

Contracted out money purchase scheme (COMPS) A defined benefit scheme (qv) whose members do not contribute to the state second pension (qv). Employer contributions must be sufficient for *protected rights* (qv) purposes, i.e. no lower than the *contracted out rebate* (qv). This will ensure that on retirement all members get at least the pension they would have received if they had not been contracted out. Otherwise the actual pension depends on the performance of the pension fund's underlying assets and is subject to IR limits as per *contracted in money purchase schemes* (qv).

Contracted out protected rights premium (COPRP) A premium paid to the state by a contracted out pension scheme in line with protected rights (qv) to secure SERPS (qv) benefits for a scheme member if the scheme ceased to be contracted out before 6 April 1997.

Contracted out rebate The amount of the national insurance contributions paid back into a pension scheme in respect of contracted out employees. The rebate is a flat rate for final salary schemes and appropriate personal pension schemes. For contracted out money purchase schemes it is age-related.

Contracted Out Salary Related Scheme (COSRS) A contracted out (qv) defined benefit scheme based on salary-related benefits. The member's pension benefits must be equivalent to, or better than, those specified under the reference scheme test (qv). This means it must provide an inflation-linked pension from age 65 up to a maximum of 5 per cent p.a. where the starting pension is worked out by taking a minimum of 1/80th of the average salary over the three years prior to retirement for each year of service in the scheme, up to a maximum of 40 years. Members' contributions are subject to normal IR limits on benefits and contributions.

Contracting out 1. Opting out of the earnings related part (S2P) of the state pension arrangements. Occupational pension schemes or appropriate personal pension plans (qv) must first satisfy contracting out conditions to ensure that they secure benefits that replace or improve upon those otherwise receivable under S2P. 2. Using exemption clauses (qv) in commercial contracts to 'contract out' of liabilities that would otherwise attach. *See* UNFAIR CONTRACT TERMS ACT 1977.

Contracting purchaser's clause *See* PURCHASER'S INTEREST CLAUSE.

Contractors' Plant-Hire Association's Model Conditions (2001) Conditions used when plant is hired out for use in the construction or civil engineering industries. To cover the risks attaching to him under CPA, the customer should insure: loss or damage to the plant on site and under his control; loss or damage to goods during loading/unloading; continuing hire charges while the plant is unable to work following loss or damage; legal liability covering injury to the driver/operator together with third party injury/damage arising from the use of the plant. The owner is obliged to supply a competent driver but the hirer is liable for his negligence. The CPA also issues a *crane hire agreement* under which the customer is responsible for planning and supervision and ensuring a safe system of work.

Contractors' plant policy Renewable cover for contractors who own, hire-in or hire-out plant (mobile plant, machinery and equipment) against unforeseen and accidental physical loss due to external causes; internal causes such as breakdown and wear and tear are excluded. The policy operates whilst at work or at rest or during dismantling or erection, loading, unloading or transit. For hired-in plant the cover includes legal liability for negligent breakdown and continuing hire charges. For hired-out plant the cover can be extended to indemnify the hirer. Cover can be arranged as a part of a contract works (qv) policy or, in some cases, motor insurance as special types.

Contracts of insurance 1. IPRU (INS) refers to: (a) fidelity bonds, performance bonds (qv), administration bonds, bail bonds (qv), customs bonds, or similar contracts of guarantee effected in return for premiums; (b) tontines (qv); (c) capital redemption (qv) contracts and pension fund management contracts when effected or carried out by a body that effects or carries out insurance contracts; (d) contracts to pay annuities on human life; (e) contracts of a kind referred to in art. 1(2)(e) of the First Life Directive; and (f) contracts of a kind referred to in art. 1(3) of the First Life Directive. 2. A contract, whereby one party, an insurer, agrees in return for a consideration from another party (the premium) to pay the insured money, or its equivalent, upon the happening of certain events. Three essentials are: the consideration (the premium), promise of payment to the insured and a specified event.

Contracts (Rights of Third Parties) Act 1999 Allows someone, not a party to the contract, to bring an action under it if: (a) the contract so provides or (b) it confers a benefit upon him, unless it appears that the contracting parties did not intend the term to be enforceable by him. Where the obligated party is aware that the third party has relied on the term, he may not rescind or vary the contract to the third party's detriment. The express terms of the contract may require the third party's consent to a variation. Insurance policies generally exclude the provisions of the Act.

Contractual liability Liability that arises as a result of a contract, as opposed to liability, imposed by common law or statute. Liability policies exclude liability for *liquidated damages* (qv) as, unlike unliquidated damages, they are agreed under contract.

Contributing interests The main contributing interests to general average expenditure (qv) are ship, freight and cargo, including specie. The only exceptions are H.M. mails, crew's effects and passengers' personal effects not shipped under a bill of lading. Otherwise the 'interests' saved contribute on their net arrived values at the place where the voyage ends.

Contribution A corollary of indemnity (qv) meaning an equitable division between insurers where two or more insurers cover the same insured and the same risk. Each insurer pays a rateable proportion of the loss either in proportion to the sums insured *(the maximum liability method* (qv)) or in proportion to their respective independent liabilities (*the independent liability method* (qv)). Insurers may avoid contributing to 'doubly' insured losses by using a *non-contribution clause* (qv).

Contribution holiday A period during which pension scheme contributions of employer and/or employee are temporarily suspended. Occurs when the pension fund is in surplus.

Contribution limits The maxima that IR allows for tax relief purposes when paid into approved occupational pension schemes, personal pension plans and retirement annuities. Contributions to personal pension schemes including self-invested personal pensions and retirement annuity contracts (qv) are based on a scale of age-related percentages of *net relevant earnings* (qv) (17.5 per cent for persons aged 35 or less up to 40 per cent for age 61 and over). Contributions to approved occupational scheme members are limited to a maximum of 15 per cent of taxable remuneration in any year regardless of age. This limit remains unchanged when contributing concurrently to a personal pension or stakeholder plan (contributions to stakeholder pensions (qv) are limited to £3,600 irrespective of age (2002/3)). Except for retirement annuity contracts (qv), all contributions are subject to the earnings cap (qv). There are no limits on employers' contributions other than those required to ensure that benefits remain inside IR maxima. *See* CONCURRENCY.

Contributions equivalent premium Payment to the state pension scheme to purchase S2P rights when a member with less than two years of qualifying service (qv), leaves a contracted out scheme. The member is then reinstated into S2P/SERPS for the whole of the contracted out period.

Contributory negligence Negligence (qv) by which a person contributes to the happening of an accident to him or contributes to the injury or damage he sustains. He is part author of his own misfortune and, under the Law Reform (Contributory Negligence) Act 1945, his damages will be reduced according to his share of the blame.

Contributory pension scheme Any pension scheme where the member makes a contribution. Compare with non-contributory schemes (qv).

Contributory value *See* GENERAL AVERAGE CONTRIBUTION.

Control of Asbestos at Work Regulations 2002 Aim at reducing asbestos exposure by obliging duty holders (employers and others) to carry out a risk assessment and declaring the amount, type and safety of asbestos in non-domestic premises they own or occupy. Employers must prepare and implement a management plan to control asbestos risks. The new regulations consolidate earlier legislation and introduce new controls on the way asbestos is handled in the workplace. The duty is owed to anyone affected by work activity. Non-domestic buildings owners contemplating refurbishment or demolition must conduct an *asbestos survey* (qv).

Control test The main test of an employer/employee relationship is the right to control how, when, where and by whom the work should be done. The 'employee' is substantially controlled and directed by the other person in the manner of doing the work. An independent contractor agrees to perform the work but not under the control of the other party. In 1952 (*Stevenson, Jordan and Harrison Ltd* v. *McDonald and Evans*) Denning L. J. illustrated the difference by distinguishing a taxi driver from a chauffeur. The other 'irreducible minimum' is the test of mutuality of obligation (qv).

Control period The period over which the standard contribution rate (qv) has been calculated to remain constant, assuming that the funding ratio (qv) at the beginning and end of the period is 100 per cent. The control period, which is normally for one year or more but which could be less, should be specified. (Source GN26.)

Controlled functions FSA functions where an individual: (a) exerts significant influence (qv); (b) deals directly with customers; or (c) deals with customer's property. The FSA's controlled functions must be performed by *approved persons* (qv). The functions are grouped as 'governing functions', 'required functions', 'systems and control functions', 'significant management functions' and 'customer functions' (qv). Certain functions are *significant influence* functions and indentified in the Table of Controlled Functions (*www.fsa.gov.uk*).

Controlled funding Method of estimating the size of the pension fund needed to secure the benefits for occupational scheme members. Each year the employer pays a premium to secure the total expected benefits at normal retirement age for the oldest employees either individually or in age groups. The insurer and the employer agree the level of funding to cover a period of years. This funding is appropriate where funds are not 'earmarked', e.g. final salary schemes (qv).

Controllers FSA definition of persons or entities owning 10 per cent or more of the shares in an authorised firm or parent company of such firm or is able to exercise significant influence over management through shareholding in such a firm or parent.

Controlling director (CD) A director who owns (or controls) at least 20 per cent of a company's voting power. In view of the influence such a person may have over his employer, special restrictions apply to a controlling director's membership of the company's pension scheme. The full details appear in Practice Notes (IR12)(1991).

Convergence The combining of traditional (re)insurance and the capital markets. Banks and insurers transfer risks to each other by securitisation (qv) and insuritisation (qv). They have borrowed from each other as part of the broader process of convergence, a visible sign of which is bancassurance (qv).

Conversion 1. Tort (qv) committed by a person who keeps property belonging to another or who disposes of it wrongfully, e.g. selling another person's car without authority. Conversion may occur deliberately or innocently. The Torts (Interference with Goods) Act 1977 extends conversion to include negligent loss of another's property by a bailee (qv). Insurance is available for motor traders who unwittingly sell stolen vehicles and solicitors (and others) who misdeliver documents (professional indemnity insurance). 2. In life insurance *convertible term policies* can be converted to either whole life or endowment policies without further evidence as to health. Whole life (qv) policies can be converted into endowment policies (qv). Also, existing policies having a surrender value can be converted to paid-up policies (qv) for reduced sums with no further premiums payable.

Convertible currency In the Lloyd's market this means any currency other than sterling, US dollars and Canadian dollars. In the company market it means any currency other than the main currencies in which the business is transacted. Convertible currency is normally accounted for in sterling.

Convertible term life policies *See* CONVERSION 2.

Cooling degree day (CDD) A measure of how much the average of the daily high and low temperature is greater than a *reference temperature* (typically 18°C or 65°F). Cumulatively CDDs measure the intensity and duration of warmth and indicate how much 'cooling' is required by, say, UK energy companies suffering poor sales during warm weather. An average daily temperature of 23°C creates 5 CDDs towards the season's aggregate. UK energy companies hedge against warm weather by purchasing *call options* (qv) indexed by CDDs. Each CDD has a notional value, the *tick* (qv), and the payout occurs when the cumulative CDDs exceed the strike (qv). *See* WINTER SEASON; HEATING DEGREE DAYS; COOLING SEASON; GROWING DEGREE DAYS.

Cooling off period 1. Under the FSA's Conduct of Business rule 6.7, it is the period allowed to a customer following his receipt of the statutory notice during which he may cancel his investment agreement. The period allowed in the case of life policies, pension contracts, appropriate personal pensions and other *cancellable investment agreements* varies between 14 and 30 days (*www.fsa.gov.uk*). 2. Periods of reflection are also allowed under the Consumer Protection (Distance Selling) Regulations, and this has implications for those selling insurance over the Internet and by other distance methods. 3. The cancellation rights (qv) of retail customers (qv) buying general insurance products are contained in Chapter 6 of the FSA's Insurance: Conduct of Business Sourcebook (qv). ICOB allows 30 days for pure protection contracts (qv) and 14 days for general insurance.

Cooling season/summer season A weather risk (qv) term covering May to September. The contract period for a weather derivative (qv) is generally based on one season or a full year.

Coordinating agent A member's agent who coordinates the administration of any particular member's affairs at Lloyd's where that member has more than one member's agent.

Co-reinsurance 1. Provision in an excess of loss treaties (qv) making the reinsured a co-reinsurer. The clause requires the reinsured to retain net and unreinsured a part of the risk, in addition to the deductible, for its own account. Example: the reinsurer covers 95 per cent of the excess layer while the reinsured accepts 5 per cent of that layer and is not authorised to reinsure it. *See* LMX. 2. Several reinsurers sharing a reinsurance contract. Each co-reinsurer has a direct contract with the reinsured.

Corporate bonds Loans to corporate entities based on a fixed rate for a fixed period. Bonds can be traded and the price usually changes when there is a change in prevailing rates of interest rates. Corporate bonds carry a higher risk than government stock (gilts) but are lower than shares as a company must pay off all debts before paying shareholders.

Corporate governance System by which companies are run and the means by which they are accountable to their shareholders, employees and the regulatory authorities. Directors are expected to run companies soundly and prudently. *See* COMBINED CODE OF CORPORATE GOVERNANCE; TURNBULL REPORT.

Corporate governance at Lloyd's Core Principles Byelaw (no. 34/96) requires honesty, transparency and integrity from managing and members' agents. The agencies are also subject to the FSA's Principles of Business that correlate closely with Lloyd's Core Principles. The board of a managing or members' agent must ensure that the business is accountable to the FSA and follows the Lloyd's Core Principles. Principle 9 emphasises the need for adequate management controls. The Lloyd's Code for Sound and Prudent Management requires that each agent is directed and managed by a sufficient number of persons who are fit and proper for the positions they hold. Sound and prudent management embraces direction and management; staffing; supervision and accountability; and compliance.

Corporate member Company admitted to membership of Lloyd's.

Corporate syndicate Lloyd's syndicate with a single corporate member.

COSHH (Control of Substances Hazardous to Health Regulations 2002/(Amendment) Regulations 2003) HSE enforceable regulations to protect workers from substances hazardous to health. Substance means any solid, gas, fume, dust or vapour and any micro-organism. The employer must, inter alia, assess, monitor and control each work situation to ensure that workers are not exposed to possibly harmful amounts of any substance connected with the work. COSHH sets out limits for a large number of hazardous substances based on *maximum exposure limits* and *occupational exposure standards.* The employee has a duty to cooperate with the employer regarding monitoring and health surveillance.

Cost and freight (CFR) Same as Cost, Insurance and Freight (qv) except that the cost of insurance is borne by the overseas buyer.

Cost, Insurance and Freight (CIF) A form of sale contract whereby the seller's price includes the cost of goods and insurance and freight charges through to the agreed destination. Consequently the seller must effect marine insurance for the entire transit.

Costs inclusive limit of indemnity A limit of indemnity under a liability policy that applies to the insured's own costs as well as damages and claimant's costs. Defence costs are commonly a part of the overall limit of indemnity applicable to directors' and officers' liability policies. *See* INDEMNITY LIMITS.

Counter guarantee/indemnity Guarantee or indemnity obtained by a surety from a bonded party. If the insurer as surety pays out under say a performance bond, redress will be sought from the bonded party or any other party providing a guarantee on his behalf. The counter guarantee is obtained even though the surety has a common law right of redress against the bonded party.

Counter life *See* CONTINGENT INSURANCE.

Counterparty risk The risk that a counterparty to a transaction will not pay when the triggering event occurs. The risk in the case of catastrophe bonds (qv) is low. The proceeds of the bond are invested in safe securities such as US Treasury Bonds and held in trust by the bankruptcy-remote SPV or a special trust. If the triggering event occurs the insurer is permitted to withdraw funds from the trust. In return the investors receive the one-year Treasury bill rate plus a premium rate.

Country damage Damage to baled or bagged cargo (e.g. cotton, coffee) caused by dirt, mud, excessive moisture from damp ground or weather, etc., occurring before the goods are actually shipped.

Country risks Another term for *political risks* (qv) insured under export credit insurance (qv).

Court Bond A bond issued to a court of law to guarantee the performance of certain duties (accounting for income, preservation of property, etc.) by a principal.

Court of Protection Bond Issued to the Court of Protection to guarantee the performance of a person responsible for the affairs of a mentally incapacitated person.

Covenants *See* RESTRICTIVE COVENANTS.

Cover/Coverage The insurance provided by the insurer for the insured or by the reinsurer for the reinsured.

Cover note A document sometimes issued by insurers pending preparation of the policy. It may be issued as evidence of more permanent cover or it may be an acknowledgement of temporary cover pending the insurer's final decision. *See also* BROKER'S COVER NOTE.

Coverholder A person authorised to accept or to issue insurance documents evidencing the acceptance of risks on behalf of Lloyd's syndicates and other insurers. A coverholder has binding authority (qv). Lloyd's requires coverholders to comply with prescribed guidelines and undergo a monitoring and review process.

Cracking, fracturing and failure of welds These risks can be covered as an extension to a boiler and pressure plant policy (qv) but the insurance is limited to self-damage. The risks apply to plant of cast-iron construction and items with welded or brazed seams. Plant such as heating boilers, ironing machines and air-heating batteries would require the extension. The cause can be internal pressure, low water, water hammer, frost, etc. A valid claim only arises when the crack or weld failure gives rise to leakage of the contents.

Craft risks The risks to cargo during transhipment or landing in small vessels.

Cranes and lifting machinery policy Policy covering blocks, conveyors and cranes of all kinds. In addition to the periodical inspection service (compulsory for most items in this category), the policy covers breakdown (qv) but may be extended to cover sudden and unforeseen physical damage (qv) at the premises or while temporarily at other premises, including the transit risk, and damage to goods lifted (excluding installed plant and machinery) and own surrounding property. Damage by extraneous causes is generally included. Other options are available.

Credit card protection insurance (CCPI) Provides cover up to £75,000 against fraudulent use of a lost or stolen credit card. The policy also provides £1,000 interest free advance if the insured is stranded overseas and includes other emergency benefits.

Credit card repayment protection (CCRP) Meets monthly repayments up to £1,000 per month for a specified period if the insured is unable to work following accident or sickness or involuntary unemployment. Life cover to secure full repayment is normally included. *See* CREDIT PROTECTION INSURANCE.

Credit default swaps A credit derivative (qv) structured as a swap. One party is a lender facing a credit risk (qv) from a third party and the counterparty in the swap agrees to insure this risk in exchange for regular periodic payments (essentially an insurance premium). If the third party defaults the counterparty insurer will have to purchase from the the insured defaulted asset. In turn, the insurer pays the insured the remaining interest on the debt as well as the principal. *See* CREDIT EVENT.

Credit derivative An over-the-counter, 'off balance sheet' (qv) instrument, derived directly or indirectly from the price of a credit instrument. They take numerous forms, including swaps (e.g. credit default swaps (qv) and options), and are used to transfer the credit risk from one party to another, e.g. banks to insurance companies (insuritisation (qv)). The amount of credit derivatives transferred to insurers rose from zero in 1998 to 30 per cent in 2002 (*www.vinodkothari.com/glossary*).

Credit enhancement Financial guarantees or other types of assistance that improve the credit of underlying debt obligations. Credit enhancement has the effect of lowering interest and improving the marketability of corporate bond issues, particularly when backed by insurance companies with high credit ratings. Financial reinsurance (qv) enhances the credit rating of the reinsured by improving ratios through 'off the balance sheet' transactions.

Credit event Event triggering the settlement of a credit default swap (qv) or total return swap (qv). The event is chosen by the counterparties and could include payment default on a reference asset or other debt obligation; insolvency or a ratings downgrade of the reference asset.

Credit insurance This covers businesses against losses due to 'insolvency' or 'protracted default' (failure to pay within 90 days of due date) of customers to whom credit has been granted. It is effectively bad debts insurance. Policies usually cover between 75 per cent and 90 per cent of the risk. The main policies: 'whole turnover (UK)', 'whole turnover (export)' 'specific account(s)', 'catastrophe', i.e. cover that is triggered once an aggregate bad debts figure has been exceeded. *See* EXPORT CREDIT INSURANCE; OVERSEAS INVESTMENT INSURANCE.

Credit life captive A captive insurance company (qv) formed by banks to insure loans to clients.

Credit life insurance A decreasing term insurance (qv) to cover the outstanding debt under hire purchase and credit sale agreements. Cover is provided under a collective policy to the creditor, e.g. finance company, to facilitate repayment on the death of any hirer or debtor. Arrears are not covered. Limits are placed on the age attained (e.g. 60 or 65) of any hirer or debtor and the length of the finance agreement (e.g. three years). Premiums are based on the average outstanding debt in accordance with returns supplied by the assured.

Credit protection insurance/payment protection insurance Protection for repayments on a personal loan, mortgage or credit card or regular financial commitments. It meets repayments for a specified period following involuntary unemployment, accident or sickness and, usually, a death benefit is added. Policies are normally sold when the loan is arranged through banks, retailers, motor dealerships, mortgage and other finance providers. *See* CREDIT CARD REPAYMENT PROTECTION.

Credit risk Risk of financial loss from a customer's or counterparty's failure to settle financial obligations as they fall due. Companies respond with credit management and may also effect *credit insurance*. Companies making bond issues may seek guarantees from insurance companies with higher credit rating through a *credit enhancement* (qv) process. The credit risk is transferable from the financial market to the insurance markets through *CDOs* and CMOs (qv).

Credit securitisation The structuring of a portfolio of credit risks into different layers. *See* CDOS; CMOS; CREDIT DEFAULT SWAPS; INSURITISATION.

Credit or insurance *See* CREDIT PROTECTION INSURANCE.

Criminal Injuries Compensation Scheme The scheme is controlled by the Criminal Injuries Compensation Authority, which administers compensation on the basis of common law damages to the victims of violent crime. The main awards are in respect of personal injury and fatal injury. There is no award for single injuries, such as a black eye. The 2001 scheme increased the level of awards, changed the formula for multiple injuries, extended eligibility to same sex partners and improved the presentation of the Tariff of Injuries (*www.cica.gov.uk*).

Critical day options Trigger events or reference points underlying a weather derivative (qv) where the payout depends on the critical conditions occurring on any day in the contract period. A critical day may be each day the temperature exceeds 25°C. The amount paid is based on the *number of critical days* occurring during the period multiplied by the tick (qv).

Critical illness policy Pays out a tax-free lump sum if, during the policy term, the insured is diagnosed with any of a range of serious conditions such as cancer, heart disease, strokes and multiple sclerosis. Even when diagnosed, the insured may live for some time so necessitating the need for financial protection while undergoing treatment and recuperation. The policy can stand alone or be added to a whole life, endowment or term insurance.

Criticial yield Yield is the interest earned on a bond, or dividend paid on shares or a fund. In the pensions industry the term critical yield refers to the investment returns needed to provide pension income for executive pension plans (qv), final salary scheme pensions, small self-administered schemes (qv), income drawdown (qv) and transfer value analysis system (qv).

Crop insurance Insurance effected by farmers against failure or reduction in output of a crop due to a specified peril (e.g. hailstorm) or a wider range of perils (e.g. adverse weather conditions).

Cross-assignment A method used in partnership insurance (qv) whereby each partner takes out a policy on his own life for the amount required, pays the premium himself and assigns the policy to his partners in order to put the money into their hands on his death or retirement. Any gain under the policy is subject to capital gains tax.

Cross frontier business *See* SERVICES BUSINESS.

Cross liabilities 1. When two blameworthy vessels collide, *liability* will be apportioned between them according to their degree of fault and, following the *running down clause* (qv), there will be two payments, i.e. cross liability. Admiralty law prescribes a single liability settlement, a method favourable to the receiving shipowner. 2. Where two or more jointly insured parties, (marine or non-marine) have legal rights against each other, the liability cover will respond as though a separate policy had been issued to each named insured. This is made possible by a *cross liabilities or severability of interest clause.*

Cross (or double) option agreement Shareholders in small companies agree that on death or retirement of a shareholder the continuing shareholders have an option to purchase the outgoing shareholder's shares. Life insurance puts money into the hands of the continuing shareholders at the relevant time to fund the purchase.

Cumulative degree days The total of degree days (qv) occurring over the period of a weather derivative (qv). The cumulative figure is multiplied by the amount of the tick (qv) to give the payout for the period, subject to the strike (qv) being breached but not exceeding any cap.

Cumulative losses *See* UNREPAIRED DAMAGE.

Current unit method An accrued benefits valuation method in which the actuarial liability is based on earnings at the valuation date. The standard contribution rate (qv) is that necessary to cover the cost of benefits that will accrue in the control period (qv) following the valuation date by reference to earnings projected to the end of that period and non-discretionary revaluation thereafter.

Curtailment Cover under travel insurances (qv) to compensate for the curtailment of the trip due to specified causes (e.g. injury to the policyholder or close relative).

Curtate annuity *See* NON-APPORTIONABLE ANNUITY.

Custody and control exclusion Public liability policy exclusion, of property in the care, custody or control of the insured. The property concerned is 'bailment' property insurable by the bailor under a first party (qv) insurances or by bailees' modified liability policies, e.g. hotel proprietors. In any event the general exclusion is overridden in respect of: (a) the effects of directors, employees and visitors, including their vehicles and contents; (b) premises (including contents) temporarily occupied by the insured for work purposes; (c) leased or rented premises; (d) third party property at premises, etc., other than the insured's premises. *See* OWN PROPERTY EXCLUSION.

Customer functions FSA *controlled functions* (qv) covering: investment adviser; trainee investment adviser; corporate finance; pensions transfer; Lloyd's adviser; customer trading; and investment management.

Customer types The FSA classifies customers as either *retail* or *commercial customers.* The former is defined as a policyholder or potential policyholder acting outside their trade, business or profession. The latter is someone who is not a retail customer. All businesses are commercial customers regardless of size. For the purpose of the rule on complaints the FSA uses the definition *eligible complainants.* This includes private individuals; commercial customers with a turnover below £1 million.; a charity with an annul income below £1 million; a trustee of a trust with a net asset value of less than £1 million.

Customers' extension An extension to a business interruption insurance (qv) that protects the insured against loss due to reduction in turnover after damage by an insured peril at a customer's premises. The cover is expressed as a percentage of the gross profit based on the significance of the customer concerned.

Customs and excise bonds Bonds are required by HM Customs and Excise to secure indemnities against loss through fraudulent or improper dealing with dutiable goods. The principal bonds include: 1. *VAT/Duty Deferment Bond.* Required from companies who import goods into the UK that are subject to VAT. The bond enables the company to defer payment of VAT or duty to the 15th day of the following month. 2. *Warehouse bonds.* Dutiable goods are held in bonded warehouses before they are required for sale and, provided they remain in the warehouse, duty is not payable. When they leave the warehouse duty becomes payable and the bond secures HMCE against loss due to default.

Customs regulations Infringements of the regulations are excluded under the Institute of War and Strikes Clauses (4.1.5) and other versions. In *Sunsport Shipping Ltd and Others* v. *Atkins and Others* (2003) the term 'customs regulations' was held wide enough to include provisions having the force of law in the country concerned as to: (a) import or export duties or licences and (b) import or export of controlled drugs and other prohibited goods, substances or materials. The words cover any law in the realm of customs and so include smuggling of prohibited goods as well as smuggling of goods subject to duty. The law extends beyond duties on imports to include criminal law. The insured's ship, upon which cocaine was discovered, was detained long enough (in excess of six months) for it to be deemed a constructive total loss within the policy. The Court of Appeal held that the exclusion applied and the insured's claim therefore failed.

Cut-off/run-off cancellation When a continuous contract is terminated under the cancelling clause (qv), the existing risks under the treaty may run-off or simply become cut-off. Run-off means that the reinsurer's liability under policies current at the cancellation date continues until each policy expires. Cut-off means that the reinsurer will not be liable for losses occurring on or after termination. The insurer usually returns the unearned premium portfolio unless the treaty is written on an earned premium basis. *See* CLEAN CUT BASIS.

Cut-through clause A reinsurance clause providing that, in the event of insolvency of the cedant, the reinsurer will be liable to the insured for his share of the loss and not to the cedant's liquidator.

Cyberliability Generic term for various types of legal liability arising from business use of the Internet and e-mail. *See* INTERNET LIABILITY.

D

Da Costa clause (blood relative clause) Industrial life clause, or 'receipt clause', allowing the office to pay a claim on death to the next of kin or beneficiary named in a will even though no grant of representation has been obtained. The sums are small and formalities kept to a minimum.

Daily sickness benefit Fixed cash benefit payable under certain health policies for each day of care (institutional or otherwise) during the insured's temporary illness.

Damages 1. *Tort* (qv). Compensation for loss. *General damages* are unliquidated, i.e. not pre-determined. The court assesses them under headings such as loss of amenity, pain and suffering and loss of future earnings. *Special damages* can be assessed with some accuracy, e.g. medical expenses, loss of earnings, damage to property. 2. *Contracts.* Damages compensate for losses flowing from the breach of contract but they may be *liquidated* (qv), i.e. stated in the contract. 3. The measure of damage relates, as far as money can, to actual losses, but *nominal damages* apply when a successful claimant has suffered no pecuniary loss. *Punitive damages* aim to punish the defendant but they are of restricted application in the UK. *See* STRUCTURED SETTLEMENTS; PROVISIONAL DAMAGES.

Dangerous Wild Animals Act 1976 Regulates the keeping of certain kinds of dangerous animals and animals with the potential to be dangerous. Licensed zoos, circuses, pet shops and research laboratories apart, anyone keeping such an animal must obtain a local authority licence. Applications may be rejected for safety and other reasons.

Data Protection Act 1998 Prevents unauthorised or inappropriate use of 'personal data' held electronically or manually. Individuals ('data subjects') are allowed access to information held about them and given redress if the Act is contravened. Organisations ('data controllers'), unless exempt, must notify the Information Commissioner of the data held and how it is used. They must follow eight data protection principles. Certain breaches amount to criminal offences and in some instances data subjects have the right to damages. Insurance responses arise under public liability, legal expenses, directors' and officers', and professional indemnity policies (*www.dataprotection.gov.uk*).

Dating back *See* BACKDATING.

Datum line cover The 'line' is the level of indebtedness that must be breached before a credit insurer is liable for the risk relating to a specific debtor.

Day in hospital Health cash plan term meaning a continuous period of hospital confinement which includes an overnight stay. The policy pays a fixed amount for each 'day' the insured is hospitalised in defined circumstances subject to a minimum number of days, e.g. three, and a maximum number, e.g. 91 days, in any benefit year. Outpatient treatment not involving an overnight stay is covered under a separate section for up to a maximum number of days, e.g. 10, in any benefit year.

'Day one' average *See* DAY ONE BASIS OF REINSTATEMENT COVER.

'Day one' basis of reinstatement cover A reinstatement cover (qv) variant. The sum insured is in two parts – the declared reinstatement value of the property at inception (day one) and an added provision for inflation (between 115 per cent and 150 per cent) during the policy and reinstatement periods. An agreed percentage of 150 per cent attracts a flat rate of 15 per cent above the normal premium. Alternatively the rate is 7.5 per cent with the premium being adjustable at the end of the year. '*Day one average*' applies the actual value at risk on 'day one' against the 'day one' declared value rather than the value at risk at the date of reinstatement against the sum insured.

Days of grace *See* GRACE PERIOD.

Dealing as an agent Includes entering into a contract of insurance with a customer on behalf of an insurer and is therefore FSA regulated as a part of *insurance selling* (qv).

'Deals as a consumer' *See* CONSUMER SALE.

Death in service benefit Tax-free lump sum payable on the death of a group life and pension scheme member while still employed prior to retirement. The benefit is a multiple (e.g. four times) of the deceased's annual earnings. The trustees pay out the lump sum and are not necessarily bound by the member's nomination as to the beneficiary. Early leavers (qv) may exercise rights under a *continuation option* (qv), to continue with life cover without evidence of health.

Death strain The mortality risk above the level of the ceding office's (qv) retention for which reinsurance may be required. On a risk premium basis this is the difference between the sum insured and retention in the first one or two years.

Debentures Securities issued by companies acknowledging long-term loans. Debenture holders are entitled to a fixed rate of interest each year regardless of company profits as it is debt capital.

Debris *See* REMOVAL OF DEBRIS (qv).

Debt 1. Underwriting measure imposed by life insurers on sub-standard lives. The debt is deducted from the sum payable on death within the term but not from any survival benefit. It may be for a fixed amount *(fixed debt)* or it may diminish each year *(diminishing debt)* eventually to nil to coincide with a *reducing extra risk* (qv) 2. Money due from one party to another. 'Trade debtors', a balance sheet item, are assets at risk through non-payment and therefore insurable under credit insurance (qv) and book debts insurance (qv).

Debtor A person who owes money to another, i.e. his creditor. The creditor has an insurable interest (qv) in the life of the debtor.

Decennial insurance Single premium ten-year (or longer) latent defects insurance indemnifying the owner against physical damage to the premises caused by an inherent defect in the design, materials, or construction of the structure. Cover includes remedial work when an inherent defect threatens the stability of the building. Subsidence, heave and landslip are covered if accompanied by damage to the structure. Insurers paying claims may acquire subrogation rights against any contractor or professional otherwise liable for the defect. The policy is assignable by the insured to new owners.

Decision notice Issued to inform a person of the disciplinary action the FSA proposes to take against him. The recipient is allowed 28 days in which to refer the matter to the FSMA Tribunal (qv). If no referral occurs the FSA issues a *final notice* stating the action to be taken and the date upon which their decision takes effect. The FSA's Decision Making Manual refers. (Visit *www.fsa.org.uk*).

Deck cargo Cargo carried outside rather than within the vessel's enclosed cargo spaces. Rule for Construction 17 (qv) provides that, in the absence of custom and trade practice, deck cargo and living animals should be insured specifically and not under the general denomination 'goods'. The insurer's knowledge is such that a mere description of the goods may be sufficient notice that the cargo will be carried on deck.

Declaration 1. A statement on a proposal form whereby the proposer affirms the truthfulness of his answers, usually to 'his best knowledge and belief'. The declaration may convert the statements into warranties which become the basis of the contract. 2. Periodic declarations of a variable, e.g. wages, made by the insured under adjustable policies (qv).

Declaration-linked basis 1. *Property insurance.* Policies covering stock that allow the insured to maintain a full insurance on fluctuating stock values without over-insuring. The insured selects an amount at risk and pays a deposit figure based on 75 per cent of that figure. Following a series of stock declarations the premium is adjusted up or down by up to 33⅓ per cent at the end of the year. 2. *Business interruption.* The insured identifies an estimated gross profit and the policy automatically allows an increase in this figure. The premium is adjusted up or down by up to 33⅓ per cent at the end of the year when the actual gross profit is known.

Declaration of health A declaration confirming continued good health, sought by a life insurer, from a proposer who, having been offered life insurance, has failed to pay the premium within the stated time or from a policyholder who wishes to revive a lapsed policy.

Declaration of value A declaration at the foot of a proposal form that the sum insured represents the full value of the property at risk. The declaration forms part of the basis clause (qv) and is commonly used in the insurance of private dwellings and their contents as an alternative to using an average clause.

Declaration policies *See* ADJUSTABLE POLICIES.

Declared value A term used in fire insurance to refer to the total cost of reinstatement as declared by the insured (*see* DAY ONE BASIS OF REINSTATEMENT COVER). The cost will include re-building and re-equipping, plus due allowance for professional fees, public authority requirements and debris removal.

Declinature A refusal by the insurer to accept a proposal for a new insurance or renew an existing policy. Refusals have to be disclosed in future applications for insurance. The right to decline at renewal does not apply to permanent contracts (qv).

Decreasing term insurance A term insurance (qv) under which the sum payable on death decreases each year by predetermined amounts. If the insured survives the whole of the policy term nothing is payable by the insurers who retain all premiums. *See* FAMILY INCOME BENEFITS; MORTGAGE PROTECTION.

Dedicated vehicle A Lloyd's corporate member that participates on one or more syndicates managed by a single managing agent (qv) (or managing agent group). It enables the corporate member to back the skills of a particular underwriter or managing agent and to participate in a class or classes of business.

Deductible A specific amount or percentage that will be deducted from all losses. Claims below the deductible are eliminated. It works in the same way as an excess (qv). A deductible of £1 million on a £5 million indemnity limits the (re)insurer's liability to £4 million. The term is mainly used in primary insurance; the reinsurance equivalent is *retention* (qv). The *deferred period* (qv) under an income protection policy (qv) is a 'time' deductible'. Compare with franchise (qv).

Deductions 'new for old' When a partially damaged vessel needs repair, the insurer is entitled to make deductions 'new for old' (Marine Insurance Act 1906, s.69). When new material replaces old material, which has depreciated by wear and tear, the shipowner must bear part of the cost of the new material. A deduction of one-third or one-sixth is made from the amount otherwise payable. In practice all Institute Hull clauses provide that an average, whether particular or general, shall be paid without deductions 'new for old'. For non-marine applications *see* NEW FOR OLD.

Deeming clause A part of the notification clause of a claims-made policy (qv). It provides that when a circumstance is notified in one year but the claim not made until a subsequent year, it will be deemed to be made in the year of notification. *See* LAUNDRY LIST.

'Deep pocket' theory Where the claimant can seek damages from more than one defendant, the claimant chooses the defendant with the greatest ability to pay, i.e. the one with 'deepest pocket'. The choice of defendant is often influenced by the insurance position.

Deep vein thrombosis (DVT) Potentially fatal formation of blood clot within a deep vein, usually in the lower limbs. Limited movement in cramped conditions, e.g. long haul flight conditions, appear to be the main cause. Air passengers making personal injury claims have to overcome the Warsaw Convention (qv) that limits compensation to 'accidents'. There is no definitive answer in English law as to whether DVT is caused by an 'accident'. Adopting the approach in *Air France* v. *Saks* (1985), a US case, a High Court decision (2002) held DVT not to be an accident for the purpose of the Convention.

Defamation Publication of untrue statements that tend to lower a person in the estimation of right thinking people. Defamation may be (a) libel, i.e. publication in a permanent form such as writing, or (b) slander, meaning a transitory publication such as the spoken word. Defamation is a tort and the aggrieved party can sue for damages if suffering special damage or for an injunction. *See* LIBEL INSURANCE.

Defeasible interest A cargo insurable interest that ceases during the transit for reasons other than maritime perils. A merchant, who is entitled to reject goods because of default by the seller, has a defeasible interest which is insurable.

Defective design Inadequate or insufficient design in premises or products. Risk management focuses upon designing out risks at the inception. In buildings, the Construction and Design Management Regulations 1994 (qv) applies, inter alia, to the design stage. HSWA 1974, s.6, places safety responsibility on designers of products (machines, etc.) for use at work. The defective design risk *may* be excluded from product liability insurance on the grounds that it is a professional negligence risk. The design risk is not excluded for retailers; they may be strictly liable for defective products under the Sale of Goods Act 1979 (qv).

Defective Premises Act 1972 Section 1 places an obligation on builders and developers to build dwellings 'fit for human habitation'. The duty is owed to all persons who acquire an interest in the dwelling for six years from when the work is completed or remedied. Section 3 removes 'caveat emptor' (qv) in selling property (this requirement is not restricted to dwellings) and makes vendors and lessors liable for negligent work on the property carried out before the sale. Section 4 makes 'repairing' landlords liable for defects of which they know or ought to have known. All public liability and household policies carry a Defective Premises Act 1972 liability extension.

Defective product For Consumer Protection Act 1987 (qv) purposes: a product where the safety is not such as persons generally are entitled to expect. A product is not considered defective merely because it is of poor quality or because a safer version is put on the market. When deciding whether a product is defective, a court takes account of all the relevant circumstances including: the manner of marketing; any instructions or warnings given; what might reasonably be expected to be done with it; the time the product was supplied.

Defective title insurance Indemnifies the prospective purchaser of land against loss occasioned from defects in the legal title arising from missing documents, etc. A title insurance policy extends for so long as the insured's interest in the property remains. The insurance is normally required by mortgagees before being prepared to grant loans where the mortgagor is at risk of a defective title.

Defective workmanship 1. *Motor trade.* Negligent workmanship on a customer's vehicle or the sale of a defective part by a motor vehicle repairer may cause an accident. The resultant liability can be insured under a motor trader's comprehensive road and garage policy, or as an extension of the *internal risks policy* (qv). 'Workmanship' means 'repair, servicing, or maintenance' and includes the pre-delivery check of a new vehicle and MOT tests. The widest available cover embraces: negligent workmanship, sale of spare parts and liability for damage to the customer's vehicle. 2. *Public liability. See* PROPERTY WORKED ON.

Defects liability period/maintenance period A pre-agreed period, commonly 12 months, starting from practical completion during which a builder must remedy, at his own expense, all genuine defects appearing in the building. The builder's liability policies should continue to run during this period.

Deferment of bonus Life insurance underwriting method for slightly impaired lives proposing for 'with profits' life assurance. Acceptance is at ordinary rates but bonuses shall not vest until maturity, or until attainment of the normal lifespan expectation.

Deferred acquisition costs Acquisition costs (qv) that are carried forward to a subsequent accounting period in order to match such expenses with the income generated.

Deferred annuity Whereby the annuity payments are deferred for a period of time, often to coincide with retirement. Compare with immediate annuities (qv) where the annuity payments commence immediately.

Deferred annuity purchase *See* AGE 75 RULE.

Deferred pension/preserved pension 1. A pension based on accrued benefits from an individual's membership of a previous pension scheme. The *preserved benefits* remain frozen until the scheme's normal retirement age for members with two or more years service. In final salary schemes (qv) the deferred pension can attract discretionary benefits. *See* DEFERRED PENSIONER. 2. The term is also used when a member takes a pension later than the normal retirement age.

Deferred pensioner A former active member (qv) of an occupational pension scheme whose benefits remain in the scheme as *preserved benefits* (qv) until transferred to a new scheme or a personal pension or drawn as a pension at a later date. *See* DEFERRED PENSION.

Deferred period/deferment period A period of delay prior to the payment of benefits in respect of any claim under an income protection insurance (qv). The period may be 4, 13, 26 or 52 weeks chosen by the insured based on the period during which full salary is payable under the employment contract. Compare with WAITING PERIOD.

Deferred premium clause AVN5A An aviation insurance clause that applies when the premium is payable by instalments. If an instalment is not paid the clause: (a) terminates cover at midnight on the day concerned; and (b) requires the payment of the outstanding balance if the claims exceeds the premium instalments paid.

Deficit clause A clause in a reinsurance or other agreement that specifies that deficits shall be carried forward and offset in arriving at any profit commission due to the reinsured. Deficits may be carried forward to extinction or for a limited period, e.g. three or five years.

Defined accrued benefits funding method An accrued benefits valuation in which the actuarial liability for active members (qv) is based on the benefits that would arise if the scheme were to discontinue at the valuation date. The standard contribution rate (qv) is the rate required to cover both the cost of benefit payments in the ongoing scheme and the accrued benefits in the event of future discontinuance at the end of the control period.

Defined benefit pension scheme Occupational scheme under which the retirement benefits are fixed by formula (e.g. 1/60th or 1/80th of final pensionable pay for each year of pensionable service). The employer undertakes to make whatever contributions, taking account of any employee contributions, are necessary to secure the pensions. Most schemes are *final salary schemes* (qv), and are subject to Inland Revenue limits (qv) if they are exempt approved schemes.

Defined contribution scheme Occupational pensions scheme where an employee's retirement benefits depend on (a) the amount of contributions and investment income on these contributions, and (b) the annuity rate available when the member retires. There is no set formula, as in the case of defined benefit schemes (qv), for determining benefits. These schemes are also called *money purchase schemes. See* INLAND REVENUE LIMITS.

Definition clause A clause whereby insurers define the meaning they intend to assign to various words and phrases in the policy. This is particularly important when the ordinary meaning of the word is not appropriate. The term 'employee' is widely defined in public and employers' liability policies with the intention of removing doubt that might otherwise cause disputes.

Degree day The measure of deviation of one day's average temperature against a standard reference temperature, e.g. 65°F or 18°C in a reference station (qv) such as London Heathrow. An average daily temperature of 23°C produces 5 degree days and measures the intensity of warmth on that day. *See* HEATING DEGREE DAYS; COOLING DEGREE DAYS; CUMULATIVE DEGREE DAYS; GROWING DEGREE DAYS.

Delay 1. An insured event under a travel insurance policy (qv) paying agreed sums if the insured's holiday departure is delayed as a result of specified occurrence, e.g. industrial action, adverse weather, aircraft breakdown, etc. 2. Late arrival of cargo at destination caused by adverse weather, mechanical breakdown or some other reason. The *marine extension clause* (8.3, Institute Cargo Clauses) extends the *warehouse to warehouse clause* (qv) to provide continuous cover during any deviation, forced discharge, reshipment or trans-shipment or other interruption beyond the control of the insured. The clause extends existing cover during the delay but does not add 'delay' as an insured peril so loss of market, etc., will not be covered.

Delay in Completion and Performance Shortfall Specialised policy for 'blue chip' construction companies with sophisticated risk management programmes. Cover provides protection against penalties incurred as a result of late completion of a contract or milestones within the contract, and the post completion *efficacy risk* (qv). Policies are customer-specific with negotiable deductibles based on cover up to US$30 million.

Delayed launch insurance An insurance to cover the extra expenses arising from the delay in launching a satellite.

Delayed turnover Postponed trade that a business interruption (qv) insurer is entitled to take into account when adjusting a claim. After trading is resumed, turnover may rise above the normal level due to postponed orders coming good. Provided this occurs within the maximum indemnity period (qv) the insurer can make due allowance in his calculation of the reduction in turnover. This adjustment is also called 'clawback'.

'Delegable' duties Where a principal delegates work to an independent contractor, and his duty in respect of that work is no higher than a duty to take reasonable care, his duties are 'delegable' and he discharges them by taking care to select a competent contractor. Certain duties are 'non-delegable' (qv).

Deliberate concealment 1. The deliberate concealment of a material fact (qv) by a proposer is a fraudulent breach of the utmost good faith (qv). 2. Limitation Act 1980, s.2, defines the term as 'the deliberate commission of a breach of duty in circumstances in which it is unlikely to be discovered for some time'. The six-year limitation period runs from time of discovery of deliberate concealment with no long-stop provision. Professional negligence errors could go undiscovered for years, but the House of Lords rejected the view that an act of negligence could amount to deliberate concealment (*Cave* v. *Robinson Jarvis & Rolf* (2002)). A contrary decision would have meant open-ended liability for negligent professionals.

Demands and needs statement The Insurance Mediation Directive requires intermediaries to give customers a statement of their demands and needs. Where advice is given, the statement must also explain the reasons for the intermediary's recommendation. The FSA's ICOB Rules will require a demand and needs statement from: intermediaries and insurers when selling to retail customers (qv), whether advice is given or not; intermediaries and insurers for advised sales to commercial customers; intermediaries only for non-advised sales to commercial customers. The statement must be given in a durable medium (qv) before the contract is concluded. However, it can be given orally: where the customer requires immediate cover or the customer requests that it be given orally. For *advised* and *non-advised sales see* ADVISING AND SELLING STANDARDS.

Demonstration and tuition An extension in motor traders' road risks policies to include driving of the trader's vehicles by prospective customers and persons undergoing driving tuition.

Demurrage 1. A penalty or storage charge for cargo or containers held beyond the allowed number of free days at a warehouse due to late collection. 2. The liquidated damages (qv) payable to the shipowner if the *lay days* (qv) allowed by the charter party (qv) for loading or discharging are exceeded. 3. Loss of hire or use of ship following collision damage. *See* DETENTION.

De-mutualisation Process of a mutual insurance company (qv) becoming a limited liability company owned by shareholders. Ex-mutual members have received substantial payments to compensate them for their loss of status.

Denial of access Business interruption (qv) extension covering loss of income due to policyholder and customers being denied access to premises following damage by an insured peril to another building, e.g. fire at adjacent premises resulting in a road block. Cover for 'non-damage' events that deny access, e.g. crowd demonstrations, are also insurable.

Dependant 1. A person financially dependent on a pension scheme member (or pensioner) but the term is defined precisely in the scheme rules. The IR automatically regards spouses and children as dependants as the later of age 18 or end of full time education/training. 2. Under employment relations legislation (right to take time off) a dependant is a husband, wife, child, parent or anyone living with the employee as a part of his family. Taking time off to deal with emergencies for dependants does not breach the employment contract. 3. *See* FATAL ACCIDENTS ACT.

Dependant's pension Pension scheme option that allows a member to sacrifice part of his own pension to secure a pension for a dependant (qv) after his death. The maximum allowable to a surviving spouse is two-thirds of the maximum member's pension at the normal retirement pension based on current earnings. If death occurs after retirement the dependant receives the percentage of the deceased member's pension as stated in the rule. *See* COMMUTATION FACTOR.

Depolarisation *See* POLARISATION.

Deposit administration scheme A *defined contribution scheme* (qv) also called a cash accumulation policy, used for employee groups or individual personal pensions. Contributions are held by the life office to accumulate with interest. When benefits become payable money is withdrawn to purchase annuities and pay lump sums. The life office carries no risk but acts as investor. The pre-retirement mortality risk is left to the scheme trustees who usually arrange separate cover.

Deposit against third party risks Motor Vehicles (Third Party Risks) Deposit Regulations 1992 provide for a deposit of £500,000 with the Accountant General of the Supreme Court by an individual or entity as an alternative to effecting compulsory motor insurance (qv) (Road Traffic Act 1988 (as amended)) .

Deposit back arrangement Amounts deposited by reinsurers with cedants to help finance the reinsurers' proportion of claims. The amount retained is usually such proportion of the agreed premium. The deposit is released annually in arrears.

Deposit company Also called a *community deposit company* it means an insurance company (other than a pure reinsurer) whose head office is not in an EC State and which has made a deposit in a member State other than the United Kingdom in accordance with regulatory requirements. If the deposit is lodged in the UK the company is called a *UK deposit company*.

Deposit premium 1. Payment under an adjustable policy (qv) to an insurer at the inception based on an estimate of fluctuating values, activities or costs that may be adjusted up or down at the end of the term. 2. In non-proportional reinsurance (qv) it is the amount paid by a cedant to a reinsurer representing all or part of premiums expected to be earned under the contract. The premium is adjusted at the end of the contract term or periodically within a multi-year contract to reflect actual premiums earned. If the parties work on an adjustable rate basis the deposit premium may be negotiated quarterly.

Depreciation The decline in value of property resulting from use, wear and tear or obsolescence. Depreciation is not covered under contracts of indemnity (qv) but insurers may issue 'new for old' (qv) and reinstatement policies (qv) thereby modifying the principle of indemnity.

Derivative A financial instrument that derives its value from an underlying asset (equity, bond or commodity) or an underlying index. A weather derivative (qv) is linked to an index derived from a weather variable such as temperature and addresses the *volume risk* of weather-sensitive firms. *Financial derivatives* are used as a tool to manage financial price risks. They consist of: *forward contracts*, tailor-made contracts to eliminate the risk of some form of price uncertainty; *futures contracts*, exchange-traded standard forward contracts; *swaps*, a package of forward contracts simultaneously arranged; *options* (qv), financial markets equivalent of an insurance policy. These contracts allow entities to hedge against future price changes or take positions to offset the impact of unwelcome price changes or other specified conditions.

Description of risk clause Some statements e.g. 'the lorry will deliver coal,' describe the risk rather than warrant it. The clause operates like an exclusion (qv) in that it suspends cover when the actual use is not as described. Cover re-attaches when normal use, i.e. delivering coal, resumes. A warranty would terminate cover, not suspend it, at the moment of breach (*Farr* v. *Motor Traders* (1920)).

Description of use Motor policies state the insurer will not be liable for loss whilst the vehicle was 'being used otherwise than in accordance with the 'Description of Use' contained in the policy. This description is also printed on the certificate of insurance. *See* CLASS OF USE.

Design risks Liability for injury, loss or damage arising out of the design, plan, formula or specification of goods. Public liability and products liability policies tend to exclude these risks where the work is done for a fee as this may indicate that the risk is more properly insured under a professional indemnity policy. Where a fee is not normally payable there is no exclusion and 'non-professionals' remain covered for third party injury or damage as defined in the policy. This is important as liability may automatically attach to 'non-professionals', e.g. retailers, under the Sale of Goods Act 1979 or the Consumer Protection Act 1987. *See* also PATTERNS, MODELS, MOULDS AND DESIGNS.

Design warranty clause A clause in the JCT Standard Form of Building Contract with Contractors Design 1998 making the building contractor responsible for the design of the building. The clause seeks to put the contractor's design liability on the same footing as that of the architect or other professional, i.e. on the basis of a duty of reasonable care. The clause does not call upon the contractor to effect insurance but the contractor's design liability can be insured in the professional indemnity market.

Designated investment business The FSA's Conduct of Business Rules (qv) relate mainly to firms carrying on 'designated investment business'. This includes dealing in, arranging and advising on shares, bonds, options and derivatives and the like and also long-term insurance (qv). It does not include general insurance contracts. *See* ICOB.

Designated professional body (DPB) Professional body so designated by the Treasury under FSMA, s.326. The Law Society, for example, supervises and regulates the *exempt professional firms* (qv) under its jurisdiction. A DPB must cooperate with the overall regulator, the FSA.

Destination clause The life policy clause identifying the persons to whom the policy moneys are payable – the insured or his executors, administrators or assigns; or possibly the representatives or assigns of the insured.

Detainment Holding back someone else's property. The *detainment clause* in the Institute War and Strikes Clauses (Hull-Time) provides that a vessel detained 12 months or more is treated as a constructive total loss (qv). However, clause 5 excludes detainment 'by or under the order of the government or other public of the country in which the vessel is owned or registered'. It is also excluded if detainment is due to infringement of any trading or *customs regulations* (qv).

Detention 1. Occurs when governmental authorities prevent a vessel and/or cargo leaving port, particularly during hostilities. 2. Where demurrage (qv) is paid for an agreed number of days any further delay is 'detention' for which the shipowner can claim unlimited damages.

Deterioration of freezer contents (household) Insurance of stock stored in a freezer and/or refrigerator against the risk of loss through deterioration following: (a) breakdown of plant; (b) non-operation of thermostatic or automatic controlling devices; (c) action of escaping refrigerant fumes from any cause; or (d) failure of the public electricity supply. *See* DETERIORATION OF STOCK.

Deterioration of stock Engineering insurance covering damage to perishable stock in cold stores directly consequent upon an accident to cooling or climatising equipment insured under a machinery breakdown policy. The widest form of cover insures loss caused by any rise or fall in temperature. *See* DETERIORATION OF FREEZER CONTENTS.

Determination of Liabilities Rules Set out in Chapter 5 of IPRU (INS). The liabilities, as calculated, are set against the assets as valued (Valuation of Assets Rules (qv)) for required minimum margin (RMM) (qv) purposes. Liabilities for general insurance business are calculated along the lines of general accounting principles and practices, but long-term business liabilities are subject to complex rules calculated by the appointed actuary (qv) guided by his professional body and the Government Actuary's Department.

Development hazard The loss development potential of a hazard (qv). Risk surveyors are concerned not only with the likelihood of a loss (the inception hazard) but whether the development of a loss will be minimal or severe. Risk mapping (qv) correlates probability and severity.

Development risks defence *See* STATE OF THE ART.

Deviation Departure of a vessel from the customary or agreed route with the intention of returning to that route to complete the voyage. Under the Marine Insurance act 1906, s.46, the insurer is discharged from liability if the deviation is made without lawful excuse. The Institute Cargo Clauses *deviation clause* protects cargo owners by 'holding covered' during deviations beyond the insured's control. A similar but more strongly worded deviation clause appears in hull voyage policies. Deviation does not apply to time policies as cover is not based on voyages.

Difference basis Business interruption insurance (qv) term used when 'gross profit' is defined as the amount by which the sum of the amount of the turnover and the amounts of the closing stock and work-in-progress shall exceed the sum of the amounts of the opening stock and the amount of the specified working expenses (qv). In short, it is *sales* minus the *cost of goods sold.*

Difference in conditions insurance A master policy purchased by a multinational company to fill the gaps in cover that may arise through differences arising in insurances purchased locally in different overseas countries. The master policy only operates for risks not covered under local policies. It 'tops up' the cover to the level desired by the organisation as a whole. See *difference in limits.* In property insurance it may take the form of an 'all risks' cover on a large risk to supplement underlying insurances arranged on a named peril basis.

Difference in limits Operates in the same way as *difference in conditions* (qv) insurance by providing excess limits of indemnity over the limits of locally arranged insurances purchased overseas.

Diminishing debt *See* DEBT 1.

Diminishing risk *See* REDUCING EXTRA RISK.

Dinghies *See* BOAT INSURANCE.

'Dip down' proviso *See* DROP DOWN COVER.

Diploma in Insurance A newly introduced (2004) examination-based qualification recognising the 'technical' development achieved by those with a growing understanding of the industry. It requires candidates to pass a 110 credit threshold. Successful CII members can apply to use the designation 'Dip CII'. *See* ADVANCED DIPLOMA IN INSURANCE.

Direct business *See* DIRECT INSURER.

Direct dealing An arrangement that enables certain motor syndicates at Lloyd's to deal directly with non-Lloyd's brokers. However, the premiums payable have to be guaranteed by, and paid through, a Lloyd's broker.

Direct insurer An insurer, as opposed to a reinsurer (qv). The direct insurer provides the primary insurance for the business community or general public with or without the involvement of an intermediary. In the US particularly, the term is also used for an insurer dealing direct with their policyholder and not through brokers or agents.

Direct liability clause *See* CUT THROUGH CLAUSE.

Directives 2002/12/EC and 2002/13/EC (Solvency I) Amend Directive 73/239/EEC (life undertakings) and 79/267/EEC (non-life undertakings) to strengthen solvency margin (qv) requirements. The new requirements (not applicable to mutuals, life or non-life, with less than €5 million annual contribution income): (a) allow Member States to establish more stringent solvency requirements; (b) increase the minimum guarantee fund (qv), (to €3 million index-linked; (c) increase the threshold levels of premiums and claims below which a higher solvency margin is required; (d) allow earlier supervisory intervention; (e) increase the solvency margin for certain volatile categories of non-life business (marine, aviation and general liability) by 50 per cent; (f) allow a life company to include up to 50 per cent of its future profits for solvency until 31 December 2009 subject to supervisory approval; (g) the division of assets, for solvency purposes, into three categories – those acceptable without limitation, those acceptable subject to limitations and those acceptable only with approval. The new measures start in 2004.

Directors Companies Act 1985, s.741 states that 'director includes any person occupying the position of director by whatever name called'. A director is therefore anyone who 'directs' (identified by function rather than title). *De jure directors* are formally appointed and registered. *De facto directors* (constructive) are never formally appointed but act openly. *Shadow directors* do not act openly, they 'lurk in the dark behind those who do', being persons 'in accordance with whose directions and instructions the directors of the company are accustomed to act' (s.741(2)). Both executive and non-executive (i.e. outsiders) have the same general legal duties. The Higgs Report (2003) on corporate governance (qv) has introduced the concept of *independent director*, i.e. a non-executive director determined by the board as being independent in character and judgement and there are no circumstances (e.g. former employee) which could affect, or appear to affect, the director's judgement. The Code on Corporate Governance also calls for the appointment of a *senior independent director* to liaise between the board and major shareholders.

Directors' and officers' liability insurance Indemnifies directors and officers for loss arising from claims against them by reason of a *wrongful act* (qv) related to their duties. The indemnity is on annual aggregate limit basis inclusive of legal costs and expenses incurred in responding to any allegation against directors and officers. Defence costs related to certain criminal or regulatory charges are also covered. The policy does not cover fines, penalties or punitive damages or, unless extended, liability as pension trustees. The insurer indemnifies the company where it has reimbursed a director or officer in relation to an insured event. The policy is *claims-made* (qv), *carries an excess* (qv) and may be extended to cover *employment practices liability* (qv). *See* ALLOCATION.

Directors' duties/liabilities A director has extensive powers to bind the company but may be personally liable for a breach of duty. The duties embrace: compliance with the Companies Acts and the Articles of Association; exercise of reasonable care and skill; and a fiduciary duty to act in good faith. Directors principally owe their duties to the company but may also owe duties to creditors and the company's employees in general. Certain sections of the Companies Acts and other legislation (e.g. Health and Safety) expose the director to criminal liability. Directors may also attract personal liability for *fraudulent trading* (qv) or *wrongful trading* (qv) or exceeding their authority. *See* DIRECTORS' AND OFFICERS' LIABILITY INSURANCE.

Directors' professional liability insurance Insurance scheme set up by the Institute of Directors for its members for up to £1 million indemnity and £25,000 insolvency defence claims and other extensive cover.

Dirty bill *See* CLAUSED BILL.

Disability 1. Disability Discrimination Act 1995 (qv) defines it as an impairment that is either physical or mental adversely affecting the person's ability to carry out day to day activities. The adverse effect must be substantial and long-term. 2. Under income protection insurance (qv) and other health policies *disability* definitions are related to occupation. Disability could mean the inability of the insured to carry out (a) his own occupation; (b) any occupation for which he is suited by education, training and experience; (c) *any* occupation; or (d) specific tasks as defined in the *activities of daily life* (qv) or *activities of daily work* (qv).

Disability benefits Benefits added to life or income protection policies. They may include *waiver of premium* (qv) during periods of disability preventing the policyholder from following his normal occupation. The term has also been applied when periodic payments following temporary disablement from working are added to a life policy.

Disability Discrimination Act 1995 DDA aims to end discrimination against disabled persons in regard to: access to goods, services and facilities; buying or renting property; employment. It is unlawful to treat the disabled less favourably than others and it is now necessary to make reasonable adjustments in the way services are provided. From 2004, service providers will have to consider adjusting the physical features of their premises where they disadvantage the disabled using the service. The law applies to employers with 15 or more employees and to service providers. Discrimination is a source of claims under employment practices liability insurance (qv). *See* DISABILITY 1.

Disability Rights Commission (DRC) Independent body created by statute to eliminate discrimination and promote equality of opportunity. Advises government, business, disabled persons and service providers. DRC is the statutory enforcement mechanism for the Disability Discrimination Act (qv) and is empowered to issue non-discrimination notices.

Disablement Physical or mental condition preventing a person from undertaking 'normal' work duties or the 'activities of daily life' (qv). 'Disablement' or 'disability' is invariably defined in the policy. *See* DISABILITY 2.

Disablement benefit The benefit payable under a personal accident or income protection insurance when the insured is either permanently or temporarily disabled. *See* PERMANENT DISABLEMENT; TEMPORARY DISABLEMENT.

Disaster recovery planning Planning centred on what an organisation needs to do after the occurrence of an untoward event, such as a fire or loss of computing facilities. Disaster recovery is more concerned with the effects of an event and minimising its negative impact than dealing with the cause. *See* BUSINESS CONTINUITY MANAGEMENT.

Disbursements Expenses incurred by the shipowner prior to sailing that will be 'lost' if the vessel does not complete its voyage. Disbursements comprise port expenses, bunkers, supplies, labour, customs fees, etc. Disbursements insurance pays for the 'lost expenses' if the vessel becomes a total loss before reaching its destination. *See* DISBURSEMENTS WARRANTY.

Disbursements warranty Hull policy clause prohibiting the insured from effecting additional insurances, including total loss of hull and machinery, other than those specified in the clause. Breach of warranty is not held covered and discharges the insurer from all liability. The clause allows the shipowner to effect policies, not exceeding 25 per cent of the insured value on disbursements (qv), increased value and anticipated freight. The warranty prevents the shipowner from fixing a low sum insured on the hull and simultaneously effecting cheap total loss only cover. Similar provisions apply to freight policies as they follow the settlements on hull policies in the event of total loss.

Discharge 1. A receipt given by a policyholder to acknowledge a loss payment and that he has no further claim on the insurer in respect of that loss. In third party claims, the insurer pays the claimant and obtains an acknowledgement to absolve the insured from all future liability relating to the cause of action concerned. 2. Unloading cargo from a vessel.

Disclaimer notices Notices displayed in public access premises such as hotels, garages, etc., or where property is left. The bailee (qv) or occupier of premises may seek to exempt or restrict liability for loss or damage to property or personal injury. The Unfair Contract Terms Act 1977 prohibits businesses from exempting their liability for death or injury resulting from negligence. Exemption of liability for loss/damage to property resulting from negligence is allowed if reasonable, but the disclaimer notice will not be effective unless it has first been brought to the attention of the bailor or other party.

Disclosure 1. Requirement under PA93 and PA95 to disclose information about pension schemes to interested parties. The principal regulations are the Occupational Pension Schemes (Disclosure of Information) Regulations 1996. 2. FSA rules that require an exempt professional firm (qv), before it provides a service that includes carrying on a regulated activity, to disclose in writing to the client that it is not authorised under FSMA. 3. The FSA obliges life insurers to advise individual policyholders that they may purchase their annuity from a different life office via the *open market option* (qv). Also life policyholders requesting surrender values (qv) must be told that they may be able to sell their policy (*see* TRADED ENDOWMENT POLI-

CIES). 4. FSA disclosure rules concern charges, remuneration and commission (Conduct of Business Rule 5.7). They oblige advisers to make consumers buying retail investment products (e.g. life insurance) aware of their status, the scope of their advice, a clear explanation of the costs of the products so that easy comparisons can be made and any connection the advisers may have to the providers. An initial disclosure document must be given at the initial point of contact and a repeat disclosure document when a product is recommended. Independent advisers have to offer the option of payment by fee rather than just commission. *See* UTMOST GOOD FAITH; STATUS DISCLOSURE; PRODUCT DISCLOSURE; DISCLOSURE OF BASIS OF ADVICE.

Disclosure of basis of advice The ICOB requirement that during the sales process an intermediary must disclose whether he advised, or provided information, on an insurance contract on the basis of: a fair analysis of the market; a selection from a limited number of insurers; or products from a single insurer. A 'fair market analysis' requires the intermediary to analyse a sufficiently large number of insurance contracts in the relevant market sector to allow it to give advice or information that is 'adequate' to meet the customer's needs. Third party intermediaries must comply whether selling to retail or commercial customers (large risks excepted), but insurers only have to comply with this disclosure if selling to retail customers. *See also* ADVISING AND SELLING STANDARDS.

Disclosure of interests The manager and executives of a Lloyd's underwriting agency, which provides recruitment and administration services for a syndicate, must disclose their interests in the insurance transactions of the syndicate in the annual report. A similar disclosure is also required of members' agents.

Discontinuance The cessation of contributions to a pension scheme leading to the scheme being wound-up or becoming a frozen scheme.

Discontinued products A product that is no longer in production. In products liability insurance (qv) such products need to be identified and brought within the business description to ensure that the 'run-off' risk is covered as the policy is 'losses-occurring' (qv). The time of damage triggers the right to an indemnity not the date of manufacture or supply.

Discounting of reserves *See* TIME AND DISTANCE POLICIES.

Discovery of ship's papers Application to court by an insurer after a loss for the production of relevant ship's documents. The order can be issued against the shipowner, a mortgagee, the insured in the case of cargo policy, insurers in the case of reinsurance, an agent who sues on behalf of his principal, an insured where the insurer seeks a return of money allegedly obtained by fraud, an assignee of policy proceeds and other interested parties.

Discovery period 1. Period within which a defalcation must be discovered and notified to the fidelity guarantee insurer (qv). The customary six month period runs from the employee's resignation, dismissal or retirement or three months from the expiry of the policy whichever occurs first. 2. *See* EXTENDED REPORTING PERIOD.

Discretionary approval ICTA 1988, s.591, allows occupational pension schemes to offer a wider range of benefits than those available under schemes entitled to mandatory approval under s.590. Discretionary approval permits enhanced pensions, higher accrual rates, higher life cover and enhanced retirement cash. IR Practice Note 12 sets out detailed rules.

Discretionary benefits Benefits that the trustees of a final salary scheme (qv) can grant to enhance a member's retirement subject to IR maximum limits. The employer could ask the trustees to enhance a member's retirement benefit on early retirement, redundancy, ill health or death in service benefits, or escalate the pension at a rate above LPI (qv). The trustees can use their discretion to award a lump sum benefit on death to any individual, not necessarily the person nominated by the member.

Discretionary scheme Occupational pension scheme where membership is by employer invitation only and where the benefits and contributions may vary from one member to another. Although discretionary, there must be equal access and no discrimination in terms of benefits on grounds of race, religion, sex or disability.

Discretionary trust policies An approach to partnership insurance to minimise the number of policies necessitated under individual trust policy arrangements (qv). Each partner effects one policy on his own life under a discretionary trust in favour of the other partners who are normally the trustees in whom the proceeds are vested. When a claim arises they are then able to apportion the proceeds among themselves to repay the deceased or retiring partner's share of the business.

Disintermediation Process of parties dealing direct without involving intermediaries, e.g. insurer sells personal lines (qv) over the Internet. Innovatory ART (qv) products are often handled directly by the contracting parties.

Disposal of abandoned vehicles policy An insurance available to local authorities to protect them in respect of their legal liability to vehicle owners whose vehicles they have removed as abandoned.

Distance non-investment mediation contract A distance contract to provide advice or information on non-investment insurance contracts, other than simply as part of the marketing stage in the sale of a contract. Specific FSA rules (*ICOB 8*) apply to these contracts with retail customers to implement the Distance Marketing Directive although such contracts rarely arise in the retail market.

Distance sales Sales that are not conducted face-to-face, such as sales through the post, over the Internet or telephone or by fax or digital television. FSA rules take account of the Distance Marketing Directive. The initial contact disclosure for telephone sales involves disclosing the name of the firm, and, if the contact is initiated by the firm, the purpose of the contact. The name of the person in contact with the customer must also be given and his link with the firm. *See* DISTANCE NON-INVESTMENT MEDIATION CONTRACT.

Distribution bonds *See* INCOME BONDS.

District of use Factor in the rating of motor insurance premiums. The incidence of vehicle accidents varies directly with the density of the population in given districts. Private car insurers generally divide the country into six districts for this purpose while commercial vehicle insurers use three districts for goods-carrying vehicles.

Divestment The provision of Lloyd's Act 1982 (qv) that the Council of Lloyd's (qv) shall not permit a Lloyd's broker to continue to act in that capacity if it is associated with a managing agent (qv).

Divisible surplus The portion of an insurance company's earning that is available for distribution to 'with-profits' policyholders in the form of bonuses.

Doctrine of priority The priority given to an assignee under the Policies of Assurance Act 1867 (qv) when a deed assigning a life policy has been executed and proper notice given. Until notice is given the assignee has no right to sue under the deed and the Act provides that the date on which notice is received shall regulate the priority of all claims – this is known as the doctrine of priority. *See* ASSIGNMENT.

Documentary credit *See* LETTER OF CREDIT.

Domestic boilers/domestic purposes Boilers not used in trade processes but this does not preclude their use in business premises exclusively for 'domestic' purposes such as central heating, supplying hot water for hand washing or use in the works canteen. The term is important as the standard fire policy provides cover for explosion damage caused by 'boilers used for domestic purposes only'. In the same way the standard fire policy covers explosion caused by gas supplied for heating, etc.

Domestic employees Unlimited liability for injury to domestic employees is covered under the household contents policy. As domestic employees are employed in a household not a business, compulsory insurance does not apply.

Domestic helpline protection *See* HOME EMERGENCY COVER.

'Doomed from the start' Lord Fraser's expression in the House of Lords case of *Pirelli* v. *Oscar Faber & Partners* (1983). Held: the cause of action, in property damage claims based on negligence, accrued at the time of the damage and not the time of discovery/discoverability for the purpose of the six-year limitation period. Lord Fraser qualified this by saying that a building could be so defective as to be 'doomed from the start' so causing the time to run from completion. Lord Fraser's qualification created the risk that owners of properties with latent defects could run out of time even before sustaining or discovering damage. The Latent Damages Act 1986 (qv) remedies the problem.

Double benefits *See* DOUBLE INDEMNITY.

Double endowment Endowment insurance (qv) whereby the amount payable on maturity is twice the amount payable on death within the policy term. It combines an endowment insurance with a pure endowment (qv) for the same sum or is structured as a term insurance for a particular sum linked to a pure endowment for double that sum. It can be offered to impaired lives as an alternative to extra premiums.

Double 'indemnity'/double accident bond Certain personal accident policies (qv) pay twice their normal benefits if the injury or death has been caused under specified circumstances, usually meaning injury following an accident involving a road or rail conveyance.

Double insurance *See* CONTRIBUTION.

Double option agreement *See* CROSS OPTION AGREEMENT.

Dreaded disease policy *See* CRITICAL ILLNESS POLICY.

Dredgers Vessels involved with sprinkling or suction, which normally work in ports or inland waterways. Cover is normally granted under the Institute Port Risk Clauses covering: 1. Loss or damage, 2. Third party liabilities except in respect of employees. A dredger proprietor with a registered office in London must effect an employers' liability insurance (qv). However, insurance is not compulsory for injury or disease suffered or contracted outside Great Britain.

Driving of other cars (DOC) A clause in the third party section of a private car policy permitting the insured to drive private type cars or motor cycles not belonging to him and not hired to him under a hire purchase agreement. If the insured parts with the insured car, the extended indemnity ceases to apply as the main indemnity then terminates. Occasionally, as an underwriting measure, the insurer may delete the extension.

Drop down cover An excess layer, umbrella liability policy (qv) or excess of loss treaty that lowers, i.e. drops down, its excess point (qv) if the limits of the underlying layer or retention have been exhausted. 'Drop downs' are subject to annual aggregate limits. The insured/reinsured may be able to absorb a given retention level on one loss but additional losses need the added protection afforded by the drop-down. 'Drop down' covers may also pick up gaps in cover as may happen in umbrella liability policies and master global policies sitting over local policies. *See* TOP AND DROP.

Dry-docking expenses The costs of entering and keeping a vessel in dry dock for repairs form a part of the repair costs. *See* COMMON CHARGES.

Dry perils The following are categorised as dry perils: aircraft, explosion, riot and civil commotion, malicious damage and earthquake. They are a group of perils, additional perils (qv), that extend the cover under a standard fire policy.

Dual membership Occurs when, following a pension sharing order (qv), an ex-spouse, in receipt of a pension credit (qv), becomes a member of the pension scheme in his or her own right alongside the member.

Dual basis payroll Method of insuring 'wages' under a business interruption policy (qv) when not included in the full payroll in the gross profit item. The policyholder insures 100 per cent of his payroll for an initial limited period, e.g. 13 weeks, but only a percentage, e.g. 25 per cent, for the remainder of the indemnity period to retain key staff. On payment of an additional premium, the insured can 'consolidate', i.e. extend the initial period of full cover for a longer period with no cover thereafter.

Dual market contracts Written in the Lloyd's market, these reinsurance contracts contain elements of more than one type of risk (e.g. marine and non-marine). The leading underwriter indicates on the slip the percentage split between the two classes.

Due diligence The process of investigation undertaken when one company is about to acquire another. It means thorough checks on a company's financial performance and its liabilities, e.g. inadequately insured losses or risks, before a transaction is completed. Reports from solicitors, accountants and insurance brokers are a part of the process. Failure to exercise due diligence could expose directors and officers to claims insurable under directors' and officers' liability insurance (qv).

Durable medium A form that allows storage of information so that it is accessible for future reference, and allows information to be produced without changes. This includes paper, floppy disks, CD-ROMs, DVDs and hard drives where e-mails are stored. *See* DEMANDS AND NEEDS STATEMENTS.

Duration of policy Where an insurance is expressed to cover the period from one particular day to another, the insurance expires at midnight on the last day unless otherwise stated. However, a policy may not run its course for the following reasons: (a) payment of the full sum under the policy discharges it; (b) agreement between the parties; (c) termination by the insured in the case of permanent contracts (life and income protection), normally by non-payment of the premium; (d) withdrawal from contract during the cooling-off period (qv); (e) determination for breach of condition or warranty.

Duration of risk Marine insurance term to denote the period during which the insurer will be liable under the policy. This may mean the duration of a voyage or the completion of a period of time depending on the type of policy concerned, voyage or time. A voyage policy on a hull continues until the ship has moored at anchor in good safety for 24 hours at the port of destination named in the policy but the policy may extend this period. In the case of goods the risk terminates when they are safely landed but this is usually extended by a transit clause (qv). The contract may terminate early if the adventure is not commenced within a reasonable period of time (Marine Insurance Act 1906, s.42(1).

Dwellinghouse A permanent structure in which the owner or tenant (or his family or servants) habitually lives and sleeps at night. A caravan or anything similar does not come within the definition.

Dynamisation The index linking of earnings to calculate pension scheme benefits or for working out *final remuneration* (qv) for the purpose of *Inland Revenue limits* (qv). The term is also used to describe *escalation* (qv).

E

Each and every loss A phrase used when a restriction, e.g. an excess, will be applied for each separate claim.

'Each for his own part and not one for the other' Maxim describing the basis on which a Lloyd's member, name (qv) or corporate accepts a share of the risk. Names, a declining category, are sole traders with unlimited liability but like corporate members have no liability for the shares of co-syndicate members.

Early leaver Occupational pensions scheme member who leaves before normal retirement age without getting an immediate retirement benefit but may qualify for a *deferred pension* (qv). Alternatively his accrued benefits could be transferred to a new scheme or used to purchase a *buy out policy (also called a Section 32 policy). See* PRESERVED BENEFITS.

Early retirement Occurs when an individual retires before the normal retirement date of the occupational pension scheme. Scheme rules and the IR usually allow immediate pensions from age 50. When early retirement is voluntary, the accrued pension rights are scaled down. Members below age 50 are *early leavers* (qv) unless granted a pension through incapacity.

Early termination insurance A derivative of *guaranteed asset protection* (qv), it covers the monetary shortfall that may arise when a car purchase finance agreement is terminated due to death or a change in the debtor's employment status through resignation, unemployment or pregnancy, or due to the vehicle being written off or stolen.

Earmarked money purchase schemes A collection of *individual arrangements (qv)* under a single trust. Each member's fund is held under a separate *earmarked insurance policy* and no other investments are allowed in this scheme.

Earmarked policy *See* EARMARKED MONEY PURCHASE SCHEMES.

Earmarking A court order compelling a pension scheme to *earmark* some or all of a member's pension scheme benefits for payment to an ex-spouse. As earmarking leaves the couple financially linked until retirement it has been superseded by *pension sharing* (qv).

Earned-incurred basis A basis for calculating the insurer's loss ratio. The claims cost estimated for a period is compared with the premiums earned for the period and expressed as a percentage thereof.

Earned premium The proportion of premium related to the period of insurance that has already run.

Earnings cap Sets a limit on how much of a person's income can be used to calculate the contribution that can be paid to, and the benefits that can be paid by, tax approved pension schemes. Contribution limits are expressed as percentages of earnings (15 per cent for occupational scheme members) subject to the annually adjustable cap, £99,000 (2003/4). The cap affects *class A members only* (qv).

Earnings related pension *See* STATE SECOND PENSION.

Earnings threshold The total amount an individual and/or his employer may pay to the individual's personal pension scheme every year, regardless of whether they have any earnings or how much they are. For 2003/4 the figure was £4,615. The threshold includes tax relief at basic rate. Individuals wishing to pay more have to justify their case by their age and earnings level.

Earthquake/earthquake insurance Natural phenomenon in the form of a violent convulsion of the earth's surface. The risks of earthquake and subterranean fire (fire of volcanic origin) are excluded from the standard fire policy. High risk areas are designated as 'earthquake zones' (qv). Earthquake cover can be obtained for either fire damage or earthquake shock damage as an additional peril (qv). Subterranean fire can also be insured in this way. The risk is sometimes securitised as a *catastrophe bond* (qv).

Earthquake zone *See* EARTHQUAKE.

E-business risk Risks originating from the conduct of electronic business both within an organisation and externally using the Internet. There are both first party risks, e.g. loss of data, breakdown of equipment causing business interruption, and third party risks. *See* INTERNET LIABILITY INSURANCE.

Ecclesiastical property Churches, chapels and their equivalents, halls, Sunday school buildings, etc. As sums insured are not easy to assess, the fire policies covering these properties are made subject to the special condition of average (qv). The Ecclesiastical Dilapidations Measures 1923 oblige the Church Commissioners to insure property, including the parsonage house, belonging to the benefice.

Economic loss In tort (qv), the term refers to losses that are 'purely' economic, i.e. those where the claimant has suffered financial damage but no personal injury or damage to property. Such losses are not generally recoverable in tort except when resulting from *negligent statements* (qv) made when a duty of care attaches, usually to a professional person, who has *voluntarily assumed responsibility* (qv). Special damage, including pure financial loss (often extra expenses), resulting from a public nuisance is recoverable in tort. The courts prefer to deal with pure economic loss in the context of contracts rather than tort. For insurance implications see *financial loss* (qv).

Economy wording A co-insurance (qv) economy measure whereby the full specification of the property insured is set out in, or attached to, the policy of the leading insurer only. The policies of the co-insurers are worded to cover the relevant proportions of the property as set out in the leading company's policy or specification.

EEA firms European Economic Area firms 'passporting' into the UK under single market directives such as the Insurance Directive. EEA firms are EU Member States plus Norway, Iceland and Liechtenstein. The FSMA 2000 (EEA Passport Rights) Regulations 2001 deal with the exercise of passport rights created under Schedule 3 of FSMA. They set out the information that must be provided to the FSA by an EEA firm exercising its passport rights. Proper notification by the EEA firm secures automatic authorisation.

Effective date/inception The starting date of a policy.

Efficacy and liquidated damages insurance Engineering policy providing contingency cover for a contractor's liability to pay liquidated damages (qv) for any delay in completion or performance failure due to contractor or supplier error in regard to work under the construction agreement.

Efficacy risk The risk that a product may fail to perform its intended function. The failure may cause physical injury or damage or a purely financial loss, e.g. loss of production time. The product liability policy does not pay to replace the product or guarantee its efficacy but liability for injury, or damage consequent upon inefficacy, is insured. Pure financial loss due to inefficacy can be insured under a *financial loss extension* (qv) of a product liability policy or under *product guarantee policy* (qv). *See* EFFICACY AND LIQUIDATED DAMAGES INSURANCE.

'Egg-shell skull rule' Test of causation in negligence (qv) making the defendant liable for damage that is reasonably foreseeable even if unexpected. The defendant 'takes his victim as he finds him'. In *Smith* v. *Leech Brain & Co.* (1961) an employee suffered a burn on the lip when splashed by molten metal. Cancer ensued at the site of a burn because of a pre-cancerous condition. The defendants were liable under the rule as liability turned on foreseeability in regard to the type, not the extent, of the injury.

Ejusdem generis rule A rule of construction. If a specific phrase is followed by a general expression then the latter will be interpreted as meaning *'of the same kind'* as the specific words. If a policy refers to 'jewellery, plate, silver, gold *or any articles*', the last three words mean 'any articles of the same valuable kind as jewellery, plate, silver and gold' and do not mean 'any articles of any kind'.

El Niño A periodic warming of the tropical Pacific ocean which affects weather around the world. El Niño results in increased rainfall in southern US and drought in the western Pacific. However, outside the tropical Pacific the effects are unpredictable and this boosts the weather derivatives (qv) market. El Niño ('little boy' in Spanish) occurs around Christmas.

Elemental perils Perils of the elements, namely storm (qv), earthquake (qv), windstorm (qv) and flood (qv).

Electrical breakdown exclusion *See* MECHANICAL BREAKDOWN EXCLUSION.

Electrical clause A fire insurance policy clause excluding loss or damage to dynamos, motors or other electrical apparatus, caused by its own overrunning, self-heating, etc. These losses are incidental to the running of electrical apparatus but consequential fire damage to other property is covered.

Electrical plant and mechanical plant Machinery, plant, motors, accessories and connections thereto powered electrically or mechanically and insurable by engineering insurers against: sudden and unforeseen damage; breakdown; explosion and collapse; accidental damage; and damage to surrounding property. Third party risks are generally covered under public liability insurance. Insurance on plant is usually coupled with in-service inspections, many of which are required by statute.

Eligibility Conditions that govern a person's right of entry into a pension scheme or right to receive a particular benefit. The conditions may relate to age, service, status and type of employment but there must be no discrimination in eligibility on grounds of sex. The Barber judgment (qv) applies to all retirement benefits earned after 17 May 1990 and is endorsed by regulations under PA95 for equal treatment between the sexes.

Eligibility period/qualifying period Period of time during which potential members of a group life scheme (qv) may join without evidence of good health.

Eligible complainants Entities protected by FSA rules contained in Dispute resolution: Complaints Handling. They are: private individuals; a commercial customer with a group annual turnover below £1m; a charity with an annual income below £1m; and a trustee of a trust with a net asset value of less than £1m.

Embedded value Actuarially estimated economic value of the in-force life insurance contracts of an insurer but excluding any value attributable to future new business. Embedded value earnings are the difference between the opening year value and the year-end value (after adjustments for any capital movements such as dividends and capital injections). The change in value measures the performance of the company's life insurance operations.

Embezzlement The conversion to his own use by an employee of property received by him on behalf of his master (Larceny Act 1916, s.17 (1)). It now falls within the definition of theft (Theft Act 1968). It is a fidelity guarantee (qv) risk, not insurable under a theft insurance except in a limited way under *money insurance* (qv).

Emergency treatment Treatment by qualified medical practitioner to an injured party following a vehicular accident on a road or public place. The Road Traffic Act compels the vehicle user to pay a specified fee and mileage expenses to the practitioner who first attends, a liability that must be insured under the motor insurance. Any payment made by this provision will not affect the insured's entitlement to no claim discount.

EMFs – Electromagnetic Fields Non-ionising radiation created by a flow of electricity. Manufactured EMFs, which have higher frequencies than those occurring from the earth's magnetic field, can affect the body tissue. Direct evidence is lacking, but health risks linked with EMFs are: impairment of the immune system, reducing the ability of the white blood cells to kill tumour cells and fight disease; adverse effects on the central nervous system, brain and glands that are connected with cancers and other physical and emotional problems; influence on body's control of cell growth; adverse effects on the skin. Magnetic fields are best dealt with by designing them out or shielding them at source. Employer's risk assessments under MHSW (qv) should include EMFs.

Employee Anyone under a *contract of service* as opposed to a *contract for services*. The difficulty in making the distinction has led to the development of legal tests. To avoid legal disputes the insurer defines '*employee*' broadly in employers' and public liability policies (the latter for the purpose of an exclusion). The definition extends to: labour gangs, sub-contractors, self-employed persons, persons hired or borrowed by the insured, volunteers, etc. The Employers' Liability (Compulsory Insurance) Act definition is: 'An individual who has entered into or works under a contract of service or apprenticeship with any employer, whether by way of manual labour, clerical work, or otherwise, whether such contract is expressed or implied, or oral or in writing.' *See* EXEMPT EMPLOYEES; EMPLOYEE/EMPLOYER RELATIONSHIP.

Employee benefits Benefits that are part of an employment package wholly or partly funded by the employer. They may include pensions, life cover, critical illness cover (qv) and income protection (qv).

Employee declaration Medical questionnaire completed by a member of a group life pension scheme when the benefits sought are in excess of the free cover limit (qv).

Employee/employer relationship An employee works under a contract of service; an independent contractor works under a contract for services. However, the courts consider the actual relationship rather than rely upon what the parties call their arrangement. The relationship affects an individual's employment rights, his entitlement to health and safety provision and also affects the employer's vicarious liability for the individual's torts. The courts use a variety of tests to determine the relationship: the control test (qv); mutuality of obligation (qv); integration test (qv); and the financial risk test (employees do not take this risk). Regard is also paid to the contractual arrangements, methods of payment, etc. Insurers write their own definition of employee (qv) into liability policies.

Employee/passengers Employers' liability policies exclude indemnity in respect of any liability covered by compulsory Road Traffic Act insurance. Consequently an employer faced by a claim from an employee injured as a passenger, in circumstances in which compulsory motor insurance applies, will claim under his motor policy.

Employee trustees Employees appointed as trustees of their employer's occupational pension scheme. Dismissal or redundancy is treated as unfair if prompted by the performance of their trustee duties. They do not have to be member-nominated employees to benefit from the protection under the Employment Rights Act 1996.

Employers' Liability (Compulsory Insurance) Act 1969/Employers' Liability (Compulsory Insurance) Regulations (1998) Employers must maintain *approved policies* (qv) with *authorised insurers* (qv). This is to cover liability for bodily injury or disease their employees may suffer in the course of their employment. Insurers must issue a Certificate of Insurance to employers who take out or renew policies. Employers must display the certificate, or a copy, at each place of business for the information of the employees, retain them for 40 years and present them for inspection by HSE. The insurance must be for at least £5 million for any one occurrence.

Employers' Liability (Defective Equipment) Act 1969 An employee, injured in the course of employment by a machine defect, no longer has to prove that his employer was negligent. The employer is strictly liable even though a third party such as a manufacturer, whether or not identified, is at fault. The employer's right of recovery, if any, against a manufacturer is subrogated to the employers' liability insurer.

Employers' liability insurance Covers the insured's legal liability for bodily injury or disease to employees (qv) if caused during the period of insurance. The policy also covers the insured's own costs and pays for solicitors' representation at inquests and courts of summary jurisdiction. Cover does not apply to injury or disease caused outside the UK except for UK-based employees. Policy extensions relate to principal's clause (qv), unsatisfied court judgements (qv) and, less frequently, retrospective cover (qv). The normal limit of indemnity is £10 million for any one occurrence. *See* EMPLOYERS' LIABILITY (COMPULSORY INSURANCE) ACT 1969.

Employers' Liability Insurance Certificate *See* EMPLOYERS' LIABILITY (COMPULSORY INSURANCE) ACT 1969.

Employer's undertaking Undertaking, in a prescribed form, whereby an employer informs an actuary whether any of the specified events, which are likely to invalidate any certificate required for contracting out, have occurred.

Empty buildings clause A clause added to a fire policy covering an unoccupied building. The insured must notify the insurer when the building becomes occupied and advise on how the building will be occupied. The insured is required to pay any extra premium that may be demanded.

'Enabling bond' A bond required by insolvency practioners under the Insolvency Practitioners Regulations (minimum £250,000) in respect of the assets to come under their control in respect of each appointment taken and which has to be detailed on monthly bordereaux submitted to the holder's bond insurer and relevant professional body.

Endorsement A clause or memorandum added to a policy embodying some alteration to the terms of the policy.

Endowment insurance A life insurance policy under which the sum insured (qv) is payable on the sooner of death or expiry of a given term of years. The policy combines savings with life protection and can be used to repay mortgages and other loans. The policy generally acquires a surrender value (qv) and loan value after a period of time. The policy can be with 'with' or 'without profits' (qv). *See* HOUSE PURCHASE SCHEMES.

Endowment mortgage *See* HOUSE PURCHASE SCHEMES.

Energy Degree Days (EDD) The aggregate of heating degree days (HDDs) and cooling degree days (CDDs). Companies at risk of extremes of high and low temperatures may use a weather derivative that pays outs on HDDs and CDDs.

Engine plant *See* ENGINEERING INSURANCE.

Engineering insurance Insurance of plant under one of four main headings: boilers and pressure plant (qv); engine plant (qv); electrical and mechanical plant (qv); and lifting machinery (qv). In addition inspection services (qv) are provided. The insurances cover self-damage (qv), damage to surrounding property, third party risks and engineering interruption insurance (qv). Also, cover is provided in connection with deterioration of stock (qv), computer risks (qv), contractors' plant (qv) and machinery erection (qv) and other miscellaneous insurances. The principal risks against which insurance is sought are explosion and collapse (qv), breakdown (qv), sudden and unforeseen physical damage (qv), fragmentation (qv) and extraneous causes (qv).

Engineering interruption loss A business interruption insurance (qv) providing an indemnity at a fixed rate per day in respect of interruptions following breakdown or unforeseen damage to installed plant and machinery or failure of the power or water supply. There are time excesses/*deductibles* (qv) or franchises (qv) applied to the indemnity period to avoid small losses, particularly temporary losses of services.

Engineering surveys Detailed surveys necessary for the underwriting of high-risk situations, e.g. pollution or environmental impairment liability cover in high-risk industries. The cost is borne by the insured directly or indirectly through higher premiums.

Enhanced annuity *See* IMPAIRED LIFE ANNUITY.

Enhanced capital requirement (ECR) Risk-based capital regime being introduced by the FSA (qv) for life and non-life insurers. Calculations are based on industry-wide assumptions *and* individual capital guidance (ICG) given to firms based on the FSA's view of how much capital would be adequate for individual firms to hold taking into account the firm's risk profile and its own assessment of their own capital needs. ICG will normally be at or above ECR and although for guidance only, the firm's not meeting the ICG figure will be expected to set out a plan to restore adequate capital. The mechanism, Individual Capital Adequacy Standards (ICAS), means that firms will hold capital more appropriate for their business and control risks and have the incentive to improve their risk management.

Enhanced ordinary charges The extra charges for the handling of insured cargo because of its damaged condition.

Enterprise risk management 'The process by which organisations assess, control, exploit, finance and monitor risks from all sources for the purpose of increasing the organisations short and long term value to shareholder' (Casualty Association). It combines a whole range of financial risks with insurance risks and seeks to optimise the manner of its risk taking.

Entrepreneurial risks General commercial and business risk that is usually accepted as a part of the firm's normal operations in the market place. Profit is the reward for entrepreneurial risks.

'Entry' Theft insurances cover loss by

'entry' when it is by *forcible and violent means* (qv). Actual entry means the insertion of any part of the body, even if it is only a finger, into the premises, but the qualifying words preclude claims when people enter without having to break down the defences of the premises.

Environment Act 1995 Main provisions: creation of the Environment Agency (England and Wales) and the Scottish Environment Protection Agency; the contaminated land regime (qv); protection of the aquatic environment; air quality management; and producer responsibility with the aim of recycling packaging waste significantly.

Environmental impact assessment (EIA) A formal assessment of the total environmental effect of a project, process, product or development. It is a legal requirement for some specific projects.

Environmental impairment liability (EIL) Claims-made policy (qv) covering legal liability to third parties for bodily injury or property damage arising out of gradual pollution. It also covers mandatory clean-up costs for both sudden and gradual pollution of the insured's own and third party sites. Cover is site-specific based on risk assessments. Multiple premises cover extends to product liability and work away risks. Some insurers reimburse voluntary costs incurred by the insured in taking emergency preventive action. Fixed premium policies can be written for up to five years. *See* CONTAMINATED LAND.

Environmental Liability Directive (ELD) Aims to establish a framework whereby environmental damage will be prevented and restoration carried out. Environmental damage is widely defined and includes water pollution, land contamination that poses a threat to human health and biodiversity damage in areas protected by European and national legislation. The person causing the damage is liable for the restoration. Insurance is not compulsory, although the proposal requires member states to encourage operators to use insurance or other forms of financial security. The proposed directive covers activities such as releasing heavy metals into water or the air, installations producing dangerous chemicals, landfill sites and incineration plants.

Environmental Management Systems (EMS) Risk management approach to eliminate/control environmental risks. The systems should cover: organisational structure, responsibilities, practices, processes and resources for implementing and maintaining environmental management. Insurers underwriting environmental impairment liability cover look more favourably on companies with EMS.

Environmental Protection Act 1990 Uses integrated pollution control to prevent pollution from emissions to air, land or water from scheduled processes. Authorisation to operate relevant processes must be obtained from the enforcing authority which for the more heavily polluting industries is HM Inspectorate of Pollution. Control of pollution to air from less heavily polluting processes is through the local authority. The regulations also place a duty of care on all those involved in the management of waste.

Equal access *See* EQUAL TREATMENT RULE.

Equal treatment rule/equal access Equal treatment legislation (PA 95, s.62) came into force on 1 January 1996 following the *Barber* judgment (qv). The main effect is that every occupational pension scheme will be treated as containing an equal treatment rule which will override any contrary provisions in the actual trust deed and rules of a scheme.

Equalisation reserve (or fund) The amount set aside to prevent exceptional fluctuations in the amounts charged to revenue in subsequent years in respect of claims of an exceptional or irregular nature (e.g. catastrophes). Amounts are added to the reserves in profitable years and released when losses are made.

Equitable assignment Assignment that does not give the assignee the right to sue in his own name. No particular form is necessary, not even writing, e.g. insured hands his life policy over to the bank as security for a loan. The assignee should notify the insurer as there may be successive assignees. Insurers in doubt as to the entitlement to the policy proceeds can pay the money into court under the Life Assurance Companies (Payment into Court) Act 1896.

Equitable interest A legal term referring to interests in property originally created and enforced by the Court of Chancery. Such an interest can arise in a number of ways such as where money has been advanced on property but no formal mortgage deed drawn up. The lender has an equitable interest and this creates an insurable interest. Similarly, a person on whose behalf property is held in trust has an insurable interest in that property.

Equity-linked life policies Life insurance policies combining life insurance with investment in equities, i.e. ordinary shares. Life insurance is linked to equity investment either through an established unit trust (qv) or unitised fund (qv) administered by the life office itself. Usually a large part of the premium is invested in the unit trust or equity portfolio, the balance provides life cover, usually *term insurance* (qv).

Erection all risks insurance A satellite market insurance covering the assembly and testing of launchers, satellites and their component parts. The testing comprises functional tests or simulated launchings, i.e. static firing of engines. The manufacturer may also be able to insure the loss of the incentive payment normally payable as a reward for the satisfactory operation of the satellite.

Errors and omissions An alternative term for professional indemnity but often used to refer to the 'newer professions', e.g. advertising agents, the media, etc. The term also describes the insurance effected by Lloyd's underwriting agents as required by Lloyd's.

Errors and omissions clause Ensures that the reinsurer is not relieved of liability if the reinsured has inadvertently made an error or omission in supplying risk information to the reinsurer. Errors and omissions must be corrected as soon as possible. Some E & O clauses apply to errors and omissions by either party. The aim is to place the parties in the position that would have existed in the absence of the error or omission.

Escalation Annual increase in the level of annuity, policy benefits or limits based on a fixed percentage or in line with an index, e.g Retail Price Index, subject to an upper limit, e.g. 5 per cent. *Dynamised pensions* have automatic increases in the pension payments or contributions. Builders' risk marine risk policy *escalate* to cover a possible increase in the insured value of the vessel under construction.

Escape clause A clause inserted into sliding scale treaties (qv) to permit the reinsurer to give notice of termination should a maximum rate become payable in any year and the cedant has the same facility if the minimum rate becomes payable in any year.

Establishment business Overseas insurance business obtained by an insurer as a result of establishing a local agent, branch office and subsidiary or associated company in foreign territories. This contrasts with *services business* (qv), i.e. non-admitted insurers who are not represented by a branch, etc., but who sell across national frontiers.

Estimated future liability In the Lloyd's annual solvency test on an open year of account, an estimate has to be made of the provision required by a syndicate to cover claims and other adjustments likely to arise from risks accepted during that year. The basis for calculation is laid down in the instructions for the guidance for auditors.

Estimated maximum loss (EML) Estimate of the maximum probable loss developing from an insured peril. It takes account of factors that will lessen the risk, e.g. fire protection, and factors that will increase the risk, e.g. combustible materials. It ignores coincidences such as all protective devices failing simultaneously with serious human error and other untoward circumstances. Insurers use EML (also called *probable maximum loss)* when fixing their retention on individual risks.

Estoppel The rule of evidence or doctrine of law that precludes a person from denying the truth of some statement formerly made by him, or the existence of facts, which he has by words or conduct led others to believe. Where an insurer continues to deal with a claim despite knowing of a breach giving him the right of avoidance, he may be estopped from denying liability (*Evans* v. *Employers Mutual* (1936)).

EU/EEA risk A risk is deemed to be located in an EU or EEA state if it is: (a) a building (and contents if insured under the same policy) situated in the Member State; (b) a motor vehicle, ship, yacht or aircraft registered in the Member State; (c) a travel policy not exceeding four months taken out in a Member State. For any other insured risk (including a life) it is an individual: (a) if the policyholder is habitually resident in the member state; (b) a business or organisation – if the establishment to which the contract relates is situated in a Member State.

EU Regulation 2027/97 Retains Warsaw Convention (qv) and Hague Protocol (qv) systems but abolishes financial limits for passenger death/injury and obliges air carriers to make advance payments to alleviate economic need. It follows the IATA Agreements (qv) and seeks to harmonise the obligations of community air carriers regarding liability for accidents to passengers given that the Warsaw Convention applies only to international flights. All defences are waived for the first 100,000 SDRs of each claim but the defence under Article 21 (proof that all necessary measures to avoid the damage had been taken) of the Warsaw Convention and Hague Protocol of contributory negligence by the passenger is retained. The Regulation lays down minimum insurance requirements.

European Accident Statement Standard form available throughout Europe in various languages. Its purpose is to get an agreed statement of facts when people are involved in road accidents to assist with the processing of any subsequent insurance claims.

European Communities (Rights Against Insurers) Regulations 2002 (ECRAIR) Any person who is a resident of an EU Member State, or Norway, Iceland or Liechtenstein, who is involved in a UK road traffic accident involving a UK registered motor vehicle or trailer may now sue the vehicle's insurer. The Insurer 'shall be directly liable to the entitled party to the extent that he is liable to the insured person'. This adds to any right he may have against the driver. ECRAIR gives effect to the 4th Motor Insurance Directive to harmonise the laws relating to civil liability in the use of motor vehicles. ECRAIR goes further than the Directive by giving the right of direct action to all UK residents involved in domestic road accidents.

European Economic Area An expanded *single insurance market* (qv) by combining the EC with the European Free Trade Area (qv) subject only to the exclusion of Switzerland. EFTA take part on the basis of all three generations of Insurance Directives (qv). Switzerland takes part only in connection with the first two generations. This gives Switzerland access to the EC's non-life market with EC insurers gaining reciprocal access to the Swiss non-life market.

European Free Trade Area Formed in 1960 and consisting of Iceland, Norway, Switzerland and (from 1991) Liechtenstein. There are no import duties between members. Former members, Britain, Denmark, Portugal, Finland, and Sweden, left to join the EC. The EC and EFTA set up a combined free trade area in 1972. A further pact created the European Economic Area (qv) in 1994.

Exceptional circumstances clause *See* SPECIAL CIRCUMSTANCES CLAUSE.

Exceptions *See* EXCLUSIONS.

Excess The amount deducted from each and every claim and borne by the insured. The excess will eliminate all claims equal to or less than the excess, and will reduce the insurer's liability for all other claims. The excess may be compulsory or voluntary in which instance the insured's premium is discounted. The excess is not to be confused with the *excess point* (qv) under layered policies. *Deductible* (qv) is an alternative term for excess, which should be compared with *franchise* (qv) sometimes called a *disappearing deductible.*

Excess aggregate reinsurance *See* AGGREGATE EXCESS OF REINSURANCE.

Excess benefits/contributions Benefits/contributions that are not subject to the rules applicable to protected rights (qv) benefits and contributions. They are provided by contributions to contracted out money purchase pension scheme (qv) or appropriate personal pension plan (qv) that are in excess of the level needed to secure protected rights benefits.

Excess floating policy A collective fidelity guarantee insurance (qv) to provide additional cover on a floating basis to supplement the specified sums insured in respect of the individual employees.

Excess insurance An insurance adding an excess layer (qv) to a primary insurance or other excess layers. It does not contribute to a loss until the limit of the primary or underlying insurances has been reached. Excess layers are used in liability insurance where the limits of indemnity of the underlying insurances do not meet the requirements of the insured.

Excess liabilities Insurance to cover the excess amount of liability for general average contributions (qv), salvage charges, sue and labour charges and three-fourths collision liability where the full amount is not covered by a hull policy. It overcomes the problem of under-insurance and the rateable reduction in an insurer's liability consequent upon a rise in value of the hull owing to a rise in tonnage values upon general average is assessed.

Excess liability insurance An insurance arranged by tour operators in connection with US and Canada fly-drive holidays. The car company effects third party cover for limits in excess of the statutory minimum for the benefit of the car users. Nonetheless the high level of damages awarded to the victims of road accidents in North America may exceed the cover provided. The purpose of excess liability insurance is to cover the liability that is uninsured under the car company's insurance arrangements.

Excess of average loss reinsurance A form of excess of loss ratio reinsurance (qv). The excess point is recalculated each year as a moving average of the loss ratio experienced over an agreed number of preceding years. The ceding office agrees to bear an agreed share of any loss in excess of that average.

Excess of line reinsurance The marine insurance equivalent of surplus reinsurance (qv). As a rule the retention is based on a table of limits graded according to the class of the carrying vessel. Retentions are based on total sums insured and not estimated maximum loss (EMLs) (qv) as in fire insurance.

Excess of loss cover Aircraft fleets can be insured on the basis that the deductible (qv) is so large that the owner is virtually his own insurer except for very large losses. The schemes can take a variety of forms, e.g. (a) the insurer paying if the claims arising from any one accident exceed a figure that is an appreciable percentage of the value of the aircraft; (b) similarly, but the excess is a percentage of the total value of the fleet; (c) the insurer paying only losses which, taken over the whole fleet during the course of the year, exceed a certain percentage of the value of the fleet.

Excess of loss ratio reinsurance/stop loss reinsurance An adaptation of an *excess of loss reinsurance* treaty (qv). The loss ratio of the cedant is 'stopped' at an agreed percentage of the premium income with the balance wholly or partly falling to the reinsurer, e.g. 90 per cent of losses in excess of 80 per cent up to 120 per cent or a given monetary amount if occurring sooner. Aggregate excess of loss reinsurance works in the same way but its entry/exit points are monetary amounts not ratios.

Excess of loss reinsurance A non-proportional reinsurance covering claims only to the extent that they exceed a certain amount or ration, e.g. a liability insurer may reinsure all losses (or a proportion thereof) in excess of £1m, the excess point, up to £2m. Excess of loss has many applications; catastrophe reinsurance (qv), per occurrence reinsurance (qv), per risk reinsurance, aggregate excess of loss (qv), excess of loss ratio (qv). Cover is normally by means of treaty.

Excess per occurrence reinsurance An excess of loss reinsurance (qv) where the reinsured's retention and the reinsurer's limit of liability apply to losses arising from a single occurrence regardless of the number of risks or policies involved. This approach may be applied to both liability and property insurances.

Excess per risk reinsurance An excess of loss reinsurance (qv) which, subject to a specified limit, indemnifies the reinsured against the amount of loss in excess of a specified retention for *each risk* involved in each loss occurrence regardless of the number of risks. The amount of risk retained by the cedant may be different for each risk transferred. A risk may be defined as a building and its contents. This form of treaty often substitutes for proportional reinsurance or supplements it, thereby protecting the cedant against the effect of underestimating *estimated maximum loss* (qv).

Excess point/attachment point In excess of loss reinsurance (qv), the insurer fixes a point up to which he will retain losses for his own account (his retention). This is the excess point as losses above this level will be payable wholly or partly by the reinsurer up to a limit, the second excess point.

Exchange of letters *See* INDIVIDUAL ARRANGEMENTS.

Exchange-traded contracts Standardised instruments that are bought and sold on a recognised exchange such as the London International Financial Futures and Options Exchange (LIFFE) (qv) which launched LIFFE weather futures products (qv), a standardised weather derivative contract, in 2001. These over-the-counter contracts are available to weather-sensitive companies wishing to hedge against the weather risk (qv).

Excluded form of loss Exclusion of a particular form or type of loss rather than a risk, e.g. fire damage to property undergoing a heating process is excluded. The risk of further damage is not excluded as the insurer will be liable for damage caused by the fire as it spreads. A public liability policy excludes liability for damage to property the insured is working on but does not exclude losses that flow from the initial damage.

Exclusion/exception A policy provision that eliminates cover in regard to specified property, persons, perils, forms of damage or particular circumstances. The excluded risks may be uninsurable, require special consideration or readily be 'bought back' if required. The exclusions may be general, i.e. across all sections of the policy, or section-specific. The insurer must prove that an exception applies unless the exclusion comes in the form of qualifying words (qv) in the operative clause (qv). *See* QUALIFIED PERILS.

Execution only The client is someone with sufficient experience and understanding of relevant investments that he places no reliance on the judgment or advice of the firm concerned. He approaches the firm or intermediary with his mind made up and asks for the transaction to be carried out on his behalf. Execution only clients forgo the cancellation rights under the Conduct of Business Rules (COB 6.7).

Executive pension plan (EPP) A money purchase discretionary occupational pension scheme principally used for directors and senior executives. An EPP can supplement any occupational scheme, but the IR maximum retirement benefit of two-thirds of pensionable earnings still applies.

Exemplary damages/punitive damages *See* DAMAGES.

Exempt approved scheme Occupational pension scheme granted exempt approval by the Inland Revenue to allow benefits up to the maximum levels as set out in the Inland Revenue practice notes (IR12). The privileges arise from ICTA 1988, s.592, and give greater flexibility than schemes approved under s.590. To qualify as exempt approved schemes they must: be established under an irrevocable trust; have a UK resident administrator; involve contributions from the employer to the scheme; and comply with the Practice Notes (IR12). Compare with Approved Scheme.

Exempt employees People who are not employees for the purpose of the Employers' Liability (Compulsory Insurance) Act 1969. They are: independent contractors; 'domestic' employees; people whose employer is related to them (husband, wife, father, mother, grandfather, grandmother, stepfather, son, daughter, grandson, etc); people who are not ordinarily resident in Great Britain and who are working in Great Britain for fewer than 14 days. In the case of offshore installations, people not ordinarily resident in the UK who work on an installation for more than 7 days are not exempt employees.

Exempt employers Certain employers are exempt from the compulsory insurance requirements of the Employers' Liability (Compulsory Insurance) Act 1969. Section 3 of the Act exempts: (a) any local authority (other than a parish council); (b) any joint board or committee whose members include representatives of any such local authority; (c) any police authority; (d) any nationalised industry and its subsidiaries; (e) certain bodies financed out of public funds; (f) employers of crews covered by insurance with a mutual insurance association of shipowners.

Exempt person Person exempt from the general prohibition in respect of a regulated activity as a result of the FSMA (Exemptions) Order 2000. *See* EXEMPT REGULATED ACTIVITIES.

Exempt regulated activities Regulated activities (qv) under FSMA that may be carried on by members of a profession that is supervised and regulated by a *designated professional body* (qv) without breaching the general prohibition.

Exempt transfers Transfers of money or money's worth that is free of liability to inheritance tax. *See* PREMIUM EXEMPTIONS; BACK-TO-BACK ARRANGEMENTS.

Ex-gratia payment A claims payment made by the insurer 'as of favour' even though there is no legal obligation to pay. Such payments are made to preserve goodwill or where the right to refuse payment is founded only on a technicality.

Exhibition insurance Insurance in respect of loss or damage to exhibits, stands and furnishings while at the exhibition and in transit to and from the exhibition. Public liability (qv) cover is added. A further option is cover in respect of exhibition expenses wholly or partly lost following damage to property on the exhibition premises or due to abandonment or interruption due to damage by fire, lightning, aircraft or explosion at the exhibition premises.

Exotic birds insurance Protects owner (who must be at least 18 years old at inception) against veterinary fees, subject to an excess, up to £5,000; accidental death from external injury; fire, lightning, storm, wind, vermin and theft. Cover includes attending and travelling to shows and exhibitions. Special provisions regarding security, heating and siting apply to external aviaries.

Exotic mammals insurance Rare animals can be covered in respect of 'vet's' fees normally up to £2,000 and subject to a £50 excess for each course of treatment. This is the core standalone cover to which additions can be made (death by accident, disease or sickness; theft, fire, storm and lightning), all subject to a 10 per cent excess, and liability cover. Escape is not covered unless facilitated by an insured peril. Insured must be at least 18 years old.

Expense ratio The fraction arrived at by dividing the amount of premiums into the amount of expenditure.

Expenses loading The amount added to a premium calculation to allow for the insurer's expenses. Other premium computation items are: contingency loading (qv), risk premium (qv) and profit loading (qv).

Expenses risk A particular risk for life companies whose relatively high fixed costs need to be recovered by the *expenses loading* (qv). The recovery therefore depends on the volume of sales. In non-life business the main expenses risk factor is the significant cost of legal expenses that arise in court settlements such as employers' liability and motor insurance injury claims.

Experience rating A method that uses past experience to establish current rates for a particular insured by adjusting normal rates up or down. In non-proportional treaties the reinsurer fixes a rate based on premiums and loss portfolios rather than exposure inherent in the business. *See* also RETROSPECTIVE RATING.

Experience refund Term used by life reinsurers to describe the profit commission that they pay to the ceding office as a refund based on the profitability of the business.

Explosion (engineering insurance) In engineering insurance explosion means the sudden and violent rendering of the plant by force of internal steam or other fluid pressure (other than pressure of ignited flue gases) causing bodily displacement of any part of the plant, together with forcible ejectment of the contents. The risk is insured by using the term explosion or collapse (qv) as a way of specifying the insured perils. They are the prinicipal risks covered in respect of boilers and steam pressure vessels under the control of the insured.

Explosion (fire and additional perils insurance) The standard fire policy covers concussion damage following the explosion: (a) of boilers used for domestic purposes. (b) in a building not forming part of a gas works of gas used for domestic purposes or for lighting. No other concussion damage is covered under the standard fire policy but fire consequent upon explosion is covered. Other explosion damage can be added as an additional peril (qv).

Explosive nuclear assemblies clause A clause in material damage and public liability policies excluding liability directly or indirectly caused by or contributed to by or arising from the radioactive toxic explosive or other hazardous properties of any explosive nuclear assembly or nuclear component thereof. *See* NUCLEAR PERILS.

Export Credit Guarantee Department (ECGD) The UK's official export credit agency under the Export Credit and Investment Guarantee Act 1991. Exporters selling UK goods and services on credit terms of less than two years now insure with private credit insurers for whom ECGD provides a number of reinsurance facilities. Direct cover from ECGD includes: *export insurance policy* (qv); *overseas investment insurance* (qv) (visit *www.ecgd.gov.uk*).

Export Insurance Policy EXIP issued by the Export Credit Guarantee Department (qv). Insures exporters against the principal political and commercial risks of not being paid in connection with *individual* capital goods, major services and construction projects. Contracts involving the sale of consumer goods or commodities on short payments are insured in the private sector. EXIP covers up to 95 per cent of the value of any loss suffered.

Exposure A term used in two senses. 1. The state of being subject to the possibility of loss. 2. The extent of risk as measured by turnover, payroll, etc.

Exposure in residence Harm of a progressive nature from a latent substance within the body even after active exposure has ceased. In asbestosis (qv) and similar contexts, it is the period during which the body incurs injury or disease as tissue reacts to the hazardous substance. *See* LONG-TAIL BUSINESS; MESOTHELIOMA.

Exposure theory A theory that equates the time of 'occurrence' of a 'long-tail' injury, such as asbestosis (qv), with the time of *exposure* to the cause of the injury for the purpose of a losses-occurring policy (qv), the *cause* meaning harmful working conditions and/or exposure to harmful substances. All insurers on risk during this exposure period are deemed to be liable for the resultant liability in proportion to their time on risk. Alternative *occurrence theories* (qv) include the *manifestation theory;* the *injury-in-fact theory* (qv); and *the triple trigger theory* (qv).

Exposure to loss premium rating Method of rating working cover excess of loss reinsurance treaties (qv) for property risks. The cedant's portfolio is analysed according to sums insured in relation to the treaty deductible. Policies with sums insured below the deductible expose the reinsurer to no risk. A mathematical formula produces a rate of premium commensurate with the degree of exposure.

Express conditions Conditions expressly stated in the policy. They may be general conditions or particular conditions, i.e. 'special conditions'. The general conditions are printed on the policy and are common to all contracts on that form. They may reinforce implied conditions (e.g. non-disclosure), deal with alterations, claims procedures, etc. Particular conditions apply to matters affecting the individual policy and are applied by endorsement (qv). In life insurance the general conditions include privileges (qv) such as loans (qv) and surrender values (qv).

Express warranty A warranty (qv) incorporated in the policy requiring the insured to do or not to do something or stating that a certain state of affairs will or not be maintained. The Marine Insurance Act 1906, s.35(1), provides that an express warranty 'may be in any form of words from which the intention to warrant is to be inferred'. Section 35(2) adds 'an express warranty must be included in, or written upon, the policy, or must be contained in some document incorporated by reference into the policy'. Section 35(3) 'An express warranty does not exclude an implied warranty, unless it be inconsistent therewith.'

Expropriation cover An insurance against the risk of losing property or rights in property when the property is seized by the government of the country in which the property is located.

Extended reporting period Period under a claims-made policy (qv) that provides a specific time, e.g. 60 days, after the policy has expired during which claims can be notified in respect of matters that occurred during the policy period. In some instances it is possible for the insured to purchase a longer period than that automatically included in the policy. The extended period does not respond in respect of claims otherwise insured. *See* DEEMING CLAUSE.

Extended terms insurance A credit insurance where the credit term exceeds 180 days.

Extended warranties (EWs) Contracts which extend the manufacturer's one year guarantee on domestic electrical goods (DEGs) and motor vehicles for between three and five years, but not general household insurance or service arrangements for central heating or alarm systems. The warranties may also cover additional risks during their term and the term of the original guarantee. Motor EWs are FSA regulated while retail sales of DEG EWs are usually exempt. All insurance-backed EWs are FSA regulated. *See* INSURED WARRANTY.

Extension clause A clause in a policy that introduces additional cover.

External company An insurance company whose head office is situated in a country outside the European Community.

External dependencies Risks attaching to a business as a result of dependencies on supplies from, or sales to, outside enitities. Loss of trade may be due to occurrences, e.g. fires, at the premises of customers and/or suppliers. Risk management involves a scrutiny of external dependencies and internal dependencies (qv). Business interruption policies (qv) can extend to cover loss of trade due to damage occurring at the premises of customers and/or suppliers, utility suppliers, loss of attraction (qv), etc.

External insurer Insurer whose head office is located outside the UK and other than an EEA insurer, a Swiss general insurer or an insurer subject to special rules.

'External means' Bodily injury, for personal accident policy purposes, must, inter alia, be caused by 'external and visible' means. This is to make it clear that the bodily injury must be due to some outside event clearly visible as distinct from internal physical defects – the words are used as the antithesis of 'internal means'. Exceptions to this strict meaning arise in connection with the inhalation of gas or the accidental taking of poison.

External member A Lloyd's underwriter who does not fall within the definition of a working member (qv).

External transfer Occurs where a pension sharing order has been made and the former spouse is not able to make an *internal transfer* (qv) to the members scheme because dual membership is not permitted. Consequently an external transfer must be applied to the pension credit.

Extinguishment damage Damage caused by water and other extinguishing agents used to extinguish and contain fires. Such damage is the natural and probable consequence of the fire and so is a part of the fire damage.

Extra charges Marine insurance term referring to the expenses incurred by the insured in proving a loss, e.g. survey fees, auction or sale charges. The insurer pays them only if the claim is admitted. However, where a survey is carried out on the instructions of the insurer, e.g. by the Salvage Association, this will always be paid by the insurer.

Extraordinary heavy weather A peril of the sea (qv). Heavy weather may be normal in certain waters and should therefore be anticipated and guarded against. They are a certainty rather than a risk. For example, storms are a daily occurrence in the Strait of Magellan around the tip of South America. When they are of exceptional severity that could not have been anticipated they become a peril of the sea and therefore insurable.

Ex-turpi causa non oritur actio 'An action does not arise from a base cause'. The rule prevents a criminal from recovering under a liability policy for injury or damage that otherwise would be within the policy. However, in *Hardy* v. *Motor Insurers Bureau* (1964), the claimant, through a right conferred by the Road Traffic Act, had a direct right of action against the insurer. Recoveries can also be made for mere acts of negligence even though criminal.

EXW (ex-works) This indicates that the price of the goods in a contract of sale is their cost at the factory gate. The purchaser assumes responsibility for the goods from that point and pays all movement costs including insurance. The contract specifies if packing is included.

F

Fac agreement Reinsurer agrees to automatically accept individual risks for a specified period (e.g. 30 days) during which time it decides whether to accept the risk on a facultative reinsurance (qv).

Fact-finding Under the FSA 'know your customer' rule (Conduct of Business Rule 5.2.5) a firm making a recommendation on a designated investment (qv) (and certain pension transactions) to a private customer must take reasonable steps to acquire sufficient personal and financial information before making the recommendation. There is no prescribed method of eliciting information but firms should have a suitable 'fact-finding' process. The document recording the information is a 'fact-find'. There are special rules for Friendly Society policies not exceeding £50 per annum or £1 per week.

Factories Act 1961 An Act, largely superseded by the Health and Safety at Work, etc., Act 1974, that extended certain common law duties of employers towards factory (qv) employees. Generally, the duties require employers to take reasonable care that the precautionary measures are not only adopted but are strictly observed. Liability is on the occupier of the *factory* (qv), unless exceptionally it attaches to the owner. Most health and safety obligations are now covered under the Health and Safety At Work, etc., Act 1974 and the Management of Health and Safety at Work Regulations 1999.

Factory Widely defined in the Factories Act 1961 (qv), s.175, the definition includes any premises, open air included, where people are employed in manual labour in activities such as manufacturing, repairing, cleaning, demolition and the slaughter of animals.

Factory mutuals US group of direct underwriting mutuals specialising in highly protected risks of large concerns on a recriprocal reinsurance basis. The objective is to provide insurance and safety engineering services for large manufacturers, substantial housing projects and public institutions.

Facultative obligatory treaty 'Fac-oblig' allows the cedant (qv) to select the risks he offers to the reinsurer who must then accept all cessions (qv) within the treaty. It is normally arranged after a surplus treaty (qv) and provides automatic facultative cover for the cedant when the surplus treaty capacity is full. It differs from a second surplus treaty only in that the cedant has a choice.

Facultative reinsurance Reinsurance (qv) on an individual risk basis; the cedant (qv) offers the reinsurance to a reinsurer who may accept or decline as he is not bound by a treaty. *See* FACULTATIVE OBLIGATORY TREATY.

Faculty of Actuaries Professional body representing actuaries in Scotland. *See* INSTITUTE OF ACTUARIES.

Fair analysis The Insurance Mediation Directive (qv) requires firms to base their advice on a *fair analysis*, meaning that they must analyse a sufficiently large number of contracts before making a recommendation. See ADVISED SALES.

Family income benefit A decreasing term insurance (qv) that, on death within the policy term, pays a regular tax-free income for the remainder of the term. There is no survival benefit. The amount of 'income benefit' per year usually remains level over the term selected but 'increasing benefit' policies can be arranged.

FAS (Free alongside ship) Seller pays all costs up to and including delivery of goods alongside the vessel and provides all documents. The risk and title then pass to the buyer who incurs the cost of loading onto the vessel and all further transit costs including insurance.

Fatal Accidents Act 1976 Enables the dependants of a person killed by the defendant's tort (qv) to claim for their financial losses and separately for bereavement. Dependants able to show a financial dependency will be able to claim provided that the deceased would have had a claim had he survived. The damages take account of earnings spent on the dependants, savings for their future, non-essentials and the value of services rendered. The bereavement claim, fixed at £10,000 per claim (fixed in 2002, reviewable), is divided equally among the eligible dependants to compensate for the non-pecuniary aspects such as emotional stress. It is *only* available to the surviving husband or wife, or, if the deceased was unmarried and a minor, to the parents.

Fault Defined in the Law Reform (Contributory Negligence) Act 1945 (qv), as 'the negligence, breach of statutory duty or other act or omission which gives rise to liability in tort, or would apart from this Act, give rise to the defence of contributory negligence'. Under the Employers' Liability (Defective Equipment) Act 1969 fault means 'negligence, breach of statutory duty, or other act or omission which gives rise to liability in tort in England and Wales or which is wrongful and gives rise to liability in damages in Scotland'. In professional liability insurance it is a 'breach of a civil duty'.

Fault liability system Legal system where an injured party can only recover compensation when able to attach fault to a third party. With the main exception of government-provided industrial injury benefits, the UK operates a fault liability system. The injured party has to prove a third party's breach of duty in order to recover damages aided in some instances by legislation creating a strict liability, e.g. the Consumer Protection Act 1987 (qv).

Faulty (or defective) design In the context of the exclusion in the contractors' all risks insurance (qv), this means: (a) a design which fails to meet the standards expected of design engineers; and (b) a design that proves inadequate but without blame or negligence attaching to the design engineer (*Queensland Government Railways* v. *Manufacturers' Mutual Insurance Co. Ltd* (1969)). The design simply has to be faulty for the exclusion to apply.

Fear of loss/fear of peril Insurers are not liable for a loss caused by action prompted by the fear of loss by an insured peril. The insured peril is the remote cause not the proximate cause (qv) of the loss. The principle does not absolve insurers from their liability for sue and labour charges, salvage charges or general average contribution when properly incurred to prevent loss from a actual or imminent peril.

Fellowship of the Chartered Insurance Institute (FCII) The highest CII qualification. The basis of election is the presentation of a portfolio of evidence of the applicant's abilities, achievements and experience. The starting point is an agreed examination. The starting point is an agreed examination benchmarked against the Advanced Diploma in Insurance (qv) or the post-1992 Associateship. The next step involves preparing a Fellowship plan including the applicant's proposals in terms of timescale and 'major achievements'. The third step is a three-year period of continuous professional development and finally the applicant must complete a business ethics programme in recognition of the possible impact their decisions may have on others. Fellows are eligible for Chartered titles (qv).

Fellowship of the Society of Financial Advisers The CII's highest qualification for financial advisers after passing 10 demanding examination papers.

Female lives Mortality rates, more favourable to women than men, enable life insurers to offer lower rates for life cover than those charged for men. Typically, insurers will deduct four years from their tabular rates (based on male lives) to find the rate for a female life.

Fencing/guarding, etc., of machinery Regulation 11 of PUWER (qv) places an absolute duty on the employer to prevent contact between people and dangerous machine parts by either preventing access or stopping the movement of the part. The following hierarchy of control must be followed 'so far as is reasonably practicable' (qv): fixed guards; other guards or protection devices; protection appliances (e.g. push sticks); information, instruction, training and supervision. This is to prevent or control exposure to mechanical hazards. Exposure to other hazards (e.g. scalds and burns, falling or ejection of articles) must also be prevented or controlled. Equipment should have clearly marked starting and stopping controls. Suitable means of isolation from sources of energy are also required. Equipment must be stable to prevent collapse or overturning and suitable lighting must provided.

FGU (from the ground up) Describes all of a cedant's losses over a period of time, including losses retained for their own account. This enables the reinsurer to assess the effect of shifts in direct underwriting experience and consider the possible effect on future reinsurance claims.

Fidelity guarantee insurance (suretyship insurance) *Commercial guarantees* (qv) protect employers against financial loss from the dishonesty of employees. *Local government guarantees* operate similarly but also cover loss due to mistakes. *Court bonds* guarantee the performance of individuals appointed by the court to handle money or other assets. *Government bonds* guarantee the performance of individuals in a position of trust given by government departments or concerned with dutiable goods for whom a *customs and excise bond* (qv) is appropriate. *See* GUARANTEE/INSURANCE-GUARANTEE.

Fiduciary The term is synonymous with trustee. A fiduciary relationship arises when one person puts trust in another *and* that other, the fiduciary, is under a duty to act in the first person's best interests in good faith without ulterior motive. Examples include partnerships, trustee and beneficiary, directors and the company. *See* DIRECTORS' AND OFFICERS' LIABILITY.

Fifth Motor Vehicle Directive Proposal (10/6/02) for motor insurance against civil liability. Main points: the minimum sum should be set at €2 million throughout the EU; three-month deadline for registration of car with foreign plates; where an accident occurs and the vehicle cannot be linked to a specific country it will be linked to the country in which the accident occurred; insurance companies claims-representatives or branch offices in Member States should be able to settle claims; a person who buys a car abroad should be able to obtain 2–4 weeks full insurance to cover the return journey to the buyer's own country.

Film finance insurance Indemnifies the insured if, at the end of a specified period, the finance he has provided exceeds the revenue collected from the production and sale of the various films known collectively as a 'slate'. The sum insured represents the entire cost of producing a slate of films, i.e. a given number, and the premium is a percentage thereof.

Film producers' indemnities Contingency insurance against pecuniary loss due to the interruption or abandonment of film through the death or incapacity of named actors or actresses.

Final average earnings *See* FINAL PENSIONABLE SALARY.

Final pensionable salary Defined in the particular pension scheme and calculated in a specified way (e.g. averaged over a limited period prior to the normal retirement date (or earlier date of leaving) or the actual final salary). The pension scheme definition is usually more restrictive than the IR's *final remuneration* (qv) definition. *See* FINAL SALARY SCHEME.

Final remuneration (IR definition) IR definition, more generous than scheme definitions, provides that the final remuneration should be not greater than either: (a) the average total earnings liable to Schedule E tax over three or more consecutive years in the 10 preceding retirement; or (b) basic annual pay of an employee liable to Schedule E tax for any one year of the five preceding retirement plus certain bonuses and commission averaged over a period and benefits in kind (qv). Adjustments can be made using dynamisation (qv). The limit affects how much of a member's earnings can be taken into account when IR calculates the maximum benefit available under an approved scheme.

Final salary scheme The main type of defined benefit scheme (qv). The pension is a proportion of final salary based on an accrual rate (qv), e.g. one-sixtieth, for each year of scheme membership plus any added years (qv). Forty years produces the maximum allowable pension. Scheme trustees must ensure that contribution levels are sufficient to deliver the pensions promised. Members can commute part of their rights into a tax-free lump seem equal to 1.5 times the final salary. *See* FINAL PENSIONABLE SALARY; FINAL REMUNERATION.

Financial Administration Foundation Certificate (FAFC) CII qualification. The only broad-based qualification specifically designed for administrative staff working in life and pensions offices.

Financial adviser Person appointed by an *independent intermediary* (qv) or *appointed representative* (qv) to provide a range of financial services. If they advise on or arrange certain types of investment (pensions, life insurance, unit trusts and shares) they and the companies they represent must be FSA-authorised. Financial advisers just advising on loans, most mortgages, general insurance or bank/building society accounts do not have to be FSA-authorised until October 2004 in the case of mortgage advisers and January 2005 in the case of general insurance and term insurance (qv) advisers. Some financial advisers sell the products of a single firm while others, *independent financial advisers* (qv), base their advice on all products in the market.

Financial derivatives *See* DERIVATIVES.

Financial guarantee insurance Covers loss from specific financial transactions and guarantees that investors in debt portfolios receive timely payment of principal and interest or guarantees in the event of default by the debtor or obligor. Financial guarantee insurances include: mortgage indemnity insurances (qv); performance bonds (qv); residual value insurance (qv). Financial guarantee cover originated in *suretyship* (qv).

Financial institutions insurance A wide range of insurances developed for the financial services industry. These include bankers' blanket bond insurance (qv), mortgage impairment insurance (qv), rogue trading (qv), operational risk (qv) and organisational liability (qv).

Financial loss cover Insures legal liability for (pure) financial loss by extending public and/or product liability cover as opposed to financial loss flowing from physical injury or damage to person or property. The extension is claims-made (qv), subject to an excess or co-insurance (qv) and has a separate annual aggregate limit of indemnity. Liquidated damages (qv) are excluded. The financial loss extension under product liability cover (qv) includes the *efficacy risk* (qv). The main insuring clause of the public liability policy covers financial loss following accidental obstruction, accidental nuisance, etc.

Financial Ombudsman Service (FOS) A 'free to consumers' dispute resolution service with three divisions: banking and loans, insurance and investment. Firms are bound when the Ombudsman makes decisions in favour of the consumer up to £100,000 plus interest, above which the Ombudsman may recommend full payment. Decisions are not binding on the consumer. FOS can also direct firms to take any steps deemed just. The FOS is funded by a general levy on all firms covered by its service. Membership is compulsory for all authorised firms. The Pensions Ombudsman (qv) operates separately.

Financial Planning Certificate (FPC) CII qualification accepted by the FSA (qv) as proof that a candidate has the level of knowledge required to become a financial adviser (qv). Holders are eligible to join the Society of Financial Advisers (qv).

Financial promotion Regime introduced under FSMA, s.21. A financial promotion is the communication, in the course of business, of an invitation or inducement to engage in an investment activity. It is unlawful if it is not made by an authorised person (qv) or has not been approved by such a person. 'Communication' embraces all forms of communication in place of previous separate rules for insurance advertisement, unsolicited calls, etc.

Financial quota share Cedant (qv) and reinsurer share the risk in agreed proportions. The cover applies to future and current years. Reinsurance commission (qv) is on a sliding scale starting with 30 per cent commission for a loss ratio of 70 per cent. For every loss ratio change of 1 per cent, the commission changes by 1 per cent. A commission that increases with the loss ratio helps the cedant when it is most needed. If the cedant has an expense ratio of 30 per cent then the cedant will have an underwriting result of zero regardless of the actual loss ratio for the year. This improves the solvency margin.

Financial reinsurance There is no clearly accepted definition but financial reinsurance is more concerned with the time value of money and financial goals than risk transfer. The intention is to stabilise the cedant's balance sheet and provide capital support. The cedant pays a premium to cover defined losses on a multi-year basis up to an agreed maximum. A profit share element converts a conventional treaty into financial reinsurance. The cedant benefits from credit enhancement (qv) by improving key ratios such as the combined ratio (qv). Specific financial reinsurance products include: time and distance policies (qv); loss portfolio transfers (qv); spread loss treaty (qv); adverse development cover (qv); blended cover (qv).

Financial Services and Markets Act Tribunal Statutory tribunal, within the Court Service, operating as a court of first instance. Persons disciplined by the FSA (qv) have the right to go to the Tribunal. The burden of proof attaches to the FSA. Usually there is an oral hearing on the substantive issues. The Tribunal's decision on fact is final but points of law may be appealed. The Tribunal can award costs against the applicant or the FSA. The Tribunal consists of a legally qualified chairman and two industry members.

Financial Services Authority (FSA) The UK's statutory financial regulator. Almost all kinds of financial services firms must secure FSA authorisation (qv). It regulates and monitors banks, building societies, friendly societies, Lloyd's, credit unions, insurance and investment firms (stockbrokers and fund managers) and independent financial advisers (qv). The FSA does not cover loans, credit and debt, and does not regulate occupational pension schemes (qv). The FSA has powers to investigate, discipline and prosecute, and can impose unlimited fines on anyone guilty of *market abuse* (qv). The FSA's four objectives are: maintaining market confidence; promoting public understanding of the financial system; protecting consumers; fighting financial crime. *See* FSA HANDBOOK. (Visit *www.fsa.gov.uk*).

Financial Services Compensation Scheme (FSCS) Compensation scheme for private customers of financial services firms that have gone out of business. If possible, FCSC transfers UK policyholders to new insurers but otherwise compensates them for their unexpired premiums. Compensation also covers unpaid claims. Compulsory third party motor insurance and employers' liability is compensated in full; in non-compulsory insurance (e.g. household or general) the first £2,000 is fully compensated with 90 per cent of the remainder. Under long term business (qv), the first £2,000 is fully protected plus 90 per cent of the value of the policy in liquidation. The scheme is funded by an industry levy.

Finite quota share Proportional multi-year reinsurance differing from a conventional quota share (qv). The insurer cedes an agreed percentage of unearned premium but the reinsurer's liability is *finite*, i.e. capped by an aggregate amount. The reinsurance is structured to assist the cedant's solvency position by paying a large amount of commission in the early stages and smaller amounts at the end.

Finite risk reinsurance Similar to financial reinsurance (qv) but has more risk transfer. It is a retrospectively rated reinsurance in which the reinsurer's liability is *finite*, i.e. capped. The multi-year contract enables the reinsurer to smooth the cedant's losses over time by providing funds for paying losses that are eventually restored to the reinsurer under an adjustable clause. The cedant gets credit enhancement (qv) by an improvement in key ratios. Investment income is an underwriting component. Finite products include: finite quota share (qv); loss portfolio transfers (qv); time and distance (qv); adverse development cover (qv); spread loss cover (qv); financial quota share (qv).

Fire Occurs where there is actual ignition that is accidental or fortuitous in origin from the insured's standpoint. The term does not include a fire lighted for a specific purpose while confined to its normal limits (e.g. in a grate), but includes fortuitous damage caused if property is inadvertently thrown or dropped onto it. A policyholder who had hidden jewellery beneath the fuel in a grate and, forgetfully, lit the fire later was able to recover. Unburned property damaged by water used for extinguishment is 'fire' damage under the proximate cause (qv) doctrine.

Fire and theft cover Named peril 'own damage' cover added to a third party motor vehicle. The property damage cover is against damage caused by fire and theft risks only. The cover could stand alone if the vehicle is out of use.

Fire certificate *See* FIRE PRECAUTIONS ACT 1971.

Fire division A section in a building formed by *fire walls* (qv) and *fire doors* to prevent a fire from spreading beyond its confines into other parts of the building. It may affect rating and the insurer's view on *estimated maximum loss* (qv). An insurer may regard a fire division as being achieved when the fire resistant (qv) rating is a given level, e.g. four hours.

Fire insurance rating System to fix premiums for fire insurance risks. The insured pays in proportion to: (a) the value at risk; (b) the degree of hazard present. The premium is the rate per cent multiplied by the sum insured. The rate reflects: (i) the trade classification, groupings of trades or sections of trades, broadly similar in experience in terms of the incidence and severity of fires; (ii) discrimination, i.e. differentiation of individual risks within a specified class due to particular features present in any individual risk; (iii) experience, meaning the relationship of losses to premiums in a given class over a period of years.

Fire map Visual record showing distribution of insured properties in a given area. Identifies possibility of catastrophic fire losses through accumulation of risk (qv).

Fire mark Plaques or medallions fixed on walls as a means of identifying the insurer of that property. The early fire insurers owned their own fire brigades and could be called to their 'own' fires. *See* FIRE PLATE.

Fire plate The successor to the fire mark (qv) used in the nineteenth and early twentieth centuries.

Fire Precautions Act 1971 A fire certificate is needed if more than 20 people are employed in the building, or more than 10 people are working other than on the ground floor, or if explosive or highly flammable materials are used or stored. Hotels and boarding houses require a fire certificate if sleeping accommodation is provided for more than six persons, or if any bedrooms are above the first floor or below ground floor. Certificates are issued by the fire authority when the owner or occupier has provided and maintained escape routes, fire fighting equipment and fire alarm systems as required. The Act overlaps with the Fire Precautions (Workplace) Regulations 1997 (qv) as amended by the Fire Precautions (Workplace) (Amendment) Regulations 1999.

Fire Precautions (Workplace) Regulations 1997 as amended by the Fire Precautions (Workplace) (Amendment) Regulations 1999 In order to comply an employer must: (a) carry out a fire risk assessment, even if holding a fire certificate (qv); (b) ensure that the fire risk can be detected and people suitably warned; (c) ensure that people can escape safely; (d) provide adequate fire-fighting equipment; (e) ensure that people know what to do in the event of fire; (f) check and maintain all fire safety equipment and provisions. Enforcement is by the local fire brigade.

Fire prevention Measures directed at reducing the incidence of fires. It includes public education, law enforcement and reduction of fire hazards and risks often at the instigation of insurers. *See* FIRE PROTECTION.

Fire Prevention (Metropolis) Act 1774 Section 83 requires insurers to ensure that fire insurance money is spent on reinstatement of buildings in England and Wales up to the sum insured if requested by any party having an interest in the property or upon any suspicion that the claim is fraudulent.

Fire protection All methods of controlling and extinguishing fires to protect property and human life from the damage and harm caused by fire. It includes construction safeguards, exit facilities, the installation of fire alarms, fire-detecting equipment and fire extinguishing equipment such as automatic sprinklers. The measures aim is to reduce the severity of the consequences of a fire. *See* FIRE PREVENTION.

Fire Protection Association (FPA) UK's national fire safety organisation. Its comprehensive services include consultancy, fire safety audits and fire risk assessments. It promotes high standards of fire safety management by working with fire, security and safety professionals in industry and commerce in both the public and private sectors. The FPA liaises closely with the government and the fire service. (Visit *www.thefpa.co.uk*).

Fire Research Station Fire Division of Building Research Establishment (qv). It carries out fire testing, fire research and provides fire and crime consultancy.

Fire resistant The extent to which material is fire resistant is measured by the time that the material or construction will withstand fire exposure as determined by a fire test that conforms with standard methods of testing. The measurements become standards for buildings regulations and other codes, e.g. 30 minutes fire resistant for internal walls in certain premises, or for insurers, e.g. four hours to achieve a *fire division* (qv) in a given risk.

Fire resurveys A follow-up survey of premises by a fire surveyor. It may be to check: if suggested improvements have been carried out; that accumulated waste has been removed; on new features, e.g. machinery, not installed at time of first survey; on changes notified to the insurer since the first survey. The whole premises are checked during a resurvey.

Fire Safety and Safety at Places of Sport Act 1987 Provides for a system of safety certification by local authorities for certain covered stands – known as 'regulated stands' – at sports grounds, and for subsequent inspections. This Act applies to all outdoor sports grounds, whatever their use, where there is a covered stand (i.e. with seated or standing accommodation) which can accommodate at least 500 spectators.

Fire survey report Prepared by a fire surveyor to assist an underwriter in considering the risk. The report, with plan, describes the premises and covers: fire hazards; fire protection; management; claims history; recommendations for risk improvement; reference to any special perils that may be required and the susceptibility of the risk to those perils.

Fire wall Floor to roof wall of incombustible materials with no doors, windows or other spaces through which a fire could pass. It needs to be sufficiently fire resistant (qv), i.e. four hours resistance, before an insurer 'compartentises' a property into separate risks. *See also* FIREWALL.

Fire waste Economic loss to society caused by fire. It embraces the direct loss of property and material damage, plus the time and cost in manufacture and other consequential losses, e.g. unemployment. The ABI and Lloyd's work closely with the Building Research Establishment (qv) and others on fire waste reduction.

Firebreak A natural or constructed barrier, such as a *fire wall* (qv) that stops or checks the progress of a fire. *See* FIREBREAK DOORS WARRANTY; FIRE DIVISION.

Firebreak doors warranty Fire insurance warranty that all firebreak doors are closed at the end of business each day.

Fireproof Literally means material or a structure that will withstand damage by fire. In practical terms in regard to a building it is taken to mean a structure built with steel and concrete or other non-combustible material that will significantly reduce both the probability of fire and its effects once started.

Firewall A logical or physical discontinuity in a computer network to prevent unauthorised access to data or resources. The secure trusted network is said to be 'inside' the wall, the insecure 'untrusted' network is 'outside'. *See* FIRE WALL.

Firm Title under which a company or partnership transacts business. Where the 'firm' is insured as in the case of professional indemnity insurance, the firm continues to be insured although the partners may change. Usually the policy indemnifies predecessors in business. Former partners are able to purchase 'run off' cover.

First aid services 1.When provided by the insured for the benefit of his employees, these services are stated to be a part of the 'Business'. *See* ANCILLARY ACTIVITIES. 2. The Health and Safety (First Aid) Regulations 1981 oblige employers to provide adequate and appropriate equipment and facilities to facilitate first aid treatment for employees and provide an 'appointed person' to take charge.

First excess The first layer of excess of loss cover (qv). Example: the first £300,000 in excess of the reinsured retention of £100,000. The term has also been used in the LMX market to refer to the first excess (i.e. additional deductible) that the reinsured retains for its own account before the excess of loss reinsurer becomes liable.

First loss policies A property insurance for an amount known to be less than the value of risk. It is used when it is inconceivable that all property would be lost in a single claim, e.g. theft of total stock of heavy steel. The insurer pays all losses up to the agreed sum insured unless the insured has understated the value at risk in which case a form of average (qv) will be applied.

First party insurance Insurance providing benefits or indemnity directly for the insured person as distinct from covering his liability to third parties. A material damage policy protecting the property owner is a first party policy.

First surplus The surplus treaty (qv) immediately above the cedant's retention (qv) and to which cessions must be made in priority to all other surplus treaties. The reinsured may arrange second and third treaties and so on.

FIS (Free into store) The seller must pay all charges, including import duty, freight and other costs including insurance to time of delivery of the goods into buyer's warehouse.

Fitness for purpose Sale of Goods Act 1979, s.14(3), implies that when goods are sold by a trader, they must be reasonably fit for the buyer's own particular purpose, provided the buyer made his purpose known (expressly or by implication) and reasonably relied on the seller's expertise. Where goods are bought for their usual purpose, notification of the buyer's purpose is implied. Fitness for purpose is also an aspect of *satisfactory quality* (qv).

Fixed commission Reinsurance commission payable at an unchanging rate with no adjustment for profit or performance on the treaty.

Fixed costs *See* STANDING CHARGES.

Fixed debt An amount deducted from a sum payable on death if death occurs within a specified term. If the life insured survives the policy term the full sum insured is payable. The fixed debt has largely been superseded by the diminishing debt. *See* DEBT 1.

Fixed objects Harbours piers, wharves, buoys and similar fixed objects with which a ship may collide. The shipowner's resultant collision liability is insured by Protection and Indemnity Clubs (qv).

Fixed rate treaty Excess of loss reinsurance treaty (qv) under which a flat rate is agreed. The rate is applied to the cedant's original gross premium income less only reinsurances paid out by the company which operate in priority to and for the benefit of the excess of loss treaty (qv). The burning cost method (qv) is used to calculate the rate. Compare with sliding scale treaty (qv).

Fixed share treaty Means quota share treaty (qv).

Fixtures and fittings Additions to buildings 'therein or thereon', usually considered a part of the building. The landlord's fixtures and fittings are insured as part of the building but if installed by the tenant they are insured as 'contents'. In regard to any particular fixtures or fittings it is necessary but not sufficient to ascertain who installed them as fittings installed by a tenant may be become landlord's fixtures. Pointers include purpose of the addition, the degree of actual attachment to the building and the terms of any lease.

Flag broker The broker who processes premiums and claims under reinsurance placed by more than one broker for the cedant.

Flag of vessel/flag of convenience Indication of the state where the vessel is registered and which is responsible for safety standards. A shipowner may choose a particular state because of less rigorous standards. Such a state is a *flag of convenience*, e.g. Liberia. Underwriters take account of the 'flag' when assessing the risk.

Flat line (or first interest) reinsurance Marine insurance whereby the reinsurer receives all of the cedant's interest up to a predetermined amount. For example, if an underwriter accepts £100,000 on a vessel and reinsures £50,000 on a first interest basis, any amount 'closed' up to £50,000 will be ceded to the reinsurer. If only £80,000 is closed to the underwriter it is his share of the risk that goes down as the reinsurer's line holds good in the sum of £50,000.

Flat premium A fixed non-adjustable premium. Sometimes used in reinsurance in respect of a portfolio of business that remains relatively unchanged over time or where a minimum premium situation applies.

Flat rate 1. An all-round rate as distinct from differential rating. The term is sometimes incorrectly used to refer to a fixed premium. 2. A reinsurance premium applicable to the entire premium income derived from the cedant from the business ceded to the reinsurer as distinct from the rate applicable to excess limits.

Flat rate scheme Defined benefit scheme (qv) where the ultimate pension benefit depends on how long the member has been in the scheme. The pension accrues at a flat rate for each year regardless of earnings.

Fleet insurance Policy on a number of vehicles operated by the same insured and rated on an experience basis, i.e. fleet rating (qv). Usually five or more vehicles constitute a fleet. The fleet itself can comprise vehicles of different classes, e.g. private cars, goods-carrying vehicles, etc. Aircraft and ships can also be insured as fleets.

Fleet rating (marine) The underwriter and shipowner agree an insured value for each vessel in the fleet. The rate is based on ownership, past claims experience and other underwriting considerations. The leading underwriter, and those who follow, write a 'line' on the highest valued vessel on the slip (qv) and a pro rata line on all other vessels in the fleet. The subsidiary insurances on freight and disbursements are also on a fleet basis.

Fleet rating (motor) Insurer compares average gross premium per vehicle with the claims cost per vehicle/year during the previous years. If the loss ratio is materially under a certain percentage, eg 60 per cent, the gross average premium may attract a fleet discount. If the loss ratio exceeds, say, 62.5 per cent, then the gross average premium will be increased. The discount or loading takes account of any trend and is applied to the insurer's tabular rate for each vehicle in the fleet. For large fleets (premiums over £100,000) rating is by burning cost (qv) or is restrospective, i.e. premiums will be based on known claims costs over a period after payment of an initial deposit premium.

Flight This is defined in policy form AVN1C (qv) as meaning 'from the time the Aircraft moves forward in taking off or attempting to take off, whilst in the air, and until the aircraft completes its landing run'.

Flight risks The risks attaching to an aircraft whilst airborne as opposed to those whilst on the ground.

Floater An item on moveable property with a sum insured that moves with the goods to wherever the property is located within a range of locations. The item 'tops up' sums insured designated to specific locations when those sums insured become temporarily inadequate.

The floater is subject to the two conditions of average (qv) and assists an insured whose distribution of goods across premises varies over time. *See* FLOATING POLICY.

Floating policy 1. *Marine.* A cargo policy covering individual shipments each of which is declared and eventually exhausts the sum insured. The arrangement has largely given way to open covers (qv). 2. *Floating insurance for building contractors.* Annual policy insures buildings of normal construction in course of erection and completion (including outbuildings, walls, etc.) up to a specific sum on the site of any of the insured's contracts.

Flood insurance Insurance against damage caused by the escape of water from the normal confines of any natural or artificial water course (other than water tanks, apparatus or pipes) or lake, reservoir, canal or dam in addition to inundation from the sea. Losses are normally subject to a minimum excess of £250. The risk is normally insured as an *additional peril* (qv) together with storm damage.

Flotsam Maritime term meaning wreckage floating on the sea (Merchant Shipping Act 1894).

Flour 'all risks' clauses Marine insurance clause for the insurance of flour as cargo. Cover is in respect of 'all risks' whatsoever but excludes damage by weevils, inherent vice, etc.

Flue gas explosion Explosion of gases in boiler flues (i.e. pipes). It is the result of ignition and not of the sudden release of internal pressure as in the case of a steam boiler explosion. The boiler and pressure plant policy (qv) can be extended to cover the explosion of gas in the furnaces or flues of the plant. Cover follows the terms of the boiler policy and therefore covers self-damage and the consequences thereof in terms of surrounding property and third party risks.

Flying risks Term used by personal accident insurers in connection with the risk of accidental bodily injury arising from flying either as a member of the crew of an aircraft or as a fare-paying passenger on a scheduled flight. The former risk is underwritten in the aviation department and the latter is covered under conventional personal accident insurance.

Follow the fortunes A proportional reinsurance principle, not always stated in the policy, under which the reinsurer shares the same fate as the cedant in regard to the underwriting and contractual risks. It does not include the cedant's commercial risk, i.e. total business risk or ex-gratia payments unless agreed or allowed under any relevant clause.

Follow the settlements A clause under which the reinsurer agrees to pay its share of the cedent's *settlements.* The reinsurer is not normally obliged to pay if the reinsured is not liable under the policy or the loss is excluded under the treaty. The clause modifies the position by requiring the reinsurer to follow the *settlement rather than the contract.*

Footsie Popular name for the FT-SE 100 Share Index, the UK's main benchmark index. It measures the daily share price performance of Britain's top 100 limited companies ranked by their size.

Force majeure Literally means 'greater force'; a clause designed to protect the insured against his failure to perform contractual obligations when caused by certain events beyond his control, such as a natural disaster or war.

Force majeure insurance Contingency cover, issued in the engineering department, in respect of a project owner's debt obligations to banks in the event of late completion or abandonment of a project due to 'force majeure' (qv). It also applies to a contractor's 'out-of-pocket' expenses when an overseas project is abandoned.

Forced sale of cargo Sale of cargo to obtain funds needed to prosecute the voyage for the common good. Any loss is admitted as a general average (qv) sacrifice. However, this only applies when cargo can be forwarded in no other way and is preferable to remaining on board until the voyage can be completed.

Forcible and violent entry Theft insurance wording to distinguish theft involving an 'attack' on the premises from theft without such an attack. The insurer generally covers 'theft following upon forcible and violent entry or followed by forcible or violent exit'. The words eliminate shoplifting or entry via an open door. The word 'violence' is used in its ordinary sense, meaning that an entry, where force might otherwise have been minimal, should be by a physical act characterised as *violent*. *See* FULL THEFT COVER.

Forecast mortality table A mortality table that takes account of anticipated changes in mortality. It indicates expected future mortality.

Foreign use (motor vehicles) Use of a motor vehicle outside the policy's normal UK territorial limits. To conform with EC law, the third party insurance must meet the minimum compulsory requirements of EC states. Insurers may automatically, or by agreement, extend cover to comprehensive cover if insured on that basis in the UK. A foreign use section is included in private car and commercial vehicle policies. *See* GREEN CARD.

Foreseeability The test of 'reasonable foreseeability' is applied in determining liability in the tort of negligence (qv). The case known as the *Wagon Mound* (*No. 1*) made the rule that damage following negligence will not be too remote if it is reasonably foreseeable. Thus foreseeability not directness is the test but see *egg shell skull rule* (qv).

Forgoing Written agreement between a pension scheme member and his employer. The former forgoes a salary increase or takes a pay cut in return for an investment by the employer of the same amount into a pension scheme.

Form of request/expression of wish Request by a pension scheme member that, on his death, the death benefits should be paid to the person(s) he has nominated in the request. The trustees are not obliged to follow the member's nomination.

Fortuitous cause/loss An accidental cause; a happening by chance. Only fortuitously caused losses are covered by insurance. A person cannot wilfully damage his property and make a claim. Neither can he claim for certainties such as wear and tear. In life insurance the fortuity is based on the date of death not its inevitability and suicide is normally excluded during the first two years.

Forum A place where disputes are heard. It usually refers to the particular court or courts having jurisdiction in the matter.

Forum of Insurance Lawyers (FOIL) Provides a forum for the exchange of information between lawyers acting predominately or exclusively for insurance clients (except legal expenses insurers) either practising within firms of solicitors, as barristers, or as in-house lawyers for insurers or self-insurers. FOIL is also an active lobbying body on matters concerning insurance litigation.

Forum rei The court of the country in which the thing or person, the subject of the action, is situated. *See* FORUM SHOPPING.

Forum shopping The selection by a claimant of a country where he prefers his action to be heard. If a choice exists the claimant 'shops around' to select the country where he is most likely to win or secure the highest award. Many UK liability policies exclude US jurisdiction.

Forward contract A privately arranged contract that specifies the price for a transaction in the future. It differs from 'futures' in that it is not standardised and is not traded on organised exchanges. Each party bears the other's credit risk.

Forwarding charges clause Institute Cargo Clause 12. Where, as a result of an insured peril, the transit is terminated short of the destination, the underwriter will reimburse the insured for any *extra charges* incurred in unloading, storing and forwarding the goods to their destination. The clause does not apply to general average (qv) or salvage (qv). Forwarding charges due to insolvency or financial default are excluded.

FOT (free on trucks)/FOR (free on rails) Seller pays all charges and loads goods on truck or rail, retaining the risk of damage until delivery to the carrier or railway agent. The buyer is responsible after such delivery and for further charges including insurance.

Foundation Insurance Test CII's starting point for newcomers to general insurance under the banner *Award in Insurance.* The single-subject course provides a basic understanding of how the market works, fundamental risk and insurance principles and procedures, and core personal and commercial insurance products. After completing FIT, candidates can proceed to the next general qualification, the *Certificate in Insurance* (qv).

Foundations clause Fire Insurance clause that provides that the value of the foundation (any part of the building below ground level) can be excluded from the buildings sum insured and is not to be included when determining the value of property at the time of a loss. The clause is used when it is considered that the foundations would not be affected by a loss.

Fourth EU Motor Insurance Directive Became law in the UK in January 2003. Principal aim is to improve the claims process for EU residents when claiming against an insurer based in another EU state. The UK's response is the Motor Insurance Database (qv) which, on being given the vehicle registration number of the third party, will be able to trace the third party's insurer.

Fragile property exclusion Breakage of fragile property is commonly excluded from 'all risks' policies (qv) but some cover can be bought back by the insured. The exclusion generally applies to 'ordinary breakage' and not breakage due to fire and theft.

Fragmentation risk/fragmentation policy (impact damage cover) The risk of damage to surrounding property by physical impact resulting from flying from any part of any insured item of plant. The risk is insurable as a named peril under engineering policies (qv) and can be combined with an inspection service.

Franchise 1. Relieves insurer of each and every loss that does not exceed a specified amount or percentage. If the limit is exceeded the loss is paid in full. The term, is distinguished from an excess (qv), the amount of which continues to be deducted for each and every loss above the specified amount. 2. The amount by which a Lloyd`s syndicate is permitted to exceed its syndicate allocated capacity. 3. *See* LLOYD'S FRANCHISE.

Fraudulent claims Claim where the insured has: (a) made false statements of fact; or (b) made statements, knowing them to be false, or not believing them to be true, or without caring whether they were true or false. Good faith, implied in all insurance contracts, requires that any claim by the insured shall be honestly made. If the insured submits a fraudulent claim all benefit, including the premium, under the policy is forfeited. *See* CHEATLINE.

Fraudulent misrepresentation Breach of the duty of utmost good faith (qv) occurring where the person knowingly makes a false statement relating to a material fact, does not believe it to be true or makes it recklessly without due regard to its accuracy. The Road Traffic Act 1988 makes it a statutory offence for a person to make a false statement or to withhold material information for the purpose of obtaining a certificate of motor insurance required by the Act.

Fraudulent trading Occurs when a company continues to trade and incur debts, when, to the knowledge of the director(s), there is no reasonable prospect of the creditors being paid. It includes a situation where there are no good grounds for believing that the company can pay its way even if the director(s) hold an opposite view. Any director guilty of fraudulent trading may be liable to contribute to the company's assets. *See* DIRECTORS' AND OFFICERS' LIABILITY.

Fraudulent withdrawals and forged signatures insurance A policy to indemnify building societies and similar institutions against losses incurred as a result of payments made in connection with fraudulent withdrawals and forged signatures. The annual premium is adjustable and is based on the annual amount of withdrawals.

Free asset ratio For UK life insurance companies only, a solvency measure calculated as available assets minus the required minimum margin (qv)/admissible assets. All other things equal, the higher the free asset ratio, the higher the level of surplus capital relative to the asset base. Reported free assets ratio are dependent on the assumptions made to value the liabilities.

Free assets Life insurance company's assets that exceed the sum of the company's liabilities and the required minimum margin of solvency (RMM). It is a measure of surplus capital once the RMM has been covered.

Free cover The maximum amount of death or disability cover which an insurer covering a group is prepared to insure for each individual without production of *evidence of health* (qv).

Free from Particular Average (FPA) A clause whereby cover excludes partial losses unless the vessel has been stranded, sunk, burned or in collision with another vessel regardless of whether such losses were actually caused by these perils. This 'major casualty' partial loss insurance is the substance of Institute Cargo Clauses (C) used particularly for bulk cargoes such as grain.

Free of capture and seizure clause (FC & S) War peril exclusion under SG policy (qv). The War Exclusion Clause is now integral to the Institute Cargo Clauses and the International Hull Clauses (qv).

Free on Board (FOB) A sales contract, mainly used for bulk cargoes (coal, grain), whereby the seller is responsible for the goods until loaded ('over ship's rail') and the buyer is responsible for all charges (including insurance) thereafter.

Free standing additional voluntary contributions (FSAVCs) *Additional voluntary contributions* (qv) to an insured defined contribution scheme (qv) that is independent of the member's occupational pension scheme. Where contributions exceed £2,400 per annum (year 2002/3) the FSAVC administrator must carry out a *headroom check* (qv) except for scheme members with net relevant earnings below £30,000 who also contribute £3,600 each year to a *stakeholder pension* (qv). An FSAVC must be used to purchase a retirement annuity with no tax-free lump sum.

Freedom of establishment The right to set up a branch, subsidiary office or similar establishment to transact business in a foreign country.

Freedom of services business The right to transact business across national frontiers with those domiciled in another country without having an establishment in that country.

Freight Reward payable to a shipowner for the carriage of goods including the profit he derives from carrying his own goods, or other people's goods but not including any passage money. *Advance freight* paid to the shipowner on a non-refundable basis is at the risk of the shipper and merged with the cargo's insured value. When freight is payable on 'out-turn' of the goods at the destination it is at the risk of shipowner and insurable by him. The term 'freight' has also been used to describe the goods themselves and has been adopted by 'freight forwarders' who handle shipments. *Chartered freight* is payable by a charterer to a shipowner and insurable by him unless paid in advance at the risk of the charterer.

Freight collision clause Clause incorporated in freight policies to cover three-fourths of the shipowner's liability for collision damage that may attach to freight. The clause is used only where freight is liable to be called upon to contribute to collision liability, i.e. where certain foreign laws may apply to the settlement. In English law freight is not taken into account in assessing the shipowner's liability for collision.

Freight contingency Insurable interest of a consignee who has paid freight on goods when delivered over the ship's rail but where the goods remain at risk until arriving at the final destination.

Freight forwarder Party that arranges the shipping of goods overseas but does not normally take possession of the goods. Freight forwarders operate under the British International Freight Association Conditions 2000. The conditions limit liability to 2 SDRs (approx.) per tonne subject to a cap based on the value of the goods. Claims should be made within 14 days of awareness of the 'event', legal actions should be brought within 9 months. The maximum liability for delay is twice the amount of carriage charges.

Freight insurance The insurance of the freight (qv) earned by shipowners. Shipowners usually insure freight for 12 months by fixing an amount that could be earned on any one round voyage. Bill of lading freight is normally paid in advance and added to the value of the goods by the cargo owner. The insurable value of freight is the gross value of freight receivable by the shipowner plus the cost of insurance. *See also* FREIGHT; FREIGHT COLLISION CLAUSE.

Freight waiver clause Clause 22 of the International Hull Clauses (11/2002) (qv) under which the insurer waives his right to freight earned or to be earned by a ship that is the subject of a constructive total loss claim (qv). *See* ABANDONMENT.

Frequency loss A type of loss that combines high probability with low impact, the predictable nature of which means that it can usually be assumed and managed, e.g. shoplifting, minor mechanical breakdowns.

Freshwater damage Cargo damaged by fresh water without the operation of a maritime peril. This risk, together with other extraneous risks such as damage by other cargo, hooks, oils and sweat may added to the policy when governed by Institute Cargo Clause (B) or (C). Clause (A), 'all risks', is already wide enough to embrace the risk. The freshwater loss/damage must be fortuitous, happening by reason of some external cause.

Friendly Societies Otherwise known as 'collecting societies' they are like industrial life companies but owned and operated for the benefit of its members. They are authorised to transact industrial life assurance as defined in the Industrial Assurance Act 1923. Friendly societies started as local organisations, distributing benefits to sick and bereaved members. They have to be registered under the Friendly Societies Act 1974 and are subject to the supervision of the FSA.

Fringe company An insurance company not regarded as one of the 'majors' by whom or for whom business is written in one of the underwriting rooms near Lloyd's.

'Frolic of his own' An act 'for one's own purposes'. It describes circumstances when an employer is not vicariously liable for the tort of his employee because the latter was not acting in the course of employment as he was 'on a frolic of his own', i.e. engaged in an activity on his own account. In *Hilton* v. *Thomas Burton (Rhodes) Ltd* (1961) demolition workers left work in the employer's van to go to a cafe. The driver, an employee of the defendants, was negligent and the foreman was killed. The defendants were not liable as the men were on a 'frolic of their own'.

From When a ship is insured 'from' the port of departure, the insurance commences when she breaks ground intending to proceed on her voyage.

Fronting The issue of a policy by an authorised insurer who cedes 100 per cent (or nearly that amount) to a second insurer or a reinsurer who is not an admitted insurer in the state concerned. The authorised insurer 'fronts' the risk for a specified fee or premium.

Frozen pension *See* DEFERRED PENSION.

Frustration clause Marine war risks cargo insurance clause stating that there is no loss because of the termination (or frustration) of the transit due to an outbreak of hostilities. The property is not irretrievably lost but is prevented from reaching its destination. There must be actual physical loss/damage to the cargo to constitute an insured loss.

FSA Handbook of Rules and Guidance Presents and gives guidance on rules made under FSMA. Each of five blocks contains sections dealing with all aspects of financial services authorisation (qv), compliance and enforcement, market structure, operation and oversight by the FSA. Block 1 sets out High Level Standards, applicable to firms and approved persons (qv). Block 2 covers Business Standards applicable to firms. Block 3 covers Regulatory Processes, i.e. authorisation (qv); supervision (qv); enforcement (qv); and decision-making. Block 4 deals with redress (qv), i.e. particularly, compensation for investors, depositors and policyholders. Block 5 covers Specialist Sourcebooks, containing specialist information on areas such as: insurance; collective investment schemes; recognised exchange and clearing houses.

FSA Returns Regulatory returns sent annually to the FSA and prepared for each regulated operating insurance company. FSA returns comprise detailed financial information on solvency, investments, business mix, claims and premiums, etc., and are publicly available. The FSA returns are prepared differently from the reports and accounts filed with Companies House.

Full buyout A concept introduced in the Pensions Bill of 2004 that will be legislated in 2005. It will oblige solvent employers who wind up defined benefit pension schemes (qv) to meet their in pension promises in full by buying out members' benefits.

Full premium if lost (FPIL) Hull policy clause making the entire premium fully earned if the insurer pays a total loss for the insured vessel, i.e. no return to the insured for the unexpired period.

Full reinsurance clause 1. Binds the reinsurer to 'follow the settlements' (qv) of the reinsured provided that the settlements are within the terms of the original policy and the reinsurance. 2. Facultative reinsurance clause that passes control over all claims settlements to the reinsurer where all or nearly all of the risk is reinsured.

Full theft cover Theft cover that goes beyond '*forcible or violent entry or exit to or from premises*' (qv) to cover any dishonest appropriation. Full theft cover is not normally available to shops or hotels, which are susceptible to casual theft.

Full Value Declared (FVD) A notation on air waybill (qv) indicating that a specific value has been declared to the carrier for the carriage of the merchandise.

Full value insurances Property insurance in which the sum insured represents the full value at risk. Where the insured completes a proposal and signs a declaration he may 'warrant' that this is the case.

Fully insured scheme A pension scheme where the trustees have effected an insurance contract in respect of each member guaranteeing benefits corresponding to those promised under the rules.

Fully paid up policies *See* PAID-UP POLICIES.

Fund A provision or reserve. Each class of insurance business has a fund based on the balance of premiums less claims and expenses after taking into account any transfer to or from the profit and loss account. In life insurance, it often means a pool of assets managed separately for asset and liability management purposes. Funds may be legally or contractually segregated which may limit the freedom of the company to switch assets between funds.

Fund account Shows how the pension scheme has dealt with members and income from investments and what investments have been bought and sold during the year. The account is compulsory.

Fundamental risks Risks of potentially wide-ranging effect on society as a whole or large segments thereof rather than individuals. They are of a catastrophic nature, e.g. war, famine, earthquake, widespread pollution and unemployment. They are generally outside the scope of private enterprise insurance with responsibility being accepted by governments. Compare with particular risks (qv).

Funded cover Prospective excess of loss treaty under which the cedant pays high premiums to the reinsurer for the purpose of paying later losses. The reinsurer deducts charges from the fund and, at the end of the contract, returns the balance to the cedant as profit commission.

Funding In regard to pension schemes it is the advance provision for future liabilities by the accumulation of assets that are normally external to the employer's business.

Funding level The comparison of a pension scheme's assets and liabilities.

Funding ratio The funding level (qv) expressed as a percentage.

Funding plan The plan to ensure that money will be available to pay out pension benefits as they fall due. It involves setting contributions at a certain level, such as the standard contribution rate (qv).

Funds at Lloyd's FAL is members' capital held in trust at Lloyd's to pay claims when premiums trust funds (qv) are insufficient. The amount is calculated at member level using the risk-based capital model (qv). The amount for individuals is equal to a ratio between 20 per cent and 30 per cent of the premiums they are permitted to write (depending on membership type, nature of risk, liquidity and resources). The ratio for corporate members is 50 per cent (except for dedicated corporate motor at 40 per cent). The funds must be maintained in value and be in a Council-approved form, i.e. readily realisable assets such as cash securities, letters of credit and bank and other guarantees. *See* LLOYD'S CHAIN OF SECURITY.

Funeral expenses insurance Pre-paid plans purchased by a lump sum or periodic payments. A plan covers the funeral director's fees and expenses and 'disbursements', i.e. doctor's fees, church fees, cost of a minister, cremation/burial fees, grave digging and cost of a plot. These plans have superseded the limited amounts available under industrial life and friendly society insurances.

Futures Short for 'futures contract' involving an obligation to buy or sell a specific amount of a commodity, currency or financial instrument at a stated price on a stated future date. The price is established on the floor of an exchange, e.g. the London International Financial Futures Exchange (LIFFE) (qv). The contracts may be traded with third parties.

G

G60 Pensions Qualification under the advanced financial planning certificate (AFPC) (qv). Demonstrates that an adviser has comprehensive knowledge of pensions matters. It also classifies an intermediary, such as an independent financial adviser (qv), as a pension transfer (qv) specialist.

GAAP accounting (Generally Accepted Accounting Principles) These principles, as practised in the UK under the Companies Act, require company accounts to give a true and fair view. There are moves towards a globally accepted GAAP for insurance accounting. GAAP is associated with *annual accounting*, which by 2005 will supersede the three-year accounting system (qv) at Lloyd's to bring them into line with insurance company accounting. *See* ANNUAL VENTURE.

Gambling policies Policies that contravene the Marine Insurance (Gambling Policies) Act 1909. It is not legal to enter into a marine insurance without a bona fide interest, or possibility thereof, in the subject matter insured. It is also an offence for a shipowner's employee, not being a part-owner, to effect a policy on PPI (qv) terms. The Act prevents gambling in marine insurance.

Game cover Specialised cover for printers and vendors of instant ticket sales and online lottery services. The policy covers: (a) contractual obligations with first party principals; (b) increased cost of failing to conform to these contracts, e.g. print re-runs; (c) printer's liability following machinery or computer breakdown, etc., not covered under an errors and omissions policy or professional indemnity policy.

Gaming Act 1845 Makes all wagering or gaming contracts null and void. An insurance on goods without insurable interest is a wager and therefore unenforceable.

GAP insurance *See* GUARANTEED ASSET PROTECTION.

GDP (Gross Domestic Product) trigger A trigger under a *contingent capital* (qv) arrangement based on trading conditions as benchmarked by changes in the growth rate of the gross domestic product in a defined trading area, e.g. Europe. The insured corporation calls in capital from an insurer when the trigger event occurs, e.g. decline in growth rates of GDP, as it will signify poor economic conditions that hit sales.

General average (GA) Loss through voluntary sacrifice of any part of the ship or cargo, or an expenditure to safeguard the ship and remaining cargo from imminent threat. General average losses include jettison, discharging cargo to refloat a ship, etc. A general average expense may occur when a ship is towed to port. An average adjuster (qv) works out the value of each 'saved interest' who then make *general average contributions*, proportionately, to the expenditure and the 'sacrificed losses'. Insurance applies to general average if incurred to avoid an insured peril. *See* GENERAL AVERAGE ADJUSTMENT; GENERAL AVERAGE AGREEMENT; GENERAL AVERAGE BOND; GENERAL AVERAGE EXPENDITURE; GENERAL AVERAGE FUND.

General average adjustment Adjustment of a general average loss usually carried out by an average adjuster (qv) appointed by the shipowner. A statement of losses, values and proportionate contributions is prepared. The cost of the adjustment is part of the general average (qv).

General average agreement Same as GENERAL AVERAGE BOND.

General average bond Document required of cargo owners, after a general average loss (qv), obtaining their agreement to pay any contribution that may become due. The bond, additional to the *general average deposit* (qv), secures release of the goods. It authorises the shipowner to draw on the funds to defray any *general average disbursements* (qv). The cargo owner obtains a *general average guarantee* from his cargo insurer who agrees to meet the insured's general average contribution.

General average contribution The contribution to general average losses (qv) by all interests at risk on the basis of their respective values. The contribution is recoverable under cargo policies if an insured peril has occurred. The insurer pays when the final account is apportioned but as this can take years a *general average deposit* (qv) is requested.

General average deposit Deposit paid by a consignee in return for delivery of the goods where the goods are subject to general average contribution. The deposit may be replaced by a general average guarantee (qv).

General average disbursements *See* GENERAL AVERAGE EXPENDITURE.

General average expenditure Expenditure, also called general average disbursements, incurred by a shipowner in connection with a general average (qv) act, e.g. hire of a tug to tow a stricken vessel to a port of refuge. Any damage to cargo during the operation is general average sacrifice. Port of refuge expenses are the most common form of general average expenditure and are recoverable from the general average fund (qv). The hull insurer is not directly liable for these expenses. They are included in the final general average adjustment and incorporated in the *general average contribution* (qv) payable by the insurer in so far as it is recoverable under the policy.

General average fund The accumulated general average deposits (qv) that are available for general average expenditure (qv) and, in due course, payment of the contributions.

General average guarantee An insurer's undertaking to pay the contribution due towards a general average fund (qv). It normally replaces a general average deposit (qv).

General average loss Sacrifice or expenditure directly consequent upon a general average act. Unless specifically agreed the insurer is not liable for any general average loss where the loss was not incurred for the express purpose of avoiding an insured peril or in connection with the avoidance of such a peril (Marine Insurance Act 1906, s.66(6)). *See* GENERAL AVERAGE.

General average sacrifice Property sacrificed for the common safety of the maritime adventure. The owner of sacrificed cargo may claim directly against his insurer under the Institute Cargo Clauses, or, after completion of the voyage, seek *general average contributions* (qv) from the 'saved interests'. *See* GENERAL AVERAGE.

General average security General average contribution (qv) is secured by a general average bond (qv), general average deposit (qv) or general average guarantee (qv). The vessel owner's interest is also secured when the cargo owner supplies documents to replace the shipowner's lien (qv) on the cargo.

General damages *See* DAMAGES.

General exceptions/exclusions Exceptions listed in a comprehensive or hybrid policy that apply to all sections of the policy. Also, each section has its own specific exceptions.

General insurance business Eighteen classes of insurance specified under FSMA (Regulated Activities) Order 2001, Schedule 1, Part I as being regulated activities (qv). They are the classes of: accident (qv); sickness (qv); land vehicles; railway rolling stock; aircraft; ships; goods in transit; fire and natural forces; damage to property; motor vehicle liability; aircraft liability; liability for ships; general liability (i.e. does not include liability relating to motor vehicle, aircraft or ships); credit; suretyship; miscellaneous financial loss; legal expenses; assistance. The classes are then grouped for accounting purposes. For example, accident and sickness classes combine to form group 1 (accident and health) and a liability (group 6) comprises liability relating to motor vehicles, aircraft, ships and general liability. *See* LONG-TERM BUSINESS.

General insurance contract Term in FSMA (Regulated Activities) Order 2001, Schedule 1, Part I, describing 18 types of general business as opposed to long-term business listed as regulated activities under FSMA, Part IV permissions. Such general insurance business (qv) include accident, aircraft, motor, legal expenses, etc.

General Insurance Standards Council (GISC) Regulates the selling, advising and servicing of its members in relation to general insurance business conducted. It is an independent, non-statutory organisation, funded by its 6,500 members who include general insurers, intermediaries, agents and those acting for them. The main purpose of GISC is to ensure that general insurance customers are treated fairly. GISC's role will be taken over by the FSA in 2005. (Visit *www.gisc.co.uk*).

General Product Safety Regulations (GPSR) 1994 A general duty is placed on all suppliers of consumer goods. They must supply products that are safe in normal or reasonably foreseeable use. Safety takes into account factors such as the product's characteristics, instructions and warnings and the categories of consumers at serious risk when using the product, particularly children. Relevant British or European standards can be taken into account in assessing safety. Breaches are punishable by fines and/or imprisonment. GPSR largely replaces the general safety requirement under Consumer Protection Act 1987 (s.10).

General prohibition FSMA, s.19, states that no person may carry on a regulated activity (qv) in the UK, or purport to do so, unless he is an exempt person (qv) or authorised person (qv). Any breach amounts to a criminal offence.

General representative A person resident in the UK designated as the representative of an insurance company with a head office outside the UK, who is authorised to act generally and accept the service of documents.

General Terms of Agreement *See* ABI GENERAL TERMS OF AGREEMENT.

General Underwriters Agreement (GUA) An agreement born out of LMP 2001 (qv) between the (re)insurers who are parties to the slip (qv) specifying the terms on which the slip leader acts as agent of the underwriters to deal with alterations, amendments and agreements.

General Works Damage *See* WORKS DAMAGE INSURANCE.

Genetic and Insurance Committee (GAIC) Set up by the government to develop criteria for evaluation of the scientific, medical and actuarial evidence available to support the use of genetic tests in insurance risk assessment and to evaluate those tests against these criteria. Members come from the insurance industry and clinical and genetic patients groups. The insurance industry has agreed a voluntary code with GAIC whose aim is to ensure that individuals do not avoid tests because they fear a result harmful to their life cover applications. *See* ABI GENETIC TESTING CODE OF PRACTICE.

Geographical limits *See* TERRITORIAL LIMITS.

Gift inter-vivos A gift made during a person's lifetime as opposed to a legacy passing on death. Inheritance tax is payable on gifts inter-vivos at a reducing rate over a seven-year period. A typical insurance solution is a decreasing term insurance (qv) that will provide funds on death during the seven-year period.

Gilts Gilt-edged securities are bonds (qv) and other loans issued by the UK government or UK local authorities, considered as safe investments. However, they are not risk free as the market price varies according to the financial climate, in particular the prevailing rate of interest.

Glass insurance Breakage of all types of glass (e.g. wired and embossed plate, figured glass, etc.). The insurers will make good or pay full replacement value, including shop fronts with lettering. Any breakage insurable under a fire policy or caused by explosion is excluded. Fixed glass in dwellings is insured under household comprehensive policies.

Glider policy Covers: loss/damage during launching, flight and landing, all subject to an excess; loss/damage while in a picketed hangar or not left unattended in the open at an approved launching site or in transit; third party injury and damage; passenger liability.

Global excess/insurance Reinsurance insurance (qv) covering all, or nearly all, of the reinsured's business, i.e. 'globally' in 'business spread' and not 'geographic' terms. The 'global' pays losses in excess of the aggregate net aggregated losses sustained by the reinsured's many departments (e.g. motor, aviation, marine, property, etc.) following one major event, such as Hurricane Betsey, that strikes simultaneously at ships, aircraft, property on land etc. Policy wording is similar to an excess of loss catastrophe reinsurance. 'Globals' can provide cover for specific risks as well as large risk accumulations.

Global insurance programme Worldwide programme enabling a multi-national to establish the same level of cover globally. It could consist of a master policy issued in the home country that results in a totally non-admitted insurance programme, i.e. no local policies. At the other extreme it is a totally admitted programme with all local entities being issued with policies and all premiums and losses being dealt with locally. Normally the programme entails: (a) a master policy arranged in the home country giving uniform cover for the whole group; and (b) local admitted policies reflecting local needs. The master policy tops up local policies to gain consistency across the group. The master policy is subject to a difference in conditions (qv) clause and a different in limits clause (qv).

Global return The return completed by Lloyd's for FSA regulatory purposes, covering the activities of all Lloyd's syndicates. When the returns are consolidated Lloyd's publish the Lloyd's market underwriting results.

Good faith Acting honestly. It means the absence of fraud, but falls short of the doctrine of utmost good faith (qv).

'Goods' In marine insurance this means 'goods in the nature of merchandise'. It does not include personal effects or provisions and stores for use on board (Marine Insurance Act 1906, Schedule, Rules for Construction of Policy, rule 17). This rule also provides that deck cargo and living animals must be specifically insured and not insured as goods unless it is customary to do so.

Goods in transit insurance Covers goods in transit by land (or by land and sea). Cover is either on (a) the *goods* protecting the owner's interest; or (b) the *liability* when a road haulier carries customers' goods. The goods owner insures 'all risks' cover up to an amount per specified vehicle or per consignment when using other transport modes. The haulier can insure on a specified vehicle basis or, on a declaration basis, by estimating annual haulage charges with a selected limit of indemnity. Cover, within the territorial limits, applies during loading, carriage, unloading or temporary garaging of vehicles or trailers. Insurance may include loss/damage to sheets, ropes, clearing up, repackaging and re-sorting following an accident. *See* ROAD HAULAGE ASSOCIATION CONDITIONS OF CARRIAGE; HAULIERS LIABILITY POLICY.

'Goods . . . in trust or on commission' 'Goods in trust', when written in a policy, does not imply a technical trust but includes holding goods as a bailee. 'Goods held on commission' has a more restricted meaning and refers to property entrusted to the insured for the purpose of sale. The phrase as a whole is wide enough to cover not only the insured's interest but also the full value of the goods. Any sum the insured recovers above his own interest is held in trust for the owners. *See* GOODS IN TRUST OR ON COMMISSION FOR WHICH THE INSURED IS RESPONSIBLE; ON GOODS.

'Goods in trust or on commission for which the insured is responsible' The addition of the phrase 'for which the insured is responsible' to the phrase 'goods in trust or on commission (qv)' restricts cover to the interest of the insured and does not extend to cover the proprietary interests of other persons in the goods. The owners of goods were not protected when a fire occurred at the insured's warehouse as the insured item protected only the warehouse proprietor's interest (*North British and Mercantile Insurance Co.* v. *Moffat* (1871).

Government bonds Required for special managers in bankruptcy, trustees under deeds of arrangement, liquidators and those concerned with dutiable goods. *See* CUSTOMS AND EXCISE BONDS.

Grace period A period (usually 15 days) for which cover continues beyond the expiry date of an annual term to allow for the payment of the premium. This privilege will be forfeited if the insured expressly or impliedly rejects the renewal terms. There is no grace period in motor or marine insurance. In life insurance a privilege condition allows 30 days of grace for the payment of the premium (other than for monthly premiums) and if the event insured against occurs within that grace period, the unpaid premium will be deducted from the policy proceeds. *See* RENEWAL.

Graded schedule scheme Pension scheme under which benefits are related to earnings in each year of membership. An alternative term is salary grade scheme.

Gradually operating causes Causes that result in loss over time, e.g. rust, corrosion and normal wear and tear. No fortuitous element is present and compensation for the reduction in value would contravene the principle of indemnity (qv). Wear and tear, etc., is specifically excluded from 'all risks' policy but 'new for old' (qv) and reinstatement policies modify the principle of indemnity.

Grammatical construction rule A rule of construction (qv) meaning that in construing a policy the ordinary rules of grammar and punctuation will apply, although a court has a discretion to correct obvious slips. The draftsmen of policies and legal documents try not to rely on punctuation to convey their meaning.

Grant of probate The legal process of proving a will, appointing an *executor* and settling an estate; but by custom, it has come to be understood as the legal process whereby a deceased person's estate is administered and distributed. Where the deceased dies intestate the deceased's *legal personal representative* is called an *administrator*.

Great Fire of London London's largest fire. It occurred in 1666 and started in Pudding Lane. It spurred the development of fire insurance. Previously fire damage compensation was funded by charitable donations and collections from guilds of craftsmen and churches. The Fire Office, formed in 1680, is generally regarded as the first fire insurance company although records indicate that fire insurance was transacted in 1667. For other historical aspects see fire marks (qv) and the Tooley Street fire (qv).

Green card Document providing evidence of cover while a vehicle is being used abroad. It contains insurance information in several languages and shows that the user's insurance meets the minimum third party requirements of all EC states. Green cards are not a legal necessity within EC states but are recognised in their own right.

Gross line The amount of insurance the insurer has on a risk before deducting the amount reinsured. Net lines plus reinsurance equals gross lines.

Gross premium method/valuation Method for placing a value on a life insurance company's liabilities that explicitly values the future office premiums payable. In addition, it usually values explicitly future discretionary benefits and future expenses. If it explicitly allows for future bonuses it may be referred to as a bonus reserve valuation. The valuation may be carried out using formula or cashflow techniques.

Gross premiums written Aggregate of all premiums falling due during the accounting year, including single premiums and portfolio premium entries after deducting portfolio withdrawals and cancellations.

Gross profit The amount, or *difference*, by which sales revenue exceeds the cost of sales, i.e. costs incurred in getting the goods ready for sale such as purchases, direct labour costs and other direct costs in manufacturing. Loss of gross profit is insured under a business interruption insurance (qv) that usually provides cover on the *difference basis* (qv). An older way of calculating gross profit was to add the net profit to the standing charges (qv) of the business.

Gross proceeds *See* GROSS VALUE.

'Gross value' Defined in the Marine Insurance Act 1906, s.71(4), as the wholesale price or estimated value ruling on the day of sale after freight, landing charges and duty have been paid. 'Gross proceeds' is the price obtained at a sale, all charges on sale being paid by the seller (Marine Insurance Act 1906, s.73).

Ground heave *See* HEAVE.

Ground risks Aviation insurance term describing the risk of damage to the aircraft while stationary on the ground.

Grounding risk Withdrawal of aircraft from service. The risk is insurable by an aircraft manufacturer under an aviation products liability policy to indemnify a manufacturer against his legal liability for loss of use pending investigation and repair of an alleged defect.

Group captives A captive insurance company (qv) formed by an association to insure the risks of its members.

Group Income Protection/Group Permanent Health Insurance Income protection insurance (qv) applied to a group, usually effected as an employee benefit. The deferred period (qv) is fixed so that the benefit becomes payable when contracted salary payments terminate or are significantly reduced. The benefit, once triggered, continues until the sooner of the end of the disability or normal retirement age.

Group insurance Insurance of a number of persons under a single contract or, if agreed, under individual contracts. Usually the persons are in the same employment or all employed or members of the same association. Group cover can be applied to various kinds of insurance, e.g. group life (qv), group accident, group legal expenses, etc.

Group life insurance Policy covering a group of lives as distinct from individuals. The group must exist for some purpose other than the insurance, e.g. employees in a firm or members of an association. The cover is often ancillary to a pension scheme but can stand alone. Policies are written as one-year term insurances (qv) with the automatic right of renewal each year subject to the terms of the contract. *See* ACTIVELY AT WORK; FREE COVER.

Group personal pensions (GPP) Personal pension plans (qv) arranged by an employer for his employees. Employers may contribute. GPPs are not occupational schemes, simply individual personal pensions grouped for administrative convenience. They are defined contribution schemes (qv) with no maximum on the retirement benefits. The employee makes his own contracting out (qv) arrangements but this will not affect national insurance contributions.

Group underwriting May occur where a parent company controls other insurance companies within its group. Group underwriting is an alternative to interchange of business within the group. Each acceptance of business is reported to a central control where a group retention is observed in accordance with a scale of group limits reflecting the group's commitments. Reinsurance may be arranged by the subsidiary or the parent. Centralised underwriting enables the group to maximise its underwriting capacity.

Growing Degree Days (GDD) Weather index calculated by subtracting a reference temperature (e.g. 50°F or 10°C) from the average daily temperature. Each degree of 'warmth' is a growing degree day (GDD). The deviations from reference temperature benchmark a biological process, such as insect development. 'Warm' temperatures necessitate the use of costly pesticides to protect crops against agricultural pests. The payout is the tick (qv) multiplied by the difference between the GDD level stated in the contract (i.e. the strike) and the cumulative GDDs for the contract period.

Growth bond/capital bond Fixed term investments, typically between three and five years, where a single premium life contract, with only nominal life cover, guarantees a minimum capital growth at maturity. It is a collective investment scheme (qv) that produces economies of scale for small investors. Investors pay tax at the basic rate and no additional tax on maturity. Higher tax payers may face a 'top slice' on any gain made on the bond.

Guarantee Promise to answer for the debt or default of another person. It is unenforceable unless evidenced in writing. The party giving the guarantee is the guarantor or surety (an insurer), the person receiving is the guarantee or creditor (e.g. the employer) and the person whose debt or performance, etc., is guaranteed is the principal (e.g. the employee). A fidelity guarantee policy (qv) may be either insurance by way of indemnity only, or a combination of both indemnity and guarantee in which case the law of insurance applies as between the insurer and the insured (the employer), but guarantee law applies between the insurer and the principal (the employee). The policy is one of 'insurance only' if effected without the constructive knowledge and consent of the principal. *See* INSURANCE GUARANTEE; PURE GUARANTEE.

Guarantee endorsement Insurance policy endorsement covering the policyholder's interest in mortgaged property providing that, if the insurer becomes insolvent, the reinsurer will pay any claim due directly to the mortgagee and/or policyholder. The endorsement is also called the mortgagee endorsement and conceptually is similar to the cut-through clause (qv).

Guaranteed annuity option The right to use the proceeds of a pension plan or insurance policy to purchase an annuity at a minimum rate guaranteed in the contract. Insurers are exposed to the risk of falling interest rates and may use derivative contracts (qv) to protect themselves against potential losses. *See also* OPEN MARKET OPTION.

Guaranteed asset protection (GAP) Pays the difference between the amount outstanding on a loan and the amount paid by an insurer if the asset, e.g. a car, is written off or stolen. It prevents the former asset owner being left with a debt. Cover is available on cars, caravans, motor cycles and light commercial vehicles and non-vehicular assets. *See* VEHICLE REPLACEMENT INSURANCE.

Guaranteed bonds *See* GROWTH BONDS; INCOME BONDS.

Guaranteed insurability A life insurance term describing the insurer's offer to provide new policies without further evidence of health. The offer is usually confined to existing policyholders.

Guaranteed Minimum Pension (GMP) Minimum pension that a defined benefit scheme (qv) must provide as a condition of *contracting out* (qv) for pre-6 April 1997 service. GMP does not apply to *money purchase contracted out schemes* (qv) as the granting of *protected rights* (qv) is the relevant contracting out provision. Where all service is post-5 April 1997 the members' benefits are protected by *limited price indexation (LPI)* (qv). Where service is pre- and post-5 April 1997, benefits are affected by GMP and LPI respectively.

Guaranteed pension The minimum pension a particular insurance policy will pay.

Guaranteed period Mininimum period for which the payment of a pension or annuity (qv) is guaranteed regardless of the annuitant's earlier death. If premature death occurs the insurer may be willing to pay the net present value of the annuity payments as a lump sum.

Guaranteed surrender value The minimum *surrender value* (qv) that an insurer will pay in the event of a life policy being surrendered. High guarantees may increase the incidence of early cancellation of savings policies, such as endowments, meaning that insurers may have to invest in readily realisable assets such as fixed interest securities.

Guest In the context of certain hotels, e.g. inns (qv), it is someone who books sleeping accommodation. The innkeeper becomes strictly liable for loss or damage to the property of a guest subject to the limitations introduced by the Hotel Proprietors Act 1956 (qv).

Guests' effects Property and effects belonging to, or the responsibility to guests, i.e. persons staying overnight at hotels and similar establishments. The proprietor of the establishment can insure the effects under a material damage policy or his legal liability for loss or damage.

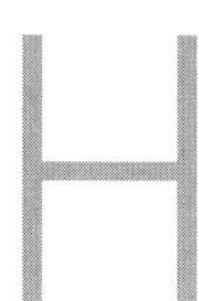

Hague Convention 1970 Convention ruling that hijacking occurs when a person on board an aircraft has unlawfully committed, or is about to commit, by force or threat, an act of interference, seizure or other wrongful exercise of control of an aircraft in flight. The Convention required every ratifying state to introduce domestic legislation to acquire jurisdiction over the offence. The state that apprehends the offender may either extradite him or her or refer the case to its own prosecuting authority. *See* HIJACKING ACT 1971.

Hague Protocol Updated the Warsaw Convention (qv) in 1955 by: extending protection to servants and agents sued by passengers dissatisfied with the Convention limits; removing some of the obstacles to claims in regard to matters such as details on tickets; removing the defence of pilot error and negligent navigation. The limit of liability to passengers doubled to 250,000 gold francs. The Protocol was introduced into the UK by the Carriage by Air Act 1961 (qv).

Hague–Visby Rules Drawn up following Brussels Protocol 1968 to replace the Hague Rules, 1924. They are appended as a Schedule to the Carriage of Goods by Sea Act 1971 (qv). The rules have been adopted by several countries to establish a uniform code of carriage of goods by sea shipped under bills of lading (qv).

Hail insurance Insurance of property against damage caused by hailstorms. It is written on buildings, their contents, and growing crops.

Hamburg Rules UN proposal in 1978 to overhaul the Hague Rules. The proposal makes the sea carrier liable for all damage to cargo regardless of cause and without limitation. The rules, opposed by the US and the UK, will come into effect when approved by 20 countries.

Hancock annuity Annuity purchased by an employer for a former employee. If the employer's clear intention was to provide an irrevocable pension for an already retired employee, when the purchase price is paid, the amount will attract tax relief (*Hancock* v. *General Reversionary & Investment Co. Ltd* (1918)).

Hangarkeepers' liability insurance *See* AIRPORT OWNERS' AND OPERATORS' LIABILITY INSURANCE.

Hard market Market in which the supply of (re)insurance is restricted in relation to the demand. Premiums increase and terms harden as (re) insurers try to become profitable.

Haulier's liability policy Covers liability for loss/damage to customers' goods; it does not cover the goods. Policies are rated on annual haulage charges. The rate varies according to the conditions of carriage and so a split is made between Road Haulage Association Conditions of Carriage (qv), CMR (qv) and estimated *unwitting* CMR (qv). Insurers require vehicles to be alarmed and usually impose security warranties that apply when the vehicles are unattended and garaged or parked overnight. Carriage of 'target goods' may attract a 'two driver' warranty. *See* GOODS IN TRANSIT.

Hazard Condition that creates or increases the probability or extent of a loss from physical sources, such as unsafe working conditions or asbestos in buildings, and moral features, such as poor attitudes. *See* MORAL HAZARD; PHYSICAL HAZARD; RISK 1.

Hazardous pursuits Certain hazardous sports and activities are excluded from personal accident insurances (qv), as they are high-risk pursuits not undertaken by all policyholders. Those who run the excluded risks can usually 'buy them back'. The 'pursuits' include: aviation (other than as a passenger on normal flights); hunting and polo; football; motorcycling; mountaineering involving the use of ropes; winter sports and others.

Hazardous waste Waste containing any substance that may create danger to: (a) the life or health of people or animals when released into the environment; or (b) to the safety of humans or equipment in disposal plants if incorrectly handled. Hazardous waste may be toxic (most pesticides, lead salts, arsenic compounds, cadmium compounds, cattle dip); flammable (e.g. hydrocarbons); corrosive (e.g. acids, alkalines); oxidising (e.g. nitrates, chromatic). Insureds knowingly involved with hazardous waste must disclose it as a material fact (qv).

Heading The insurer's name and address at the top of the policy form.

Headroom check Check to ascertain that a member's free standing additional voluntary contributions (FSAVC) (qv) do not exceed the IR's maximum of 15 per cent of pensionable earnings (qv) for an occupational scheme. The check applies to members with contributions of more than £2,400 gross per annum (January 2003 figure). The earnings cap (qv) applies to the headroom check if it applies to the main benefits.

Health and Safety at Work, etc., Act 1974 Legal framework to promote high standards of health and safety at work. It sets out general duties employers have towards employees, customers and the general public. It also sets out the duties that employees have towards themselves and their colleagues. The duties are based on the ideal of 'so far as is reasonably practicable' (qv) meaning the time, cost and difficulty to avoid or reduce a risk have to be balanced against the degree of risk itself. Persons with five or more employees must have a written safety policy. The law is enforced by HSE (qv) inspectors or environmental health officers. Where problems exist they may issue improvement notices (qv) or prohibition notices (qv). Criminal prosecutions can be against companies and individuals. *See* HEALTH AND SAFETY COMMISSION; HEALTH AND SAFETY EXECUTIVE.

Health and Safety Commission The HSC and the Health and Safety Executive (qv) administer the Health and Safety at Work, etc., Act 1974 (qv) and are a focus of initiative for all matters relating to health and safety at work. HSC consists of representatives of both sides of industry and the local authorities. It is responsible for developing policies in the health and safety field, and for making proposals to the appropriate minister. When HSC takes action it can: (a) issue guidance on specific industries or processes; (b) publish an Approved Code of Practice (qv); (c) propose statutory regulations or changes in existing regulations.

Health and Safety (Display Screen Equipment) Regulations 1992 Apply to all workstations using display screen equipment (VDUs) and habitual users of such equipment. The employer must analyse each workstation to assess the risks to health. There are minimum requirements for each workstation based on the equipment, the environment and the interface between users and equipment. The Regulations call for the planning of regular breaks, eye tests at the request of employees, corrective appliances, training and information on health and safety. A breach is criminal and also supports civil actions.

Health and Safety Executive (HSE) A separate statutory body appointed by the Health and Safety Commission (qv) that works in accordance with the advice and guidance given by the Commission. The Executive also enforces legal requirements and provides an advisory service to both sides of industry. The major inspectorates in the health and safety field are within the Executive.

Health and Safety (First Aid) Regulations 1981 Cover the requirements for first aid provision in the workplace.

Heating Degree Day (HDDs) A unit of temperature in a weather derivative (qv) measuring how low the average daily temperature is relative to a reference temperature, usually 18°C or 65°F. A baseline of 18°C minus an average temperature of 13°C gives 5 HDDs signifying how much heating is required that day by a weather-affected trader, e.g. pavement café. The payout is a specified notional amount, i.e. the tick, multiplied by the difference between the HDD level specified in the contract (the strike) and the cumulative HDDs for the period. HDDs are used as a hedge against 'cooler' summers by leisure companies, beverage suppliers, etc. Compare with cooling degree days (qv). *See* COOLING SEASON; HEATING SEASON.

Heating processes Process involving the application of heat such as drying, baking and cooking. The term is significant in fire insurance as damage to any property undergoing a heating process is an excluded form of loss (qv). It is not an excluded risk, as any fire damage that flows from the damage to the heated property will be covered by the policy.

Heating season/winter season Weather risk term meaning November to March. Weather derivatives (qv) may run for just one season or a full year. *See* COOLING SEASON.

Heave Upward movement of land that can result from the expansion of the clay sub-soil after the removal of trees or other vegetation or from the natural movement of earth and rock. Heave is usually insured when *subsidence* is also covered.

Hedge A conservative strategy used to limit financial loss by effecting a transaction that offsets the underlying position. A hedge correlates with the risk so a profit made on a futures (qv) or option contract (qv) mitigates the loss on an investment or activity. *See* WEATHER DERIVATIVES.

Height clause Restrictive endorsement (qv) in liability insurance operating as an exclusion or a warranty to regulate the height at which work may be undertaken. For example, a public liability policy may exclude work at heights in excess of 40 feet. Compulsory employers' liability legislation does not prohibit the use of restrictive trade endorsements. As an alternative the policy may exclude work on particular types of buildings such as blast furnaces (qv).

Held covered (H/C) 1. Cover granted by marine insurers under the 'held covered' clause to protect the insured in circumstances to which the policy does not otherwise apply such as when the vessel navigates in waters not permitted under the Institute Warranties (qv). Cover is conditional upon the insured giving the insurer prompt notice and paying any reasonable additional premium. 2. Insurers may 'hold covered' pending completion of the formal arrangements.

High risk property A term in household contents policies, typically defined as: 'jewellery, precious stones or articles made of gold, silver or other precious metals, clocks, watches, photographic equipment (not for commercial use), binoculars, telescopes and the like, musical instruments, antiques, curios and works of art, stamps and coin collections'. They are high value/small bulk items attractive to thieves. The purpose of the definition is to assign to such property a separate sum insured, e.g. £5,000, as a sublimit of the overall contents figure and a single article limit, e.g. £1,500.

Highly protected risk (HPR) Risks of the highest quality in terms of physical hazard. Loss prevention measures may include automatic sprinkler systems, haylon systems, water hydrants and fire and smoke alarms addressing both probability and severity of loss. HPR risks benefit from lower premiums.

Highway authorities Highways Act 1959 transferred the duty to repair highways to the Secretary of State for the Environment or the appropriate local authority according to the road classification. Formerly, a local authority was not liable for injuries caused to highway users by its own non-feasance (e.g. non-repair of the surface) but this rule was abolished by the Highways (Miscellaneous Provisions) Act 1961). Previously there had been liability for misfeasance only.

Hijacking Forcing a pilot to fly aircraft to an unscheduled destination. The normal aircraft 'all risks' policy excludes hijacking. Politically motivated hijacking and sabotage can be insured by a separate war risks policy. Hijacking of lorries has been a concern for goods-in-transit insurers but the risk is not excluded. 'Carjacking' is the same thing but applies when cars are forcibly taken from their drivers.

Hire purchase clause Motor insurance clause protecting the interest of any hire purchase company that has financed the purchase of the insured's vehicle. The clause may appear in other property policies.

Hit and run drivers *See* UNTRACED DRIVERS.

Hold Harmless Agreement A contractual arrangement whereby one party assumes the liability of another party. The effect is to transfer the potential financial loss. A tenant may hold his landlord 'harmless' against claims by injured third parties. The term is synonymous with 'indemnity agreement' but some purists make a distinction. They regard 'hold harmless' as paying 'on behalf' of the indemnitee while 'indemnity' means reimbursing him *after* he has first paid the loss himself. It is customary for public and employers' liability policies to provide a *principal's clause* under which, subject to policy terms, any indemnity granted by an insured to his principal, is covered by insurance.

Holistic risk management A rigorous, coordinated approach to risk management within an organisation. The aim is to identify, prioritise, quantify, mitigate and finance risk from all sources that threaten the achievement of both strategic and financial objectives. The financial and 'insurance' risks are integrated in a single programme. Alternative terms *enterprise risk management* and *financial risk management* could be construed more narrowly.

Home business Business underwritten in the UK for UK residents.

Home country control Principle of EC insurance regulation under which an insurance company that conducts business in several Member States is subject only to the licensing and supervision of its home country. *See* SINGLE EUROPEAN LICENCE.

Home emergency cover Covers emergencies involving the roof, drains, plumbing, heating, electrics, vermin etc. Features 24 hour call out and up to £250 for call out charges, parts, materials and VAT. Separate benefit for overnight accommodation if needed.

Home foreign business General insurance business underwritten in the UK relating to risks situated outside the UK. Marine, aviation and transport business and treaty reinsurance is normally excluded from this definition. See also *services business* (qv) and *non-admitted insurer* (qv).

Home income plans Equity release schemes such as *lifetime mortgages* whereby an elderly person mortgages his or her house to an insurance company or other institution to fund an annuity (joint life and survivor annuity (qv) for couples). Mortgage interest is met from the annuity instalments (or deferred until death) leaving an income for the homeowner(s). The loan, up to 80% of the value, and any rolled-up interest is repaid on death but the estate benefits from any capital appreciation. Compare with *home reversion plan* (qv).

Home responsibilities protection (HRP) Entitlement to the basic state pension (qv) for persons unable to accept regular employment because they are caring for children or a sick or disabled person at home.

Home reversion plan Like home income plans (qv), but the house is sold outright to the insurance company in return for an immediate annuity and a life tenancy. The sale price is below market value and the insurance company or institution purchasing the property benefits from any increases in property value. After death nothing remains for any dependants.

Home service assurance *See* INDUSTRIAL LIFE ASSURANCE.

Homogenisation The structuring of an insurance portfolio to make the exposure within it more similar, e.g. through the use of surplus treaty reinsurance (qv).

Honour policies *See* POLICY PROOF OF INTEREST (PPI).

Hospital Defined in health insurances and hospital cash plans as 'a privately owned or National Health Service hospital with facilities for medical and surgical treatment registered in the UK with a local authority in accordance with the Public Health Acts'. Some types of establishment are not included in this definition: residential nursing homes, convalescent homes, hospices, health hydros, nature cure clinics and similar establishments or private beds registered as nursing homes.

Hospital cash plan Low cost alternative to private medical insurance (qv) providing fixed cash benefits for various circumstances. For example, *hospital day care* is selectable in the range £12 to £48 per day up to 10 days in a year; *hospital in-patient treatment* ranges from £18 to £72 per day up to 91 days per year or longer in some cases. Other sections provide benefits for dental treatment, optical requirements, parental stay, acupuncture, stress counselling, etc. Exclusions: pre-existing medical conditions (qv); war; intentional self-injury; alcohol or drug abuse; pregnancy or childbirth; mental diseases, disorders or breakdown; nuclear radiation; cosmetic surgery; treatment for infertility or pregnancy termination; AIDS; confinement for domestic reasons.

Hospital payments Payment of hospital treatment fees, for in-patient or outpatient treatment up to specified amounts, by an insurer who has made a third party payment to a road accident victim. The insurer's obligation arises from the Road Traffic Act 1988, s.157, and is regardless of any admission of liability. Vehicle owners who have made deposits against third party risks (qv) or obtained securities against third party risks (qv) also have to make these payments.

'Hostilities' Does not imply war but means acts or hostility or operations of hostility. They must be carried out by persons acting as agents of an enemy government or of an organised rebellion and not by individuals acting on their own initiative.

Hot explosion The sudden release of energy from an extremely rapid combustion of chemicals, gas or a cloud of dust.

Hot work permits Permits are incorporated into safe systems of work to minimise the fire risk. Work activities for which insurers are likely to require a hot work permit include: (a) work in hazardous environments; (b) work in confined spaces; (c) work near combustible materials, liquids and gases; (d) work on drums and tanks. The permit imposes high standards of fire protection. *See* BURNING WARRANTY.

Hotel Proprietors Act 1956 An Act which defines an inn (qv), restricts strict common law liability for the property of a guest (qv), sets limits of liability at £50 any one article and £100 any one guest, and provides that there will be no strict liability for vehicles and their contents, or horses or other animals and their equipment or harness. The innkeeper loses the benefit of the limits of £50 and £100 if he fails to display the notice in the Schedule to the Act in a conspicuous place. Displaying the notice is not an admission that the establishment is an inn. The financial limits do not apply to property that has been deposited, or offered for deposit, for safe custody.

Hours clause A catastrophe excess of loss clause that treats multiple losses originating from the same cause (e.g. a hurricane), and occurring during within a specified time (typically 72 consecutive hours), as a single loss occurrence. If treated as individual losses the probability is that most would fall below the level of the deductible. The reinsured is allowed to choose the date/time for the commencement of any consecutive hours period and allowed to divide the catastrophe into two or more loss occurrences.

House of Lords Highest court in the UK. It is the Supreme Court of Appeal from the Court of Appeal in England and the Superior Courts of Scotland and Northern Ireland. Appeals are heard by the Appellate Committee, which usually consists of five, or three, Law Lords. They give written judgments. Since its Practice Statement in 1966 it is not bound by its previous decisions, but they do bind the lower courts.

House purchase schemes Life insurance is used in connection with house purchase but endowment mortgages are no longer popular. The homeowner bought a policy (sum insured equal to mortgage debt) to run parallel with the mortgage, paying interest and premiums until, on death or maturity, the policy proceeds repaid the loan. The 'low cost endowment' used an endowment with profit policy with a sum insured below the mortgage amount in the expectation that bonuses would accrue sufficiently to produce a full repayment. Any shortfall due to premature death was covered under a decreasing term policy. The underperformance of many endowments are leaving housebuyers with a debt at the end of the term, leading to accusations of mis-selling.

House Rebuilding Cost Index Recognised index of changes in the cost of rebuilding houses produced by Building Cost & Information Service Ltd of the Royal Institute of Chartered Surveyors. It is used by insurers of buildings under household insurances as the basis of automatic increases in the sum insured on renewal where the policy concerned is subject to indexation (qv).

Household The term, according to the decision in *Oldfield* v. *Scott and Jackson (third party) (Oldham County Court, 24 July 2002)*, refers to persons with whom the policyholder normally resides at home. Miss Oldfield's injury was caused by her holiday companion, Scott, who arranged travel insurance that excluded claims by members of the insured's household. Oldfield did not reside with him and was not therefore a member of his household. The insurer could not benefit from the exclusion. The term is defined in some policies.

Household buildings cover Most insurers allocate fixed or maximum sums insured that are usually index-linked. Cover may be on an accidental basis in respect of buildings, outbuildings, etc. Additional coverage areas include: alternative accommodation following insured damage; trace and access faults; lock replacement; property owners' liability; emergency repairs. There will invariably be an *unoccupancy clause* (qv).

Household contents cover Contents are defined and can be insured 'new for old' (qv) or on an indemnity basis (qv) against named perils or against 'accidental damage' basis. Sums insured are fixed at the outset but index-linked. There is limited cover for contents in the open and theft from outbuildings. Additional coverage areas include: alternative accommodation; loss of water; freezer contents; temporary removal; business equipment; personal liability; occupiers' liability; employers' liability for domestic employees. The policy contains an *unoccupancy clause* (qv). High risk property (qv) is subject to an inner limit sum insured and a single article limit.

Household insurances Private dwellings insurance on buildings and contents. Policies are either 'comprehensive', i.e. covering a range of named perils, or on the wider accidental damage basis. 'New for old' (qv) cover is available in connection with contents. *See* HOUSEHOLD BUILDINGS COVER; HOUSEHOLD CONTENTS COVER; HIGH RISK PROPERTY.

Household removal insurance Covers the contents of a house during the house removal process. Household contents policies apply only to property 'temporarily removed'; also they do not apply to furniture removed to a depository. Removal is usually 'all risks' cover and may be subject to a condition that the removal or the packing is carried out by professional removers. Cover applies for up to seven days but may be restricted to 48 or 72 hours.

Housekeeping Fire underwriters' and surveyors' term for the general management, tidiness and cleanliness aspects of a risk.

Hovercraft insurance Amphibious vehicles insurable against accidental, fire and theft. Cover operates during road transit in trailer or on low loader. Third party and passenger liability applies. Special terms apply for racing and/or business use. The Hovercraft (Civil Liability) Order 1986 amends earlier legislation in matters relating to civil liability for injury to passengers and loss/damage to baggage.

Hull/hull insurance Structural framework of a vessel, aircraft, hovercraft or boat, or anything that floats or moves. Permanently moored floating devices (except offshore structures for oil production) such as floating lighthouses, buoys and markers are not normally insured in the marine hull market. 'Hull' originally meant insurance on the ship and its masts but not the machinery, ship's stores, nets, ropes, equipment and bunkers. The policy now covers *hull and machinery* including *disbursements* (qv) and a *running down clause* (qv). Risk factors in marine insurance include: year of construction; type (tanker, tug, etc); tonnage; construction; flag; trade; trading limits (coastal, ocean going); propulsion; socio-economic environment. Ships are normally insured for yearly periods under the Institute Time Clauses (qv) or the International Hull Clauses (qv).

Hull syndicate A marine insurance syndicate that specialises in hull insurance to the exclusion of other forms of insurance.

Hundred per cent treaty basis Method to reduce the work and expense in preparing reinsurance treaty accounts. It obviates the preparation of separate accounts each showing the reinsurer's individual proportion of premiums and losses. Instead a statement shows the hundred per cent treaty amounts of every item on the account with a copy submitted to each reinsurer with only its proportion of the final balance shown thereon. *See* CLEAN CUT BASIS (qv).

Hurricane A violent windstorm covering a large area. It usually originates at sea, with winds circulating at tremendous velocity around a 'centre' that in itself moves fairly slowly. In view of its range in time and space, hurricanes are brought within the hours clause (qv) in catastrophe excess of loss treaties.

Hybrid scheme 1. Occupational pension scheme in which the ultimate benefit depends which, of two combined elements performs better, a final salary scheme (qv) or a money purchase scheme (qv). 2. An occupational scheme that offers money purchase benefits to some members and final salary benefits to others.

Hybrid small self-administered scheme Self-administered pension scheme with insurance policies among its assets.

Hybrid solution Integrated risk cover (qv) triggered by reference to insurance loss experience and/or financial losses.

IATA Inter-Carrier Agreements on Passenger Liability Following the 1995 Kuala Lumpur conference the IATA Inter-Carrier Agreement (IIA) waived limits on liability for injury to passengers. Subsequently, the IATA Implementing Agreement (MIA) waived the defence in Article 20 (all necessary measures to avoid the damage had been taken, etc.) of the Warsaw Convention (qv) up to 100,000 SDRs but the original Article 22 limits should remain in respect of public liability insurance or similar bodies. All UK carriers are required through their air transport licences to increase their limits to 100,000 SDRs. *See* INTERNATIONAL AIR TRANSPORT ASSOCIATION and EU REGULATION 2027/97.

IBNeR *See* INCURRED BUT NOT ENOUGH REPORTED.

IBNR *See* INCURRED BUT NOT REPORTED.

Identification clause Clause stating that the policy and schedule will be read together and that any word or expression to which a specific meaning has been attached shall have the same meaning wherever it appears.

Ill-health early retirement Occurs when a pension scheme member in poor health retires early. The pension may be higher than the amount that would have been achieved by an early retirement for other reasons.

Illustration A life, pensions or investment estimate given in respect of the returns a person might get on their contributions or investment. It usually shows the expected outcome for different levels of growth. The actual returns may be higher or lower than the estimates provided. The illustration is an 'invitation to treat' not an offer.

IMB Piracy Reporting Centre International Marine Bureau's centre started in 1992 following the growth in piracy on the oceans. It maintains a round the clock daily watch and, working with law enforcement, reports suspicious shipping movements, piracy and armed robbery at sea anywhere in the world. It publishes information on the Internet that puts ships' masters on the alert. Weekly piracy report and other details can be viewed on *www.iccwbo.org/ccs/menu_imb_piracy.asp*. *See* PIRACY.

Immediate annuity An annuity that commences payment to the annuitant (qv) at the end of the first prescribed payment period after the payment of the purchase price.

Immediate care annuity Purchased life annuities to fund the care of the elderly entering residential or nursing homes at a time of need. The annuity takes the form of tax-free payments to the care provider as it is a part of their taxable income. Immediate care annuities are 'designated investments' and therefore subject to the FSA's Conduct of Business Rules (qv). The annuities may be linked to the Retail Price Index.

Immediate cause This means the proximate cause (qv), i.e. the nearest cause in efficiency and not the nearest in time. Bacon summarised this by saying, 'it were infinite for the law to consider the cause of causes, and their impulsions one of another, therefore, it contenteth itself with the immediate cause, and judgeth of acts by that, without looking to any further degree'.

Immediately Has been held to mean 'with all reasonable speed considering the circumstances of the case' (*Re Coleman's Depositories Ltd and Life and Health Assurance Association* (1907). In *Farrell* v. *Federated Employers Insurance Association Ltd* (1970) a writ served on 7 January 1966 was not given to the insurer until 3 March 1966. Lord Denning MR said that 'with all reasonable speed would mean by the end of January at the latest'. Insurers often require notification of a claim *immediately* and, under liability policies, require the insured to forward every writ, notice, letter or other document served on him *immediately* on receipt.

Immobiliser clause Goods in transit (qv) clause requiring vehicles to be fitted with an approved anti-theft device that is put into effective operation when the vehicle is left unattended. The particular wording of the clause is important. *See* ALARM SYSTEM IN OPERATION.

Impact damage agreement Cost-saving agreement that operates when a motor vehicle collides with immobile property (e.g. buildings and fences) that may be insured against impact damage. The terms of the agreement vary between insurers but normally the motor insurer pays 75 per cent of the damage to immobile property regardless of actual liability.

Impact damage cover 1. Engineering insurance term insuring 'damage by physical impact to surrounding plant or property belonging to the insured or held in trust by the insured or on commission or for which the insured is responsible resulting from fragmentation of any part of any insured item of plant'. The cover can be applied to: boilers and pressure plant; cranes and other lifting machines; lifts and hoists; and electrical and mechanical plant. 2. An additional peril (qv) included in a 'named peril' household policy. It covers impact damage caused by vehicles or aircraft or anything dropped therefrom. Damage caused by falling trees and branches is also covered. 3. Impact cover is also added to named perils commercial property insurance and covers the risk of third party (and sometimes own) vehicles and animal damage to the insured property.

Impaired capital A US term describing the financial position of an insurer whose net current assets are less than its fully paid-up shares.

Impaired life annuity An enhanced annuity (qv) granted to a person with a shortened life expectancy. Serious health conditions, e.g. cancer, heart disease, as well as some lifestyle habits may bring annuitants into this category.

Impaired lives Persons with health conditions that limit their life expectancy. They cannot secure life insurance on normal terms but get better annuity rates.

Implied conditions/terms Contractual terms that by law are tacitly binding and do not have to appear in the contract. Conditions can be implied by statute (e.g. Sale of Goods Act 1979 (qv)). The following conditions are implied in insurance contracts: (a) that the subject matter of insurance is in existence at the date of effecting the policy; (b) that the insured has an insurable interest; (c) that the parties observe utmost good faith towards each other at all material times and in all material particulars; and (d) that the subject matter of insurance is so described as to clearly identify it and define the risk undertaken by the insurers.

Implied warranty A warranty (qv) which by law is tacitly understood to be binding and does not have to appear in the policy. The Marine Insurance Act 1906 (ss.39, 41) implies: (a) that under a voyage policy (qv) the vessel will be seaworthy at the commencement of the voyage; and (b) the legality of the insured adventure. In a voyage policy on goods or other moveables there is a further implied warranty at the commencement of the voyage that the ship is reasonably fit to carry the goods, etc., to the intended destination (s.40).

Importation of average A clause in a policy, not subject to average (qv), whereby average can be imported if the policy is liable for a loss also covered by another policy that is subject to average. The policies then contribute on an equal footing.

Improvement notice Issued by HSE inspectors ordering that Health and Safety at Work, etc., Act 1974 (qv) contraventions be remedied within a specified time. The notice is served on the person deemed to be contravening the legal provision, or on any person on whom responsibilities are placed, e.g. an employer, an employed person or a supplier. The person may be prosecuted instead of, or in addition to, being served with a notice. Insurers usually provide cover in respect of prosecution defence costs.

Imputed knowledge Knowledge of one party that is deemed to be possessed by another because of their relationship. An insured may wish to impute knowledge to the insurer on the grounds that their agent actually possesses that knowledge. In insurance, the position is complicated because for some purposes the intermediary acts as agent of the insurer while for others (e.g. carrying out instructions to effect the insurance) he is agent of the insured. The party relying upon the doctrine of imputed knowledge must prove the existence of an agency in relation to the point at issue.

Inadequate design *See* FAULTY DESIGN.

'In an efficient condition' Motor insurance policyholders must take 'all reasonable steps to maintain in efficient condition the vehicle'. The insured will be excused if, having taken reasonable steps, a defect causes an accident. The negligence of a garage employee does not breach the condition unless there was negligence by the insured in delegating the work to an incompetent (*Liverpool Corporation* v. *T. & H.R. Roberts* (1964)). What is 'reasonable' depends on the facts. *See* UNROADWORTHY.

In and out policy/all in policy Fidelity policy for banks and other financial institutions, e.g. stockbrokers dealing in securities. The insurance applies to all or some of the following instruments: bonds, debentures, stocks, scrip, shares, transfers, certificates, coupons, warrants, cash, cheques, bank notes, bills of exchange, promissory notes, title deeds or other valuable documents. Cover is in respect of loss arising from dishonesty by employees, customers or others.

'In connection with' This phrase was said to mean 'connected with, subserving and being ancillary to' (*Hatrick & Co.* v. *R* (1923)). The test was applied in *Kearney* v. *General Accident* (1968) when an employee fell while painting roof trusses of a building. The employers' liability policy excluded 'any work *in connection with* roofs other than of private dwellings and/or shops . . . of not more than three floors'. The judge considered that the painting of the trusses and the underside of the outer cover was 'connected with, subserving or ancillary to' work in connection with the roof.

In force A policy is in force from the time of inception until the time of expiry unless previously cancelled.

In rem Legal right or action against 'the thing' as opposed to the person (in personam). It includes a maritime lien that a salvor may have against the saved property (vessel or cargo). Admiralty law allows a salvor to arrest or seize property to enforce his legal right rather than arresting or seizing the owner, whose identity is often not known. The seized property is security until the claim is settled or until acceptable security is substituted. The salvor may relinquish his right to hold property and take up an action *in personam* for the value of the salvage award.

'In respect of any one accident' *See* ANY ONE ACCIDENT.

'In transit' The goods in transit insurer covers goods while in transit and temporarily housed during the course of transit. Transit begins when the goods start to move, i.e. when they are loaded. The insurer was liable when goods were stolen from a loaded vehicle on his premises even though the journey had not commenced. The argument that the goods were not *in transit* failed (*Sadler Bros. Co.* v. *Meredith* (1963). In *Crows Transport* v. *Phoenix* (1965) it was held that, unless the policy otherwise provides, transit commences the moment the carrier accepts the goods. Transit does not end when the vehicle reaches its destination. In *Tomlinson* v. *Hepburn* (1961) it was held that transit only came to an end when the unloading was completed.

'Inability to attend to business of any kind' *See* DISABILITY 2.

Incapacity pension A pension payable, subject to scheme rules, to members whose illness prevents them from working normally. The pension helps to offset any fall in income.

Inception date The date on which the insurance becomes operative.

Inchmaree Clause Clause 2.2 of the *Perils Clause* of the International Hull Clauses (1/11/02) named after a ship that suffered uninsured damage (1887) following a crewman's negligence. The clause supplements the *perils of the sea clause* (Clause 2.1) by adding cover for loss or damage to the vessel caused by the so-called *Inchmaree perils*: bursting of boilers, latent defects in hull machinery, cargo handling accidents, repairer's negligence, crew negligence and barratry of master, officers and crew.

Inchmaree perils *See* INCHMAREE CLAUSE.

Incidental business Business written by a Lloyd's syndicate formed to write one class of business but which falls into another class. This is permissible within specified limits.

Incidental non-marine Non-marine insurance underwritten by a marine insurer that is supplementary or incidental to his marine business.

Income and Corporation Taxes Act 1988 Governs the approval and tax treatment of both personal and occupational pension schemes. Section 590 deals with mandatory approval for occupational pension schemes but most schemes are approved as *exempt approved schemes* (qv) that give greater flexibility in terms of the benefits.

Income benefit 1. An amount paid annually (or more frequently) under a family income benefit policy (qv) from the time of death to the end of the agreed term. 2. An amount paid monthly (or weekly) under a policy covering disablement from working due to accidental injury or sickness. *See* SICKNESS BENEFITS.

Income bonds/distribution bonds Single premium life policy paying a guaranteed income for a fixed term, three to five years. At maturity most schemes return the original capital but there are more complex schemes where the return of capital depends on the performance of the underlying assets. A basic rate tax payer is allowed a tax-free income of 5 per cent per annum.

Income drawdown/withdrawal Withdrawal of pension scheme benefits before using balance of fund to purchase a compulsory annuity. Members of small-administrated pension schemes, personal pension schemes and occupational schemes with money purchase benefits (qv) or additional voluntary contributions can delay the purchase of a pension until age 75 while withdrawing regular sums from their pension fund subject to certain maximum and minimum amounts. The individual can still take a tax-free lump at retirement leaving the balance for drawdown and the retirement annuity purchase by age 75.

Income protection/permanent health insurance *A permanent contract* (qv) that, after a *waiting period* (qv), pays an income for so long as the policyholder is unable to work due to accident or illness up to a given age, usually retirement. The maximum benefit is circa 60 per cent of pre-disability income and may be level or index-linked. A proportionate benefit is paid to persons returning to work but forced to take lower paid jobs. Income protection cover is available for individuals and groups. Benefits can be immediate or deferred until a certain time has passed. *See* DEFERRED PERIOD.

Incontestable clause/indisputable clause Policy provision often included in life policies whereby the insurer agrees not to challenge the validity of a policy because of alleged misstatement by the insured after the policy has been in force for a stipulated period, usually two or three years.

Incorporate Name Limited liability company operating as an underwriting member at Lloyd's.

Incoterms (International Chamber of Commerce Terms of Sale) Standardised international trade contracts defining the obligations in a sale. These terms deal with expenditure, place (delivery) and time (when goods and transit risks pass from seller to buyer). *See* FOB, FOR, CIF, EXW.

Increase in cost of working An expense that is insured under a business interruption insurance (qv). It is the additional expense necessarily and reasonably incurred for the sole purpose of reducing the shortfall in turnover during the indemnity period (qv). For example, the business may have to rent alternative premises and/or pay overtime to make up for lost production. The insurer will not pay for increased costs in excess of the loss of the gross profit that the extra costs have served to avoid.

Increased value policy (I/V) Covers an excess amount over the insured value of the property, hull or cargo. The insurance stands alone for a separate agreed amount in excess of the agreed value and is written as a total loss only cover. In the case of cargo I/V covers increases in value during the currency of the underlying policy. Hull policies limit the amount of I/V cover in excess of the agreed hull value.

Increasing extra risk A life insurance term to describe an extra risk that increases with the passing of time, e.g. being overweight or chronic bronchitis.

Increasing term insurance Term insurance (qv) for individuals uncertain as to future life insurance requirements. A five-year policy may offer without further evidence of health options to: extend the policy term; increase the sum insured by 50 per cent; convert to a whole life or endowment subject to an age limit of 60.

Incurred but not enough reported (IBNeR) An expression used by insurers when referring to the inadequate *reserving* (qv) of past claims.

Incurred but not reported (IBNR) At the end of an accounting period, the insurer creates a reserve to cover the estimated cost of losses that have occurred but have not yet been reported. The 'INBR' reserve is quite significant in liability insurance as many claims have a 'long tail' (qv). The regulatory authority prescribes the form in which INBR claims must be included in the *FSA returns* (qv).

Incurred claims or losses The total of paid and outstanding claims arising in a period. The term is also used, for the purpose of claims statistics, where, for given accident (qv) or policy years (qv), the incurred claims are compared to earned premiums in order to assess the underwriting profitability for each class of business.

Incurred loss ratio Incurred losses (qv) stated as a percentage of earned premiums (qv).

Indemnification aliunde Doctrine meaning indemnity from 'another source'. It must be distinguished from subrogation (qv). If the insured receives any sum, before or after a loss, that reduces his actual loss, he must credit the insurer with that sum. For example, an employer holding salary otherwise due to a defaulting employee must deduct the relevant sum from any claim under a *commercial guarantee* (qv).

Indemnity 1. Security against financial loss. An insurance principle designed to place an insured in the same financial position after a loss that existed immediately before the loss. An 'exact financial compensation' may be denied by an inadequate sum insured (qv), indemnity limit (qv), excess (qv) or franchise (qv). The principle cannot be applied to life insurance (qv) and personal accident (qv), termed 'benefit policies' (qv), as the payments are based on specific benefits not indemnity. The leading case on indemnity is *Castellain* v. *Preston* (1883) (qv). *Subrogation* (qv) and *contribution* (qv) are corollaries of indemnity. 2. Non-insurance risk transfer, via contracts, where one party agrees to make good the loss of another by the inclusion of indemnity agreements otherwise called *hold harmless agreements* (qv). *See* PRINCIPAL'S CLAUSE; INDEMNITY AGREEMENT.

Indemnity Agreement *See* INDEMNITY 2; HOLD HARMLESS AGREEMENT.

Indemnity commission Commission advanced by a life company to an intermediary on the understanding the company can clawback the whole or part of the commission if the policy lapses within a specified period of time.

Indemnity limits Imposed by liability (re)insurers to put a ceiling on their potential liability. Public liability insurers usually limit their liability in respect of the damages and claimant's costs arising from any 'one occurrence' with no limit for the period of cover. In addition the insurer pays the insured's own costs but some liability policies are 'costs inclusive' (qv). Under products liability and professional indemnity policies it is usual to impose annual aggregate limits with no per-occurrence limit. Some policies may contain both per-occurrence and annual limits. 'Inner' or 'sub-limits' may be applied to particular forms of loss (e.g. financial loss cover (qv)).

Indemnity period/the maximum indemnity period In a business interruption insurance (qv), it is the period beginning with the occurrence of the damage and ending not later than the end of the period stated in the policy as the *maximum indemnity period*, e.g. 24 months. The period reflects the time needed to restore the business to its pre-loss trading level and is chosen by the insured.

Independent financial adviser (IFA) Adviser able to offer a full range of products from financial services companies or from a selected panel on grounds of merit. IFAs may work on their own account or for firms. Key principles they must follow include: 'know their client' (qv) by means of a fact find (qv) to form a comprehensive view of the client's needs in order to offer 'best advice' (qv). IFAs can be remunerated by commission and/or fees. He must give full details at the outset of fees and, under the FSA's (qv) *disclosure* rules (qv), full details of any commission they will receive on recommended transactions. Regulated by the FSA, they must contribute to an industry wide compensation scheme.

Independent liability method When contribution (qv) arises the insurers contribute 'rateably' to the loss. Under the independent liability method each insurer's liability is calculated as if the other policy did not exist. The insurers then, particularly in liability insurance and non-concurrent policies (qv), calculate their contribution to the loss in proportion to their individual liabilities. Example: Liability insurer A's policy limits liability to £1 million and B's limit is £0.5 million. The loss is £180,000. Independently each insurer is liable for £180,000 and each therefore contributes £90,000 (50 per cent) to the loss. Insurer B would benefit from the *maximum liability (or pro rata) method* that apportions claims in proportion to limits of indemnity or sums insured (2:1 in this case) meaning A would pay £120,000 and B £60,000.

Independent range Two (or more) policies, each covering a range of risks, are of independent range when each covers property of a specific description that is within the non-identical range of the other. The policies overlap in that they have common ground (e.g. Policy 1 insures stock in buildings A, B, and C; Policy 2 insures stock in A and B only).

Independent trustee Trustee unconnected to the pension scheme, its members or the employer. Such an appointment may be compulsory when an insolvency practitioner has taken over from an employer (PA 1995, ss.22–26).

Index A means of continually measuring the movement of a particular set of statistics over periods of time. Most unit trust fund managers measure their fund's performance against that of an appropriate 'benchmark' index with the aim of at least matching or beating its progress. Weather derivatives (qv) are based on movements in an underlying index.

Index-based products Option contracts based on an index. The value of a derivative is derived from the underlying index as in the case of weather derivatives (qv). Variations between the actual losses and those derived from the index creates the basis risk (qv).

Index linked *See* INDEXATION.

Index tracking An index tracking fund aims to follow a particular index as closely as possible, not necessarily aiming to beat it. It invests only in the companies that make up that index. Index tracking removes the need to employ fund managers and so reduces charges.

Indexation A method whereby benefits or sums insured are increased periodically by a factor derived from an index of prices or earnings. Household building sums insured are linked to a rebuilding cost index and contents cover increases annually in line with an index reflecting replacement costs. Regulations oblige exempt approved schemes (qv) to increase pension payments for post April 1997 service by at the least the appropriate percentage taken from the retail price index up to 5 per cent per annum but this cap reduces to 2.5 per cent in 2005 under what is called limited price index (LPI). LPI does not apply to AVCs and FSAVCs. *See* ESCALATION; STABILITY INDEX CLAUSE.

Indirect business 1. Business transacted with the insurer through an intermediary such as a broker or agent. 2. Business accepted by way of reinsurance.

Indisputable clause Same as INCONTESTABLE CLAUSE.

Individual arrangement (IA) Occupational pension scheme for a named employee. The scheme is insured and is normally established by an exchange of letters between the employer and employee. Where the letter does not incorporate a declaration of trust it is linked with a formal declaration of trust to ensure that the arrangement is legally enforceable. IAs are Inland Revenue approved.

Individual bonds/mini bonds Enable individual investor to pursue own objectives by way of a separate fund.

Individual Capital Adequacy Standards (ICAS) Mechanism in calculating enhanced capital requirements (ECR) based on an industry-wide assumptions to allow for differences in the risk profiles of individual firms of insurers, both life and non-life. ICAS operates through Individual Capital Guidance that is usually set above ECR and will be affected by whether firms' risk assessment processes follow all the FSA's guidance. *See* RISK-BASED CAPITAL.

Individual pension account (IPA) Personal pension scheme where the individual holds money in an individual pension account. The money is invested in a selection of investments, including shared funds such as unit trusts This makes it possible to invest in stocks and shares and spread risks. Movement in share prices can be tracked daily in the financial press in order to monitor the value of the pension fund. It is relatively simple to transfer pensions savings from one scheme to another.

Individual trust policies for partners Each partner effects life insurance on his own life in trust for his partners. A separate policy is required for each partner to ensure that each has funds with which to purchase a share of the deceased (or retiring) partner's part of the business.

Industrial accident Social security case law definition: 'an accident arising while he is doing what his contract obliges him to do, and because of the risk created by what his contract obliges him to do. The accident must therefore be one which happens while he is within what has been called the scope or ambit of his work'. An electrician injured while driving to work was held not to have had an industrial accident. An employee who has suffered an industrial injury does not have to satisfy the national insurance contributions for statutory sick pay and benefits.

Industrial all risks insurance Covers accidental loss, destruction or damage to the property, except as excluded (e.g. faulty or defective design, inherent vice, latent defects, explosion of boilers, sonic bangs, collapse and others that may be applicable in real terms to certain categories of equipment). Many of the exclusions can be bought back. The property insured is industrial and commercial plant and equipment. Cover is often arranged on a first loss basis (qv).

Industrial disease A disease or illness suffered by an employee as a result of working on an industrial process or in harmful working conditions. Benefits are payable by the state under the Social Security (Industrial Injuries) (Prescribed Diseases) Regulations 1985 as amended. The victim may also be able to sue the employer for negligence or breach of statute. Prescribed diseases include asbestosis (qv) and mesothelioma (qv); silicosis (mines and quarries); byssinosis (respiratory, cotton); tenosyniovitis (conveyor work, pottery); lead poisoning (glass, scrap metal, lead); cancer; dermatitis; occupational deafness including tinnitus.

Industrial injuries benefit A social security benefit payable tax free to employees who either (a) suffered an accidental injury arising in the course of work; or (b) contracted a prescribed disease or prescribed injury while working. It is a no fault compensation scheme running parallel with any rights the injured party may have against his employer. Benefits include the *industrial injuries disablement benefit* (qv) payable for loss of capacity through an industrial accident (qv) or prescribed disease. Payments are based on the percentage disablement caused by the injury, e.g. 40 per cent disablement attracts £46.72 per week (2003).

Industrial life assurance Low value life and savings policies issued by industrial life offices and friendly societies. Premiums were formerly collected at regular intervals, e.g. weekly/fortnightly, from the homes of the policyholders. Premiums are now generally paid by monthly bank mandate.

Inefficacy Clause *See* EFFICACY RISK.

Inevitable accident An accident that could not have been avoided by the exercise of ordinary care, caution and skill. It therefore amounts to a defence against claim of negligence or refers to a situation where negligence cannot be proved against the defendant.

Infectious disease, murder and closure extension Clause in a business interruption policy (qv) to protect the insured against interruption due to infectious and contagious disease (AIDS is not covered), discovery of vermin at the premises, closure by a competent authority due to defective drains and sanitation, murder or suicide, or food poisoning affecting persons at the premises. This extension is particularly relevant for public access risks such as hotels, etc., and will cover cancellation of bookings due to an outbreak of notifiable infectious or contagious diseases in the area.

'Inflammable' Easily set on fire. Any property which by its presence increases the risk of fire is inflammable. It has to do with the inherent nature and qualities of the goods.

Inflation rate risk The risk that significant increases in the inflation rate will have a disproportionate effect on insurers, e.g. the inflation factor built in to long-tail liability claims may outweigh the general economic level of inflation. Inflation is also of importance in health and medical insurance as the claims inflation may be higher than economic inflation.

Informa Group Created out of the 1995 merger between Lloyd's of London Press Ltd (qv) and IBC Ltd. The previous publications, Lloyd's List (qv), Lloyd's Shipping Index (qv), Lloyd's Casualty Week (qv) are now part of the Informa Group's family of products and services. The website *www.infformamaritime.com* sets out comprehensive details. *See* LLOYD'S MARINE INTELLIGENCE UNIT.

Infringement of rights insurance Insurance against legal liability for inadvertently infringing a copyright, patent or trademark.

Ingestion damage Aircraft damage caused when foreign objects (e.g. stones from runway, birds) are drawn into the airtake by the suction of the engine and rotate around in contact with the rotating compressor blades. The risk applies mainly to turbo-jet and turbo-propeller engines. Even slight damage necessitates completes stripping of the engine. The aircraft policy covers the damage subject to a sizeable excess but excludes progressive deterioration. Cover responds to sudden damage necessitating immediate repair.

Inherent vice Deterioration, damage or wastage in the product itself by natural processes without the operation of any external agency. The resultant damage or reduction in value is not fortuitous and therefore outside the scope of insurance. Many property insurances, including 'all risks' covers, exclude inherent vice to put the matter beyond doubt.

Inheritance tax (IHT) A UK tax on capital wealth or assets transferred to other persons (except a spouse) within the seven years preceding the benefactor's death. There are certain exemptions from IHT, e.g. gifts out of income; gifts to support certain relatives in need. Life insurance is used to both minimise and pay the tax. Liquid funds from a policy obviates the forced disposal of assets to fund the tax liability. The first £255,000 is in a 'nil rate' tax band (2003).

Injury-in-fact trigger A theory seeking to trigger a long-tail injury (qv) (e.g. asbestosis) only into those losses-occurring liability policies (qv) or policy periods during which there was *actual* occurrence or development of the injury. It ignores exposure (qv) to the risk of injury and the manifestation (qv) of it. No liability is attached to policies in force during which there was no progression of the injury but the theory is difficult to apply. *See* TRIPLE TRIGGER THEORY.

Injury to the environment An important interference with the environment caused by a modification of the physical, chemical or biological conditions of water, soil and/or air in so far as these are not to be considered to be damage to property or death or physical injury. The authorities seek to make the polluter pay (qv) on a strict liability basis for this and other forms of injury and damage.

Injury to working partner's clause Employers' liability policy clause that brings liability for injury to the proprietors of a partnership within the policy. If a partner is injured at work due to the negligence of an employee or another partner, a standard employers' liability policy will not operate but the clause brings such injury into the policy subject otherwise to its terms and conditions. Consequently the premium is calculated as if all partners were employees, i.e. their earnings must be included in the estimate and declarations relating to wages and salaries.

Inland marine insurance A development from marine insurance covering inland transit exposures on road, rail or inland water. It includes goods in transit, carrier's liability, property in the possession of bailees and movable equipment and property. In the US it may include fixed structures such as bridges and tunnels that are normally included in property insurance.

Inland Revenue Limits The contribution and benefit limits that must not be exceeded under approved pension schemes (qv), which receive valuable tax relief. Contributions, including AVCs (qv), cannot exceed 15 per cent of annual earnings before deductions for tax and national insurance. For members joining after May 1989 the earnings themselves are subject to the earnings cap (qv). The maximum pension benefit under approved occupational schemes, defined benefit (qv) or defined contribution (qv), is the same, i.e. two-thirds of final remuneration (qv).

Inland Revenue Savings and Pensions Share Schemes (IRSPSS) Took over responsibility for pensions work, including personal pensions, from the Pensions Schemes Office in April 2001. IRSPSS is also responsible for savings products, employee share schemes and any continuing MIRAS issues.

Inn Defined in the Hotel Proprietors Act 1956, s.1(3), as a hotel, i.e. 'an establishment held out by the proprietor as offering food, drink and, if so required, sleeping accommodation, without special contract, to any traveller presenting himself who appears able and willing to pay a reasonable sum for the services provided . . . and who is in a fit state to be received'. The words 'without special contract' are important and mean that an 'inn' is any establishment 'open to all and sundry', i.e. it does not pick and choose its guests. The proprietor assumes special legal responsibilities (*see* INNKEEPER'S LIABILITY). For legal purposes hotels are either inns or private hotels (qv).

Innkeeper The proprietor of an inn (qv).

Innkeeper's liability An *innkeeper* has a legal duty to provide food and accommodation to anyone who appears able to pay and is in a fit state to be received, provided facilities are available. The innkeeper's liability for property belonging to a guest (someone who has booked sleeping accommodation) is strict but provided the notice in the Schedule to the Hotel Proprietors Act 1956 is displayed the strict liability is limited to £50 any one article and £100 any one guest. The limits do not apply if the innkeeper has been guilty of negligence or other fault or the property was deposited for safe keeping. There is no liability if the guest caused the loss. Other customers are mere travellers and liability for their effects is governed by ordinary legal rules.

'Innocent' capacity Acceptance of insurance or reinsurance business at very favourable but inadequate rates without a proper study or understanding of the risks involved. New and inexperienced insurers have been accused of providing innocent capacity and the naive acceptance of whole portfolios of business.

Innocent misrepresentation Unintentional supply of misleading information relating to a material fact (qv) in breach of the duty of *utmost good faith* (qv). Where the insurer exercises the right of avoidance ab initio (qv), the risk does not attach and the full premium must be returned. Under industry code of practice, insurers agree not to avoid policies issued to private individuals where the innocent misrepresentation is in the nature of a technicality.

In-orbit insurance Covers the operational phase of a satellite risk.

Inquest Judicial enquiry before a jury into any matter, particularly violent or sudden deaths. Liability insurers pay for the solicitor's fee for representation at any inquest or fatal enquiry (qv) where the liability for the death may be the subject of indemnity under the policy. The insured (or his legal personal representatives) must give immediate notice once they have knowledge of an impending inquest or fatal enquiry. Proper representation of the insured is important and the insurer can also obtain copies of the coroner's depositions.

In-scheme AVCs Additional voluntary contributions (qv) by a pension scheme member to an insurance company or building society chosen by his pension scheme, or to the scheme itself.

Insolvency clause Clause, common in the US, whereby the reinsurer agrees, in the event of the cedant's insolvency, to pay its obligations to the liquidator or other specified party.

Insolvency of other reinsurers clause Treaty clause that the loss to the reinsurer shall not be increased due to the inability of the reinsured to secure a reinsurance recovery from another reinsurer.

Inspection classes Refers to the different types or classes of plant and machinery in connection with which engineering insurers provide an inspection/examination service. Broadly, this means: boiler and pressure plant; lifts, cranes and lifting machinery; and electrical and mechanical plant. *See* INSPECTION SERVICES; STATUTORY EXAMINATIONS.

Inspection of records clause Reinsurance clause allowing reinsurer to inspect the reinsured's records relating to transactions under the contract. The right of inspection extends beyond the end of the contract for so long as the reinsurer has a remaining liability.

Inspection services Engineering insurance normally includes an inspection service by engineer surveyors. There are detailed statutory requirements that call for periodic inspections of boilers and pressure vessels, lifts, cranes and other lifting plant, etc. The service usually runs in conjunction with insurance on the item concerned. The insured can opt for more than the basic statutory service. A full technical service includes advice, reports, tests and the like.

Institute Cargo Clauses 1/1/82 There are three types: (a) Institute Cargo Clauses (A) cover 'all risks' of loss or damage, subject to the specific exclusion of certain non-fortuitous losses; (b) Institute Cargo Clauses (C) covers loss or damage reasonably attributable to named major casualties (fire, explosion, stranding, sinking, etc.); (c) Institute Cargo Clauses (B) cover is as per C above but adding 'earthquake, volcanic eruption or lightning' and 'wet damage' from the sea, lake or river but also covering theft, shortage or non-delivery. All three sets cover general average sacrifice or contribution, salvage and sue and labour charges and contain the war exclusion (qv) but (A) does not exclude piracy. The clauses are no longer tied to the *memorandum* (qv).

Institute Clauses Standard sets of clauses drafted by the Technical and Underwriting Committee chaired by the International Underwriters Association of London (qv). They are used in the main forms of marine insurance and air cargo insurance written in London and beyond. The clauses often override the provisions of the Marine Insurance Act 1906 and, when added to the MAR 91 form (qv), they govern the extent of the insurer's risk. The current Institute Cargo Clauses (qv) were introduced on 1 January 1982. The most recent International Hull Clauses date from 1 November 2002 (qv).

Institute Container Clauses The Institute Container Clauses (Time) provide 'all risks' cover subject to the exclusion of named non-fortuitous losses. Loss or damage to the container's machinery is covered only when the container is a total loss or the damage is caused by a named (major) peril. Ordinary damage (scrapes and bumps) is not covered. Confiscation is excluded under the War Risks Exclusion but is insured under the Institute War and Strikes Clauses Containers – Time.

Institute Freight Clauses Apply a 3 per cent franchise to all partial loss claims, other than those for general average.

Institute of Actuaries Professional body representing actuaries in England and Wales. Formed in 1848 it received its Royal Charter of Incorporation in 1884. *See* FACULTY OF ACTUARIES.

Institute of London Underwriters Founded in 1884 the ILU has a worldwide influence, but membership is confined to companies underwriting in the London market. It is now a part of the International Underwriters Association (qv) where its work in compiling and revising the standard Institute Clauses (qv) continues.

Institute of Risk Management IRM is an educational body and members' organisation for risk management professionals. It seeks to represent an increasingly broad and diverse set of stakeholders on a worldwide basis. The IRM's key objectives are: education; qualifications; good practice; and partnership. It has combined with AIRMIC and ALARM to publish the Risk Management Standard (qv).

Institute Time Clauses A revised version of the Institute Time Clauses (Hulls) was issued on 1 November 1995. ITC hull clauses work on a *named perils* basis and each clause has its own name, e.g. Perils Clause. Cover for war and strikes for hull insurance can be obtained under the Institute War and Strikes Clauses (Hulls–Time). As the cover is intended for an annual contract, war and strikes cover can be cancelled at short notice (seven days) or even automatically. The International Hull Clauses 1/11/02 (qv) are the latest revision, but the 1995 version is still used as underwriters choose from the alternative versions case by case.

Institute warranties Standard trading limits for ships not engaged in regular services. Used in hull insurances, the warranties mainly restrict navigational areas as without them the underwriter risks granting cover unwittingly in hazardous areas worldwide. Breach of warranty is *held covered* (qv), subject to payment of an additional premium and any change of conditions imposed by the underwriter. Five warranties spell out restrictions on areas as to times of year when restrictions apply while a sixth restricts the carriage of Indian coal in terms of both time and place.

Institutional investors Institutions such as insurance companies, pension funds, unit trusts, investment trusts and banks who invest on behalf of their policyholders and private investors. They provide an indirect way for investment by individuals in a range of securities including equities.

Insurability *See* INSURABLE RISK.

Insurable interest A principle of insurance whereby a policy is not valid unless the insured person stands to suffer a financial loss if the insured event occurs (e.g. loss or damage to property or creation of a liability), or benefit from the non-occurrence of the event, i.e. the property being preserved or no liability being created. Generally, an insurable interest must exist when the policy is issued *and* at the time of loss except in the case of marine insurance, when interest is required only at the time of loss, and in life insurance when interest is required only at the inception. *See* GAMBLING ACT; POLICY PROOF OF INTEREST.

Insurable risk Risk capable of being insured. A risk is only insurable when: (a) it is measurable in financial terms; (b) an insurable interest (qv) exists; (c) it exists in large homogeneous groups (see risk combination (qv); (d) the probability of loss can calculated; (e) it is a pure risk (qv); (f) it is of a fortuitous nature; (g) it is not against public policy to insure it; (h) the premium is a reasonable premium in relation to the individual's financial risk; (i) it is not so widespread that it is beyond the scope of commercial insurance as with certain fundamental risks (qv). An uninsurable risk (qv) is one that fails to meet some or all of these elements.

Insurance Insurance is risk financing (qv), risk transfer (qv) and risk combination (qv). By combining a large number of exposure units into a group the insurer can predict the probability of loss with a reasonable degree of accuracy for the group as a whole and so spread the loss over the group. The degree of uncertainty for the group is reduced but not for an individual member. The individual transfers his risk of loss to the insurer who *finances* the risk in return for a premium. The insured substitutes the certainty of a premium for an unknown loss in regard to *insurable risks* (qv). *See* CONTRACT OF INSURANCE for the legal definition.

Insurance agent *See* AGENTS; IMPUTED KNOWLEDGE.

Insurance bonds A term often used to describe *investment bonds* (qv). They contain an insurance element and are single premium policies issued by insurance companies.

Insurance broker A full-time intermediary offering a service on the basis of professional expertise and competence. The broker offers advice and arranges the insurance normally as agent for the insured but is usually remunerated by a commission from the insurer. From January 2005, insurance brokers will be regulated by the FSA.

Insurance Business Rules FSA (qv) rules relating to the conduct of insurance business. The FSMA empowers the FSA to make rules prohibiting an authorised person (qv), who has permission to effect or carry out contracts of insurance, from carrying on a specified activity. Another rule empowers the FSA to make rules in relation to contracts entered into in the course of carrying on long-term insurance business (qv) particularly in regard to linked-policies (s.141(4)). It means that where the FSA has determined that a particular index is no longer permissible it can stop new policies being linked to that index. It can also require that existing linked policies should substitute a new index for the prohibited one.

Insurance companies Insurance suppliers incorporated under the Companies Act. This includes: 1. Proprietary companies, i.e. limited liability companies generally constituted under the Companies Act with a subscribed share capital. The shareholders have the ultimate rights to the profits, but in the case of a life insurance company provision has to be made for a share of the profits to go to 'with profits' policyholders. 2. Mutual companies. These are notionally owned by the policyholders who share in the distributable profits in proportion to the sums assured and conditions of their policies. Such companies have been common in life insurance but some have demutualised.

Insurance Companies (Legal Expenses Insurance) Regulations 1990 Provisions that state the insured person under a legal expenses policy has the right to choose his own solicitor. The regulations also deal with the conflict of interest that would arise if the legal expenses insurer acting for the claimant was also the liability insurer for the defendant sued by that claimant.

Insurance: Conduct of Business Sourcebook (ICOB) Rules applicable to an insurance intermediary (qv), including an insurer, when carrying on insurance mediation (qv) for a customer in relation to a non-investment insurance contract or entering into a distance non-investment mediation contract with a retail customer. The rules also apply to insurers when acting as product providers and managing agents at Lloyd's in relation to non-investment insurance contracts. ICOB also applies to: a firm which communicates or approves non-investment financial promotion; motor vehicle liability insurers and the Society of Lloyd's for that type of business. ICOB does not apply to reinsurance and large risk contracts (qv) for commercial customers.

Insurance Directives Three generations of both life and non-life directives The first directives paved the way for any insurer authorised in any Member State to set up a branch, agency or establishment in any other EC state, without restriction by the host, subject only to the host's regulatory requirements, now largely harmonised. The second generation created free movement of insurance services within the EC by abolition of restrictions to sell across national boundaries. The third generation completed the move towards a single insurance market by abolishing the right of a host nation to insist upon authorising insurers established in other Member States. Authorisation in one state became a Single European Licence (qv), allowing an insurer, without authorisation from any other state: (a) to establish elsewhere; and (b) to sell into other states from establishments outside those states. Post-authorisation regulation is carried out by the insurer's home state to complete the twin aims of single licence and home country control. *See* FOURTH MOTOR INSURANCE DIRECTIVE.

Insurance history Previous insurance record of the insured or proposer. Unsatisfactory insurance history is material (utmost good faith (qv)) and must be disclosed to the insurer. Where proposal forms are used, it is customary for the insurer to include questions about present insurances; previous declinatures; imposition of special terms or increased premiums by previous insurers; refusals to renew; cancellations.

Insurance intermediaries Firms carrying on an insurance mediation activity including an insurer, for example when it advises on or arranges its own non-investment insurance contracts or those of another insurer through its own sales force. *See* INSURANCE: CONDUCT OF BUSINESS RULES.

Insurance-linked securities (ILS) A way of transferring insurance risk to the capital market by way of securitised bonds, e.g. catastrophe bonds (qv) and life bonds (qv). They are attractive to investors as they have a high yield and lack correlation with other assets. Losses caused will be unconnected with economic downturns. There are three types of trigger for ILSs: indemnity (actual losses of bond-issuing insurer); index (benchmarking of loss estimates); or parametric (qv).

Insurance-linked swap Swap transaction under which the investor receives fixed payments for an agreed term in return for a promise to pay a specified amount if an insurance-related event, e.g. earthquake, occurs.

Insurance mediation Defined under the Insurance Mediation Directive (qv) as any of the following: (a) introducing, proposing or carrying out other work preparatory to the conclusion of contracts of insurance; (b) assisting in the administration and performance of such contracts, in particular in the event of a claim; and (c) concluding contracts of insurance. These activities become regulated activities (qv) in 2005.

Insurance Mediation Directive Approved by the European Parliament in September 2002 concerning insurance and reinsurance intermediary regulation. Its aim is to create a system of registration based on the following professional requirements: (a) in possession of the necessary general, commercial and professional knowledge and ability; (b) of good reputation; (c) in possession of professional indemnity insurance or any comparable guarantee against liability for professional negligence; (d) having *sufficient financial capacity* (qv) for those intermediaries who handle client account money. This is similar to the GISC (qv) matrix of regulation. Once intermediaries are registered in their home country they will be free to provide services in other EC states. *See* MEDIATION ACTIVITIES.

Insurance penetration Measures and monitors trend of insurance purchases as a percentage of gross domestic product in a particular country. It is an indicator of the importance of insurance generally or a particular line of insurance. Higher penetration rates are achieved in the developed countries.

Insurance premium tax (IPT) Tax on general insurance premiums. Current (2003) standard rate is 5 per cent of gross premium but 17.5 per cent (introduced in April 1997) for travel and extended warranties on vehicles and some domestic appliances. Most long-term insurance is tax exempt, as is reinsurance, insurance for commercial ships and aircraft and insurance for commercial goods in international transit. Premiums for risks located outside the UK are also exempt, but they may be liable to similar taxes imposed by other countries.

Insurance selling An FSA regulated activity covering *arranging* (qv) the purchase of insurance policies; *advising* (qv) on insurance policies; *dealing as an agent* (qv). Assisting in the administration and performance of policies is also regulated.

Insured The party insured under the policy. Also known as the policyholder.

Insured personal pension Pension under which an insurance company manages the assets of the plan. The fund managers have to be FSA (qv) authorised. This authorisation also applies to private managed funds (qv) but not self-invested personal pensions (qv) or small self-administered schemes where the investment decisions are the responsibility of the member.

Insured scheme Pension scheme under which the pensions and other benefits are secured solely by insurance policies or annuity contracts managed by the insurance company. Compare with *managed fund policy* (qv).

Insured warranty An extended warranty (qv) where the cover is supplied by an authorised insurer and therefore subject to FSA regulation. Service-backed warranties provide repair cover that is not insurance backed. When issued on domestic electrical goods the retailers concerned may be exempt from FSA authorisation and regulation takes the form of a code of conduct (e.g. British Retail Consortium Code of Practice). Motor EWs are regulated by the FSA.

Insured's representative clause Clause in liability policies to the effect that in the event of the insured's death the insurer will continue the cover in favour of the deceased's personal representatives subject to compliance by them with the terms of the policy. *See* PERSONAL REPRESENTATIVE.

Insurer The term used by the FSA to describe a product provider in relation to non-investment insurance contracts. When the term insurer is used, it does not relate to the activity the insurer conducts as an intermediary.

Insurer concerned Insurers who, under the Motor Insurers' Bureau's (qv) Unisured Drivers Agreement (qv), settle a third party claim because at the time of the accident a policy, albeit invalid, issued by them was in force in respect of the defendant. The payment is made notwithstanding that the defendant, by reason of breach of policy, had no valid right to indemnity under the policy. As insurer concerned they have a right of recovery against the uninsured motorist himself.

Insurer's option Material damage insurers reserve the right to provide the indemnity by monetary payment, repair, reinstatement or replacement. In the absence of an option the insured could demand a cash payment. The insurer loses the option if he fails to exercise his alternative rights in a reasonable period of time. An insurer who has indicated his preference may be estopped from choosing an alternative course.

Insuring clause Same as operative clause (qv).

Insuritisation The transfer of financial risk from the capital to the insurance market. A bank securitises a portfolio of corporate bonds or loans known as collateralised debt obligations (qv) or through a portfolio of credit default swaps (qv). A special purpose vehicle (qv) buys the CDOs and passes them through to (re)insurers who are significant investors in subordinated debt based on relatively homogenous assets such as residential mortgage loans, credit card receivables or car loans. Other examples: residual value insurance (qv), revenue guarantee products (qv) and other customised financial products. Other risks transferred to the insurance market have included project finance and royalty streams embracing film, franchises, drugs and music. The insurer forfeits repayment of interest and/or capital if there is default on the loans.

Insurrection A revolt against civil authority or established government. It has been defined as a 'rising of the people in open resistance against established authority with the object of supplanting it'.

Insur-sure Services Ltd Formed in 2001 to unify the back office support for the London Insurance Market. It is owned by Lloyd's (25 per cent), the International Underwriting Association (25 per cent) and by Xchanging (50 per cent). The company has combined the separate processing and settlement operations of Lloyd's Policy Signing Office (qv) and the IUA's London Processing Centre (qv) into a single service for syndicates, insurance companies and brokers. The company also has an e-business infrastructure to enable market participants to continue to compete effectively globally. Xchanging is a company owned by General Atlantic Partners LLC, a leading investor in IT, Internet and Internet-enabled business.

Integrated Lloyd's Vehicle (ILV) Holding company owning/controlling both a managing agent *and* also a corporate member (qv) as a supplier of capacity (qv) to the managing agent's syndicate(s). Lloyd's regulations prevent the two companies combining into one. An ILV providing 100 per cent of the capacity is virtually an insurance company operating at Lloyd's. ILVs can acquire capacity (qv) by way of (a) capacity auctions (qv); (b) acquisition of a fellow corporate member; (c) direct offers to other members. Much of the new capital has come from insurance and reinsurance companies, and institutional and other investors, based principally in Bermuda, the US and the UK. ILVs are relatively low-cost insurance operations. The Chairman's Strategy Group (qv) recommended that all managing agents and syndicates should become ILVs.

Integrated pollution control (IPC) The IPC regime, under Part 1 of the Environmental Protection Act 1990, applies an integrated approach to the environmental regulation of certain industrial activities. Emissions to air, water and land must be considered together. The IPC regime has regulated polluting processes by issuing (or refusing) permits that are shortly being phased into the new Integrated Pollution and Control Regime. (Visit *www.environment-agency.gov.uk*).

Integrated risk products The integrating in a single multi-year contract of conventional insurance risks with financial and commodity risks. Where the risk transfer element is minimal they are akin to financial reinsurance (qv) with the aim of smoothing losses over time. Multi-covers and blended covers are integrated products.

Integrated vehicle See integrated Lloyd's vehicle (ILV).

Integration Reduction of a person's pension by part or all of the pension they will receive from the basic state pension (qv). *See* STATE OFFSET PENSION.

Integration test A test used in the employee/employer relationship (qv). It seeks to establish whether a person works on their own account or as an integral part of the employer's organisation. The test is likely to succeed if the relationship is a continuing one between the parties. If the individual's activities are restricted to one employer and the individual carries no financial risk the individual may be deemed to be an employee. Denning L. J. compared a taxi driver with a chauffeur to make this point (*Stevenson, Jordan and Harrison Ltd* v. *McDonald and Evans*).

Intellectual property The general term for intangible property rights which are a result of intellectual effort. Patents, trademarks, designs and copyright are the main intellectual property rights. *See* INTELLECTUAL PROPERTY ASSET PROTECTION; INTELLECTUAL PROPERTY LITIGATION PROTECTION.

Intellectual property asset protection Cover that focuses on the revenue streams generated by Intellectual Property (IP) rights and their perceived value. The basis of indemnity is tailored to individual circumstances, and will vary from: (a) reimbursement of research and development costs – for IP still in development; (b) loss of projected future earnings where products are newly launched; (c) loss of profit calculated on historic earnings – for mature products. A legal audit takes place before cover is granted.

Intellectual property litigation insurance Covers businesses against the legal costs and damages that can arise from an IP litigation action. The scope of cover varies but generally embraces: 1. *Exploitation agreements* in terms of the fees and expenses in enforcing the contractual terms inherent in agreement. Cover may include defence costs when the insured has unintentionally breached an agreement. 2. *Defence* fees and expenses incurred in defending a claim by a third party that the products or processes used or sold by the insured infringe IP rights. Cover may include the damages that the insured would pay if the defence is unsuccessful. 3. *Invalidity/ownership* – professional fees and expenses in defending challenges to ownership, validity or title to IP where rights have already been granted. 4. *Pursuit* fees and expenses pursuing those who have infringed the insured's IP rights.

Intention of parties rule A rule of construction (qv). Where possible the words of the policy must be construed liberally so as to give effect to the intention of the parties. In insurance the parties intend to make an insurance contract and any interpretation that is contrary to the real intention of the parties is not to be adopted.

Interest clause 1. Reinsurance clause under which the reinsurer and the reinsured share any interest awarded on damages in proportion to their respective shares of the actual loss in those cases where the reinsured's net loss exceeds a given level, e.g. £250,000. In long-tail liability business large claims may take years to settle and interest may be awarded. 2. Treaty clause describing the business and limits covered.

Interest profit The profit attributable to a life insurer earning a higher rate of interest than that assumed at a previous valuation. The profit becomes a part of the surplus.

Interest rate risk Risk that changes in interest rates will affect the resale value of debt securities held in a fund portfolio, e.g. a pension fund. There is an inverse relationship between the rate of interest and the value of the underlying security such as a bond.

Interim bonus Life insurance bonus calculated and paid at the time of a claim on with profits policies maturing or becoming the subject of a death claim during the interval between two bonus declarations.

Interim trust deed Allows a pension scheme to be set up on the basis of very general terms. The detailed rules are set up later in a definitive trust deed.

Interlocking clause Clause applicable to 'risks attaching' reinsurances (qv). The clause allows apportionment of a loss between years of account when a loss arises on policies attaching to different underwriting years. This is achieved by proportionately reducing the deductible and the reinsurer's liability for each of the two years by the percentage that the loss to each year of account bears to the total amount of the loss.

Intermediary A 'middleman' through whom the insurance is arranged.

Intermediary clause Treaty clause that identifies the intermediary who negotiated the agreement. Most clauses shift all credit risk to reinsurers by providing that: (a) the reinsured's payments to the intermediary are deemed to be payments to the reinsurer; and (b) the reinsurer's payments to the intermediary are not payments to the reinsured until received by the reinsured.

Internal control All of the policies, procedures and processes established to ensure that business objectives are achieved in a cost effective manner. The Turnbull Report (qv) on Compliance with the Combined Code of Best Practice in Corporate Governance requires the board in a listed company to give high level meaningful information in its annual report on, inter alia, its responsibility for internal control and confirm that there is an ongoing process for identifying, evaluating and managing significant risks.

Internal dependencies A business interruption (qv) term referring to internal activities and situations which, if interrupted by material loss or damage, would adversely affect the firm's ability to maintain turnover. One small machine could be of such strategic importance it could hinder or stop production runs. Compare with EXTERNAL DEPENDENCIES.

Internal dispute resolution System which must be included in an occupational pension scheme for dealing with members' concerns and complaints. It must be used by a member before taking a case to the Pensions Ombudsman (qv) or OPAS (qv).

Internal risks insurance Motor trader's version of a public liability policy but adapted to cover custody and control of customers' cars, the sale of parts and defective workmanship, if required.

International Air Transport Association (IATA) Promotes safe, regular and economical air transport and is a means of collaboration amongst air transport operators. IATA has drawn up standard conditions relating to the carriage of passengers and baggage setting out limits of liability. Carriers are always free to use their own conditions. The IATA Inter-Carrier Agreement on Passenger Liability (qv) has 'modernised' the Warsaw Convention (qv).

International Association of Insurance Supervisors (IAIS) Represents insurance supervisory authorities from about 100 jurisdictions. It promotes cooperation among insurance regulators; sets international standards for insurance supervision; provides training for its members; coordinates work with regulators in other financial sectors and international financial institutions. (Visit *www.iais.org*).

International Civil Aviation Organisation (ICAO) Sets standards and makes recommendations for international air navigation. The international aspects involved make a high level of standardisation and cooperation between nations essential.

International Convention on Civil Liability for Bunker Oil Pollution Damage 2001 Fills gap arising from 1992 CLC (qv) regime that compensates only for oil pollution spillages from the cargo or bunkers of *laden oil tankers*. The Convention extends civil liability to pollution caused by oil spills from the bunkers of general cargo ships. The Convention follows 1992 CLC in most respects and includes compulsory insurance. The strict liability of CLC has already been extended to non-tankers and tankers in ballast in the UK by the Merchant Shipping (Salvage and Pollution) Act 1994 (qv).

International Hull Clauses (IHC) (01/11/02) Standard clauses that are used with the MAR 91 form (qv). IHC reflects current practices, the increased importance of the International Safety Management Code (qv), flag states and classificiation societies (qv) in connection with ship safety. The pollution hazard clause (qv) has been extended. The new clauses emphasise the consequences of breaching policy conditions. Part 1 sets out the Principal Insuring Conditions, Part 2 sets out additional frequently required clauses including Clauses 40 to 44 (4/4ths collision liability, fixed and floating objects, returns for lay up, general average absorption and additional perils otherwise excluded in Part 1) only apply when agreed by the underwriter. Part 3 contains claims provisions.

International Maritime Bureau First International Chamber of Commerce anti-crime bureau and has observer status with Interpol and cooperates with governments and law enforcement agencies generally. Its task is to prevent fraud in international trade and maritime transport, reduce the risk of piracy, assist law enforcement agencies, protect crews and investigate insurance losses. *See* IMB PIRACY REPORTING CENTRE.

International Maritime Organisation (IMO) United Nations Agency for setting standards on ship safety and prevention of oil pollution connected with which it is responsible for international conventions. It has headquarters in London. The UK's annual subscription is based on ship's tonnage on the UK and Red Ensign registers.

International motor insurance certificate *See* GREEN CARD.

International Safety Management Code (ISM) Concerns safe operation of ships and pollution prevention. ISM is mandatory under the International Convention for Life at Sea. It applies to: passenger ships (including high speed craft), ro-ro passenger ships, oil tankers, chemical tankers, gas carriers, bulk carriers of 500 gross tonnage or above, high speed cargo craft of 500 tonnage or above, cargo ships and mobile offshore drilling units of 500 tonnage or above. The 'Company' (shipowner, manager or bareboat charterer) must establish and implement a safety management system and obtain a Document of Compliance (DOC) every five years that is also audited annually. Non-compliance means automatic termination of the hull and machinery policy (Clause 13 International Hull Clauses (qv)). Policies usually protect the interests of innocent mortgagees for a limited period. *See* INTERNATIONAL SAFETY MANAGEMENT CODE ENDORSEMENT.

International Safety Management Code Endorsement Applies to cargo policies to exclude cover whenever the cargo is carried in non-ISM Code certified vessels or whose owners do not hold a Document of Compliance at the time of loading. The exclusion does not apply where the policy has been assigned to an innocent third party who has bought the cargo in good faith.

International Sharing Agreement An agreement between motor liability insurers and 'own damage' insurers applicable to accidents involving vehicles registered in different EC states when one is insured for 'own damage'. Regardless of liability, the liability insurer and the own damage insurer share the 'own damage' indemnity on a fixed basis. The agreement reduces the costs inherent in an international claim.

International Underwriters' Association of London (IUA) Formed in 1999 by the merger between the Institute of London Underwriters (qv) and the London and Reinsurance Market Association to bring together marine, non-marine and reinsurance interests. The IUA is the world's largest representative body of wholesale and reinsurance. The IUA runs the Technical and Underwriting Executive Committee to which other committees, including the Clauses Sub-Committee and the Pollution Group, report.

International Union of Aviation Insurers Represents the interests of aviation insurers in 31 different countries, providing a central office for the circulation of information between members. The Union also seeks to provide a better understanding and conduct of international aviation including space risks. Membership is open to pools, groups or associations whose participants are engaged in aviation insurance on a direct or reinsurance basis. In exceptional circumstances aviation insurance companies may be considered for membership.

Internet liability/cyberliability insurance 1. Anyone connected to the Internet for business faces the risk of claims for libel, slander, breaches of intellectual property and confidentiality rights. The policy pays for legal liability and defence costs arising out of 'e-activities' broadly meaning 'the transacting, disseminating or enabling the marketing, buying, selling or distribution of goods, services or information through electronic networks'. Additional clauses cover cost of replacing records, financial losses due to fraud, legal fees for enforcing intellectual property rights, loss of profits due to interruption in trading through viruses, hacking, etc., claims by employees, brand protection, etc. 2. Internet service providers insure their Internet liability arising out of the provision of Internet services. Risk management is an important response to all Internet risks.

Internet Weather Derivatives Exchange (I-Wex.com) Information and research portal for global weather derivatives (qv) market. Gives access to LIFFE trading and the OTC weather risk market. It is a consortium formed between Intelligent Finance Systems Ltd, LIFFE (qv), and World-wide Intellectual Resources Exchange Ltd (WIRE) (qv). The portal contains weather data from all major contract sites worldwide.

Interruption reports Reports on the potential for interruption of a business as a result of fire, breakdown or any other peril covered or to be covered; the business interruption (qv) equivalent of a fire survey. The report covers: (a) the effect of 'damage'; (b) how long it will take to recover from the interruption; (c) how the insured might be assisted to keep the business going during the period of interruption. The report assists in fixing the rate and assessment of the estimated maximum loss (EML) and risk improvement. The report should take account of *external dependencies* (qv).

Intervening cause (novus actus interveniens) New cause that intervenes into a sequence of events that is not the reasonable, natural or probable consequence of the preceding cause. It breaks the chain of causation. Even if the chain started with an insured peril there will be no liability for losses occurring after the occurrence of the intervening cause which changes the outcome and destroys the cause and effect relationship between the insured peril and the loss. *See* PROXIMATE CAUSE.

Introducer In terms of the conduct of *designated investment business* (qv) an individual appointed by a provider firm or *appointed representative* (qv) whose role is simply to effect introductions or distribute non-real time financial promotions e.g. leaflets and brochures. The introducer should not give any investment advice except discreet advice to the effect that the client should consider making an investment and recommending a suitably authorised individual or firm he or she may consult. *Introducing* is also regulated under ICOB (qv) as part of arranging non-investment insurance contracts.

Introducer approved representative An *appointed representative* (qv) appointed by a provider firm and whose scope is limited to: effecting introductions; distributing non-real time financial promotions, e.g. leaflets, brochures. Such a representative can have an unlimited number of principals (qv).

Introducing *See* INTRODUCER.

Intruder alarm warranty Warranty whereby the insured under a commercial policy must: install an intruder alarm system as specified; inspect and maintain the system in accordance with specified standards by a NACOSS or other approved installer; put the system into full and effective operation whenever the alarmed portion of the building is closed or unattended. All keys must be removed from the premises when closed or unattended except for a part of the premises residentially occupied.

Inure to the benefit of Means taking effect for the benefit of a particular party. Reinsurance contracts may provide that other reinsurances, applied first to the loss, are to 'inure to the benefit of' the reinsurer. If the other insurances are to be disregarded they 'inure to the benefit' of the reinsured.

Investment bonds *See* SINGLE PREMIUM BONDS; GROWTH BONDS; INCOME BONDS; MANAGED BONDS; WITH PROFITS BONDS.

Investment income The part of an insurer's income that comes from the interest and dividends on its investments in financial assets (e.g. equities and government bonds) and the return on any other investment (e.g. property) into which it has put its funds.

Investment insurance *See* OVERSEAS INVESTMENT INSURANCE.

Investment report Sets out details of investments held by a pension fund and the buying and selling transactions that have taken place. It explains why the particular investments were chosen and why changes were made in the investment portfolio.

Investment risk The risk that the rates of investment returns anticipated in insurance and investment calculations are not achieved.

Investment trust A company that invests in stocks and shares bought with the capital subscribed by shareholders, retained profits and loan finance. The shares of the trust are available only to the extent that existing shareholders are prepared to sell the whole or a part of their holdings.

'Inward' reinsurance *See* ASSUMED REINSURANCE.

IPRU (FSOC) Interim Prudential Sourcebook for Friendly Societies. It sets rules, principles, guidance on how to comply with a requirement, evidential provisions (high-level guidance containing examples on compliance) and directions on minor. The rules, etc., arise from FSMA and powers devolved upon the FSA (qv). The rules have the status of law and principles, while lacking legal status, are effectively as powerful. IPRU (FSOC) will become integrated in the new Integrated Sourcebook.

IPRU (INS) Interim Prudential Sourcebook for Insurers. This comprehensive document sets out rules, principles and directions applicable to insurers. The rules, etc., are derived from FSMA and/or the powers of the FSA. Rules have legal status but principles, though effectively as powerful, do not. The Sourcebook gives guidance on how an insurer should comply with its various obligations. *Evidential provisions* give high-level guidance and examples on compliance. Separate sourcebooks exist for Lloyd's, Friendly Societies, banks, investment businesses and building societies. IPRU (INS) will become incorporated in the new Integrated Sourcebook.

ISAs Individual Savings Accounts provide tax-free saving. Individuals can invest a total of £7,000 per year. From this figure, £1000 may go into life insurance, £3000 into cash deposits and £3000 into stocks and shares in a maxi-ISA. The other maxi-ISA combines cash and/or life insurance with stocks and shares as long as the entire package is provided by one company. Mini Cash ISAs and Mini Stocks and Shares each have a limit of £3,000. Mini Insurance ISA's have a £1,000 limit.

Issue risk policy Covers the risk of loss to a reversioner (the owner of property which will revert to him on the determination of a particular estate, e.g. death of a life tenant) caused by the birth of a child to the life tenant. The policy is on an indemnity basis.

Issuer risk Risk of financial loss if the issuer of a security (bank or corporation) defaults on repayments or interest and/or capital repayment.

I-Wex *See* INTERNET WEATHER DERIVATIVES EXCHANGE.

J

Jane's 'All the World's Aircraft' Annual publication containing information of value to underwriters. It contains photographs, descriptions and performance details of the majority of civil and military aircraft and engines in current production and/or under development.

Janson clause Clause that may be added to a hull policy in circumstances where hull particular average claims (qv) are likely to be frequent. The policy is made 'free of particular average' (qv) if the partial loss does not equal or exceed 3 per cent of the insured value. The insured warrants that he will remain uninsured for the 3 per cent.

Jason clause A clause appearing in a contract of affreightment when disputes may be subject to US law. The clause obligates the owners of cargo to contribute to general average in cases of danger, damage or disaster resulting from faults or errors in navigation or in the management of a vessel or its machinery, provided that the owner shall have exercised due diligence to make the vessel in all respects seaworthy, and to have it properly manned, equipped and supplied. The clause avoids the consequences of a US court decision which held that a shipowner could not recover cargo's proportion of general average arising out of a negligent navigation or error in management.

JCT 21.2.1. Non-negligent cover An insurance in the joint names of Employer and Contractor for the benefit of the Employer. It secures 'non-negligent' liability cover and damage to any property other than the contract works and site materials caused by collapse, subsidence, heave, vibration, weakening or removal of support or lowering of the ground water arising out of the works. The insurance is usually required when work involves existing buildings or is close to them. *See* JOINT CONTRACTS TRIBUNAL.

Jetsam Cargo or goods that sink when jettisoned. Term also applies to such goods when washed ashore.

Jettison Deliberate throwing overboard of cargo or parts of the ship. If done in time of peril, this is a *general average sacrifice* (qv) but is also recoverable as a direct claim on the policy.

Jewellers' block policy Covers jeweller's stock, goods in trust and bank notes on an 'all risks' basis on the premises, in the vaults or in transit. The policy extends to cover premises, trade and office fixtures and fittings against a wide range of perils. The policy contains strict limits for specified types of losses.

Joint and several liability *See* JOINT TORTFEASORS.

Joint Cargo Committee A joint committee of Lloyd's and the IUA (insurance companies) concerned with the general welfare of marine cargo insurance and the Institute Cargo Clauses. It makes recommendations to the market to provide a framework for the underwriting of cargo business.

Joint Contracts Tribunal (JCT) A company concerned for over 70 years with producing suites of standard contracts and guidance notes for the construction industry. JCT has nine constituent bodies representing the key professions and associations from both the public and private sectors. The contracts range from simple house extensions through to major public construction projects. *See* JCT CLAUSE 21.2.1. NON-NEGLIGENT COVER. (Visit *www.jct.co.uk*).

Joint Excess Loss Clauses 1/1/97 Main set of clauses for the excess of loss reinsurance of London Market syndicates and companies. They are the only standard set of clauses but are sufficiently flexible to have a wide application.

Joint Excess of Loss Committee Run by Lloyd's and the IUA (qv) to promote standardised wordings and clauses for excess of loss reinsurance contracts.

Joint Hull Committee A joint committee of the the IUA (qv) and Lloyd's (qv), to which the IUA provides the Permanent Secretary, concerned with the general wellbeing of the marine hull market. It reviews and updates the Hull Institute Clauses in consultation with the market. It has also set up Education and Marketing, Wordings and Technical, Statistics and Information, Maritime Industry Liaison and Finance sub-committees. It has established monthly market briefings to report on the work of the committee and to inform the market on current technical and safety issues. Administers *joint hull understandings* (qv).

Joint Hull Returns Bureau A bureau under the auspices of the Joint Hull Committee (qv) that handles and approves applications from shipowners for returns of premium, e.g. laid-up returns.

Joint hull survey A hull survey undertaken jointly by a surveyor representing the insurer and another surveyor representing the insured.

Joint Hull Understandings A market agreement to provide a framework for the underwriting of hull business in London. The agreement is administered by the Joint Hull Committee (qv). The aim is to achieve some uniformity of practice by means of recommendations, but the understandings do not provide rates or a basis of rating. The understandings are reviewed annually and set guidelines on the treatment of renewals of business regarded as unsatisfactory.

Joint insureds/joint names policy Two or more persons whose interests are insured under the same policy. It appears to be an established principle that, in respect of any particular risk, one insured cannot sue a joint insured under the same policy against the same risk. However, in liability insurance it is customary to add a cross liabilities clause (qv).

Joint life and survivor annuity Annuity (qv) on two or more lives that continues until the death of the last survivor.

Joint life annuity Annuity (qv) on two or more lives that ceases on first death.

Joint life insurance Life insurance policy dependent on two or more lives that becomes payable on the first death. Policies may be whole life, endowment or term. *See* LAST SURVIVOR INSURANCE.

Joint surveys Fire surveys undertaken by two surveyors. Where a risk is very large and shared by two or more insurers (co-insurance), the lead insurer undertakes the survey but may involve the insurer holding the next largest proportion. One insurer may survey the building and the other surveys the contents. It may also occur where a fire surveyor is accompanied by a specialist surveyor (e.g. sprinkler leakage specialist). In other instances, the company surveyor may be accompanied by the broker's surveyor.

Joint Technical and Clauses Committee (JTCC) Formed by the Aviation Insurance Office Association (AIOA) and Lloyd's Aviation Underwriter's Association (LAUA). It is mainly concerned with the drafting of wordings and clauses.

Joint tortfeasors Two or more persons who are jointly and severally liable for the same tort (qv). It means that the claimant can sue both (or all) of them or recover the whole of amount of any one regardless of the extent to which each participated. A tortfeasor held wholly liable for the damage has a right of contribution from other tortfeasors liable for the same injury/damage (Civil Liability (Contribution) Act 1978 (qv)). Vicarious liability (qv) is a principal instance of joint tortfeasors.

Judicial delay insurance A special scheme insuring against the additional costs incurred by a litigant following the delay or postponement of a court hearing. Cover operates for non-appearance of the judge, a presiding official or counsel due to illness or for any other reason.

Judicial review insurance Policy indemnifying the insured in the event of the insured's planning consent being made subject to a judicial review hearing and the insured's intended development prevented or delayed.

Jumbo risk Policy of insurance written with exceptionally high limits.

Jurisdiction/jurisdiction clause The authority of a court to hear and decide cases. Jurisdiction is determined by the geographic location of the court and the subject matter of the case. A *jurisdiction clause* in liability policies usually means that the policy will respond only to an action brought in Great Britain, Northern Ireland, the Channel Islands or the Isle of Man. Another common approach, less restrictive, is simply to exclude claims that are the subject of US and Canada jurisdiction.

Justification Defendant may plead that the actions that form the basis of the case against him were justified. In a libel case, the plea of justification admits the publication of the defamatory words but pleads that they are true in substance and in fact.

Keeper The person made liable under the Animals Act 1971, s.2. (qv). The keeper is the person who owns the animal or has it in his possession, or is the head of the household of which a member under the age of 16 owns it or has it in his possession. If a person ceases to own or have possession of the animal he will remain the keeper until another person becomes the keeper. A person who takes possession of an animal to prevent it from causing damage or to return it to its owner does not, merely by so doing, become a keeper.

Key features document Document that the FSA requires should be given to any person considering the purchase of a life insurance policy or joining a pension scheme before they make their decision. The document is presented in such a way that the consumer will be assisted in making comparisons with the different providers' offerings for the type of investment concerned.

Keyman insurance Insurance protecting an entity against financial loss caused by the death or disability of a 'key' person. The loss is the estimated cost of lost business, abandoned projects and replacement of the individual. Some lenders require keyman insurance before lending to small companies which rely on one or a few key people. Keyman insurance products include life and/or health insurances.

Keys clause Theft cover clause stating the 'cash in safe' cover will not operate if the safe keys are left on the premises when the premises are closed for business.

Kidnap and ransom insurance Reimburses insured for ransom paid to kidnappers and pays for professional assistance to help negotiate with the kidnappers. Cover is effected by corporations on named individuals or by 'celebrities'. The policy is subject to a per-person or annual aggregage limit of indemnity and is subject to a substantial deductible or co-insurance clause. It is a condition of the policy that its existence is never disclosed. Banks cover 'forced withdrawals' from its vaults and money to secure the release of a banker or member of his family. Kidnap and ransom cover is also available at Lloyd's for valuable bloodstock.

Knock for knock agreement A forbearance agreement between two motor insurers that in the event of an accident involving their respective insureds each would carry its own loss in terms of accidental damage repairs regardless of liability. The agreement has been replaced by the memorandum of understanding (qv).

'Know your customer' FSA's COB Rule 5.2 requires a firm to take all reasonable steps to elicit the personal and financial information needed to enable them to discharge their services properly from the client's perspective. *See* FACT FINDING.

L

Label clause Marine cargo clause limiting liability on a claim to payments for reconditioning of the cargo, the cost of new labels and re-labelling.

Labour gangs Gangs of individuals whose leader, the labour master, negotiates work and payment with an employer. The work is usually casual in the construction industry, agriculture or horticulture. As the gang usually works alongside the employer's staff, they are brought within the employers' liability policy definition of 'employees'. The definition includes: 'labour masters and persons supplied by them . . .'

Labour-only sub-contractors Sub-contractors, often in the building trade, who contract to supply work not materials. They are within the employers' liability policy definition of 'employees' similar to *labour gangs* (qv).

Landed value Market value of cargo at destination on the final day of discharge from the carrying vessel.

Landslip Property insurance peril held to mean 'a rapid downward movement under the influence of gravity of a mass or rock or earth on a slope'. The word *rapid* may in some cases give way to the concept of the 'slow accident'. Pressure built up over time before pushing over a wall may be landslip (Ombudsman view). Landslip is insured as an additional peril (qv) alongside subsidence (qv) and heave (qv). In all forms of cover, normal land settlement and coastal erosion are excluded together with damage to boundary walls, gates and fences unless the buildings are damaged at the same time.

Lapse/lapses risk A policy lapses when it is not renewed for a further term. Revival of lapsed life policies may occur under a non-forfeiture clause (qv).The *lapses risk* in life business means a lower level of recovery of fixed costs. Where up-front commission is paid it becomes more difficult to recover.

Lapse ratio The percentage of policies, in force at the beginning of the year, that lapse by non-renewal, surrender or cancellation during the year. Insurers who have to constantly replace lapsed policies have relatively high acquisition costs. Life companies use the ratio as an indicator of marketing performance. The converse is *persistency* (qv).

Large risks *Large risks* with commercial customers that are located in the European Economic Area are *not* subject to the Insurance: Conduct of Business rules (qv) on standards of advice. They are insurances embracing: (a) railway rolling stock, aircraft, ships, goods in transit, aircraft liability and liability of ships; (b) credit and suretyship, where the policyholder is engaged professionally in an industrial or commercial activity or in one of the professions and the risks relate to such activity; (c) land vehicles (other than railway rolling stock), fire and natural forces, other damage to property, motor vehicle liability, general liability and miscellaneous financial loss, in so far as the policyholder exceeds at least two of the following three criteria: (i) balance sheet total – €6.2 million; (ii) net turnover – €12.8; (iii) average number of employees during the year – 250.

'Last straw'/'death blow' cases Final link in a chain of events closest in time to the loss but not closest in efficiency. In *Leyland Shipping Co.* v. *Norwich Union* (1918) a torpedoed ship later sunk following a storm, the 'last straw', but the proximate cause (qv) of the loss was the torpedo damage. The insurer was not therefore liable as the policy excluded war risks. An undamaged ship would have survived the storm.

Last survivor annuity *See* JOINT LIFE AND SURVIVOR ANNUITY.

Last survivor insurance Life policy on two or more lives under which the sum insured is payable on the last death. They are used in connection with leases granted for the lifetime of two or more people. Policies are usually whole of life or endowment.

Late entrant Individual joining a group life and pension scheme beyond the date at which he was automatically eligible for membership.

Late retirement Actual retirement of a pension scheme member after his normal retirement age.

Latent Damages Act 1986 Partly nullifies the House of Lords decision (*Pirelli* v. *Oscar Faber & Partners* (1983)) that when property damage occurs the limitation time runs from the time of damage. The Act adds a further three years' limitation period from the date the damage was reasonably discoverable subject to a 'long stop' provision of 15 years from the act of negligence. The claimant's knowledge of the damage or capability of reasonably discovering it, follows the 'knowledge' requirements of the Limitation Act 1980 (qv).

Latent defect An existing defect that is not apparent or discoverable by reasonable care. For the purpose of *decennial insurance* (qv), latent defects are 'defects which have occurred at the time of construction but do not manifest themselves until some substantial time afterwards'.

Latent defects insurance *See* DECENNIAL INSURANCE.

Latent disease Disease that may lie dormant or undiscovered for years before being diagnosed or discovered, e.g. asbestosis (qv). *See* LONG-TAIL LIABILITY.

Launch insurance Covers a spacecraft during the launch phase. The cover is material damage on an 'all risks' basis and includes the risk of malfunctioning. The policy runs from the initial ignition until the spacecraft reaches its correct and final orbit and its systems fully checked before it begins the commercial operations for which it was intended.

Laundry list List of past events (e.g. all house surveys by a particular person) that could lead to claims under a professional indemnity claims-made policy. By notifying the event in advance of any claim the insured seeks to have the event deemed as a'claim made during the policy period' even though the policy, at time of claim, may have lapsed. The 'laundry list' may be a sufficient notification but insurers may contend that the list is too broad to protect the insured against any specific claims. Each case turns on its own facts (*Hampton* v. *Field*).

Law of large numbers The larger the number of exposure units considered, the more closely will the losses occurring match the underlying probability of loss. Insurance uses the law to predict future losses with an acceptable degree of accuracy to facilitate the spreading of risk among homogeneous groups.

Law Reform (Miscellaneous Provisions) Act 1934 Enacts that on death all actions subsisting against the deceased, or vested in him, survive against or for, his estate. The estate can claim damages for the period between the accrual of the cause of action and the date of death. Damages are calculated 'without reference to any loss or gain to the estate consequent upon the death' so annuities previously payable and life insurance now payable are disregarded. Awards under the 1934 Act are the same regardless of claims under the Fatal Accidents Act (qv), under which there is to be no duplication of damages.

Lay days Number of days allowed in a charterparty that a ship may use a dock for loading/unloading before demurrage (qv) is payable to the shipowner. The lay days may be either (a) fixed as to number; or (b) indeterminate as being dependent on the circumstances, e.g. 'according to the custom of the port'.

Layer/layering A horizontal stratum of cover within a structure of layers. For example, a primary insurer covers £100,000, the first excess insurer covers the next layer up to £200,000, the second excess insurers takes in excess of £200,000 up to £300,000 and so on. Layering spreads the risk among insurers or reinsurers and is applied to both property and liability insurances. *See* EXCESS INSURANCE.

Lay-up return/laid-up return The return of premium allowed under the *returns clause* (qv) by marine insurers when the vessel is out of use.

Leaching Process by which organic matter and soluble pollutants is washed out of a layer of soil, or dumped material, by percolating rainwater. Causes pollutants to enter the ground and groundwater. It causes gradual pollution (insurable only under environmental impairment liability cover (qv)). The material washed out is called *leachate.*

Leading underwriter agreement An agreement that allows for certain changes in conditions to be agreed by the leading Underwriter without the agreement of all subscribing Underwriters. The LUA is being superseded by the *General Underwriters Agreement* (qv) although it remains possible to incorporate the LUA into the new LMP slip. *See* GENERAL UNDERWRITERS AGREEMENT.

Leading underwriter/insurer 1. Lloyd's underwriter or company recognised as a specialist or as having the greatest capacity in a particular class of business. They are first to take a portion of the risk and quote a rate of premium. Other underwriters follow by accepting portions of the risk. On large risks it may be necessary to select two/three specialist leaders. 2. The insurance company on a co-insurance policy who has accepted the largest share of the risk and accepts responsibility for the survey and administration of the insurance.

Leakage 1. *Marine policies* cover leakage caused by maritime perils. Leakage may also be an insured peril but this will not include loss from ordinary leakage occurring in liquids by evaporation, soaking into the container or other natural causes except to the extent that the loss of liquids (e.g. palm olives or molasses shipped in bulk) exceeds a certain amount or percentage. This is known as *ullage.* 2. *Household.* Leakage of oil from any fixed heating installation under both buildings and contents insurances is covered.

Leasehold redemption policy *See* CAPITAL REDEMPTION POLICY.

'Left unattended' Goods in transit term restricting cover when vehicles are *left unattended.* Whether a vehicle is left unattended is a question of fact. A vehicle was held to be unattended when its driver was in a shop for 15 minutes quite unable to watch over the vehicle. In *Starfire Diamonds* v. *Angel* (1962) 2 Lloyd's Rep. 213, the Court of Appeal held that a car was left unattended when the driver left his car in a lay-by while urinating behind some bushes 37 yards away. He saw a man on the far side walking away with a suitcase from the car but was not in a position to attempt to frustrate any attack on the vehicle. *See* ORDINARY MEANING RULE.

Legal assignment An assignment (qv) that permits an assignee to sue in his own name. The Policies of Assurance Act 1867 allows the assignee to sue on the policy provided he has given notice to the insurer in writing. The policy must be endorsed or the assignment must be by separate instrument. *See* EQUITABLE ASSIGNMENT.

Legal costs extension A liability policy clause indemnifying the insured against his own defence costs if incurred with the insurer's consent. These costs are borne by the insurer *in addition* to damages and claimants' costs that are subject to the specified limit of indemnity. The legal costs form a part of the indemnity limit only if the limit is *costs inclusive* (qv).

Legal expenses insurance An insurance for individuals, families and businesses to enable them to meet the cost of defending or pursuing certain civil actions. Cover is also available for defending prosecutions and an allowance is made for attendance expenses in connection with court hearings or similar proceedings. *See* COMMERCIAL LEGAL EXPENSES; MOTOR LEGAL EXPENSES.

Legal liability Liability attaching to a party because of the breach of a legal duty or by way of statute. Employers' liability (qv), public liability (qv) insurances, etc., insure *the legal liability* of the insured and not the injury, damage or loss suffered by the third party. If there is no legal liability there will be no payment to an injured claimant. The allegation of liability is sufficient to give the insured access to the insurer's help by way of defence costs and claims handling.

Legal personal representative Person who administers the estate of a deceased person. If nominated in a will, the person is an executor. A person appointed by the court is an administrator. As personal actions survive the death of a person, liability policies indemnify the insured's legal personal representatives.

Legionellosis Infections caused by legionella. Legionnaires' disease is a life-threatening form of pneumonia caused by legionella pneumophila bacteria. The business risks are: closure during outbreak investigation; clean up costs; claims from employees and third parties; business interruption when nearby attraction closes due to outbreak. Property owners may suffer void periods and lower rents. Relevant statutory requirements include HSWA and Management of Health and Safety at Work Regulations 1992 (qv). Insurance solutions include business interruption cover (qv), clean up costs cover and legionellosis liability (qv).

Legionellosis liability insurance A claims-made policy (qv) covering liability for third party injury caused by legionellosis arising out of the business. The risk arises from recirculating hot and cold water systems. Insurers regard third party claims as 'gradual pollution' claims and thus exclude them under public liability insurance. Cover is granted under legionellosis liability cover. The employers' liability policy responds to legionellosis claims as specific diseases cannot be excluded under this compulsory form of insurance.

Letter of credit (L/C) A document issued by a bank, at the buyer's request, guaranteeing payment to the seller upon receipt by the bank of shipping and documents validating the delivery of goods. L/Cs are also used on a 'standby' basis to secure recoverables from non-admitted reinsurers to enable the cedant to reduce its provision for unauthorised reinsurance in its statutory statement.

Lettered rules York–Antwerp Rules (qv) that are prefixed by a letter rather than a number. The lettered rules apply only when it is impossible to apply the numbered rules.

Level premium system/level annual premium system Life insurance premiums are the same amount each year and do not increase as age increases. The premiums charged in the early years are more than sufficient to cover the mortality risk and so contribute to a reserve. In later years the reserve is used at a time when the level annual premium is insufficient to cover the mortality risk.

Levy 1. General levy is paid by all occupational and personal pension schemes covered by the Pension Scheme Registry (qv). The amount depends on the number of members. This levy funds the Registry, the Pensions Ombudsman (qv) and Opra (qv), including grants made by Opra to OPAS (qv). 2. The compensation levy is a part of the levy paid by the occupational pension schemes eligible for compensation. It pays the compensation and expenses of the Pensions Compensation Board (qv).

Liability insurance Insurance against the legal obligation to pay compensation and costs to third parties and employees for loss, injury or damage. Liability may arise through negligence (qv); strict liability (qv); breach of statutory duty (qv); breach of contract (qv). Key liability policies include employers' liability (qv), public liability (qv), products liability (qv), professional indemnity (qv) and directors' and their duties (qv).

Liability sequence Four distinct stages apply to liability claims. 1. The cause (e.g. spillage of toxic chemical onto grazing land) – the *initial act.* 2. The effect (cows ill after grazing) – the *occurrence.* 3. Discovery of injuries – the *manifestation.* 4. Action – *the making of a claim.* The sequence may be lengthy or virtually instantaneous e.g. workman burns down a house. Any one stage may be used to trigger a claim. Public liability policies are usually *occurrence* policies (qv), i.e. the injury/damage must occur within the policy period regardless of the time of the initial act or of the claim. In long-tail (qv) disease claims and gradual pollution many years may separate the 'occurrence' from the 'manifestation'. Professional indemnity insurance is 'claims-made'(qv), a stage 4 trigger. *See* OCCURRENCE TRIGGER THEORIES; TRIPLE TRIGGER THEORY. See Figure 5.

Libel Publishers may insure against libel, slander and innuendo. Professional indemnity policies have a libel extension. *See* INSURANCE.

Licensed Lloyd's advisers In-house or independent advisers who advise corporate members on their underwriting commitments. They work in the same way as members' agents work for *names* (qv).

Lien The right to hold someone's property as security for the performance of an obligation. A broker who, as agent, pays the premium and receives the policy, may retain it under the broker's lien until reimbursed. These rights depend on proper performance by the agent of his duties. The lien does not usually apply to money due from another broker or sub-agent. In life insurance *lien* means debt (qv). A carrier's lien which operates in a similar way to protect a carrier when freight (qv) is payable at destination.

Life, accident, sickness and unemployment insurance (LASU) Creditor insurance (qv) under which a death benefit is added to protection against loss of income following accident, sickness and unemployment.

Life Assurance Act 1774 Made insurances on the lives of persons or events (ships or merchandise excepted) null and void if the person benefiting had no interest. It also made it unlawful to issue policies without naming the person for whose benefit the policy is issued. It further provided that no greater amount than the value of the interest could be recovered under the policy meaning the amount of interest at inception not the time of claim. *See* INSURABLE INTEREST.

Life Assurance Companies (Payment into Court) Act 1896 Enables a life insurance company, unable to obtain a satisfactory discharge for the policy proceeds, to pay them into court.

Life bonds The borrowing of money from the capital market through the sale of bonds by a *special purpose vehicle* (qv).

Occurrence policy

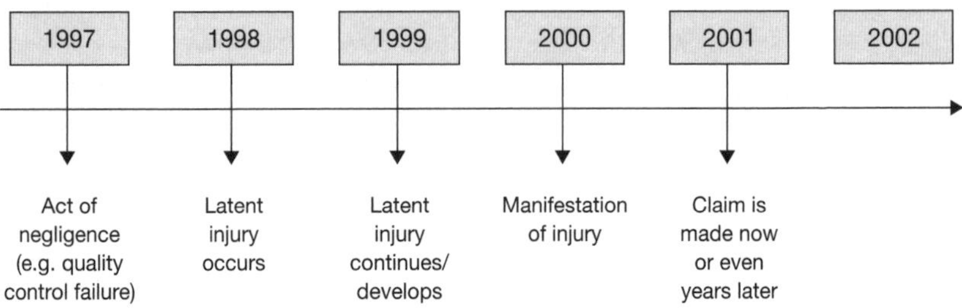

The policy in force in 1998 and 1999 is triggered even if lapsed. Insurers on risk in 2000, time of manifestaton, and 2001 (or even years later), time of claim, will not be liable.

Claims-made policy

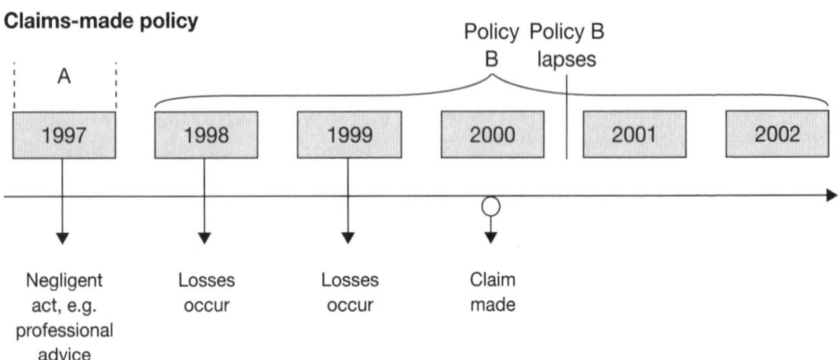

Claims-made policies (e.g. gradual pollution and professional indemnity) are triggered by the time of claim, provided incident is after the retroactive date (qv). If the 'retro' date is 1 January 1998 (the inception date) there will be no cover for the 1997 incident. If subsequent to 'retro date' policy B will apply if the claim is made before 31 December 2000 or if cover terminates before the end of any *extended reporting period* (qv).

Figure 5. Liability sequence – occurence policy v. claims-made policy

The bonds are secured against the anticipated surplus from a portfolio of life insurance or pensions policies. The surplus will be used wholly or partly, depending on whether there are shortfalls in the anticipated surplus, to meet repayment and interest obligations. The SPV arranges reinsurance to provide liquidity where the surpluses are not adequate to pay the bondholder. *See* SECURITISATION.

Life expectancy The average number of years that a person of a given age may be expected to survive. *See* MORTALITY TABLE.

Life fund *See* LIFE INSURANCE FUND.

Life insurance A policy that pays a specified sum on death or upon the life insured surviving a given term of years depending on the type of policy. Insurances are on lives where the contract is not one of indemnity but of an ultimate claim. In the UK *ordinary life* insurance means all life business that is not within the term *industrial life* assurance (qv). The principal life contracts are: endowment (qv); whole life (qv); and term (qv) insurance. Each type can be adapted or combined to meet a variety of circumstances.

Life Insurance Association (LIA) Association (23,000 individual members) with objectives to: (a) promote communication, participation and education within the life insurance industry; (b) improve business standards and heighten professionalism in the selling of life insurance via a professional code; (c) sponsor courses, seminars, etc., to increase awareness of the activities of the life industry; (d) promote understanding with government, the FSA (qv) and other bodies.

Life Insurance Council (LIC) Operates as part of the ABI (qv) dealing specifically with the life insurance industry. Its elected management committee reports to the full council, which in turn reports to the Board of the ABI.

Life insurance fund The accumulated savings and contributions of policyholders held against the life companies' liabilities to pay future claims. The funds are increased yearly by premiums paid and investment income received, less payments made to policyholders, management expenses (including commission), taxation and transfers to shareholders' funds (qv), where appropriate. Life funds are credited with all or part of any capital appreciation in asset values.

Life insurance (satellites) Life insurance in the satellite insurance market refers to an 'all risks' insurance in respect of total or partial loss during the operating life of the satellite.

Life insured The person whose life is the subject-matter of the life insurance contract. If A effects a policy on the life of B, his partner, B is the life insured. This is a 'life of another' policy (qv).

Life of another policy A life policy taken out by one person on the life of another in whom he has an insurable interest at inception.

Lifetime mortgage A mortgage aimed at those who own property but have no income. A mortgage is raised on the property and either: (i) an annuity is purchased and the mortgage, plus interest which is added to the original loan, is repaid on sale of the property, often after the death of the borrower; or (ii) less frequently, the loan is repaid on death or sale together with a fixed percentage growth in the property value with interest paid during the mortgage term. Lifetime mortgages are FSA-regulated when the mortgage meets the definition set down in the legislation.

LIFFE The London International Financial Futures and Options Exchange, the financial and non-financial derivative exchange that launched LIFFE Weather Futures (qv) in 2001. (Visit *www.liffe.com*). *See* EXCHANGE TRADED CONTRACTS.

LIFFE Weather Futures Standardised exchange-traded weather derivatives launched by LIFFE (qv) for companies seeking to manage weather risk. LIFFE's contracts are written for London, Paris and Berlin creating a basis risk (qv). The weather index is the monthly mean of *daily average temperature* (qv) not degree days (qv). The instruments are traded freely and are therefore liquid as well as being transparent as live bids and offers can be seen and made in real time on LIFFE Connect.

Lift policy Covers breakdown (qv) but can be extended to cover sudden and unforeseen physical damage (qv) to the plant at the premises, temporarily elsewhere and in transit between the two. It also covers damage to own surrounding property resulting from fragmentation (qv), damage to goods being lifted (excluding installed plant and machinery) and third party risks.

Lifting Operations and Lifting Equipment Regulations 1998 (LOLER) Regulations relating, inter alia, to the initial installation of certain lifting equipment. The employer must then appoint a 'competent person' to inspect the lifting equipment at agreed intervals. The inspection is often performed by insurance companies. LOLER covers lifts, cranes, lifting and handling machinery in all workplaces. The provisions of PUWER 1998 (qv) apply to lifting equipment.

Lifts and hoists The cover provided under a lift policy (qv) is applicable to items such as: electric or hydraulic passenger and goods lifts, manual goods lifts and service lifts, paternosters, motor vehicles lifting tables, and builders', coal, coke, cupola hoists.

Lightning An insured peril added to a standard fire policy to cover damage by lightning. It is independent of the fire peril. No ignition is necessary.

Limit of indemnity/liability The maximum sum an insured may collect, or for which an insured is protected, under the policy. It is a 'sum insured' under property insurances but a 'limit of indemnity' under liability policies. The liability limit may be: per policy, per event, per occurrence, per year, per 'originating cause' or, by way of sub-limit, per specified type of loss. *See* COSTS INCLUSIVE INDEMNITY; COMBINED SINGLE LIMIT.

Limitation Act 1980 Specifies the maximum periods from the accrual of the cause of action for which claims will be heard before becoming statute-barred. The main periods are: six years for simple contracts and claims for personal property; 12 years for contracts by deed or concerning real property and land; and three years for personal injury (but the court can extend this period (s.11)). If the claimant is unable to take action at the time of accrual because of a disability (e.g. mental incapacity), the time runs from when the disability ends. By s.11 the time runs from the cause of action or when the claimant first had significant knowledge of his right of claim and the identity of the defendant. The Latent Damages Act 1986 (qv) deals with latent damage cases.

Limited binding authority A binding authority (qv) that does not permit the coverholder (qv) to underwrite risks on behalf of a Lloyd's syndicate without prior agreement or confirmation by the syndicate.

Limited conditions reinsurance (LCR) Reinsurance where the cover provided is more limited than cover under the primary policy. Example: a hull is insured 'named perils' including partial loss under the primary policy but reinsured 'total loss only' (qv). LCR safeguards the reinsured's treaty programme from a major loss by redirecting the total loss claim to LCR, normally arranged facultatively.

Limited premium life policy A life policy under which the premium is payable for a limited period only and not the full duration of the policy term; e.g., a whole life policy may be written with premiums terminating at age 65 while the policy remains in force.

Limited Price Indexation (LPI) *See* INDEXATION.

LIMNET Means the London Insurance Market Network, a computerised network. It merged under WISE (World Insurance E-Commerce) (qv) with two other leading electronic networks in 1999.

Line 1.The proportion of risk accepted by a (re)insurer. In reinsurance the cedant's retention is a 'line' and the capacity of a surplus treaty is a multiple of the 'line'. A £50,000 retention and a ten-line surplus treaty creates reinsurance capacity of £500,000 enabling a risk of £550,000 to be accepted. 2. The amount accepted by an underwriter when signing a slip is called the 'written line'. 3. Term describing a category of insurance as in 'personal lines', i.e. insurances by individuals in their private capacity (e.g. household, private car, etc.).

Line of credit A method of risk financing (qv) involving the agreement of a bank to provide finance to fund losses as they occur. Contingency funds arranged in this way may reduce a firm's borrowing capacity and restrict its investment potential but may be advantageous for firms with a good credit rating. The lender charges for guaranteeing the standby line of credit. If not used there will be no additional charge. *See* CONTINGENT CAPITAL.

Line slip Arrangement whereby underwriters or companies and a broker agree, for a specified type of risk, that the broker only needs to approach the leading and second underwriter who accept or reject each risk on behalf of all the underwriters concerned in their agreed proportions. This is used when a broker places a large number of similar risks with the same group of underwriters.

'Liner allowances' *See* OVERTIME; TEMPORARY REPAIRS.

Lines to stand A condition whereby a broker secures an underwriter's commitment on the monetary amount of his acceptance, even though on closing, this line may represent an increased percentage of a reduced limit. This will happen if the placement is not completed and allows the broker to place 100 per cent of a smaller amount not exceeding the monetary amount with the underwriter. This happens when the broker has doubts about the availability of the capacity for full placement.

Linked assets Long-term business (qv) assets by reference to which linked benefits are determined. These assets are separated from the other long-term business assets of the company.

Linked benefit The value of the rights conferred under a life policy or collective investment scheme by reference to the value of specific assets or fluctuations in an index of the value of such assets, e.g. unit trust holdings.

Linked-life insurance (or life-linked) Investment schemes offered by life insurers in which premiums paid by the policyholders as investors are used partly to purchase life insurance and partly to purchase units in a unit trust (qv) or unitised fund (qv). The proceeds or benefits payable will be the greater of the guaranteed sum insured or the value of the units accrued. *See* UNIT-LINKED LIFE INSURANCE.

Linked qualifying service Linking together of a member's pension benefit and period service in one scheme with the benefits the member earns in a new scheme. The previous benefits are transferred. The qualifying service in the two schemes is linked.

Liquidated and ascertained damages Damages specified in a contract representing a genuine pre-estimate of compensation due for an anticipated breach of contract, (e.g. delay in completion). They are usually expressed in agreed sums per week. Liquidated damages are only levied when reasons for delay do not entitle the party concerned to an extension of time. Liability insurers specifically exclude any liability to pay liquidated damages or penalties.

Liquidation Legal process of winding up insolvent companies. The liquidator endeavours to recover the maximum sums due to the company for the benefit of the creditors and other stakeholders (qv). He may recover from the directors if they are personally liable to the company for any breach of duty. Liquidators have to carry out their duties with skill and care. Special *enabling bonds* (qv) are available for insolvency practitioners so that cover becomes automatic whenever needed. Liquidation may lead to claims under a *directors' and officers' liability insurance* (qv).

Liquidity risk The risk that an individual or business will be unable to meet its financial obligations from its cashflow. This may lead to an entity having to quickly convert assets into cash at considerable loss or becoming insolvent.

Listed vehicle Lloyd's corporate vehicle listed on the London Stock Exchange.

Livestock insurance Insurance of livestock against death through accident or disease. Insurances usually relate to horses and cattle, but pigs and sheep can be covered. A fresh proposal is obtained each year. The main categories are: horses; hunters and polo ponies; foaling risks; bloodstock; cattle; transit and show risks; castration.

LLD Abbreviation for the Lloyd's Sourcebook performing a similar function for Lloyd's as IPRU (INS) does for insurance companies.

Lloyd's London-based major insurance marketplace that originated from Edward Lloyd's coffee house after the Great Fire of London in 1666. It became a meeting place for persons interested in shipping and marine insurance. Lloyd's became incorporated by statute in 1871 and is now controlled by the Lloyd's Act 1982 (qv) with oversight from the FSA (qv). Lloyd's provides facitities for its members who underwrite risks by participating with others in syndicates. The Society of Lloyd's (qv) is directed by the Council of Lloyd's (qv) with operational responsibility in the hands of the Lloyd's Franchise Board (qv). Business is transacted through accredited Lloyd's brokers.

Lloyd's Act 1982 Outcome of the Fisher Report on the effectiveness of Lloyd's powers of self-regulation. Led to the formation of the Council of Lloyd's (qv) to assume the rule-making and disciplinary functions previously vested in Lloyd's membership as a whole. The Act incorporates the proposal that Lloyd's brokers should divest themselves of their interests in underwriting agencies. The Council now exercise its powers subject to FSA (qv) oversight.

Lloyd's advisers Advise corporate members (qv) of Lloyd's. They recommend their members to particular syndicates. Dedicated vehicles (qv) do not use Lloyd's advisers. The Lloyd' Advisers Bye-law governs registration and regulation of Lloyd's advisers. Advisers must show that they have sufficient skill, competence and experience to advise on syndicate participation and must satisfy Lloyd's on their approach to syndicate analysis. The Council of Lloyd's has discretion to determine whether an existing or prospective Lloyd's adviser is 'fit and proper'.

Lloyd's agents A worldwide network of agents who supply the shipping intelligence for publication in Lloyd's List (qv) and Lloyd's Shipping Index (qv). They also arrange for inspections and reports on reported losses. Many are authorised to settle claims and get involved with non-marine insurances, notably aviation and travel claims. There are over 400 agents and 500 sub-agents. A Lloyd's agent is not a 'legal agent', he acts on his own account and is not authorised to receive notice of abandonment (qv).

Lloyd's American Trust Fund Trust fund maintained in the US by Lloyd's underwriters since 1939. All premiums received in respect of policies issued by the underwriters in US dollars are vested in Citibank as trustee for the benefit of the holders of such policies.

Lloyd's Aviation Publication covering aviation loss, surveying and adjusting. It also provides operational and maintenance studies and aircraft valuations for both operators and the financial services industry. *See* BLUE BOOK.

Lloyd's Aviation Underwriters' Association (LAUA) A specialist group of aviation underwriters who combine to represent their common interests in consultation with the Committee of Lloyd's, government departments, etc. It maintains close links with company market and aviation insurers throughout the world. It publishes Lloyd's policy forms and is represented on the joint technical and clauses committee.

Lloyd's brokers Accredited brokers able to enter the underwriting room at Lloyd's and place risks. All applicants for accreditation must be members of the

General Insurance Standards Council (GISC) (qv) but in 2005 will come under FSA regulation. They are required to carry professional indemnity insurance (qv). They must also comply with the LMP 2001 Principles (qv) and interface with Lloyd's business systems. The accreditation process has other high standard requirements. Lloyd's brokers also place risks with insurance companies. *See* LOCAL BROKERS.

Lloyd's Canadian Trust Fund Trust fund created into which Lloyd's underwriters must pay all of their Canadian dollar premiums. The fund is held by the Royal Trust Corporation of Canada.

Lloyd's Casualty Week Lloyd's Marine Intelligence Unit (qv), provides weekly reports on marine, non-marine and aviation casualty information. Insurers, shipowners, cargo owners, shipping agents and others are able to find information on catastrophic events, labour disputes, seizures and arrests, natural disasters and other categories of unforeseen events that affect shipping, transport, trade, or insurance. The Unit analyses world casualties and their impact.

Lloyd's Central Fund A fund available to meet claims when *premium trust funds* (qv), *Funds at Lloyd's* (qv) *and members' means* (qv) have proved insufficient. All syndicates pay into this fund annually at a rate set by Lloyd's centrally. The fund is backed by reinsurance that pays out if claims exceed £100 million in any one year up to £350 million. The *central fund callable layer* provides further funds (total value of £300 million) that Lloyd's can call upon from syndicates' premium trust funds. *See* LLOYD'S CHAIN OF SECURITY.

Lloyd's 'Chain of Security' Chain underpinning the ability of Lloyd's to pays its claims. The first link is the *premiums trust funds* (qv); the second is *Funds at Lloyd's* (qv); the third is *members' means* (qv); the fourth is the *Lloyd's Central Fund* (qv). This is all supported by *Lloyd's long-term financial security* (qv). The FSA (qv) has proposed that the Financial Services Compensation Scheme (qv) would act as a last resort if the Lloyd's Central Fund (qv) could not finance a claim following the insolvency of a Lloyd's syndicate.

Lloyd's, classes of business Lloyd's underwrites five main classes of business: marine, non-marine, motor, aviation and term life.

Lloyd's Code for Sound and Prudent Management Requires that Lloyd's agencies should be directed and managed by a sufficient number of persons who are fit and proper for their positions. There also has to be proper staffing, supervision and accountability and compliance. The Code specifically requires the involvement of non-executive directors of suitable calibre and enough in number to carry sufficient weight in the board's decisions. *See* CORPORATE GOVERNANCE AT LLOYD'S.

Lloyd's Codes Handbook Codes of conduct detailing how underwriting agents (qv) can best meet their responsibilities under Lloyd's Core Principles (qv). All codes originate as regulatory bulletins (qv). The codes, supplementary to the Council's byelaws (qv), promote best practice. Compliance is strong evidence of the adequacy of the underwriting agent's procedures. The various entities at Lloyd's must also comply with FSA (qv) codes.

Lloyd's, Conduct of Business Registered members of Lloyd's (qv) must adhere to certain standards of conduct of business set out in byelaws and codes. The FSA's Conduct of Business Sourcebook includes a chapter on Lloyd's (qv).

Lloyd's core compliance activities Set out in regulatory bulletin 025/96. A managing or members' agent's compliance oversight officer must concern himself that his firm meets the regulatory requirements in respect of: operating procedures; in-house rules; notification requirements; advisory services; regular monitoring/internal audit; complaints procedures; staff training; names' compliance (members' agents); compliance review.

Lloyd's Core Principles Lloyd's equivalent of the FSA's Principles for Business (qv). They have much common ground (e.g. integrity; skill, care and diligence; market conduct; conflicts of interest) without being identical. Differences are mainly in terms of focus. The FSA emphasises customers' interests whereas Lloyd's focuses on 'conduct towards members' reflecting differences between personal financial advice and the underwriting of a wide range of risks.

Lloyd's corporate members Companies with limited or unlimited liability admitted to membership at Lloyd's. They engage managing agents but are not obliged to use a member's agent. Corporate members originally participated across a spread of syndicates but regulatory changes enable them to dedicate their total capacity to a single syndicate. The corporate member and its managing agent may both be owned by an integrated Lloyd's vehicle (qv). Other corporate structures are *spread vehicles* (qv) and *dedicated vehicles* (qv).

Lloyd's, Corporation of When incorporated under the Lloyd's Act 1871 no distinction was made between the Corporation and the Society of Lloyd's (qv). The Corporation has historic links with Edward Lloyd's eighteenth-century coffee house, a meeting place for underwriters, shippers, etc. The Corporation does not underwrite business but is the platform from which business is done. The Corporation's departments include the commercial directorate, market supervision, legal services, worldwide markets, IT, education and training, compliance and authorisations.

Lloyd's, Council of Created by the Lloyd's Act 1982 (qv), the Council manages and supervises the Lloyd's market. It is the internal regulator of Lloyd's subject to the overriding supervision of the FSA (qv). The Council has six working, six external and six nominated members. The appointment of the nominated members has to be confirmed by the Governor of the Bank of England. Lloyd's members select the remaining members. The Council makes decisions, issues resolutions, requirements, rules and byelaws (qv), but now delegates a range of issues to the Lloyd's Franchise Board (qv).

Lloyd's Fire Policy This policy varies from the standard fire policy in that fire caused by explosion is covered.

Lloyd's Form of Salvage Agreement Known as Lloyd's Open Form (LOF), administered by Lloyd's Salvage Arbitration Branch, it is a contract between the salvor ('the contractor') and the shipowner. It is impracticable for the agreement to be signed by the numerous cargo owners normally involved. The Agreement operates on a 'no cure – no pay' basis and provides for the appointment by Lloyd's of an arbitrator to decide on the amount to be paid. The Agreement also permits a maritime lien (qv) to the salvor.

Lloyd's franchise Lloyd's Franchise Board (qv), acting through executive directors, is franchisor, contracting with *managing agents* (qv). The franchisor provides agreed service standards and the franchisee must promote and protect the Lloyd's brand, security and licences and prepare an annual business plan. Lloyd's assists with business plans and ways to improve results but can impose constraints on syndicates and ultimately remove a franchisee from Lloyd's. The franchisee contributes to the Lloyd's central fund (qv). *See* LLOYD'S FRANCHISE BOARD.

Lloyd's Franchise Board The Board, acting as franchisor, is accountable to the Council of Lloyd's (qv). It sets the franchise strategy, profitability targets and high standard risk management It provides guidelines for all syndicates and operates a business planning and monitoring process. The Board is also responsible for supervision and solvency of the Lloyd's franchise (qv); operating through key sub-committees, it replaces the Lloyd's Market Board and Regulatory Board.

Lloyd's franchisee Each managing agent (qv) is a franchisee running an independent specialist insurance or reinsurance business within the framework set by the Lloyd's Franchise Board (qv).

Lloyd's Introductory Test An examination introduced at Lloyd's by Bye-law No. 8 of 1985. Each new entrant to the Room must take the test soon after starting at Lloyd's.

Lloyd's Law Reports Maritime and insurance cases heard in the English courts but include important Scottish, Commonwealth and US decisions. The reports are an important source of commercial law information as about 80 per cent of the reports are not published in other law reports.

Lloyd's licences Licences that permit Lloyd's to undertake insurance business in other countries (60 in 2003). The licences and eligibility relate to direct insurance, but reinsurance can be undertaken in many other territories. In some instances (e.g. Argentina, Ecuador, Mexico in 2003) the licences relate only to reinsurance.

Lloyd's Life Assurance Ltd A separate company established in 1971 by Lloyd's underwriters to offer life insurance schemes through insurance brokers.

Lloyd's List International Daily publication of news regarding shipping and aviation matters (shipping movements, marine and aviation casualties, fires) read worldwide by management from transport and associated industries. It also reports on ships sales, purchases, launchings, chartering, offshore industry and the tanker and dry cargo markets. The List is now published by Informa (qv).

Lloyd's Loading List Provides exporters and freight forwarders with a valuable guide to cargo-carrying services available from UK and European ports. It is now compiled by Informa (qv).

Lloyd's long-term financial security The total resources of Lloyd's and its members, it equalled £21.9 billion in 2002. Lloyd's has paid every valid claim for over 300 years. Lloyd's is rated A (excellent) by A.M. Best (April 2002) and A (strong) by Standard and Poors (May 2002). All Lloyd's syndicates benefit from the ratings accorded to Lloyd's regardless of individual performance.

Lloyd's Marine Policy (MAR 91) Standard policy containing schedule setting out: name of insured; subject-matter insured; premium; summary of pertinent clauses (e.g. Institute Cargo Clauses A (qv)), endorsements, special conditions and warranties. Importantly the policy states '*The Attached Clauses and Endorsements Form a Part of this Policy.*' The International Underwriting Association of London produces a parallel policy, the IUA Marine Policy.

Lloyd's Market Association (LMA) Represents underwriting businesses at Lloyd's. Brings together five previously separate associations: Lloyd's Underwriters' Association (LUA), Lloyd's Underwriters' Non-Marine Association, Lloyd's Underwriting Agents' Association, and Lloyd's Market Association (previously the Lloyd's Corporate Capital Association). Each retains its own identity while using the LMA structure in dealing with Lloyd's and the regulators. Two-thirds of the LMA budget is used to provide technical support for the marine, non-marine and aviation markets. The LMA's key partners are the London Insurance Market Brokers' Committee and the International Underwriting Association (qv). The LMA represents its members on international bodies.

Lloyd's Market Intelligence Unit (LMIU) Provides a family of shipping industry products covering: global shipping movements updated daily; casualties as they happen; ownership, and Protection and Indemnity Clubs – changes as they happen; vessel characteristics; new construction; a combination of the above; a maritime consulting business. (Visit *www.lloyds.miu.com*). LMIU is a division of Informa (qv).

Lloyd's members' margin *See* REQUIRED MEMBERS' MARGINS (LLOYD'S).

Lloyd's members' means *See* MEMBERS' MEANS.

Lloyd's membership A Lloyd's member is either a *name* (qv) or a *corporate member* (qv) who supplies the capital to underwrite risks at Lloyd's. They delegate the underwriting of business to *managing agents* (qv) and members' agents provide a link with syndicates. New names are no longer admitted and by 2005 remaining names should have converted to limited liability. Each member maintains *funds at Lloyd's* (qv). The *integrated Lloyd's vehicle (ILV)* is the principal route for new capital. Names now operate mainly through *members' agents pooling arrangements (MAPA)* (qv). Corporate members include companies, investment institutions and international insurance companies, and Scottish limited partnerships. *See* MEMBERS' ANNUAL SOLVENCY TEST.

Lloyd's Motor Underwriters' Association (LMUA) Association working on behalf of motor syndicates to place motor cars into groups according to the degree of hazard and cost of repair for the purpose of rating motor risks. The ABI's Motor Committee of the Association carries out the same work.

Lloyd's of London Press Ltd Corporation of Lloyd's (qv) subsidiary that became the Informa Group on its merger with IBC Ltd in 1995. Informa has continued to collect, process and publish the enormous volume of information received from Lloyd's agents and other worldwide connections. The best known publication is Lloyd's List International (qv).

Lloyd's Policy Signing Office LPSO was created to facilitate the checking and signing of policies prepared by Lloyd's brokers on behalf of underwriters. It also performs a number of other functions such as central accounting. LPSO's work has been transferred to the Insur-sure Services Ltd (qv).

Lloyd's Register LR's principal marine business is that of a classification society (qv) for ships. It sets standards of quality and reliability during design, construction and operation. A ship's hull and machinery must conform with the standards laid down and are inspected to ensure that they comply. Formerly known as Lloyd's Register of Shipping, the new name reflects the wide-ranging services supplied to other industrial sectors. (Visit *www.lr.org*).

Lloyd's, regulation of The external regulator, the FSA (qv), delegates to the Council of Lloyd's (qv), the internal regulator. The Council must maintain an effective delegation of responsibilities for the purpose of carrying out the Society's regulatory functions so that the Council can adequately control them. The Society deals cooperatively with the FSA in carrying out those regulatory functions and notifies the FSA when proposing byelaw changes. The byelaws (qv) are supplemented by Core Principles for Underwriting Agents (qv) and various codes. The FSA will regulate Lloyd's brokers from 2005. *See* MARGIN OF SOLVENCY; REQUIRED MARGIN (GENERAL BUSINESS); REQUIRED MARGIN (LONG TERM BUSINESS).

Lloyd's Shipping Index A unique daily record of the details and latest worldwide movements of more than 23,000 merchant vessels. The report includes details of ownership changes and casualty histories. The information is provided by Lloyd's Market Intelligence Unit (qv).

Lloyd's, Society of Lloyd's Act 1871 incorporated Lloyd's as a 'Society and Corporation' without distinguishing between the two. However, FSMA, s.190, specifically makes *the Society* an authorised person (qv) enabling the FSA (qv) to make rules and take disciplinary action against it. The FSA can issue directions to members of the Society or (s.193) direct the Society, through its Council (qv), to impose obligations on its members. The Society is often said to comprise those individuals and entities that are for the time being members of Lloyd's plus the legal rights and all property that collectively belongs to them.

Lloyd's solvency requirements There is an annual solvency test for members and one for Lloyd's as a whole. A member's agent is responsible for ensuring the ongoing solvency of his member's business. Direct corporate members are responsible for their own solvency. Lloyd's must maintain *net central assets* at a prescribed level (LLD 11.2.1). Central funds must be sufficient to cover (a) any shortfall in the assets of a member when less than the sum of the liabilities and the member's margin; and (b) any adjustment required when overall assets as a whole are less than liabilities. The solvency of managing and members' agents is governed by the normal law relating to limited liability companies. *See* REQUIRED MINIMIMUM MARGIN.

Lloyd's Survey Handbook Reference book setting out information of loss or damage caused to a large number of commodities. Authoritative views are expressed as to the principal causes of loss or damage. The book is valuable to firms and professionals in both shipping, including cargo handling, and insurance, and anyone involved in handling cargoes.

Lloyd's syndicate Group of underwriting members whose syndicate is run by a managing agent (qv) whose active underwriter (qv) accepts risks on behalf of the syndicate. Each syndicate member takes an agreed share of the risk strictly for his own account. Each syndicate is given its own number and is allowed to underwrite up to an allocated premium limit in any given year. At present a syndicate is formed for an underwriting year as an *annual venture* (qv), now being phased out.

Lloyd's underwriter *See* ACTIVE UNDERWRITER.

Lloyd's Underwriters' Association Formed in 1909 it is concerned with the

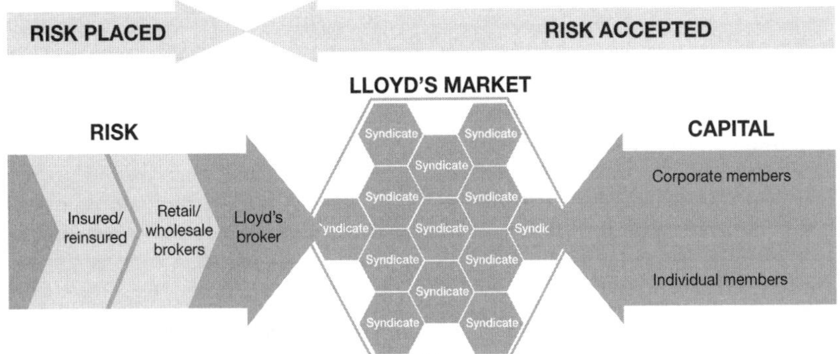

Figure 6. Insurance at Lloyd's

Source: Diagram of insurance at Lloyd's

underwriting, technical and administrative problems that arise in Lloyd's marine market. It liaises closely with Lloyd's Insurance Brokers' Association, the International Underwriters' Association (qv) and the Liverpool Underwriters' Association. Now part of the London Market Association (qv).

Lloyd's Underwriting Agents' Association (LUAA) Protects the interests of underwriting agents (qv) and liaises with Lloyd's. It reports to its members on matters raised by the Council or franchise board (qv). The LUAA has no regulatory power but is represented on both standing and ad hoc committees. Now part of the London Market Association (qv).

Lloyd's World Market Directorate Maintains Lloyd's worldwide trading status. It manages Lloyd's overseas offices, deals with overseas compliance, accredits Lloyd's brokers, promotes Lloyd's and develops its portfolio of licences. It also runs a Business Intelligence Centre with wide-ranging information services. Its electronic and paper-based resources cover insurance markets, companies, news, legal information, etc.

LMP Slip Born out of *London Market Principles 2001* (qv). *See* SLIP.

Loading 1. Adjustments made to the risk premium, i.e. pure premium (qv), to calculate the premium. Loadings include allowances for office expenses, profit and loss escalation. 2. An increased charge as an underwriting measure in respect of a higher normal risk. 3. Placing goods on a vessel or vehicle. In marine, goods in transit, commercial vehicle and public liability cover, the acts of loading and unloading may signify the moment that the risk attaches or terminates. A 'loading/unloading' clause provides a dividing line between the public liability policy and commercial vehicle third party section.

Loan insurance *See* LOAN PROTECTION POLICY.

Loan protection policy Policy providing a benefit to help the policyholder meet his loan obligations during periods of incapacity through sickness or accident or through unemployment following redundancy. It is a creditor insurance (qv).

Loan to Value (LTV) The amount of a mortgage expressed as a percentage of the property value or purchase price. A mortgage of £75,000 on a £100,000 property value would mean a LTV of 75 per cent.

Loanback A loan facility generally available under a personal pension scheme. Common uses of the loan include purchase of house or business premises (pension mortgages), or new machinery, or meeting short-term requirements. The policyholder has to provide security for the loan, as the pension policy cannot be used for this purpose. A first or second charge on property is normally taken but the lender may take other forms of security. The loan does not have to be repaid until retirement at which time it is financed out of the tax-free lump sum available at that time.

Loans (life policies) Whole life and endowment policies include a privilege clause undertaking to grant a loan up to 90 per cent or 95 per cent of the surrender value (qv). The rate of interest is determined at the time of the loan. Repayment can be made at any time or when the policy matures. Meanwhile interest and premiums are payable. An alternative way of securing a loan on a life policy is to use it as collateral security (qv) when borrowing from a bank.

Local authority indemnity A policy issued to local authorities to provide an indemnity in respect of third party claims following errors and omissions in respect of local land charges, etc., and notices issued in connection with them.

Local brokers/producing broker Lloyd's term for an unaccredited broker who accesses the Lloyd's market through an accredited broker.

Local government bond A guarantee to a local or public authority required under the Local Government Act 1972, s.114, in respect of loss of money or other property due to the dishonesty of officials employed by the authority.

Location clause Cargo insurance clause in open covers (qv) limiting cover at any one location during transit when the goods are not on the oversea vessel. Shipments may accumulate at one port and the clause limits the insurer's liability to an amount for any one loss in any one location.

London insurance market Rarely defined, but usually means the international insurance business written in London. It consists of: 1. Home foreign, namely direct overseas business written in the UK. 2. International reinsurance (large volumes of business generally come from the US). 3. Marine and aviation. 4. US excess and surplus lines business. London market premiums earn a gross income about equal to that derived from UK 'domestic' commercial business and UK personal lines business.

London Market Excess of Loss (LMX) Excess of loss reinsurances of Lloyd's syndicates and London companies that accept business in the *subscription market* (qv). Reinsurances of Lloyd's motor and employers' liability insurances are not part of the subscription market and are not therefore LMX. The concept of LMX originally centred around whether the business included *assumed reinsurance* (qv) or US business.

London Market Principles 2001 Optimisation of client service with a more open and efficient operating environment by enhancing the clarity of contracts and payment terms. LMP updates are published periodically. The Principles have been drawn up jointly by Lloyd's, the International Underwriters' Association (IUA) (qv) and the Lloyd's Insurance Brokers' Committee (LIBC) (qv). 'One stop' processing for the entire London market has been facilitated through Insur-sure Ltd (qv) together with electronic trading through WISE (qv).

London Processing Centre (LPC) Created by the International Underwriting Association (qv) as the centralised policy signing and claims processing bureau for the international insurance company market in London. It set up a central settlement system for members' and brokers' accounts known as LIPS (the LPC Irrevocable Payment System) and settled most claims electronically using the LPC's Claims and Loss Advice Settlement System (CLASS). These services transferred to Ins-sure Services Ltd (qv) in 2001.

London Underwriting Centre (LUC) Premises near Lloyd's providing underwriting rooms for leading insurance and reinsurance companies. The companies take up leases and some make LUC their main London office. At peak times there are between 3,500 and 4,000 broker-visits a day (normally it is 2,000 to 2,500) to the LUC, which also houses the International Underwriting Association (qv). All tenants benefit from computer-based communications linking to the world market. Full network facilities and other electronic systems are available.

Long service benefit Benefit payable at normal retirement age under the preservation requirements of PSA93 with which short service benefit must be compared.

Long-tail liability Liability for an injury, e.g. *asbestosis* (qv), that takes many years before it is discovered and reported as a claim. As most policies are written on a *losses-occurring basis* (qv) it is necessary to trace the insurer on risk at the time of occurrence. Gradual pollution is also a cause of long-tail liability. *See* LIABILITY SEQUENCE; OCCURRENCE THEORIES.

Long Term Agreement An agreement by the insured to renew a policy on the original terms for a given term of years, e.g. three, in return for a premium discount.

LTAs are separate contracts and if the insurer offers amended cover, the insured can avoid renewals. LTAs are most common in commercial insurance.

Long-term business Schedule 1 of FSMA 2000 (Regulated Activities) Order 2001, as amended by the FSMA (Regulated Activities) (Amendment Order) (No 2) Order 2003, lists nine classes of long-term business as regulated activities. I. Life and annuity. II. Marriage and birth. III. Linked long-term. IV. Permanent health. V. Tontines. VI. Capital redemption. VII. Pension fund management. VIII. Collective insurance, etc. IX. Social insurance. There are 18 general insurance business (qv) classes listed as regulated activities.

Long-term care bonds Investment bonds designed to cover the cost of care in old age. They can be used to cover 'residential home' cost as well as the expenses incurred when care takes place in the home (i.e. residence) of the individual. *See* LONG-TERM CARE INSURANCE.

Long-term care insurance Contributes to the cost of residential or home care for persons unable to perform the '*activities of daily life*' (qv) because of a disability or age-related condition. Pre-funded insurance plans are available for the healthy with no immediate care needs. Immediate plans are arranged only when care is actually needed and this often involves the purchase of an immediate care annuity payable directly tax-free to the host care home.

Loss A claim under a policy. The financial loss caused to the insured by the occurrence of the event insured against. Certain 'loss' definitions such as *constructive total loss* (qv) are contained in the Marine Insurance Act 1906.

Loss adjuster Independent claims expert engaged by insurers to investigate claims and assess the true extent and value of any loss. Loss adjusters are not engaged for smaller, routine losses. The relevant professional body is the Chartered Institute of Loss Adjusters.

Loss adjustment expense (LAE) The expense incurred by a cedant (qv) in the defence and settlement of claims but not its overhead expenses. The definition of LAE depends on the terms of the reinsurance contract.

Loss assessor A person, sometimes called a public loss assessor, with specialist knowledge, appointed by the insured to assess his claim and negotiate a settlement with the insurer or insurer's representative, e.g. loss adjuster (qv).

Loss development The difference between the initial estimate of a loss and the amount estimated at a later date or the amount paid on settlement at which point it is the difference between the amount reserved and the amount paid.

Loss occurrence 1. Occurrence of a single loss. 2. An occurrence of several losses arising out of the same incident or catastrophe in accordance with a policy definition such as an hours clause (qv) or claims series clause (qv).

Loss of attraction Extension to a business interruption policy covering loss of gross profit due to damage to a nearby attraction that draws passing trade to the business. It is an *external dependency* (qv). Fire damage at the main store in a shopping mall will reduce sales in neighbouring shops.

Loss of documents Documents vary in nature and value. Material damage policies provide cover only in respect of the cost of the materials and the cost of labour in reinstating the documents. There is no cover for consequential loss. Professional indemnity policies cover 'all risks' on the insured's own documents and those for which the insured is responsible. They also cover the insured's legal liability for loss of documents. *See* COMPUTER SYSTEM RECORDS.

Loss of engagements The marine equivalent of 'loss of use'. A shipowner, who loses the use of his ship through an insured peril insures for 'loss of engagements'.

Loss of expectation of life claims As a separate head of claim it was abolished by the Administration of Justice Act 1982. However, if the claimant's expectation of life has been reduced, any award for pain and suffering may take account of the claimant's anguish caused by his awareness of this reduction.

Loss of hire insurance Insurance for shipowners who may lose a charter as a result of a casualty. The insurance pays an amount per day for a certain number of days per year (e.g. 90, but could be 360) once a 'time deductible', e.g. 14 days, has been exceeded. Cover follows the International Hull Clauses (qv) but excludes total loss.

Loss of licence policy Covers commercial pilots against the risk of temporary grounding or loss of licence on medical grounds. The amount payable is a multiple of the pilot's annual salary cover. The underwriting factors are: type of flying done; geographical limits; flying experience and type of aircraft flown; previous health record; previous licence invalidations.

Loss of specie A change in the nature or character of cargo, vessel or other property (e.g. bicycle crushed by steamroller) so that it is no longer the type of property that was insured. *See* ACTUAL TOTAL LOSS.

Loss of use Inability to use property, e.g. a motor car, during period of repair or replacement. Some insurers provide temporary replacement cars under comprehensive policies. Otherwise the loss, which is consequential, is not covered under material damage insurance and this is often reinforced by a loss of use exclusion. 'Loss of use' may be claimed against a negligent third party. Under houshehold policies the cost of alternative accommodation is covered when the property cannot be occupied following insured damage. *See* LOSS OF USE (AVIATION).

Loss of use (aviation) An insurance to safeguard an aircraft owner against loss of earning capacity when the aircraft is laid-up for repair following an accident. The benefit is as an amount per day subject to a time excess (qv). Cover operates only when a claim is admitted under the hull policy.

Loss portfolio The liability of an insurer for the unexpired portion of the in-force policies or outstanding losses or both for a specified segment of the insurer's business for which reserves have been made. *See* LOSS PORTFOLIO TRANSFER; LOSS PORTFOLIO ENTRY; LOSS PORTFOLIO WITHDRAWAL.

Loss portfolio entry A reinsurer may accept, at inception or renewal of a treaty, responsibility for the cedant's loss portfolio (qv) from the previous year(s). The reinsurer thus pays losses for a contractually defined set of earlier losses in return for the unearned premium.

Loss portfolio transfer (prospective) Transfer of loss portfolio (qv) in respect of claims on the cedant's future business. The terms are adjustable according to the volume of business. The reinsurance recoveries follow the loss pattern of the cedant. The effect is to transfer liabilities to the balance sheet of the reinsurer in return for a premium reflecting the time value of money with the timing and investment risks being assumed by the reinsurer. The cedant replaces unknown liabilities with a known cost and this helps clean up the balance sheet especially if a merger or acquisition is involved. It is an *alternative risk transfer* (qv) product.

Loss portfolio transfer (retrospective) Transfer of incurred losses (loss portfolio (qv)) from an insurer to a reinsurer who receives a premium based on the net present value of losses, loaded for profit, expenses and timing. The reinsurer invests the premium over the time taken to settle the claims. Transfers allow an insurer to improve financial ratios or exit a line business. It is a finite risk solution (qv). *See* LOSS PORTFOLIO ENTRY.

Loss portfolio withdrawal At the end of a reinsurance period, or at the cancellation of a reinsurance contract, the reinsurer can be relieved of responsibility for claims outstanding at that time by paying the cedant a proportion (e.g. 90 per cent) of the outstanding claims.

Loss prevention The measures taken to reduce the probability of the occurrence of a loss. Compare with POST-LOSS MINIMISATION.

Loss rating *See* EXPERIENCE RATING.

Loss ratio The ratio of losses paid and outstanding to premiums. The lower the loss ratio the more satisfactory the outcome and the greater the amount available for commissions, administration costs and profit.

Loss reserves 1. An amount set aside to provide for outstanding claims, reported and not reported. 2. A reserve deposited by a reinsurer with the reinsured to cover outstanding claims. It is often done by way of irrevocable letter of credit in connection with US treaties and contracts.

Loss retention clause Requires the ceding company (qv) to retain a proportion of the loss to the reinsurers (qv) once an agreed loss ratio (qv) has been exceeded.

Losses carried forward *See* DEFICIT CLAUSE.

Losses-occurring policies *See* OCCURRENCE; LIABILITY SEQUENCE; OCCURRENCE TRIGGER THEORIES; TRIPLE TRIGGER THEORY.

Losses occurring reinsurance Covers losses occurring during the period of the treaty regardless of the date of the claim. The reinsurer's liability is triggered by an occurrence within the treaty period even though the underlying policy may have been incepted before the treaty commenced as in long-tail claims (qv). Compare with claims-made reinsurance and risks attaching (qv).

'Lost years' The years by which a person's life expectancy is reduced following injury caused by another person. *During his lifetime* the claimant is able to recover as a separate head of damages for the loss of earnings during the 'lost years' (*Pickett* v. *British Rail Engineering Ltd* (1980) A.C. 136). However, the legal representatives of a deceased person can no longer recover damages under this head for the estate (Adminstration of Justice Act 1982 (qv)).

Low cost endowment A combination of with-profit endowment and decreasing term insurance introduced as a part of *house purchase schemes* (qv).

Low start endowment insurance Variation of low cost endowment (qv) under which the premiums in the early years are low on the understanding that later premiums will be at a higher than normal level to compensate for the early years reduction. The aim is to assist a person with a limited income but who has prospects of good future salary increases. The sum insured and bonuses are not affected by the low early premiums.

Lower earnings limit Minimum a person must earn in any pay period before they have to pay national insurance. Reviewed annually.

Lowering of ground water A 'nuisance' peril that may create liability for third party property damage. Construction industry firms face this risk, which can also cause damage to the contract works and the insured's own property. Insurance can be arranged under JCT clause 21(2)(1) 'non-negligent' cover (qv). Ground water is water occupying the pores and crevices of rock and soil as opposed to surface water. Where the work of the contractor lowers the ground water the stability of buildings may be undermined leading to a nuisance (qv).

Lump sum Method of settlement where the claimant or beneficiary receives the entire proceeds of the policy at once rather than in instalments. Life policies are usually settled in this way.

Lump sum certificate Certificate 'transferring' pension scheme must supply when a member transfers to another scheme. The certificate shows the maximum available from the transfer payment (qv) for the new pension.

Lutine Bell The bell from HMS Lutine, a captured French vessel, lost in 1799 when carrying bullion much of which was recovered in 1857–8. The bell now hangs in the 'Room' at Lloyd's above the Caller's Rostrum and is rung to call attention to very important announcements such as casualties and arrivals of missing ships. It is rung once for bad news and twice for good news.

M

Machinery consequential loss insurance *See* ENGINEERING INTERRUPTION LOSS.

Machinery erection insurance An engineering insurance catering for contractors and others who move, erect or install plant and machinery. The cover enables the contractor to meet his contractual obligations and cover can extend to: testing operations; maintenance period liability; constructional plant and equipment used in connection with the contract; manufacturers' guarantee for repairs or replacements from manufacturing defects.

Made good The sums paid to a general average fund (qv) to make good losses incurred by the general average act.

Mainstream financial activity The FSA regulates professional firms that carry on mainstream financial activity as per the Regulated Activity Order. It includes direct advice to clients on investment and pension products, discretionary investment management and certain types of corporate finance activities such as listing and public offers. Broadly it means standalone investment advice as opposed to advice as an adjunct to the provision of professional services, e.g. legal services. Such firms must become *authorised professional firms* (qv). A professional firm not conducting mainstream financial activity, whose advice is incidental to a professional activity, can become *an exempt professional firm* (qv) regulated by a *designated professional body* (qv).

Maintenance bond Performance bond (qv) under which the surety guarantees that the contractor will fulfil his obligations during the maintenance period (qv) that follows completion.

Maintenance period The period after completion of a construction contract during which the contractor is responsible for maintenance issues and defects. During this period (commonly 12 months), the contractor should maintain his insurance as required by contract. Different levels of cover are available (visits maintenance, extended maintenance guarantee maintenance) depending on the specifics of the contract. *See* JOINT CONTRACTS TRIBUNAL; CONTRACT WORKS.

Maintenance warranty A fire policy clause requiring the insured to maintain the premises in a good and substantial state of repair during the currency of the policy.

Major syndicate transaction Where a mandatory offer (qv) has resulted in the major stakeholder in a Lloyd's syndicate holding at least 90 per cent or more of syndicate capacity, the managing agent may seek permission from the Council (qv) to compulsorily acquire the remaining part of the capacity from the minority interests. (Byelaw 18/97).

Malicious damage Unlawful damage committed by individuals motivated by ill will in circumstances not amounting to a riot (qv). Riot cover normally extends to cover damage caused by malicious persons acting on behalf of a political organisation. Malicious damage can be covered more generally as an additional peril (qv) subject to an excess and the exclusion of loss by theft.

Malpractice insurance Describes the professional indemnity insurance (qv) issued to doctors, nurses, surgeons, hospitals and practitioners of complementary therapists. The term is also used more generally in the US as an alternative for professional indemnity (qv).

Managed fund A unit-linked fund (qv) or insurer managed fund in which transactions in the underlying assets are decided by the fund manager. Normally fund managers invest in a spread of all types of assets as opposed to a specified type of asset.

Management of Health and Safety at Work Regulations 1999 (MSHW) Regulations principally concerned with risk assessment, management, health surveillance, use of competent assistance and provision of information and training for employees. Employers and the self-employed must carry must out a risk assessment and have arrangements for effective planning, organisation, control, monitoring and review of their preventative and protective measures. Employers with five employees or more must record their assessments. Regulatory breach is a criminal offence and, by an amendment, it is intended to allow civil claims against the employer.

Managing agents Corporate bodies responsible for running Lloyd's syndicates. They appoint the active underwriter (qv) and the staff. The *managing agent's agreement* sets out the duties, powers and remuneration of the agent and obligations of the member. Since 2003 managing agents have been granted franchises (qv) to operate within Lloyd's. Some even provide capital to the syndicates they manage in which case they become corporate members (qv). Lloyd's has published a number of codes of practice for managing agents.

Mandatory approval The IR must approve an occupational pension scheme that meets the requirements of ICTA 1988, s.590(3). The benefit under such schemes (approved schemes (qv)) must be a pension on retirement at a specified age between 60 and 75 not exceeding one-sixtieth of final remuneration for each year of service up to a maximum of 40. Cash commutation must not exceed three-eightieths of final remuneration for each year of service. A widow(er)'s pension in death after retirement must not exceed two-thirds of the employee's pension. These and other restrictions result in most schemes preferring *exempt approved scheme status* (qv).

Mandatory offer An offer that a Lloyd's member or group of members holding 75 per cent of a syndicate's capacity must make to acquire the syndicate's residual capacity. In practice it means that corporate members aligned to a syndicate are obliged to make an offer to buy out the unaligned members who are not obliged to accept. *See* MAJOR SYNDICATE TRANSACTION.

Manifestation theory *See* OCCURRENCE TRIGGER THEORIES; TRIPLE TRIGGER THEORY.

Manual Handling Regulations 1992 MHR apply to virtually every form of employment. Employers should avoid manual handling whenever 'reasonably practicable' otherwise they must make a risk assessment based on the task, the load, the environment and the person. The employer's duty is to make the task safe while the employee should use the systems of work for handling operations. A breach by the employer amounts to a criminal offence and may provide the basis for an injured employee to claim damages.

Manuscript policy A written policy based on the specific needs of a large commercial insured such as a major airline. The standard policy form is not suitable and at the request of the broker or risk manager the manuscript policy is drawn up.

MAR 91 Policy form used in the London market to which the standard Institute

Clauses must be attached. The form sets out the agreement to insure in simple terms leaving cover to be defined by the standard clauses.

Margin of solvency Surplus of insurer's realisable assets over its liabilities. General insurers and long-term insurers must demonstrate a *required minimum margin* of solvency (RMM). For a general insurer this is the higher of two results, one based on annual premiums (the premium basis), the other based on the average of three years' claims (the claims basis). Also an insurer must ensure that the margin does not fall below the guarantee fund. One-third of the required margin of solvency constitutes the *minimum guarantee fund (MGF)*. The MGF for a general insurer varies according to the class of business up to €3 million for motor, aviation, general, credit and suretyship (less for mutuals). RMM also varies, according to class, for long-term business. For life business this is €3 million for proprietary companies (less for mutuals). *See* ASSET RULES; DETERMINATION OF LIABILITY RULES; MINIMUM GUARANTEE FUND.

Marine and Aviation Insurance (War Risks) Act 1952 Empowers the UK government to reinsure British ships and aircraft against war risks and, when in the UK, cargo, foreign ships and aircraft. In the absence of an alternative, the government can also provide primary war risk insurance if the UK is at war. This is important as war risks cover in the commercial markets is subject to cancellation at short notice at time of war or terrorism. The government used its powers during the Gulf war and again following 'September 11'. It formed a company, Troika, to provide war and terrorism cover for airlines and service providers pending the return of commercial reinsurers to the war risks market.

Marine and aviation risks exclusion Public liability exclusion of risks insurable in the marine and aviation markets. The exclusion is of liability arising out of the ownership, possession or use by by the insured of aircraft, hovercraft or watercraft other than barges, motor launches and non-powered craft used on inland waterways. The ownership or use of small craft is not excluded. Also the insurer modifies the exclusion so that any contingent or vicarious liability associated with craft not owned or operated by the insured is covered.

Marine cargo certificate of insurance Evidence that an individual consignment is insured. Banks will only discount bills of exchange on the production of this certificate.

Marine clause A fire insurance clause excluding property which is insured or would but for the existence of the fire policy be insured by a marine policy except for any excess beyond the amount which would be paid by a marine policy.

Marine extension clause (MEC) Cargo policy clause extending the warehouse to warehouse clause (qv). It provides continuous cover during any deviation (qv), delay (qv), reshipment, trans-shipment or other interruption in the course of transit beyond the control of the insured. The policy is extended during the delay but does not add delay as an insured peril.

Marine insurance Marine Insurance Act, s.1: 'a contract whereby the insurer undertakes to indemnify the assured, in manner and to the extent thereby agreed, against marine losses, that is to say, the losses incident to marine adventure'.

Marine Insurance (Gambling Policies) Act 1909 *See* GAMBLING POLICIES.

Maritime adventure Defined in the Marine Insurance Act 1906 as existing where (i) tangible property is exposed to loss by maritime perils (qv), (ii) any pecuniary interest, etc., is thereby endangered, or (iii) any third party liability incurred. To be insurable, such adventure must be lawful.

Maritime lien Right of a salvor to hold the property that has been saved pending payment of the salvage award. Under the Lloyd's Form of Salvage Agreement the lien is discharged when the owner of the salved property provides a general average deposit (qv), general average guarantee (qv) or some other form of general average security (qv). *See* IN REM.

Maritime perils Means: 'perils consequent upon, or incidental to, the navigation of the sea, that is, perils of the sea (qv), fire, war perils, pirates, rovers, thieves, capture, seizure (qv), restraints and detainments of princes and peoples, jettisons, barratry (qv), and any other perils, either of the like kind or which may be designated by the policy' (Marine Insurance Act 1906).

Market abuse Behaviour in relation to qualifying investments which, by the 'regular user test', is likely to be regarded as abusive, particularly if: the behaviour is considered to be based on information that is not generally available (misuse of information); the behaviour is considered to give a false or misleading impression of the supply, demand, price and value of investments; or the behaviour is likely to distort the market in investments in question. The sanctions are criminal and civil. (Visit *www.fsa.gov.uk*).

Market agreement Voluntary agreement among insurers to establish cost saving practices. Insurers enter into claims agreements to avoid expensive arguments about liability or quantum when each insurer insures a party involved in the same accident. The agreements work best when each insurer writes a similar account so that, overall, the net amount that one insurer would owe another under normal legal processes is insignificant compared with the savings gained. *See* MEMORANDUM OF UNDERSTANDING (qv).

Market capacity *See* CAPACITY.

Market captive The parent of a captive insurance company (qv).

Market level adjustment Adjustment applied to actuarial liability (qv) to reflect the difference between the market value and the actuarial value of the assets.

Market overt The rule, that a person who bought goods in 'market overt' (an open market) acquired a good title even if the goods were stolen, has been abolished by the Sale of Goods (Amendment) Act 1994. The so-called 'thieves charter' prejudiced the real owners of the goods and frustrated the subrogation rights (qv) of theft insurers.

Market share liability A principle whereby all manufacturers of a particular type of product share liability for its injurious nature in proportion to their market shares for that particular product. The principle is adopted in some US courts where the cause of the harm cannot be traced to particular manufacturers.

Market wordings database A collection of wordings created from duplicate wordings being registered by Lloyd's brokers. It means that more wordings are available to other brokers and underwriters.

Married Women's Policies of Assurance (Scotland) Act 1880 The Scottish equivalent of the Married Women's Property Act 1882 (qv).

Married Women's Property Act 1882 Allows a married woman to effect a policy on her own life or the life of her husband for her separate use. The Act further provides that a policy effected by a man on his own life for the benefit of his wife and/or children, creates a trust (qv) in favour of the stated objects. The policy proceeds do not form a part of the husband's estate or become subject to his debts. The same applies when a wife takes out the policy for benefit of her husband and/or children. The Act creates a trust of life policies where, apart from the Act, they would not be created and gives special protection against creditors.

Martial law The suspension of ordinary law due to war and rebellion. It is not a law in the proper sense but the exercise of will by a military commander who takes the responsibility for suspending ordinary law to ensure safety of the state. It is illegal in time of peace but, by inference, lawful in times of war or civil commotion. Insurance policies may exclude losses during a period of martial law.

Matching risk The risk that liabilities and assets are not properly matched. The risk arises from mismatches related to currency and timing, interest rate risk and inflation risk. It is of major importance to life insurers as mismatching could lead to the sale of investments to meet claims as they fall due at a time of low values. In regard to annuities it is necessary to match annuity liabilities with investments of a similar pattern, e.g. fixed income securities. The FSA prescribes asset and liability valuation rules aimed at minimising this risk.

Material damage insurance The insurance of tangible property as distinct from the insurance of persons (life and limb), rights, pecuniary interests, and liability. Fire, theft, motor, cargo and hull policies are all policies that are entirely or partly of a material damage nature where the subject matter of insurance takes the form of tangible property. The property can usually be insured against named perils or on an 'all risks' or accidental damage basis.

Material damage proviso Business interruption insurance (qv) proviso requiring that, before a claim can be allowed, a material damage claim must be admitted; the absence of such insurance would prolong the interruption. When the interruption results from damage at external premises, e.g. the supplier's, the only requirement is that the damage should have been caused by an insured peril. *See* CUSTOMERS' EXTENSION; SUPPLIERS' EXTENSION; LOSS OF ATTRACTION; DENIAL OF ACCESS; EXTERNAL DEPENDENCIES.

Material fact A fact that would influence the judgement of a prudent underwriter in deciding whether to accept a risk for insurance and on what terms. The proposer has a duty to disclose material facts at the inception, at renewal and in respect of mid-term alterations where there has been a change in risk. Examples: motor insurance – details of young drivers; industrial activities – heating processes and previous claims.

Maternity cash benefit A benefit payable under some private health insurances at a specified rate, e.g. £250 for each child, after the policy has been in force for at least 10 months.

Mathematical reserves Provision made by an insurer to cover liabilities (excluding liabilities which have fallen due) arising under or in connection with contracts for long-term business.

Maturity The end of the term of an endowment insurance.

Maximum approvable benefit The maximum pension benefit a member can receive under an approved scheme (qv). This does not apply to personal pensions (qv) or simplified defined contribution schemes. The maximum amount varies according to whether the member is a Class A, Class B or Class C member (qv).

Maximum liability method *See* INDEPENDENT LIABILITY METHOD with which it is compared.

Maximum possible loss (MPL)/maximum foreseeable loss (MFL) The largest possible loss that could occur given the worst combination of circumstances. Under a fire policy the worst case scenario would be a fire in circumstances where the automatic sprinklers and fire extinguishers failed, and the fire brigade came late to the scene. A further coincidence might be a fully stocked warehouse containing high value combustible goods. Compare with *estimated maximum loss (EML).*

Means *See* LLOYD'S MEMBERS MEANS.

Mechanical breakdown exclusion Motor insurers exclude mechanical and electrical breakdown from the 'own damage' section of a comprehensive policy. If the breakdown, e.g. brake failure, causes an 'own damage' accident, the damage will be covered but not the repair of the brake. However, if the breakdown is the result of failure to observe the reasonable care condition (qv) the insured may get no cover except for the compulsory insurance elements of his policy and then subject to the insurer's right to recover the amount paid.

Mechanical Breakdown Insurance 1. Covers the cost of breakdown of household appliances or motor vehicles. 2. *See* AVIATION MECHANICAL BREAKDOWN INSURANCE.

Mediation An alternative dispute resolution (qv) approach to settling disputes. An impartial mediator helps the parties to negotiate. The process is not binding unless or until the parties reach agreement, after which the final agreement can be enforced as a contract.

Mediation activities Activities set out in the Regulated Activities Order 2001 (qv) as amended. The activities are: (a) introducing, proposing or carrying out other work preparatory to the conclusion of contracts of insurance; (b) concluding contracts of insurance; (c) assisting in the administration and performance of contracts of employment, particularly in the event of a claim. The FSA does not intend to regulate claims handling on behalf of insurance companies, expert appraisal or loss adjusting. Travel insurance sold as part of a holiday package is not a regulated mediation activity. *See* INSURANCE MEDIATION DIRECTIVE.

Medical attendant's report Report from proposer's doctor under non-medical schemes (qv) involving life cover.

Medical Defence Union Ltd Mutual non-profit organisation owned by its members – health professionals (doctors, dentists, etc.) providing: conduct of legal proceedings, risk management advice and professional indemnity insurance up to £10 million for any legal liability based on injury due to clinical negligence. Cover applies within the UK and in respect of 'Good Samaritan' acts worldwide. An *individual assistance policy* offers cover on personal injury following malicious attack, loss/damage to professional equipment and legal defence costs (health and safety, data protection, tax investigations). The customised *practice policy* is a buildings and contents policy including employers' liability (qv), an item on drugs and medical stock and an emergency helpline.

Medical expenses insurance *See* PRIVATE MEDICAL INSURANCE.

Member-nominated director Person who becomes a director of a corporate trustee and is chosen by the members of an occupational pension scheme.

Member-nominated trustee(s) *See* MEMBER TRUSTEES.

'Member of a household' *See* 'ANY MEMBER OF THE INSURED'S HOUSEHOLD'.

Member to member liability *See* MEMBERS' CLUBS.

Member trustees/member-nominated trustees Trustees appointed specifically in their capacity as scheme members whose appointments have been influenced by other members. This includes selection by a trade union. Not all member trustees are member-nominated trustees within the meaning of PA 1995. Under PA 1995 occupational scheme members have the right to select at least one-third of the trustees, unless the members have approved an alternative proposal by the employer. Previously the employer alone could appoint or remove trustees.

Member's agent Advises Lloyd's members on their underwriting commitments and links them to their syndicates.

The *member's agent's agreement* sets out the duties, powers and remuneration of the agent and the obligations of the member. Advising on syndicate participation is regarded as financial advice and is therefore regulated by the FSA. Members' agents must also adhere to the Lloyd's Code of Conduct for Members' Agents.

Members' Agents Pooling Arrangement (MAPA) Allows Lloyd's members to participate in more syndicates than normally possible. The members' agents pool underwriting capacity and the members spread their risk by taking smaller lines across more syndicates. A minimum of five members' agents must participate in each MAPA with no more than 10 per cent of MAPA capacity being allocated to any one syndicate. Corporate members wishing to participate must appoint a member's agent in order to do so.

Members' annual solvency test procedure Each Lloyd's member must have sufficient assets to meet liabilities plus a prescribed margin (see *required minimum margin (general business* (qv)) and *required minimum margin (long-term business* (qv)). If there is a shortfall the member must provide additional assets. The members' Funds at Lloyd's (qv) usually covers the deficiency. Ultimately Lloyd's must show the FSA (qv) that it has sufficient assets to cover any aggregate shortfall of all members after the prescribed surplus tests.

Members' clubs Voluntary associations of individuals. They must sue or be sued in the names of the members of the committee, or the officers, on behalf of themselves and all other members. Members are liable only to the extent of their subscriptions. Public liability insurances cover add the personal liability of members as well as member to member liability.

Member's margin *Required minimum margin of solvency* (qv) for a Lloyd's member calculated in accordance with FSA rules for general business and long-term business. *See* ANNUAL SOLVENCY TEST; MEMBERS' ANNUAL SOLVENCY TEST; REQUIRED MINIMUM MARGIN.

Members' means In addition to members' Funds at Lloyd's (qv), members must prove that they have sufficient net eligible means (at least £350,000 in 2002) to commence or continue underwriting. This wealth is called upon if the premium trust funds (qv) and Funds at Lloyd's (qv) prove insufficient.

Member's normal contribution Member's regular payment to the pension scheme as set out in the scheme's rules.

Membership termination Discontinuance of membership in an organisation or group. Terminates membership eligibility under a group policy or employee benefit scheme due to end of employment or other change in circumstances. Under group life policies the departing member may benefit from a continuation option (qv).

Memorandum, The Clause referring to particular average (qv) used in the discarded SG form (qv). The object was to free underwriters from liability for particular average in respect of certain classes of goods that were particularly susceptible to damage by insured perils. In respect of other goods and the ship and the freight, it applied a franchise (a percentage of damage) which had to be reached before a particular average claim was payable by the insurer.

Memorandum of Association Document lodged at Companies House setting out the objects and the powers of a company incorporated under the Companies Act. Any acts outside the objects clause are *ultra vires* and therefore invalid. Directors making 'contracts' that are ultra vires may be personally liable. *See* DIRECTORS' AND OFFICERS' LIABILITY.

Memorandum of Understanding (motor insurance) Voluntary agreement between motor insurers replacing the knock for knock agreement (qv). Insurers, whose respective insureds have been involved in a collision, agree, when liability attaches to their insured, to pay the other insurer's accidental damage claim without contesting the amount claimed. This saving in administrative costs is a part of the *reduction in paper work exchange.*

Memorandum of Understanding (MoU) Framework for the relationship between the FSA (qv) and the Financial Ombudsman Service (FOS). It reflects the fact that whilst each is operationally independent, they need to cooperate and communicate constructively with each other in order to carry out their respective functions effectively. A similar undertaking links the FSA and the Financial Services Compensation Scheme (qv).

Merchant Shipping Act 1995 A consolidating Act dealing with, inter alia, liability for oil pollution, compulsory insurance, the International Oil Pollution Compensation Fund and the liability of shipowners and others. The Act embodies the 1976 Convention on the Limitation of Liability for Maritime Claims. It also enables the government to act when a shipping casualty threatens large scale oil pollution in UK waters. Government-caused damage to vessels is covered under the International Hull Clauses (qv).

Merchant Shipping and Maritime Security Act 1997 Section 16 adds to s.192 of the Merchant Shipping Act 1995 a provision enabling the Secretary of State to regulate compulsory third party liability insurance for all British merchant ships and foreign ships visiting British ports.

Merchant Shipping (Salvage and Pollution) Act 1994 Extends strict liability for oil pollution damage to all ships carrying persistent oil whether as fuel or cargo. In the event of discharge or release the shipowner is strictly liable for: damage outside the ship by contamination; the cost of preventative measures; and damage caused by the preventative measures. The right of shipowners to limit their liability is not affected. The Act recommends liability insurance but, unlike CLC (qv), does not make it compulsory.

Mesothelioma Malignant industrial disease caused by asbestos exposure. Tumours erupt from the mesothelial cells in the linings of the lungs. It is a terminal condition and life expectancy, once the condition has been diagnosed, averages 12 to 18 months. The long-tail (qv) from exposure to diagnosis is between 20 and 50 years.

Metal Workers' Extension Extension applying the insured's fire policy cover on plant and machinery to the premises of any machine maker, engineer, founder, metal worker, customer, agent or subcontractor and whilst in transit by road, rail or inland waterway in Great Britain and Ireland. The extension does not apply to premises occupied by the insured and has a maximum liability under the extension and a maximum any one location.

Mid-tail business Any class of business that has a 'run off' (qv) of more than three years but less than ten years. *See* LONG-TAIL BUSINESS.

Military or usurped power This includes 'not only the acts of foreign enemies engaged in warfare within the realm or of subjects of the Crown engaged in internal warfare, but also the acts done by forces of the Crown in repelling the enemy or suppressing a rebellion. There must be something in the nature of warfare, something more in the nature of war or civil war than of riot or civil commotion'. The risk is excluded in standard property insurance on the grounds that governmental authorities are responsible for law and order.

Minimum benefit/pension Minimum benefit set in a pension scheme. It means that a member, whose actual pension falls below the minimum, will receive the minimum amount.

Minimum contributions Contributions payable to an appropriate personal pension scheme (qv) or to a FSAVC (qv) scheme by the DWP in respect of a member who has contracted out (qv). The contributions are the flat rate rebate plus the age-related rebate of national insurance contributions and basic rate tax relief on the employer's share of the rebate where paid into a personal pension plan. The term also describes any minimum amount that a member must contribute in order to be a member of an occupational or personal pension scheme, or in order to make additional voluntary contributions (qv).

Minimum Funding Requirement (MFR) MFR is intended to provide security for members of defined benefit schemes (qv) in the event of their employer becoming insolvent and making further contributions to the scheme. Schemes must hold a minimum level of assets to meet its liabilities and set out a time scale within which any underfunding must be addressed. An MFR valuation must be conducted by the scheme actuary at least every third year. Following the Pensions Bill (February 2004) MFR will be replaced in 2005 by scheme-specific funding requirements allowing schemes greater flexibility in developing funding strategies appropriate to their circumstances. The Bill also introduces the concept of *full buyout* (qv) that will affect solvent employers who wind up their defined benefit schemes.

Minimum guarantee fund (MGF) Minimum reserves required by an insurance company. An insurer's required minimum margin of solvency must not fall below the MGF. MGF for *general business* is €2 million (or €3 million for motor, aviation, general liability, credit and suretyship). This is reduced by 25 per cent for mutual associations. The MGF for life insurance undertakings is €3 million but is reduced by 25 per cent for mutual associations. The new levels of MGF under Directive 2002/12/EC (qv) do not apply to mutuals with less than €5 million of annual contribution income. The FSA calls for a short-term plan if the MGF rule (rule 2.9) is breached. The new MGF levels are index linked in line with inflation. *See* MARGIN OF SOLVENCY.

Minimum income guarantee Tops up the income of pensioners receiving less than the minimum income by pension credits.

Minimum payments Minimum amount an employer is allowed to contribute to a contracted out money purchase pension scheme (qv). The amount contributed secures protected rights (qv) for the members. It consists of a flat rate rebate of national insurance contributions and corresponds to the reduction in NI contributions that applies in respect of employees who are contracted out.

Minimum reserve Nominal amount reserved against a claim that has been reported to an insurer but without sufficient information to enable the insurer to make a reasonable assessment of the potential liability. *See* IBNER.

Minority buyouts The compulsory purchase of residual syndicate capacity by a member, or group of members, holding 90 per cent or more of the syndicate capacity after a mandatory offer (qv). *See* MAJOR SYNDICATE TRANSACTION.

Mirror syndicate A syndicate with the same constitution as another syndicate managed by the same managing agent (qv).

Misfeasance The improper performance of a lawful act, e.g. repairing a road negligently. Compare with non-feasance (qv).

Mis-selling Mis-selling has been described by the FSA (qv) as a failure to comply with the FSA Rule Book and its broad Principles of Business (qv). The term does not appear in the FSA Handbook but it commonly refers to an advised sale of investment products to consumers which does not meet the

Handbook requirements for suitability (qv) or 'know your customer obligations'. The emphasis is on the suitability of the recommendation for the individual and not the investment performance of the product. If suitability was established at the time of sale, and the required explanation of risk was given, then the consumer dissatisfaction about investment returns achieved gives no ground for an allegation of mis-selling.

Missing beneficiaries' indemnity Executors, administrators or trustees may wish to distribute an estate among the available beneficiaries even though a beneficiary may be missing. The indemnity enables them to proceed knowing that they will be indemnified against claims if the missing person reappears.

Missing document indemnity A transaction may depend upon a life insurance policy, share certificate or other document that is missing. An indemnity given by an insurer may enable the transaction to proceed as the insured is then covered against any loss resulting due to another person subsequently producing the document and basing a claim upon it.

Missing ship Ship deemed to be missing when, after extensive enquiries, it is officially posted as 'missing' at Lloyd's. It is then considered an 'actual total loss' and both hull and cargo claims are settled accordingly. During peacetime the cause of loss is deemed to be an insured peril but war peril during wartime.

Mixed policy Marine policy covering the subject-matter for the voyage and a period of time thereafter, such as a period in port.

Mixed syndicates Lloyd's syndicates made up of both corporate and individual members. Generally spread vehicles (qv) write on these syndicates alongside names (qv). *See* PARALLEL SYNDICATES.

Model Rules Specimens produced by the OPB (qv) and/or the Inland Revenue for certain categories of pensions to facilitate approval (qv) and/or the issue of a contracting out certificate or an appropriate scheme certificate.

Modified contribution rate *See* RECOMMENDED CONTRIBUTION RATE.

Money/Money insurance An insurer's definition of money includes cash, bank notes, cheques, postal orders, postage stamps, national savings certificates and holidays with pay stamps, luncheon vouchers and VAT purchase invoices. Cover is 'all risks' subject to specific limits depending on the circumstances of the loss, e.g. from a locked safe or a directors home. Insurers normally cover personal assault and theft by employees, primarily a fidelity guarantee (qv) risk, is covered only if discovered within 14 days.

Money laundering The process of making dirty money (money obtained illegally) legitimate through a process of placing, layering and integrating that money into the financial system.

Money purchase scheme A defined contribution scheme (qv) where the member's contributions (and those of the employer) are invested to build up a pension fund from which a retirement annuity and other benefits can be taken subject to IR limits (qv). The contributions are usually a percentage of the member's earnings.

Monoline insurer Separately capitalised insurer that focuses wholly on one type of business, e.g. bond credit insurance. They are product speciality insurers often working on a wholesale basis.

Monte Carlo simulation Mathematical technique that produces numerical solutions for differential equations. It is used extensively in finance for such tasks as pricing derivatives (qv) or estimating the value at risk of a portfolio. It is also used in insurance and risk management, typically to solve problems that require the calculation of one or more statistics of a probability distribution.

Moral hazard Character, habits and actions of insureds and others (e.g.

employees, associates) that influence the possibility and extent of a loss. Carelessness, unreliability, poor lifestyle, dishonesty are the unfavourable characteristics that insurers guard against or avoid. Compare with physical hazard (qv).

Morbidity/morbidity table Relative incidence of disease and accidents in a well-defined class or classes of person. It is set out in statistics based on actuarial practice called a *morbidity table* and used by health and life underwriters.

'More specific insurance clause' A non-contribution clause. Two policies may cover the same property and same interest, one in specific terms and the other in general terms. To prevent contribution (qv), the clause provides that a more specific insurance operates first when a claim occurs. 'More specific' refers to the range of property covered and not the range of perils.

Mortality cross-subsidy The amount shared out among long-living annuitants that is derived from the insurer's profit derived from those who die shortly after taking out the annuity. Annuities are a way of 'insuring' against outliving one's capital. The cross-subsidy is cumulative over time and exposes those who defer their annuities, as with *income drawdown* (qv), to *mortality drag* (qv).

Mortality drag The additional rate of return that investments left in a fund, such as *income drawdown* (qv), have to generate above the yield on an annuity in order for income drawdown to provide a higher overall retirement pension. Over time it becomes very difficult for the return on the fund to beat that from an annuity.

Mortality profit The additional surplus in a life fund due to the actual mortality rate being more favourable than that assumed at an earlier valuation.

Mortality table An instrument by which the probabilities of life and probabilities of death can be measured. The basis is the ratio of the number of persons dying at any age to the number of persons alive at the beginning of the year of that age. Mortality and interest rate factors enable actuaries to produce life insurance 'net premium' calculations.

Mortgage impairment insurance. Indemnifies mortgage lenders against loss due to 'portfolio' properties sustaining uninsured or under-insured damage. The policy is triggered when damage is due to perils against which the mortgagor was required to insure. The policy also responds if the insured mortgagor is unable to recover under his policy for reasons such as insolvency of the insurer concerned. The insured is also protected against its own negligence in failing to maintain a valid insurance as required by any mortgage deed.

Mortgage indemnity insurance. *Financial guarantee insurance* (qv) covering a mortgage lender for any loss incurred when the mortgagor has defaulted and the property is sold for less than the amount of the loan. A Lloyd's syndicate wishing to underwrite mortgage indemnity on ships or aircraft must first obtain approval from the War, Civil War and Financial Guarantee Committee.

Mortgage payment protection insurance (MPPI) Meets mortgage payments when the borrower suffers accidental injury, sickness or unemployment. No benefit is payable for the first two months. The policy may provide lump sum benefits for accidental death or critical illnesses (qv).

Motor accessories Additional items on or in the vehicle. The 'own damage' section of a comprehensive car policy covers accessories while in or on the car or in the insured's private garage. In the case of goods-carrying vehicles the accessories have to be on the vehicle.

Motor breakdown cover Roadside recovery assistance. The insured chooses either breakdown relating to *his vehicle* on an any driver basis, or relating to *himself* on an any vehicle basis as a driver or passenger. He also chooses a level of cover.

Motor Committee of the Association of British Insurers A committee that mirrors the Lloyd's Motor Underwriters' Association (qv). Their combined dialogue is called the Motor Conference.

Motor conference *See* MOTOR COMMITTEE OF THE ASSOCIATION OF BRITISH INSURERS.

Motor insurance Insurance of motor vehicles and liabilities arising from the use of vehicles. *Comprehensive policies* cover loss/damage to the insured's vehicle, liability to third parties and other sections depending on the type of vehicle. *Third party fire and theft* covers third party risks plus loss/damage to the insured's vehicle if caused by fire and theft. *Third party only* is limited to third party risks only. *Act only cover* is less extensive than third party only as cover is limited to the compulsory insurance requirements of the Road Traffic Act 1988 (qv). Most policy forms have a foreign use (qv) section. The principal vehicle types are: private cars; commercial or goods-carrying vehicles; agricultural and forestry vehicles; motor trade; motorcycles, mopeds; and special types (e.g. mobile plant).

Motor insurance certificate Proof of insurance in accordance with the Road Traffic Act 1988 (qv) in the form required by law. The certificate must be delivered to the insured party otherwise, for Act purposes, the insurance is not effective (s.147(1)). When cover is cancelled the certificate must be returned to the insurer within seven days or a lost certificate declaration completed.

Motor Insurance Database (MID) Set up to combat uninsured driving. Contains information about registered vehicles, policyholder and insurance details. Mandatory data for privately insured vehicles is supplied by insurers. Fleet owners and motor traders must also supply details. MID links with the Police National Computer helping fast identification of uninsured drivers and assists fraud enquiries. MID is managed by Experian for the Motor Insurers' Information Centre (qv).

Motor Insurance Information Centre (MIIC) Wholly owned subsidiary of the Motor Insurers' Bureau (qv) that tackles the crime of uninsured driving. MIIC has created the Motor Insurance Database (qv) – the platform for achieving its objective. This database also enables the MIIC to fulfil the role of national information centre as required by the Fourth EU Motor Insurance Directive (qv) to make cross-border claims less onerous. (Visit *www.miic.org.uk*).

Motor Insurers' Anti-fraud and Theft Register (MIAFTR) ABI-based computerised log of all total loss and theft of vehicle claims. Insurance companies and Lloyd's participate in the scheme, which assists in tracing and recovering vehicles. MIAFTR links directly with DVLA facilitating loss history checks by the public. It also checks vehicles against hire purchase information to ascertain if the insured still has a debt.

Motor Insurers' Bureau (MIB) Private company established to enter into Agreements with the government to compensate the victims of negligent uninsured and untraced motorists. Every insurer underwriting compulsory motor insurance is obliged to become a member and contribute to the funding. The UK Guarantee Fund compensates victims of the motorists concerned when there is no other source of compensation. MIB also acts as the UK Green Card Bureau to ensure that the system operates satisfactorily in the UK. *See* UNINSURED DRIVERS AGREEMENT; UNTRACED DRIVERS AGREEMENT.

Motor Insurers' Bureau Uninsured Drivers Agreement *See* UNINSURED DRIVERS AGREEMENT.

Motor Legal Expenses Helps the motor insured to: (a) pursue uninsured loss claims, including personal injury, against third parties; (b) defend motoring prosecutions; (c) handle disputes regarding vehicle sales, repairs, etc; (d) access a legal helpline. Cover may extend to free car hire, replacement car facility and rescue/recovery in the UK.

Motor Trade Policies *See* COMPREHENSIVE ROAD AND GARAGE POLICY; ROAD RISKS; INTERNAL RISKS.

Motorised waterborne craft Liability arising from use of waterborne craft is excluded in public liability policies as per the *marine and aviation exclusion* (qv). In *Bankers Insurance Co. Ltd* v. *South and Another* (2003) a jet ski was held to be a motorised craft so the liability under the policy was excluded. Jet ski liability is also excluded under personal liability insurance (qv).

'Movables' In marine insurance this means 'any movable tangible property, other than the ship, and includes money, valuable securities and other documents unless the context or subject-matter indicates otherwise' (Marine Insurance Act 1906, s.90).

Multi-appliance policy An extended warranty (qv) covering domestic appliances as chosen by the insured and is not related to a particular contract of sale as with a *connected contract*. The policy is renewable annually and is usually issued by an insurer and not a retailer.

Multi-insurers Marine and transit insurance term used where a single movement of goods involves different insurers in different parts of the transit.

Multi-parent captive Captive insurance company (qv) formed to meet the common needs of a group of independent companies or professional practitioners.

Multi-peril US term describing a policy covering a range of perils as opposed to one covering a single peril or restricted range of perils. The UK equivalent is comprehensive (qv).

Multi-trigger/dual trigger programme Two separate events combine to trigger a payment by the insurer only when the second event occurs. The latter is frequently linked to a metric or index outside the control of the insured in order to avoid moral hazard (qv) but correlates closely with the policyholder's financial interests. For example, a dual trigger policy for a private hospital's medical malpractice risk pays: (a) if the actual malpractice claims exceed a certain amount only if (b) the hospital's equity portfolio value falls below a specified level during the same period.

Multi-year, multi-line covers Contracts running for more than one year, not subject to annual renewal, that 'bundle' more than one class of business. Such policies produce a saving for the insured as losses over longer periods, (e.g. five years), are more predictable than losses over one year and the insurer reduces the contingency loading accordingly.

Multi-year contract Policy that runs for a fixed number of years. At Lloyd's any 'non-cancellable' policy running in excess of 18 months is called 'multi-year'.

Multiple benefit scheme *See* HYBRID SCHEME 2.

Mutual insurance company An insurance company owned by its policyholders, i.e. having no shareholders, formed by deed of settlement or registered as a company limited by guarantee. Funds are raised by premiums. The profits in life companies being shared among the policyholders usually as higher life insurance bonuses. An additional levy or call is imposed to meet losses if premium contributions are insufficient. Mutuals may be established for any class of business or they may be limited to members of a particular trade. Some former mutuals are now registered companies. Mutuals are often best known through *Protection and Indemnity Clubs* (qv) but are also found as the providers of professional indemnity cover for their members. *See* DEMUTUALISATION.

Mutuality of obligation One of two irreducible minimum requirements before a contract of employment exists (*Court of Appeal in Montgomery* v. *Johnson Underwood Ltd* (2001) – an agency worker case) The Courts ruled that there must be an obligation on the employer to provide work and on the employee to accept it. One of the leading cases concerned waiters who worked at various catering functions. They did not work continually but would be telephoned and offered a particular job. The Court found that the employer did not have to offer them the work nor did they have to accept it. This meant they were not employees due to lack of mutuality of obligation. The second irreducible requirement is covered by the *control test* (qv). *See* EMPLOYEE/EMPLOYER RELATIONSHIP.

N

'Nail-sick' roofs Loss adjusters' term to describe a situation where the nails holding down roof slates or tiles have rusted causing the slates or tiles to slip in high winds.

Nail to Nail Term denoting that transit insurance on paintings runs from the moment it is removed from the wall on which it is fastened to the time it is rehung in its new location.

Name An alternative term for an individual underwriting member (qv) of Lloyd's. Names face unlimited liability but are being phased out at Lloyd's following the introduction of corporate membership.

Name limit The maximum amount a property insurer will cover for a named insured in respect of property at any one location such as a warehouse. The balance is ceded under a surplus reinsurance treaty.

Named driver basis A basis upon which motor traders road risks policies (qv) can be rated, often suitable for small garages. Cover operates only when vehicles are being driven by one of the drivers named in the policy.

Named drivers Persons named in a motor insurance policy as being the only drivers permitted to drive under the policy.

Named peril policy A policy covering named or defined perils rather than 'all risks' (qv) of loss or damage. A loss is admissible only when matched against a named peril. *See* ADDITIONAL PERILS.

Named steamer Marine term used when underwriters of an open cover (qv) require that cover will only attach if they are advised of, and approve, the specific carrying vessel before each declaration.

National Approval Council of Security Systems (NACOSS) An independent inspectorate for the intruder alarm industry whose approval of an intruder alarm company is often mandatory if systems are to be accepted by theft insurers.

National Association of Pension Funds (NAPF) Promotes workplace pensions. Its priority is to ensure a regulatory and fiscal environment which encourages the provision and take-up of employer-sponsored pensions, as well as sound stewardship of pension fund assets. (Visit *www.napf.co.uk*).

National Health Service (NHS) Cash Benefit A benefit payable in cash to a person insured under a private medical insurance (qv), who is treated in the public ward of an NHS hospital. The cover applies if a medical specialist recommends particular hospital treatment covered by the policy.

National insurance Part of the UK social security system providing benefits in various forms, i.e., sickness, industrial injury, unemployment, pensions, maternity and death. Apart from contracting out (qv) provisions participation is compulsory for designated categories of people. The rates of contribution vary according to class but are standard within each class. Contributions are deducted from earnings in the case of employees whose employers also contribute.

Natural hazard A hazard caused by natural forces that may be climatic, oceanographic or geological in nature. Contrasts with man-made hazard.

Natural premium method Outmoded method of charging life insurance premiums. Each premium is related to the current risk of death and therefore increases year by year. At later stages the premiums often become prohibitive as there is no reserve or surrender value (qv). It differs from assessmentism (qv) in that no allowance is made for expenses. The level annual premium system (qv) overcomes the problem of the natural premium system.

Navigation risks The risks arising when a vessel is navigating or at sea as distinct from the risks arising in port or when the vessel is laid up.

Negligence A tort (qv) meaning 'the omission to do something which a reasonable man, guided upon those considerations which ordinarily regulate the conduct of human affairs, would do, or doing something which a prudent and *reasonable man* would not do'. A claimant must show that: (a) the defendant owed him a duty of care (qv); (b) he was in breach of that duty; (c) the breach caused him injury or damage that was not too remote. The reasonable man has been described as the 'man on the Clapham omnibus' and someone 'who does not have the agility of an acrobat or the wisdom of a Hebrew prophet'. Persons professing special skill, e.g. solicitors, must use the customary skill of their profession.

Negligence Clause *See* INCHMAREE CLAUSE.

Negligent misstatement/statement Misleading statements made in circumstances in which a duty of care exists. (qv). They often cause 'pure' economic loss (i.e. financial loss unconnected with physical injury or damage). Claimants, not in a contractual relationship with professionals, must establish a tort liability on the basis that the defendant breached a duty of care causing loss. This is the only certain circumstance in which the law recognises a liability for pure economic loss in negligence. The basis of liability has been that the person making a statement outside a contract has 'voluntarily assumed the risk' and, having done so, must exercise reasonable care. *See* NEGLIGENCE; PROFESSIONAL INDEMNITY INSURANCE.

Net central assets Assets comprising the fourth link in the Lloyd's chain of security (qv). On 31 December 2002 they amounted to £563m (the central fund of £467m plus other Society assets of £87m). They are the central assets of Lloyd's less the liabilities of the Society (less the liabilities of the members) valued in accordance with the Lloyd's Sourcebook (LLD 9 – 15). For margin of solvency purposes they must cover, in the aggregate: members' defined deficiencies on general and long-term business, the Society's required minimum margin and the excess (if any) of €3,000,000 (when converted at a designated rate to sterling) over the sum of members' margins for long-term business and the amount of any increase in the Society margin invoked under the relevant rule. If net central assets fall below the required amount, the Society must inform the FSA.

Net line US term meaning the amount of risk that an insurer retains for his own account without reinsurance. More widely a 'net line' underwriter accepts business mainly with the intention of ceding all or nearly all of it by way of reinsurance. The underwriter effectively acts in effect as a fronting company or agent.

Net line underwriter *See* NET LINE.

Net loss The amount of the loss absorbed by an insurance company after deducting all recoveries from reinsurance (qv), subrogation (qv) and salvage (qv). These net retained losses can be funded internally out of cash flow or specially dedicated assets. Externally they may be funded out of lines of credit or, in the case of proprietary companies, the issue of new securities.

Net premium income This is usually taken as gross premium income less premium returns and rebates, reinsurance premiums, and often production costs, brokers'/ agents' commission, etc.

Net relevant earnings The income that can be used to assess the maximum contribution that can be made to a personal pension scheme by the self-employed or employees in non-pensionable employment. In the case of the self-employed this is income (tax schedule D) less business expenses. For the employed it is income (tax Schedule E) including profit-related pay and taxable benefits.

Net retained lines clause Allows the reinsured to effect other reinsurances in priority so that the treaty itself protects only the net account, e.g. the treaty comes into play after proportional or facultative cessions. The *insolvency of other reinsurers clause* is embedded within this clause.

Net retention The amount retained by the reinsured for its own account after co-insurance, proportional or facultative reinsurance have been taken into account. *See* NET RETAINED LINES CLAUSE.

Net risk The remaining residual risk after the intrinsic hazards of the business or organisation have been reduced in terms of nature, scale and probability of occurrence by the precautions taken by the insured. Ascertaining the net risk is a part of risk assessment.

New business strain Occurs when the early years' premiums under a contract, less the initial expenses and any early claims, are not sufficient to cover the reserve, plus any explicit required solvency margin, that the company wishes to set up. An expanding life insurer may find that the unexpired premium reserve is increasing faster than it is being released making it difficult to achieve the required margin of solvency. *Zillmerization* (qv) allows for this situation. Reinsurance on a *risk premium basis* (qv) is another possible solution.

New entrant contribution rate The amount estimated as being sufficient to provide pension benefits for future entrants, including any contribution required from the members.

New for old policies Cover for household contents where an item lost or destroyed would be replaced with a new item, with no deduction for wear and tear. It is 'replacement as new' but if the 'new' is superior to the 'old' the insured pays for 'betterment'(qv). Business insurance equivalent is the *replacement clause* (qv). Sums insured must represent full replacement costs.

NHS indemnity An indemnity provided by the Crown to pay for the financial consequences of alleged negligence on the part of medical practitioners occurring in NHS hospitals. It does not cover private practice, 'Good Samaritan' acts or other work undertaken outside the practitioner's NHS contract and neither does it include General Medical Council or disciplinary hearings or any criminal charges resulting from clinical practice work in the NHS.

'Night' A goods in transit policy warranted that vehicles would be in 'locked garages at night', except when employed on night journeys, but then never left unattended (*A. Cohen & Co. Ltd* v. *Plaistow Transport Ltd (Graham, Third Party)* (1968)). McKenna J. stated, obiter, that night should be construed by reference to lighting up time.

Night risk clause Goods in transit clause to warrant that vehicles left loaded overnight must not be unattended unless locked and immobilised in accordance with any such provision in the policy. It may also be required that such vehicles be left either in a building or yard, which is also securely closed and locked, or in an attended official car park. *See* NIGHT.

Nil certificate Certifies that a transfer value (qv) is not to be used to provide retirement benefits in lump sum form, such as on a transfer from an FSAVC scheme (qv).

Nipple leakage Leakage through the failure of the nipple joints of boiler or pressure plant. The cost of repair can be covered as an extension to a boiler and pressure plant policy (qv). The extension covers 'self damage' only. Damage consequent upon the leakage is not covered as separate water damage cover is available under burst pipes cover (qv). *See* ADDITIONAL PERILS.

No claim bonus discount/bonus (NCD) A reward for not claiming under a policy. For each motoring claim-free year it means a progressive reduction on the following year's motor insurance premium until a four/five maximum year has been reached. Maximum discounts are in the range 60–65 per cent but if a claim occurs the insured drops back down the scale. Once the insured has four years' NCD he can pay extra for a *protected no claim bonus*. The bonus is then guaranteed provided there are no more than two claims in any period of five years. NCDs are available from some household insurers

No cure, no pay When a salvor attempts to preserve property endangered by a maritime peril, he does so voluntarily and receives no payment for it unless he is successful. Any remuneration received is known as 'salvage charges' (qv). *See* also LLOYD'S FORM OF SALVAGE AGREEMENT.

No fault liability system An injured person receives compensation up to a specified amount without having to prove fault (e.g. negligence) against a third party. In the UK certain industrial injury benefits are payable automatically under the social security regardless of fault. In some countries road accident victims secure compensation without having to prove fault but the UK operates a fault liability system in most areas of injury/damage.

'No risk no premium' Where the risk has not been run by the insurer any premium paid by the insured must be returned to him (*Tyre* v. *Fletcher* (1777)).

Noise at Work Regulations 1998 Oblige an employer to prevent damage to the hearing of workers from 'noise doses' above the prescribed level. A risk assessment (qv) must be carried out whenever an employee is likely to be exposed to this risk.

Nominal damages *See* DAMAGES.

Nomination Nomination to the trustees by a pension scheme member as to the person to receive any death benefit following his death. The trustees are not obliged to follow the nomination. This is also called 'expression of wish' or 'form of request'. Nominations are also made by policyholders to friendly societies as to the person to be paid in the event of their death. The nomination binds the society up to a specified amount. Most life nominations come under the Married Women's Property Act 1882 (qv).

Non-admission of liability clause Liability policy clause prohibiting the insured from compromising or settling any claim or admitting liability without the written consent of the insurer. The clause is not contrary to public policy and the insurer does not have to show that he was prejudiced in order to rely on it.

Non-admitted insurer An insurer that is not authorised to write insurance in a given jurisdiction.

Non-apportionable annuity An annuity under which the payments end with the final payment preceding death. No pro rata amount is paid to cover the period between that payment and the time of death.

Non-avoidance of compulsory insurance Authorised motor insurers and employers' liability are restricted in their ability to avoid liability under policies covering compulsorily insured liabilities. Where a claim is met solely because of the non-avoidance provisions the insurer has a right of recovery against the insured.

Non-cancellable policy *See* PERMANENT POLICIES.

Non-concurrent policies Separate policies covering the same property but where the overlap is not complete as one policy may be specific (insures A) and the other more general (insures A, B and C). If A is damaged contribution (qv) may arise subject to the two conditions of average (qv).

Non-consumer sales A non-consumer sale takes place when the purchaser buys the goods for his business. All business-to-business transactions are non-consumer sales. The seller is permitted to exclude his liability for the implied terms under the Sale of Goods Act 1979, fitness for purpose and satisfactory quality, provided that the exclusion clause passes the test of reasonableness (qv). Compare with consumer sales (qv).

Non-contribution clause *See* MORE SPECIFIC INSURANCE CLAUSE.

Non-contributory Pension schemes and employee benefit plans when the cost is wholly borne by the employer. The term does not apply to contributory schemes under which contributions are suspended during a contribution holiday.

Non-delegable duties Duties of a personal nature. The person responsible has a duty to see that proper care is taken and, even though he may engage a contractor to carry out the duties, he remains liable for any breach of duty. For example, a principal may engage a contractor to perform acts involving strict liability (qv) as in *Rylands* v. *Fletcher* (qv).

Non-delivery Loss in which the entire shipping package and its contents fail to arrive at its destination. Compare with short delivery (qv).

Non-disclosure Innocent non-disclosure by the proposer before the insurance contract has been concluded. If it relates to a material fact (qv), the insurance will be voidable ab initio (qv) at the option of the insurer. If the insurer exercises the option the full premium will be returned. *See* UTMOST GOOD FAITH.

Non-exempt activities order FSMA, s.327(6) states that activities must not be of a description, or relate to an investment of a description, specified in an Order made by HM Treasury for the purposes of this sub-section. This coupled with the restricted activities of the designated professional bodies (qv) will prohibit exempt professional firms (qv) from carrying on specific types of regulated activity.

Non-forfeiture clause Life policy clause that keeps the policy in force out of the surrender value for a limited period, after the grace period (qv) and continued non-payment of the renewal premium. The policy may remain open for one year or until the surrender value has been exhausted. If a limited period applies, any balance remaining is paid to the insured or used to buy a paid-up policy (qv). When the non-forfeiture period ends a revival clause (qv) may apply.

Non-invalidation clause A clause that can be added without charge to a fire policy. It protects the property owner against a breach of warranty by a tenant provided that the owner was not aware of the breach and he advises the insurers as soon as he becomes aware of it.

Non-investment insurance contract A general insurance contract (qv) or a pure protection contract (qv) but which is not a long-term care insurance contract (qv). Such contracts are governed by *Insurance: Conduct of Business Rules* (qv) except travel insurance sold as a part of a holiday package (a decision to be reviewed in 2007).

Non-mainstream regulated activity Regulated activity (qv) of an *authorised professional firm* (qv) in relation to which certain conditions (5.2.1, The Professional Firms Sourcebook) are satisfied. This includes a condition making the regulated activity *incidental* to the provision of professional services. FSA requirements are modified or disapplied so that the supervision in regard to the activities is equivalent to that which applies to the exempt regulated activities (qv) of exempt professional firms (qv).

Non-medical insurance/non-medical limits Life insurance arranged without the proposer being medically examined. The insurer requests a medical report from the proposer's doctor with the proposer's permission. Life offices have their own non-medical underwriting limits expressed in terms of age and sum insured, and type of policy.

Non-negligent cover *See* JCT CLAUSE 21.2.1.

Non-participating policy An alternative term for a non-profit policy (qv) also called a without profits life insurance policy.

Non-pensionable earnings Earnings such as overtime and bonuses not taken into account when calculating pension scheme benefits or contributions.

Non-pensionable employment Employment where either the worker chooses not to join an occupational pension scheme or there is no available scheme for him to join. Earning from such employment can be included in net relevant earnings (qv).

Non-profit policy A life insurance policy that does not participate in the divisible surplus (qv) so that the amount payable is the sum insured only. Alternatively called a non-participating policy.

Non-proportional reinsurance Reinsurance in which the cover is not in direct proportion to the reinsured's loss as in quota share (qv) and surplus treaties (qv). The reinsurer accepts liability wholly or partly on individual losses or losses on the whole account when they exceed an excess point (an attachment point) subject to an upper limit. Most non-proportional reinsurances are structured around *excess of loss reinsurance* (qv). *See* EXCESS OF LOSS RATIO; EXCESS PER OCCURENCE; EXCESS PER RISK.

Non-standard construction Buildings of unusual construction or incorporating materials more combustible than those used in standard construction (qv). They fall below 'grade 2', i.e. buildings made of predominately non-combustible materials. The fire insurer is likely to increase the premium, and may restrict the cover and impose conditions or warranties.

Normal expenditure exemption Expenditure that is regular, out of income and does not reduce the transferor's normal standard of living, can be transferred from one person to another free of inheritance tax. Life insurance premiums may qualify for this exemption.

Normal pension age (NPA) Earliest age at which a pension scheme member becomes entitled to receive full retirement benefits other than the guaranteed minimum pension (qv). This definition is relevant for preservation (qv) and contracting out purposes. Each scheme has its own NPA; members retiring earlier normally get a reduced pension.

Normal pension/retirement date Date applicable to an occupational pension scheme member as specified in the scheme rules. It is the date when a member becomes entitled to receive his retirement benefits and is usually the date of reaching that stated NPA.

Normal retirement age (NRA) The age at which a person holding a particular post normally retires.

'Nose' Colloquial term describing the period between the retroactive date (qv) and the inception date of a claims-made policy (qv). Claims arising from occurrences within this period but made during the policy period will be within the policy. Occurrences preceding the retroactive date are not within the 'nose' and not therefore covered regardless of when claimed.

Not to inure clause Clause 15 (Benefit of Insurance Clause) of the Institute Cargo Clauses provides that the insurance is not to inure for the benefit of the carrier or other bailee. Contracts of carriage or bailment may provide that the carrier or bailee will have the benefit of any insurance on the goods. The aim is to deny insurers their subrogation rights against the carrier or bailee. The 'not to inure clause' protects the insurer by negating this contractual provision.

Notice of abandonment A condition that must precede a constructive total loss (qv). If the insured fails to give notice to the marine insurer, the loss can only be treated as partial unless an actual total loss is proved (Marine Insurance Act 1906, s.62). An underwriter who accepts the notice admits liability for the loss. Notice is not necessary where it would not benefit the insurer. *See* ABANDONMENT.

Notice of Cancellation (Reinsurance) *See* CONTINUOUS TREATY.

Notice of loss/occurrence *See* NOTIFICATION CLAUSE.

Notification clause Sets out the procedure the insured must follow on becoming aware of an occurrence that may lead to a claim. Notice may be required 'immediately' (qv), 'as soon as possible' or within a specified time. The notice should include information as to the occurrence and, in the case of liability insurance, the insured is cautioned not to admit liability. The condition is a condition precedent to liability. *See* LAUNDRY LIST.

Notional reinstatement value scheme *See* 'DAY ONE' OF REINSTATEMENT COVER.

Novation The agreement to substitute a new contract for an existing one. It happens when insurers agree to transfer a policy from one person to another as, for example, when insured property changes hands. The insurer's consent is required as most contracts of insurance (life and marine contracts excepted – see assignment (qv)) are personal contracts.

Novus actus interveniens A new act intervening. It breaks the chain of causation. *See* PROXIMATE CAUSE.

Nuclear Energy Insurance Cover against property damage, liability and accident in connection with the operation of nuclear energy installations. Cover is available, including damage cover on the installations themselves, from a single atomic energy insurance pool, the British Nuclear Insurers created by the British Insurance (Atomic Energy) Committee for the UK market as a whole. The pool currently comprises 13 insurance companies and 40 Lloyd's syndicates. As a result most policies (marine, aviation and insurances of the person excepted) contain a radioactive contamination clause (qv) and an explosive nuclear assemblies clause.

Nuclear Installations Act 1965 Governs liability and compensation for nuclear damage for which a UK nuclear licensee is responsible. The Act requires compensation to be paid for damage to persons or property up to £140 million (reviewable). The operator's strict no-fault liability runs for 10 years after the incident, the government accepting liability for 20 years thereafter. Each operator must be insured in respect of his liability under an insurance approved by the DTI before a licence will be granted. *See* NUCLEAR PERILS.

Nuclear perils The risks of injury to persons or damage to property caused by radiation from nuclear reactor sites or by nuclear matter in the course of carriage.

Nuisance Sir Frederick Pollock defined it as 'a wrong done to man by unlawfully disturbing him in the enjoyment of his property or, in some cases, the exercise of a common right'. There are two kinds of nuisance. A public nuisance is a crime, e.g. causing a road obstruction, and is actionable only by individuals suffering special damage (something more than other affected parties, e.g injured by the obstruction not just inconvenienced). A private nuisance, a tort (qv), is an unlawful interference affecting the occupier's use or enjoyment of his property. Private nuisances are invasions by noise, smell, water or smoke to the point where it is unreasonable. Public liability insurance covers accidental obstructions and other forms of nuisance.

Numbered rules The York–Antwerp rules (qv) that are pre-fixed by numbers. They are applied in priority to the lettered rules.

O

Obligatory treaty A reinsurance treaty under which the original insurer must cede and the reinsurer must accept all risks falling into the class of business covered by the treaty.

Oblige line An alternative term for accommodation line (qv).

Obligee The person or firm protected by a bond. In a performance bond (qv) it is the property developer.

Obligor The person, also called the principal, giving the bond to the obligee (qv). In a performance bond it is the contractor, i.e. the party bound under the bond.

Obsolete buildings clause Applies a form of reinstatement insurance to buildings upwards of 50 years old that cannot be rebuilt in a like manner after a claim. The insurer agrees that, in the event of substantial loss, they will replace the 'old' with a new building or purchase an alternative building as a replacement. The sum insured should reflect this cost and partial losses may be dealt with on a reinstatement or indemnity basis.

Obsolete parts clause Clause applied by motor insurers when the subject-matter insured is a car no longer in production. The clause limits the liability of the own damage (qv) insurer for the cost of replacing any unobtainable part to the maker's last list price plus the current cost of fitting.

'Occupation' Occupation means vocation, profession, trade or calling in which the insured is engaged for reward or profit. Where there is an exclusion relating to particular occupations in a health or accident policy this does not preclude the insured from carrying out acts or duties connected with the ordinary daily acts associated with occupations in general. Occasional acts do not amount to an occupation (*Berliners* v. *Travelers Insurance Co.* (1898)). *See* DISABILITY.

Occupational classes A method of rating whereby the usual premium is based on the insured's occupation. This is underwriting by occupation (qv), and is used in personal accident insurance (qv) where as many as five occupational classes segment risks according to the degree of hazard present in the occupation. Extra-hazardous occupation calls for special consideration. Occupational underwriting lies at the heart of many insurance schemes, e.g. motor insurance for civil servants.

Occupational deafness An industrial disease caused by noise exposure. It is an insidious disease affecting the inner ear. Many workers are exposed to this risk and years may pass before they become aware of the situation. The disease's long-tail (qv) potential has serious implications for employers' liability insurers. The disease is incurable but preventable and has attracted attention from the legislators through the Noise at Work Regulations 1998 (qv).

Occupational hazard A condition in an occupation that increases the peril of accident, sickness or health problem.

Occupational pension scheme A scheme organised by an employer or on behalf of a group of employers to provide pension benefits for one or more employees on leaving service or on death or retirement.

The scheme is run by trustees and can be contributory or non-contributory (qv). Schemes are either *defined benefit schemes* (qv) or *defined contribution scheme* (qv). *See* EXEMPT APPROVED SCHEMES.

Occupational Pensions Board (OPB) Statutory body responsible for: issuing contracting out or appropriate scheme certificates for pension schemes that meet the necessary requirements; ensuring that guaranteed minimum pensions and protected rights are secure; and ensuring that equal access and preservation requirements are satisfied. OPB's involvement extends to the enforcement of disclosure of information to scheme members and advising schemes as to the extent to which their rules comply with overriding legislation and advising schemes on certain rules regarding early leavers, etc.

Occupational split A group insurance term indicating the occupational split of the company's workforce, e.g. 30 per cent clerical, 70 per cent manual.

Occupier The Occupiers' Liability Act 1957 (qv) contains no official definition. The term, one of convenience, denotes a person who has a sufficient degree of control over premises to put him under the 'common duty of care' (qv) to lawful visitors. Control is the decisive factor and it is immaterial that the occupier has no interest in the land. The occupier's control does not preclude others from being liable, e.g. repairing landlords (q.v). *See* COMMON DUTY OF CARE; OCCUPIERS' LIABILITY ACT 1984.

Occupiers' Liability Act 1957 The occupier (qv) owes the 'common duty of care' (qv) to lawful visitors. The Act gives particular guidance on how to accommodate the different needs of visitors, e.g. being prepared for children to be less careful than adults. The occupier can expect persons exercising a trade to guard against risks incidental to their trade. He will not be liable for the negligence of independent contractors unless negligent in selecting them or checking their work. Account is also taken of all the circumstances, including warnings of dangers to ascertain if they been sufficient to make visitors reasonably safe. The occupier cannot (Unfair Contract Terms Act 1977 (qv)) use a notice or a contract to exclude liability for negligence leading to personal injury. *See* OCCUPIERS' LIABILITY ACT 1984.

Occupiers' Liability Act 1984 Section1(3)(4) provides a statutory duty of care owed by occupiers to trespassers. A duty is owed if the occupier is aware of danger and knows (or has grounds to believe) that the trespasser may be in the danger area. The duty is to take such care as in all the circumstances is reasonable to see that the trespasser does not suffer injury. Appropriate warnings may discharge the duty. The duty is built around the 'common duty of humanity' (qv), which took into account, along with the occupier's skill and resources, his actual knowledge of the trespasser's presence or likelihood of it. The duty is less onerous than the common duty of care (qv) owed to lawful visitors.

Occurrence Generally an event that results in an insured loss. Specifically, an event that triggers a 'losses-occurring' liability policy that covers injury or damage occurring during the policy period even if the claim is brought after the policy has expired. The occurrence may be a single accident or, by policy definition, injuries to multiple victims due to exposure to the same harmful conditions on a continuing basis (*claims series clause* (qv)) or adverse events all occurring within a specified time (*hours clause* (qv)). Contrast with *claims-made policies* (qv). *See* OCCURRENCE TRIGGER THEORIES; LIABILITY SEQUENCE.

Occurrence Trigger Theories Liability policies are triggered by insured events 'occurring' during the policy period. Difficulty in pinpointing the time of occurrence of latent diseases and gradual pollution has produced theories, not universally accepted, from the US: 1. *Exposure theory.* Injury is simultaneous with first exposure. All insurers on risk during the exposure period are liable on a time on risk basis; 2. *Manifestation theory.* Injury is deemed to occur when it is first diagnosed. Only the policy in force at time of discovery is liable – this theory is rarely applied. 3. *Injury In Fact Theory.* Policies are triggered only if in force when an actual injury occurs or progresses. No liability is triggered during dormant periods. 4. *Triple Trigger Theory/Continuous Trigger Theory.* Injury is deemed to occur at time of first exposure, during continuing exposure *and* at time of manifestation. Any policy in force at any stage will be liable. Issues also arise as to how limits of indemnity should be applied. *See* OCCURRENCE; STACKING OF LIMITS.

Ocean marine A US term describing the insurance of seagoing hulls, cargoes and liabilities. This distinguishes those insurances from inland marine and sometimes from inland waterway hull, cargo and liability insurances.

Odd time Most policies are issued for terms of one year renewable annually. Wherever the first period of insurance is longer than a year there is 'odd time' for which a pro rata charge is made.

Off Balance Sheet Resources and transactions that do not show on the balance sheet. It involves financing other than by equity or debt. It occurs in a variety of circumstances notably: (a) where a financial institution provides an operating lease that makes a fixed asset available to the firm in return for regular rental payments. The use of the asset is acquired but no capital expenditure has taken place and so does not appear on the balance sheet; (b) where a company securitises available assets and markets them to investors through a special purpose vehicle (qv) in the form of bonds secured on the underlying assets. It transfers the assets to the SPV but retains use of them as income generators. They 'come off the balance sheet' to improve the return on investment and other financial ratios. *See* SECURITISATION.

Officers Companies Act 1985, s.744, gives a limited definition: 'officer, in relation to a body corporate, includes a director, manager or secretary'. Not everyone with the title 'manager' is sufficiently senior to be an 'officer' who must have a level of authority over the affairs of the whole company in a given area of activity. The term officer includes the company secretary and auditor. *See* DIRECTORS' AND OFFICERS' LIABILITY.

Offset The state pension offset. A member's pensionable earnings or a member's pension are reduced to take account of the amount of state pension a member will receive.

Offset Clause Agreement between the reinsured and the reinsurer that debits and credits between them may be set off against each other with payment only of the balance. Premiums due to the reinsurer may be set off against claims payments due to the reinsured. Offsetting becomes important if one of the parties becomes insolvent.

Offshore insurance Branch of marine insurance covering installations and activities connected with the offshore exploration and production of oil or gas by mobile and non-mobile installations. The risks run from the construction on land, the pipelines and pumping stations up to and including the operation period.

Oil pollution See Merchant Shipping (Salvage and Oil) Act 1995, Merchant Shipping Act 1995, the Oil Pollution Compensation Fund Convention 1971 and pollution clause.

Oil tankers Vessels carrying oil in bulk. The risk of oil pollution has resulted in compulsory liability insurance for vessels carrying more than 2000 tons.

The Merchant Shipping (Oil Pollution) Act 1971 as amended by the Merchant Shipping Act 1974 requires such ships to have a certificate of insurance before they can enter or leave a UK port or terminal.

Omnibus clause An 'indemnity to other persons' clause in a liability policy. The motor insurance policy, for example, indemnifies permitted drivers (qv), passengers and employers.

'On goods' An unqualified reference to insurance on goods covers both the beneficial interest of the insured and, if they belong to someone else, the liability of the insured to the owner. It does not cover the owner's proprietary interest unless the policy names the insured as the commercial trustee and describes the property as belonging to a named third party. (*Hepburn* v. *Tomlinson (Hauliers) Ltd* (1966)).

'One disaster or casualty' clause Same as an HOURS CLAUSE.

One-third new for old Under the Marine Insurance Act when new material replaces old in ship repairs, the shipowner is required to bear part of the cost of new materials; a deduction of one-third or one-sixth is made from the amount payable. In practice the International Hull Clauses (qv) provide that claims are payable without deduction new for old.

Onus of proof The obligation on an insured to prove that the insured event has occurred or the obligation on an insurer to prove that an exception applies. If the insurers allege lack of utmost good faith preceding the issue of the policy the onus of proof attaches to them.

OPAS (Occupational Pensions Advisory Service) Grant-aided organisation giving free help to members of the public with problems on personal or occupational pension schemes. OPAS does not advise state schemes. OPAS involvement in dispute resolution must be exhausted before cases can be referred to the Pensions Ombudsman.

Open cover/policy 1. Cargo insurance for insureds who ship goods on a regular basis. The contract covers all sendings within the scope of the policy at agreed rates. The insured must declare each shipment to facilitate the issue of certificates. Premiums are debited monthly or quarterly. The policy is not subject to a fixed term but can be cancelled subject to 30 days notice. 2. Marine reinsurance facility whereby the reinsurer takes a share of any business of a defined type that is offered by the cedant. It works in the same way as the open cover for cargoes (see 1. above).

Open market A term referring to a risk placed in the open market as opposed to one that is covered under a binding authority, line slip or treaty.

Open market option Pension scheme member's option to use his fund to buy an annuity (qv) from any insurance company in the open market. The member is able to search for the best available annuity rate.

Open pilot warranty Aviation clause setting out the minimum acceptable qualifications for a pilot not named on the policy. A named pilot or one who 'meets the open' affirms to the insured that the pilot's use of the aircraft will not invalidate the cover. It does not automatically give cover to the pilot under the liability section of the policy.

Operating ratio A ratio that monitors an insurer's overall trading performance. It has three components: (a) the loss ratio, i.e. total losses and claims handling costs as a percentage of net premium income; (b) the expense ratio, i.e. underwriting expenses as a percentage of premium income; (c) investment income ratio, i.e. net investment income on funds contributed by policyholders as a percentage of net premium earned. The operating ratio is the result of deducting the investment income ratio from the sum of the loss ratio and expense ratio.

Operational risk/operational risk insurance. 'The risk of direct or indirect loss resulting from inadequate or failed internal processes, people and systems or from external events' (Basel Committee on Banking Supervision 2001). The definition includes the legal risk but excludes strategic and reputational risk. It encompasses: 'people' risks (ineffective management); internal and external fraud; failure to comply with laws and regulations; damage to physical assets; business disruption through IT failure; transaction processing failures; and outsourcing weaknesses. The move towards operational risk management is FSA-driven. Firms will have to comply with the policy on systems and control from 2004. Financial businesses are able to insure against the risk by purchasing a 'basket' insurance, with fewer exclusions, over and above the more traditional insurances. The basket includes cover under: professional indemnity; directors' and officers' liability; broad form crime and computer crime; unauthorised trading; employment practices liability; pension trust liability; organisational liability (qv); broad form external fraud.

Operative clause/insuring clause clause Policy clause that (subject to conditions) sets out the insurer's responsibilities in terms of losses or events in respect of which he will have to provide an indemnity (qv) or payout under a benefit policy (qv).

Opra (Occupational Pensions Regulatory Authority) Opra supervises a range of legal requirements affecting occupational pensions including stakeholder pensions (qv). It also supervises employers who make employer or employee payments into personal pensions. Opra can take action where carelessness or negligence could put a scheme at risk. It collects the levy (qv) that funds Opra, OPAS (qv), and the Pensions Ombudsman (qv) while also running the Pensions Registry (qv). The sale and marketing of personal pensions and stakeholder pensions is supervised by the FSA (qv). In 2005 Opra will be replaced by the *Pensions Regulator* (qv). *See* PENSION PROTECTION FUND.

Option Derivative financial instrument under which the payment of a sum of money gives a right, not an obligation, to buy or sell something at an agreed price on or before a specified date.

Ordinary annual contributions Term used in Practice Notes (IR12) to denote annual contributions payable to an occupational pension scheme by the employer on a common basis, e.g. a fixed amount or a fixed percentage of the payroll. Compare with *special contributions* (qv).

Ordinary breakage Breakage (not associated with any named perils) of fragile cargo which is regarded as inevitable during transit. It is generally excluded unless caused by the vessel or craft being stranded, sunk, burnt or in collision. The *Replacement Clause* (qv) deals with breakage of machinery.

Ordinary meaning rule Rule of construction. Words in a policy must be construed in their plain, ordinary and popular meaning, and not in their strictly philosophic or scientific meaning. However, the context may make it clear that the words must, to carry out the intention of the parties, be understood in some special sense. Legal and technical terms are to be given their strict legal meaning unless the policy shows a different intention.

Organisational liability A broad form of cover with high attachment points for financial businesses such as banks. It covers liability for losses whether arising from professional services or not, unless excluded. The burden is on the insurer to show that an exclusion applies. The exposures include, inter alia, sales practices; anti-competitive practices/price fixing; discrimination; contractual interference; punitive and multiple damages (catastrophe basis); Internet liability. The basket of cover follows the operational risk insurance (qv).

Original coverage The insurance transacted between the primary insurer and the original insured in contrast to the insurance the primary insurer obtains from a reinsurer.

Original terms reinsurance Reinsurance of life insurance at the same rate of premium and subject to the same conditions as those of the ceding office. The reinsurer is liable for a proportion of the original policy throughout its duration. In the event of surrender or alteration of the original policy, the reinsurer follows the practice of the ceding office and the conditions of the underlying policy. The reinsurer also follows the rate of bonus declared by the cedant under with profits policy.

Originating Cause A claims series clause (qv) term. The meaning has been interpreted in a number of ways but where a series of individual claims are unified by a common cause, that cause may be regarded as the originating cause. An insured may seek to rely on this provision to reduce the deductibles (qv) payable and reach the minimum level at which the insurers' obligation to pay commences. A primary layer insurer may seek to aggregate multiple claims to limit its exposure to its retention level. A financial institution mis-sold pensions but was not allowed by the House of Lords to treat the poor training of their representatives as the common cause and could not therefore aggregate the losses to breach the £1m deductible. The poor training was background only; the real cause of the 22,000 losses (maximum was £35,000) was the failure of the representative to give *best advice* (qv) to each claimant individually.

Outstanding claims advance A payment made under a reinsurance contract or treaty whereby an advance payment is made in respect of outstanding claims that will come into account in a subsequent periodic settlement when the actual claim amount has been determined.

Outstanding claims reserve An amount reserved based on the estimated amount needed to meet incurred claims that have not yet been finally settled.

Outstanding losses or claims The total of losses or claims that have been notified but at a given time are still outstanding and as such are only estimated amounts.

Outwards reinsurance Reinsurance of Lloyd's syndicates.

Over-age additional premium Additional premium on an open cover (qv) applied to a cargo which is carried by a vessel over 15 years old or which is outside the scope of the classification clause (qv). It may also be applied for breach of navigational warranties (Institute Warranties (qv) where the ship is over 15 years.

Over-insurance Insuring property for more than its actual value. It can be inadvertent or fraudulent. The penalties for under-insurance can cause the insured to over insure but the use of declaration policies (qv) enables insureds with fluctuating sums insured to overcome the problem.

Over-the-counter (OTC) derivatives A derivative, sold by a financial intermediary, tailored to particular risk financing needs rather than being exchanged-traded. I-Wex OTC Weather Risk Market allows 'open access' enabling a company to submit all details, barring price, of the weather risk they seek to hedge. Others search the database with a view to making offers.

Overall premium limit Maximum amount of business a Lloyd's member may write based on the member's Funds at Lloyd's (FAL) (qv). The limit is allocated to syndicates in proportions agreed between the member and the member's agent.

Overcarriage Marine insurance term in reference to a situation where certain goods are not discharged at the destination port but are 'overcarried' and discharged on the homeward voyage. This amounts to deviation (qv) and the risk ceases when the vessel sails on from the port of destination still carrying the goods.

Overclosing The acceptance by an underwriter of a larger amount than originally agreed with the broker.

Overdone slips A slip (qv) that is oversubscribed. The acceptances obtained by the broker exceed the amount of business available. It may be done intentionally by a broker seeking access to a wider market in the future. When it occurs the line written by each underwriter is reduced proportionately (short-closing (qv)).

Overdue risk An overdue ship. When a ship is overdue, the underwriter on risk may seek a reinsurance with other marine syndicates at a cost. Both the insurer and the reinsurer have access to the latest shipping intelligence provided by Lloyd's.

Overfunding Pension scheme with assets exceeding those required to meet liabilities. *See* ACTUARIAL SURPLUS.

Overheating Excessive heating. If a boiler or self-fired pressure vessel accidentally suffers a general deficiency of water while working, severe damage may be caused to the boiler shell, firebox, etc. The risk is insurable as a whole or, in the case of a multi-tubular boiler, limited if desired to the overheating of the tubes only. The cover is for 'self damage' only and is put into effect as an extension of the boiler and pressure plant policy (qv).

Overlap The parallel payments that occur when, following the pensioner's death within the guaranteed pensions period, the payment of the pension runs concurrently for a time with a dependant's pension.

Overlapping policies *See* NON-CONCURRENT POLICIES.

Overriding commission 1. An additional commission payable to particular intermediaries who introduce a large volume of profitable business to the insurer. 2. Discount granted by a reinsurer to an intermediary or cedant to cover the cedant's overhead expenses. To prevent a ceding office from writing business and reinsuring 100 per cent as a full-time activity for the sake of the underwriting commission, established reinsurers usually insist that the cedant retains a reasonable proportion of the business for their own account.

Overriding of implied terms rule A rule of construction (qv) to the effect that where there is a contradiction between express and implied terms the express words will prevail.

Overseas deposits Deposits required under local legislation to be made by insurers in overseas countries for the protection of locally based policyholders.

Overseas investment insurance The ECGD (qv) provides political risks cover against expropriation, war and restrictions on remittances. Breach of contract cover is also considered case by case. Cover protects investors in terms of equity in, or loans to, foreign enterprises. Bank portfolio loans cover is also available to banks in support of bank lending to overseas projects where there is no UK sponsor or UK export. The initial duration of ECGD cover is 15 years.

Overseas Personal Liability A public liability policy extension indemnifying any director or employee (including family members) of the insured during temporary visits anywhere in the world on the insured's business. The extension applies to 'off duty' activities outside the scope of the main indemnity clause.

Overtime When overtime is worked to merely expedite the repairs so that the owner may more speedily employ the ship, the excess cost is not recoverable from the insurer. However, where liners with advertised sailing dates are involved the insurer admits the overtime expenditure. 'Liners' means passenger and cargo vessels.

Overwriting of premiums Occurs where the volume of business written on behalf of a Lloyd's member exceeds allocated premium limit (qv). In response Lloyd's demands additional security to back the additional risks underwritten. The increase may be the result of poor administration, a fall in exchange rates or coverholders (qv) writing larger volumes of business than expected under binding authorities (qv).

'Own branders' Suppliers who put their own name on the product and give the impression that they are producers. Such suppliers are 'producers' for the purpose of the Consumer Protection Act 1987 (qv) and may be strictly liable for the damage as defined by the Act.

Own damage A term used to describe loss or damage to the insured's own vehicle under a motor insurance policy. An 'own damage' excess may apply under the 'loss or damage' section of the policy.

Own Property Exclusion Excludes liability under liability insurance for 'damage to property owned or occupied by or in the care, custody or control of the insured or any servant . . .' 'Owned property', though excluded, is not in any event within the operative clause (qv) of a legal liability policy. Such property is normally insured under first party insurance (qv). There is legal liability for property not belonging to the insured that is in his custody of control. *See* CUSTODY AND CONTROL EXCLUSION.

P

PA(90) A select mortality table based on data in respect of pensioners that is used in pensions work. The *minimum funding requirement* (qv) mortality basis is PA(90) rated down two years, but experts suggest that it should be rated down by 12 years to reflect improvements in mortality.

Package policy Combines different insurances in one document for one insured. Example: Shopkeepers' policy covers property, business interruption, money, liability covers, etc.

Packaged products FSA term that distinguishes policies made up of risk *and* investment elements (e.g. life policy, unit trust) from 'pure' investment business (e.g. gilts (qv)). Product providers dealing with private customers must highlight particular product features in a way that helps the customer make comparisons between different products.

Paid losses or claims The total amount of losses or claims that have been settled during a given period (before adjusting for outstanding claims).

Paid-up policy Policy granted by life insurer for a reduced amount based on premiums already paid with no further premiums payable. The reduced sum is payable on death under paid-up whole life policies and an on death or maturity in the case of endowments. Paid-up pensions are called 'preserved pensions (qv)'.

Paid-up scheme Pension scheme under which contributions have ceased. Assets continue to be held and used by the administrator in accordance with scheme rules.

Pair and set clause Stipulates that, in the event of loss or damage to any article forming a part of a pair or set, the claim will reflect the value of the lost item and not the reduced value of the pair or set.

Parallel syndicate Lloyd's syndicate consisting of a single corporate member (qv) operating alongside one or more mixed syndicates (qv) participating in all the same risks on a proportionate basis.

Parametric trigger Physical trigger applicable to a catastrophe bond (qv) based on an occurrence at a specified place *and* of specified severity. A bond might be contingent upon on the *magnitude* of earthquake activity in and around *Tokyo* as measured by the Japan Meteorological Agency. If the event occurs, investors sacrifice their capital and/or interest. The trigger is based on a natural catastrophe model estimating a wide variety of parameters based on incomplete data and knowledge.

Paramount clauses/exclusions International Hull Clauses that are stated to be paramount and override anything inconsistent with them. These clauses embrace exclusions of: war; strike; malicious acts; nuclear risks.

Parol evidence Word of mouth evidence in court. While not generally admissible to contradict the written policy, there are exceptions that allow the parties to bring evidence that they contracted otherwise than in accordance with the terms used to express their agreement, e.g. the policy was obtained by fraud.

Part IV Permission Permission given by the FSA under Part IV FSMA to carry on regulated activities.

Part of Reinsurance term indicating that the reinsurer is accepting part only of the original risk and making it clear that in the event of a short closing (qv) he will not be prepared to accept the whole of the risk.

Partial disablement An injury or sickness that prevents the insured from performing fully his normal occupation activities. The insured can perform some parts of his duties or work in less demanding circumstances. The partial disablement benefit is less than the total disablement equivalent.

Partial loss A loss that does not destroy the insured property or damage it beyond economic repair. *See* PARTICULAR AVERAGE.

Partially approved scheme Pension scheme where part is approved by the IR. This might arise where some members are employed overseas and not therefore paying UK taxes.

Partially repaired damage Where a ship is only partially repaired, the insured is entitled to the reasonable cost of such repairs plus an allowance for the reduction in the ship's market value because of the failure to effect full repairs. The aggregate must not exceed the cost of full repairs (Marine Insurance Act 1906, s.69(2)). *See* UNREPAIRED DAMAGE.

Participating policy A with profits policy (qv).

Particular average A partial loss of the vessel or cargo, including total loss part of the shipment, caused by an insured peril and which is not subject to a *general average loss* (qv); it falls on 'particular' property as opposed to general average which is loss relating to *all interests.* The term does not include *particular charges* (qv). The term has been replaced in the Institute Clauses by *partial loss*, but the original term is used in marine insurance circles.

Particular average adjustment Calculation of reduction in value of cargo insured under *valued policies* (qv) following insured damage. The gross sound and damaged values are compared to find the percentage reduction in value to be applied to the agreed value to give the amount of the claim. Where percentages cannot be agreed the damaged goods are sold. The difference between the sound value and the sale price gives the relevant percentage. Total loss of part of the cargo is based on the proportion of the insurable value that the part lost bears to the insurable value as a whole.

Particular charges Marine term describing expenses (excluding salvage charges and general average) incurred by or on behalf of the insured for the safety/preservation of the subject matter. They are added to the particular average (qv) claim if related to an insured loss. Examples: survey fees, fumigating damaged cargo.

Particular risk A risk that has restricted consequences. Motor accidents will normally only directly affect people within the vicinity. *Fundamental risks,* e.g. mass unemployment, affect society as a whole. Particular risks are susceptible to loss control. Fundamental risks lead to government schemes, e.g. social security.

Particulars of claim The Civil Procedure Rules term for setting out details of the amount of the claim.

Partnership insurance Life insurance to protect business partners against the withdrawal of capital and meeting the financial obligations that arise on death or retirement of a partner. Various combinations of life insurance can be used. The aim is to ensure that the money gets into the right hands at the right time, while minimising costs and taxation liabilities.

Party wall Wall separating two buildings, but which is not regarded as an effective fire shield unless it passes through the roof and conforms with Building

Control, which allows for differences in building material. *See* FIRE DIVISION.

Passenger indemnity The indemnity granted at the insured's request under third party motor cover to passengers for accidents they cause. The indemnity applies to private car and commercial vehicle policies.

Passenger liability The liability of the user or driver of a vehicle, ship or other conveyance towards passengers in respect of injury or damage to their property. Liability may be governed by common law, contract, statute or international convention. Passenger liability insurance for motor vehicles is compulsory under the Road Traffic Act 1988.

Passing off This tort (qv) is the pretence by one person that his goods or services are those of another. The person whose business interests suffer has a right of action in damages or for an account, and for an injunction to restrain the defendant (qv) in the future. It is possible to insure under *intellectual property litigation insurance* (qv) against liability for having inadvertently infringed a third party's intellectual property rights.

Passive breaches of utmost good faith Innocent *non-disclosure* of a material fact and *concealment,* deliberate withholding of a material fact (qv).

Passive management A fund management strategy that seeks to match the return and risk characteristics of a market segment or index by mirroring its composition. Also called *passive portfolio strategy.*

Passport cover Travel insurance (qv) compensates the insured in the range £300 to £500 for the expense of replacing a lost passport.

Past service Member's period of service with the employer before joining the pension scheme or before a particular date. The benefit allowed in respect of previous service is called *past service benefit.*

Past service reserve Method of calculating the value of a member's pension scheme benefits. It takes account of reserves in a final salary scheme to cover future salary increases due to inflation and career enhancement.

Patterns, models, moulds and designs Under a material damage policy the liability for loss of such items is limited to the cost of reproducing them. The consequential loss, e.g. loss of market, is not covered unless specially arranged.

***Pawsey* v. *Scottish Union & National* (1907)** Produced classic definition of *proximate cause* (qv): 'proximate cause means the active, efficient cause that sets in motion a train of events which brings about a result, without the intervention of a force started and working actively from a new and independent source'. *See* CONCURRENT CAUSES; LAST STRAW CASES; INTERVENING CAUSES; REMOTE CAUSE; CONSECUTIVE CAUSES.

Pax Abbreviation of 'passengers' as used on aviation slips.

Pay as may be paid Reinsurance term indicating that the reinsurer will pay without questioning the insurer's liability under the original insurance.

Pay as paid policy Livestock policy under which the insurer pays the insured a given percentage of any compensation received from the government as compensation for the compulsory slaughter of their animals to prevent the spread of a disease, e.g. foot-and-mouth.

Pay as you go (PAYG) Method whereby pension scheme payments are made out of current income as they fall due rather than by previous funding. The state pension schemes operate in this way.

Pay Back 1. Rating method. The underwriter bases his price on expected loss frequency over a period of time. If a loss is forecast every five years, the risk premium (qv), ignoring expenses and profit margins, is the limit of cover divided by five, giving a five-year pay back. When quoted as a percentage of the limit, the rate is termed 'rate on the line', the inverse of *pay back*, so 20 per cent means five-year pay back. 2. Pay back to reinsurer following a major loss or losses. The renewal premium is increased for a period during which time the contract is in 'pay back'.

'Pay on behalf of' Liability insurance (e.g. directors' and officers' (qv)) indicating that the insurer will pay defence costs on behalf of the insured. Where the insurer's promise is to 'indemnify', the obligation is to reimburse the insured's outlay instead of paying 'up front'.

'Pay to be paid' *See* PROTECTION AND INDEMNITY CLUBS.

'Paying passengers' Passengers who get a 'lift' in someone else's vehicle and make a contribution towards the running costs. *See* CAR SHARING.

Payment protection insurance (PPI) Gives protection for repayments on a personal loan, mortgage, credit card or other regular commitments. *See* CREDIT PROTECTION INSURANCE.

Payment schedule Details as to the amount and time of payment of contributions to a pension scheme. A schedule is compulsory for money purchase schemes (qv).

Payroll cover 'Payroll' includes salaries, wages and remuneration of all kinds including national insurance, bonuses, holiday pay and other payments pertaining to salaries and wages. Payroll may be insured in full as a part of the gross profit item in a business interruption insurance (qv) but the *dual basis payroll* (qv) provides an alternative approach.

Peak value clause Marine cargo clause applied to cotton cargoes providing that the sum insured will be based on the highest value in the cotton market at the time of loss.

Pecuniary loss insurance Pecuniary means 'relating to money'. Pecuniary loss insurances are those that protect the insured's financial rights or interest such as revenue or receivables. This includes: business interruption insurance (qv), book debts (qv), legal expenses (qv) and fidelity guarantee (qv).

Penalty 1. A punishment like a fine or monetary payment. It is against public policy (qv) to allow a person to insure against fines but legal defence cover is available under liability and legal expenses insurances. Penalties along with liquidated damages (qv) arising under contract are commonly excluded under liability policies. 2. The nominal sum payable by an obligor, an insurer, on breach of a condition in a bond (qv).

Pension A lifetime payment to a person during his retirement years having previously been an active member (qv) of a pension scheme and/or become entitled to a state pension.

Pension cost Amount allocated to the employer's profit and loss account for his pension contributions over the period that scheme members are expected to work.

Pension credit Amount in a pension credited to the former spouse of a pension scheme member following a pension sharing order (qv). Compare with pension debit (qv).

Pension debit The reduction of a member's pension by a certain percentage following a pension sharing order (qv) that matches the *pension credit* (qv) awarded a former spouse. It is based on the cash equivalent transfer value (qv) in regard to the order.

Pension drawdown *See* INCOME DRAWDOWN.

Pension fraction The fraction used in working out a member's pension entitlement in a final salary scheme (qv). The pension may be one-sixtieth for each year of pensionable service up to a maximum of two-thirds of final salary.

Pension fund 1.The accumulated assets of a pension scheme. 2. Amount built up in an individual's pension scheme while an active member (qv) to fund his retirement benefits. The fund value depends on the level of contributions and investment earnings. Final salary schemes (qv) have a notional cash equivalent transfer value (CETV) which is calculated actuarially to give the fund value that would arise in the event of the member leaving the scheme at the date of the calculation.

Pension fund withdrawal *See* INCOME DRAWDOWN.

Pension funding methods Methods used at each valuation (qv) to fix the contribution rate for the scheme. A number of different types of methods exist. The accrued benefit method (qv) and the projected benefit method (qv) are popular in the UK.

Pension guarantee A legally binding undertaking from the pension provider that payments to a pensioner will continue for a given term, or up to a specified amount, regardless of the pensioner's earlier death.

Pension liberation schemes/trust busting Schemes under Opra (qv) investigation as they are tainted with dishonesty. Promoters advertise that they are able to turn an individual's pension fund into an immediate tax-free cash. They often use offshore facilities, invent a fictitious employer's identity to secure a transfer from the individual's pension scheme and take 20–30 per cent of the fund in the process.

Pension mortgage Interest-only mortgage where interest payments run parallel with payments into a personal pension fund. The capital is repaid out of the tax-free cash option available at retirement, usually permitted between ages 50 and 75, which period is taken into account when fixing the mortgage term.

Pension Protection Fund (PPF) A UK protection scheme operative from 2005 for *defined benefit schemes* (qv) and hybrid schemes whose employers become insolvent leaving the pension scheme unable to pay its liabilities. Pensioners will be guaranteed 100% of their pensions and non-pensioner members will be guaranteed 90% of their accrued pensions. PPF is funded by a levy on all relevant private sector schemes. *See* MINIMUM FUNDING REQUIREMENT.

Pension revaluation The application to the preserved benefits (qv) of early leavers of indexation (qv), escalation (qv) or the award of discretionary increases. PSA93 imposes a minimum level of revaluation in the calculation of guaranteed minimum pension (qv) and of other preserved benefits.

Pension Review The Pension Transfer and Opt Out Review instituted by the Securities and Investment Board (now replaced by the FSA) in 1994 and now an s.404 scheme (qv).

Pension scheme A means by which an individual can make pension provision. This may be either collective or individual and with or without the involvement (by means of contributions or otherwise) from the individual's employer. Technically, the term is used to refer to a *personal pension scheme* (qv) or a *free standing additional voluntary contributions scheme* (qv) that has been approved by the Inland Revenue. The term *company pension scheme* is often used to describe *occupational pension schemes.*

Pension scheme statement of recommended practice (SORP) Rules that set out how the accounts of an occupational pension scheme must be calculated and written.

Pension Schemes Act 1993 (PSA93) Many of its regulations were brought into force in 1997, covering aspects of occupational and personal pension schemes.

Pension Schemes Registry A part of Opra (qv), PSR lists the occupational schemes covered by Opra (qv) and helps members trace schemes with which they have lost touch. It also enables Opra to check that every scheme has paid its levy (qv).

Pension sharing order Enables divorcing couples to share their pensions following a court order at the time of the divorce. The arrangement will reduce the value of the member's pension rights by a specified percentage (the pension debit) and an equivalent amount *pension credit* will be transferred to the ex-spouse. Pension sharing does not apply to the basic state pension (qv), unmarried couples or to separated couples.

Pension sharing/splitting Splitting of pension benefits between a divorced couple means 'a clean break' instead of remaining financially linked until retirement age as happens with earmarking (qv). The ex-spouse is entitled to a *pension credit* that remains in the member's current scheme or is transferred to a separate pension arrangement; most pension schemes insist upon the latter. The split means each can decide, within IR limits, when to take their pensions. but the ex-spouse is subject to the member's chosen retirement date. The original term *pension splitting* now called *pension sharing* (qv).

Pension splitting *See* PENSION SHARING.

Pension transfer Transfer of the cash value from one approved pension scheme to another. A transfer payment is made to the member's receiving scheme.

Pensionable earnings 1. *See* NET RELEVANT EARNINGS. 2. Pensionable earnings/salary are the earnings on which pension scheme benefits and contributions are calculated as defined in the scheme rules. Normally it refers to total PAYE earnings from the employer for the relevant tax year and therefore includes bonuses, overtime, commissions and benefits in kind. Some final salary schemes may restrict 'pensionable earnings' to the member's basic salary; definitions vary so full PAYE (P60) earnings are not necessarily the scheme's pensionable earnings.

Pensionable salary Definitions are by scheme rules. In a final salary scheme it is not necessarily the salary in the last year of service. *See* PENSIONABLE EARNINGS.

Pensionable service The years of service used by an employer for calculating entitlement to pension benefits from an occupational pension scheme. Scheme rules define the eligible periods and types.

Pensioneer trustee An independent trustee whose appointment is mandatory to secure approval for a small self-administered scheme (qv). The pensioneer is then not allowed to resign unless an immediate replacement is available.

Pensioner members People receiving a pension from an occupational pension scheme.

Pensioner trustees Pensioner members (qv) appointed as trustees.

Pensioner's rights premium The payment to the state by a private pension scheme when it ceases to be contracted out (qv) of a defined benefit scheme (qv). It enables the state to provide the guaranteed minimum pension (qv) for scheme members (or pensioners over state pension age).

Pensions Compensation Scheme Scheme that pays compensation to members of occupational pension schemes when assets have fallen in value due to dishonesty or employer insolvency. The scheme is run by the Pensions Compensation Board under parliamentary jurisdiction. Compensation is funded by a levy on occupational pension schemes.

Pensions managed fund Occupational pension scheme not managed by the firm itself but either by an insurance company, which receives the premiums, invests them for the benefit of the fund, and pays out the pensions, or by external investment managers.

Pensions Management Institute (PMI) Formed in 1976 to promote professionalism amongst those involved with pension scheme management and consultancy. It sponsors the national vocational qualification (NVQ) in pensions administration and is generally concerned with maintaining high standards within the pensions industry.

Pensions Ombudsman (PO) Decides complaints and disputes about the way pension schemes are run (maladministration). Complaints on sales/marketing fall to the FSA (qv). PO is an independent, impartial adjudicator whose decision binds all parties and can be appealed only on a point of law. PO does not become involved in a dispute between a member and his scheme until normal dispute resolution and OPAS (qv) involvement have been exhausted. (Visit *www.pensions-ombudsman.org.uk*).

Pensions Regulator Replaces Opra (qv) in 2005 when it takes over the regulation of occupational pensions and specific functions of personal pensions and stakeholder pensions. It is also assuming new functions. The Regulator will be funded by a levy on relevant schemes. The Pensions Regulator Tribunal will be established to handle references from determinations by the Regulator. There will be a new criminal offence for failing to attend on a witness summons before the Tribunal.

Per occurrence *See* EXCESS PER OCCURRENCE REINSURANCE.

Per risk *See* EXCESS PER RISK REINSURANCE.

Percentage adjustments A term describing a percentage increase or decrease to give effect to changes in fire insurance premium rates to reflect changes in the experience of the various classes of risk.

Percentage of fire loss Form of business interruption policy (qv) under which the insurer pays a percentage of the amount paid for the material damage claim. The percentage is based on the relationship between the interruption sum insured and the total fire sum insured. The policy is an *excess fire policy* not one of indemnity.

Performance bond Common in the construction industry, the surety protects the project owner by guaranteeing that the contractor will perform his contractual obligations. If the contractor defaults, the project owner (the obligee) calls upon the surety to pay damages (the additional costs of completing the work) up to the amount of the bond. The surety (the obligee) has recourse against the contractor (the principal). The bond may incorporate a *payment bond* guaranteeing that the contractor will pay sub-contractors and for the contract materials. *See* MAINTENANCE BOND; RETENTION BOND; STREET WORKS BOND.

Peril A contingency, or fortuitous happening, which may be covered or excluded by the policy.

Perils of the seas Refers only to *fortuitous* accidents or casualties of the seas and does not include the ordinary action of the wind and waves (MIA1906, Rule for Construction 7). Sinking, foundering of ship at sea, collisions or unintentional stranding are not mentioned but are 'perils of the sea'. Something which may happen at sea, not something that must happen, is the criterion. *See* PERILS ON THE SEA.

Perils on the sea Perils that could occur at sea, e.g. fire, violent theft by persons outside the vessel, but could also occur elsewhere. They are perils added to 'perils of the sea' as named perils.

Period policy *See* TIME POLICY.

Permanent contracts/policies Life and *income protection policies* (qv) policies to which the insurer is committed for a number of years, e.g. 20 years or to age 65. Renewal is at the option of the insured only. The insurer comes off risk only when the agreed period has elapsed.

Permanent health insurance *See* INCOME PROTECTION.

Permanent partial disablement Disability benefit payable when an injury leaves the insured working on a reduced basis as opposed to not working at all. The impairment is ongoing. The benefits are a proportion of the permanent total disablement (qv) benefit.

Permanent selection The exclusion from a group of lives of persons of a certain type with the result that the mortality rate of the group will differ compared to the population norm. Example: persons suffering from chronic diseases may be excluded from a group of lives acceptable for life insurance at ordinary rates of premium with the result that the insured group will have a lighter mortality rate.

Permanent total disablement (PTD) Condition, other than one relating to loss of sight or limb, that attracts a lump sum benefit payable when the insured is unable to follow any occupation or gainful employment. Some policies allow the PTD benefit if the insured's disablement prevents him from following his normal occupation not any occupation (e.g. injured ex-footballer becomes journalist).

Permitted investments Types of investments that pension trustees operating under trust deed rules are permitted to make. *See* TRUSTEE ACT 2001.

Permitted maximum The legal name for the earnings cap (qv).

Perpetual insurance Fire insurance method under which the insured pays a deposit in a lump sum or in instalments based on a percentage of the value of the property at risk. The insurer invests the sum paid in order to accrue interest from which claims will be paid. The insured can end the arrangement by withdrawing his deposit.

Persistency The renewal quality of insurance policies, particularly life policies. High persistency means that a high proportion of policies stay in force until the end of the policy term. Low persistency means a high percentage of lapses.

Person guaranteed The person, also called the principal, whose fidelity or undertaking is the subject of a fidelity guarantee or a bond.

Personal accident/sickness insurance An *accidents only* policy pays lump sum benefits following permanent total or partial disablement (qv), dismemberment or death caused by an *accident* (qv) and weekly benefits for temporary total disablement. The policy is renewable annually but similar cover is available under travel policies (qv). Hazardous pursuits (e.g. mountaineering) are excluded but can usually be bought back. A weekly/monthly benefit can be added for total disablement through sickness – a *personal accident and sickness policy. See* CONTINTENTAL SCALE; INCOME PROTECTION.

Personal contracts Insurance contracts are personal contracts, i.e. they depend upon trust and confidence. Consequently insurance policies are not assignable without the insurer's agreement. However, commercial and other circumstances dictate that marine and life policies are not considered to be personal contracts.

Personal injury Intended by insurers to mean bodily injury embracing physical or psychiatric harm, disease or illness. A strict interpretation of *personal injury* includes intangibles such as injury to feelings resulting from defamation, personal data abuse and false arrest. Insurers may prefer to use the term 'bodily injury' (qv) in certain policies.

Personal legal assistance A section of a commercial legal expenses insurance (qv) to provide similar cover for directors, partners and key personnel and their families in respect of private matters.

Personal liability insurance A household contents extension indemnifying the insured (and resident family members) against legal liability for third party injury or damage resulting from acts or omissions occurring in a private capacity. Cover excludes liability arising from: business or profession; land or buildings; motor vehicles.

Personal lines Insurances bought by individuals for their personal insurance needs; e.g. private car, household, travel and pet insurances.

Personal pensions Pensions for the self-employed and persons not in an occupational scheme. Tax relief is based on *net relevant earnings* (qv). Retirement can be at any time between 50 and 75. A tax-free lump sum (25 per cent of fund) is available at retirement. If income drawdown (qv) is used, the balance must fund a compulsory retirement annuity by age 75. Personal pensions can be used for contracting out (qv). The term also applies to *retirement annuity contracts* (qv), set up before July 1988.

Personal property/belongings Part of the household contents definition generally specified as 'valuables and personal items' belonging to the insured or his family. Personal items are items worn, used or carried about the person in everyday life. Personal belongings exclude, inter alia: money and credit cards; mechanically propelled vehicles; bicycles, caravans, bicycles, etc; fragile items; business and trade goods. Money, pedal cycles and specified articles can be insured under separate sections.

Personal Protective Equipment at Work Regulations 1992 (PPE) Suitable personal protective equipment must be provided unless the risk is adequately contained. PPE must be maintained in good repair and steps taken to ensure that it is used correctly. The need for PPE must be assessed and information given on its use. A breach is criminal and a civil claim can be founded on a statutory breach (qv).

Personal recommendation For the purpose of ICOB (qv), it is the advice given to a specific person (including the advice given to a group of people).

Personal representative *See* LEGAL PERSONAL REPRESENTATIVE.

'Persons at work' Under the Health and Safety at Work, etc., Act 1974 (qv) it means: 'all persons at work', whether employers, employees or self-employed, are covered except domestic servants in a private household. The Act extends to many not covered by the previous legislation, e.g. self-employed, those employed in education, health services, leisure industries and in some parts of the transport industry.

Pet insurance Covers domestic pet owners against financial consequences (veterinary fees) of accidental injury to the pet, illness and third party liability. Comprehensive cover extends to loss or theft, cancellation of holidays, cost of advertising, payments of rewards. Death benefit does not apply to elderly animals. Domestic pet cover is not available for racing dogs, guard dogs, working dogs or dogs registered under the Dangerous Dogs Act 1991 (qv). *See* EXOTIC BIRDS; EXOTIC MAMMALS.

Phantom vessel Typically a vessel that has no valid classification, i.e. it is not registered with any recognised ship registry and is used as a vehicle for fraud on cargo owners. In *Nima Sarl* v. *Deves Insurance Co. Ltd* (2002), the Court of Appeal disallowed the insured's claim as the vessel, considered by the insurer to be a phantom, never intended to sail for the destination named in the policy. The risk did not attach.

Phased retirement Pension option allowing the member to 'phase in' retirement by drawing segments from his fund at intervals. Each withdrawal funds an annuity and a tax free lump sum and builds up the pension payments. The main constraint is the *age 75 rule* (qv). This option, also called '*staggered vesting phased retirement*', should be compared with income drawdown (qv).

Physical hazard A hazard that arises from the material, structural or operational features of the risk itself apart from the persons associated with it (moral hazard (qv)). In fire insurance, physical hazard concerns construction, heating, security and use of premises. *See* STANDARD CONSTRUCTION.

Pilferage Theft unaccompanied by any attack on the premises often by persons lawfully on the premises. Pilferage is not usually covered under commercial theft policies; losses are low impact, high probability losses and therefore suitable for risk assumption (qv) and risk prevention (qv), particularly by retailers. Pilferage by employees is a fidelity guarantee insurance (qv) risk. In the marine cargo clause it has been held as: 'the taking of a small part of the goods rather than of the whole'. *See* FULL THEFT INSURANCE.

Pirates/piracy An assault on a vessel, cargo, crew, or passengers at sea by marauders, who owe no allegiance to a recognised flag, acting for personal gain. It includes acts of rioters who attack a ship from the shore and passengers who mutiny. Piracy is insurable under the Institute War Clauses. The risk is a serious concern of the International Marine Bureau (qv) which has it own definition of piracy.

Pivotal age Age for a contracted out (qv) pension scheme member when, and if, it is advantageous to return to the state second pension (qv).

Plain English A 'campaign' joined by a number of insurers to combat criticism that policies are written in almost incomprehensible language. These insurers endeavour to use language their policyholders regard as easier to understand.

Plain form of policy A policy without clauses attached like the defunct S.G. (ship and goods) form used by Lloyd's from 1799 until 1983. It remained in use because all of its words and phrases had been defined in the courts. The current *MAR form* (qv) expresses the agreement to insure and adds detailed cover through the Institute Clauses.

Planned risk assumption Risk financing (qv) whereby the business treats losses as normal operating expenses recovered through the prices charged for their products or services. The risks are not assumed unwittingly. The method is appropriate for low impact high frequency losses.

Plant and machinery insurance Boilers, pressure, lifting equipment, etc., are all subject to statutory inspection at preset intervals. Insurers provide these and other inspection services in respect of: boilers and pressure vessels; lifts; cranes and lifting plant; and electrical and mechanical plant. Risks covered: sudden and unforeseen damage including the key perils of breakdown, explosion and collapse; and working environment risks such as operator error, frost fracture, overheating and collision. Other risks covered: malicious acts; loss or damage to surrounding property through explosion or *fragmentation* (qv). Cover can be extended to cover engineering consequential loss (qv) caused by damage to plant and machinery.

Plate glass insurance *See* GLASS INSURANCE.

Pleasure boat insurance A category of marine hull policies covering various forms of watercraft used for private purposes. Types of vessel include: yachts, including sail boats; outboard motors; and jet skis. The basis of cover is usually hull and liability.

Plural tenancy risk Premises occupied by a number of different tenants. The situation may present fire hazards due to: 1. Trades of widely different character under one roof. 2. Different standards of cleanliness. 3. Frequent changes of tenants without notice to the insurer. 4. Poor upkeep of fire extinguishing appliances in the absence of clear responsibility. 5. Risk of insecure and badly kept heating appliances in some parts of the building. If there is no fire division between the individual risks, the rate for the whole is fixed by reference to the highest-rated tenant.

Plurality of risk This exists when a fire insurance covers more than one building or range of buildings each with its own separate sum insured.

Pluvius insurance *See* WEATHER INSURANCE.

Points basis A system of rating motor traders' road risks policies (qv) by allocating a certain number of points for each feature of the insured's business (e.g. number of vehicles; number of persons permitted to drive; number of trade plates, etc.). The insured submits an annual declaration in respect of these activities.

Polarisation/depolarisation The concept of polarisation was introduced by the pre-FSA regulators making it mandatory for financial advisors to be either independent or tied to one company. The FSA has depolarised and restricts an authorised representative to one principal for investment business for retail clients while able to access the products of other providers through their principal. There is no limit on the number of principals in regard to commercial customers. Authorised persons are not restricted as to number of principals in regard to non-investment general insurance contracts but the principals enter into a multiple-principals agreement to facilitate the supervision of the authorised person concerned.

Policies incepting basis A reinsurance treaty written on the basis that the reinsurer's liability is based on when the underlying policy was effected and not whether the loss occurred or was notified.

Policies of Assurance Act 1867 An Act enabling the assignee of a life policy to sue in his own name provided that he has an equitable right to the proceeds and has given the insurer written notice of the date and purpose of the assignment. The assignee has no title until notice is given and will find that 'priority of notice regulates the priority of the claim'. The assignment can be by endorsement or separate document.

Policy Written evidence of the contract between the insurer and the insured. Under the contra proferentem rule (qv) ambiguity will be construed against the insurer as the document writer.

Policy proof of interest (PPI) Policy whereby the insurer waives proof of insurable interest when settling a claim. The policy is unenforceable as it is a wagering contract but is otherwise valid. PPI policies are significant in maritime trade where cargo changes ownership and it would be difficult to prove an interest at a particular time. A PPI clause is attached to the policy, otherwise known as an 'honour policy', peculiar to marine insurance.

Policy reserve *See* LEVEL ANNUAL PREMIUM SYSTEM.

Policy summary A document in durable medium (qv) that FSA rules require intermediaries to give retail customers, setting out the main benefits, exclusions and limitations of the policy and other information.

Policy year 1. The period between inception or renewal date and expiry of an annual policy. 2. A term used for certain loss statistics, it relates to the calendar year or accounting year in which the commencement date of the policy falls and may include policies issued for varying periods of time.

Policyholder The person, otherwise called the insured (qv), in whose name the policy is issued.

Policyholders' equity A large part of the investment earnings of non-life insurers comes from the administration of what is called the 'policyholders' equity' in the assets of the company covering the unearned premium reserve (qv) and outstanding claims.

Policyholders' funds *See* TECHNICAL RESERVES.

Political risk There is no single definition but usually means a risk that is subject to political decisions and therefore beyond the firm's control. Political risk must be carefully distinguished from commercial risk (changes in production, prices, interest rates, currency rates, etc.). They fall into five groups: confiscation; expropriation and nationalisation; currency inconvertibility; contract frustration; and war and civil unrest. Insurance cover is available for each group with confiscation, expropriation and nationalisation being the most readily available and contract frustration being the most difficult risk to place. The *Export Credit Guarantee Department* (qv) has a vital role in the insurance of political risk but there is also private sector provision. See *credit insurance* (qv); *export credit* (qv); *financial guarantee* (qv) and *overseas investment insurance* (qv).

Polluter pays principle Equates the price charged for using environmental resources with the cost to society. Charges may be direct through taxes on pollution-generating processes or indirect through the purchase price of licences entitling the holder to generate specific quantities of pollutants. Another approach is to make polluters strictly liable for the injury/damage that they cause, leaving them to carry the risk or undergo the scrutiny of an insurer. *See* ENVIRONMENTAL PROTECTION ACT 1995.

Pollution Damage to land, water, property or the atmosphere by the disposal of waste materials or the release of toxic, corrosive, ionising, irritating, thermal or other noxious or offensive substances. The environment can also be impaired by noise or vibration. Pollution causes direct (bodily injury, damage to crops) and indirect (loss of profits due to business interruption and clean-up costs) costs. Statutory control comes through the Environmental Protection Acts 1990–95 invoking 'the polluter pays principle' (qv).

Pollution clause Public liability clause excluding liability for pollution and contamination unless caused by a sudden, identifiable and unexpected incident 'happening in its entirety at a specific time and place during the period of insurance'. All pollution/contamination arising out of one incident is deemed to take place at the time of the incident. The clause is more widely used than SEPTIC (qv). The aim is to exclude *gradual pollution* from the cover. *See* ENVIRONMENTAL IMPAIRMENT LIABILITY; POLLUTION INSURANCE.

Pollution Hazard Clause Covers loss or damage to the vessel following governmental action to prevent or mitigate a pollution hazard or damage to the environment or threat thereof. The government's act must flow directly from damage to the vessel for which the underwriter is liable. (Clause 5 International Hull Clauses (qv)).

Pollution insurance 1. *First party insurance* (qv) indemnifying the insured in respect of expenses incurred in extracting pollutants from land or water on his own site(s) when their release results from an insured loss. Cover may be added to material damage insurance or marketed as *pollutant clean up and removal insurance.* 2. *Pollution liability insurance* covers the insured's legal liability to third parties for bodily injury, property damage or clean up costs on third party sites. Cover may be the result of 'sudden and accidental pollution' as per the *pollution clause* (qv) or *accidental nuisance,* a term in the operative clause of the public liability policy, that usually applies to the accidental escape of pollutants, smells, etc. and includes liability for pure financial loss. *Environmental impairment liability* (qv) provides the widest cover as it applies to gradual pollution cover and may be combined with first party cover. 3. The *debris removal clause* (qv) brings the cost of removing or decontaminating contaminated items within the scope of material damage insurance. Similarly smoke damage following fire is a form of contamination and will be covered under material damage insurance. 4. *See* 1992 CLC.

Polychlorinated biphenyls (PCBs) Non-flammable liquids formerly used in heat exchangers, electrical condensers, hydraulic and lubricating fluids, and various inks and paints. Most uses of these highly toxic chemicals have been curtailed. Leakage of PCBs in food production led to widespread food poisoning in Japan and leading US authorities have classified PCBs as probable human carcinogens. The chemical is lethal to fish and harmful to wildlife.

Pool A combination of insurers in a specific class of insurance in which they agree to share the premiums and losses. Pooling is used for exceptionally heavy risks, e.g. atomic energy risks.

Pool Re (Pool Reinsurance Co. Ltd) Government-inspired mutual company authorised to transact reinsurance for property and business interruption and related classes. By agreements with the government Pool Re provides its members (major insurance companies and Lloyd's) with reinsurance cover for losses from commercial property damage in Great Britain caused by acts of terrorism. Members offer 'defined' terrorism cover (qv) where they insure the property against fire and explosion and they reinsure their terrorism portfolio with Pool Re. Pool Re is a party to a retrocession (qv) with HM Treasury who will indemnify Pool Re against its reinsurance liabilities to members subject to exceptions and deductions for expenses. In 2003 the market for terrorism became fully competitive, rates previously set by Pool Re having been lifted with wider terrorism cover, i.e. 'all risks', also becoming available. *See* TERRORISM; TERRORISM COVER.

Port of refuge expenses Common form of general average expenditure (qv) arising when a ship enters a port of refuge following a casualty or general average damage to the ship. If the entry is due to accidental damage, only the expenses of entry into port and discharging the cargo, if necessary for the purpose of repairs, are allowed in general average. If entry follows general average damage, the following are also allowed: warehouse rent during repairs; cargo reloading costs; outward port charges.

Port risks insurance 'All risks' cover for vessels laid up in the sheltered location for an extended period or for smaller vessels working only in and around the port.

Portability The ability of a pension scheme member to take his accrued pension entitlements with him from one job to another. This obviates the need to change policies and incurs only the minimum penalties.

Portfolio A defined body of: (a) insurance policies in force, a premium portfolio; (b) outstanding losses, loss portfolio (qv); (c) company investments, investment portfolio.

Portfolio reinsurance The transfer by cession of an entire portfolio of policies from a cedant to a reinsurer. It may be prompted by the cedant wishing to exit a particular line of business. Alternatively the reinsurer assumes a percentage of the entire portfolio of the cedant's business in a selected line or all lines of business.

Portfolio return Ceding offices resume the insurance of a portfolio of business from the reinsurer to whom they had previously ceded it.

Portfolio run-off Continuing the reinsurance of a portfolio (qv) under a cancelled treaty until all premium is earned or all losses settled or both.

Portfolio Transfer The transfer of general or life insurance business, usually involving many individual policies, from one insurer to another. Transfer applications must be approved by the court (FSMA, s.107). The FSA (qv) monitors the progress of the application to ensure that policyholders (of both transferor and transferee) are treated fairly and remain secure. An FSA-appointed independent expert reports on the impact on both sets of policyholders.

Positions policy/bond *See* COMMERCIAL GUARANTEES.

Possible maximum loss Compare with estimated maximum loss (qv). *See* MAXIMUM POSSIBLE LOSS.

Post 89 member *See* CLASS A MEMBER.

Post-loss funding Contingent capital (qv) arrangement whereby the funding to pay for a loss is obtained after the loss by means of guaranteed equity or debt finance. The financial institution giving the guarantee receives a commitment fee from the insured. The *loss* is defined in conventional insurance terms. Post loss funding is alternative risk transfer (qv).

Post-loss minimisation The steps taken to contain a loss to a minimum amount (loss protection (qv)). The property salvaged from a fire may have a sale value or be restored. Property is removed from burning buildings and protected against the elements and theft. Where personal injury or disease is concerned, appropriate support can shorten periods of disablement suffered following injury and trauma. *See* REHABILITATION.

Postponed retirement Continued employment of pension scheme members beyond their normal pension date (qv). Subject to scheme rules they continue as *active members* (qv) and commence their pension at a later date.

Power Presses Part IV of PUWER 98 (qv) contains specific regulations for power presses. Each power press should have an associated guard or protection device and be thoroughly examined at least every 12 months if it has a fixed guard, otherwise six monthly, and inspected daily to ensure that it is safe. This work should only be performed by a competent person and records should be kept.

Practice Notes (IR12) (PN) IR notes on discretionary approval of occupational pension schemes.

Pre-Action Protocols Part of the Civil Procedure Rules covering claims procedures and timetables in respect of: personal injury; clinical negligence; defamation disputes; professional negligence; construction and engineering disputes. The objects are to encourage the early exchange of full information about the claim; to enable the parties to avoid litigation by agreeing a settlement; and to support the management of proceedings. The Protocols lead to a 'cards on the table' approach.

Preamble *See* RECITAL CLAUSE.

Precipice bond A single premium, high income bond, typically for five years, under which the full return of capital depends on a stock market-measure (e.g. FTSE 100) performing to a minimum level over the life of the product. If the index/measure under-performs investors may not receive a full return of capital; the return drops ever lower as the index/measure continues to fall (the 'precipice effect'). The FSA requires firms to give clear explanations of the risks involved and follow certain other requirements.

Precipitation Rainfall and snowfall. *See* PRECIPITATION COVER; SNOWFALL COVER.

Precipitation cover Weather derivative (qv) with a reference point based on an expected rainfall level in a specific location over a defined period. If the point is exceeded, certain entities, e.g. a theme park, will suffer poor sales and receive a payout based on the accumulated deviations above the rainfall index multiplied by the tick (qv). If the actual rainfall level does not exceed the reference point (or strike (qv)) there is no payout; the only cost to the firm is the premium paid in return for the protection granted. *See* PRECIPITATION SWAPS; SNOWFALL COVER.

Precipitation swaps Two parties exchange payments streams by reference to an underlying index based on rainfall or snowfall. A snow-clearing local authority could enter into a swap with a ski resort. In the event of snow *above* the reference point, the extra cost of snow clearing is funded out of the income stream of the ski resort. The converse would also apply. The upside risk of one party pays the downside risk of the other.

Pre-existing medical condition A physical or mental condition that existed prior to the effective date of the insured's health-based insurance. The policy usually excludes claims where a condition, the subject of medical treatment or consultation within one year prior to policy inception, has contributed to the claim. If, after two years of insurance, a pre-existing condition has not necessitated further treatment, the exclusion will not usually apply.

Pre-launch insurance Satellite insurance providing 'all risks' insurance from the completion of the assembly until the launch. The policy operates while the satellite is in storage and transit and also covers third party risks. The cover continues until the intended time of the launch engine's ignition. If the launch is aborted the policy may become operative once again.

Pre-loss minimisation *See* LOSS PREVENTION.

Premises risk Liability for injury/damage arising from ownership or occupation of premises. The 'premises risk' is covered under public liability insurance. For some types of business, e.g. hotels and cinemas, it is the central risk. In other cases, e.g. electrical contractors, the risk is minimal as most work is done away from the premises. *See* also PUBLIC ACCESS RISKS; OCCUPIERS' LIABILITY ACT 1957; OCCUPIERS' LIABILITY ACT 1984.

Premium advice note A note sent by a broker to an insurer or policy signing office when the broker's client has been debited with the premium or credited with a return premium.

Premium earned As premiums are payable in advance it follows that at any one time, e.g. end of the financial year, most policies will have an unexpired term to complete. The premium earned is the pro rata share of the premium relating to the period that has expired.

Premium exemptions Premiums paid during a person's lifetime on his own life may be regarded as normal expenditure out of income and therefore exempt from inheritance tax. Such premiums are not 'normal expenditure' if an annuity was purchased on his life unless they were not associated operations, i.e back to back (qv). Policies and annuities are not regarded as associated operations if, first, the policy was issued on full medical evidence of the insured's health, and, secondly, it would have been issued on the same terms if the annuity had not been bought.

Premium/expense ratio A ratio that relates expenses to net premium earned.

Premium income limit Otherwise called the *overall premium limit* it is the limit that, in respect of a Lloyd's member, represents the maximum underwriting capacity that can be allocated to one year of account. *See* OVERWRITING OF PREMIUMS.

Premium overwriting *See* OVERWRITING PREMIUMS.

Premium Portfolio The unearned premium debited to an outgoing reinsurer (loss portfolio withdrawal (qv)) and credited to the incoming reinsurer as in loss portfolio entry (qv).

Premium rate Amount charged for each unit of insurance or variable associate, e.g. turnover, reflecting the level of activity. The rate varies according to the degree risk (e.g. high, medium, low) and breadth of the cover. The rate may be per class or a rate per cent (or per mille).

Premium value Valuation of a long-term insurance policy for the pension scheme's accounts. It is based on how much the scheme has to pay for each member. The actuary or accountant may opt for a modified premium value, i.e. one that excludes the insurance company's setting up charges.

Premiums reducing policy Marine insurance policy effected by shipowners on the insurance premiums paid on their ships. In the event of loss of a vessel, the owner will lose the unearned premium. The premiums reducing policy runs concurrently with other relevant policies.

Premiums trust fund Trust fund into which all premiums received by a Lloyd's member must be placed. The fund is available for the payment of claims, reinsurance premiums, syndicate expenses and, when an account has been closed, for the payment of any profit due to the member. Each member has a sterling fund, a US dollar fund and a Canadian dollar fund. The funds are the first link in *Lloyd's chain of security* (qv).

Prepayment Payment in advance. Occurs when the employer's pension contributions exceed the actuarial calculation as being the contributions required. The prepayment, is shown in the employer's (not the pension scheme's) accounts as an asset.

Present value Current value of future payments. It is calculated by deducting an amount for interest, and taking account of how likely it is that the money will be paid. Also called capitalised value.

Preservation *See* PRESERVED BENEFITS.

Preserved benefits/pension Benefits granted to an occupational pension scheme member on leaving before normal pension age based on benefits already earned. The benefits are 'frozen' and become payable when the member retires. In the case of a contracted out scheme the preserved pension must be in accordance with the *guaranteed minimum pension* (qv) and be transferable.

Pressure plant Plant designed to contain gas or vapour, such as steam, under pressure. The majority of items have to be inspected under statutory provisions. A steam boiler is an example. The principal risk is explosion and/or collapse.

Pressure Systems Safety Regulations 2000 The aim is to prevent injury from the hazard of stored energy due to system failure. Pressure system users/owners must show that they know the safe operating limits, mainly pressure and temperature, of their pressure systems, and that the systems are safe under those conditions. They need to: (a) have a suitable written scheme of examination before the system is operated; (b) ensure that the pressure system is examined in accordance with the written scheme; (c) ensure that the scheme is certified by a competent person.

Prevention of access *See* DENIAL OF ACCESS.

Primary exposure An aviation insurance term to describe risks which, although serious, are not potentially catastrophic.

Primary insurance The insurance granted by an insurer to the original insured. If the insurance required exceeds the primary insurer's retention, the insurance up to the retention is called the primary layer, or the first layer, or is called the underlying insurance.

Primary liability This principle is bound up with subrogation (qv). Where the same loss or damage becomes the subject of a claim under both a first party policy (qv) covering the owner's interest and another person's liability for that loss/damage, the liability insurer ultimately pays for the loss as their insured is *primary liable.* The property owner has no direct claim against the liability owner, only against the third party.

Primary reinsurance clause A clause under which the reinsurer agrees to pay losses directly to the insured. The clause is rarely used.

Principal 1. One who authorises an agent, to act on his behalf. If an agent purports to act on his own behalf, his principal is called an undisclosed principal. 2. A principal debtor is one who owes a debt that is guaranteed by a surety. 3. A sum of money put out at interest. 4. An authorised firm that accepts regulatory responsibility for contracted *appointed representative* (qv) firms and individuals. The principal must report its contracted agreement with an AR to the FSA for inclusion in the FSA Register. *See* PRINCIPAL'S CLAUSE.

Principal employer The employer who has special rights and responsibilities, e.g. appointing trustees, when a number of employers combine to run a pension scheme.

Principal's clause A clause in a public or employers' liability extending the insured's policy to provide an indemnity, where any contract so requires, to any principal in like manner to the insured. The principal (qv) must observe the terms and conditions of the policy and agree that conduct and control of any claims shall be vested in the insurer. The clause meets the requirements made of contractors to indemnify their Employers in accordance with Joint Contract Tribunal (qv) contracts.

Principal's cover A phrase used when the principal (i.e. the employer) and not the contractor arranges the insurance even though the standard form of contract, e.g. Joint Contract Tribunal, normally places insurance obligations on the contractor. It often means a combined contractors' 'all risks' public liability being effected. This arrangement is sometimes called 'wrap-up cover'.

Principles for Business Eleven principles detailed in Block 1 of the FSA Handbook (qv). They are a general statement of the fundamental obligations of firms under the regulatory systems. The principles embrace, inter alia, standards of care, integrity, customer relationships based on trust and dealing with the regulators in an open and cooperative manner. Breaching a principle makes a firm liable to disciplinary action. (Visit *www.fsa.gov.uk*).

Priority liabilities Priority to pay some liabilities, e.g. guaranteed minimum payments, before others when a pension scheme is wound up. If the assets are insufficient to meet all liabilities the *priority rule* applies. The trustees must follow this scheme rule in deciding the order in which they settle scheme liabilities.

'Priority of notice regulates the priority of claim' *See* POLICIES OF ASSURANCE ACT 1867.

Private hire vehicle Passenger seating vehicles having not more than 12 seats and used for the carriage of passengers for hire or reward but, not being authorised to ply for hire from the streets and designated places, are hired direct from the insured's premises or instructions issued therefrom.

Private hotel A convenient term to distinguish hotels from those run as inns (qv). It is an establishment, which, unlike an inn, picks and chooses its guests. The proprietor's responsibilities for guests (qv) and their property are not governed by any special legal rules. The normal laws of tort, contract and bailment will apply.

Private managed funds A normal insured pension but having a fund link that is unique to the individual or partners in a business. The life insurance company owns the assets of the funds which are therefore subject to regulatory control so the individual cannot manage the fund as can happen with self-investment personal pensions (qv).

Private medical attendant's report *See* MEDICAL ATTENDANT'S REPORT.

Private medical insurance 1. Insurance that enables the insured to gain access to medical treatment, with benefits including: a private en-suite room in hospital; surgeon's and other specialists' fees;

out-patient treatment, including physiotherapy; day care treatment, including diagnostic and surgical procedures. 2. An integral part of a typical *travel insurance* (qv).

Private pension scheme Any non-state pension scheme The main types of private pension schemes are: occupational pension schemes (qv), personal pension schemes (qv), stakeholders pensions (qv).

Private personal liability A public liability extension to indemnify the insured and his employees in respect of their personal liability (qv) while abroad on 'business' but in connection with 'off duty' activities. Where the insured is an individual the cover also applies within the usual country of residence.

Private warnings Issued by the FSA to approved persons (qv) and firms when formal disciplinary action is under consideration.

Privilege conditions These are life insurance policy conditions conferring concessions on the insured such as paid-up provisions (qv), surrender values (qv), grace period (qv) and non-forfeiture (qv).

Pro rata liability method Also called *maximum liability method.* See *independent liability method* (qv) with which it is compared.

Probability The science of the measurement of chance. In the theory of probability, certainty is represented by unity. The probability of an event that is not certain is a fraction – the smaller the chance of the event happening the smaller the fraction. Insurance, by combining large numbers of similar exposure units, can predict the probability of the insured event with greater accuracy than is possible with small groups or individuals. Mortality tables (qv) help actuaries predict with a high degree of accuracy the probabilities of males and females dying at each age by observing a large number of lives. *See* RISK COMBINATION.

Probable maximum loss *See* ESTIMATED MAXIMUM LOSS.

Probationary period/qualifying period *See* WAITING PERIOD.

Proceeds of policy scheme Money purchase scheme (qv) that purchases an insurance policy for each member. The proceeds of the policy buys the member's pension.

Product disclosure ICOB (Chapter 5) requirement that the retail customer should receive key information before the contract is concluded. Retail customers must also have up to date information in the event of changes to policy terms, conditions or the premium. There is also a requirement for product disclosure for commercial customers at the point of sale and renewal. Disclosure for packaged products (qv) is covered in ICOB (Chapter 6).

Product extortion insurance Indemnifies the insured for a proportion of loss due to the payment of extortion demands or for recalling a threatened or contaminated product or destroying such a product.

Product guarantee insurance/efficacy cover Covers the insured's legal liability to replace, rework or recover products that have failed to perform their intended function after delivery to a customer. The policy is claims-made (qv) with co-insurance as standard, and product recall (qv) as an option. The policy may back up the insured's written guarantee to his customer for a one-off product such as chemical plant or be used to support a guarantee of a company's products (e.g. wall ties).

Product liability (financial loss) *See* FINANCIAL LOSS.

Product liability exclusion Exclusion of liability arising from 'products' (qv) supplied by the insured. This can appear both in public liability and professional indemnity policies. The risk is insured under a products liability policy (qv).

The dividing line between the products and public liability policies is important. In the public liability policy the exclusion does not apply to products still in the insured's custody and control.

Product liability insurance Insures legal liability for damages, claimants' costs and own costs for accidental injury or damage caused by 'products' (qv) supplied by the insured. The policy is 'losses-occurring' (qv) with an annual aggregate limit of indemnity. Cover is worldwide in respect of products supplied from the UK. The efficacy risk (qv) is not covered but is included under a financial loss extension (qv). The insurer is not liable to replace defective products or for product recall (qv). *See* RETROSPECTIVE COVER; VENDOR'S INDEMNITY; BATCH CLAUSE; CONSUMER PROTECTION ACT 1987; PRODUCT GUARANTEE.

Product recall exclusion A product liability (qv) exclusion of the cost incurred by the insured in recalling injurious products from customers and distributors. The costs are insurable under product recall insurance (qv). *See* also PRODUCT RECALL PLAN.

Product recall insurance An 'extra expense' cover indemnifying the insured for costs incurred in recalling a product suspected of being injurious to customers and users. Recall costs include communications, transport, warehousing, inspection, overtime, even destruction and so on. Cover is triggered by the decision of the insured to recall the product because of its potentially harmful nature. Cover applies to accidental causes not design faults. Companies should maintain a product recall plan (qv).

Product recall plan A manufacturer's plan to enable him to action a product recall (qv) situation immediately on becoming aware that it is necessary or prudent to withdraw a dangerous product. Tracing, identifying and handling products need to be pre-planned to minimise cost and risk. The plan is a vital risk management tool.

Product tamper insurance Protects manufacturers who are the victims of product contamination or the threat thereof. The insurance pays the cost of stock destruction, business interruption and product rehabilitation. There is no cover for third party injury (*see* PRODUCT LIABILITY INSURANCE) or extortion payments (*see* PRODUCT EXTORTION INSURANCE). Consultancy services are usually available through the insurer. Food manufacturers and leading retailers are the most likely victims.

Professional fees legal protection A legal expenses insurance for professional fees (including those of a firm's accountants) for representing the insured's interests in the event of being subject to an in-depth investigation by the IR. Also covered are appeals against VAT assessments made by HM Customs and Excise. Cover includes personal protection for individual directors, partners and the self-employed where there is likely to be overlap of the investigation into the individual's own affairs. Cover usually extends to include the cost of fees that may be incurred by the insured in dealing with PAYE Audit Investigations.

Professional indemnity insurance (PI) Claims-made (qv) cover protecting 'professionals' against civil liability arising from a breach of professional duty subject to an annual aggregate limit. Insured's own costs are covered in addition. The policy eliminates claims due to matters occurring before the retroactive date (qv) and occurrences and claims reported after expiry unless reported within *an extended reporting period* (qv). Extensions include loss of documents cover. *See* PROFESSIONAL FEES LEGAL PROTECTION; PROFESSIONAL NEGLIGENCE; MEDICAL DEFENCE UNION.

'Professional negligence' The neglect of a professional duty of care by a professional. It is a negligent act, error or omission that, if it causes a loss, will make the professional liable in law to a client or third party to whom duty is owed. (*See Hedley Byrne* v. *Heller & Partners* (1964)). *See* PROFESSIONAL INDEMNITY INSURANCE; VOLUNTARY ASSUMPTION OF THE RISK.

Professional (or independent) trustees Professionals who provide trustee services as a business.

Professional sports teams exclusion Cover in respect of professional sports teams is a standard exclusion in a personal accident catastrophe excess of loss reinsurance cover. The sums insured are high and there is an accumulation risk.

Profit commission A commission based upon a pre-defined formula intended as an incentive and reward. Examples are: (a) the commission received by an underwriting agent from the syndicate members at Lloyds as a reward for profits; (b) the commission received by a cedant from a reinsurer as a reward for the ceding of profitable business.

Prohibited conditions Conditions in a compulsory insurance policy (motor and employers' liability) that are prohibited for the purpose of the legislation (e.g. 'things to be done after the event' such as reporting the incident and not admitting liability).

Prohibition notice 1. Prohibits the continuation of work until specified improvements have been carried out. Notices are issued by HSE inspectors. Contravention of the order risks prosecution for the employer and/or company officers responsible. 2. An order by Opra (qv) banning an individual from being a trustee of one particular occupational pension scheme.

Project financing/limited recourse finance A technique whereby a major project is insured by the ECGD (qv) with reference to the viability of the project and its cashflow rather than by reference to the general financial strength or creditworthiness of the buyer or borrower. The foreseen earnings provide the essential security for the lender and the insurer.

Project insurance A policy used with large construction projects. The principal effects a policy on the project as a whole to avoid the multiplicity of policies that occurs when each party arranges his own insurance. The policy applies to the more conventional material damage and liability policies (except employers' liability and motor risks which are governed by legislation), but does not usually include professional indemnity risks.

Projected accrued benefit method Required by the Pension Scheme Surpluses (Valuation) Regulations 1987 and relates only to the calculation of the actuarial liability (qv). The actuarial liability is based on service up to the valuation date and allows for projected earnings. Actuarial assumptions and methodology are prescribed in the regulations. Except in certain prescribed circumstances the longest period for eliminating any statutory surplus (qv) is five years.

Projected unit method Accrued benefits method used to calculate the actuarial liability for active members (qv) either as at the valuation date or as at the end of the control period (qv), taking account of all types of decrement. The method allows for projected earnings up to the date of assumed retirement, date of leaving or death, as appropriate.

Promissory A word at the foot of a proposal form. The proposer agrees that the proposal and declaration shall be 'held to be promissory and shall be the basis of the contract'. Although the proposal specifically makes the statements 'promissory', they do not necessarily constitute continuing warranties (qv), making the contract voidable if contravened at any time during the policy period. The term emphasises that the proposal answers amount to express conditions (i.e. warranties in insurance parlance) as distinct from mere representations so that the replies are taken as statements of fact and not of intention. The expression may reinforce the fact that the completed proposal form and declaration form the basis of the contract (qv).

Properly maintained Health and safety legislation requires floors, stairs etc., 'shall be of sound construction and be properly maintained.'

Property damage In an insurance policy it means physical damage to tangible property as opposed to financial loss, even if flowing from the damage, or bodily injury. It does not refer to 'property' in the sense of a right of ownership.

Property damage excess An excess (qv), usually £250, in a public liability policy applicable to claims involving loss or damage to material property.

Property in the insured's custody or control *See* CUSTODY AND CONTROL EXCLUSION.

Property legal protection cover Cover for legal costs and expenses incurred in pursuit or defence of civil actions against third parties resulting in physical damage or interference to the property and/or pecuniary loss. Cover is available for both individuals and businesses separately or as a part of a general legal expenses cover. A Buy-To-Let version of cover is available.

Property Owners' Combined Insurance Package policy incorporating 'standard cover', with optional add-ons, for commercial property investors. The policy takes account of the particular needs of such investors by way of special features, e.g. full cover on vacant premises, subject to security; automatic cover for newly acquired premises and alterations and improvements to existing premises; lock replacement. Employers' liability (qv) and property owners' liability form part of the standard cover with legionellosis liability (qv) as an optional cover.

Property owners' liability policy Covers the legal liability of the owner of property to third parties sustaining injury or property damage.

'Property worked on' exclusion Public liability (qv) exclusion of the insured's legal liability for damage to 'that part of any property being worked on where the loss or damage is the direct result of such work'. The intention is to exclude defective workmanship and the clause effectively operates as an excluded form of loss (qv) and not an excepted risk because any consequential damage will be covered.

Proportional reinsurance The cedant and the reinsurer share the risk in agreed proportions, either fixed (quota share treaty) or variable (surplus treaty) based on the ceding office's retention and the sum insured. The reinsurer shares proportionally the premiums earned and the claims plus certain expenses incurred by the ceding office. Proportional reinsurances may be arranged facultatively or by treaty and they may include: quota share reinsurances (qv); surplus treaties (qv); facultative/obligatory treaties (qv); reinsurance pools (qv).

Proportionate benefit *See* INCOME PROTECTION INSURANCE; REHABILITATION BENEFIT.

Proposal form A form completed by a party seeking insurance. It enables the insurer to assess the risk, prepare the policy, and set up the administration. *See* BASIS CLAUSE.

Proposer The prospective insured, i.e. the party proposing to effect an insurance, by the completion of a proposal form.

Proprietary companies Insurance companies constituted under the Companies Acts or by Royal Charter. The proprietors of a company are the shareholders who have supplied the capital. They look to the directors (qv) and officers (qv) to manage the company and safeguard its assets.

Prosecution clause Fidelity guarantee policies (qv), such as commercial guarantees, include a clause requiring the employer to assist the insurers in bringing a civil action in the name of the insured employer for recovery of the loss. The use of the term 'prosecution clause' has been criticised as it normally relates to criminal proceedings.

Prospective benefits valuation method Method under which the actuarial liability (qv) is the present value of: (a) the benefits for current and deferred pensioners and their dependants, allowing for any future increases; and (b) the benefits which active members will receive for both past and future service, allowing for projected earnings up to their expected leaving dates and, if appropriate, increases thereafter, less the present value of future contributions in respect of current members at the standard contribution rate (qv).

Prospective excess of loss cover Finite risk (qv) cover under which future losses are paid by the financial reinsurer and funded in a smoothing process in the ensuing years. *See* SPREAD LOSS TREATY.

Prospective reserve A life or health insurance reserve estimated to be sufficient to pay future claims. It is the amount designated as a future liability to meet the difference between the present value of projected future benefits and expenses as well as the present value of future premiums.

Prospective service Length of potential service of a member up to a future age or date. This is used in some instances in working out IR limits on early retirement and by some schemes for other purposes, e.g. calculating incapacity pensions or spouse's pensions.

Protected cell company A single entity that segregates its assets between different cells. Each cell is used by a company whose risks are not sufficiently large to justify forming their own captive (qv) but they get the benefits of self-insurance. The 'offshore' legislation, under which PCCs operate, was originally designed for rent-a-captives (qv) but is now applied more widely.

Protected no claim discount *See* NO CLAIM DISCOUNT.

Protected rights Pension under a money purchase arrangement arising from being contracted out scheme. The benefits are derived from the minimum equivalent payments (qv) that would otherwise have been paid to the state second pension (qv) but for the contracting out.

Protected rights annuity Pension purchased with the money from protected rights (qv).

Protected risk A risk which, as a result of the insurer's advice or insistence, is protected by loss prevention measures as in fire insurance (e.g. sprinkler leakage system installed) or theft insurance (e.g. intruder alarm installed).

Protection *See* LOSS PREVENTION and PROTECTION AND INDEMNITY CLUBS.

Protection and Indemnity Clubs Mutual associations protecting shipowners in respect of risks not covered in the marine insurance market. The shipowner enters his vessel on a tonnage basis that determines his levy or call (qv) at the beginning of the financial year. If claims are heavy a further levy may be demanded. The most important P & I classes are: 1. Protection. Covers shipowner in respect of liability for loss of life or personal injury, damage to immobile objects, one-quarter Running Down Clause (qv), oil pollution and life salvage. 2. Indemnity. The basis is 'pay to be paid' (qv) and means reimbursing shipowners who have indemnified cargo owners for damage caused by negligence of the crew. There are two other classes: war risks and freight war risks. P & I Clubs accommodate 90 per cent of the world's merchant tonnage. *See* BAIL CLAUSE.

Protection maintenance clause Commercial policy clause requiring that all or specific protections agreed at the commencement of the policy be maintained in full and efficient working order throughout the currency of the policy. If the clause is interpreted as a warranty (qv), the cover terminates from the date of breach and the insurer does not have to show a cause and effect relationship between a breach and a loss. In some instances the breach has been held to be a suspension of cover so that when compliance is resumed subsequent losses will be covered. *See* DESCRIPTION OF RISK CLAUSE.

Protest A marine insurance claims document in the form of a statement sworn by a ship's master before a notary giving details of the casualty. He 'protests' innocence of blame for loss or, or damage to, the ship or cargo. If fuller information is required, a further statement, an extended protest, is made.

Protracted default Credit insurance term describing a long overdue payment, e.g. failure by a debtor to pay the insured within 90 days of the due date. Protracted default is an insured event.

Provision 1. An amount retained as reasonably necessary to provide for asset depreciation, or any liability or loss which is likely to be incurred. 2. In a pensions context, the unfunded obligation to provide employees' pensions and shortfall of funding payments over the amount calculated by the actuary as being his estimate of the costs of providing pensions. Pensions costs in employers' accounts should be actuarially assessed and included in the employer's balance sheet under 'provisions for liabilities' as 'pensions and other similar obligations'. 3. Term in a policy, contract or statute.

Provision and Use of Work Equipment Regulations 1998 *See* PUWER 1998.

Provision for unearned premium *See* UNEARNED PREMIUM.

Provisional damages Where there is a chance that, in the future, an injured person will suffer serious deterioration in his condition, the court is empowered to issue a declaratory judgment, which, in the event of such deterioration, enables the plaintiff to apply for a review of the original award. Where the declaration is made, the damages awarded are provisional.

Provisional premium The premium charged under an adjustable policy (qv) at the inception.

Provisioning risk The risk that insurance company accounting provisions may be set at a lower level than is actually required. It misleadingly enhances the company's financial situation upon which inappropriate underwriting decisions could be made. The capital available may not be sufficient to support the type or level of business that is accepted.

Proviso clauses Any term or clause in an insurance policy that describes its benefits, cover stipulations, conditions, limits or exclusions.

Proximate cause The insurer is liable only for loss *proximately caused* by an insured peril not loss caused by an *excepted* or *uninsured peril*. It is the dominant cause not the *remote cause* (qv). The insurer will be liable if the sequence between an insured peril and the loss is unbroken (i.e one link in the chain is the natural and probable consequence of the previous link). If the initial cause in an unbroken chain is an excepted peril, the excepted peril is the proximate cause notwithstanding that it triggers an insured peril. As well as operating sequentially with other perils, the insured peril may run as a concurrent cause (qv) with other perils. *Pawsey* v. *Scottish Union and National* (1907) (qv) sets out a classic definition. *See* IMMEDIATE CAUSE; INTERVENING CAUSE; LAW STRAW CASES.

Prudent underwriter An underwriter who underwrites risks on a reasonable basis and who is neither unduly apprehensive nor duly incautious. The concept of the prudent underwriter is at the heart of the fundamental principle of utmost good faith (qv) as a fact will be judged to be material (see material fact) if it is one that would have influenced the judgement of a prudent and experienced underwriter in his assessment of the risk. The assertion that the particular underwriter would have been influenced by it does not make it a material fact and the fact that another would have ignored it does not prevent it from being material. The test is objective.

Prudential regulation Deals with the financial management and viability of a firm. It is aimed at ensuring that company failures do not endanger the stability of the financial markets or cause financial loss for the customers of that firm. The FSA sets the standards for the maintenance of capital resources proportionate to a firm's risks. The provisions will shortly be incorporated into a single Prudential Sourcebook .

Pseudonym An abbreviation or set of letters used at Lloyd's for the purpose of identifying syndicates or brokers.

Public access risks It is a situation where the public may come in large numbers to the premises, e.g. sports grounds, theatres, department stores, etc. *See* PREMISES RISK.

Public authorities clause Material damage clause covering the extra cost of reinstatement that arises solely in consequence of a public authority or European Community requirement. The cover applies to property damaged by an insured peril including undamaged portions of the affected building but not undamaged buildings. The sum insured should take account of the potential extra costs.

Public Liability Insurance (PL) Losses-occurring policy (qv), subject to a limit for any one occurrence, indemnifying the insured in respect of legal liability for third party injury and property damage arising from the business. Insured's own costs are covered. The policy has a number of extensions (e.g. motor contingent liability (qv), data protection) and excludes risks (e.g. employers' liability, covered under other policies) normally covered under other policies. *See* POLLUTION CLAUSE.

Public policy The law will not enforce an insurance which is against public policy, i.e. a policy with a mischievous tendency and therefore injurious to the state or the community. Insurance contracts without insurable interest are in effect wagering contracts and are therefore contrary to public policy and void.

Public sector pension scheme The occupational scheme for employees of central government; local government; nationalised industries; other state organisations. Scheme rules are defined by statute. The accrual rate is one-eightieth for each year of service with a maximum pension of 40/80ths.

Public sector transfer arrangements System used by a transfer club made up mainly of public sector pension schemes. A transfer club is where several schemes deal with transfer payments in the same way.

Public Utilities Clause Extends a business interruption insurance (qv) to provide an indemnity in respect of interruptions due to damage by an insured peril at the premises of a specified supply authority.

Punitive damages/exemplary damages *See* DAMAGES.

Purchased life annuity An annuity (qv) purchased under a contract approved by the IR or by an individual out of his own capital. They are taxed as investments – the capital content is tax-free and the interest content is treated as unearned income. Exempted from these provisions are all annuities secured under approved pension schemes of any nature, including retirement annuities under the current legislation (ICTA88). These are taxed as earned income on the total of each instalment.

Purchaser's interest clause Fire insurance clause to protect the interest of the purchaser of property if, at the time of loss, the insured property is the subject of an uncompleted contract of sale. The policy covers the interests of the purchaser and vendor up to the completion. The clause refers to buildings only and only to the extent that the property is not otherwise insured by the purchaser.

Pure captive A captive insurance company (qv) that confines its underwriting to the risks of its parent company.

Pure endowment Life policy that pays the sum insured if the life insured survives the policy term but nothing in the event of earlier death.

Pure protection contracts Contracts that are a sub-category of *long-term insurance contracts*, e.g. critical illness (qv) and income protection (qv), in respect of which: (a) the benefits are payable only on death or in respect of incapacity due to injury, sickness or infirmity; (b) the benefits are payable on death (other than accidental death) only where death occurs within 10 years of the date on which the person in question was first insured, or where death occurs before that person attains a specified age not exceeding 70 years; (c) the contract has no surrender value, or the consideration consists of a single premium and the surrender value does not exceed the premium; (d) the contract makes no provision for conversion or extension causing it not to comply with (a), (b) or (c); and (e) the contract is not one of reinsurance. These contracts are governed by the *Insurance: Conduct of Business rules* (qv). Long-term care is regulated as an investment product and therefore excluded from the definition.

Pure risk Uncertainty as to whether a loss will occur. With a pure risk there is no possibility of gain; the outcome is loss or no change. Such risks are static and inherent in the environment, e.g. fire, but can be minimised by risk management (qv). Compare with speculative risk (qv).

Pure year figures The figures relating to premiums, claims, etc., refer only to the particular year of account. Figures relating to business written in earlier years but transferred into that year are excluded.

Put option Gives the buyer/holder the right, but not the obligation, to sell to the issuer the underlying instrument or, in the case of a weather derivative, the cash value of a weather data index such as degree days (qv). Put options are also called floors or weather floors.

PUWER – Provision and Use of Work Equipment Regulations 1998 Provisions to enhance the safe provision and use of work equipment. The Regulations place general duties on employers and list minimum requirements for work equipment to deal with selected hazards in any industry. 'Work equipment' includes everything from a hand tool, through machines of all kinds, to a complete plant such as a refinery. Part IV has specific requirements for power presses (qv). *See* FENCING OF MACHINERY.

Qualified peril Peril that has to be interpreted against the backdrop of qualifying words. The insured must show that his loss was caused by the peril as qualified. The standard fire policy contains qualified perils – fire is covered only if not occasioned by or happening through, riot and civil commotion. An insured must therefore show that his fire damage was 'fire damage *not* caused by riot or civil commotion'. *See* ONUS OF PROOF.

Qualifying period *See* WAITING PERIOD.

Qualifying policy A life insurance policy certified by the Inland Revenue as complying with the 'Qualifying Policy Regulations'. Proceeds on maturity or death will be tax exempt.

Qualifying service Length of time an employee has to work for an employer before becoming eligible to join the employer's pension scheme. Also refers to the service to be taken into account to entitle a member to a 'short service benefit'.

Qualifying year A year when somebody has paid national insurance every week. If necessary an individual can clear any arrears by a single payment. No payment is required in respect of weeks credited to persons in receipt of social security benefits.

Quantum The monetary amount payable in damages or to an insured under an indemnity contract.

Quantum of interest Occurs when two parties have a simultaneous insurable interest in the same subject-matter. The buyer of cargo may insure the cargo, but the seller may also insure his contingent interest to guard against default by the buyer. Dual but not identical insurable interest also arises with mortgagors (full interest) and mortgagees (interest to the extent of the loan).

Quarter days Four days in the year once linked to the renewal of annual policies and other transactions. Fire and accident insurers extended the first period of annual insurances to the nearest quarter day. In England and Ireland – Ladyday (25 March); Midsummer (24 June); Michaelmas (29 September); Christmas (25 December). In Scotland: Candlemas (2 February); Whitsun (15 May); Lammas (1 August); Martinmas (11 November).

Queen's Counsel Clause A professional indemnity clause whereby the insurer agrees to pay any claim without requiring the insured to contest it unless a QC advises that it can probably be successfully defended.

Quota share reinsurance (QSR) Basic form of proportional reinsurance. Allocates risk, losses and loss adjustment expenses (qv) between the cedant (qv) and the reinsurer on a *fixed percentage basis* defined in terms of the policy limit and subject to an allowance for the cedant's expenses. QSRs boost the cedant's capacity and reduce the volatility of earnings.

Quotation slip A slip upon which a Lloyd's underwriter presents terms for consideration by the proposer without either party being committed to a transaction.

Radioactive contamination The contamination of any material, surface, environment or person by radioactive substances such as alpha particles or gamma rays. Radioisotopes used in industry (e.g. medicine, food, pasteurisation) are generally of low power with a short life. The risk is insurable if the UK's Atomic Energy Authority standards for the use of radioisotopes are strictly observed. Product and public liability policies exclude loss or damage from ionising radiations or contamination from any nuclear fuel or waste from the combustion of nuclear fuel. *See* NUCLEAR PERILS.

Rate *See* PREMIUM RATE; FLAT RATE.

Rate of gross profit The rate of gross profit earned on the turnover during the financial year immediately before the date of damage, i.e. the ratio of gross profit to turnover. A business interruption policy (qv) pays the amount produced by applying the rate of gross profit to the reduction in turnover (qv). Gross profit (qv) is calculated on the 'difference basis' (qv).

Rate on line A percentage arrived at by dividing reinsurance premium by the reinsurance limit, e.g. £5 million excess of loss cover with a premium of £1 million gives a rate on line of 20 per cent; the inverse, known as payback, is a period of five years. Rate on line is used to assess the adequacy of the contract rate.

Rateable contribution The basis upon which an insurer must contribute to a loss when contribution (qv) applies. *See* INDEPENDENT LIABILITY METHOD.

Rating groups (cars) ABI (qv) recommendations as to which of 20 groups each car model should be allocated as a factor in determining the premium. The allocation is based on car characteristics in terms of performance, design, safety, value and likely repair/replacement costs.

Ratings The evaluation of credit risk attaching to securities and institutions by established rating agencies such as Best's (qv), Standard and Poor's (qv), and Moody's Investor Services. *See* CREDIT ENHANCEMENT.

Ratio decidendi The principle on which the case is decided. It makes the decision a precedent for the future development of the law.

Ratios The following ratios are important for monitoring performance or calculating premiums: 1. Burning ratio. Insurance claims as a percentage of total premiums for current policies. 2. Claims (or loss) ratio. Incurred losses in relation to earned premiums. 3. Expense ratio. Insurers' total expenses in relation to written premiums. 4. Combined or composite ratio. Sum of (2) and (3), a figure below 100 per cent indicating that an underwriting profit has been achieved.

Raw materials Materials acquired for manufacturing purposes. The item on raw materials in a manufacturer's fire insurance is valued at market value immediately prior to the loss. Once worked upon but not yet incorporated in a finished product, the materials become part of 'work in progress' which takes account of labour costs and other direct expenses incurred.

Reasonable care/precautions condition Condition requiring an insured to take reasonable precautions to prevent accidents and safeguard property. The clause is not usually construed as a warranty (qv), enabling the insurer to repudiate the liability irrespective of a causal connection between the breach and the loss (*Lane* v. *Spratt* (1970)). A liability policy is triggered by the insured's negligence (qv) and so it would be repugnant to avoid liability because of the insured's lack of care except, depending on the facts, where lack of care amounts to recklessness.

Reasonable construction rule A rule of construction (qv) to the effect that where there is ambiguity the reasonable construction is to be preferred.

Reasonable Despatch Clause/Avoidance of Delay Clause Institute Cargo Clause making it a condition that the insured shall act with reasonable despatch in all circumstances under his control. Cover runs while the goods are in ordinary transit but if the insured chooses to interrupt the transit, the insurance terminates at the place of the interruption.

Reasonable man The objective test in negligence (qv) is based on the 'acts or omissions' of the reasonable man – the 'man on the Clapham omnibus who does 'not have to possess the wisdom of a Hebrew Prophet or the agility of an acrobat'. No person is an 'insurer' of his fellow men – there has to be fault, which, in negligence, means falling below the standard of the reasonable man.

Reasonableness *See* TEST OF REASONABLENESS.

'Reasonably practicable' Regulation 12(3) of the Workplace (Health, Safety and Welfare) Regulations 1992 (and other regulations): 'all floors, steps, stairs, passages, and gangways shall, *so far as is reasonably practicable*, be kept free from any obstruction and from any substance likely to cause a person to slip'. This is the lowest of the duties (compare with *properly maintained* (qv) and *all practicable steps* (qv)). The occupier can weigh the cost against the risk and the expected efficacy of the measures. Reasonable practicability is considered stricter than negligence and it is for the employer to prove that compliance was impracticable.

Rebate Only Personal Pension Personal pension built up solely of national insurance contribution rebates paid by DWP to the pension provider. It applies whenever a member has elected to contract out of the state second pension (qv) by means of a personal pension but makes no actual contributions.

Rebellion 'The taking up of arms traitorously against the government of the state. It is a graver form of insurrection (qv) for general purposes in which there is usurped power amounting to treason'. (F.H. Jones).

Rebuilding cost The cost of rebuilding premises following its destruction by an insured peril. The amount, taking into account professional fees and debris removal, should represent the sum insured under a buildings reinstatement insurance. The ABI's guide on buildings costs is drawn from the 'Guide to House Rebuilding Costs' published by the Building Cost Information Service of the Royal Institution of Chartered Surveyors.

Received for shipment bill The bill of lading issued prior to shipment stating the particulars of goods and their apparent condition. Under the Carriage of Goods by Sea Act 1971 (qv) such a bill may be demanded by a shipper from the shipowner.

Reciprocal duty A duty, such as the *duty of utmost good faith* (qv) that attaches to both contracting parties.

Reciprocal health agreements UK agreements with other countries entitling travellers in those countries to obtain free or reduced rate medical attention under local national health provisions. As a travel policyholder bears the first portion of a medical expenses claim, the UK traveller should produce form E111 (obtainable from the Department of Social Security) to receive a full indemnity in the event of receiving treatment.

Reciprocity Exchange of reinsurance business between reinsurers. Each accepts the cessions from the other to stabilise the accounts or reduce costs. Direct insurers may also enter into exchanging its home business with an equivalent amount of foreign business from another direct insurer. The reciprocity could be 100 per cent or a proportion of the business.

Recital Clause The opening clause of the policy reciting names of the parties and stating that the insured has applied for the contract of insurance. The clause is also called the 'Preamble'.

Recognised occupations *See* APPROVED OCCUPATIONS.

Recommended contribution rate Pension scheme actuary's recommendation as to the standard contribution rate (qv). Usually involves adjusting the current standard contribution rate to allow for differences between the actuarial liability (qv) and the actuarial value of assets taking into account the objectives of the funding plan.

Record of payments Record of amount and frequency of contributions made through the employer's payroll to a personal pension provider. It must show: deductions from pay; the employer's contribution; and the date by which contributions must be received by the provider. The due date for employee contributions must be no later than the 19th of the month following deduction. Providers not in receipt of contributions within 30 days of due must inform Opra (qv).

Recourse indemnity/ECGD recourse indemnity obligation insurance A policy that responds when an ECGD-backed buyer credit loan agreement coincides with a supplier default on the connected export contract. In the absence of insurance, the ECGD's right of recourse would cause the loss to fall on the exporter.

Recoveries Amounts the insurer can recoup after paying for a loss. It may be the result of: sale of salvage; exercise of subrogation rights (qv); or reinsurance recovery.

Rectification Process of rectifying a policy document that fails to represent the terms agreed between the parties. If an insured feels that a mistake has been made in the policy he may seek rectification and apply to the court if the insurer refuses. To succeed he will have to show that the policy does not represent the agreement and is not true evidence of the contract.

Recurrent single premium method *See* SINGLE PREMIUM METHOD.

Recurring clause Income protection (qv) clause defining the period that must elapse before a recurrence of a prior disablement claim will be regarded as a new claim, to be admitted for benefits only when any newly commenced deferred period (qv) has ended. If the recurrence is within the defined period, the renewed disablement is regarded as a continuation of the prior claim.

Red line clause Cargo policy clause printed in red to remind the insured of his obligation to preserve his right of recovery against a carrier or bailee for the benefit of the insurer.

Reducing extra risk A life insurance term referring to an extra risk which is at its greatest at the inception (qv) and then decreases, e.g. tuberculosis after treatment.

Reference scheme Theoretical pension scheme to which reference is made to ensure that members of contracted out salary related schemes post-April 1997 will receive as much in benefits as under the reference scheme to comply with PSA93, s.12B. The scheme actuary must certify that the scheme meets these benchmark requirements.

Reference scheme test *See* REFERENCE SCHEME.

Reference station Station whose statistics are used for the purpose of calculating average daily temperatures (qv) and other meteorological variables for the purpose of weather derivatives (qv). All such contracts are based on the actual observations of one or more stations.

Refrigerator insurance Engineering insurance covering breakdown and/or accidental damage to plant and the resultant damage to own surrounding property. A monetary excess applies. The policy is suitable for refrigerating machinery used with cold rooms or chambers for the storage of frozen or chilled goods or in connection with air conditioning units for the control of temperature in offices and other buildings.

Registrar of Occupational and Personal Pension Schemes Runs Pension Schemes Registry (qv) as a part of Opra (qv).

Regulated activity Any type of business falling within the scope of FSMA. The Act contains a general prohibition (qv) on the carrying out of such an activity in the UK unless it is authorised or *exempt* (qv). The wide-ranging activities include: accepting deposits; acting as a trustee in an authorised unit trust scheme; effecting or carrying out insurance contracts; dealing in investments as principal or agent; managing the underwriting capacity of a Lloyd's syndicate as a managing agent; arranging deals in contracts of insurance written at Lloyd's, etc.; agreeing to carry on a regulated activity which is carried on by way of business. Insurance mediation will be regulated from 2005. (Visit *www.fsa.gov.uk*).

Regulated classes of insurance The 18 classes of general business subject to regulatory control under the Financial Services and Markets Act 2000 (Regulated Activities) Order 2000. *See* GENERAL INSURANCE BUSINESS.

Regulated retail activity An FSA term describing one or more of the following activities: mortgage arranging or advising; the sale or administration of general insurance or pure protection contracts (qv); retail investment activities. All firms carrying on regulated retail activities have to comply with FSA reporting requirements.

Regulatory bulletin Form in which Lloyd's publishes codes to help underwriting agents meet the regulatory and other responsibilities flowing from the Core Principles for Underwriting Agents (qv). The bulletin is then included in the Codes Handbook (qv).

Regulatory business plan Written plan prepared by the managing agent for each Lloyd's syndicate and submitted to the Lloyd's franchise board (qv). The franchisor monitors approved plans against performance. The managing agents, as franchisees, must prepare an annual business plan in accordance with the long-term profitability target and the guidelines published by the franchisor. A *syndicate business forecast* (qv) must be attached to the business plan. Plans are also required by the FSA for insurance intermediaries.

Regulatory Decisions Committee (RDC) Takes most of the FSA's enforcement decisions following independent investigations and recommendations from the enforcement staff whose work is separated from the decision-taking function. The RDC seeks agreement from the party affected by issuing warning notices (qv) and decision notices (qv), but the recipient may take his case to the Financial Services and Markets Tribunal (qv).

Regulatory processes FSA regulation encompasses: authorisation (qv), supervision, enforcement (qv) and decision-making (qv).

Regulatory risk The risk that a regulated entity fails to meet the requirements and expectations of its regulatory authority responsible for enforcing rules, codes and practices. The FSA has considerable authority and could vary the permission granted to authorised persons and firms leaving them unable to carry on regulated activities.

Rehabilitation Restoring the physical and/or mental capabilities of an injured person through counselling, therapy or education. The aim is to return that person to a normal way of life or an early return to work, or rehabilitate them in a new earning capacity. Some liability insurers provide claimants with early access to rehabilitation services without prejudice to their position on liability.

Rehabilitation benefit/proportionate benefit Reduced benefit payable under an income protection insurance (qv) when an insured returns to work on reduced earnings as a result of a disability. The benefit starts only after 13 weeks of total incapacity and when a full claim has been admitted.

Rehabilitation of Offenders Act 1974 Means that 'spent' convictions need not be disclosed to insurers as material facts (qv). The rehabilitation period is five years for non-custodial sentences, seven years for custodial sentences exceeding 6 but not exceeding 30 months. Sentences over 30 months do not become 'spent'. An agent or previous insurer who is aware of a spent conviction must not disclose it.

Reinstatement 1. A *reinstatement condition* attached to a commercial property policy to provide that a claim may be based on full repair or replacement cost without deduction for depreciation subject to certain conditions. Many household policies contain a reinstatement clause allowing 'new for old' (qv) settlements subject to conditions and excluded forms of property. Where a 'new' item is superior to an 'old' item the insurer, commercial or household, may replace it provided the insured contributes to the 'betterment'. 2. Most property policies give the insurer the option to settle a claim by money, repair, reinstatement or replacement. Once the insurer opts for reinstatement it becomes an obligation to restore the property substantially to its pre-loss conditions even if its means exceeding the sum insured. 3. Following a claim, the sum insured or limit of indemnity is reduced by the amount concerned. A 'reinstatement of sum insured (or limit of indemnity) clause' automatically restores the sum insured after a loss. *See* REINSTATEMENT AVERAGE.

Reinstatement average Means average (qv) as applied to a policy subject to the reinstatement clause (qv). Average will not apply if the sum insured is equal to 85 per cent or more of the value at risk at the time of reinstatement. The sum insured should therefore allow for the period of insurance plus the time estimated for rebuilding. Losses settled on an indemnity basis remain subject to normal pro rata average.

Reinstatement by the insured An insured may be obliged to reinstate by statute or by contract under certain provisions in the Trustee Act 1925, s.20(4), (qv) or the Law of Property Act 1925 s.108(3).

Reinstatement clause/memorandum *See* REINSTATEMENT 1.

Reinstatement of data Computer insurance indemnifying the insured in respect of the cost of reinstating data contained in the data-carrying material following accidental erasure, accidental failure of the public electricity supply when exceeding 30 minutes, and the insured being denied access to the premises or use of the computer because of loss/damage to other property in the vicinity. Other losses can be added to the cover.

Reinstatement premium protection Reinsurance treaty provision enabling the reinsured to purchase, at inception, automatic restoration of full policy limit after a claim. It removes the uncertainty associated with negotiating the premium after a loss has occurred.

Reinstatement (reinsurance) A reinsurance clause restoring cover to the level existing prior to the occurrence of a loss.

The number of reinstatements to be allowed is usually negotiated when the treaty is placed. Reinstatements may be free or charged at a percentage of the treaty premium. Reinstatement applies mainly to *risk excess of loss treaties* (qv) covering property, marine and aviation business, and all forms of catastrophe excess of loss treaties.

Reinstatement under statute *See* FIRE PREVENTION (METROPOLIS) ACT 1774.

Reinsurance Process whereby a reinsurer (qv) agrees to indemnify an insurer, the cedant, against all or part of the loss that the latter may sustain under the original policy or policies it has issued. Reinsurance provides a secondary system of risk spreading reducing the potential losses that could attach to insurers. Reinsurers themselves may reinsure, a process known as *retrocession.* Under EU regulation, the use of reinsurance lowers the *required minimum margin* (qv). Reinsurance may be proportional (qv) or non-proportional (qv) and arranged either on a facultative (qv) basis or by treaty (qv).

Reinsurance clause Clause that distinguishes a reinsurance policy from an underlying marine insurance. The concluding words of the clause are 'to pay as may be paid thereon' meaning that the reinsurer is liable only for losses actually covered by his policy regardless of claims paid on the original policy. Many reinsurances are more restricted than the original policy and the clause must then be qualified by terms such as 'but against Total Loss only'.

Reinsurance commission An allowance expressed as a percentage of the reinsurance premium made by the reinsurer for all or part of the cedant's acquisition and other costs. The commission may include a profit factor for the cedant. *See* OVERRIDING COMMISSION; PROFIT COMMISSION; MARINE REINSURANCE COMMISSION.

Reinsurance pools An organisation of reinsurers through which particular types of risk (e.g. certain categories of sub-standard lives seeking life cover) are underwritten with premium losses and expenses shared in agreed proportions. Pooling creates the advantage of averaging over a large number of similar risks.

Reinsurance to close An agreement under which Lloyd's underwriting members who are members of a syndicate for a *year of account* (qv) to be closed are reinsured by underwriting members who comprise that or another syndicate for a later year of account against all liabilities arising out of insurance business underwritten by the reinsured syndicate. The practice will end when Lloyd's moves to GAAP accounting (qv).

Reinsured/reassured The party that is reinsured, i.e. the ceding office or cedant.

Reinsurer A reinsurance company that only writes business with insurance companies, or a primary insurance company that also writes reinsurance contracts for other insurers; the expressions *reinsurance inwards* and *reinsurance outwards* refer to the acceptance and placing of reinsurance respectively.

Reinsuring clause The clause in a reinsurance contract that sets out the terms under which a claim can be made. It is the reinsurance equivalent of the operative clause (qv).

Rejection insurance Covers loss due to goods being rejected or condemned by the governmental authorities of the importing state. Insurance is arranged by exporters of consumer goods, including food, that may be perceived to have a health risk. Cover is conditional upon high standards of quality control in the country of origin.

Relevant benefits Financial benefits provided on death or retirement, other than permanent health benefits or sums payable on accidental death in service, that are relevant to an occupational pension scheme for the purpose of 'exempt approved' status. IR 12 (Practice Notes) sets out the detail.

Relevant earnings *See* NET RELEVANT EARNINGS.

Remediation Cleaning-up and restoring land that has become contaminated. Costs can be recovered under first party insurances and liability to third parties may be covered under environmental impairment liability (qv). Local authorities can compel owners/occupiers to remediate contaminated land (qv).

Remote cause A non-dominant cause linked to a chain of events that culminates in a loss. The remote cause facilitates the loss rather than causes it. In *Marsden* v. *City & County Assurance Co.* (1865) a fire broke out and a mob assembled and broke plate glass windows in neighbouring premises with a view to looting. The action of the mob, not the fire, was the proximate cause (qv).

Remoteness of damage Describes the lack of a sufficiently direct connection between the wrong complained of and the injury alleged to have been sustained. 'Negligent' defendants are not liable for damage that is too remote.

Removal of debris clause Property insurance clause extending cover to include costs of clearing away debris, dismantling, shoring and propping up following insured damage. Sums insured are normally increased by 5–7.5 per cent to allow for these expenses.

Removal or weakening of support accorded to land or buildings A construction industry and civil engineering risk which will generally constitute a nuisance (*Bower* v. *Peate* (1876)) making the creator or person who authorised the nuisance liable for the damage without proof of negligence. *See* JCT 21.2.1 NON-NEGLIGENT COVER; COLLAPSE INSURANCE.

Remuneration Total payments from the employer for the year assessable as income under Schedule E but excluding anything arising from the acquisition/disposal of shares or interest in shares. In regard to Class A members (qv) any pay in excess of the *earnings cap* (qv) will be disregarded in assessing allowable contributions to approved pension schemes.

Renewable term insurance Term insurance (qv) that carries an option to renew for a further specified period of years without evidence of good health.

Renewal The continuance of a policy beyond its initial period. Most policies, permanent contracts (qv) excepted, are renewable by mutual consent and allow 15 days' grace period (qv) except in marine insurance. *See* RENEWAL NOTICE.

Renewal notice Document issued by an insurer to invite renewal (qv). In the case of Lloyd's (qv) the renewal notice comes from the broker. A motor insurance renewal incorporates a temporary motor insurance certificate to ensure there is no gap in Road Traffic Act cover.

Rent-a-captive Specialised form of captive (qv) for businesses seeking the benefits of internal funding without incurring the costs of forming their own captive. A rent-a-captive is formed by a group of investors and operated as a business. Insureds wishing to participate 'rent' space, i.e. get their own account, in the captive.

Repetitive strain injury *See* WORK-RELATED UPPER LIMB DISORDERS.

Replacement An option when an insurer settles a claim under a contract of indemnity. The goods supplied must be equivalent to the lost goods in nature and quality. If in a superior condition betterment (qv) applies. Insurers may gain by getting discounts on replacement goods. Replacing goods rather than paying cash discourages fraud. 'New for old' policies (qv) modify the principle of indemnity.

Replacement clause Marine cargo clause providing that in the event of loss/damage to any part of a machine carried as cargo, the sum recoverable will not exceed the cost of replacing and fitting including forwarding charges. This avoids a possible total claim on a machine simply because a particular replacement part is not obtainable.

Reporting excess of loss Specific 'working' excess of loss cover. The reinsured must 'report' each and every risk in the account (usually cargo) that exceeds the excess point in the contract. The reinsured pays a premium on the amount of the exposure above the excess point at an agreed rate or percentage of the reinsured original rate.

Reporting of Injuries, Diseases and Dangerous Occurrences Regulations 1995 Regulations requiring employers and the self-employed to report specified occupational injuries and diseases to the HSE. These include fatal accidents, accidents causing major injuries or more than three days' absence from work, work-related diseases and dangerous occurrences.

Representation Statement made by the insured to the insurer before the contract is concluded. If relating to a material fact (qv) it must be true. If relating to a matter of expectation or belief it is true if made in good faith. Representations are often converted into warranties by a basis clause (qv) at the foot of the proposal form.

Reputation risk The risk that relates to the organisation's reputation and public perception of the organisation's integrity, efficiency and effectiveness. The principal response is reputation risk management (qv) but indirectly most forms of property and business interruption (qv) are important in helping a firm to sustain its presence and therefore reputation. *See* TRADE NAME RESTORATION.

Reputation risk management This is part of the culture and processes that are directed towards the effective management of potential opportunities and threats to the organisation achieving its objectives through maintaining and enhancing its reputation. The processes will involve preparing business continuity, crisis management and disaster recovery plans, and a sound communication plan designed to work with the media and other stakeholders. Case histories show that companies who demonstrate an ability to overcome a crisis actually enhance their reputation and share value.

Request note A document whereby an insurer presents a reinsurer with particulars of a risk proposed for facultative reinsurance (qv). The reinsurer may respond with a *take note* (qv) stating the amount of reinsurance undertaken.

Required minimum margin (RMM) The minimum margin of solvency (qv) required at all times of regulated general and long-term insurers. Firms in breach must provide a plan to restore their financial position. The FSA (qv) definition of RMM is effectively a weighted average of provisions (life insurance) or premiums/claims in non-life business, but the FSA, taking its 'realistic approach', looks at the way RMM, often conservative, has been calculated. *See* SOLVENCY MARGIN.

Res ipsa loquitur 'The thing speaks for itself.' The maxim applies whenever it is improbable that an accident would have occurred without negligence on the part of the defendant. The court infers negligence and the defendant has to disprove it.

Reserve premium/retained premium The proportion of the reinsurance premium payable that has been retained by the cedant to assist in financing the reinsurer's share of the cost of settling claims.

Reserve value Name given to the technical life insurance reserve that arises from the level annual premium system (qv).

Reserves *See* FREE ASSETS; TECHNICAL RESERVES.

Reserving Process of estimating or calculating amounts to be allocated to cover outstanding claims and unexpired risks. Insurers use an actuarial approach or a computerised program for the purpose. The reserved amount is adjusted whenever new information on a claim is received.

Reset mechanisms Applies to some ART (qv) products enabling them to be varied following the occurrence of loss(es). It also refers to risk modelling techniques whereby the premium payable under a multi-year contract is automatically adjusted by reference to the claims record and changes in the prevailing market and economic conditions.

Residual value insurance A financial guarantee insurance (qv) that protects a lessor against unexpected declines in the market value of leased equipment (vehicles, aircraft, heavy machinery) upon termination or expiration of the lease agreement. The insurance helps the lessor manage the *asset value risk* inherent in leasing.

Resilience test Regulatory test imposed on UK life insurers to ensure that they can withstand a specific fall in equity market values without breaching their required *margin of solvency* (qv). The result is embedded in the calculation of technical provisions instead of being presented as solvency capital. The appointed actuary (qv) is expected to apply his own judgement in considering matters relevant to the test.

Respondentia Ancient form of loan, similar to bottomry (qv), but secured on the cargo only and repayable only if the cargo is saved.

Restricted employer-related investment PA95, s.40, restricts investment by the pension fund in this type of investment to 5 per cent of the scheme assets. SSAS (qv) is an exception.

Restrictive covenant Condition in a property-related deed that limits the use or development of land/buildings by subsequent purchasers. The encumberance affects the marketability of the title and creates a risk, insurable under a restrictive covenant indemnity (qv), for anyone who infringes it.

Restrictive covenant indemnity Indemnifies the insured in the event of any third party attempting to enforce a restrictive covenant (qv). The breach may be either an existing breach or a forthcoming development of the property of which the insurers were aware at inception. Mortgagee's interests and successors in title are automatically covered. The single premium policy runs in perpetuity and includes the insured's costs in defending a claim.

Restrictive endorsements Liability term excluding liability arising out of particular work circumstances, e.g. builder's policy may exclude work more than 40 feet in height or working on high structures like blast furnaces. There is nothing in compulsory employers' liability legislation to prohibit such restrictions (*Dunbar* v. *A & B Painters* (1985)), but they are not favoured and more likely to be applied to public liability cover.

Retail customer A policyholder or potential policyholder acting outside his trade, business or profession. FSA rules require that retail customers be supplied with: a policy summary; price information; details on how to claim; policy document; renewal information; details of mid-term changes. All private individuals are *eligible complainants* (qv) from a complaints perspective.

Retail Price Index (RPI) UK index of consumer prices widely used for *indexation* (qv). There are several variants from the headline rate such as RPIX, i.e. prices excluding mortgages.

Retained benefits Member's benefits from previous occupational schemes, personal pension schemes (qv) or retirement annuity policies (qv). Where the existing scheme has an accrual rate (qv) better than one-sixtieth per year, retained benefits, when taken with existing benefits, must not exceed two-thirds of final remuneration (qv), i.e. the maximum under a tax approved scheme.

Retention The amount retained by an insurer and not ceded to a reinsurer. In surplus treaty reinsurance the retention is referred to as a *line* and the capacity of the treaty is expressed as multiple of the line. In risk management the term retention, or *risk retention* (qv) refers to self-insured amounts.

Retention bond Given by an insurer on behalf of a contractor in exchange for the release of retention monies from the employer or main contractor. The bond is equal to the monies released and is circa 2.5 per cent of the construction contract value. *See* PERFORMANCE BONDS.

Retirement annuity policies/contracts (RAPs) Replaced by personal pension plans in 1988 but pre-88 plans still run. They restrict the holder to retirement at age 60 or after. Retirement at 50 is possible only if transferring to a personal pension but the tax-free cash entitlement is calculated differently. RAPs, also called *Section 226 annuities,* are not subject to the earnings cap (qv).

Retirement options They may include: purchase of an annuity; commutation of part of pension for tax-free lump with reduced retirement annuity; phased retirement (qv); income drawdown (qv); self-investment up to age 75; leave the fund fully invested until age 75.

Retroactive date Date that defines the extent of cover in time under claims made liability policies (qv). Claims resulting from occurrences *prior* to the retroactive date are not covered notwithstanding the notification of claims during the policy period. Retroactive dates are commonly stated to be the inception date of the first year of cover. *See* 'NOSE'.

Retroactive insurance Cover for a loss that has already occurred, e.g. a major fire, but for which the severity of the loss is uncertain. The insured pays a high premium to substitute certainty for the uncertain outcome. The insurer is attracted by the investment potential of a high premium pending settlement of the claims.

Retrocedant/retrocedent *See* RETROCESSION.

Retrocession/retrocessionaire The transaction when a reinsurer (the retrocedant) reinsures parts of his risks (the retrocession) with another reinsurer (the retrocessionaire).

Retrospective cover Liability policy extension bringing within a losses-occurring policy (qv) on a claims-made basis (qv) bodily injury or damage caused prior to the inception of the policy but for which no previous policy can be traced. 'Retro' cover closes gaps in the insured's insurance history but does not respond to shortfalls in cover in traced insurances. 'Retro' cover should embrace the insured's previous activities as the current business description may not apply.

Retrospective excess of loss Finite risk cover (qv) for IBNR (qv) losses under which the reinsured pays a premium for the (partial) assumption of losses that exceed the accumulated reserves. Contracts may be structured as: stop loss treaties (qv), working excess of loss treaties (qv) or catastrophe excess of loss basis (qv).

Retrospective rating A system when the rate to be charged for the (re)insurance is determined at the expiry of the policy taking account of the experience during the policy period subject to a maximum and minimum premium.

Return premium Refund to the insured by law (e.g. liquidation of insurer) or by contract. If the risk does not attach the insurer runs no risk and must return the premium. Once the risk has attached the insured is not entitled to any return except under a contractual provision, e.g. adjustable premium, cancellation or laying up of vessels or vehicles.

Revaluation *See* PENSIONS REVALUATION.

Revalued earnings scheme Scheme benefits are based on revalued earnings, i.e. index-linked earnings for a given period.

The state second pension (qv) is a revalued earnings scheme.

Revenue limits IR imposed maxima on benefits and contributions when calculating maximum benefits in approved occupational schemes (qv). Limits vary according to Class A, B and C membership (qv).

Revenue undertaking Written undertaking by scheme administrator promising to notify IR in the event of certain circumstances or before taking specified actions, e.g. undertaking that benefits will not exceed IR maximum approvable limits.

Reverse liability Legal expenses insurance item. If the insured is awarded damages for personal injury or damage to property and payment is not made within a given time (e.g. three months) then the insurer will pay in full up to £1 million. The employers' liability section – unsatisfied court judgements (qv) – pays the amount of the award if the insured would have been entitled to an indemnity had the award been made against him in respect of an injured employee. *See* UNRECOVERED DAMAGES.

Reversionary annuity Annuity payable to one person (e.g. surviving spouse) upon the death of another (other spouse). If the former dies first, the premiums are forfeited.

Reversionary bonus A sum added periodically during the currency of a with profits life insurance which becomes payable at the same time and in the same circumstances as the sum insured.

Revival clause Allows the holder of a lapsed life policy to apply for a revival notwithstanding that the grace period (qv) and the non-forfeiture period (qv) have both expired. The period allowed is one or two years from the days of grace. The policyholder must pay a revival fee, the overdue premiums plus interest and submit evidence of health as required by the office.

Riding Establishments Act 1970 Any person holding a licence to run a riding establishment must have public liability insurance. The insurance indemnifies the licensee against legal liability for any injury sustained by any person who hires a horse or who is being instructed. The insurance must also cover the liability of the insured and hirer for third party bodily injury.

RINET (Reinsurance and Insurance Network) Brussels-based electronic network created by a consortium of mainly European reinsurers and insurers. RINET was a part of the merger that formed WISe (qv) in 1999.

Riot Needs five elements: (a) it must involve at least 12 persons (three at common law, 12 by the Public Order Act 1986 making it a criminal act); (b) all must have a common purpose; (c) there must have been an inception or execution of that common purpose; (d) they must intend to help one another by force if necessary against any person who may oppose them in the execution of their common purpose; (e) force or violence must be used in such a manner as to alarm at least one person of reasonable firmness and courage. This definition originated in *Field* v. *Receiver of the Metropolitan Police* (1907). Riot is often insured as an additional peril (linked with malicious persons) under property insurances.

Riot, civil commotion Riot (qv) has an exact legal meaning. Riot and civil commotion (qv) are mentioned in the operative clause (qv) of the standard fire policy as excluded perils. Cover can be obtained as an additional peril, sometimes linked with damage caused by labour or political disturbances or vandals or malicious persons.

Riot, civil commotion, strikes, locked-out workers, labour disturbances and malicious persons Group of perils added to a fire policy. Damage caused in these ways embraces fire damage and other forms of damage, e.g. wrecking and looting, but not losses caused by war and allied perils. The insured must give notice of claim within seven days to assist the subrogation rights of insurers in their claim against the police authority under the *Riot (Damages) Act 1886* (qv) that allows 14 days for the particulars of the occurrence to be notified. The normal riot wording restricts damage caused maliciously to damage caused by malicious persons acting in connection with any political organisation. *See* MALICIOUS DAMAGE; TERRORISM.

Riot (Damages) Act 1886 Any person suffering riot damage can claim compensation from the police authority but only to the extent that the compensation exceeds an insurance claim. Insurers who have paid a claim can exercise subrogation (qv) rights against the police in their own name.

Risk 1. The possibility or chance of harm, injury or damage. It is influenced by *hazards* (qv) present in a situation. Some definitions distinguish *pure risks* (the outcome is 'loss or no change') from *speculative risks* (qv) which range from 'loss to gain'. A distinction is also made between *insurable* (qv) and *uninsurable risks.* 2. A risk may also be the subject-matter (qv) insured or the peril insured against. 3. An insurance company's risk is uncertainty regarding the cost of a particular claim and depends on the *underwriting risk* (qv) and the *timing risk* (qv) or both. *See* RISK ANALYSIS.

Risk analysis Systematic use of information to determine the probability of an occurrence and the severity of its consequences. This leads to informed decisions as to how particular risks should be managed. Risk mapping (qv) facilitates the process.

Risk assessment 1. Collective reference to: risk identification (qv), risk analysis (qv) and risk evaluation (qv), i.e. an overall process in risk management (qv). 2. Legal requirement under health and safety regulations. *See* MANAGEMENT OF HEALTH AND SAFETY AT WORK REGULATIONS 1999; COSHH.

Risk assumption An informed decision to accept the likelihood and consequences of a particular risk. This is planned risk assumption. A supermarket chain may choose to carry the risk of loss or damage to plate glass windows given that it has a spread of risk and the maximum possible loss is small relative to their resources. Deductibles (qv) and self-insurance (qv) are forms of risk assumption.

Risk aversion/risk averter An attitude of an individual or organisation with a preference for avoiding risk whenever possible. A *risk averter* prefers a definite premium, even though it may exceed the loss expectancy, to unknown losses. If the loss expectancy's monetary amount is £50, a risk averter will pay, say, £75 when the loss possibility range is £0–£5,000.

Risk avoidance An informed decision not to become involved with, or continue with, a risk situation. The potential loss is regarded as greater than the potential value of the risk-creating activity, e.g. using PCBs (qv) in manufacturing processes, building on flood plains.

Risk-based capital (RBC) A measure of the capital required to absorb any unexpected losses that result from the risks an organisation assumes in regard to its business and operational activities. In insurance RBC management means an insurer calculates the capital needed to support different classes of business. Overall RBC is expressed as a ratio, the total capital of the company divided by the company's RBC as determined by formulae. The FSA has proposed that insurers will be required to hold the higher amount of minimum capital requirement as set out in the EC Directives and *enhanced capital requirement* (qv), a more risk sensitive calculation specified by the FSA.

Risk benefits Pensions term describing benefits that are not pre-funded and that are often insured on an annual basis, which usually means death or disability benefits.

Risk bundling Risk financing (qv) approach that allows a company to benefit from its own diversification across the different classes of risk, and over time through the use of captives (qv) or multi-line, multi-year programmes.

Risk classification Underwriters combine individual risks into groups or 'classes'. This facilitates the underwriting process and enables individual proposals to be considered in the light of the class to which they belong. Some classes, e.g. total abstainers, mature applicants, may receive preferential treatment while others may belong to an excluded class, e.g. a motor insurer might exclude jockeys or others with a high exposure.

Risk combination Homogeneous groups of risks among whom the losses of the few can be distributed. There is no substantial advantage in two people combining to share each other's losses, reciprocity (qv) excepted. It is only by large homogeneous groups combining through insurance that makes it possible to apply the law of large numbers (qv). Risk combination is at the heart of insurance. 'The loss lighteth rather easily upon many than heavily upon few' (Elizabethan Act 1601).

Risk control Implementation of risk treatment decisions. Individuals will be made responsible to see that the control measures are implemented and maintained in accordance with agreed timescales. Monitoring risk and their control measures is a vital part of an iterative process.

Risk distribution/diversification Risk reduction techniques that spread risks geographically or by line of business to avoid the problems of risk accumulation or overdependence on a particular class of business. The object is to increase the number of mutually independent risks.

Risk elimination Means risk avoidance (qv).

Risk evaluation/measurement A process to establish risk management priorities by comparing the level of controllability or other criteria. Risk mapping (qv) is a useful tool for prioritising risks by placing them on a risk profile and revealing which threats require management time and resources.

Risk excess An excess of loss reinsurance contract that is limited to property risks. The reinsured is protected within his overall exposure on an individual risk basis, i.e. the limit and the deductible apply to 'each and every loss on each and every risk'.

Risk financing Risk management techniques to provide funding for losses after they have occurred. Some risks are retained and paid out of normal cash flow, reserves or a formal self-insurance scheme, the ultimate of which is a captive insurer (qv). Insurance is a common external source of finance while non-insurance risk transfer through *hold harmless agreements* (qv) and financial instruments such as *weather derivatives* (qv) also entails external financing. There are numerous *alternative risk transfer products* (qv) that offer a range of solutions, particularly for firms active in the financial and capital markets.

Risk identification The initial risk management (qv) step to identify the firm's exposure to risk. It entails: reviewing all relevant data on business assets, activities and personnel; and checking financial statements, including the balance sheet and the loss of profit and loss accounts, to identify potential sources of loss. Other techniques include interviewing, in-house workshops, observation and preparing flow charts to show all operations of the organisation and all loss-possibility situations in the purchase-process-distribution sequence. Risk identification makes it possible to prepare a *risk inventory* (qv).

Risk inventory/register A record of all risks identified during the risk management process. Each risk is described, classified by type and assessed in terms of its potential in terms of severity and probability. The proposed control or responses measures are noted together with details of the 'risk owner', i.e. the manager or employee responsible for implementing the control measures and monitoring the risk. The 'owner' is given a target date for implementation or other designated action.

Risk management The purpose of risk management is to limit the organisation's exposure to risk to an acceptable level taking account of probability of the loss occurring, its impact or both. The principles can be directed at limiting adverse outcomes or achieving desirable ones. Procedures involving risk identification (qv); analysis and measurement of risk (risk assessment); selection of control measures and measures of financing risk (risk treatment (qv)); implementation of control; monitoring and updating control measures. Risk control and risk financing (qv) are at the heart of an iterative process aimed at reducing the likelihood and severity of loss.

Risk management and systems and control From 2004 (Integrated Prudential Sourcebook) firms must have written policies setting out the risks that they face and their strategy for managing and controlling those risks. As a minimum they will need clear policies to cover credit, market, liquidity, operational and group risk and, for insurers, specific risks relating to underwriting, claims provision and claims management. The policies must be endorsed and monitored by the firm's managing body, e.g. the board.

Risk Management Standard Launched in 2002 by the Institute of Risk Management (qv), the Association of Insurance and Risk Managers (qv) and ALARM (qv), it provides a formalised risk management framework to meet the requirements of working risk managers. The standard is accessible free of charge on the organisations' respective websites.

Risk manager Person appointed to carry out risk management (qv) on behalf of an industrial or other organisation. Risk managers may join the Association of Risk Managers in Industry and Commerce (AIRMIC)(qv) or the Institute of Risk Management or ALARM (qv) if in the public sector.

Risk Mapping/risk profiling A graphical depiction of a select number of risks analysing them in terms of probability and severity. The horizontal axis illustrates the probability of loss, high or low, while the vertical axis plots severity, high impact or low impact, two categories in each case (as in the diagram below) to give four categories. Some models use four impact categories and six probability categories. Obviously high probability/high impact losses cannot be tolerated while low probability/low impact losses can be paid out of cashflow. All risks plotted should be reviewed, controlled and financed.

Risk measurement *See* RISK EVALUATION.

Risk neutralisation Risk financing (qv) method which combines some of the features of risk retention and risk transfer. It involves an arrangement to offset one risk by taking a counterbalancing position on another risk. This happens with *futures* (qv), *weather derivatives* (qv) and *weather swaps* (qv), which have elements of risk transfer and risk retention.

Risk ownership Part of the risk management process that allocates responsibility at a senior level for managing key risks. The allocation of risk is supported by a mechanism for reporting issues ultimately to the senior person who has overall responsibility for risk management.

Risk premium The pure premium needed to cover the expected risks but with no allowance for expenses, commission and

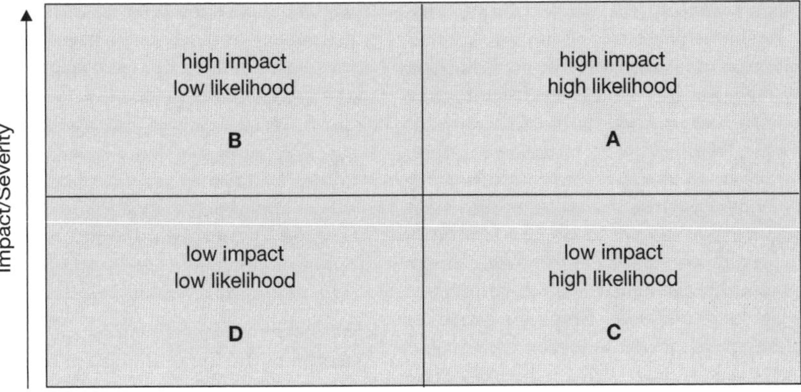

Figure 7. Risk mapping – How to prioritise risks

contingencies. It is the amount of premium required to cover the risk, taking account of the average claim amount and average claim frequency.

Risk premium method reinsurance Also called *yearly premium method* it is a form of life reinsurance under which the risks, but not the reserves, are transferred to the reinsurer for a premium that varies each year with the amount at risk and the ages of the life insureds. The cedant retains all investment content.

Risk profile Analysis of (re)insurer's business that tabulates risks into bands of similar values, showing the number of risks in each category, average values, aggregate values and aggregate premiums, etc.

Risk purchasing group (RPG) Alternative risk transfer term that refers to collective insurance buying.

Risk reduction Measures introduced into an insured organisation to mitigate the effects of risks that cannot realistically be avoided altogether. Measures vary according to the situation but the installation of burglar alarms, sprinkler leakage systems and implementation of quality control procedures are all examples.

Risk register *See* RISK INVENTORY.

Risk retention The term used to describe the self-insurance assumed by an entity by means of *deductibles* (qv) on conventional insurances or by choosing not to insure at all.

Risk retention groups Member-owned liability insurance companies. Set up in the US in the face of a 'hard market' (qv), a number of trade associations or groups of companies combined to form risk retention groups as allowed under the Liability Risk Retention Act 1986. The groups operate as insurance companies limited to writing liability covers for groups with a common interest. RRGs require members to capitalise the company. Many of the groups focus on pollution liability or product liability.

Risk retention techniques Risk assumption (qv) techniques.

Risk tolerance The amount of risk that an investor, individual or business is willing to assume to achieve a specific goal. Risk tolerance is a function of financial capacity, willingness to take risks and the overall profile of the business or individual. The risk profile can be plotted on a risk map, i.e. a probability/impact matrix. Financial services professionals need to understand the risk tolerance levels of their clients. *See* Figure 7.

Risk transfer One party transfers the financial effects of his loss to another party. In insurance the insured transfers the possibility of loss to the insurer in return for the premium. Other forms of risk transfer can be found in contracts and leases that are used to transfer risk from one party to another to the extent permitted by law (*see* UNFAIR CONTRACT TERMS ACT 1977). Risk transfer of a different kind occurs where an activity is transferred from one party to another, e.g. the sub-contracting of a hazardous process to another party, but this could also be termed an example risk avoidance (qv).

Risk treatment Decision stage of risk management when the firm decides how to respond to risk. The options include risk transfer (insurance and non-insurance), risk financing (qv); reduction, avoidance, prevention, control, etc. This is followed by implementation.

Risks attaching Excess of loss reinsurance covering losses on policies issued or renewed during the treaty period until they expire. The attachment point is the key.

Road Haulage Association Conditions of Carriage 1998 Conditions whereby hauliers accept liability for loss, misdelivery or damage for goods unless an exception (e.g. inherent vice, Act of God) applies. Liability is limited to £1,300 per tonne not exceeding the value of the consignment. Physical loss, misdelivery or non-delivery must be notified within 7 days and a claim made within 14 days of termination of the transit. Other losses need to be notified and claimed within 28 and 42 days respectively. All liability ends if the goods owner does not commence legal proceedings within one year from commencement of the transit. Liability for consequential loss (qv) is capped at the amount of the carriage charges. There is no liability for livestock, bullion, money, precious metals, etc., unless specially agreed. *See* HAULIERS' LIABILITY.

Road Rescue cover Offered by some private car insurers as part of the car insurance. Covers the cost of call-out and roadside repairs (subject to exceptions), vehicle recovery to a garage, hire car to continue a journey or return home, rail fare to cover cost of collecting the car after repair, transportation of the car and occupants to destination or home or overnight hotel accommodation up to specified limits.

Road Risks insurance Motor trade policy permitting driving of own and customers vehicles on a road or temporarily garaged during a journey. Use of vehicles is restricted to motor trade use and social, domestic and pleasure. There are wide ranging options for driving by the insured, the insured's spouse, employees and friends and named additional drivers. Further extensions include loan and hire, unaccompanied demonstration, private hire or windscreen cover. Cover can be comprehensive, third party fire and theft or third party. Risks on the insured's premises are covered under internal risks policies (qv). *See* POINTS BASIS; NAMED DRIVER BASIS; TRADE PLATE BASIS.

Road Traffic Act 1988, Part VI (Compulsory Insurance Requirements) It is unlawful to use, or permit use of, a motor vehicle on a *road* without a third party policy or security (qv) (s.143). Minimum cover is liability for death or injury and for property damage up to £250,000 under a policy issued by an authorised insurer belonging to the Motor Insurers' Bureau (qv) and meeting EC requirements. The policy must also cover *emergency treatment* (qv). The insurer's right to avoid an 'Act' claim is restricted (s.148). *See* ACT ONLY POLICY; CAR SHARING; MOTOR INSURANCE CERTIFICATES.

Robbery Stealing by force or threat of force (Theft Act 1968, s.8).

Rogue trading Covers financial institutions for direct financial losses caused by traders acting outside their authority. Unauthorised trading means trading which at the time of trade is: (a) in excess of permitted financial limits; or (b) outside of permitted product lines; or (c) not with a designated counterparty. The policy does not cover simple errors or losses caused by traders acting on behalf of third parties and that part of any loss that is deemed to have been authorised. Cover is usually arranged in conjunction with a *bankers' blanket bond* (qv).

Room, The The underwriting room at Lloyd's.

Rovers Same as pirates.

Royal Society for the Prevention of Accidents (Ro.SPA) Ro.SPA's accident prevention work is supported by the ABI and individual insurance companies in financial, technical and information terms.

RPI escalation Rate of annual increase in respect of annuity and pensions payments to help them maintain purchasing power. The annuity payments increase in line with increases in the retail price index, a cost of living index, subject, usually, to a cap of 5 per cent per annum. This contrasts with a level annuity that remains unchanged no matter how long it runs.

Rules for Construction of Policy Twelve rules set out in the Schedule to the Marine Insurance Act 1906 for the purpose of interpreting the marine insurance policy. The rules relate to such phrases as 'lost or not lost' (qv); at and from; from; from the loading thereof; safely landed; touch and stay; perils of the sea; pirates; thieves; restraint of princes; barratry; all other perils; average unless general; stranded; ship; freight; and goods.

Run-off account A year of account of a Lloyd's syndicate which has been left open after the date at which that account would normally have been closed by reinsurance. *See* OPEN YEAR.

Run-off cancellation A reinsurance provision under which the reinsurer, despite cancellation of the treaty, remains liable under policies still current at the date of cancellation.

Run-off liability The potential liability of a losses-occurring liability insurer (qv) in respect of occurrences that occurred while they were on risk being reported as claims after the expiry of their policy. Contrast with claims-made policy (qv) where the run-off risk attaches to the insured who may be faced with a claim after the policy has terminated. *See* LONG-TAIL.

Run-off licences Granted by Lloyd's to certain run-off companies and managing agents to conduct the run-offs of Lloyd's syndicates. These run-offs arise from *open years* (qv) not closed by *reinsurance to close* (qv).

Running Down Clause (the Collision Clause) An International Hull Clause (qv), officially called 3/4ths Collision Liability. It extends the policy to cover three-fourths of the shipowner's legal liability to damage to other vessels, freight and their cargo, and general average where the insured vessel has collided with another vessel. Up to 3/4ths of legal costs are also payable. Settlements are on a cross-liability basis. The remaining part and other risks (e.g. loss of life) are insured in Protection and Indemnity Clubs (qv).

'Running landing numbers' For the purposes of particular average (qv) each series is to be made up of packages landed consecutively. *See* TAIL SERIES.

Running-off A situation where an insurer is no longer underwriting new business but continues to meet its liabilities under existing contracts that are running off.

***Rylands* v. *Fletcher* (1868)** A case creating a strict liability for an occupier of land who brings and keeps on his land a 'mischievous thing' that later escapes and causes damage or injury no matter how careful he has been. In recent times unsuccessful attempts have been made to apply the rule in *Rylands* v. *Fletcher* to secure compensation on a strict liability basis for pollutants that have seeped from the defendant's land. The strict liability rule arises only when there has been 'non-natural' use of the land.

S

S2P *See* STATE SECOND PENSION.

Sabotage Wilfully doing illegal damage or other malicious acts to disrupt the insured. Term originated in France from the word, French 'sabot' or wooden shoe, which disgruntled workers would use to damage property.

Sacrifice *See* GENERAL AVERAGE SACRIFICE.

Safe place of work At common law means a place of work that an employer has made reasonably safe. He does not have to eliminate every conceivable risk if the burden of doing so is unduly onerous. The duty is higher than the *common duty of care* (qv) under the Occupiers' Liability Act 1957. *See* WORKPLACE REGULATIONS.

Safe system of work System of work that, in pursuance of his common law duty, an employer has made reasonably safe. The term may include: physical layout of the work, sequence of the work, the provision of warnings and notices, and the issue of special instructions. A system may have to be modified as circumstances change. The employer must take reasonable care to see that the system is followed. The duty applies to work that follows a regular pattern but may also apply to single operations.

'Safely landed' The risk on goods and moveables continues until they are safely landed in the customary manner and within a reasonable time after arrival at the port, otherwise the risk under the insurance ceases (Marine Insurance Act 1906, Schedule, Rules for Construction, rule 5).

Safety policy Clear plan that *every* employer must have for keeping the workplace safe. Those employing more than five workers at a time must have a *written safety policy* (HSWA, s.2). The policy must cover how safety is to be maintained and kept up to date, and the employer must ensure that every employee knows the content of the policy.

'Said to Contain' Disclaimer noted on a bill of lading (qv) that the vessel carrying the cargo did not verify the type, quantity or condition of the cargo when the vessel received the loaded and sealed container.

Sailing warranty Implied warranty in a voyage policy on a ship that the voyage will proceed with reasonable despatch. Unreasonable delay may increase the hazards so permitting the insurer to avoid the policy.

Salary grade scheme A career average scheme (qv) under which the member's benefits earned each year depend on an earnings range rather than an exact amount. All persons in the band receive the same benefit.

Salary sacrifice scheme Pension arrangement in writing under which the employee agrees with the employer to forgo part of his earnings in return for a corresponding contribution by the employer to the scheme.

Sale of Goods Act 1979 As amended by the Sale of Goods Act 1994, the Act implies, inter alia, in contracts for the sale of goods by a business, that the seller promises that the goods will of *satisfac-*

tory quality (qv), will be *as described* and will be *fit for purpose* (qv). The seller as a trader will be liable for any breach that causes injury but may have recourse against his supplier. The *Unfair Contract Terms Act 1977* (qv) restricts the exclusion or limitation of liability in relation to these terms depending on whether it is a consumer sale (qv) or a non-consumer sale (qv).

Salvage 1. Property saved from a misfortune on land or at sea. 2. An *award* payable to a third party, known as a *salvor,* for services rendered to preserve maritime property from an insured peril, provided that the salvor acted voluntarily and the property has been threatened by a maritime peril at sea. Insurers contribute to the award in so far as the peril was insured.

Salvage agreement Entered into by parties in a salvage situation. The salvor (qv) then acts under contract instead of voluntarily and so forfeits his rights to salvage charges. However, if subscribing to the Lloyd's Standard Form of Salvage Agreement (qv), the 'no cure, no pay' *condition* is preserved. The successful salvor receives either the sum fixed in the agreement or the amount awarded by a Lloyd's-appointed arbitrator.

Salvage Association (SA) SA negotiates salvage contracts when instructed by the shipowner following a loss. It provides expert advice, organises surveys (worldwide) of hull and cargo, including oil industry damage, and supervises salvage operations. British Maritime Technology Ltd acquired SA in 2001.

Salvage award *See* SALVAGE 2.

Salvage charges The insurance term for *salvage award* (qv). Compare with SUE AND LABOUR CHARGES; SISTERSHIP CLAUSE.

Salvage loss The loss incurred when goods damaged by a marine peril are sold at an intermediate port because it is considered they will be worthless by the time of reaching the original destination. The underwriter pays a total loss but takes credit for the net proceeds of the sale.

Salvage value Estimated monetary amount that could be realised by selling damaged property, cargo or the vessel.

Salvor A person who saves property. In maritime law salvors have a lien on property saved. *See* SALVAGE.

Satellite Any manmade body, including spacecraft, launched by rocket into space and put into orbit around the earth. The use of satellites for communications has been greatly extended and the aviation insurance industry has developed a range of policies to meet the risks. *See* SATELLITE/SPACE INSURANCE.

Satellite consequential loss insurance Consequential loss cover following physical loss or damage to a satellite. Media and telecoms companies rely upon satellite transmission on a daily basis and service interruptions are costly. Cover can be effected at any time during the lifespan of the satellite.

Satellite/space insurance Cover for satellites is related to four phases of the satellite's lifespan. The erection period is covered under erection all risks (qv), the period from completion of assembly to launch is covered under pre-launch insurance (qv), the launch itself is insured under launch insurance (qv) and during its working life it is covered under life insurance (qv). Other insurances available are satellite consequential loss (qv) which can be effected during any phase, third party liability (qv) and extra expenses from delayed launch (qv).

Satellite third party insurance Covers liability for physical damage and bodily harm to third parties both on the ground and in space caused, for example, by satellites colliding or launch failures.

Satisfactory quality The Sale of Goods Act 1979 (qv) term whereby the seller promises that the goods are of *satisfactory quality.* This means reaching a standard that a reasonable person would regard as satisfactory, taking into account the price and any description. Aspects of quality include fitness for purpose, freedom from minor defects, appearance and finish, durability and safety. *See* FITNESS FOR PURPOSE; PRODUCT LIABILITY; UNFAIR CONTRACT TERMS ACT 1977.

Schedule 3 Order Issued annually when the government specifies the amount by which *preserved benefits* (qv) should increase between a member leaving a scheme and their normal pension date (qv). The name is taken from PSA93, Schedule 3.

Schedule of contributions Special payment schedule aimed at ensuring that the pension scheme will not have an actuarial deficiency during the period concerned. Defined benefit schemes, because of the minimum funding requirement (qv), must maintain a schedule signed by an actuary containing contribution rates and payment dates.

Schedule policy The part of an insurance policy that sets out the detail that is specific to the individual contract. The information includes: name and address of insured, policy inception date (qv), the period of insurance and the premium.

Scheme actuary Actuary appointed by the trustees or managers of an occupational pension scheme under PA95, s.47.

Scheme administrator Person appointed to manage a pension scheme who must ensure that the scheme is operated in accordance with the requirements of the authorities and its own trust deed and rules. The appointment is mandatory for exempt approved schemes. The administrator may have to give certain *revenue undertakings* (qv).

Scheme auditor Occupational pension scheme auditor appointed by the trustees or managers under PA95, s.47.

Scheme rules Rules relating to a particular pension scheme. All members have the right to see the full scheme rules.

Scheme service The period of employment with one or more connected employers. *See* CONTINUOUS SERVICE.

Scheme trustees Individuals or independent institutions that are responsible for the management of a trust in accordance with the trust deed. Scheme trustees have the power to select any investment they wish in order to adhere to the trust deed. Their activities come under the jurisdiction of Opra (qv) who may remove or suspend a trustee.

School fees insurance Various investment, savings and insurance schemes to ensure that a parent will be able to meet educational costs when they arise. The range of policies that can be built into the parents' plan include endowment (qv), critical illness (qv), income protection (qv) and special policies such as reimbursement of fees when illness prevents the child from attending school.

Scorching Damage to property caused by heat but unattended by ignition. Without ignition there is no fire damage within the meaning of the fire policy. Scorching consequent upon fire will be covered under the doctrine of proximate cause (qv).

Seasonal increase clause Clause automatically increasing sums insured on property during stated periods that reflect seasonal factors.

Seasonal risk A risk or an increase in risk that attaches during only a part of the year.

Seaworthiness The reasonable fitness of a vessel in all respects to encounter the ordinary perils of the contemplated voyage, properly crewed, provisioned and equipped. Seaworthiness is implied in voyage policies, but not in time policies (qv). A shipowner's right of claim under a time policy is prejudiced if he knowingly goes to sea in an unseaworthy condition. Cargo policies waive breach of the warranty except where the insured is privy to the unseaworthiness.

Seaworthiness admitted clause Cargo clause whereby the insurer admits that no claim will be repudiated on the grounds of unseaworthiness. The clause does not prevent the insurer from proceeding, in the name of the insured, against a carrier who is liable for the loss. The clause also ensures that the insured is not prejudiced by the carrier's wrongful act.

Second loss insurance A policy that contributes to a loss only when the loss exceeds the sum payable by a more specific insurance. *See* AVERAGE/TWO CONDITIONS OF AVERAGE.

Second surplus treaty A supplementary treaty to a first surplus treaty. Cessions may only be made to the second surplus after the capacity of the first treaty has been satisfied.

Secondary exposure Exposure to risk indirectly through association with a person more directly exposed. Mrs Gunn died of mesothelioma caused by inhaling asbestos dust from her husband's working clothes (*Gunn* v. *Wallsend Slipway & Engineering Co. Ltd* (1989)).

Secret commission A commission taken by an agent without the consent of his principal. It is a breach of good faith and the agent forfeits his rights against the principal. An employee who secretly accepts a commission on his employer's insurance commits a crime (Prevention of Corruption Act 1906).

Section 32 buy-out An insurance policy, taking its name from the Finance Act 1981, s32, into which pension scheme leavers may transfer their *preserved benefits* (qv).

Section 32A policy Insurance policy that secures the *protected rights* (qv) of an active or deferred pensioner on the winding up of a *contracted out money purchase scheme (qv).*

Section 226 policy *See* RETIREMENT ANNUITY.

Section 404 scheme order The UK Treasury order under an FSMA s.404 scheme following an FSA 'report and review' proposal on the alleged widespread or regular failure by authorised persons to comply with rules relating to a particular kind of activity (e.g. mis-selling of pension schemes).

Section schemes An s.53 scheme (PSA93, s.53) is an occupational pension scheme that used to be contracted out (qv) and still has a guaranteed minimum pension scheme or protected rights. An s.590 scheme (ICTA88, s.590) is an occupational scheme that gets mandatory approval (qv). An s.608 scheme is an occupational scheme approved before 6 April 1980 but not approved under the new code. Consequently no contributions have been made since 1980.

Securitisation A means by which self-liquidating financial assets such as loans and mortgages are packaged by a business as bonds and sold through a special purpose vehicle (qv) to capital market investors. The business continues to service the securitised assets although the credit risk has been transferred to investors whose concern is the creditworthiness of the assets not the business which granted the loans. *See* SECURITISATION OF INSURANCE RISK.

Securitisation of insurance risk Transfer of insured risks from the insurance market to the capital market through a special purpose vehicle (qv). The SPV sells bonds on the proviso that it can default on interest and/or capital repayments if the insured risk, e.g. a hurricane, occurs. The retained amounts fund the losses of the (re)insurer. Securitisation has provided alternative sources of capital when reinsurance capacity has been in short supply. *See* CATASTROPHE BONDS; INSURITISATION.

Segmentation *See* CLUSTER POLICY.

Segregated fund Part of the pension scheme's assets managed by an external investment manager. These investments are separated from the remaining assets controlled by the fund's investment manager. The segregated fund often indicates an individual portfolio of stocks and shares as opposed to a pooled fund (qv).

Seizure Exclusions in the Institute Cargo Clauses and International Hull Clauses warrant the policy 'free of capture, *seizure*, etc.' Seizure means 'every act of taking forcible possession, either by lawful authority or by overpowering force'. None of these elements were present when Dominican Republic customs officials stole cars due for transshipment (*Bayview Motors Ltd* v. *Mitsui Fire & Marine Insurance Co. Ltd* (2002), 1 Lloyd's Rep 652).

Select mortality table A mortality table based on selected lives only and not the general population, e.g. lives accepted for insurance.

Select rate of mortality This occurs when rates of mortality are differentiated by age and duration. Most mortality tables used in life insurance have two or three periods of select mortality.

Selection against the insurer *See* ADVERSE SELECTION.

Selection of lives Life insurance practice of categorising lives as standard, substandard or declined. The object is to guard against anti-selection, as the substandard lives have the greatest incentive to insure, disturbing the mortality balance. Standard lives attract normal terms while sub-standard (i.e. impaired) lives (qv) are rated according to their impairment.

'Self damage' Actual damage to the insured item from internal rather than external causes. It features in some engineering insurance (qv) policies.

Self-drive hire Hiring out of vehicles for short periods allowing customers to drive. The self-drive policy defines acceptability in terms of both vehicles and drivers. *See* WAIVER OF DAMAGE.

Self-insurance The payment of losses as they become due by an individual, partnership or corporation that retains all or part of its own risks. High frequency/low impact losses are paid out of cash flow. In other cases the firm retains the first portion of other losses to be paid out of reserves and insures the excess of the retention. Self-insurance is distinguished from non-insurance because it represents a formalised accrual of liabilities. *See* PLANNED RISK ASSUMPTION; CAPTIVE INSURANCE COMPANY.

Self-invested personal pensions (SIPPs) Personal pensions that allow the individual to select where his contributions, within limits, should be invested. The investment opportunities include stocks and shares, unit and investment trusts, insurance company funds, deposit accounts and commercial property. Certain investments (e.g. works of art) are prohibited. Individuals must have *net relevant earnings* (qv) and will receive tax relief on contributions at the highest marginal rate. Group arrangements are common. SIPPs are offered by insurance companies and stockbrokers. *See* SELF-INVESTMENT.

Self-investment The investment of the asset of an occupational pension scheme approved under Chapter I in employer-related investment. A 5 per cent limit is imposed by PA95 and the IR imposes separate restrictions on self-investment by small self-administered schemes.

Self-managed funds (SMFs) Earmarked schemes (qv) where the policies are linked to an investment fund. The investment fund is normally selected by the employer or trustees but held in the name of the insurance company.

Seller's interest Policy effected by a seller of cargo to protect his contingency interest in the event that the buyer's policy fails to respond to a loss. *See* QUANTUM OF INTEREST.

Semi-obligatory reinsurance Treaty under which only one of the parties has an obligation. The cedant may be obliged to offer all risks of the given class but the reinsurer will not be bound to accept them (obligatory–facultative). Conversely, the reinsurer may obliged to accept all risks that the cedant chooses to offer (facultative–obligatory).

Senior captive A captive insurer that has developed into a normal insurer taking risks from the market generally.

Sentimental loss Occurs when *sound* cargo is sold at a reduced price because of an unfavourable association with goods, part of the same cargo (e.g. tea), damaged by an insured peril. The 'sentimental' loss on the sound goods is uninsured.

Sentimental value The value that a person attaches to property based on feelings of emotion and affection not monetary values. Such values cannot be expressed in financial terms and cannot therefore be insured.

'SEPTIC' (single event pollution trigger insurance clause) Clause reading 'All pollution or contamination which arises out of one Event shall be deemed to have occurred on the date that the insured first becomes aware of the circumstances which have given or may give rise to Pollution or Contamination.' The clause was intended to bring gradual pollution into public liability policies, but the restricted reinsurance market meant little take up. *See* POLLUTION CLAUSE.

SERPS (State Earnings-Related Pension Scheme) Replaced by the Second State Pension (S2P) (qv) in 2002 as the earnings-related part of the statement retirement scheme. Rights built up under SERPS are protected.

Service risk A life insurance/personal accident underwriting term for the higher risk of accidental death of members of the armed forces.

Services business Overseas (re)insurance business that is transacted in the UK. This cross-frontier business contributes significantly to the UK's balance of payments. In the EC it is the right of an insurer to sell insurance cross border into other Member States. It does not apply to business accepted under full binding authorities (qv) held by coverholders (qv) in the Member State where the risk is located.

Services clause Clause in a fire policy on buildings in respect of the cover provided on items such as telephones, gas, water pipes and cabling which are partly outside the building. The cover is 'accidental damage' and applies to property belonging to the insured or that for which he is responsible.

Set-off Clause *See* OFFSET CLAUSE.

Settled policy A policy forming the subject of a trust (qv).

Settlement 1. An agreement to resolve a dispute. 2. A payment of an account or claim. 3. In respect of buildings it means movement in a lateral direction but in practice it is not so restricted. Every new property settles on its foundations and the stresses and strains of this movement cause cracks in the plaster and other minor damage. It is not easy to distinguish subsidence (qv) damage from settlement damage. 4. A document, such as a deed or will, defining the way of succession to land or other property or enjoyment of the rents and profits thereof.

Seven-day clause An hours clause (qv) based on seven days. Some catastrophe occurrences may last for this period, expressed often as 168 consecutive hours rather than seven days.

Severability Provision in a directors' and officers' liability policy that the wrongful act or knowledge of one director or officer is not to be imputed to another for the purpose of utmost good faith (qv) or application of a policy exclusion. Each insured person is treated as having arranged his own cover.

Severe Inflation Clause *See* STABILITY CLAUSE.

Shadow director *See* DIRECTORS.

Shareholders' share purchase *See* CROSS OPTION AGREEMENT (qv).

Short service benefit Pension benefit which must be kept for an early leaver (qv) of a pension scheme in order to meet the preservation (qv) requirements of PSA93.

Ship The First Schedule (rule 15) of the Marine Insurance Act 1906 states that the term 'includes the hull, materials and outfit, stores and provisions for the officers and crew, and in the case of vessels in a special trade, the ordinary fittings requisite for the trade, and also, in the case of a steamship, the machinery, boilers, and coals and engine stores, if owned by the assured'.

Ship construction *See* BUILDER'S RISK POLICY.

Ship value This is usually agreed each year between the shipowner and the leading underwriter.

Shipowner's liability The liability of a shipowner for loss, injury or damage to others or the property of others arising in tort, contract or under statute. *See* PROTECTION AND INDEMNITY CLUBS; RUNNING DOWN CLAUSE.

Shipped bill Bill of lading (qv) issued after the goods have actually been loaded. Under the Carriage of Goods by Sea Act 1971 (qv) a shipper may demand such a bill from the shipowner. Normally done by adding the name of the vessel and the date of shipment to the received for shipment bill (qv).

Shipping costs *See* FREIGHT.

Shop insurance A business insurance for retailers who can acquire a package policy (qv) with standard cover or a tailor-made insurance policy covering a range of risks in one document based on sections of cover chosen by the insured.

Short closing The practice by a broker overplacing the risk, i.e. securing acceptances that exceed the available cover so that, on closing, the line written by each underwriter is reduced proportionately.

Short delivery The quantity of cargo delivered is less than the bill of lading quantity (qv).

Short period An insurance for less than 12 months. The premium charged is higher than pro rata.

Short-tail Insurance business where it is known that claims will generally be notified and settled quickly. Contrast with LONG-TAIL.

Sick building syndrome A building where a significant number of occupants have experienced illness and discomfort attributable to the accumulation of air pollutants and contaminants (e.g. radon, micro-organisms). The problems originate from the circulatory deficiencies of the building's air conditioning system.

Sickness benefit A weekly or monthly benefit available as an add-on to the accident only (personal accident (qv)). When the add-on exists, the policy is called a personal accident and sickness policy (qv). The sickness benefit is normally for up to 52 weeks.

Signed Line Underwriter's participation in a risk after the lines have been short-closed (qv) from the *written line* (on the slip (qv)) to 100 per cent of the amount at risk.

Significant influence The influence that an approved person (qv) has over any of the *controlled functions* (1 to 20 in the FSA's table of controlled functions). Persons with *significant influence* must: (a) take reasonable steps to ensure that the firm's regulated business is so organised that it can be controlled effectively; (b) exercise due skill, care and diligence in managing that business; and (c) take reasonable steps to ensure that the business complies with relevant regulatory requirements. (Visit *www.fsa.gov.uk*).

Signing down *See* SHORT CLOSING.

Silent risk A risk or insurance in respect of premises where no activities are currently undertaken and no machinery used.

Simple reversionary bonus A bonus added to a with profit life insurance policy expressed as a percentage of the sum insured only. Bonuses once declared are guaranteed and are paid with the sum insured at death or maturity.

Simplified defined contribution scheme (SDCS) Money purchase scheme (qv) with additional limitations, e.g. lump sum not to exceed twice final remuneration. IR no longer considers applications for SDCSs but existing schemes continue.

Simultaneous payments clause A reinsurance clause binding the reinsurer to pay a claim simultaneously with the direct insurer's payment to the original insured.

Single article limit A limit on the maximum an insurer will pay in respect of any one article which has been insured under a general description, e.g. personal possessions/belongings. A collective sum insured may not fully reflect the aggregate of the values at risk. The single article limit encourages the insured to insure high value items separately for appropriate amounts.

'Single European Licence' *See* SINGLE INSURANCE MARKET.

Single insurance market Market allowing EC insurers to set up *establishment business* (qv), e.g. branches, in any other state without being subject to host state restrictions. Also an insurer authorised in its home state can engage in *service business* (qv) by selling freely across national frontiers. The EC has published three generations of Insurance Directives (qv). The effect is to make EC insurers subject to *home country control* (qv) creating an authorisation known as the 'Single European Licence'.

Single liability When two ships collide, the shipowner with the greater share of the blame pays the other the difference between their respective liabilities; according to maritime law there are not two liabilities. However, marine hull policies provide that claims shall be settled on the basis of cross liabilities (qv).

Single market agreement Any agreement that extends across a single market, i.e. marine, aviation or non-marine, only. They may be joint agreements between Lloyd's underwriters and insurance companies. Examples include *leading underwriters' clauses (qv)* in all three markets, the 'companies collective signing agreement' (non-marine) (qv) and the Marine Waterborne Agreement (qv).

Single passport EC term for *single European licence* (qv).

Single premium An insurance under which a 'one off' premium secures cover for a long term, even in perpetuity as for a restrictive covenant indemnity (qv).

Single premium bonds/insurance bonds Life company single premium contracts providing a lump sum investment with limited cover for medium- to long-term capital growth. They are a collective investment alternative to a unit trust. Special tax rules allow limited tax free withdrawals but capital growth is subject to higher rate income tax. The bonds may guarantee income or growth. Bonds may be categorised as: managed bonds (qv); with profits bonds (qv); equity bonds (qv) or income bonds (qv).

Single premium method A pensions method of determining the premiums payable under an insurance contract with the object of meeting within each year the cost of benefits relating to that year.

Sinking fund policy *See* CAPITAL REDEMPTION POLICY.

Sistership clause If two ships in the same ownership collide, the clause confers on the insured the same rights as if the two vessels were separately owned and separately insured. An appointed arbitrator apportions liability on that basis.

Skey Forms Questionnaires adopted at Lloyd's and the LMX to give an overview of the reinsured's account. They are regarded as providing the minimum needed for the purpose of a reinsurance submission. Charles Skey, a Lloyd's non-marine underwriter, created the forms.

Sleep easy covers Catastrophe reinsurances at very high, even unlikely levels, that create an extra degree of security against events of unexpected severity.

Sliding scale premium/treaty A reinsurance premium under a non-proportional treaty based on burning cost for the period subject only to agreed minimum and maximum amounts. *See* ESCAPE CLAUSE.

Sliding scale reinsurance commission A scale of commission payable under a treaty where the amount of the commission varies inversely with the loss ratio subject to a maximum and minimum.

Slip Document submitted by a Lloyd's broker to underwriters containing particulars of a risk proposed for insurance. The leading underwriter signifies his acceptance and the broker seeks further acceptances until the risk is fully subscribed. Insurance companies and Lloyd's syndicates may appear on the same slip. LMP slips have been introduced following LMP 2001. The slip's standardised layout is to clarify responsibilities and timescales and deliver certainty at point of contact. The slip can incorporate either the *General Underwriters' Agreement* (qv) or *Leading Underwriters' Clauses* (qv). *See* SLIP EPS; SLIP POLICY; SLIP CREATION GUIDELINES.

Slip agreement An addition to the slip (qv), expressing the underwriter's agreement to an issue agreed by the underwriter after his initial acceptance.

Slip creation guidelines Best practice guidelines enabling brokers and underwriters to develop their own pro-formas to ensure the slip contains clear and complete information relating to the risk, its administration and procedures for agreement of claims and endorsements. They ensure clarity of contract terms and responsibilities.

Slip EPS (Electronic Placing Support) Allows risks to be written electronically.

Slip leader The insurer on the placing slip identified as leader. Under LMP 2001 (qv), the slip leader has responsibility for coordinating contract and claims management and administration.

Slip policy A signed *slip* (qv) that has been adapted to serve as a policy in place of a formal document where either the insured or reinsured does not require one.

'Slow accident' A latent gradually progressive disease (e.g. asbestosis). The term accident is used as the 'fortuity' is in the outcome rather than the cause which is often exposure on a continuing basis to harmful work conditions. Pollution damage caused gradually over time by seepage is also regarded as a 'slow accident'. *See* LOSSES-OCCURRING; TRIPLE TRIGGER THEORY; INJURY IN RESIDENCE.

Small claims pool Funds pooled by all Lloyd's syndicates out of which all small claims are paid.

Small self-administered scheme (SSAS) Occupational pension scheme where: all assets are pooled in a central fund; benefits are paid from those central funds; and trustees have wide powers of investment. They may be insured, i.e. held centrally in insurance policies only, or self-administered where the funds are held centrally in investments outside policies, e.g. in property, shares, loans. There must be fewer than 12 members, one of whom is a controlling director (qv). The appointment of a pensioner trustee (qv) is mandatory for exempt approved status.

Snowfall cover Weather derivative (qv) based on expected level of snowfall in a given location over a specific time. Snowfall above the reference level may impose additional costs on snow-clearing local authorities, who hedge the risk with a call option (qv). Levels below the reference point reduce revenues at the ski resort, which hedges with a put option (qv). The former receives a payout at high levels of snow, the latter at low levels. *See* PRECIPITATION COVER; SUNSHINE COVER.

'So far as is reasonably practicable' Certain legally imposed 'health and safety duties' have to be carried out in this way. It means that a particular risk can be balanced against the time, trouble, cost and physical difficulty of taking measures to avoid the risk. If the cost and effort are disproportionate to the risk, the parties can run the risk without taking the alternative steps. The greater the risk, the greater must be the effort before it is considered disproportionate. If both the consequences and extent of risk are small, insistence on great expense would not be reasonable. Compare with 'all practicable steps' meaning 'capable of accomplishment regardless of cost but dependent on state of knowledge at time.' *See* PROPERLY MAINTAINED.

Social, domestic and pleasure use A class of use (qv) in private car insurance.

Socially responsible investment (SRI) Occupational pension scheme trustees are required to include a statement in the Statement of Investment Principles (qv) on the extent to which social, environmental or ethical considerations are taken into account in the selection, retention and realisation of investments.

Society margin (Society of Lloyd's) Required minimum margin (RMM) for the Society of Lloyd's. It must maintain the RMM it would have been obliged to maintain under IPRU(INS) (Margins of solvency) had it been an insurer carrying on all the *general insurance business* carried on by its members, but eliminating inter-syndicate reinsurance (the Society guarantee fund). The Society must cover any shortfall out of its *net central assets* (qv).

Society of Fellows Created by the Chartered Insurance Institute to encourage continuing study by Fellows of the Chartered Insurance Institute. Its wide-ranging objectives include stimulating research and contributing to the enhancement of the CII as a professional body.

Society of Financial Advisers (SOFA) Part of the Chartered Insurance Institute (qv), it is the UK's leading professional and educational body for financial advisers. SOFA has the largest number of members qualified to an advanced level in financial planning. It encourages professional development through qualifications, conferences, seminars, etc. There are four levels of SOFA designation. The entry level qualification is the Financial Planning Certificate (qv). The penultimate level is the Associateship – ASFA necessitating six Advanced Planning Certificate (qv) subjects, three of which give access to professional membership, MSFA. The highest level is Fellowship – FSFA after four additional subjects, making ten in total and is subject to five years' relevant experience. (Visit *www.sofa.org)*.

Soft market A market in which there is a ready supply of insurance. Competition among insurers drives premium rates down and terms and conditions ease as insureds find themselves able to negotiate better terms.

Sole purpose test IR rule that the sole purpose of any pension scheme is to provide a pension for its members. Those responsible for the scheme must take account of the rule in managing the scheme. Breaches that disadvantage members or connected persons (qv) attract serious penalties.

'Solely and independently of any other cause' Phrase that qualifies the term 'accidental bodily injury' in personal accident insurances. The phrase excludes injury or disablement where a pre-existing condition has contributed to the onset of the disablement or prolonged its duration. A gall stone sufferer died when accidentally struck. Independently of each other neither the medical condition or the blow would have killed him.

Solvency An insurer is solvent for regulatory purposes when its assets exceed its liabilities by the *required minimum margin* (qv). The FSA prescribes methods for the valuation of assets and liabilities for the purpose of showing regulatory solvency. The actual solvency margin is the excess of assets over liabilities. *See* FREE ASSETS; SOLVENCY I; SOLVENCY II.

'Solvency I' Directives *See* DIRECTIVES 2002/12/EC and 2002/13/EC.

Solvency II Ongoing review of solvency regulation that appears likely to lead to the implementation of a risk-based capital (qv) model for solvency purposes in the EC in the next few years.

Solvency margin *See* MARGIN OF SOLVENCY; REQUIRED MINIMUM MARGIN SOLVENCY TEST.

Solvency test 1. The test to show that the insurer or underwriter is complying with FSA solvency requirements by comparing the available solvency margin with the required minimum margin (qv). 2. Actuarial calculation to determine whether an occupational pension scheme's assets are sufficient to pay the benefits to members.

Sonic bangs clause A sonic bang is the result of pressure waves caused by aircraft travelling at sonic or supersonic speeds. The exclusion of damage caused by sonic bangs is found in all property insurances. In motor insurance the exclusion applies only to the any 'own damage' cover that may apply.

South American Clause Cargo clause defining termination of cover on South American shipments. It overrides both the warehouse to warehouse clause (qv) and the marine extension clause (qv) and extends cover after discharge from the overseas vessel. Cover terminates on the soonest of: (a) delivery at the final warehouse at the named destination; (b) 60 days after discharge from the vessel; or (c) 90 days after discharge from the vessel on shipments by way of the Magdalena River.

Space insurance *See* SATELLITE/SPACE INSURANCE.

Special circumstances clause Business interruption policy (qv) clause whereby a claims adjustment may take account of the trend of the business, variations or other special circumstances. The aim is to produce a figure representing, as nearly as possible, the results that would have been achieved but for the interruption. The clause is also called the 'exceptional circumstances clause' or 'bracketed provisions'.

Special condition of average *See* AVERAGE.

Special contributions Extra payments by an employer into an occupational pension scheme for a period not exceeding three years or as a single premium. This may purchase new benefits or cover an actuarial deficiency. Compare with ordinary contributions (qv).

Special drawing rights (SDRs) An international reserve asset that measures and compares the changing value of international currencies. An SDR is expressed daily by reference to a basket of currencies and is used in international conventions (e.g. Warsaw Convention) and conditions of contract as a measure of value or limit of liability.

Special perils *See* ADDITIONAL PERILS.

'Special purpose' captive Captive insurance company formed to finance a particular exposure. It provides an in-house facility for financing risks where conventional insurance is costly or difficult to obtain. Such exposure may include professional indemnity, credit or insolvency risks, product guarantee, warranty or other 'special situations'.

Special purpose vehicle (SPV) Independent trust or captive created to act as a conduit through which an insurer can transfer insurance risk to the capital market. The SPV sells bonds to investors who will sacrifice principal and/or interest if a defined catastrophe occurs. The SPV like a reinsurer uses the sacrificed funds to indemnify the insurer. The SPV is bankruptcy-remote and holds legal rights over the assets transferred. SPVs do not just apply to insurance-related transactions.

'Special relationship' *See* NEGLIGENT STATEMENT.

Special types Generic term used by motor insurers to describe vehicles or mobile plant designed for special purposes, e.g. bulldozers, diggers, etc. They may be insured under motor (particularly for Road Traffic Act purposes), engineering or public liability policies. 'Tool of trade' risk is covered when they are used on site.

Special waiver clause Professional indemnity clause whereby the insurer agrees not to exercise their right of avoidance where the insured shows that any non-disclosure (qv) or misrepresentation of facts or untrue statement at inception or any subsequent renewal was entirely innocent. Where the non-disclosure prejudices any claim, the insurer is able to reduce the amount payable to the sum that would have been payable in the absence of such prejudice.

Specie Marine term meaning any cargo with a value/weight ratio exceeding that of silver. The term covers gold bullion, other precious metals, precious stones, bonds, share certificates, money in coin and currency in notes. Specie does not include objets d'art or fine arts such as porcelain, sculptures and paintings.

Specification Usually it amplifies the schedule (qv) and gives details of the breakdown of the total sum insured shown in the schedule. Additional clauses may also appear in the specification.

Specifics Items that are specific to a particular insurance and not generally applicable. There may be specific exclusions or additions to cover.

Specified working expenses/uninsured working expenses Expenses itemised as *not* being insured under a business interruption policy (qv). They vary directly with turnover and are not at risk when a fire curtails business. For example, packing expenses cease when a business is not producing goods and should not therefore be insured as a part of the gross profit (qv).

Speculative risk A risk where the outcome may range from loss to gain. The prospect of gain induces businesses to take risks. Businesses control speculative risks by means of sound business practices such as hedging, market research, internal controls, etc., and forming limited liability companies. Insurance is not available to protect firms against insolvency. *See* HOLISTIC RISK MANAGEMENT; ENTERPRISE RISK MANAGEMENT.

Spent convictions *See* REHABILITATION OF OFFENDERS ACT 1974.

Split annuity A combination of a single premium immediate annuity (qv) and a single premium deferred annuity (qv) whereby the premium is split between the two. The immediate annuity provides a current income, only part of which is taxed, while the deferred annuity accumulates over time to the original total premium invested.

Spontaneous combustion Self-ignition of combustible material by the internal development of heat. The standard fire policy excludes damage to property by its own spontaneous combustion but damage caused in any resultant fire spread is covered.

Spread loss Aggregate excess of loss *financial reinsurance* (qv) under which premiums, under a multi-year contract, are paid during the good years to build up a fund from which losses are recovered in poor years. Premiums accumulate in an investment fund as well as additional premiums paid if losses exceed the fund balance. Cover is fixed on a *per year basis,* often stop loss. The key is to stabilise the cedant's losses over time.

Spread vehicle Corporate member or a group of corporate members writing alongside individual members on a spread of syndicates across the market.

Spreader clause An aviation policy clause providing that if the declared number of passengers is exceeded, the insurer's limit of liability per passenger will be automatically reduced.

Sprinkler leakage insurance Covers damage caused by the accidental discharge of water from a sprinkler leakage system. The installation attracts reduced premiums from the fire insurer but introduces the accidental discharge risk.

Spurious selection This occurs when the results of an investigation appear to indicate an unexpected variation in mortality due to selection. It may be due to statistical faults in the data or abnormal experience.

Stability clause/index clause Clause that adjusts the retention and limit provisions of an excess of loss reinsurance in accordance with the fluctuations of a published wage or price index. The clause apportions the effect of inflation proportionately between the parties. This protects the reinsurer who, on the basis of unadjusted retention, would suffer the full effects of inflation. The *severe inflation clause* is a variant that invokes the index only if inflation exceeds an agreed level, e.g. 20 per cent.

Stacking of limits Applying the limits of more than one *losses-occurring policy* to an occurrence, loss or claim. It may occur when the same long-tail injury is deemed to have occurred in each of a number of years causing the limits of those periods to be aggregated to produce a higher limit than the insurer intended. Insurers use *claims series clauses* (qv) in order to attempt to trigger all claims from 'one original cause' into a single year.

Staggered vesting phased retirement *See* PHASED RETIREMENT.

Stakeholder pensions Personal pensions with strict limits on cost, access and terms targeted at the mass market. Even non-earners can contribute up to the maximum of £3,900 per year (2002/3) with contributions net of tax even if no tax is paid. Occupational scheme members earning up to £30,420 or less may contribute concurrently to the scheme.

Stakeholders People or organisations who may be affected by, or perceive themselves to be affected by, risk creating decisions or activities. Stakeholders can be internal (e.g. employees) or external (e.g. shareholders, regulatory bodies, customers).

Standalone corporate syndicate Syndicate with a single corporate member and which does not write business in parallel with any existing syndicate. The syndicate writes business solely for its own account and is supported by a single underwriting corporate member, the sole source of capital. Lloyd's does not generally allow a standalone syndicate to be established unless it brings new capital to the market.

Standard & Poor's Claims Paying Ability Rating A rating based on S & P's assessment of the financial capacity of an insurance company and its ability to meet its claims obligations. There are two ranges of ratings: (a) secure range: AAA to BBB; and (b) vulnerable range BB to CCC.

Standard construction Property insurance term referring to buildings constructed of brick, stone or concrete and roofed with slates, tiles, metal, asbestos, concrete or sheets or slabs of incombustible mineral. This is abbreviated to 'bsst'. Broadly this means buildings of incombustible materials (Grade 1) insurable at standard rates. Lloyd's uses the term *massive construction*. *See* NON-STANDARD CONSTRUCTION.

Standard contribution rate Contribution rate (employer and employee) appropriate to a particular funding method (e.g. prospective benefit method (qv)) ascertained by a valuation before taking account of any actuarial surplus (qv)/actuarial deficiency (qv). The rate is normally expressed as a percentage of the pensionable pay.

Standard excess An excess (qv) that is written into the standard or basic policy such as the young and inexperienced drivers excess in motor policies. Other excesses, voluntary or compulsory, may be added

Standard lives Proposers acceptable for life insurance on normal terms because there is no evidence to show serious ill health. *See* SELECTION OF LIVES.

Standard policy A policy form in general use.

Standard turnover Business interruption (qv) term meaning the turnover (qv) during the 12 months immediately before the date of the material damage. The liability of the insurer for loss of gross profit (qv) is determined by applying the rate of gross profit (qv) to the reduction in turnover being the difference in turnover between the standard turnover and the turnover achieved during the indemnity period (qv).

Standing charges A business interruption (qv) term describing the ongoing costs, i.e. fixed costs or costs that do not decrease proportionately with turnover. They must be paid by the business notwithstanding the curtailment of trading. These expenses, e.g. rent, are at risk and therefore payable out of gross profit, the main item insured under the policy.

Standstill An engineering policy added to erection all risks or contractors all risks cover when a construction project enters a period of inactivity, i.e. goes on 'standstill'. The policy is on a named peril basis.

State Earnings-Related Pension Scheme *See* SERPS; S2P.

State of the art/development risks defence Defence whereby a 'producer' can avoid Consumer Protection Act 1987 (qv) liability. If, at the time of supply, the state of scientific and technical knowledge was not such that a producer of similar products might have been expected to discover the defect if it had existed while there were products under his control, there will be no liability under the Act. It is no defence to show that the producer was unaware of the risk because of no prior accidents. The defence only applies when there has been some technical or scientific advance since the time of supply that subsequently enable the defect to be identified (*Abouzaid* v. *Mothercare (UK) Ltd* (2001)). The producer must show that the defence applies.

State pension age Age from which state pensions are payable, 65 for men and 60 for women. The pension age for women is being phased to reach 65 over the period 2010 and 2020.

State pension offset The reduction in pension or pensionable earnings to achieve integration (qv).

State Second Pension (S2P) Replaced SERPS (qv) in 2002 providing a more generous additional state pension for low and moderate earners and certain carers and people with long-term disability. S2P gives employees earning up to £24,600 (2002/3 terms) an improvement over SERPS whether or not contracted out (qv). Most help goes to persons in the lowest of three earning bands, i.e. up to £10,800.

Statement of Investment Principles (SIP) Written statement by occupational scheme trustees of the principles governing their investment decisions. Trustees must have regard to advice from a suitably qualified person, consult with the employer and publicise the existence of the statement to members as required under PA95, s.35. The legislation protects UK-domiciled private policyholders.

Statement of Principles for approved persons (SP) The FSA sets out four *Statements of Principles* that apply to *all approved persons* (qv) to ensure that they undertake their roles efficiently and with integrity in carrying out *controlled functions* (qv). Three additional principles apply to approved persons performing significant influence functions (qv). Approved persons in breach of the principles face disciplinary action. SP is different from *Principles of Business* (qv) that apply to firms only.

Status disclosure 1. With exceptions, firms conducting regulated activities (qv) must take care to ensure that every letter (including electronic equivalent) which it or its employees send to a private customer must disclose that it is 'authorised and regulated by the Financial Services Authority'. 2. The FSA requires firms to disclose details of the services they provide and appropriate information on the products which are being sold.

Statute-barred A civil claim that cannot be brought because it is outside the time permitted by statute (Limitation Act 1980 (qv)) is 'statute barred'. *See* also the LATENT DAMAGES ACT 1986.

Statute of Frauds 1677 Largely superseded by other enactments but s.4 remains. It provides that no action shall be brought upon a guarantee unless the agreement is in writing and signed by the party to be charged, or his agent. See unenforceable contracts (qv) for the effect on contracts of fidelity guarantee (qv).

Statutory absolution *See* REHABILITATION OF OFFENDERS ACT 1974.

Statutory declaration A written statement of facts under the Statutory Declarations Act 1835 declared as being true before a commissioner or magisterial officer. In policy claims conditions the insurer calls for proofs of loss (qv) and may demand statutory declarations to verify the truth of an insured's claim.

Statutory discharge The discharge by a pension scheme member who has exercised his statutory right to a cash equivalent under PSA93, s.99 on leaving the scheme. An alternative to cash is a *statutory transfer* (qv).

Statutory examinations Examinations of boilers, steam and air receivers, hoists and lifts, and other plant and equipment in pursuance of a range of legislative requirements. The relevant legislation lays the inspection frequency, e.g. steam boilers 14 months, cranes and chains, ropes and lifting tackle 6 months. Inspections have to be carried by a 'competent person'.

Statutory exclusions The Marine Insurance Act 1906, s.55, lists several losses for which underwriters are not liable unless the policy otherwise provides. The exclusions are: wilful misconduct; delay; wear and tear, ordinary leakage and breakage, inherent vice or loss caused by rats or vermin; injury to machinery not caused by maritime perils.

Statutory notices procedures The FSA in its decision-making role has statutory powers to issues *warning notices (qv)* and *decision notices (qv)*. As a supervisory authority it is empowered to issue a *supervisory notice* which may order immediate action on the part of an authorised person or indicate that the matter concerned is open to review.

Statutory transfer Occurs when a pension scheme member exercises his legal right to call upon his previous pension scheme to make a transfer payment to a new scheme.

Stipulation Policy condition that does not go to the root of the contract. A breach does not affect the insurer's contractual liability but does entitle him to sue for damages. The requirement that an insured should submit a wages declaration under an adjustable policy is a stipulation.

Stock endorsement A fidelity guarantee insurance (qv) endorsement to extend the policy to cover loss from misappropriation or improper dealing with stock-in-trade by the person guaranteed.

Stocks and shares ISA Individual ISAs (qv) that invest in stocks and shares. For this purpose, stocks and shares include: unit trusts; investment trusts; open ended investment companies; investments on any recognised Stock Exchange; corporate bonds; shares held in a savings-related share option scheme; and gilts (qv).

Stop loss treaty *See* EXCESS OF LOSS RATIO TREATY.

Storage risk Fire insurance term in respect of warehouse storage of property in bulk. The risk depends on the nature of the goods and any increase in risk due to the way they are stored. Even non-hazardous goods may be rated-up when stored in bulk.

Storm The Shorter Oxford Dictionary states: 'A violent disturbance of the atmosphere, manifested by high winds, often accompanied by heavy falls of rain, hail or snow, by thunder and lightning and (at sea) by turbulence of the waves. Hence sometimes applied to a heavy fall of rain, hail, or snow, or to a violent outbreak of thunder and lightning, unaccompanied by strong wind'.

Stranding Occurs where a vessel takes the ground in an unusual manner and remains hard and fast for an appreciable length of time owing to some extraneous and accidental cause and not in the ordinary course of navigation.

Strategic risk Group of risks impacting on strategy and long-term plans of the organisation. The risk groups include: market and customer trends; economy/policitical stability; competition; tactical decisions (investments, mergers, etc.); achieving predicted performance; major catastrophe/incident, including reputational risk; ethics, culture; corporate governance (qv). They demonstrate the need for holistic risk management (qv).

Street works (or Road and Highways Act) bond A performance bond (qv) that guarantees to a highway authority that a building developer will fulfil his obligation to construct roads on the estate or area of his development. The bond is usually 100 per cent of the construction costs involved.

Stress A demand on physical or mental energy. It can cause a breakdown in a person's physical or mental health. Employees, whose stress is caused by their employers' breach of duty, may bring actions in the civil courts for damages or, if linked to dismissal, compensation may be awarded by an employment tribunal. The risks come under employers' liability insurance (qv) and/or employment practices liability insurance (qv). Employers need to include stress in their risk assessment (qv) and educate employees in stress management.

Strict liability Liability even when there is no proof of negligence. It may arise at common law, e.g. the rule in *Rylands* v. *Fletcher* (1868) (qv), or by statute as in the case of the Consumer Protection Act 1987 (qv). The rationale is that the person creating a recognised 'dangerous situation' should be liable without proof of fault for the consequences. Defences to strict liability are very limited.

Strike The level of the index used in a weather derivative (qv) above or below which the writer of a call or put option starts to pay the holder. For example the strike on a weather derivative may be based on the excess of 100 Heating Degree Days (qv).

Strikes clauses The Institute Strikes Clauses (Cargo) (1/1/82) cover loss or damage to cargo by: (a) strikers, locked-out workmen or persons taking part in labour disturbances, riots or civil commotions; and (b) any terrorist or any person acting from a political motive. Under the Institute War and Strikes Clauses (Hulls – Time) similar cover is included with the addition of damage by '*any* person acting maliciously'. Shipowners face the prospect of cover being cancelled at short notice but voyages underway are permitted to complete their transit.

Structured settlements Arrangement between the claimant and the defendant's liability insurer whereby the lump sum payment for future losses is replaced by periodic payments for a fixed period or until the claimant's death. They may be index-linked, varied or 'structured' during the period. The insurer uses the 'lump sum' to buy an annuity that funds tax-free payments to the claimant. The court has no power to order such a settlement (Damages Act 1996, s.2).

Subject approval no risk (SAPNR) A phrase used by an underwriter when he feels that the proposer may not accept the terms indicated on the slip. The effect is that the proposer's confirmation of acceptance is required promptly before the risk can attach.

Subject-matter of the insurance This is the object, property or potential liability described in the policy and to which the insured must be so related as to have an insurable interest (qv). For example, the subject-matter of marine insurance is the actual vessel or cargo. Compare with subject-matter of the insurance contract (qv).

Subject-matter of the insurance contract This is the insured's interest in the subject-matter of the insurance (qv). The insurer cannot guarantee to restore the goods or cancel a liability but they can protect the insured's interest against financial loss.

Subject Premium *See* BASE PREMIUM.

Subject to average A phrase against an item or sum insured to indicate that in the event of under-insurance average (qv) will apply.

Subject to survey A phrase to indicate that the insurer's acceptance of a risk is provisional pending completion of a survey by the office's fire surveyor.

Subrogation The right of the insurer who has granted an indemnity (qv) to take over any recovery rights the insured may have against third parties liable for the same loss. A *subrogation condition* in the policy enables the insurer to take action in the insured's name before paying the claim. Subrogation may arise under contract, tort or statute (Riot (Damages) Act 1886 (qv)). Example: insurer paying for a car damaged by a third party's negligence can pursue the third party.

Subrogation condition *See* SUBROGATION.

Subrogation waiver The agreement by an insurer that he will not pursue his subrogation rights in specified circumstances.

Subscribers Lloyd's members who seek access to syndicates where capacity is available. They submit bids to the *capacity auctions* (qv) stipulating, in multiples of 0.1p per pound of capacity, the price they are willing to pay. Subsequently, bids are matched against tenders to determine the capacity to be transferred and the price of the transaction.

Subscription market A market, such as Lloyd's, where Underwriters accept shares of an insurance (or reinsurance) coverage on a co-insurance (or co-reinsurance) basis in contrast to markets where a single insurance carrier will accept the whole of the offer.

Subsidence Damage to buildings due to a movement of land on which the property is situated. Insurance against subsidence, landslip and heave (qv) is available on residential and commercial buildings either as a named peril or under accidental damage cover. The cover excludes normal land settlement, coastal erosion and damage to walls, gates and fences unless the buildings are damaged at the same time. Normally a £1,000 excess will apply.

Substances hazardous to health They are: any substance that has by law to be labelled as 'very toxic', 'toxic', 'harmful', 'irritant' or 'corrosive'; substances for which a maximum exposure limit (MEL) has been set or an occupational standard has been set. They include harmful micro-organisms, substantial quantities of airborne dust or other substances that create comparable health hazards, including: dusts, fumes/gases, solvents, resins, pesticides, acids, alkalis, mineral oil and contaminants such as arsenic and phenols. *See* CONTROL OF SUBSTANCES HAZARDOUS TO HEALTH REGULATIONS.

Substituted expenses Expenses incurred to prevent or reduce a loss for which the marine insurer would have been liable. The expenses may not qualify as general average expenditure (qv) but they can substitute for expenses that do qualify. If the substitution shows a saving, the substituted expenses are allowed in general average (qv).

Subterranean fire It refers to a fire of volcanic origin but would embrace a fire in a coalfield or oil well. The risk, and earthquake, are excluded from the standard fire policy but are insurable in the UK as an additional (special) peril.

Sudden and unforeseen physical damage The widest form of material damage cover under engineering insurance policies. It includes breakdown risks (qv), including electrical and mechanical breakdown, and accidental damage. In short the damage can be from internal or external causes.

Sudden death clause Reinsurance treaty clause requiring or permitting termination of the contract in the event of a change in control of the ceding office, the insolvency of either party and certain other defined events.

'Sudden, unintended, unexpected' pollution *See* POLLUTION CLAUSE.

Sue and labour charges Expenses voluntarily incurred by the insured for the preservation of property; this would include payments under pre-arranged salvage contracts. Sue and labour are distinguished from salvage charges leading to awards to salvors acting independently of any contract. *See* SUE AND LABOUR CLAUSE.

Sue and labour clause Clause in the Institute Cargo Clauses and in the International Hull Clauses reminding the insured to act at all times as though uninsured. The clause makes sue and labour charges (qv) recoverable from the marine insurer in addition to any admissible claim even a total loss claim as it is deemed by the Marine Insurance Act, s.78(1), to be a *supplementary contract.*

Sufficient financial capacity The Insurance Mediation Directive (qv) requires that all insurance intermediaries should have sufficient financial capacity. The aim is to protect customers against the inability of an intermediary to transfer the premium to the insurer or to transfer the amount of a claim or return the premium to the insured. The implementation must take one of the following forms: the transfer of customers' money through strictly segregated accounts; setting up a guarantee fund; payments to the intermediary being treated as payments to the insurer but payments to the intermediary not being treated as payments to the insured; intermediaries to have permanent financial capacity equal to 4 per cent of the sum of the annual premiums received, subject to a minimum of €15,000 (£9,400). The UK may adopt any combination of these four measures.

Suicide clause Clause in a life insurance policy enabling the insurer to avoid the contract if death occurs by suicide within a specified time (one or two years of inception). Some offices omit the exclusion altogether.

Suitability (FSA Conduct of Business Rule 5.3). This builds on *know your customer* (qv). The provider or independent intermediary must take reasonable steps to recommend an investment *suitable* for the customer. This applies when advising private customers, managing occupational schemes or stakeholder schemes, or promoting personal pensions schemes to groups of employees. The suitability requirements are especially stringent for packaged policies (qv) to private customers. Most suitability requirements call for a formal *suitability letter* to the customer explaining the reason for the recommendation. The letter must summarise the main consequences and any possible disadvantages of the transaction.

Suitability letter *See* SUITABILITY.

Sum insured The amount specified as the maximum amount that the insurer will pay under the policy. The limit is normally set by the insured and should set the full value at risk or, in some household policies, the full value of replacement, otherwise *average* (qv) may apply. The sum insured is normally used as the basis for calculating the premium.

Summary jurisdiction/proceedings Proceedings relating to criminal offences tried summarily by magistrates. Employers' liability and certain other liability policies pay for the solicitor's fee for representing the insured in a court of summary jurisdictions, provided the circumstances of an injury or event relate within the scope of the policy.

Summer *See* COOLING SEASON.

Sums insured in force The total face value of life policies currently in force.

Sunk This means the vessel must be fully submerged.

Sunrise clause A clause occasionally found in casualty reinsurance or claims-made contracts that provides coverage for losses reported to the (re)insurer during the term of the current contract, but resulting from pre-inception occurrences. Sunrise clauses are used to reactivate coverage that no longer exists due to the existence of a sunset clause. (*See* SUNSET CLAUSE).

Sunset clause Reinsurance or claims-made policy clause restricting cover to losses reported within a restricted period after the expiry of the policy. The period may be short, a 'mini tail', e.g. 60 days, or longer, e.g. three years for certain reinsurance contracts. *See* EXTENDED REPORTING PERIOD.

Sunshine cover Weather derivative (qv) based on the number of hours sunshine recorded in a given location over a specified period. Holiday resort businesses receive a payout when the recorded hours of sunshine are below the reference point and exceed the strike (qv). *See* PLUVIUS POLICY.

Supplier default cover A credit insurance term to describe an insurance against loss due to the insolvency of a supplier.

Suppliers' extension Business interruption (qv) policy that protects the insured against loss of gross profit following damage by an insured peril at the premises of a supplier, named or unnamed. Cover is expressed as a percentage of the gross profit to reflect the significance of the supplier(s).

Supply of Goods and Services Act 1982 (as amended) Any goods supplied under contracts governed by the Act must conform to the implied terms stated in the Sale of Goods Act 1979 (qv).

In addition any service provided must be carried out: (a) with reasonable skill and care; (b) for a reasonable price (unless a price has been agreed); (c) within a reasonable time (unless time is made of the essence, i.e. a date has been agreed at the time of making the contract).

Surety/suretyship *See* SURETYSHIP INSURANCE.

Suretyship insurance The insurer (the surety) provides a bond (qv) to guarantee the fulfilment of the obligations of its client (the obligor) to a third party (the obligee) derived from a contract relating to goods, services and performance. *See* CONSTRUCTION BONDS; COURT BONDS; GOVERNMENT BONDS; FIDELITY GUARANTEE.

Surplus 1. An accounting expression to describe the excess of income over expenditure of mutual companies rather than profit. 2. The amount ceded by way of reinsurance after the direct office has fixed its retention (qv). 3. In life insurance, the difference between assets and liabilities as revealed at the annual valuation, out of which bonuses are paid to with profits policyholders. 4. Pension fund surplus. The retirement benefits of final salary scheme members may be enhanced as a result of a surplus in their fund. ICTA, s.603, obliges the trustees to eliminate any surplus above the calculated statutory surplus. The retirement benefits can be improved or the employer may be permitted a contribution holiday (qv) or given a refund subject to tax at a rate of 40 per cent.

Surplus share treaty (SST) Proportional treaty that allocates risk, losses and premium on a variable-percentage basis between the cedant and reinsurer. The cedant's retention is a fixed monetary amount for each policy but the percentage reduces as the policy limit increases. Where the retention, called a line, is not exceeded, 100 per cent of the risk is retained by the cedant. The treaty capacity is expressed as a multiple of the cedant's line; a retention of £3m plus a four line treaty (£12m) means that the cedant is able to accept up £15m without recourse to further reinsurance facultatively or by a *second surplus treaty*. See Figure 8.

Surrender 1. The act of terminating an existing life insurance (whole life or endowment) and receiving the current surrender value (qv) in cash. 2. A pensions term to describe allocation (the giving up of part of a pension in return for a pension payable to the member's spouse or dependants) or commutation (qv).

Surrender value The cash due when a life insured terminates his policy before maturity. The existence of a reserve makes the payment possible but due allowance is made for expenses and the cover granted. Often there is no surrender value during the first two years.

Suspension order Opra (qv) suspension of a named person from continuing to act as a trustee of any occupational pension covered by the order (PA95, s.4). The trustee will be able to resume if the order is removed.

Swaps An alternative risk transfer between two parties having risks in the opposite direction. An insurer might swap a windstorm exposure with a building contractor who gets work if windstorm occurs. If it does not occur, the contractor's excess capacity is compensated from the insurer's additional profit following favourable claims experience.

Swaps (weather) Agreement between parties with diverging interest to exchange payment streams based on an underlying rate, index, instrument or asset and a 'notional amount'. An ice cream manufacturer wants a warm summer while an overseas tour operator expects a cool summer to boost his sales. If the temperature is above the reference temperature, 18°C, the ice cream company pays the tour operator out of their enhanced revenue. No premium

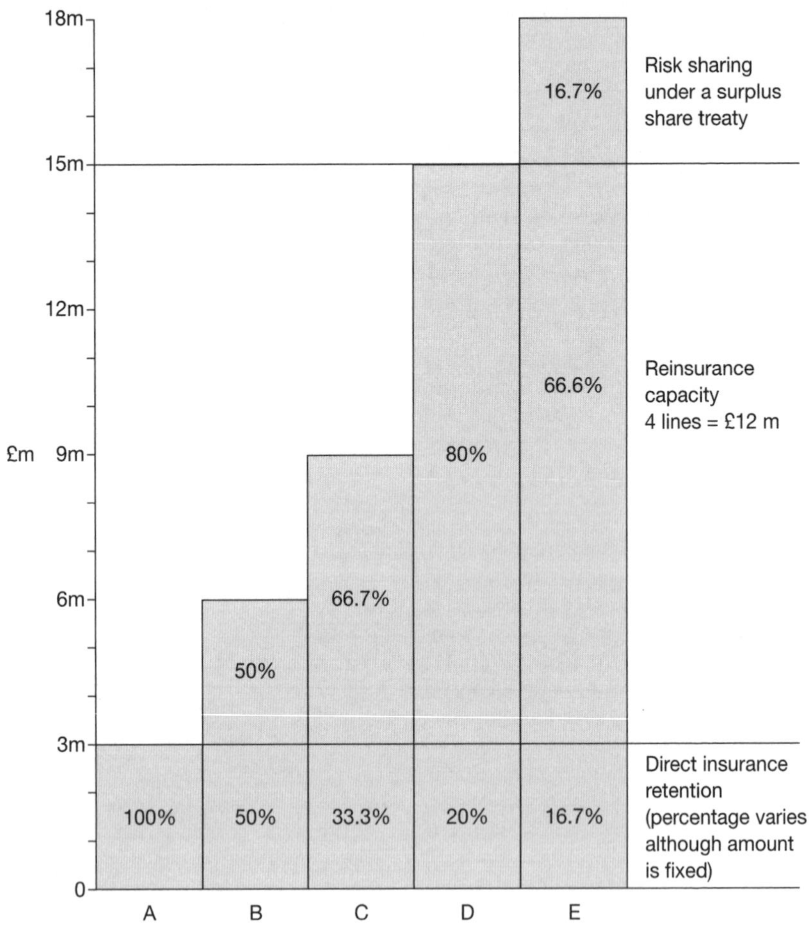

Figure 8. Surplus share treaty

changes hands, the upside risk of one party pays the downside risk of the other.

Sweat damage Damage to cargo caused by water condensing from humid air inside a container or the hold of the ship due to a fall in outside temperature.

Switching investments Most insurance companies issuing investment bonds and unitised funds (qv) offer a variety of investments linked to property, equity, managed and fixed-interest funds, and sometimes cash or gilt funds. In return for a fee most will permit the holder to switch his investment from one fund to another. As the money remains invested in the same life policy liability to tax does not arise as happens when shares are sold.

Sympathetic damage Where damaged cargo taints other cargo, the resultant loss is known as sympathetic damage. If the original damage was occasioned by an insured peril without any intervening cause then the sympathetic damage is covered by the policy. Goods liable to cause this type of damage include: hides and skins, certain cheeses, guano and carbon disulphide.

Syndicate A grouping of Lloyd's underwriters. *See* LLOYD'S SYNDICATES.

Syndicate allocated capacity The maximum amount of business that can be written by a Lloyd's syndicate, based on the capacity of all members of the syndicate.

Syndicate business forecast Document that must accompany the *regulatory business plan* (qv) covering business forecasts for the open years and the coming financial year. The forecast has to be in a standard electronic form.

Syndicate pseudonym The unique number issued to each syndicate at Lloyd's and by which it is subsequently identified. When subscribing to a risk an underwriter adds his syndicate number for transfer onto all documentary and computer entries. Each syndicate is allocated a unique three letter pseudonym to add to the syndicate number. The Lloyd's central accounting facility rejects any entries where the number and the pseudonym are not compatible.

Syndicate quota share reinsurance Provides a way for participation in risks underwritten at Lloyd's from outside the Lloyd's market. Lloyd's allows a syndicate to enter into quota share reinsurance (qv) with a non-Lloyd's reinsurer that it has approved. The reinsurance itself: (a) must not exceed 20 per cent of syndicate capacity although higher levels may be specially agreed; and (b) must relate to categories of business representing at least 15 per cent of the syndicate's capacity.

Syndicate stamp A document setting out the names of, and share taken by, the members of a Lloyd's syndicate. It defines the constitution of the syndicate for each year of account and must be registered at Lloyd's.

Synopsis sheet A Lloyd's term referring to a document presented in a non-marine claims settlement.

System of check System used by an insured to check on the work, honesty and accuracy of persons whose fidelity is insured under a fidelity guarantee insurance (qv). Under a *positions policy* (qv), individuals are not identified so the system of check on procedures and supervision becomes the key underwriting factor.

System of work *See* SAFE SYSTEM OF WORK.

T

Table of definitive numbers The list of underwriters showing the percentage, i.e. the signed line, each has accepted on the risk described in the policy. The list is attached to the policy.

Table of limits Table setting out different retentions (qv) for various classes of risk, defined by type, quality or other criteria. It is frequently used in surplus treaty reinsurance (qv).

Tail 1. A period beyond the expiry of an insurer's liability policy during which the insurer remains liable for losses that occurred during the policy period. *See* LONG-TAIL. 2. In the context of claims-made policies (qv) 'tail' means an *extended reporting period* (qv) or *discovery period.*

Tail series Marine cargo term referring to the last packages to be discharged which total an insufficient number to reach the agreed 'series' for the application of a franchise or a deductible.

Taint damage Damage to cargo the result of being stowed close to other cargo that has adversely affected it.

Take note A document issued in facultative reinsurance (qv) by a reinsurer indicating acceptance of a risk offered in the request note submitted by a cedant.

Target risk A very large risk that attracts the attention of brokers and insurers because of its size. It becomes widely offered in the market place. The term also describes a risk that is offered to many insurer because of its undesirable, hazardous features.

Targeted money purchase scheme Defined contribution scheme (qv) indicating the amount of benefit it proposes to pay. There is no obligation to pay this amount but the intention influences the level of contributions.

Tariff Minimum premium rates drawn up by a trade association for a particular class of business.

Tax havens Low tax areas offshore, particularly attractive to captives (qv). Bermuda tops the list followed by the Cayman Islands, Guernsey, Gibraltar and the Isle of Man. Taxes on profits are deferred until they are repatriated. Formation is more straightforward and, given that captives will have one main or only customer, this is appropriate as the procedures in the developed countries are stringent as their aim is to protect the general public.

Technical insolvency Impairment of an insurance company's assets to the point where it no longer maintains the required margin of solvency (qv) but which would not make a non-insurance company insolvent.

Technical reserves Funds available to the insurer to meet future claims on insurance that has been underwritten. In the UK the reserves must include: the unexpired premium reserve (qv); the unexpired risk reserve (qv); outstanding claims reserve; reserve for claims incurred but not yet reported (IBNR). Common prudence might call for additional reserves, e.g catastrophe reserve.

Technical words meaning rule Rule of construction meaning that where technical or legal words are used in a policy they are to be given their strict technical legal meaning unless the policy shows a different intention. Example: Four armed men stole cash from the insured. There was no other disturbance in the area, but technically there had been a 'riot' the definition of which (at that time) required only that there should be three persons with a common purpose threatening violence. The exclusion of 'riot' applied.

Technological changes risk Risk related to the rapid development of new technologies. Certain changes may have a significant impact on health and therefore employers' liability claims, e.g. repetitive strain injury (qv), from inceased use of visual display units. Technological changes have also impacted on the effectiveness of distribution channels leading to more insurance, especially personal lines (qv), being sold and serviced electronically. This could adversely affect insurers and intermediaries more reliant on traditional methods.

Technology risk Relates to failure of technology, e.g. systems failure, poor data quality, software problems, etc.

Temporary absence Absence from work through illness or employer-approved temporary leave of an active member of an occupational pension scheme. During the absence retirement benefits continue to accrue and the member remains covered by the death in service benefit for a maximum of 30 months for illness-related absence and 12 months for other employer-approved reasons. Females taking maternity leave are treated as having been in continuous service.

Temporary annuity An annuity (qv) under which the payments to the annuitant will cease at the end of a given period or at death whichever shall occur the first.

Temporary disablement The insured's inability to continue working for a period following accidental injury or sickness. Most personal accident policies (qv) provide a weekly/monthly benefit for a total or partial disablement for the duration of the disablement up to a maximum period, e.g 104 weeks in the case of accident.

Temporary insurance/assurance *See* TERM INSURANCE.

Temporary removal clause Commercial insurance clause covering items, other than stock, while temporarily removed for cleaning, renovating, repair or similar purposes to any situation in the UK or Republic of Ireland subject, normally, to a 10 per cent limit of the sum insured. Household policies cover contents in a bank, safe deposit or occupied house or in any other building where the insured or a family member is living or employed or carrying for up to 90 consecutive days subject to restrictions.

Temporary repairs Where a ship is temporarily repaired with a view to economy, or because there is no alternative, insurers pay for both the temporary and subsequent repairs not exceeding the insured value. Temporary repairs for the shipowner's convenience are not allowed except for liners running to advertised sailing schedules.

Tenant's liability The liability of a tenant under contract or tort for loss or damage to the premises leased to him. The custody and control exclusion (qv) in a public liability policy is overridden in connection with property leased to the insured to give cover. The tenant's liability section of a household contents policy indemnifies the insured in respect of liability for buildings damage when caused by insured peril.

Tender bond *See* BID BOND.

Tender clause International Hull Clause enabling the insurer to take tenders for repair after notification of a loss. The insurer can decide where repairs are carried out and veto a particular place of repair or particular ship-repairing firm. The insurer makes an allowance (30 per cent of insured value) for time lost between invitations to tender and acceptance.

Tenderers Lloyd's members wishing to surrender their capacity (qv). They enter a tender bid into the capacity auction (qv), stipulating the minimum amount (the floor limit), in multiples of 0.1p per pound of capacity they are prepared to accept. Subsequently, tender bids are matched against bids submitted by subscribers (qv) to ascertain the amount of capacity to be transferred and the price of the transaction. *See* CAPACITY TRANSFER MARKET.

Term insurance/temporary insurance Life policy that pays the sum insured only if death occurs within the policy term. If the life insured survives the term, there is no survival benefit. Decreasing term insurance (qv) and convertible term insurance (qv) are forms of term insurance.

Terminal bonus An additional bonus added to existing life insurance benefits when a 'with profits' policy becomes a claim by death or survival of the policy term. *See* BONUSES.

Terminal funding Pension arrangement, not common in the UK, except for a discretionary payment to meet the present value of a benefit when that benefit is due to commence.

Terminal illness The onset of a terminal illness is treated under some life policies as an insured event. It means that the sum insured is paid prior to death.

Termination of adventure clause In certain circumstances, e.g. war, the shipowner is able to terminate the contract of affreightment at a place other than the original destination. Provided notice is given to the cargo insurer and any additional premium paid, the goods are held covered until sold and delivered at the place of termination or during forwarding or delivering to the policy destination to a limit of 60 days after discharge at the final port.

Termination of risk Under a voyage policy (qv) this is when the ship has safely moored at anchor for 24 hours at the stated port of destination. To prevent overlap with the succeeding policy which normally runs 'at and from' (qv), that policy is claused 'no risk to attach until expiry of the previous policy'. Under the ordinary form of cargo policy the risk terminates upon the goods being safely landed at the port of destination but account has to be taken of the clauses that normally extend the cover. *See* WAREHOUSE TO WAREHOUSE.

'Terms to be agreed' (t.b.a.) Indication on a slip (qv) that certain contract terms have to be finally agreed. Marine underwriters commonly accept the risk at a rate to be agreed although other aspects of the risks, e.g. commencement date, can be covered by the term. An alternative term 't.b.a. l/u' means 'to be agreed with the leading underwriter (qv)'.

Territorial limits Geographical limits within which the insured event or loss must occur. Example: A public liability policy (qv) applies to occurrences within Great Britain, Northern Ireland, the Channel Islands or the Isle of Man plus temporary visits overseas for manual or non-manual work. Cover may be subject to a jurisdiction clause (qv).

Terrorism 1. The Pool Re (qv)/HM Treasury definition for (re)insurance purposes is: 'an act of any person acting on behalf of or in connection with any organisation which carries out activities directed towards the overthrowing or influencing of any government de jure or de facto by force or violence'. 2. Terrorism Act 2000, s.1 (qv): an act of terrorism is any *specified action*, the use or threat of which is designed to influence any government or to intimidate the public in order to advance a political religious or ideological purpose. The *specified actions* are actions which: (a) involve serious violence against a person; (b) cause serious damage to property; (c) endanger a person's life (other than the person committing the act); (d) create a serious risk to the health or safety of the public; or (e) are designed to interfere with or seriously disrupt an electronic system.

Terrorism Act 2000 Permanent UK-wide anti-terrorist legislation. It has a new definition of terrorism (qv) that applies to all kinds of terrorism.

Terrorism cover From 2003, means: insurance, not exceeding 12 months in total and written as per the general cover to which it attaches, and otherwise in accordance with the Pool Re (qv) Underwriting Manual, to cover all losses subject to certain terms and conditions and excluded losses (war, including riot and cyberterrorism). The reinsurance cover is now 'all risks' (extended from fire and explosion) irrespective of the original policy perils. The direct insurer may still insert a terrorism exclusion limiting the scope of the cover obliging the insured to 'buy back' to the level offered by Pool Re. Insurers may now modify their definitions of terrorism. Previously insurers linked terrorism with acts 'for political, religious, ideological or similar purposes'. Pool Re's definition links only to organisations seeking to overthrow governments. Cover offered by companies will come into line with that offered by Pool Re.

Terrorism Risk Insurance Act 2002 (TRIA) US statute to stimulate a competitively priced insurance market for terrorism insurance cover prompted by the events of 11 September 2001.

Test of reasonableness Means that a trader who uses an exclusion clause has to show that it is 'fair and reasonable' (Unfair Contract Terms Act 1977 (qv)). The court decides but, under the test, considers whether the clause can be shown to be 'fair and reasonable' considering the circumstances known to the parties at the time the contract was made. It considers the bargaining strength of the parties and other relevant circumstances.

Thatcham (Motor Insurance Repair Research Centre) World-leading automotive research and technology centre. It provides the automotive and insurance industries with valuable commercial information. (Visit *www.thatcham.org* for ratings on car security, safety factors, etc.)

Theft Act 1968 An Act that changed the legal definitions set out in the Larceny Act 1916. The new definitions caused insurers to adopt their own definitions of 'theft' rather than import definitions from the Act. *See* FORCIBLE AND VIOLENT MEANS.

'Thieves' According to the Marine Insurance Act 1906, Rule of Construction number 9, the term 'thieves' does not cover clandestine theft or a theft committed by any one of the ship's company, whether crew or passengers. The peril in a marine policy appears to cover loss or damage by assailing and violent thieves. Institute Cargo Clauses B and C do not cover any form of theft. The International Hull Clauses 1/11/02 cover (clause 2.1.3) covers 'violent theft from persons outside the vessel' and in 2.1.5 'piracy' is covered.

Third Motor Insurance Directive, Directive 90/232 Requires mutual recognition within all EC states of compulsory motor insurance arranged in another EC state. Where a vehicle is involved in an accident in another member state and the compulsory insurance requirements of the two states are at different levels, the higher level will apply. Road Traffic Act 1988, s.145(3), provides that compulsory insurance must cover UK liability and that of another EC state where an accident occurs.

Third Non-Life Directive 1992 Completed the move to a single market by creating freedom of establishment. It abolished the right of an EC state to insist upon authorising the activities of an insurer established in another state whether established in the host state or selling directly into it from an establishment elsewhere in the EC.

Third Parties (Rights Against Insurers) Act 1930 If an insured becomes insolvent after incurring a liability to a third party but before compensation is paid, the rights in his liability policy vest in the third party. The third party's claim against the insurer is no better than the insured's claim so the insurer could, for example, plead that the policy was voidable due to a breach by the insured.

Third party 1. Someone other than the policyholder who has been injured or whose property has been damaged. 2. Person brought into legal proceedings by the defendant as being a person considered wholly or partly liable for the loss, e.g. retailer joins manufacturer in a product liability case. *See* CIVIL LIABILITY (CONTRIBUTION) ACT 1978; THIRD PARTY PROCEEDINGS.

Third Party Fire and Theft Differs from third party motor (qv) only in that it covers damage to the vehicle if caused by fire or theft or attempt at theft. *See* MOTOR INSURANCE COMPREHENSIVE COVER.

Third party insurance Synonymous with public liability, it distinguishes cover from a policy covering liability to employees. In aviation insurance the term third party insurance distinguishes general third party cover from legal liability to passengers in the insured's own aircraft. A captive company in the open market also uses the term in connection with the insurance business for parties other than its parent company. Marine third party liability is the primary business of Protection and Indemnity Clubs (qv).

Third party motor cover Covers liability for third party (qv) injury and property damage, including emergency treatment, and liability for accidents caused by passengers. The policy exceeds the level of cover required under Road Traffic Act compulsory requirements that require cover only in connection with vehicles used *on a road or other public place*. The normal third party policy is not so restricted.

Third party notice/proceedings Process by which the defendant in a civil action may obtain a court order to include a third party in the proceedings because he seeks a remedy or indemnity from that party. A retailer faced with a product liability claim might seek to join the manufacturer in the action, perhaps prompted by the insurer in pursuing subrogation rights (qv). This avoids the costs of a separate action. *See* THIRD PARTY 2.

Third party sharing agreement Market agreement between participating motor insurers. Where two motorists are involved in an incident and third parties are injured, the insurers agree not to apportion blame but share third party claims equally. Any injury to the driver of either vehicle or any injury to any employee of the insured is excluded by the agreement.

3/4ths Collision Liability Clause *See* RUNNING DOWN CLAUSE.

Three-year accounting system Lloyd's system whereby an underwriting year is not closed until the end of the third year following inception of the underwriting year and all premiums and claims for that year are accounted to that year. An account opened on 1 January 2003 will be open until 31 December 2005. A reserve for outstanding claims liability is then carried forward to the next open year by a *reinsurance to close* (qv). Lloyd's is now moving to 'annual accounting', the approach used by insurance companies.

Threshold conditions Minimum conditions that a firm must satisfy to gain and retain FSA authorisation (qv) to undertake regulated activities (qv). The conditions relate to: legal status; office location; claims representative; resources; suitability.

Tick A payment per unit of deviation recorded in a weather index. For example, £2,500 per Heating Degree Day is the tick, meaning a payout based on £2,500 times the number of HDDs in excess of the strike (qv). *See* WEATHER DERIVATIVES.

Tied annuity option Option to use the proceeds of a pension plan to buy an annuity from the insurer concerned at its current market rate as an alternative to taking the guaranteed annuity option (qv). *See* also OPEN MARKET OPTION.

Time and Distance Policies Discounting mechanism using an aggregate excess of loss cover (qv). The reinsurer agrees to pay the cedant a fixed schedule of payments at future dates in return for an initial premium representing the net present value of the scheduled losses. The contracts are a form of financial reinsurance (qv) with little or no risk transfer. The principal uncertainty is date of settlement and this makes the arrangement attractive to long-tail insurers.

Time charter The charterer has the use of the vessel for a specified time. The shipowner supplies the crew and the provisions.

Time deductible/excess An excess (qv) or deductible (qv) expressed in terms of hours or days as opposed to a monetary amount. Under an engineering consequential loss policy (qv) it is customary to exclude the first 24 hours (or some other period) of any period of interruption following damage to or breakdown of plant or machinery.

Time loss insurance Form of business interruption insurance (qv) that pays an amount for each day's stoppage of the business. The system is used on occasions in some engineering consequential loss policies based on time lost following machinery breakdown.

Time on risk A period during which the insurer has been on risk for an insurance that has been discontinued.

Time policy A policy that insures the subject-matter, normally a hull (qv), for a stated period of time (Marine Insurance Act 1906, s.25(1)) as opposed to a specific voyage. Hull risks are usually insured in this way using the International Hull Clauses or the earlier Time Clauses.

Timing risk 1. Risk attaching to an insurer that losses become payable earlier than expected. This prevents the insurer from earning his anticipated investment income or requires the premature liquidation of assets or raising loans to satisfy the claims. Financial reinsurance methods (qv) are primarily concerned with allowing insurers to smooth out losses over time. 2. The risk that an investor buys or sells investments at the wrong time.

Tinnitus A noise in the ears that may accompany loss of hearing. Tinnitus may have a significant effect on the damages awarded in claims based on occupational deafness (qv).

Tmax The maximum temperature for a given day as defined by 12:00 a.m. to 12:00 p.m. *See* AVERAGE DAILY TEMPERATURE.

Tmin The minimum temperature for a given day as defined by 12:00 a.m. to 12:00 p.m. *See* AVERAGE DAILY TEMPERATURE.

'To pay as cargo' A buyer with an interest in cargo that is in transit may arrange a policy supplementary to the cargo insurance. This will be worded 'to pay as cargo' for an increased value as the amount under the cargo policy may be inadequate to protect the buyer's interest. The phrase means that the supplementary policy will contribute pro rata to any claim paid by the primary insurer. *See* INCREASED VALUE.

'To pay as may be paid' A reinsurance clause term indicating that the reinsurer will follow claims paid on the original policy but only in so far as the reinsured is legally liable to make the payment.

Tonner reinsurance 1. Form of total loss only reinsurance of: (a) vessels over or between specified tonnages; or (b) aircraft over or between specified hull values and/or seating capacities. The policies are effected on *policy proof of interest* (qv) without the benefit of salvage to the insurer. 2. An aviation reinsurance under which the reinsurer agrees to pay a fixed amount if an air crash results in a stated number of deaths.

Tontine bonus method A method of distributing bonuses to 'with profits' life insurance policyholders which has been used in the US but not in the UK. There are variations but the general principle is that declared surpluses are retained for ultimate distribution to the policyholders who survive a certain fixed period.

Tool of trade risk Risk arising out of the use of a special type (qv), such as a mobile digger, as a tool of trade, i.e. used for its intended function, digging, lifting etc. This risk is distinguished from the road risk necessitating compulsory third party motor insurance. Tool of trade risks are of a third party nature, e.g. liability for damage to underground cables, and insurable under commercial motor, public liability or engineering insurances.

Tooley Street fire London's second largest fire (1861) is a landmark in the development of fire insurance. It highlighted inadequacies in both the method of pricing fire insurance and fire-fighting arrangements. Differential rates of charges were introduced to penalise unsatisfactory features and reward favourable ones.

Top and drop layer/arrangement *Drop down cover* (qv) means the unexhausted limit of the top layer of excess of loss cover drops down to a stated lower layer(s) to respond to further losses when that layer is exhausted. The reinsured uses a *back up policy* (qv) to cover the risk of the top layer itself being exhausted by an earlier loss. The risk can be mitigated by not combining too many layers in one top and drop arrangement when the total amount of cover is limited. Top and drop may be *whole account* or *class specific*. Dropping to the bottom of the programme is termed 'cascade'. *Top and step* is a variation, the top layer only drops to reinstate the immediate underlying layer.

Top and step *See* TOP AND DROP LAYER.

Top-up cover *See* GAP; VEHICLE REPLACEMENT COVER.

Tornado A storm of wind of extreme violence. It originates in a funnel-shaped cloud that rotates. The barometric pressure may drop so severely and rapidly that buildings may actually explode from within.

Torrey Canyon Disaster A major disaster that alerted all countries to the risks and dangers of oil pollution. On 18 March 1967 the Torrey Canyon (a Liberian oil tanker) went aground 24 kilometres north east of the Scilly Isles liberating her cargo of crude oil. On 24 March 1967 there was a 64 kilometre long oil slick with an average width of 16 kilometres off Lands End. The Merchant Shipping (Oil Pollution) Act 1971 was passed in order to make oil pollution insurance compulsory for certain tankers.

Tort Wrongful act, apart from breach of contract, that causes damage or harm to others for which compensation or other remedies may be obtained in a civil action. Negligence (qv) and nuisance (qv) are common torts.

Tortfeasor The party who commits a tort (qv).

Total cost of risk Insurance premiums paid for the benefit of risk transfer (qv), costs of resources engaged in the risk management process, i.e. risk evaluation, risk control, etc., including public sector fire and police authorities, uninsured losses and self-insured losses make up the total cost of risk.

Total earnings scheme Career average scheme (qv) meaning that a member's pension is worked out as a fraction of their total earnings while being a member of the scheme.

Total loss Subject-matter of insurance is lost, destroyed or damaged beyond economic repair. See actual total loss (qv) and constructive total loss (qv).

Total loss of part Marine cargo provision whereby the loss of whole package in loading or discharge or the loss of a whole craft load shall be treated as a total loss of that part of the cargo and consequently will not be subject to a franchise.

Total loss only Marine insurances, particularly hull facultative reinsurances, are sometimes arranged on the basis that the (re)insurer is liable only in the event of a total loss. Cover may or may not include arranged or compromised total losses, sue and labour charges, and salvage charges.

Total return swap Term from the equity derivative markets to describe a swap under which one party pays all dividends received from, and the periodic appreciation in, a specified share and the other pays interest plus periodic depreciation in that share. The technique is now applied to credit derivatives as a means of selling the credit risk.

'Touch and stay at any port or place whatsoever' A marine clause which only permits the vessel to call at the customary ports on the voyage and at ports for purposes connected with the voyage. Such calls do not amount to deviation (qv).

TOVALOP Means 'Tanker Owners' Voluntary Agreement Concerning Liability for Oil Pollution'. An agreement, supported by most tanker owners worldwide, whereby owners agree to pay for clean-up costs incurred by governments in respect of oil discharged from tankers belonging to the owners. Each member insures his liability under the Agreement.

Tow and assist clause International Hull Clause (10.2) stating that the vessel will not be towed except where towing is customary or the ship is in need of assistance to the first place of safety. It is also provided that the ship shall not undertake towage or salvage services under a previously arranged contract.

Tracing services 1. Tracing service provided by Opra (qv) through Pensions Registry Scheme (qv). It helps former pension scheme members track pension scheme memberships relating to earlier employment periods. Mergers and acquisitions over time may make tracing former memberships difficult for individuals. 2. DWP runs a tracing service to help schemes trace information on their deferred pensioners. 3. Employers' Liability Code (qv).

Trade association clauses The International Underwriters' Asssociation (qv) has drafted standard clauses for a number of trade associations to give them the comprehensive cover they require. The trades affected include: rubber, timber, coal, sugar and flour.

Trade contents This term often appears as an insured item under the combined policies effected by small businesses. It may bring together in one sum stock, trade fixtures, fittings and machinery. An alternative is to cover stock separately while combining other forms of trade property into a single figure under the title trade contents.

Trade endorsements Endorsements (qv) to reflect the requirements of a trade, or category of risk, within a particular trade. They may be restrictive or expansive. *See* RESTRICTIVE ENDORSEMENTS.

Trade name restoration (TNR) Food-borne illness damages the reputation and therefore income stream of restaurants and similar businesses. TNR provides protection and crisis management against the financial costs of: (a) food-borne illness business interruption; (b) adverse media; and (c) reputation crisis management.

Trade plate basis A method of rating motor traders' road risks policies. The insurer charges a flat rate for each set of trade plates. Cover is limited to vehicles carrying a set of specified trade plates. Alternative methods of rating: named plate basis (qv) and points basis (qv).

Trade wastes Wastes of organic and inorganic origin discharged by industrial and commercial concerns. Organic wastes are discharged on a considerable scale by the food industries: canneries, dairies, breweries, abbatoirs and fish-meat factories. Other significant waste generators include paper-mills, tanneries, petro-chemical works, textile manufacturers and laundries. Inorganic wastes include acids, alkalis, cyanides, sulphides and the salts of arsenic, lead, copper, chromium and zinc. Underwriters concern themselves as to the methods of waste disposal used by firms as considerable pollution damage and cleaning up costs can arise. Any discharge of waste into the air, soil or water can create major problems not least for liability insurers. *See also* WATER POLLUTION.

Traded endowment policy (TEP) Endowment policy (qv) that has been sold by the original policyholder to an investor before the policy matures. The policy is assigned to the new owner who pays all future premiums but who ultimately receives the policy proceeds. The insurer is notified of the assignment. The original owner 'trades' his policy when the market value exceeds the surrender value (qv).

Trading Warranties. 'Trade' in marine insurance means where the vessel navigates. Underwriters control navigation risks by means of the Institute Warranties (qv).

Transfer club Group of employers and occupational schemes that have agreed to deal with transfer payments (qv) in the same way.

Transfer credit The benefit purchased for a member when a transfer payment (qv) is made by his ex-pension scheme to his new scheme. Pensionable service in the old scheme is linked to service in the new scheme.

Transfer of business A procedure whereby an insurance company can, subject to supervision by the FSA, transfer its rights and obligations under policies issued to another insurer without obtaining the formal consent of the policyholders concerned.

Transfer payment Amount paid by one pension scheme to another when its former member joins another occupational pension scheme or starts a personal pension to which his benefits are transferred. The transfer payment may be made in accordance with the scheme rules (qv) or in the exercise of a member's right under PSA93.

Transfer value The value of a pension in a previous employment when transferred to a new employer's pension scheme. An occupational scheme is not bound to accept a transfer value.

Transit Clause/Duration Institute Cargo Clause 8 (1/1/82) incorporating the *warehouse to warehouse clause* (qv). Cover attaches when the goods leave the warehouse, etc., at named place of origin, continues during the ordinary course of transit, and ceases on soonest of arrival at place of storage at named destination or 60 days after discharge. If the intended destination is altered after discharge, cover ceases on commencement of transit to new destination, unless it has already ceased under the above conditions. The clause allows for trans-shipment (qv).

Transit insurance *See* GOODS IN TRANSIT INSURANCE.

Trans-shipment Transfer of goods from one vessel or conveyance to another, often contracted for in 'through' bills of lading. The Transit Clause (qv) provides continuity of cover following any forced discharge, reshipment or trans-shipment or during any permitted variation provided the original destination is unchanged.

Travel insurance Wide choice of policies for the business and holiday traveller. A typical policy covers loss or theft of luggage; loss or theft of money and documents; cancellation of holiday due to unforeseen circumstances; delayed departure; personal accident benefits; passport cover (qv); liability insurance and emergency medical benefits; together with other options depending on the type of holiday or trip. Cover can be on an individual, group or family basis, single trip or annual policy. Special policies are available for winter sports and other hazardous pursuits.

Treaty firm Firm whose head office is situated in an EEA state (qv) other than the UK and which is incorporated in that state. Automatic authorisation (qv) is given, subject to conditions that include a 'consent notice' from the home state regulator, to firms exercising EC Treaty rights. Authorisation by the home state regulator provides the firm with a 'passport' to carry on business in the UK. *See* SINGLE INSURANCE MARKET.

Treaty reinsurance Under treaty arrangements the cedant agrees to offer, and the reinsurer agrees to accept, all risks of a defined class. This enables the cedant to grant immediate cover for 'large' risks without first seeking the reinsurer's consent. *See* QUOTA SHARE; SURPLUS LINE; EXCESS OF LOSS, and compare with FACULTATIVE REINSURANCE.

Trespass A tort (qv) committed with 'force and violence' on the person, property or rights of another. All three types are actionable per se without proof of damage unlike *nuisance* where the interference is indirect and requires such proof. Wrongful interference with goods is covered in the Tort (Interference with Goods) Act 1977. Liability policies do not cover intentional acts but most public liability policies cover liability from accidental trespass, false arrest, false imprisonment and invasion of privacy. Some cover also exists in respect of loss of documents under professional indemnity policies.

Trigger The event or circumstances that activates the insurer's liability to the insured under the policy. Contrast losses-occurring (qv) liability policies with claims-made (qv) policies. *See* LIABILITY SEQUENCE; TRIPLE TRIGGER THEORY; GROSS DOMESTIC PRODUCT TRIGGER; MULTI-OVAL TRIGGER.

Triple trigger theory/continuous trigger theory An *occurrence trigger theory* (qv) that charges the loss against *any* policy in force from the time of first exposure to a harmful situation to the time of manifestation of the injury or disease. *Triple* is derived from: (a) initial exposure; (b) continuing exposure (injury-in-residence); and (c) manifestation. The theory triggers *any* policy for its full limit not just a share. The insured can select which policies should respond with the possibility of *stacking limits* (qv), aggregate limits of indemnity from different policy years. The theory has not been uniformly adopted across the US, its birthplace. Other theories, e.g exposure theory (qv), injury-in-fact theory (qv), and the manifestation theory (qv), have also found favour. Insurers use a *claims series clause* (qv) in order to trigger continuing losses from one original cause into the policy year of first occurrence. *See* also BATCH CLAUSE; LIABILITY SEQUENCE.

Trivial pension Small pension that can be encashed without affecting IR approval.

True monthly premiums Life insurance premium that is paid monthly and is not an instalment of an annual premium. Consequently when death occurs there is no deduction from the claim payment in respect of the premiums that would have been payable had the policy run its full term in the year of death.

Trust An arrangement under which property is transferred to a person called the trustee or several such persons. Trustees are under an obligation to keep the property or deal with it for the benefit of others, the beneficiaries. The trust is created by a trust deed. Occupational pension schemes are set up under trust deeds. *See* PARTNERSHIP; MARRIED WOMEN'S PROPERTY ACT 1882; TRUST POLICIES.

Trust deed The legal document setting out the responsibilities of the trustees, i.e. holders of property, and the rights of the beneficiaries. In the case of unit trusts (qv) the trust deed concerns the trustees and the fund managers and lays down the framework within which managers must operate.

Trust policy A policy that forms the property to be held in trust for the beneficiary. People whose capital is used in their business or profession often effect whole life insurances on trust under the Married Women's Property Act 1882 (qv) for the protection of dependants putting the policy beyond the reach of creditors. A child's deferred insurance could also be arranged in trust for a child under the same Act. *See* PARTNERSHIP INSURANCE.

Trustbusting A colloquial term for *pension scheme liberation services* (qv).

Trustee Act 1925, s.20(4) Money recovered under an insurance on property held in trust may be applied by the trustee (or by the court) in reinstating the property, but the consent of any person whose consent is necessary under the trust instrument must be obtained.

Trustee Act 2000 An Act that gives pension scheme trustees powers to invest trust funds freely, largely irrespective of what powers are given by the deed, but introduces a range of further duties to ensure that all beneficiaries' interest are protected with greater diligence. The Act applies to trusts established after 1 February 2001.

Trustee(s) The person or persons (corporation or individual) appointed to carry out the terms of a trust (qv). A trustee has an insurable interest in respect of the legal right or interest in the trust property vested in him if permitted or directed by the trust deed.

Trustees' undertaking Given by the trustees to the scheme actuary. This results in the trustees having to provide such information as the actuary may require and any items prescribed by regulations and professional guidance published by both the Institute and the Faculty of Actuaries.

TUPE-Transfer of Undertakings (Protection of Employment) Regulations 1981 Provide that the acquirer of a business takes over the employees involved on their existing terms and conditions so that they can sue the new employer as if still employed by their original employer. Liability for accidental injury is also transferred but the insurer who pays is the one receiving the premium at the time of the accident (*Bernadone* v. *Pall Mall Services* (2000) and *Haringey Health Care Trust* v. *NHS Trust*).

Turnbull Report Guidance published in 1999 to assist the directors of UK listed companies in complying with the internal control requirements of the Combined Code on Corporate Governance (qv) to which 'Turnbull' is appended. Includes guidance on risk management related to operational risk (qv) and compliance risk as well as financial risk. *See* CORPORATE GOVERNANCE.

Turnover The monetary value of sales in a period of time. The figure reflects the level of activity in a firm or organisation and may be used to measure exposure (qv) as in products liability. *See* ADJUSTABLE POLICIES; STANDARD TURNOVER.

Twenty-fourths method A method of computing the unearned premium reserve (qv). It is assumed that, on average, policies run from the middle of the month of inception. The appropriate number of twenty-fourths of premiums relating to the policies commencing in each month is then carried forward as unearned.

Two-risk warranty A warranty used in catastrophe excess of loss reinsurance (qv) to ensure that the reinsurance is not invoked unless at least two distinct risks are involved. Involvement in single losses applies to working cover excess of loss treaty (qv). The warranty is used in life, personal accident, catastrophe property and reinsurance in the London excess market (LMX).

U

Uberrimae fidei Latin phrase meaning 'of the fullest confidence'. *See* UTMOST GOOD FAITH.

UK Equities Usually means ordinary shares issued by a UK incorporated company, not being an investment trust, and which are quoted in the official list of a recognised stock exchange in the UK or traded on the Alternative Investment Market.

UK Margin of Solvency Insurers whose head office is not in the UK must maintain a margin of solvency (qv) and a UK margin of solvency. *See* SOLVENCY MARGINS.

Ullage The loss of liquid, also called trade loss, when shipped in bulk or in casks, and occurring during a voyage as a result of shrinkage or evaporation. Consequently, the insurer pays only for leakage losses in excess of a stated figure. *See* LEAKAGE.

Ultimate net loss clause 1. The amount that a reinsured can recover under an excess of loss reinsurance (qv). This is usually defined as all payments in respect of the claim, including loss adjustment expenses (qv) but excluding the reinsured's office expenses, less recoveries by way of salvage, other reinsurances or otherwise. The clause allows payment to the reinsured before all recoveries have been made and before the *ultimate net loss* has been determined. 2. In an *umbrella liability policy* (qv) it is the amount actually paid or payable for which the insured is liable (including or excluding defence costs) after deducting recoveries and reinsurance that inure to the benefit of the contract.

Ultra vires Beyond the power. An action outside the proper authority of a corporation or a director or officer for which they may be liable.

Umbrella arrangement Permission granted by a Lloyd's broker to a non-Lloyd's broker who uses the name, pseudonym, etc., of the Lloyd's broker to place business with or on behalf of underwriting members. The non-Lloyd's broker must intend becoming a Lloyd's registered broker within three years and confine the arrangement to one Lloyd's broker. The non-Lloyd's broker must undertake to submit to all Lloyd's bye-laws and regulations. The Lloyd's broker is responsible for premiums due to the underwriting members.

Umbrella brokers A broker operating in the Room (qv) at Lloyd's under an *umbrella arrangement* (qv).

Umbrella cover Takes the form of excess of loss reinsurance treaty to protect the reinsured against an accumulation of retained losses arising from one event under different classes of businesses. Example: A storm causing widespread losses affecting property, motor, marine and aviation accounts. Alternative terms: whole account (qv); back-up cover (qv).

Umbrella liability policy Liability policy with high limits covering over the top of underlying, primary, liability insurances subject to a self-insured retention. Cover is usually broader than the primary cover and may have a *drop down provision* (qv).

Unaligned member Lloyd's syndicate member who has no connection with the controller of the managing agent of that syndicate.

Unallocated assets Pension scheme assets that have not yet been used to provide pension benefits.

Unapproved scheme Occupational pension scheme that is not approved by the Inland Revenue. It forgoes the tax advantages of approved schemes.

Underfunding Occurs where a defined benefit scheme's assets are less than its accrued liabilities. Under the minimum funding requirement (qv) the employer and the trustees must agree a schedule to eliminate the deficit over a five-year period. Extra contributions from the employer may correct the position.

Under-insurance Occurs when the amount of insurance is less than the full value of the property insured and means that the insured pays a smaller premium than that required as the rate is fixed on the basis of full values being insured. It leads to partial loss claims being scaled down by *average* (qv). *See* FIRST LOSS POLICIES.

Underlying layer The basic or primary layer of coverage, the initial policy that will respond to the covered loss. Only when the limits of the underlying policy have been exhausted will the other respective layers of insurance respond, as with the case of an excess or umbrella policy in liability insurance.

Underwriter Term originated in Lloyd's coffee house when merchants signed their names at the foot of a slip to signify acceptance of a part of a maritime risk. The term is used to refer to an insurer or an individual skilled in the process of selecting risks for an insurance company or Lloyd's syndicate. *See* ACTIVE UNDERWRITER.

Underwriter's guarantee *See* GENERAL AVERAGE GUARANTEE.

Underwriting Process of evaluating and pricing risks proposed for insurance. Risks are often considered in the context of the class of business that the insurer underwrites and the insurer decides whether a particular risk is acceptable and, if so, whether the normal terms and conditions will apply. The underwriter monitors the classes of business underwritten and regularly reviews rates and strategies.

Underwriting agency A registered underwriting agent is a firm or company managing and carrying out underwriting for an insurance company or Lloyd's syndicates if permitted by the Council of Lloyd's. Lloyd's distinguishes between a managing agent (who manages one or more syndicates) and a members' agent who acts for members in other capacities and may introduce them to syndicates run by managing agents. Most agents conduct both functions.

Underwriting capacity/limit The maximum amount an insurer or reinsurer is willing to accept in the event of a single loss in a given period. It also refers to the aggregate amount accepted in any one location or in a given period of time. The limit may be set by internal guidelines, by the regulatory authorities, or by restrictions agreed with a reinsurer or co-insurer.

Underwriting excess of loss reinsurance An alternative term for working cover excess of loss (qv).

Underwriting policy clause Obliges a reinsured to consult with, or seek approval from, the reinsurer when proposing to make material changes to established acceptance and underwriting practices.

Underwriting profit/loss Money earned or lost by an insurer in its underwriting (qv) activities as distinct from money earned from investments. Also called a technical profit calculated by earned premiums less losses, loss adjustment costs and other underwriting expenses incurred.

Underwriting reserves *See* TECHNICAL RESERVES.

Underwriting risk The risk that underwriting results will deviate adversely from the risk allowed for in assessing the premiums required to cover the pure risks accepted by the insurer. Poor underwriting decisions have an adverse impact on profitability.

Underwriting year For accounting and classification purposes it is the treaty year in which a contract was written or renewed. Applies to proportional reinsurance (qv). *See* UNDERWRITING YEAR SYSTEM.

Underwriting year system Method in proportional treaty reinsurance (qv) whereby all premiums and losses relating to an *underwriting year* (qv) are accounted to that year regardless of when such losses arise or when such premiums and losses are paid.

Undiscovered loss clause Cargo clause providing cover for losses that are not discovered until the boxes are opened after the termination of the risk. Externally the box or package appears in good condition, but contains *concealed damage.*

Unearned Premium Insurance *See* AVIATION UNEARNED PREMIUM INSURANCE.

Unearned premium/unearned premium reserve That part of the premium or reinsurance premium applicable to the unexpired portion of the policy. The unearned premium reserve is the accounting provision at a specific time that reflects the total amount of unearned premiums. The effect is to write down current profits by the reserve and carry it forward as income in the next financial year.

Unenforceable contract A contract defective only in the sense that it cannot be enforced by direct legal action. The contract is otherwise valid and subsisting, so a transferee of property gains a good title and any deposit paid may be retained. A contract of fidelity guarantee (qv) not in writing would be unenforceable (the Statute of Frauds).

Unexpired risk reserve Provision to safeguard the insurer against any deficiency in the unearned premium reserve (qv). The risk reserve also allows for possible claims under contingency policies that run in perpetuity and do not lend themselves to annual apportionment.

Unfair Contract Terms Act 1977 Governs a trader's ability to restrict his liability. Any clause restricting negligence liability for death/injury is void. The following clauses will be void unless *reasonable*: (a) those attempting to restrict negligence liability for loss or damage to property; (b) standard term clauses limiting liability for breach contract; (iii) those requiring a consumer to indemnify any other party for negligence or breach of contract. It also provides that a trader cannot exclude a consumer's statutory rights under the Sale of Goods Act 1979 (qv). The Act lays down a *test of reasonableness* (qv). Insurance policies are exempt from the Act.

Unfair dismissal A statutory claim (Employment Rights Act 1996) entitling eligible employees to a compensation award by a tribunal. Dismissal is unfair if the employer fails to bring it within one of five permitted reasons: viz; conduct; capability; redundancy; illegality; or some other substantial reason. Employers can insure under Employment Practices Liability Insurance (qv). Compare with wrongful dismissal (qv).

Unfair Terms in Consumer Contract Regulations 1999 Stipulates that a term which has *not* been individually negotiated in a consumer contract is unfair if it causes *a significant imbalance* in the rights and obligations of the parties to the consumer's detriment. The Director General of Fair Trading must consider any complaint made to him about the fairness of any contract term drawn up for general use The Regulations apply generally and so affect all insurance contracts with private individuals, but terms defining the product are not covered. This means that an insurer can limit the cover by including an excess (qv). Other insurance terms may be deemed unfair.

Unfunded scheme A 'pay as you go' pension scheme that does not acquire and build up assets to fund the pension. State pensions are unfunded.

Unfunded Unapproved Retirement Benefits Scheme (UURBS) Pension arrangement for which IR approval is not sought and under which there is no pre-funding. The employer provides benefits out of income for employees earning more than the earnings cap (qv). *See* FUNDED UNAPPROVED RETIREMENT BENEFITS (FURBS) (qv).

Uniform accrual The method of determining benefits for early leavers (qv) under the terms of the 'preservation' conditions of social security legislation. Retirement benefits are treated as being earned equally over the period of potential pensionable service to normal pension date.

Uniform bonus system *See* UNIFORM COMPOUND REVERSIONARY BONUS; UNIFORM SIMPLE REVERSIONARY BONUS.

Uninsurable risk A risk that cannot be insured because an essential condition is not present. It may: (a) lack insurable interest; (b) defy quantification; (c) entail widespread losses (e.g. war damage to property on land); (d) create excessive cost; (e) be speculative; (f) may reflect certainty rather than uncertainty; (h) be contrary to public policy.

Uninsured drivers Drivers not covered by third party insurance as required by the Road Traffic Act 1988. Their injured victims can secure compensation under the Uninsured Driver Agreement 1999 (qv). The Third Motor Insurance Directive 90/232 requires the victim to bear the first £175 of property damage, but there is no recovery for a person who knowingly enters an uninsured or stolen vehicle.

Uninsured Drivers' Agreement 1999 Agreement between the Motor Insurers Bureau (qv) and the government whereby the MIB compensates the victims of negligent uninsured drivers who had no insurance or only defective insurance. In the latter instance the vehicle insurer deals with the victim's claim but has a right of recovery against the negligent motorist. *See* UNTRACED DRIVERS AGREEMENT.

Uninsured losses/uninsured loss recovery Losses not covered by a first party insurance (qv) such as an accidental damage excess under a comprehensive car insurance and cost of hiring an alternative car. The losses may be recoverable from a negligent third party.

Uninsured standing charges clause Business interruption clause (qv) providing that, if any standing charge (qv) is not insured, a proportionate reduction will be made in the increased cost of working part of the claim.

Uninsured working expenses *See* SPECIFIED WORKING EXPENSES; BUSINESS INTERRUPTION INSURANCE.

Unistatus annuity rates Same rates regardless of marital status, gender or having dependants or not.

Unit allocation In a unit-linked insurance contract, it is the percentage of the premium that is used to buy units. It varies according to the charging structure of the policy and the age of the policyholder.

Unit-linked annuity Annuity (qv) where the payment to the annuitant is linked to the performance of underlying assets, e.g. a particular investment fund. Performance depends on current investment market conditions. A pension scheme member taking a particular view on the value of the underlying assets could opt for such an annuity.

Unit-linked life insurance Life policy in which profits depend on the performance of units in an invested fund. Part of the premium purchases guaranteed life cover but most is invested in a fund that invests in unitised funds. The policyholder's investment is expressed in units of the underlying investment vehicle and their value can rise or fall. At maturity the policyholder receives the net value of all units purchased for him or the units themselves.

Unit trust Collective investment where investors (unitholders) obtain an interest in a fund by purchasing units from the managers knowing that they can resell their units to the managers at a price reflecting the stock market's value of the trust's investments on the day. FSA (qv) authorised trusts are empowered to sell units directly to members of the public. Many unit trust schemes are unit-linked life insurance (qv) schemes. *See* UNIT TRUST SECTORS. (Visit *www.investmentfunds.org.uk*).

Unit trust sectors For purposes of performance comparison, UK unit trusts are divided into sectors according to their investment objective. For example, the Income Funds sector's objective is 'immediate income', the Growth Sector seeks capital protection while the Specialist Fund sector provides options for investors who want to invest in a single country, e.g. Japan, or pursue a single theme, e.g. technology.

Unitised with profits business An approach which combines the 'with profits' concept with the management structure of a unit-linked life policy (qv). Policyholders receive units in the 'with profits' fund and units are priced depending on an annual *reversionary bonus*. A terminal bonus is added at maturity. Most UK 'with profits' business is written on a unitised basis.

Universal average The application of average to commercial and industrial fire risks on a widespread basis so that virtually no policy is issued without being subject to some form of average.

Unlimited liability A situation where an individual such as a sole trader or partner is liable to the full extent of his personal wealth for business debts. Contrast with a shareholder of a company whose liability is limited to the capital he has agreed to subscribe. Names at Lloyd's have unlimited liability. The intention is to switch all Lloyd's underwriting capacity to corporate members.

Unliquidated damages Damages that are assessed by the court. Unlike liquidated damages (qv) they are not agreed in advance and included in a contract. Unliquidated damages are the main component of liability insurance claims.

Unoccupancy clause Household insurance clause defined in terms such as 'your home has not been lived for more than 60 consecutive days'. Cover is restricted and may be subject to regular visits by the insured as well as central heating being turned off or drained. Under commercial policies the requirements vary, but, as a minimum, cover will not operate if, without the insurer being informed, premises are left unoccupied or unused for 30 consecutive days. Some policies make special requirements as to water supply and may call for minimum temperature 10°C during the winter, or for the services to be shut down.

Unplanned risk assumption Risk assumption (qv) that is not the result of a conscious decision. Risks are assumed inadvertently and are usually inconsequential.

Unrecovered damages Damages awarded by the court against a defendant who has failed to pay. Reverse liability (qv) and unsatisfied court judgments (qv) are insurance solutions to this problem.

'Unrepaired damage' If a damaged ship is not repaired, and has not been sold, then, when cover expires, the insured can claim the reasonable amount of depreciation resulting from the unrepaired damage not exceeding the cost of repairs of the damage (Marine Insurance Act 1906, s.69(3)). If an unrepaired vessel later becomes a total loss by an insured peril during the same policy term, the insurer is liable for the total loss only (s.77(2)). If the total loss occurs in a subsequent period, the insured is able to recover both the unrepaired damage and the total loss if both are caused by insured perils.

Unreported claims *See* IBNR FOR CLAIMS INCURRED BUT NOT YET REPORTED.

'Unroadworthy' Means not fit for the road. The term is not confined to soundness of the vehicle. Packing eight people into a Ford Anglia made it unroadworthy (*Clarke* v. *National Insurance & Guarantee Corporation Ltd* (1963)).

Unsatisfied court judgments An award of damages to an individual that remains unpaid. An employers' liability policy pays for unsatisfied court judgments awarded against third parties in favour of employees injured in circumstances to which the employers' liability policy would have applied had the employer been the party liable. The insurer will pay the damages if they are unsatisfied six months after judgment provided no appeal is outstanding. It is a condition that the employee's rights are assigned to the insurer. *See* REVERSE LIABILITY.

Unspecified working expenses Expenses that are insured as a part of the gross profit item under a business interruption insurance (qv). They relate to expenses that will continue despite the interruption in the business, e.g. rent and interest payments. *See* SPECIFIED WORKING EXPENSES.

Untraced Drivers Agreement Agreement between the Motor Insurers' Bureau (qv) and the government under which the MIB compensates the personal injury victims of negligent motorists who remain untraced. The deliberate running down of victims is outside the scheme as compensation is available from the Criminal Injuries Board (qv).

Unvalued policy Property insurance in regard to which the amount to be paid on a total loss has not been agreed. The parties fix a sum insured representing the insurer's maximum liability otherwise claims are to be dealt with on an indemnity basis subject, often, to pro rata *average* (qv). Marine Insurance Act, s.16, provides a basis of valuation for the insurance of hulls, cargoes and freight, etc., which, in the absence of any agreed value, must be used for the purpose of indemnifying the insured. Hulls and cargoes are invariably insured under valued policies (qv) but freight is generally insured under unvalued policies. *See* VALUATION CLAUSE.

'Unwitting CMR' Unknowing participation by a carrier in a CMR contract. Occurs when a road carrier accepts goods for part of a European road carriage between different countries when a single CMR contract governs the complete carriage. Each successive carrier, even if not crossing a national frontier, becomes a party to the contract and liable under CMR (qv) even if not aware of the contractual situation.

Uplifted 60ths (accelerated accrual) Occurs when the member of an approved occupational pension scheme is permitted to accrue benefits at a rate above the normal one-sixtieth of final salary for each year of service. The IR scale uses a scale for this purpose. Acceleration is available to members who have continuous rights prior to 17 March 1987.

'Use' of motor vehicles 'Use' is not synonymous with 'drive'. 'Use' implies an element of control, management or operation. An employee driving his employer's vehicle is using it but so too is the employer for whose benefit the journey is undertaken. Both parties must therefore be covered for the purpose of compulsory insurance under the Road Traffic Act 1988.

Usurped power This is: '(a) invasion by foreign enemies to give laws and usurp the government, or (b) internal armed force in rebellion assuming the power of government by making laws and punishing for not obeying those laws. Usurped power involves organised tumult or open warfare, and must be something more than action by a mere unorganised rabble; it implies a more or less organised body with more or less authoritative leaders'. (F.H. Jones).

Utmost good faith (uberrimae fidei) An obligation of the insured to disclose *material facts* (qv), i.e. facts that would influence the insurer before accepting the contract. The insurer must reciprocate but in practice the duty weighs more heavily on the insured. A breach by the insured makes the contract voidable *ab inito* (qv) at the insurer's option. Breaches may be through *concealment* (qv); *non-disclosure* (qv); *fraudulent misrepresentation* (qv); *innocent misrepresentation* (qv). The duty is pre-contractual but revives at renewal and to certain mid-term alterations affecting the risk. *See* CONTINUING DUTY OF UTMOST GOOD FAITH.

Valuables *See* HIGH RISK PROPERTY.

Valuation 1. A statement or certificate confirming the value of items of insured property, usually prepared by an independent professional. 2. In life insurance this is the annual assessment of the insurer's assets and liabilities in the manner required by the valuation regulations (qv). 3. An actuarial valuation (qv) when an actuary compares pension scheme assets and liabilities. He works out the level of contributions required to create sufficient money to ensure that the pensions due to members will be funded. In the case of defined benefit schemes, there must be an actuarial valuation every third year.

Valuation Clause Provides consistent basis for determining insured value of a shipment under an open cover (qv) relating to cargo at the time the risk attaches.

Valuation date Date used for the actuarial valuation. The figures produced will relate to this date.

Valuation-linked scheme A fire insurance scheme under which the insured chooses an inflation rate for the policy year and for each year the work of reinstatement may be necessary.

Valuation method The approach used by the actuary in carrying out an *actuarial valuation* (qv). See *accrued benefits valuation method* and *prospective benefits valuation* (qv).

Valuation of Assets Rules Rules in IPRU (INS) showing how, for required minimum margin (qv) purposes, an insurer's assets must be valued. Generally assets are valued at market value as prescribed in the rules but insurers must now apply the *resilience test* (qv) as a safeguard against changes in value of assets. Where an asset cannot be valued in a prescribed way it must be omitted from the margin of solvency (qv) calculation. The rules restrict the proportion of total assets held in any one asset or asset class. The assets eligible to cover solvency requirements comprise three groups: those that may be accepted without limitation; those subject to some limitation; and those acceptable only with FSA approval.

Valuation report Report on an actuarial valuation (qv). Also called an actuarial report.

Value The worth of something in money terms. The standard fire policy offers to pay the insured the 'value of the property' and the average clause (qv) refers to the 'value of the property at the time of fire'. Following the rules of construction the term will be given its ordinary meaning and the word will be given the same meaning wherever it appears in the policy unless a contrary intention is shown by express words or definitions contained in the policy. Under unvalued policies (qv) value generally means market value unless the policy is written on a reinstatement basis (qv). Marine insurance policies are generally issued on a valued policy (qv) basis.

Value added tax cover Credit insurance cover applying to the VAT content of sales invoices.

Valued as original A marine reinsurance term making the reinsurance contract a *valued policy* (qv) and ensuring that the value is the same as in the original policy.

Valued policy Contract under which the insurer agrees at inception to pay a stated sum in the event of a total loss without allowance for depreciation or appreciation. Partial losses are dealt with on an indemnity basis. Marine insurers issue valued policies on cargo (partial losses dealt with pro rata) and hulls (total loss only). Where a valued policy is not issued, e.g. open covers (qv), a valuation clause (qv) is used.

Variable annuities An annuity (qv) contract under which the payments to the annuitant will vary with the value of an underlying investment portfolio or linked to a cost of living index.

Variation of permission FSA has power to vary a firm's Part IV permission (qv) on its own initiative. The grounds for exercising this power are set out in FSMA, ss.45–47.

Vehicle replacement insurance Like *guaranteed asset protection* (qv) – *GAP* – the policy pays out in the event of the vehicle being written off or stolen, but the benefit payable is the difference between the insurance company pay-out and the original invoice value. Cover is suitable for motorists who have wholly paid for their cars or paid large initial deposits. Policies run for two or three years as selected by the insured subject to a maximum benefit of £10,000.

Vendor's indemnity Products liability policy (qv) extension to indemnify any independent vendor of the insured's product. The indemnity does not apply where the third party injury/damage arises from certain activities, e.g. intentionally changing the physical or chemical make-up of the product, undertaken by the vendor.

Vested rights Pensions term meaning: (a) benefits to which active members (qv) would be unconditionally entitled on leaving service; (b) the preserved pension benefits for deferred pensioners; (c) pensions entitlement of current pensioners; including, where appropriate, the related benefits for spouses or other dependants.

Vesting bonus Bonus declared in respect of, and allotted to, with profits life policies. Once declared it is said to 'vest' and is added to the life insurance benefit and the existing bonuses. All vested bonuses become payable under the same conditions as the sum insured. With profits benefits once added are guaranteed.

Violent entry *See* FORCIBLE AND VIOLENT ENTRY.

'Violent means' A qualifying term in a personal accident insurance in regard to the 'accidental external means' (qv) causing 'death or disablement'. 'Violence' emphasises the insurer's intention to avoid liability for gradually operating causes of an internal nature. The degree of violence is not of any consequence. The smallest degree will suffice.

'Visible means' Emphasises the importance to the insurer of restricting personal accident cover to bodily cause by accidental external means. Anything which is external is also visible. Exceptions to this strict meaning arise in connection with the accidental taking of poison or the inhaling of gas. If a person consumes poison when they intend to take a prescribed medicine, the act is at least visible and a fortuitous element is involved.

Void contract Without legal effect. All fraudulent contracts are void. The Gaming Act 1845 (qv) rendered all gaming contracts null and void. Insurances without insurable interest are wagering contracts and therefore void.

Voidable contract A contract is voidable if one party has the option of treating it as void. If he elects to treat it is as binding, then both parties will be bound. Insurance contracts secured by the insured's misrepresentation or non-disclosure are voidable at the insurer's option.

Volenti non fit injuria 'To him who is willing there can be no injury.' No action in tort is sustainable by a person who has expressly or impliedly assented to the risk, i.e. he cannot enforce a right that he has voluntarily waived. There is no consent when a person acts under a moral or legal constraint or when rescuing a person endangered by a third party's negligence.

Volume risk The effect of demand for a product or service on revenue. Energy sector sales fall during warm winters regardless of price. Heating fuels are bought because it is cold not because prices are low. Weather derivatives (qv) are used as a hedge against the volume risk.

Voluntary assumption of responsibility test Following *Henderson* v. *Merrett Syndicates Ltd* (1994), this test has been accepted as the correct basis of liability where issues of a duty of care and economic loss arise as they do in professional negligence cases. The giving of advice and providing a service call of a duty of care when the party concerned assumes or undertakes a responsibility to another. In this case the managing agents at Lloyd's owed a duty of care to names (qv) who had suffered disastrous financial losses following the negligent management of the syndicates.

Voluntary contributions certificate Issued by an FSAVC scheme to the member as evidence of his membership and contributions to the IR.

Voluntary excess An excess (qv) for which the insured volunteers in order to get the benefit of a reduced premium.

Voluntary schemes Pension, life insurance or other benefit schemes in which the members select the type and level of benefits they require from the range available. The members pay the contributions and premiums. The collective nature of affinity groups and trade unions means the members get better terms than they would as individuals.

Voyage policy Marine policy covering the subject-matter from the port of departure to destination irrespective of any time element. In practice the Institute Cargo Clauses (Clause 8 the Duration Clause) includes a time element by a provision to extend cover to up to 60 days after discharge from the vessel.

Wagering policy A policy effected without insurable interest (qv) is a wager, but policy proof of interest policies (PPI) (qv) are used in practice. The Life Assurance Act 1774 enacts that all policies shall be null and void if the insured has no interest (see insurable interest (qv)) in the event insured against or if made by way of wagering or gambling.

Wages Wages may be insured under business interruption insurance (qv) as an unspecified working expense (qv) or left uninsured as a *specified working expense* (qv). Wages are also a key variable in employers' liability and other *adjustable policies* (qv). *See* and compare PAYROLL COVER; DUAL BASIS PAYROLL.

'Waiters' The uniformed staff of the Corporation of Lloyd's, who perform general duties, wear red gowns and are known as 'waiters' reminiscent of the coffee house from which Lloyd's originated.

Waiting period 1. The prescribed amount of time, e.g. 30 days, following the issue of the policy that must pass before the policy will respond to an insured event. Income protection policies (qv) eliminate any disability due to sickness that commences during the waiting period. Disability commencing subsequently will be covered under the policy's normal terms that will generally include a *deferred period* (qv). 2. The period of employment that must elapse before a new employee can join his company pension scheme or group life scheme.

Waiver clause Marine insurance clause that entitles both the insurer and the insured to take measures to prevent or reduce loss without prejudice to their respective rights. They do not by their actions take up a fixed position on *abandonment* (qv) or a *constructive total loss* (qv).

Waiver of premium Health/life policy option whereby the insurer waives premiums when the insured is incapacitated through sickness or disability. Similar provisions are available in personal pension schemes when the provider agrees to credit ongoing premiums for the benefit of the scheme member.

War 'Armed conflict of states in which each seeks to impose its will upon the other by force. It is not a blind struggle between mobs of individuals without guidance or coherence, but a conflict of organised masses moving with a view to cooperation, acting under the impulse of a single will and directed against a definite objective.' (F.H. Jones).

War and civil war risks exclusion agreement Non-marine insurance companies and Lloyd's underwriters agreed not to cover the consequences of war risks on land. Consequently the government provides cover in times of war. A standard exclusion of war (and civil war) appears in non-marine policies other than life. War risks cover is available in the marine and aviation markets. *See* WAR RISKS INSURANCE; WATERBORNE AGREEMENT.

War risks/perils Fundamental risks (qv) connected with political and related matters capable of causing widespread damage. War risks are excluded from material damage policies covering property on land and more usually covered under central government schemes. War perils include: war (qv), civil war (q.v), rebellion (qv), insurrection (qv), usurped power (qv), military or usurped power (qv), civil commotion (qv), martial law (qv). *See* WAR AND CIVIL RISKS EXCLUSION ON AGREEMENT.

War risks insurance Cover on *ships or cargo* against war risks, derelict mines, torpedoes, bombs etc. (qv). Cover is under the Institute War Clauses (Cargo) and the Institute War and Strikes Clauses (Hulls-Time). Cargo is covered under a voyage policy (qv) only *while on board* the oversea vessel except for restricted cover while in craft. War risks *and* strikes cover for hulls is on a time policy (qv) but cover terminates automatically if there is war between the major powers, or the vessel is requisitioned, otherwise it can be terminated at seven days' notice. Open covers (qv) and floating policies (qv) are also subject to seven days' cancellation. The waterborne agreement (qv) brings marine insurance into line with non-marine insurance (i.e. excludes war risks on land-based property). *See* WAR AND CIVIL WAR EXCLUSION AGREEMENT; WAR RISKS.

War risks policies (aviation) War, hijacking and similar risks are underwritten in a specialist market and in the marine and aviation market. Cover for war risk liabilities is underwritten in the aviation market only.

Warehouse to warehouse clause Clause within the Duration Clause of the Institute Cargo Clause providing that cover attaches when the cargo leaves the warehouse at the starting place and ends at final port on the basis of the soonest of delivery: (a) at final warehouse at named destination; (b) at any other warehouse elected by insured at, or prior, to destination; or (c) 60 days after discharge overside at final destination.

Warning notice Disciplinary notice detailing the FSA's proposed course of action in regard to alleged unsatisfactory conduct by an authorised person. The recipient can respond by stating why no action should be taken against him. If unconvinced the FSA can proceed to a decision notice (qv). *See* PRIVATE WARNINGS.

Warranted free from particular average Marine insurance term applied when the policy does not cover partial loss other than a general average loss (qv). Since the introduction of the Institute Cargo Clauses (1/1/82), the words 'particular average' no longer appear in policies but the term lives on in marine insurance circles where its meaning is well known.

Warranty A condition that must be complied with literally. A breach precludes the insured from recovering under his policy, although the loss may not have been affected by the warranty. Insurance warranties may consist of undertakings that certain things shall be done (waste removed from premises daily) or things shall not be done (certain changes in risk factors) or a declaration whereby the insured affirms or negatives a certain state of affairs, e.g. representations in a proposal form.

Warsaw Convention A 1929 agreement (updated by the Hague Protocol 1955) that limits the liability of airlines in the event of 'accidents' on *international flights*. In 1966, the top limit was increased to $75,000 for personal injury except in the event of the airline's 'wilful misconduct'. This limit no longer applies to EC carriers following the EC Regulation 2027/97. Other carriers have also contracted out of the Convention's injury limits. The Convention, which also limits liability on luggage, continues to apply in some situations. The IATA Inter-Carrier Agreements on Passenger Liability (qv) has 'modernised' the Warsaw Convention principally by increasing or removing the limitations on passenger liability for injury or death, revising the basis for airline liability and simplifying 'travel documents'. *See* IATA.

Waste Warranties Warranty (qv) under commercial fire insurance cover requiring the insured to take specific action to control waste. Examples: all oily and/or greasy waste remaining in the building overnight to be kept in metal receptacles with metal lids and removed from the building once a week; warranted all combustible trade waste and refuse be removed from the building every night; warranted all sawdust, shavings and other refuse be removed from the buildings every night.

Waterborne Agreement Marine market agreement whereby underwriters will cover goods against *war risks* (qv) while they are actually on the overseas vessel subject to a 15 day time limit after arrival at the destination. Limited cover applies while the goods are in craft en route between the ship and the shore and, also during trans-shipment. The agreement is given effect in the *Institute War Clauses (Cargo)* by the Waterborne Clause.

Waterborne Clause *See* WATERBORNE AGREEMENT.

WBS (Without benefit of salvage) Marine insurance term whereby the insurer forgoes the benefit of the salvage. Tonner reinsurance contracts (qv) are written both WBS and PPI (qv) to obviate questions of legal enforceability when salvage is clearly impossible.

Wear and tear Arises out of the normal use of property and is excluded from property insurances although would not, in any event, be embraced by terms such as 'accidental damage'. However, 'new for old' policies disregard wear and tear in claims settlements. *See* REINSTATEMENT POLICIES.

Weather derivative A security, swap or option whose value is directly related to weather events over a specified time in a specified location. Weather derivatives pay cash flows depending on occurrences such as deviations from average temperature, precipitation levels, etc. Companies use weather derivatives as a hedge against weather conditions damaging to their trade, e.g. pavement café suffers during a cool summer and may acquire heating degree days (qv). *See* COOLING DEGREE DAYS; WEATHER SWAPS; WEATHER INDICES; ENERGY DEGREE DAYS; GROWING DEGREES; PRECIPITATION.

Weather indices The underlying index upon which weather derivatives are based. The two main temperature indices are heating degree days (qv) and cooling degree days (qv). Other weather variables: maximum or minimum temperature; critical temperature events (temperature passing a defined value); rain and snowfall; windspeed.

Weather insurance Insurance for the promoter of an outside event, e.g. outdoor play, that depends on specific weather conditions. The policy pays if, for example, a preset rainfall level is exceeded leading to cancellation or reduced attendance. *See* ABANDONMENT OF EVENT; WEATHER RISK; PLUVIUS POLICY.

Weather-linked bond Like a catastrophe bond (qv) it transfers the insurance risk to the capital market. Bond investors sacrifice their interest and/or capital if weather conditions deviate from a reference point. The insurer may, for example, hedge against a prolonged spell of extreme cold capable of triggering an excessive number of weather-related claims.

Weather risk 1. Adverse effect on corporate costs or revenue of the non-catastrophic effect of weather that deviates from normal conditions; e.g. poor heating energy sales due to mild winter. Weather-sensitive businesses use weather derivatives (qv). 2. Risk of injury/damage by high severity/low probability events such as severe windstorm. Insurance is the usual response. 3. Adverse effect on insurers' underwriting results following widespread losses through hurricane, tornado, flood, etc.

Reinsurance is the traditional response, but catastrophe bonds (qv) or swaps (qv), and other alternative risk transfer products, are also used. *See* also WEATHER INSURANCE; PLUVIUS INSURANCE.

Weather risk management The weather risk (qv) is managed by hedging against poor sales volume and/or increased costs caused by unwelcome weather conditions. Weather derivatives (qv) supplement existing risk management tools. The main weather risk management products are structured as caps (*see* CALL OPTIONS), floors (*see* PUT OPTIONS), swaps (qv) and collars (qv).

Weather Risk Management Association (WRMA) Trade association for companies and organisations wishing to manage the risks associated with unwelcome weather. WRMA promotes the industry, provides forums, including an annual conference, for discussion and interaction with others associated with financial weather products.

Wet perils Certain named perils added to a fire insurance policy (qv). The perils are: storm (qv); flood (qv); burst pipes (qv); sprinker leakage (qv).

Wet risk Lloyd's term for non-marine risks, i.e. it is not connected with hulls, marine cargoes or maritime liability, but has a maritime association. Examples include the insurance of dock and port structures, offshore oil and gas structures, bridges, wharves and dams.

Whiplash injury Neck injury suffered by drivers and passengers of motor vehicles caused by their sudden involuntary body movement due to a collision. The cost to motor insurers is £600 million to £700 million each year. The ABI (qv) has commissioned research under the title, 'Prevention and Management of Whiplash Neck Injury'.

Whistle blowing 1. The reporting in writing to Opra (qv) by an actuary or an auditor of an occupational pension scheme where they suspect that a breach of certain rules has occurred. Others may report such breaches but the actuary and the auditor have a legal duty to do so (PA95, s.48). 2. The FSA can accept whisteblowing information from insiders in regulated firms by virtue of its prescribed regulator status under the Public Interest Disclosure Act 1999. The Act protects 'whistleblowers' from reprisals and secures compensation for victims for revealing serious wrongdoing.

White labelling Term that applies when a firm, e.g. broker, labels and sells an insurance product under its own name when it is the product of another firm, e.g. an insurer. The FSA does not restrict this practice but has issued a guidance note to say that firms should make clear to the customer the identities of both the insurer and the intermediary and should ensure that their communication with the customer is clear, fair and not misleading.

Whole account cover Refers to excess of loss treaty (qv) protecting the whole of the reinsured's written business or the whole of a category, such as the liability account rather than arranging separate protections for public liability, employers' liability, third party motor, etc. Whole account cover has many layers, is often on a co-insurance basis and may take care of *disasters and clashes* (qv).

Whole policy rule Rule of construction meaning that the whole of the policy must be looked at and not merely a particular clause. Where a proposal is expressly incorporated in a policy by the terms of the policy, the two should be read together.

Whole turnover insurance A credit insurance (qv) whereby the insured insures the whole of his sales ledger rather than insure selectively on the basis of named accounts.

Wholesale broker A broker who places risks with Lloyd's or with insurance companies on behalf of other brokers, i.e. subbrokers who are customer-facing and therefore, unlike the wholesaler, subject to ICOB rules. Wholesale brokers normally attract business as they are able to secure better policy terms and conditions than the sub-brokers. Wholesale brokers who are Lloyds-accredited provide a route to the Lloyd's market for other brokers and may operate under binding authorities (qv).

Widow's/widower's guaranteed minimum pension (WGMP) A contracted out occupational pension scheme must pay at least this amount in pension benefits to the surviving spouse of a member who dies. This applies for any benefits earned pre-April 1997. WGMP does not apply to a scheme that has contracted out under protected rights rules.

Wilful blindness The ignorance which occurs when a person deliberately and wilfully refrains from inquiring into a situation or deliberately disregards a situation in the hope of profiting from it. It applies to assignees for value who seek to gain advantage by giving notice of an assignment under the Policies of Assurances Act 1867 (qv) ahead of previous assignees they know or suspect to exist who have not yet given notification. This conduct is not permitted as a means of an assignee gaining priority.

WIN (World Insurance Network) Formed by leading international insurance brokers to exploit the use of Internet technology to place risks internationally while also continuing to place business manually. In June 1999, WIN merged with LIMNET (qv) and the RINET (qv) to form WISe (the World InSurance – E-commerce) (qv).

Wind risk The risk that wind speed variations will reduce the volume of electricity generated by wind farms and therefore sales for wind power companies. The risk can be managed by a weather derivative (qv) based on *wind power indices (WPIs)*. The average value of the index over any 12-month period is 100 in a normal year. An annual value of 95 indicates that the index is 5 per cent below normal for the region and leads to a payout. Wind farm developers, operators and financiers may all hedge against the wind risk.

Winding up Closing of an occupational pension scheme, usually done by buying annuities for all members, including deferred annuities (qv). Alternatively all assets and liabilities can be transferred to another scheme in accordance with the scheme rules and any relevant laws. There are statutory provisions to determine when winding up commences for statutory purposes (Occupational Pension Schemes (Winding Up) Regulations 1996, Regulation 2 (SI 1996/3126)).

'Windscreen' breakage Under private comprehensive car policies, insurers agree that, if a claim for damage consists solely of damage to the windscreen or windows, payment will be made without prejudice to the insured's entitlement to no claim discount (qv).

Windstorm (including tornado and cyclone) insurance Insurance against damage done to property by unusually high winds or cyclone or hurricane. The risks are usually insured as additional perils, but it is possible to insure against these perils alone.

Winter *See* HEATING SEASON.

WISe (World InSurance – E-commerce) 1999 merger of three electronic networks: WIN (qv) created by international brokers, LIMNET, the London market network successful at transmitting accounting transactions, and RINET, a consortium of mainly European (re)insurers. Membership of WISe is also available to captives, loss adjusters and third party suppliers. The activities of the three merged networks are grouped under two main programmes. WISe Trusted Trading focuses on a legally regulated environment for electronic trading. WISe Data Exchange focuses on facilitating the exchange of administrative transactions. WISe operates on a non-profit basis from Brussels, London and New York. Its work with electronic data standards was transferred to ACORD (qv). WISe aims to 'facilitate the use of electronic commerce to improve client service, reduce processing and administrative costs and provide maximum scope for competitive trading'. By April 2003, WISe had attracted 50,000 registered users.

With average if amounting to 3 per cent Clause limiting recovery of partial losses under a marine policy to those reaching a franchise of 3 per cent (the customary level for commodities) of the insured value.

With average irrespective of percentage Allows full recovery of all partial losses due to a named peril in a marine policy. No franchise based on a percentage of the value applies.

'With privity of the assured' An expression from the Marine Insurance Act 1906, s.39(5), meaning that a shipowner, while not having knowledge regarding the soundness, i.e. seaworthiness (qv), of his vessel is not entitled to turn a 'blind eye' to the situation.

With-profits annuity The annuity payment follows the fortunes of the value of the underlying assets. Consequently income can rise or fall. The fund may benefit from increased bonuses declared in future years and the annuitant selects at the outset a future bonus rate, typically up to 5 per cent of the fund, but if the selected rate is not achieved the income will fall. Some providers offer guaranteed minimum income payments.

With-profits bond Single premium life policies invested in the insurer's with profits fund made up of investment in company shares, fixed interest securities, commercial property, cash, etc. High tax payers can benefit by withdrawing 5 per cent each year for 20 years without an immediate tax liability as the IR treat it as a return of capital. Annual reversionary bonuses are added and a terminal bonus (qv) is paid out at maturity.

With-profits policies Whole life policies (qv) and endowment policies (qv) that attract bonuses representing a share in the profits (see divisible surplus (qv)). The bonuses are declared each year and become a guaranteed addition to the sum assured at death or maturity.

With proportion Indicates that if an annuitant (qv) dies before the next annuity payment is due, a pro rata payment will be made in respect of the period from the last payment to the date of death.

Withdrawal reinsurance *See* REINSURANCE WITHDRAWAL.

Without prejudice Phrase used during the negotiations of third party claims settlements indicating that liability is not admitted. Statements and offers made 'without prejudice' cannot subsequently be used in evidence at court proceedings.

Without profits policies Whole life (qv) or endowment policies (qv) that guarantee a fixed sum on death or, in the case of endowments, survival without any bonus (qv) addition. They are also called non-participating policies as they do not participate in the insurer's profits.

Without proportion Indicates that if an annuitant dies (qv) during the interval between two annuity payment dates, there will be no payment for the period between the payment preceding death and the date of death.

Wording As Expiring Term used in slips (qv) to indicate that the general terms and conditions of an expiring treaty will be incorporated on renewal for the following year.

Wording As Underlying Term used in slips (qv) for upper layers of excess of loss treaties to indicate that the general terms and conditions will be as per the lower layers.

Work away risk Describes a public liability risk where the main hazards stem from the work undertaken by the insured on third party premises. Electricians, plumbers, etc., install, repair or carry out maintenance on the premises of others. Visits to the insured's premises by customers are not a major feature of the risk.

Work in progress 1. Property item at risk of loss or damage by fire, etc., usually included in the policy schedule. The sum insured is based on the cost of raw materials plus the cost of labour and other resources used in creating the product up to the time of loss. Completed products insured as stock.

Work-related Upper Limb Disorders (WRULDs) A condition or disorder relating to many areas of the body, including muscles, tendons, joints, etc. Areas affected include the neck, shoulders, arms, elbows, hands and fingers. Tenosynovitis and carpal tunnel syndrome are particular sources of employers' liability claims. WRULDs should be considered as part of the risk assessment carried out under MHSW (qv).

Working cover/layer First layer of an excess of loss treaty above the reinsured's retention. The attachment point (qv) is relatively low in order to accommodate relatively frequent claims to protect the reinsured's normal daily exposure on the basis of any one event or risk. Premiums are generally based on prior years' loss experience calculated on an automatic scale. Compare with buffer layer (qv) and catastrophe layer (qv).

Working excess of loss per event Retention and cover apply to the sum of all losses from the same event; unlike a catastrophe excess of loss there is no *two risk warranty* (qv) and the deductible is low enough to be triggered by a single risk.

Working excess of loss per risk Deductible and cover are applied individually for each risk regardless of whether losses are caused by a single event.

Working in progress cover Credit insurance protecting a manufacturer who has committed resources to enter into contracts with suppliers against losses due to default by the prospective customer.

Working layer *See* WORKING COVER.

Working member A Lloyd's underwriter principally occupied with the conduct of business at Lloyd's by working for a Lloyd's broker or underwriting agent.

Working partners *See* INJURY TO WORKING PARTNERS CLAUSE.

Workplace (Health, Safety and Welfare) Regulations 1992 Regulations, imposing duties on employers and those in control of workplaces (mining and construction sites excepted), aimed at: (a) health and safety in the workplace covering the environment in which employees are expected to work (ventilation, temperatures etc.); (b) design and maintenance of the premises (condition of floors, traffic routes, etc.); and (c) welfare facilities. The Regulations apply to all parts of the workplace including outdoor workspace. A breach of the Regulations is criminal and also provides the basis for a civil action.

Works Damage Insurance An engineering insurance relevant to businesses producing manufactured goods with installed plant and machinery which may, along with the manufactured goods, suffer accidental damage in the factory. The property is insured against damage following accidental external impact, including falling, toppling, overturning or dropping at the location. The policy usually extends to cover customers' property undergoing repair or renovation and, in certain circumstances, loading and transit cover in respect of new products may be included. The policy carries an excess (qv) and exclusions relate to fire and additional perils (qv), theft, faulty workmanship, electrical and mechanical breakdown, loading for despatch, the initial installation or final removal (these are insured as transit risks).

World-wide Intellectual Resources Exchange Ltd (WIRE) A leading provider of Internet-based markets for international insurance, reinsurance and alternative risk transfer (ART) (qv). In 1999, WIRE launched Artemis, a portal site, acting as a repository for news and information for the ART market of which weather trading is a key part.

Wrap-up cover An owner-controlled insurance programme covering all liability interests in a large construction project. The cover is arranged by the owner (the principal) whose interest is protected as well as those of contractors, sub-contractors, suppliers, architects, etc. The intention is to reduce overall insurance costs. *See* PRINCIPAL'S COVER.

Write business To provide the insurance cover.

Written lines *See* SIGNED LINES. It is otherwise called a closed line (qv).

Written premium Premium income in respect of business written during the financial year regardless of the portions earned.

Written words prevail over printed word rule Rule of construction (qv). Where there are both written and printed words in a policy, the policy is to be construed as a whole, but the written words are more specific than the printed word and will therefore prevail in the event of inconsistency. The written or typewritten words are specially inserted to show the intention of the parties.

Wrongful act Loss arising from any wrongful act is the insured event under a directors' and officers' liability insurance (qv). It is defined within the policy in these terms: 'any actual or alleged breach of duty breach of trust neglect error misstatement omission breach of warranty of authority or other act done wrongfully attempted by any Director (qv) or Officer (qv)'.

Wrongful conversion *See* CONVERSION (qv). The wrongful conversion section of the motor trader's policy covers the insured for: (a) the loss which occurs when a vehicle, purchased from a person who is not the true owner, is reclaimed by the true owner or to whom compensation has to be paid; and (b) loss following the sale of a vehicle in circumstances where the trader is unable to pass a valid title to the purchaser who may claim damages against the trader. The insurance is conditional upon the trader carrying out a check on possible hire purchase agreements that may be in force before parting with his cheque. The trader generally carries the first 20 per cent of any loss.

Wrongful Dismissal The dismissal of an employee when the employer is in breach of contract. The employee can found a common law action on the breach. An employee, summarily dismissed in breach of his notice and other contractual entitlement, will have a claim for damages unless the dismissal was justified under the employment contract. The risk is insurable by the employer under employment practices liability insurance (qv) and legal expenses insurances (qv). Compare with unfair dismissal (qv).

Wrongful trading A director who trades on knowing that there is no reasonable prospect that the company will avoid going into liquidation, paying its debts and the winding up expenses is guilty of wrongful trading. The Insolvency Act 1986, s.214, provides that a civil remedy may lie against the director who may then become personally liable to contribute to the assets of the company for the benefit of creditors. *See* DIRECTORS' AND OFFICERS' LIABILITY INSURANCE.

Yacht insurance Special policy insuring yachts, cabin cruisers, inboard motorboats and sailing ships. They are vessels used for pleasure not commercial purposes. The policy covers accidental loss or damage to the vessel, salvage charges, sue and labour charges and liability to third parties including passengers.

Year of account 1.The year to which a risk is allocated and to which all premiums and claims in respect of that risk are attributed. The year of account of a risk is determined by the calendar year in which it is first signed. A year of account is normally closed by reinsurance to close (qv) at the end of 36 months. The system will come to an end when GAAP accounting (qv) takes over. 2. In reinsurance it is a method of accounting to a proportional treaty whereby all premiums and losses accounted during the year in question are accounted to that year regardless of the year of origin of the cession or of the date of loss. Contracts accounted on this basis are usually closed at the end of each year by a portfolio transfer (qv) into the following year.

Year of occurrence Accounting system under which the insurer allocates all premiums to the relevant treaty year according to the dates they are due, while all losses are entered according to the date of the occurrence.

York–Antwerp Rules Revised in 1974, a set of rules, incorporated in contracts affreightment and adopted by leading maritime nations, to govern the methods of applying *general average.* The 1994 amendment provides that in certain circumstances measures taken to prevent or minimise damage to the environment by pollutants (e.g. oil spills) will be allowed in *general average* (qv).

Young/inexperienced driver's excess A standard excess (qv) which imposes an 'own damage' excess in respect of certain drivers of cars, commercial vehicles, and motor cycles. An inexperienced driver is a person over 25 year of age, with a provisional licence. A young driver is under 25 years of age.

Z

Zero-Beta Asset An investment that does not correlate with an index or market results.

Zero-Coupon Bond A bond under which no coupon payments are made. A single redemption payment is made at the end of the term.

Zillmerisation A process whereby an adjustment is made in the actuarial valuation of long-term business to take credit for the future recovery of the costs of acquiring new business.

Zone system System developed by the National Association for Insurance Commissioners in the US for the triennial examination of insurers. Teams of examiners are formed from the staffs of several states in each of the geographical zones. The results of their examinations are then accepted by all states in which an insurer is licensed, without the necessity of each state having to conduct its own examinations.

Appendix 1

Marine abbreviations

A

A1 First class.

aa After arrival; always afloat.

All ER All-England Law Reports.

ABS American Bureau of Shipping (classification society).

ACV Air cushion vehicle (hovercraft).

AGWI Atlantic/Gulf/West Indies.

AHF American hull form.

aoa Any one accident.

aob Any one bottom.

aol Any one loss.

aos Any one shipment.

aov Any one vessel.

aovoy Any one voyage.

AP Additional premium; annual premium; agricultural produce.

APL As per list.

Appd or h/c Approved or held covered at a premium to be agreed.

AR (or A/R) All risks.

Arr.TL Arranged total loss.

Atl Atlantic.

ATL Actual total loss.

Aux Fitted with auxiliary engine(s).

Av Average.

B

BBcl Both to blame collision clause.

Bdi Both days inclusive.

Bdx Bordereaux.

B/E bill of exchange; bill of entry.

B/G Bonded goods.

B/L Bill of lading.

BR Builder's risk insurance.

BV Basis of valuation; Bureau Veritas (classification society).

B/V Book value.

BW Bonded warehouse.

C

CFR Cost and freight.

CIF Cost, insurance and freight.

cgf rec Credit given for recovery.

CIM Convention International pour les Marchandises par Chemin de Fer (International Convention concerning Carriage of Goods by Rail).

CMR Convention Marchandises Routiers (International Convention concerning Carriage of Goods by Road).

COGSA Carriage of Goods by Sea Act.

C/P Charter party; custom of port (grain trade).

CPA Claims payable abroad.

CPD Charterer's pay dues.

CRO Cancelling returns only.

CTL Constructive total loss.

CTO Combined transport operator.

C/V certificate of value.

C/VO Certificate of value and origin.

D

D/C Documentary credit; deviation clause.

DCOP During currency of policy.

DD Damage done.

Dis or disbts Disbursements.

DK Deck.

dpv Daily pro rata.

DRC Damage received in collision.

D/V Dual valuation.

DWT Deadweight tonnage.

E

e & ea Each and every accident.

e & el Each and every loss.

e & eo Each and every occurrence.

EFT Electronic funds transfer.

ERV Each round voyage.

EXQ Ex quay.

EXS Ex ship.

EXW Ex works.

F

faa Free of all average.

FAS Free alongside.

FCL Full container load.

fcsrcc Free of capture, seizure, riots and civil commotion.

fc & s free of capture and seizure.

FCV Full contract value (used in building risks).

FDO For declaration purposes only.

FEU Forty foot equivalent unit (size of container).

FFO Fixed and floating objects.

FGA Foreign general average.

FIA Full interest admitted.

FOB Free on board.

FOC Flag of convenience.

FOD abs Free of damage absolutely.

FOR Free on rail.

FOS Free on steamer.

FOT Free on truck.

FPA abs Free of particular average absolutely.

FPIL Full premium if lost.

FRO Fire risk only.

fsl Full signed line (insurance).

FVC Fishing vessel clauses.

fwd Forward; fresh water damage.

G

GA (or G/A) General average.

GA con General average contribution.

GAD General average deposit.

GADV Gross arrived damaged value.

GASV Gross arrived sound value.

Grs Grains; gross.

GRT Gross registered tonnage.

GS Good safety.

H

H/C held covered at premium to be arranged.

H & M Hull and machinery.

hk Hook damage.

h & o Hook and oil damage.

HW High water.

HWD Heavy weather damage.

I

IBC Institute Builders' Clauses.

ICC Institute Cargo Clauses.

if In full.

IFC Institute Freight Clauses.

In trans In transitu (in transit).

I/o in and/or overdeck.

iop Irrespective of percentage.

IHC International Hull Clauses.

ITC International Time Clauses.

IUA International Underwriters' Association.

IV Increased value.

IVC Institute Voyage Clauses.

IYC Institute Yacht Clauses.

J

JHU Joint Hull Undertakings.

J & lo Jettison and loss overboard.

J & wo Jettison and washing overboard.

Jett Jettison.

K

KHz Kilohertz.

Kt Knot.

L

L and DS Live and dead stock.

LATF Lloyd's American Trust Fund.

LCL Less than container load.

ldg Loading.

Ldg and dly Landing and delivery.

LC London clause (chartering); label clause.

LNYD Liability not yet determined (used in collision cases).

LOH Loss of hire.

Ltg Lighterage.

ltr Lighter.

L/U Leading underwriter; laid up.

LO/LO Lift on/lift off.

M

Machy Machinery.

MD Malicious damage.

MIA Marine Insurance Act.

MIP Marine insurance policy.

M/R mate's receipt.

MSA Merchant Shipping Act.

MSC Manchester Ship Canal.

MV Motor vessel.

N

NA Net absolutely; North America.

N/A No advice; not applicable.

N/C New charter.

ND Non-delivery; no discount.

N/E. Not entered.

NRAD No risk after discharge.

NRAL No risk after landing.

NRAS No risk after shipment.

NRTOR No risk till on rail.

NRTWB No risk till waterborne.

NUR Not under repair.

NV Norske Veritas (classification society).

O

O/b on or before.

OBO Ore/bulk/oil carrier.

OC Open cover; off cover.

O/c Open charter.

O/D open deck.

OGR Original gross rate.

ORB Owner's risk of breakage.

ORL Owner's risk of leakage.

O/S open slip.

P

PA Particular average.

PC Profit commission.

P Chgs Particular charges.

PD Property damage; port dues.

PI Personal injury.

P & I Protection and indemnity.

PIA Peril insured against.

Pkg Package

PL Partial loss.

Poc Port of call.

Por Port of refuge.

PP Parcel post.

P/P Pier to pier.

PPI Policy proof of interest.

PT Premium transfer.

Q

Qlty Quality.

QRs quantity restrictions.

Qty Quantity.

R

R & CC Riots and civil commotion.

RDC Three-fourth running down clause.

rd Running days.

RI Registro Italiana (classification society).

R/I Reinsurance.

RLN Running landing numbers.

rob Remaining on board.

ROD Rust, oxidisation and discolourisation.

Ro/ro Roll on/roll off carrier.

ROW Removal of wreck.

RP Return of premium.

RTBA Rate to be agreed.

Ry or rly Railway.

S

S Salvage.

SA Salvage Association.

S/A subject to acceptance (insurance).

S and FA Shipping and forwarding agent.

S and L Sue and labour.

SANR Subject to approval, no risk till confirmed.

SBT Segregated ballast tanks.

S/C Salvage charges.

SD Sea damage; small damage.

Sd Short delivery.

SDR Special drawing rights.

SG Policy Ship and goods policy form.

Shpt Shipment.

Sk Sack.

SL Salvage loss.

S/L Cl Sue and labour clause.

Sld Sailed.

S/o Shipowner.

SOL Shipowner's liability

S & p Seepage and pollution.

SR & CC Strikers, riots, and civil commotions.

SRL Ship repairer's liability.

SS or str Steamer.

SSO Struck submerged object

Strd Stranded.

SV Sailing vessel.

SWD Sea water damage.

T

T/A Transatlantic.

T and s touch and stay.

TCATLVO Total and/or constructive loss and/or arranged total loss of vessel only.

TCH Time hire charter.

TEU Twenty foot equivalent unit (shipping container or size)

Thro' B/L through bill of lading.

TL Total loss.

TLO Total loss only.

Tonn Tonnage.

TPL Third partly liability.

TP & ND Theft pilferage and non-delivery.

T/S Trans-shipment.

U

U/C Under construction.

ucb Unless caused by.

U/D Under deck.

UK/C United Kingdom/Continent.

ULCC Ultra large crude carrier.

UNCITRAL United Nations Commission on International Trade Law.

UNCTAD United Nations Conference on Trade and Development.

UNL Ultimate net loss.

U/R Under repair.

V

VC Valuation clause.

vd Valued.

VLCC Very large crude carrier.

Vop Value on policy.

W

WA With average.

WB Water ballast; way bill.

WBS Without benefit of salvage.

Whf Wharf.

WOB Washing overboard.

WP Without prejudice.

WRO War risk only.

Wtd Warranted.

WW worldwide.

X

XS Excess.

XS Loss Excess of loss reinsurance.

T

YAR York–Antwerp Rules.

Yt Yacht.

Appendix 2

Abbreviations and short forms – pensions

ACA Association of Consulting Actuaries.

AGM Annual General Meeting.

APC Auditing Practices Committee.

APL Association of Pensions Lawyers.

APPS Appropriate Personal Pension Scheme.

APT Association of Pensioneer Trustees.

ARP Accrued Rights Pension.

AVC Additional Voluntary Contribution.

BE Band Earnings.

CA Certified amount.

CA Companies Act.

CCA Current Cost Accounting.

CEP Contributions Equivalent Premium.

CGT Capital Gains tax.

CIF Common Investment Fund.

CIMPS Contracted-in Money Purchase Scheme.

CIPS Contracted-in Pension Scheme.

CIR Commissioners of Inland Revenue.

COE Contracted Out Employment.

COMPS Contracted Out Money Purchase Scheme.

COPRP Contracted Out Protected Rights Premium.

COSRS Contracted Out Salary-related Scheme.

CPA Compulsory Purchase Annuity.

CPIC Company Pensions Information Centre.

CT Corporation tax.

DIS Death in Service.

DBPS Defined Benefit Pension Scheme.

DDT Definitive Deed Trust.

DPB Designated Professional Body.

DWP Department of Work and Pensions.

ECON Employer's Contracting Out Number.

EF Earnings Factor.

EGM Extraordinary General Meeting.

EPB Equivalent Prevention Benefit.

ERI Employer Related Investment.

FA Finance Act.

FSA Financial Services Authority.

FSAVC Free Standing Additional Voluntary Contributions.

FURBS Funded Unapproved Retirement Benefits Scheme.

GAAP Generally Accepted Accounting Principles.

GAD Government Actuary's Department.

GMP Guaranteed Minimum Pension.

GPPP Group Personal Pension Plan.

HC Historical Cost.

HRP Home Responsibilities Protection.

ICTA Income and Corporation Taxes Act.

IFA Independent Financial Adviser.

IHT Inheritance Tax.

IPA Individual Pension Arrangement.

IR Inland Revenue.

ISA Individual Savings Account.

ITD Interim Trust Deed.

LEL Lower Earnings Limit.

LIC Life Insurance Council of the ABI.

LPI Limited Price Indexation.

LRP Limited Revaluation Premium.

MFR Minimum Funding Requirement.

NAPF National Association of Pension Funds.

NPA Normal Pension Age.

NRA Normal Retirement Age.

NRD Normal Retirement Date.

NRE Net Relevant Earnings.

OMO Open Market Option.

OPAS The Pensions Advisory Service.

OPB Occupational Pensions Board.

Opra Occupational Pensions Regulatory Authority.

PA95 Pensions Act 1995.

PSA93 Pensions Schemes Act 1993.

PAYG Pay As You Go.

PIL Payment in Lieu.

PLA Purchased Life Annuity.

PMI The Pensions Management Institute.

PN Practice Notes.

PO Pensions Ombudsman.

PPS Personal Pension Scheme.

PRP Pensioners Rights Premium.

PUP Paid Up Pension.

RPI Retail Price Index.

S2P State Second Pension.

SCON Scheme Contracted Out Number.

SERPS State Earnings-related Pension Scheme.

SI Statutory Instrument.

SIPP Self Investment Personal Pension.

SOI Statement of Intent.

SORP Statement of Recommended Practice.

SPA State Pensionable Age.

SR State Regulation.

SSAP Statement of Standard Accounting Practice.

SSAS Small Self-administered Scheme.

SSB Short Service Benefit.

SSP State Scheme Premium; Statutory Sick Pay.

TV Transfer Value.

UEL Upper Earnings Limit.

UURBS Unfunded Unapproved Retirement Benefits Scheme.

WGMP Widow's/Widower's Guaranteed Minimum Pension.

Appendix 3

Glossary of special terms

A fortiori much more; with stronger reason.

Ab initio from the beginning.

Actio personalis moritur cum persona a personal action dies with the person (Common law rule now largely superseded by statute).

Actus Dei nemini facit injuriam the Act of God prejudices no one.

Ad hoc for a special purpose.

Ad idem of the same mind.

Ad valorem according to the value.

Aliunde from elsewhere (e.g. Indemnification aliunde).

Ats. (ad sectam) at the suit of.

Bona fide in good faith.

Causa proxima non remota spectatur the immediate, not the remote, is to be considered.

Caveat emptor let the buyer beware.

Cestui (pl. cestuis) que trust the beneficiary under a trust.

Ceteris paribus other things being equal.

Chose in action a personal right of property, which can be enforced only by action, e.g. debt.

Consensus ad idem in perfect agreement.

Damnum loss or damage.

Damnum absque injuria loss without wrong.

De die in diem from day to day.

De facto as a matter of fact.

De jure as a matter of law.

De minimis no curat lex the law does not concern itself with trifles.

De novo anew.

Delegates no post delgare a delegate cannot delegate (an agent may not delegate his authority).

Duress actual or threatened violence, or imprisonment.

Ejusdem generis of the same kind.

Ex delicto arising out of wrongs.

Ex gratia as of favour.

Ex hypothesi from the hyposthesis.

Ex parte on the one side; action by one party in the absence of another.

Ex turpi causa no oritur action an action does not arise from a base cause.

Exempli gratia (e.g.) for example.

Factum est for example.

Force majeure superior power.

Ibidem. (ibid.) in the same place.

Id est (i.e.) that is.

In camera not in open court.

In re in the matter of.

In status quo in the former position.

In transitu on the way; in passing.

Infra below.

Inter alia among other matters.

Inter vivos during life; between living persons.

Intra vires within the powers of.

Lex loci the law of the place.

Lex mercatoria mercantile law.

Lex non scripta the unwritten, or common, law.

Lex scripta the written law; statute law.

Mala fide in bad faith.

Mutates mutandis the necessary changes being made.

Nemo dat quod no habet no one can give what is not his.

Novus actus interveniens a new act intervening.

Obiter by the way.

Obiter dictum a saying by the way (as in a judgment without creating a precedent).

Pari passu with equal step; equal ranking.

Passim in various places; here and there.

Pendente lite while litigation is pending.

Per capita by heads; by the number of individuals.

Per se by itself.

Pro tanto for so much.

Qua in the capacity of.

Quantum amount.

Quantum meruit as much as he earned.

Qui facit per alium facit per se he who acts through another is deemed to act in person.

Quid per quo something in return for something (literally 'what for what'); a mutual consideration.

Ratio decidendi the reason or ground for a judicial decision.

Respondeat superior let the principal answer.

Scienter knowingly (e.g. the owner of an animal knows of its dangerous propensities).

Sine die without fixing a date.

Sub judice under consideration.

Sui generis of its own kind.

Sui juris without disability.

Supra above.

Uberimma fides utmost good faith.

Uberimmae fidei of the utmost good faith.

Ultra vires beyond the legal power.

Vis major irresistible force (Act of God).

Viva voce by word of mouth (oral testimony).

Volenti non fit injuria that to which a man consents cannot be considered an injury.

Appendix 4

Insurance industry associations, bodies and related organisations

American Institute for CPCU (AICPCU) Insurance Institute of America (IIA) *www.aicpcu.org.*

American Insurance Association (AIA) *www.aiadc.org.*

Arson Prevention Bureau *www.arsonpreventionbureau.org.uk.*

Associated Scottish Life Office Scottish Mutual (*www.scottishmutual.co.uk*);

AEGON; Scottish Life; Scottish Widows: Standard Life.

Association of Average Adjusters (AAA) *www.average-adjusters.com.*

Association of British Insurers (ABI) *www.abi.org.uk.*

Association of Burglary Insurance Surveyors (ABIS) *www.abis.org.uk.*

Association of Consulting Actuaries *www.aca.org.uk.*

Association of Independent Financial Advisers (AIFA) *www.aifa.net.*

Association of Insurance and Risk Managers (AIRMIC) *www.airmic.com.*

Association of Investment Trust Companies (AITC) *www.aitc.co.uk.*

Association of Pensions Lawyers *www.apl.org.uk.*

Association of Personal Injury Lawyers (APIL) *www.apil.com.*

Assurance Medical Society *www.assurancemedicalsociety.org.uk.*

British Bankers Association (BBA) *www.bba.org.uk.*

British Fire Services Association *www.bfsa.org.uk.*

British Insurance Brokers Association (BIBA) *www.biba.org.uk.*

British Insurance Law Association (BILA) *www.bila.org.*

Chartered Institute of Loss Adjusters (CILA) *www.cila.co.uk.*

Chartered Insurance Institute (CII) *www.cii.co.uk.*

Committee of European Securities Regulations (CESR) *www.europefesco.org.*

Council of Mortgage Lenders (CML) *www.cml.org.uk.*

Criminal Injuries Compensation Board *www.cica.gov.uk.*

Department of Work and Pensions *www.dwp.gov.uk.*

Disability Rights Commission (DRC) *www.drc-gb.org.*

Federation of European Risk Management Association *www.ferma-asso.org.*

Financial Services Authority (FSA) *www.fsa.gov.uk.*

Financial Services Compensation Scheme (FSCS) *www.fscs.org.uk.*

Financial Services Practitioner Panel *www.fs-pp.org.uk.*

Fire Mark Circle *www.firemarkcircle.fsnet.co.uk.*

Geneva Association *www.genevaassociation.org.*

General Standards Insurance Council (GISC) *www.gisc.co.uk.*

Global Association of Risk Professionals (GARP) *www.garp.com.*

Government Actuary's Department (GAD) *www.gad.gov.uk.*

Headway – the brain injury association *www.headway.org.uk.*

Health and Safety Executive (HSE) *www.hse.gov.uk*

Inland Revenue (IR) *www.inlandrevenue.gov.uk.*

Institute for Global Insurance Education *www.igie.org.*

Institute of Actuaries *www.actuaries.org.uk.*

Institute of Directors *www.iod.com.*

Institute of Financial Services (IFS) *www.ifslearning.com.*

Institute of Insurance Brokers (iB) *www.iib-uk.com.*

Insurance Advisory Board (IAB) *www.insuranceadvisoryboard.com.*

Insurance Information Institute *www.iii.org.*

Insurance Institute of London (ILL) *www.iilondon.co.uk.*

Insurance Services Office *www.iso.com.*

Internal Market Directorate General *www.europa.eu.int/dgs/internal-market/index/.*

International Association of Insurance Supervisors (IAIS) *www.iaisweb.org.*

International Federation of Health Plans *www.ifhp.com.*

International Credit Insurance and Surety Association (ICISA) *www.ucisa.org.*

International Maritime Organisation (IMO) *www.imo.org.*

International Association for the Study of Insurance Economics *See* Geneva Association.

International Union of Aviation Insurers *www.iuai.org.*

International Union of Investment and Credit Insurers *www.berneunion.org.uk.*

International Underwriting Association (IUA) *www.iua.co.uk.*

Investment and Life Assurance Group (ILAG) *www.ilag.co.uk.*

Investment Management Association *www.investmentuk.org.*

LGSA Marine *www.lgsamarine.co.uk.*

Lloyd's America *www.lloydsamerica.com.*

Lloyd's of London *www.lloyd's.com.*

London Market Insurance Brokers' Committee (LMBC) *www.lmbc.co.uk.*

London Market Principles 2001 (LMP2001) *www.lmp2001.com.*

Loss Prevention Certification Board (LPCB) *www.brecertification.co.uk.*

Motor Accident Solicitors' Society (MASS) *www.mass.org.uk.*

Motor Conference *www.abi.org.uk/Public/Consumer/Motor/MotorConference.htm.*

Motor Insurance Repair Research Centre *www.thatcham.org.*

Motor Insurance Information Centre *www.miic.org.uk.*

Motor Insurers' Bureau (MIB) *www.mib.org.uk.*

National Security Inspectorate (NSI) *www.nsi.org.uk.*

Offshore Group of Insurance Supervisors (OGIS) *www.ogis.net.*

Pensions Management Institute (PMI) *www.pensions-pmi.org.uk.*

Pensions Ombudsman *www.pensions-ombudsman.org.uk.*

Pensions Policy Institute *www.pensionspolicyinstitute.org.uk.*

PEP and ISA Management Association *www.pima.co.uk.*

Personal Injury Bar Association *www.piba.org.uk.*

SIPP Provider Group *www.sipp-provider-group.org.uk.*

Spinal Injuries Association (SIA) *www.spinal.com.*

Staple Inn Actuarial Society *www.sias.org.uk.*

UK Forum for Genetics and Insurance *www.ukfgi.org.uk.*

UK Pensions Industry's Technical Website *www.ariesps.co.uk.*

Worshipful Company of Insurers *www.wci.org.uk.*

Portals and web pages

Artemis (Alternative Risk transfer portal) *www.artemis.bm.ht/.*

World Insurance Portal *www.rsx.co.uk.*